W9-BUT-918

Worldmark Modern Conflict and Diplomacy

Worldmark Modern Conflict and Diplomacy

VOLUME 2

JAPANESE INVASION OF CHINA TO YUGOSLAV WARS

GALE
CENGAGE Learning

Detroit • New York • San Francisco • New Haven, Conn • Waterville, Maine • London

© 2014 Gale, Cengage Learning

WCN: 01-100-101

Worldmark Modern Conflict and Diplomacy

Ceres Publishing Services LLC, Cynthia Brantley Johnson, Editor

Project Editor: Elizabeth P. Manar

Editorial Staff: Deirdre Blanchfield, Kathleen J. Edgar, Jason Everett, Debra Kirby, Kimberley McGrath

Rights Acquisition and Management: Ashley M. Maynard, Robyn V. Young

Imaging: John Watkins

Product Design: Kristine Julien

Composition: Evi Abou-El-Seoud, Mary Beth Trimper

Manufacturing: Wendy Blurton

Indexing: Laura Dorricott

Gale
27500 Drake Rd.
Farmington Hills, MI, 48331-3535

ISBN-13: 978-1-57302-726-7 (set)
ISBN-13: 978-1-57302-727-4 (vol. 1)
ISBN-13: 978-1-57302-728-1 (vol. 2)

This title is also available as an e-book.
ISBN-13: 978-1-57302-729-8
Contact your Gale, a part of Cengage Learning sales representative for ordering information.

For product information and technology assistance, contact us at
Gale Customer Support, 1-800-877-4253.
For permission to use material from this text or product,
submit all requests online at **www.cengage.com/permissions.**
Further permissions questions can be emailed to
permissionrequest@cengage.com

Cover photographs: Images of flags © ArtisticPhoto/Shutterstock.com; Image of Palestinian protester © Jaafar Ashtiyeh/AFP/Getty Images; Image of Nobel Laureate Aung San Suu Kyi © Ragnar Singsass/Getty Images; Image of Sudanese people at displacement camp © Marcus Prior/AFP/Getty Images.

While every effort has been made to ensure the reliability of the information presented in this publication, Gale, a part of Cengage Learning, does not guarantee the accuracy of the data contained herein. Gale accepts no payment for listing; and inclusion in the publication of any organization, agency, institution, publication, service, or individual does not imply endorsement of the editors or publisher. Errors brought to the attention of the publisher and verified to the satisfaction of the publisher will be corrected in future editions.

LIBRARY OF CONGRESS CATALOGING-IN-PUBLICATION DATA

Worldmark modern conflict and diplomacy / Cynthia Johnson, editor.
    pages cm
    Summary: "Worldmark Modern Conflict and Diplomacy presents easy-to-understand information on 90 global conflicts and diplomatic efforts in 2 volumes. The set will cover specific conflicts that have had a truly global impact, as well as the efforts and organizations focused on solving these conflicts. Arranged alphabetically, each of the approximately 90 entries will cover the origins of a conflict or diplomatic effort, its current status, and its wide-ranging impact on the world. Topics include historical and current conflicts from World Wars I & II to Al-Qaeda and the Arab Spring, as well as diplomatic efforts such as the United Nations and the Nobel Peace Prize. The set includes material on recent events in places ranging from Kosovo to Myanmar to South Sudan to the Palestinian Territories"—Provided by publisher.

    Includes bibliographical references and index.
    ISBN 978-1-57302-726-7 (set) — ISBN 1-57302-726-X (set) —
ISBN 978-1-57302-727-4 (v. 1) — ISBN 1-57302-727-8 (v. 1) —
ISBN 978-1-57302-728-1 (v. 2) — ISBN 1-57302-728-6 (v. 2)
    1. International relations—History—20th century—Encyclopedias—Juvenile literature. 2. International relations—History—21st century—Encyclopedias—Juvenile literature. 3. Diplomacy—History—20th century—Encyclopedias—Juvenile literature. 4. Diplomacy—History—21st century—Encyclopedias—Juvenile literature. 5. World politics—20th century—Encyclopedias—Juvenile literature. 6. World politics—21st century—Encyclopedias—Juvenile literature. 7. Military history—20th century—Encyclopedias—Juvenile literature. 8. Military history—21st century—Encyclopedias—Juvenile literature. I. Johnson, Cynthia, 1969- , editor.
    D443.W675 2014
    327.1'6—dc23
                                                      2013047114

Printed in the United States of America
1 2 3 4 5 6 7 18 17 16 15 14

Table of Contents

VOLUME 1

VOLUME 2

Introduction

The first half of the 20th century brought two major world wars, the first of which was so terrible it was considered to be the "War to End All Wars." World War I (1914–18), like the wars that preceded it, involved long, hard battles fought over each foot of land with combatants often face-to-face with their enemies. Despite the belief that the world had learned its lesson and would never again experience such devastation, only a few decades later, World War II (1939–45) had begun, spreading the conflict even wider and involving atrocities on a unimaginable scale in the form of the Holocaust. By the close of that war, much of the world map had been redrawn, and colonialism was fading.

As the old empires began to fall apart following World War II, independence movements emerged in former colonies, leading to violent separations and tenuous new identities. In Algeria, a brutal war for independence from France provided a framework for both other independence movements and for the tactics used in attempts to stop them. The bloodshed frequently did not end with independence, as many of the newly independent countries devolved into civil warfare—often multisided and involving rapidly shifting alliances.

Much of the division in these new countries was based on a complex mix of ethnic and economic ties, where historically favored groups fought to maintain their status while other groups demanded a foothold. Sometimes this warfare resembled traditional civil wars, with two defined sides and a clear front, but more often allegiances were less clear, and the distinction between soldier and civilian was blurred in guerrilla warfare.

As guerilla warfare became more common, the influence of major powers in local wars also became clear. The East and the West, particularly the Soviet Union/China and the United States/United Kingdom, often fought what were described as proxy wars in countries such as Vietnam, Argentina, and Afghanistan. That these were often hidden wars—undeclared and camouflaged under the guise of being "advisory"—only exacerbated animosities.

Combatants in the last century had access to a larger array of weapons, including nuclear weapons, which were used for the first time in World War II in a devastating U.S. attack on Japan that resulted in the deaths of some 200,000 people and brought about Japan's swift surrender. These weapons remained a major aspect of the emerging Cold War and many regional conflicts since, and though they have not been used again in warfare, the threat of their use has shadowed many subsequent conflicts. Chemical weapons, not new in concept but expanded in practice, became more common, and were first used on a large scale by Germany in the trench warfare of World War I. More recently, sarin gas was used to kill Syrian civilians in 2013, allegedly by the Syrian government. The effectiveness and efficiency of chemical weapons make them unacceptable to the international community, though other modes of killing are just as lethal. New technologies have provided additional methods for killing at a distance, including remote operated drones, which have been used most notably in Afghanistan.

Yet at the beginning of the 21st century, weapons of mass destruction and killing via drone strikes were not the causes of the majority of deaths in conflict zones. Much of the violence has been internal rather than international, due to political, ethnic, and religious differences. In 2011 the Arab Spring overturned the rule of several longstanding dictators in various Middle Eastern countries, yet several of the countries, such as Egypt and Libya, have continued to experience internal turmoil and violence long after their leaders were toppled. Years after the movement began in Syria, civil war continued to rage in early 2014 as rebel forces fought against long-time leader Bashar al-Assad and amongst each other.

Increasingly, as the 21st century progressed, new organizations—not based in nationality or ethnicity—emerged. Some were violent. Al-Qaeda, a pan-ethnic and pan-national, religion-based terrorist organization, crosses countries and continents with its membership and acts of violence. Loosely linking together what would have previously been separate, often poorly guided and funded organizations, al-Qaeda gained more power to act and to generate fear. Likewise, large criminal organizations, such as drug cartels, bring fear and destruction to their communities when they put economics before parochial interests. Dedicated to making money and moving product at the expense of families, friends, and countrymen, drug cartels move to wherever the money is, leaving a path of destruction and terror along the way.

In response to violent conflicts throughout the world, humanitarian organizations were established to help address the needs of those affected by such events. These non-profit organizations, such as the International Committee of the Red Cross and Red Crescent, provide victims of war, conflict, and natural disasters with food, shelter, medical help, and other assistance. Some of these organizations also work to hold warring participants to humane standards of behavior and alert the world to the magnitude of the human tragedy involved in war-torn areas.

While the last century brought a proliferation of types of warfare and weapons, it also saw a similar expansion in methods of resolving conflict. Major international organizations dedicated to preserving peace, ensuring mutual protection from enemies, and resolving disputes emerged. The Nuremberg Trials following World War II gave form to a judicial means for holding countries and their leaders responsible for atrocities that would otherwise go unpunished. The International Criminal Court has held an increasing number of perpetrators responsible for actions that are widely regarded as incompatible with a civilized society.

In some of the countries most divided by civil conflict and brutality, a new process was created to help populations heal. In South Africa following the fall of its apartheid system, the "Truth and Reconciliation Commission" sought to bring to light the horror of the past in order to allow a coming together for the future. This approach has been used in many countries prior to and after the South African commission, with more than 30 established since the 1970s.

In a few cases, the movement toward a new, democratic order has been achieved through non-violent means. In Tunisia, where the Arab Spring began with mass protests in 2010, the new government passed a constitution in 2014 that seems to provide the hope of a more open and inclusive society.

Worldmark Modern Conflict and Diplomacy profiles nearly 100 of these exemplars of warfare, peacemaking, and negotiations. From the Japanese invasion of Manchuria in 1937 to the Arab Spring that swept through the Middle East and North Africa beginning in 2010 and continued to have impacts years later, *Worldmark Modern Conflict and Diplomacy* presents a roadmap of the evolution of the sometimes stumbling attempts to recreate society and provides students and readers the foundation for understanding and engaging in critical analysis and discussion of these attempts.

The Editors

Acknowledgments

The editors at Cengage extend their thanks to the following scholars and researchers for their expertise and contributions to *Worldmark Modern Conflict and Diplomacy*: Thomas Carson, Yahya Chaudhry, Dave Eisenstadter, Laurie Hillstrom, Joseph P. Hyder, J.D., Adrienne Wilmoth Lerner, J.D., Brenda Wilmoth Lerner, K. Lee Lerner, Dr. John E. Peterson, and Kathleen Wilson.

Using Primary Sources

The definition of what constitutes a primary source is often the subject of scholarly debate and interpretation. Although primary sources come from a wide spectrum of resources, they are united by the fact that they individually provide insight into the historical *milieu* (context and environment) during which they were produced. Primary sources include materials such as newspaper articles, press dispatches, autobiographies, essays, letters, diaries, speeches, song lyrics, posters, works of art—and in the 21st century, electronic media communications, such as Web logs (blogs)—that offer direct, first-hand insight or witness to events of their day.

Categories of primary sources include:

- Documents containing firsthand accounts of historic events by witnesses and participants. This category includes diary or journal entries, letters, email, newspaper articles, interviews, memoirs, and testimony in legal proceedings.

- Documents or works representing the official views of both government leaders and leaders of other organizations. These include primary sources such as policy statements, speeches, interviews, press releases, government reports, and legislation.

- Works of art, including (but certainly not limited to) photographs, poems, and songs, including advertisements and reviews of those works that help establish an understanding of the cultural environment with regard to attitudes and perceptions of events.

- Secondary sources. In some cases, secondary sources or tertiary sources may be treated as primary sources. For example, if an entry written many years after an event, or to summarize an event, includes quotes, recollections, or retrospectives (accounts of the past) written by participants in the earlier event, the source can be considered a primary source.

Analysis of Primary Sources

The primary material collected in this volume is not intended to provide a comprehensive or balanced overview of a topic or event. Rather, the primary sources are intended to generate interest and lay a foundation for further inquiry and study.

In order to properly analyze a primary source, readers should remain skeptical and develop probing questions about the source. Using historical documents requires that readers analyze them carefully and extract specific information. However, readers must also read "beyond the text" to garner larger clues about the social impact of the primary source.

In addition to providing information about their topics, primary sources may also supply a wealth of insight into their creator's viewpoint. For example, when reading a news article about an event, consider whether the reporter's words also indicate something about his or her origin, bias (an irrational disposition in favor of someone or something), prejudices (an irrational disposition against someone or something), or intended audience.

Students should remember that primary sources often contain information later proven to be false, or contain viewpoints and terms unacceptable to future generations. It is important to view the primary source within the historical and social context existing at its creation. If for example, a newspaper article is written within hours or days of an event, later developments may reveal some assertions in the original article as false or misleading.

Test New Conclusions and Ideas

Whatever opinion or working hypothesis the reader forms, it is critical to then test that hypothesis against other facts and sources related to the incident. For example, it might be wrong to conclude that factual mistakes are deliberate unless evidence can be produced of a pattern and practice of such mistakes with an intent to promote a false idea.

The difference between sound reasoning and preposterous conspiracy theories (or the birth of urban legends) lies in the willingness to test new ideas against other sources, rather than rest on one piece of evidence such as a single primary source that may contain errors. Sound reasoning requires that arguments and assertions guard against argument fallacies that utilize the following:

- false dilemmas (only two choices are given when in fact there are three or more options);
- arguments from ignorance (*argumentum ad ignorantiam*; because something is not known to be true, it is assumed to be false);
- possibilist fallacies (a favorite among conspiracy theorists who attempt to demonstrate that a factual statement is true or false by establishing the possibility of its truth or falsity. An argument where "it could be" is usually followed by an unearned "therefore, it is.");
- slippery slope arguments or fallacies (a series of increasingly dramatic consequences is drawn from an initial fact or idea);
- begging the question (the truth of the conclusion is assumed by the premises);
- straw man arguments (the arguer mischaracterizes an argument or theory and then attacks the merits of their own false representations);
- appeals to pity or force (the argument attempts to persuade people to agree by sympathy or force);
- prejudicial language (values or moral goodness, good and bad, are attached to certain arguments or facts);
- personal attacks (*ad hominem*; an attack on a person's character or circumstances);
- anecdotal or testimonial evidence (stories that are unsupported by impartial observation or data that is not reproducible);
- *post hoc* (after the fact) fallacies (because one thing follows another, it is held to cause the other);
- the fallacy of the appeal to authority (the argument rests upon the credentials of a person, not the evidence).

Despite the fact that some primary sources can contain false information or lead readers to false conclusions based on the facts presented, they remain an invaluable resource regarding past events. Primary sources allow readers and researchers to come as close as possible to understanding the perceptions and context of events and thus to more fully appreciate how and why misconceptions occur.

Chronology of Events

1863 The International Committee of the Red Cross (ICRC) is founded in Geneva, Switzerland, to provide impartial medical assistance to all those injured in war.

1885 European powers meet in Berlin, Germany, to discuss how to divide up the continent of Africa. They eventually create 50 European-ruled colonies with boundaries that disregard longstanding traditional governments and tribal, ethnic, and linguistic ties.

1893 The disputed border between Afghanistan and Pakistan, known as the Durand Line, is created via an agreement between the Afghani monarchy and the British colonial government of Pakistan. More than a century later, the border region remains one of the most dangerous and troubled areas in the world.

1895 Japan defeats China in the First Sino-Japanese War.

1898 The United States helps Cuba defeat Spain and gain its independence in the Spanish-American War.

1901 The first Nobel Prizes are awarded, including the Nobel Peace Prize to Frederic Passy and Jean Henri Dunant. Passy's work supported organized international conflict resolution. Dunant's depiction of the Battle of Solferino in 1859 inspired the creation of the International Committee of the Red Cross.

1901 In December, the first wireless message is transmitted across the Atlantic Ocean, via a telegraph system designed by inventor Guglielmo Marconi.

1904 Ground is broken on the Panama Canal, connecting the Atlantic Ocean to the Pacific Ocean.

1904 The Russo-Japanese War begins. The Empire of Japan and the Russian Empire fight over Manchuria and Korea. This is considered the first imperial war.

1904 The Trans-Siberian Railway is completed, connecting Moscow with the Sea of Japan. It is the longest railway line in the world.

1905 Japan defeats Russia in the Russo-Japanese War and gains control of the South Manchurian Railroad.

1905 The Russian Revolution of 1905 breaks out with mutinies against military leadership and worker strikes. It results in a new constitution in 1906 establishing a limited constitutional monarchy and a multiparty system.

1906 Finland becomes the first European country to give women the right to vote.

1907 The Second Hague Peace Conference establishes 10 rules of war, most of which are violated during the coming First World War (1914–18).

1908 Three-year-old Pu Yi becomes Emperor of China until his abdication in 1912. He is later briefly restored to the throne as the leader of the puppet state of Manchukuo.

1908 The Young Turks revolt against the Ottoman Empire, restoring the parliament.

1909 Japan's Prince Ito, a four time prime minister, is assassinated by a Korean nationalist.

1911 A group of revolutionaries in southern China launches a successful revolt that ends the imperial system. The Xinhai Revolution establishes the Republic of China, led by the newly formed Chinese Nationalist Party, or Kuomintang.

1913   South Africa passes the Native Land Act, which requires the nation's majority black population to live on 13 percent of the total land area, while the remaining 87 percent is reserved for the minority white population. This law forms a cornerstone of the apartheid system.

1914   On June 28, a radical Serb named Gavrilo Princip assassinates Archduke Franz Ferdinand, heir to the throne of Austria-Hungary, on the streets of Sarajevo. The murder sets off a chain reaction of events that quickly draws the major powers of Europe into what will become World War I.

1914   The first shots of World War I are fired on July 28, one month after the assassination of Archduke Franz Ferdinand.

1914   Ernest Shackleton, a polar explorer, launches the Imperial Trans-Antarctic Expedition. His ship becomes trapped in ice and is slowly crushed, though the explorers escape with no loss of human life.

1914   The Panama Canal officially opens on August 15. One of the largest and most difficult engineering projects ever undertaken, it greatly reduces the time required for ships to travel between the Atlantic and Pacific Oceans.

1915   The failing Ottoman government attempts to rid what is present-day Turkey of Armenians, leading to the deaths of more than a million people. The massacre, often called the Armenian Genocide, becomes a contested political issue that has repercussions into the 21st century.

1915   The Second Battle of Ypres in western Belgium is fought in the spring and becomes the first time Germany uses poison gas on a large scale. The German Army's release of chlorine gas on April 22 causes 6,000 Allied casualties, many of whom die within 10 minutes of exposure.

1917   The United States formally enters World War I.

1917   Russian Tsar Nicholas II is forced to abdicate, ending imperial rule in Russia and eventually leading to the rise of the Bolshevik party, led by Vladimir Lenin.

1918   A virulent strain of Spanish Flu sweeps across the world, killing an estimated 20 to 40 million people.

1918   Tsar Nicholas II of Russia, his wife, and their five children are executed to prevent the royal family from ever regaining power.

1919   The Treaty of Versailles is signed on June 28, ending the war between Germany and the Allied Powers of France, Russia, and Great Britain.

1920   Following the end of World War I, the League of Nations is established. A precursor to the United Nations, the League's primary objective is to maintain world peace.

1920   The United States ratifies the Nineteenth Amendment to the Constitution, which grants women the right to vote.

1922   British-controlled Ireland is divided into the predominantly Catholic Republic of Ireland, which becomes an independent nation, and the predominantly Protestant Northern Ireland, which remains part of the United Kingdom. Following the partition, armed groups such as the Irish Republican Army (IRA) engage in a decades-long guerilla war to unite Ireland.

1925   Adolf Hitler publishes *Mein Kampf,* detailing his political views and plans for Germany.

1929   The U.S. stock market crash in late October plunges the nation into the Great Depression. The severe economic downturn soon spreads to other Western industrialized countries.

1930   Mohandas Gandhi leads the Salt March starting on March 12. The 240-mile march sparks acts of civil disobedience against the British Raj and becomes an important milestone in the Indian independence movement. Gandhi's nonviolent approach is later emulated in many movements around the world, including the American civil rights movement of the 1960s.

1930   The USSR, under Josef Stalin, begins collectivizing agriculture—abolishing individual farms in favor of large-scale collectives—leading to massive food shortages and famine.

1931	Japan invades and occupies the three northeastern provinces of China (called Manchuria), setting the stage for the Second Sino-Japanese War.
1931	The Convention for the Regulation of Whaling is the first international treaty enacted for the purpose of conserving a natural resource.
1933	The Nazi Party comes to power in Germany with the election of Adolf Hitler in January.
1934	Mao Zedong, commonly called Chairman Mao, leads the Red Army of the Chinese Communists on what becomes known as the Long March. Women, children, and the ill and elderly are left behind to be executed by the Kuomintang as party leaders make their way south to regroup as a guerrilla force.
1936	Japan signs the Tripartite Agreement, forging an alliance with Germany and Italy that becomes known as the Axis Powers during World War II.
1936	The Spanish Civil War begins, pitting Spanish Nationalists (aided by Nazi Germany and Fascist Italy) against Republicans or Loyalists (aided by the United States, the Soviet Union, and several Western European nations). The Nationalist victory has a significant impact on the balance of power in Europe, helping create the conditions that lead to World War II.
1937	Japan captures the Chinese capital of Nanjing on December 13. Over the next six weeks, Japanese military forces conduct a brutal campaign known as the Rape of Nanjing, during which they torture, rape, and murder hundreds of thousands of Chinese civilians.
1938	German troops march into neighboring Austria on March 12 to annex the country on behalf of Adolf Hitler's Third Reich. The Anschluss (annexation) becomes a pivotal moment in the movement toward World War II.
1938	A coordinated series of attacks against Jews throughout Nazi Germany and Austria kills more than 90 people and leads to the arrest and detention in concentration camps of about 90,000. The night of violence becomes known as Kristallnacht (Crystal Night) after the broken glass that lines the streets from smashed windows.
1939	Germany and the Soviet Union sign the Molotov-Ribbentrap Pact, a 10-year non-aggression treaty that allows Hitler to move forward with plans to invade Poland without fear of war with the Soviets. Hitler later violates this treaty when he invades the Soviet Union on June 22, 1941.
1939	Germany invades Poland on September 1, prompting a declaration of war by France and Great Britain two days later that marks the formal start of World War II (1939–45).
1941	On June 22 Germany and its allies launch an invasion of the Soviet Union code-named Operation Barbarossa.
1941	Imperial Japan bombs the U.S. naval base at Pearl Harbor, Hawaii, on December 7, prompting the United States to enter World War II.
1941	In a bid to capture the city of Leningrad, Russia, Germany launches a blockade of the city. The 872-day Siege of Leningrad results in the deaths of approximately 1.5 million people.
1942	On April 9, Japanese soldiers force 80,000 Filipino and American prisoners to march 65 miles to Camp O'Donnell in the Philippines. The prisoners are subjected to horrific physical abuse and there are a huge number of fatalities. The Bataan Death March is later judged to be a war crime.
1942	More than 100,000 Japanese Americans are forced to relocate to internment camps in the U.S. interior, ostensibly to prevent them from aiding the enemy.
1942	A secret U.S. government initiative to produce the first atomic bomb begins. In addition to building the first atomic bombs, the Manhattan Project gathers information on German nuclear capabilities.
1943	The Jewish Resistance in Warsaw, Poland, fights Nazi efforts to transport the remaining Jews to the Treblinka extermination camp. The Warsaw Ghetto Uprising is eventually crushed by the Germans, and the Ghetto is liquidated by May 16.
1944	On June 6 Allied troops land along a 50-mile beach in France in an effort to free

the country from Nazi occupation. By the day's end the Allies have lost more than 9,000 soldiers but gained a foothold in Normandy.

1944 Soviet Premier Joseph Stalin deports nearly the entire ethnic Chechen population to Siberia and present-day Kazakhstan. About 60 percent die during the forced exile.

1945 Germany surrenders to the Allies on May 7 to end World War II in Europe.

1945 Fifty nations meet in San Francisco, California, to draw up the charter for what will be the United Nations. The UN officially comes into existence on October 24.

1945 At the Potsdam Conference, the victorious Allies divide Germany into four military occupation zones controlled by France, Britain, the United States, and the Soviet Union. The Soviet zone evolves into Communist East Germany, while the other three zones become democratic West Germany.

1945 The United States drops atomic bombs on the cities of Hiroshima and Nagasaki in Japan. Japan surrenders on August 15, ending the war in the Pacific.

1945 Ho Chi Minh and other Viet Minh nationalists declare independence from French colonial rule and create the Democratic Republic of Vietnam.

1945 War crimes trials of prominent leaders of Nazi Germany begin in the city of Nuremberg, Germany. The International Military Tribunal trials result in death sentences for 12 men as well as clarification about what constitutes a war crime. Twelve additional trials, lasting until 1949, are held to convict others, including judges and doctors, involved in atrocities committed during the war.

1946 Determined to reclaim its former colony, France sends troops to Vietnam and launches what becomes known as the First Indochina War.

1946 The International Court of Justice (ICJ) begins operating in April from its permanent seat in The Hague, Netherlands. The ICJ hears cases brought by one nation against another on a variety of matters, including territorial disputes, environmental issues, genocide, and the legality of the use of force in war.

1946 The International Whaling Commission (IWC) is established to enforce a moratorium on commercial whaling.

1947 The United States launches the European Recovery Program, known informally as the Marshall Plan. The program is designed to rebuild the economies of Europe, partially in order to stop the spread of communism.

1947 British India is divided along religious lines to create Hindu-majority India and Muslim-majority Pakistan. Both countries claim the territory of Kashmir, which becomes the cause of several major wars and an ongoing military standoff between the two nuclear-armed nations.

1948 The United Nations passes its Convention on the Prevention and Punishment of the Crime of Genocide (CPPCG).

1948 Soviet troops blockade West Berlin in an attempt to force its citizens to accept Communist control. The United States and Great Britain respond with the Berlin Airlift, during which British and American pilots successfully supply the city with food and fuel via airdrop for nearly a year until the blockade is lifted.

1948 On May 14 David Ben-Gurion announces the establishment of the State of Israel. The following day, Egypt, Syria, Transjordan, and Iraq invade Palestine to begin the 1948 Arab-Israeli War.

1948 The National Party (NP) gains control of the South African government and makes apartheid an official policy. Apartheid requires strict racial segregation and provides many social, political, and economic advantages to minority whites.

1949 On August 29, the Soviet Union successfully tests its first fully functional nuclear weapon, initiating an arms race with the United States.

1949 On October 1, Chairman Mao declares the creation of the People's Republic of China, a Communist nation. Members of the deposed Kuomintang reestablish the Republic of China in Taiwan.

1949 The North Atlantic Treaty Organization (NATO) is established to further the national security of its members.

1949 The fourth and final Geneva Convention is completed. The conventions guide the conduct of nations in wartime and form the cornerstone of modern humanitarian law.

1950 The Korean War begins, pitting Communist North Korea (backed by China) against U.S.-supported South Korea. The three-year conflict costs the lives of more than one million Korean and Chinese people as well as almost 37,000 American troops.

1950 Joseph R. McCarthy, U.S. Senator from Wisconsin, dramatically pronounces that hundreds of communists are employed in the U.S. State Department. Amid the anticommunist hysteria known as the Red Scare, hundreds of U.S. citizens are accused of being communist sympathizers and subpoenaed to appear before the House Un-American Activities Committee (HUAC).

1953 Julius and Ethel Rosenberg are executed on June 20. After a controversial trial, the American husband and wife were convicted of espionage for selling atomic secrets to the Soviet Union.

1953 The armistice ending the Korean War leaves the border between North and South Korea in virtually the same place as it was before the war started.

1954 Nationalists launch the Algerian War of Independence in response to years of French repression.

1954 Viet Minh fighters defeat the French Army in the pivotal Battle of Dien Bien Phu, ending French colonial rule in Vietnam.

1954 The Geneva Peace Accords ending the First Indochina War formally divide Vietnam at the 17th Parallel to create Communist North Vietnam and U.S.-supported South Vietnam.

1955 The Warsaw Pact—a mutual defense treaty between Communist states of Central and Eastern Europe—is signed on May 14.

1956 Soviet leader Nikita Khrushchev ends the forced exile of ethnic Chechens and allows them to return to their native land.

1956 President of Egypt Gamal Abdel Nasser announces a plan to nationalize the Suez Canal, initiating what becomes known as the Suez Crisis. Israel, Great Britain, and France respond by sending troops and warplanes to regain control of the important waterway, which connects the Mediterranean and Red seas.

1957 The European Economic Community is established to create a common market in Europe. The common market allows for easier trade and the movement of labor across the borders of member countries.

1958 The Communist Party of China launches its "Great Leap Forward" initiative to transform the country from a largely agrarian economy to a largely industrial one. The Great Leap Forward program is enforced through suppression of dissent and forced labor and results in the deaths of more than 20 million people.

1959 The Antarctic Treaty is drafted. The agreement is designed to keep the massive continent open for scientific research and prohibit nuclear testing, radioactive waste disposal, and other military activities.

1959 Basque separatists form Euskadi Ta Askatasuna (ETA; Basque Homeland and Freedom). ETA pursues a path of armed resistance for more than five decades in an effort to gain independence from Spain.

1959 Fidel Castro's communist forces oust the U.S.-supported government and take control of Cuba, launching Castro's 50-year rule and Cuba's antagonistic relationship with United States.

1960 Cyprus gains its independence from Great Britain, but tensions between Greek and Turkish Cypriot communities erupt into violence, resulting in a divided nation.

1960 The Organization of the Petroleum Exporting Countries (OPEC) is founded. The organization works to coordinate oil prices among the member countries and ensure a steady supply of oil on the world market.

1961 Adolf Eichmann—the man responsible for organizing the mass deportation of Jews to extermination camps in Nazi Germany—is captured by Israeli Mossad agents in Argentina, where he has been living since the end of the war. Brought to Israel to face charges of crimes against humanity and war crimes, he is executed in 1962.

1961   The CIA sponsors a military invasion of Cuba on April 17. When the American invaders are overwhelmed by local militia, the Bay of Pigs becomes a humiliating defeat for the United States and an image-burnishing victory for Cuban leader Fidel Castro.

1961   East German authorities prevent free movement between East and West Germany first by erecting a barrier of barbed wire, and later by building a wall. The heavily fortified, 96-mile long Berlin Wall becomes a tangible symbol of the period of East-West political and military rivalry known as the Cold War.

1962   Following a brutal, eight-year war, France agrees to grant Algeria its independence. On October 8 Algeria becomes the 109th member of the United Nations.

1962   Soviet leader Nikita Khrushchev orders the construction of missile silos in Cuba that will be capable of delivering weapons to U.S. cities. President John F. Kennedy responds by establishing a naval blockade of Cuba to prevent Soviet arms shipments. While the crisis is resolved peacefully, the tense standoff is generally considered the closest the world has come to nuclear war.

1963   After the majority of African countries gain independence from former European colonizers, African leaders meet to establish the Organization of African Unity (OAU).

1963   In the wake of the Cuban Missile Crisis, a "hot line" is established between the United States and the Soviet Union to ensure that a future breakdown in communication does not lead to warfare.

1963   An estimated 250,000 people participate in the March on Washington for Jobs and Freedom on August 28, which culminates in civil rights leader Martin Luther King Jr. making his famous "I Have a Dream" speech.

1963   U.S. President John F. Kennedy is killed by an assassin's bullet while riding in a motorcade in Dallas, Texas.

1964   The U.S. Congress passes the Civil Rights Act. This landmark legislation prohibits discrimination on the basis of race, color, religion, sex, or national origin in the areas of education, employment, and public accommodations.

1965   On March 7 a group of peaceful voting-rights marchers are attacked by white law enforcement officers in Selma, Alabama. The violent repression convinces the U.S. Congress to pass the Voting Rights Act, which secures minority voting rights and marks the end of the African-American civil rights movement.

1965   The United States commits military troops to Vietnam, where North Vietnamese Army forces and Communist guerilla fighters are attempting to overthrow the U.S.-friendly government of South Vietnam. American troops will remain in Vietnam for almost ten years fighting what becomes an unwinnable, unpopular war.

1967   Ernesto "Che" Guevara is killed in Bolivia. An Argentine doctor, author, and Marxist revolutionary, Che becomes a worldwide symbol of rebellion.

1967   On June 5 Israel launches a surprise pre-emptive attack against Egyptian air fields where neighboring Arab states had massed troops. In what becomes known as the Six-Day War, Israel wins a decisive victory and takes control of the Gaza Strip, Sinai Peninsula, West Bank, East Jerusalem, and the Golan Heights.

1968   A brief period of political liberalization and increased freedom for citizens of Czechoslovakia begins on January 5. The Prague Spring reforms are halted when the Soviets send troops to occupy the country.

1968   On March 16 U.S. Army soldiers kill between 300 and 500 unarmed civilians in the hamlet of My Lai in South Vietnam. The My Lai Massacre prompts global outrage and serves as a rallying point for opposition to the war in Vietnam.

1968   The Nuclear Non-Proliferation Treaty (NPT) attempts to prevent the spread of nuclear weapons technology and forms the basis for international monitoring and inspections conducted by the United Nations International Atomic Energy Agency.

1971   The Indo-Pakistani War results in the secession of East Pakistan and the creation of the independent nation of Bangladesh.

1971 Idi Amin's brutal and erratic eight-year reign as president of Uganda begins.

1972 Leaders of the United States and Soviet Union sign the strategic arms limitation treaty (SALT I) on May 26.

1972 During the Olympic Games in Munich, Germany, members of the Palestinian terrorist group Black September kill two Israeli Olympic athletes and take nine more hostage. During a failed rescue attempt, the terrorists kill all nine hostages.

1972 U.S. president Richard M. Nixon makes a historic visit to China, helping China become an accepted member of the global community.

1972 One of the first and most significant international environmental treaties, the Stockholm Declaration, is issued from a United Nations conference.

1973 On January 27 the United States and Vietnamese Communist forces sign a peace agreement ending U.S. involvement in the Vietnam War. American troops are withdrawn from the country without achieving a clear victory.

1973 General Augusto Pinochet assumes leadership of Chile in a military coup. During his 17-year rule, he suppresses dissent and imprisons or tortures thousands of Chileans.

1973 Arab members of OPEC place an embargo on oil exports to the United States, partly in response to U.S. support of Israel. The embargo causes the cost of oil and petroleum-based products such as gasoline to triple almost overnight.

1974 One of the deadliest attacks of the decades-long Troubles in Northern Ireland occurs on November 21, when the Irish Republican Army (IRA) bombs two London pubs, killing 21 people and injuring almost 200.

1975 The Vietnam War ends in a communist victory when North Vietnamese Army forces capture the South Vietnamese capital of Saigon.

1975 The Khmer Rouge takes over Cambodia. Approximately 2 million Cambodians will die under the brutal rule of dictator Pol Pot.

1976 A series of protests and riots known as the Soweto Uprising brings inequality in South Africa to international attention. At least 176 people are killed, including many children, during clashes between demonstrators and police.

1976 Argentina's infamous "Dirty War" begins when President Isabel Perón is deposed on March 23. The military junta that takes over the government initiates a brutal crackdown against suspected political opponents, and more than 30,000 people are killed or simply disappear over the next seven years.

1978 The Camp David Accords forge a historic peace treaty between Israel and Egypt. Israeli Prime Minister Menachem Begin and Egypt's President Anwar Sadat share the Nobel Peace Prize for achieving this breakthrough.

1979 The Iranian Revolution culminates in the overthrow of a pro-Western, liberal monarchy led by Shah Mohammad Reza Pahlavi. Ayatollah Ruhollah Khomeini assumes control of Iran and institutes a conservative Shia theocracy.

1979 On November 4 supporters of Ayatollah Ruhollah Khomeini storm the American embassy in Iran and take 66 Americans hostage. Though 14 are later allowed to leave, 52 remain in captivity for 444 days before being released.

1979 A Marxist revolution led by Sandinista rebels overthrows the U.S.-backed government in Nicaragua.

1979 The Soviet Union invades Afghanistan in December in an effort to crush radical Islamist opposition to the pro-Soviet government.

1980 Polish labor leader Lech Walesa initiates worker strikes at shipyards in Gdansk on April 30. The strikes quickly spread across the country to form the Solidarity Movement.

1980 Seeking to take advantage of post-revolutionary chaos in Iran, Iraqi President Saddam Hussein launches a military invasion on September 22. This action marks the beginning of the eight-year Iran-Iraq War.

1980 Archbishop Oscar Romero of El Salvador is assassinated on March 24. As a proponent of liberation theology, a Roman Catholic movement aimed at helping the poor and addressing inequality, Romero had campaigned against human rights abuses by the Salvadoran government and military.

1981   Egypt's President Anwar Sadat is assassinated after he negotiates a peace treaty with Israel in 1979. He is succeeded by Hosni Mubarak, who leads the country until he is deposed by the Egyptian Revolution in 2011.

1982   When Argentina invades the Falkland Islands, Great Britain launches a military response. The Falklands War only lasts two months before Argentine forces surrender and the archipelago returns to British control.

1983   A bloody coup in the Caribbean island nation of Grenada prompts a controversial U.S. invasion. Within a matter of weeks, American forces prevail and restore Grenada's constitutional government.

1985   Soviet leader Mikhail Gorbachev introduces new policies called *glasnost* and *perestroika,* which allow greater freedoms for the people of the Soviet Union.

1986   U.S. President Ronald Reagan and members of his administration are implicated in a political scandal dubbed the Iran-Contra affair. The complicated arrangement involves sending weapons to Iran in exchange for the release of American hostages held in Lebanon, and using proceeds from the weapon sales to support Contra rebels in Nicaragua.

1986   The Lord's Resistance Army (LRA), led by warlord Joseph Kony, launches its 25-year reign of terror in northern Uganda. One of the tactics employed by the LRA is the abduction of between 60,000 and 100,000 children, with girls forced into service as sex slaves and boys initiated as soldiers.

1987   The Montreal Protocol on Substances that Deplete the Ozone Layer calls upon UN member nations to completely phase out chlorofluorocarbons (CFCs) and other ozone-depleting substances by 2010.

1988   A military junta takes control of Burma and changes the nation's name to the Union of Myanmar.

1988   After eight years of war and terrible damage done to both sides, Iran and Iraq accept a cease-fire agreement on August 20.

1988   Saddam Hussein's regime carries out the Anfal campaign against the Kurdish population of northern Iraq. During this genocidal campaign, the Iraqi military uses chemical weapons on Kurdish civilians.

1988   The U.S. Navy shoots down Iranian Air Flight 655 over the Strait of Hormuz, killing all 290 passengers aboard, after incorrectly identifying the aircraft as an F-14 Tomcat fighter.

1988   Pan Am Flight 103 is destroyed by a terrorist bomb over Lockerbie, Scotland, on December 21. Libyan nationals with ties to Libyan leader Muammar al-Qadhafi are later charged with the crime.

1988   The Belfast Agreement, or Good Friday Agreement, provides the framework for a power-sharing government in Northern Ireland and ends the period of violent conflict known as The Troubles.

1989   After a brutal and costly decade-long entanglement, the Soviet Army withdraws from Afghanistan in defeat, allowing Islamist extremists and Afghan warlords to take control of the country.

1989   The fall of the Berlin Wall, a potent symbol of Cold War tensions, allows unrestricted travel between East and West Germany for the first time in almost 30 years.

1989   Student-led demonstrations in Beijing's Tiananmen Square receive widespread popular support until they are brutally repressed by the Chinese military and hundreds or perhaps thousands of unarmed civilians are killed.

1989   The Atlacatl Battalion, a Salvadoran Army unit trained at the U.S. Army's School of the Americas, massacres six Jesuit priests who had promoted social justice and service to the poor.

1989   Islamic extremist Ayatollah Khomeini of Iran issues a fatwa (religious decree) against British-Indian author Salman Rushdie, demanding that he be executed for blasphemy over content in his novel *The Satanic Verses.*

1989   On June 4, the once-banned Solidarity Movement wins control of the Polish government in national elections.

1990   South African anti-apartheid activist Nelson Mandela gains his freedom after being held as a political prisoner since 1964.

1990   On October 3 West and East Germany are formally reunited as the Federal Republic of Germany.

1991   The once-powerful Soviet Union dissolves into 12 independent republics, officially bringing the Cold War to an end.

1991   Taiwan renounces its claims to the Chinese mainland and asks the international community to recognize it as an independent nation. Chinese leaders make it clear that any nation that recognizes Taiwanese independence will lose all international relationships with mainland China.

1991   A U.S.-led coalition achieves a quick victory in the Persian Gulf War, forcing Iraq to end its occupation of neighboring Kuwait.

1991   Kurdistan becomes an autonomous state within Iraq with its own local government and parliament. Iraq's Kurdish population later supports the U.S.-led invasion of Iraq that overthrows President Saddam Hussein in 2003.

1991   Civil war breaks out in Sierra Leone. Over the next decade, a series of military and civilian governments, assisted by British and UN forces, fight a rebel group called the Revolutionary United Front (RUF). The bloody conflict claims the lives of more than 50,000 people.

1992   The Chapultepec Peace Accords bring an end to civil war in El Salvador. The 12-year conflict takes 75,000 lives, many of them civilians.

1992   The UN Conference on Sustainable Development, popularly known as the Earth Summit, is held in Rio de Janeiro in June. It produces major environmental treaties on biological diversity, climate change, and desertification.

1993   The European Union (EU) is founded to link Western European nations together economically. It gradually grows to include most of Eastern Europe.

1993   Radical Islamic terrorists detonate a truck bomb beneath the World Trade Center in New York City, killing six people and injuring more than 1,000.

1993   Following the death of longtime head of state Fèlix Houphouët-Boigny, Côte d'Ivoire's political situation becomes extremely unstable, with coups and fighting between various rebel groups throughout the country.

1993   South African leaders F. W. de Klerk and Nelson Mandela are jointly awarded the Nobel Peace Prize for their work to end apartheid.

1994   Anti-apartheid activist Nelson Mandela becomes president of South Africa.

1994   The Rwandan Genocide begins on April 6. Over the next three months, approximately 500,000 members of the ethnic Tutsi group are killed by members of the ethnic Hutu group.

1994   The North American Free Trade Agreement (NAFTA) creates a single free trade zone between Canada, the United States, and Mexico.

1994   Palestine Liberation Organization (PLO) leader Yasser Arafat and Israeli Foreign Minister Shimon Peres and Prime Minister Yitzhak Rabin share the Nobel Peace Prize for their roles in forging the Oslo Accords, which provide a framework for creating a Palestinian state.

1995   On March 20 members of Aum Shinrikyo, a Japanese religious cult, release sarin gas in five coordinated attacks in the Tokyo subway system. Thirteen people die and hundreds are injured.

1995   Timothy McVeigh and Terry Nichols, both U.S. citizens and anti-government activists, detonate a truck bomb at the Alfred P. Murrah Federal Building in Oklahoma City, Oklahoma, on April 19. The domestic terrorist act kills 168 people, including 19 children.

1995   To begin the healing process in post-apartheid South Africa, the Promotion of National Unity and Reconciliation Act establishes a Truth and Reconciliation Commission to investigate violations of human rights and allow both victims and perpetrators to testify.

1995   The North Atlantic Treaty Organization (NATO) responds to ethnic violence in the former Yugoslavia by initiating a bombing campaign in Bosnia and Herzegovina.

1995   Twenty years after the end of the Vietnam War, Vietnam and the United States reestablish normal diplomatic relations.

1996   Guatemala's 36-year civil war ends. The conflict claims the lives of 100,000 people and displaces more than a million others.

1996   On August 23, al-Qaeda leader Osama bin Laden issues a fatwa (official order from an Islamic leader) calling for jihad (holy war) against the United States in response to the presence of U.S. troops in Saudi Arabia.

1996   The Taliban takes control of Afghanistan. They rule according to a strict interpretation of Islamic law that is enforced through intimidation and violence.

1996   The eight nations with territory in the Arctic, along with indigenous people of the region, form the Arctic Council to serve as a forum for promoting cooperation on issues of concern, such as sustainable development and environmental protection.

1997   The Kyoto Protocol to the United Nations Framework Convention on Climate Change attempts to limit the effects of global climate change by calling on nations to reduce the amount of carbon dioxide and other greenhouse gases they emit.

1997   A British nonprofit organization publishes *Islamophobia: A Challenge for Us All*. The book warns of growing discrimination against Muslims and popularizes the term "Islamophobia."

1997   The Chemical Weapons Convention (CWC), a treaty banning the use, production, acquisition, and stockpiling of chemical agents for use in warfare, becomes international law.

1998   The signatories of the Antarctic Treaty enact the Protocol on Environmental Protection to the Antarctic Treaty, also known as the Madrid Protocol, to ban resource exploitation and require strict environmental assessments and emergency preparedness for all activities on the continent.

1998   Hostile neighbors India and Pakistan both conduct nuclear weapons tests, demonstrating to the world that they possess nuclear capability.

1998   Terrorist bombings strike the U.S. embassies in Kenya and Tanzania on August 7 and bring Osama bin Laden and his al-Qaeda organization to public attention.

1999   Responding to widespread ethnic violence in the former Yugoslavia, NATO launches major combat operations in Serbia on March 24.

1999   On April 1 Canada establishes a new territory called Nunavut as a home for the indigenous Inuit people.

2000   Responding to a public outcry about "blood diamonds" financing civil wars in African, the world's largest diamond enterprise, De Beers of South Africa, offers guarantees that none of its diamonds will come from war zones.

2000   Al-Qaeda terrorists attack the American Navy destroyer U.S.S. *Cole* in Yemen.

2001   On September 11 members of the radical Islamic terrorist group al-Qaeda hijack passenger airliners and intentionally crash them into the World Trade Center towers in New York City and the Pentagon in Washington, D.C. The 9/11 attacks claim nearly 3,000 lives.

2001   In response to the 9/11 attacks, Congress passes the U.S.A. Patriot Act. The controversial act gives law enforcement personnel greatly expanded power to search and monitor personal information and communications with the aim of preventing terrorism.

2001   The United States and NATO invade Afghanistan on October 7, after the Taliban government refuses to hand over Osama bin Laden and expel the rest of the al-Qaeda terrorist network.

2001   The International Criminal Court (ICC) is established to secure justice for perpetrators of the most serious international crimes, including genocide, crimes against humanity, war crimes, and crimes of aggression.

2002   In his State of the Union address on January 29, U.S. President George W. Bush announces his intention to respond to the 9/11 attacks by fighting a "war on terror." He describes North Korea, Iran, and Iraq as an "axis of evil" and claims that these nations threaten world security by developing weapons of mass destruction and aiding terrorist groups.

2002   The U.S. Department of Homeland Security (DHS) is established to help protect the nation from domestic threats, especially terrorism.

2002   The United States begins the controversial practice of detaining suspected terrorists at Guantànamo Bay Naval Base in Cuba.

2002   The U.S. government argues that the Geneva Conventions do not apply to terrorists because they are not soldiers representing a nation. This argument is used to justify the alleged torture and other inhumane treatment of suspected terrorists in the interest of national security.

2002   The euro replaces national currencies in 11 European Union member states.

2002   The African Union (AU) is founded to find solutions to many of the major problems facing modern Africa. The AU eventually grows to include 54 participating members (all of the African continent except Morocco), though some members have been suspended.

2002   Fuerzas Armadas Revolucionarias de Colombia (Revolutionary Armed Forces of Colombia, or FARC) rebels kidnap presidential candidate Ingrid Betancourt. She is held captive for six years before Colombian soldiers posing as humanitarian aid workers secure her release.

2003   The government of Sudan arms Janjaweed militias to crush a rebellion and mount a campaign of ethnic cleansing against non-Arabs in Darfur, resulting in the deaths of tens of thousands of civilians.

2003   A U.S.-led coalition invades Iraq and overthrows its leader, Saddam Hussein. The Iraq War and the lengthy U.S. occupation that follows fail to create a stable, democratic Iraq.

2003   The largely nonviolent "Colour Revolution" takes place in Georgia, Ukraine, Kyrgyzstan, and other countries in the former Soviet Union and the Balkans, as well as the Philippines.

2004   The Bolivarian Alliance for the Americas (Alianza Bolivariana para los Pueblos de Nuestra America or ALBA) is established to foster social, political, and economic cooperation between Latin American countries and Caribbean island nations based on socialist principles.

2004   The single largest expansion of the European Union occurs with the addition of 10 countries (including eight from the former Soviet bloc) on May 1.

2004   The United Nations Security Council provides an official definition of terrorism in Resolution 1566.

2006   North Korea conducts its first nuclear test in defiance of international attempts to curtail its nuclear capabilities.

2006   Ellen Johnson Sirleaf is elected president of Liberia. The Nobel laureate becomes the first female head of state in Africa.

2006   Mexican President Felipe Calderón launches a crackdown on drug cartels and their trade. The resulting drug war in Mexico leaves more than 60,000 people dead and threatens to destabilize the country.

2006   On September 8, the UN adopts a Global Counter-Terrorism Strategy that focuses on addressing the social, political, and economic conditions that are conducive to the spread of terrorism.

2007   A disputed election sparks violence between rival ethnic groups in Kenya. More than 1,000 people are killed and hundreds of thousands displaced.

2007   A new, more peaceful era in Irish history begins on May 8, when Protestant leader Ian Paisley becomes first minister of Ireland and Catholic leader Martin McGuinness becomes deputy first minister of Northern Ireland.

2007   Experts link global climate change to persistent droughts, corresponding shortages of food and water, and violent conflicts over these resources in the African nations of Darfur, Somalia, Côte d'Ivoire, and Burkina Faso.

2007   The Aral Sea, once the world's fourth-largest lake, shrinks to 10 percent of its original size due to pollution and misuse. The loss of this Eastern European natural resource is regarded as one of the world's worst ecological disasters.

2008   On February 13, Australian Prime Minister Kevin Rudd offers a national apology to the Stolen Generations, a group of roughly 100,000 Aboriginal children who were forcibly removed from their homes between 1910 and 1970 and placed with white families in a government-sponsored effort to assimilate them.

2008   Kosovo declares its independence from Serbia on February 17. The European Union and the United States support Kosovo's secession, but Serbia and Russia strongly oppose it.

2008	Russian troops invade Georgia in August, purportedly to support South Ossetia in its effort to break away from Georgia.
2008	Kuomintang Party candidate Ma Ying-jeou is elected president of Taiwan after campaigning to improve relations with China.
2008	Pro-Tibet protesters repeatedly disrupt the ceremonial global tour of the Olympic Torch on its way to the Summer Games in Beijing, China.
2009	The Bolivarian Alliance for the Peoples of Our America (ALBA) approves the creation of its own currency, the SUCRE, to replace the American dollar in regional trade among nations in Latin America and the Caribbean.
2009	U.S. President Barack Obama pledges support to the Mexican government to help combat drug trafficking.
2009	In September, record melting of polar sea ice allows two German merchant ships to become the first in modern history to travel across the Arctic Ocean through the Northeast Passage.
2009	The Sri Lankan Civil War comes to an end after 26 years of fighting between ethnic Tamil separatists, known as the Tamil Tigers, and the military forces of Sri Lanka. The United Nations estimates that between 80,000 and 100,000 people died in the conflict.
2010	A UN-backed tribunal indicts four former members of the Khmer Rouge for genocide, crimes against humanity, and war crimes in connection with the deaths of up to two million people in Cambodia between 1975 and 1979.
2010	Following the self-immolation of a Tunisian street vendor, the Arab world erupts in protests demanding greater freedom and democracy. Several longstanding dictators are overthrown during what becomes known in the Western media as the Arab Spring.
2010	President Barack Obama orders a surge of 30,000 additional American troops to Afghanistan in an attempt to stabilize the Afghan government and facilitate an eventual U.S. withdrawal.
2010	Sebastián Piñera, a Harvard-educated, free-market-friendly, billionaire economist, is elected president of Chile. He takes office on March 11, less than two weeks after a massive earthquake devastates parts of the country.
2010	An explosion on the *Deepwater Horizon* oil rig kills 11 workers and spills 5 million barrels of oil into the Gulf of Mexico, destroying marine ecosystems and devastating fishing and tourism industries.
2010	France, which is home to the largest Muslim population in Western Europe, enacts a law making it illegal for Muslim women to wear the full-face coverings called burqas in public.
2011	Arab Spring protests force Egyptian President Hosni Mubarak to step down on February 11, ending his 30-year rule.
2011	On March 30, the military junta that has ruled Burma for more than 20 years hands over power to an elected civilian government led by President Thein Sein.
2011	On May 2 U.S. Navy SEALs storm a fortified compound in remote Abbottabad, Pakistan, and kill Osama bin Laden. The head of the al-Qaeda terrorist organization had been sought by the United States and its allies since the 9/11 attacks.
2011	The Syrian Civil War begins in July, as rebel forces fight to overthrow Syrian President Bashar al-Assad. More than one million refugees flee to neighboring countries over the next three years.
2011	In August, the U.S. Department of Defense announces that a CIA-operated drone strike has killed a top-ranking al-Qaeda leader, Atiyah Abd al-Rahman, in a mountainous region of Pakistan.
2011	Rebel forces supported by Western powers kill Libyan dictator Muammar al-Qadhafi in the city of Sirte on October 20. The rebels secure control of Libya and hold free elections the following year.
2011	U.S. Secretary of Defense Leon Panetta declares the mission in Iraq officially over, and the last American soldiers leave Iraq on December 18.
2011	An all-time high of 308 humanitarian aid workers are killed, kidnapped, or injured around the world. A majority of these violent events take place in Sudan, Afghanistan, Pakistan, and Somalia.

2011   A U.S.-flagged container ship, the *Maersk Alabama,* comes under attack by Somali pirates along the dangerous 1,880-mile (3,000-kilometer) coast of Somalia. The ship's captain, Richard Phillips, is rescued by U.S. Navy SEALS after being taken hostage.

2011   Mexican President Felipe Calderón requests assistance from the United Nations General Assembly in Mexico's increasingly desperate fight against powerful drug cartels.

2011   Following a referendum that won approval from nearly 99 percent of voters, South Sudan formally separates from Sudan and becomes an independent nation.

2012   Over the strong objections of the United States, the United Nations General Assembly tacitly acknowledges Palestinian statehood by voting overwhelmingly to grant Palestine "Observer Nation" status.

2012   In May, the nation of East Timor concludes a long and brutal war for autonomy from Indonesia and makes a peaceful transition of power to an elected government.

2012   On September 11, the terrorist organization Ansar al-Sharia attacks the U.S. diplomatic mission in Benghazi, Libya, killing four American diplomats, including U.S. Ambassador to Libya J. Christopher Stevens.

2012   On November 24, the Basque separatist group ETA announces that it will permanently disband and enter negotiations with France and Spain.

2012   The Arctic polar ice cap reaches its lowest level since records have been kept.

2013   A domestic terrorism incident occurs in the United States on April 15, when two homemade bombs explode at the Boston Marathon, killing 3 people and wounding at least 180 others.

2013   A new skyscraper, called One World Trade Center, is completed in May on the site of the twin towers that were destroyed in the 9/11 attacks.

2013   A military coup in July removes the increasingly religiously extremist, but democratically elected, president of Egypt, Mohamed Morsi.

2013   On August 21 Syrian military supporters of embattled president Bashar al-Assad allegedly use sarin gas to kill hundreds of people around Damascus.

2013   Responding to reports that the Syrian military used nerve gas, the United States declares its intention to supply direct, lethal military aid to Syrian rebels.

2013   The Islamist group al-Shabab attacks the upscale Westgate Shopping Mall in Nairobi, Kenya, taking hostages and killing more than 60 civilians.

2013   The humanitarian relief organization Doctors Without Borders/Médecins Sans Frontières announces in August that it will close down its operations in Somalia because the country has become too dangerous.

2013   U.S. Army private Bradley Manning is convicted on 17 charges, including aiding the enemy, for his role in a massive leak of confidential military and diplomatic records related to the wars in Iraq and Afghanistan.

2013   Edward Snowden, an American computer analyst who had worked for the National Security Agency, leaks information about covert intelligence programs to a British newspaper.

2013   Argentine Cardinal Jorge Mario Bergoglio becomes Pope Francis. His elevation to the papacy brings renewed attention to the role of the Catholic clergy during Argentina's "Dirty War."

2013   North Korean leaders declare the 1953 armistice agreement that ended the Korean War invalid and claim that a state of war exists with South Korea.

2014   The United Nations Commission on Human Rights in North Korea releases a report accusing North Korea of crimes against humanity and recommends prosecution of the country's top leaders by the International Criminal Court (ICC).

Japanese Invasion of China

🌐 Introduction

On September 18, 1931, a bomb went off in Mudken, China, near the South Manchurian Railroad, owned by Japan. The bomb caused only minor damage, but the Japanese used the attack to justify invading China. The Japanese began bombing a nearby Chinese garrison, and very quickly had occupied Mudken. This was the beginning of Japan's occupation of three northeastern provinces of China called Manchuria, and it set the stage for a full-scale war with China in 1937. But the bomb that started the war was not planted by the Chinese. It is believed that several Japanese military officers plotted together to stage the bombing as a prelude to war with China.

Japan, once a highly isolated nation with little contact with the outside world, had undergone a period of rapid industrialization and modernization beginning in 1868, when the country came under the rule of the Meiji emperor. There were emperors of Japan before that time, but they were only figureheads—the real power resided with military governors called shoguns. The Tokugawa Shogunate had existed from 1600 to 1867.

One of the pivotal events that led to the downfall of the shogunate was the appearance of U.S. naval officer Commodore Matthew Perry (1794–1858), who arrived off the coast of Japan with a fleet of warships in 1854 and, through threat of force, opened the nation to international trade. The massive ships and superior weaponry of the U.S. fleet awed the Japanese and damaged the credibility of the shoguns.

Under the Meiji emperors, Japan was transformed and radically militarized. All men were required to serve in the Japanese military for four years upon reaching age 21. Old class systems were abolished. Factories and shipyards were built, infrastructure was improved, and the Japanese eagerly sought out Western technology.

Hand in hand with this rapid modernization and militarization was a surge in nationalism. The positive aspects of nationalism include patriotism and a sense of national unity. The negative aspects include feelings of superiority and antipathy over other cultures, feelings that sometimes led to war.

🌐 Historical Background

Japan and China, the two major powers in East Asia, have a long history of conflict. In 1894 and 1895, Japan tested its new military might in the First Sino-Japanese War, largely over which of the two countries, China or Japan, would control Korea. The Japanese won, humiliating China. In 1904 and 1905, Japan defeated Russia in the Russo-Japanese War, gaining control of the South Manchurian Railroad. In 1910, Japan annexed Korea. Japan's expansion was part of a policy of invading neighboring countries in order to provide a buffer of protection for Japan. The three Chinese provinces of Manchuria provided this buffer, but were also attractive since they were rumored to contain bountiful natural resources. By this time, the Japanese had developed great confidence in their military strength.

By 1930, Japan, along with the rest of the world, was facing a depression. The Great Depression, which devastated the world's economy leaving millions destitute, began with the U.S. stock market crash of 1929 and continued until the early-1940s. At the same time, Japan's population was growing, and its nation, on a series of islands in the Pacific Ocean, had limited space and resources. The Japanese wanted more space to support their growing population. In 1930, Japan had about 64.4 million people.

However, China had a population of almost half a billion people, and a huge expanse of land. China was much less developed than Japan, but had a rich—and long—history. The Japanese were also proud of their nation and ethnicity, so much so that many believed that

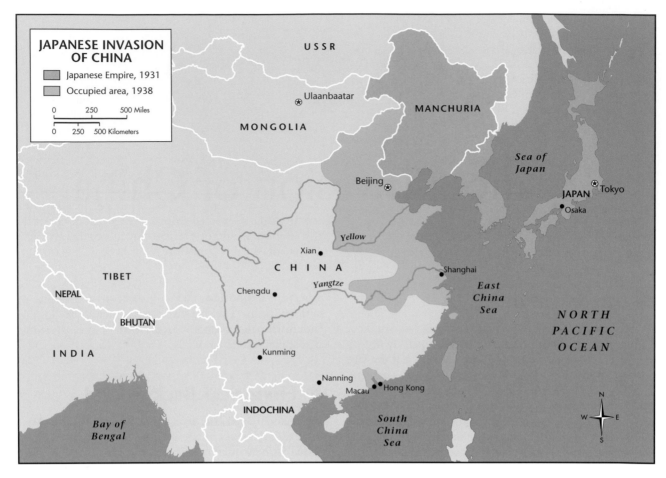

JAPANESE INVASION
OF CHINA

▨ Japanese Empire, 1931

▨ Occupied area, 1938

0   250   500 Miles

0   250   500 Kilometers

all other ethnicities were inferior to the Japanese. This led to disdain for the Chinese, and it enabled the brutality that took place during the Second Sino-Japanese War.

China's Civil War

In 1931 China was led by Chiang Kai-Shek (1887–1975), a nationalist who was fighting a war to remove the emerging Communists from China. Earlier, when the Qing Dynasty collapsed in 1911, China fell under the control of several regional warlords, who battled for territory. In an effort to reunify the country, Sun Yat-sen (1866–1925) fought the warlords and occasionally made common cause with the emerging Communist Party of China (CPC), also known as the Chinese Communist Party (CCP). Following reunification, the nationalists (Kuomintang) and the CCP vied for control of China. The Chinese Civil War was fought from 1927 to 1950, but the two sides temporarily came together in 1937 to fight the Japanese.

The Chinese Civil War required significant resources, and Chiang had a goal of first unifying the country by pacifying the Communists before engaging with Japan. Although the escalation of the war with Japan eventually led Chiang to ally the nationalists with the Communists, he initially did not expend many

resources to protect China, making Manchuria an easy target for the Japanese.

Mudken Incident

The Japanese wanted to dominate China, but government officials in Tokyo did not want Japan to appear to be the aggressor. Government officials appeared willing to wait for the inevitable conflict, but the troops on the ground were not. The Kwantung Army, an elite group within the Imperial Japanese Army, was ready for action, even if it meant sabotage. The Mudken Incident was not the army's first attempt to incite war.

The Kwantung Army had allied itself with Zhang Zuolin (1875–1928), a warlord the army had helped put in power. After becoming disillusioned with Zhang in 1928, the Kwantung Army blew up his train. The hope was that the bombing would spark anti-Japanese protests, and give the Japanese an excuse to invade. However, there were no protests, and, therefore, no pretense for invasion.

In 1931 they tried again. The Kwantung Army prepared bombs that would appear to be directed at Japan's South Manchurian Railroad, while fortifying its positions from which to strike back at the Chinese. The government in Tokyo attempted to stop the plot, sending a messenger with a note telling the Kwantung to stand down, but someone sympathetic to the Kwantung informed the army that orders to stand-down were coming. Before the army could receive the official orders, military personnel detonated the bombs, creating a pretense to launch their attack. The army then "struck back" at the Chinese.

Invasion

Japan invaded Manchuria, pretending to protect itself from attacks while downplaying its interest in keeping the captured territory. China, meanwhile, appealed to the League of Nations, the new international body that was a precursor to the United Nations. Initially, the League of Nations did nothing. When the league finally voted against Japan's invasion, with Japan casting the only dissenting vote, Japan resigned from the United Nations.

The league commissioned an investigation into the Mudken Incident. The report, issued in December 1931, was named the Lytton Report, after the chair of the investigating committee, V.A.G.R. Bulwer-Lytton (1876–1947), the 2nd Earl of Lytton, in the United Kingdom. The Lytton Report concluded that Japan had instigated the war by staging the bombing.

Japan sought to control Manchuria, and did so brutally. Observers reported that the Japanese routinely bombed civilian locations and fired on fleeing survivors. Once the Kwangtun Army had secured Manchuria and the occupation was completed, the government in Tokyo supported the new country, now separated from China. Manchuria officially became a Japanese puppet state.

Occupation

The region of Manchuria, which takes its name from the indigenous people, the Manchus, was renamed Manchukuo. The Japanese installed Pu Yi (1906–1967) as the ruler. As a child, Pu Yi had been emperor of China—in fact the last emperor of China—until his abdication in 1912, when he was six years old. While Pu Yi had some symbolic significance for some Chinese, he served at the pleasure of the Japanese. Reportedly, Pu Yi frequently challenged the Japanese in private, but in public he was submissive.

Japan claimed to have no designs on other Chinese territory, but it continued to battle the Kuomintang, making and breaking truces, and slowly increasing its territory in China. In 1933 the Japanese signed the Tanggu Truce, stopping their advance just short of China's Great Wall, a more than 5,500-mile (8,850-kilometer) fortification created over centuries starting as early as 700 BC. Strategically well positioned in 1935, Japan suggested that China officially recognize Manchukuo and join with them to fight communism. Despite the Kuomintang's fervor to defeat communism, the group declined Japan's offer. However, Chiang remained completely focused on defeating the Communists, rather than repelling the invaders.

Alliance with the CCP

Others did not share Chiang's single-minded focus on defeating the CCP, and viewed Japan as a greater—and more immediate—threat. In 1936, Chiang was abducted by a group of his military officers, who demanded that he fight the Japanese instead of the Chinese Communists. They called on Chiang to ally himself with the CCP to protect China. Chiang conceded, and the Chinese nationalists and Communists formed a united front against the Japanese.

On July 7, 1937, shots were exchanged between the Japanese and the Chinese at the Marco Polo Bridge southwest of Beijing. The Kwantung Army, concerned that its garrison might be overrun, sent in reinforcements. Chiang ordered troops to the region, declaring the Chinese would not retreat. Japan decided to teach China a lesson and ordered a major assault, quickly capturing Beijing and the surrounding area.

Japan hoped that China would concede defeat quickly, but China opened another front. Japan's army was much better equipped, but the Chinese had many more troops. The battle raged for months, with Nanjing (also spelled Nanking) finally falling to the Japanese in December 1937. Although Japan had occupied Manchuria since 1931 and fought numerous battles with the Kuomintang, the Marco Polo Bridge Incident is considered the event that kicked off what is called the Second Sino-Japanese War (1937–45)—and the complete invasion of mainland China.

The Rape of Nanjing

The Japanese set their sights on the capital of China, Nanjing. Chiang realized he could not hope to win at Nanjing and withdrew most of his troops, leaving the city's residents

---

FOREIGNERS IN OCCUPIED CHINA

Although China has the reputation for being closed to foreigners, before the Communists won the civil war, there were fairly extensive communities of foreigners living in China. Some of the foreigners were missionaries, sent to convert the Chinese to Christianity. Others were businesspeople and diplomats.

Most foreigners lived in compounds with others of the same nationality, separated from the Chinese. However, there was considerable interaction between the Chinese and the foreigners, including some that was considered scandalous.

One scandal that shook the city of Beijing as it awaited the invasion of the Japanese was the murder of a 17-year-old English schoolgirl named Pamela Werner. She was living with her father, a scholar and former British diplomat, in Beijing (then called Peking) when she was murdered and horribly mutilated. Her body was found the morning after she left home on her bicycle to go ice skating.

The murder, the cover-up, and the botched investigation shook the confidence of foreigners in China, who had felt protected from the expected brutality of the coming Japanese invasion.

Japanese infantry and cavalry troops march through the triple arched chungsun gate that leads to Nanjing (Nanking), capital of China. The capture of the city was one of the principal objectives of the invading Japanese forces following the fall of Shanghai. *© Bettmann/ Corbis/AP Images*

inadequately defended. The Japanese captured Nanjing on December 13, 1937. The invasion of Nanjing was notorious for the level of violence and brutality committed by the Japanese. During the six weeks following Nanjing's fall to Japan, the Japanese military killed several hundred thousand civilians and unarmed soldiers. Japanese newspapers described a contest between two Japanese officers to see who would be the first to kill 100 people with a sword. When they both surpassed the goal, they upped the target to 150.

In addition to the brutal killings and torture, an estimated 20,000 women were raped, many repeatedly. Infants and senior citizens were raped. Pregnant women were raped and then killed with a bayonet through the stomach. The rapes were an organized effort, with soldiers searching door-to-door for females.

The level of cruelty was astounding. At what is called the Straw String Gorge Massacre on December 18, 1937, the Japanese killed 57,000 former soldiers at one time, dumping most of them in the Yangtze River.

The Rape of Nanjing, also called the Nanjing Massacre, remains a contentious issue between the Chinese and the Japanese. Some Japanese officials claim the reports of violence were exaggerated, although official Japanese records have been destroyed. Although many Japanese nationalists continue to deny the massacre happened, in 1995 the Japanese prime minister and the emperor both offered apologies and condolences.

Blockade and Stalemate

For the next several years, Japan made hard-fought gains into China, and it sought to force China's surrender. China refused to surrender, although its territory was dwindling. China, though under-equipped, had many more soldiers, and so fought a war of attrition, making each foot Japan gained costly in terms of the number of people lost.

Japan attempted to further isolate nationalist-controlled China by instituting a blockade preventing any goods from reaching the area. However, the events

Chinese prisoners being buried alive by their Japanese captors outside the city of Nanjing (Nanking), during the infamous Rape of Nanjing. © *Bettmann/Corbis/AP Images*

leading to World War II (1939–45) had begun, and the sides that would fight the war started taking shape. Japan signed the Tripartite Agreement in 1936, allying itself with Germany and Italy. The group of nations that would align to become the Allies (including the United Kingdom and the United States) in the war—those concerned primarily with stopping German aggression in Europe—now had an incentive to help Japan's enemies. The United Kingdom and the United States worked to open routes and deliver supplies to the Chinese.

The next several years were largely a stalemate in the Second Sino-Japanese War. On December 7, 1941, a confident Japan launched a surprise attack on the U.S. naval base at Pearl Harbor, Hawaii, killing some 2,400 Americans. Until that time, the United States had refrained from joining World War II. A day after the attack, however, the country officially entered the war. Fighting U.S. troops in the Pacific ultimately forced the Japanese to divert attention away from China.

Following the German surrender in May 1945, Japan was defeated by the Allies and officially surrendered in September of that year. The terms of Japan's surrender were such that it ceded all captured territory, including the provinces of Manchuria captured in 1931. It was also forced to dismantle its military. After Japan's defeat by the Allies, the Soviet Union occupied parts of Manchuria, which were not returned to China until after the 1969 Sino-Soviet Border Conflict.

⊕ Impacts and Issues

Japan and China continue to be suspicious of one another and are often hostile. Along with the memory of the invasion itself is an anger at Japan's denial of responsibility for the aggression. The racial distain exhibited during the invasion—and for many years before and since—has exacerbated the distrust between the nations. Despite the post-World

Soong Mei-Ling (1897–2003), wife of Chiang Kai-Shek, the Chinese nationalist leader, looks over the victory headlines after the surrender of Japan in World War II. © *Keystone/Getty Images*

War II dismantling of the Japanese military, China remains wary. Even trade between the two countries—both economic powerhouses—remains anemic.

The Communists emerged greatly strengthened following the Japanese invasion, and the Kuomintang and CCP renewed their civil war from 1946 to 1950. Manchuria served as a base for the Communists, who were victorious. The Communists isolated China for decades following their ascension, committing a host of atrocities against their own people. The Kuomintang retreated to Taiwan, where they established the Republic of China. The People's Republic of China asserts its claim to Taiwan, but Taiwan is, for all practical purposes, autonomous.

⊕ Future Implications

Eighty years after the Mudken Incident, China held ceremonies to commemorate the event that began 14 years of occupation by the Japanese—an event that the Chinese refer to as their time of national humiliation. Many analysts believe that China's foreign policy—that of a very proud and nationalistic people—can be best understood as a response to a series of humiliating defeats, culminating in the brutality inflicted by the Japanese during their invasion.

Rifts in Japan and China's relationship continue to occur on occasion, including the 2012 and 2013

territorial dispute over uninhabited islands in the East China Sea. (The islands are called Diaoyu in China and Senkaku in Japan.) Amid rising tensions, Chinese patrol boats and Japanese ships have reported confrontations in the area. In an effort to strengthen its claim to the islands that are also claimed—and administered—by the Japanese, China created an air defense zone, which was disputed by Japan and its ally, the United States.

SEE ALSO *Chinese Revolution; Korean Conflicts; World War II*

BIBLIOGRAPHY

Books

Tamanoi, Mariko. *Memory Maps: The State and Manchuria in Postwar Japan.* Honolulu: University of Hawaii Press, 2009.

Yamamura, Shin'ichi. *Manchuria Under Japanese Dominion.* Philadelphia, PA: University of Pennsylvania Press, 2006.

Young, Louise. *Japan's Total Empire: Manchuria and the Culture of Wartime Imperialism.* Berkeley: University of California Press, 1999.

Periodicals

Caffrey, Patrick J. "Transforming the Forests of a Counterfeit Nation: Japan's 'Manchu Nation' in Northeast China." *Environmental History* 18, no. 2 (April 2013): 309.

Lone, Stewart. "Japan and Imperialism, 1853–1945." *Asian Studies Review* 36, no. 2 (June 2012): 289-290.

Web Sites

"Nanjing Massacre." *History.com.* http://www.history.com/topics/nanjing-massacre (accessed December 23, 2013).

Ogura, Junko, and Jethro Mullen. "Fresh Anti-Japanese Protests in China on Symbolic Anniversary." *CNN,* September 19, 2013. http://www.cnn.com/2012/09/18/world/asia/china-japan-islands-dispute/index.html (accessed December 22, 2013).

Tisdall, Simon. "China Escalates Islands Dispute with Japan." *The Guardian,* November 24, 2013. http://www.theguardian.com/world/2013/nov/24/us-warns-beijiing-island-dispute-senkanus (accessed December 23, 2013).

Yan, Alice, and Johnny Tam. "10,000 Gather to Recall Victims of Nanjing Massacre: As Tensions Rise Between China and Japan, in the City of Nanjing They Were Grieving for Those Who Died in a Previous Conflict Between the Two." *South China Morning Post,* December 14, 2012. http://www.scmp.com/news/china/article/1104877/10000-gather-recall-victims-nanking-massacre (accessed December 23, 2013).

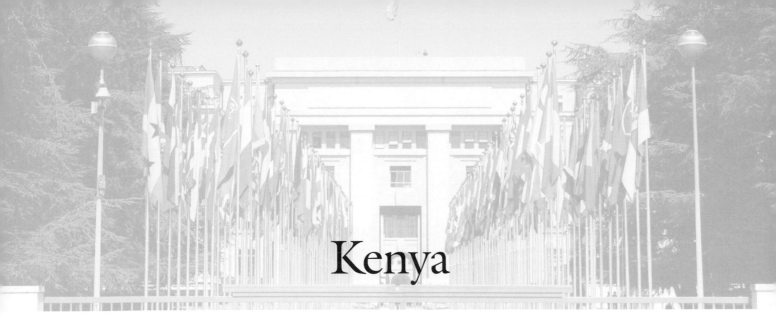

Kenya

⊕ Introduction

In 2007, following a contentious election with an equally contentious outcome, violence erupted in Kenya. People were dragged from their houses and hacked to death with machetes as rival ethnic groups supporting different presidential candidates took up arms and began fighting. More than 1,000 people were killed and hundreds of thousands displaced.

The violence appeared to stem from longstanding disputes over land and political power among Kenya's diverse ethnic peoples. In March 2011, the International Criminal Court (ICC) in The Hague indicted six leaders, including members of the opposing political camps, for orchestrating the post-election rampages. Two years later, two of the six suspects, Uhuru Kenyatta (1961–) and William Ruto (1966–), were elected President and Vice President of Kenya, respectively.

⊕ Historical Background

Situated in eastern Africa, Kenya's southeastern shores border the Indian Ocean. The country is bordered by Tanzania to the southwest, Uganda to the due west, Sudan to the northwest, Ethiopia to the due north, and Somalia to the east.

Kenya is home to roughly 44 million people as of 2013. The African tribal groups that comprise the Kenyan population generally fall into three major cultural and linguistic groups: Bantu, Nilotic, and Cushitic. Around 70 percent of Kenya's population is Bantu, with the Kikuyu tribe making up the largest proportion of this group (around 22 percent). Other prominent tribes include the Luo, Luhya, and Kalenjin.

Independence

Kenya was under the rule of the British Empire from the late 19th century until declaring its independence in 1963. In the 1950s, an anti-colonial uprising led by Kikuyus, known as the Mau Mau rebellion, besieged the country. Jomo Kenyatta (1889–1978), a leader of Kenya's nationalist movement, was jailed for nine years after being convicted on dubious charges of involvement with the Mau Mau insurgency. Kenyatta became the nation's first leader after independence. A Kikuyu who favored capitalism and was educated and lived for 15 years in the West, Kenyatta attempted to unite the diverse nation by including representatives of different political and ethnic groups in his administration. Kenyatta chose as his first Vice President Jaramogi Oginga Odinga (c. 1911–1994), a Luo socialist. Tensions arose within the administration because of their differing views, and Oginga Odinga split off to form his own party. In 1969, Kenyatta's government banned Oginga Odinga's party and formed a one-party system that remained intact until 1992.

Kenyatta died in 1978, and his Vice President, Daniel arap Moi (1924–), became Kenya's second President. Moi, an authoritarian leader, remained in office for 24 years. In 1992, Moi finally allowed multiparty elections, but the first election was plagued with gang violence that left more than 3,000 dead in the Rift Valley. Moi held onto his office until 2002, when he was forced to step down by a constitutional mandate.

In 2002, Mwai Kibaki, a Kikuyu, ran for President against Moi's chosen successor. For his campaign, Kibaki teamed up with Raila Amolo Odinga (1945–), a Luo, and son of Oginga Odinga. According to Raila Odinga, Kibaki also informally agreed to form a power-sharing government. Once he had been elected President, however, Kibaki decided not to share power with Raila Odinga, eventually eliminating Raila Odinga's supporters from his administration.

During Kibaki's administration, Kenya's economy rose from a state of near-collapse to healthy growth. The media became more open, and universal compulsory

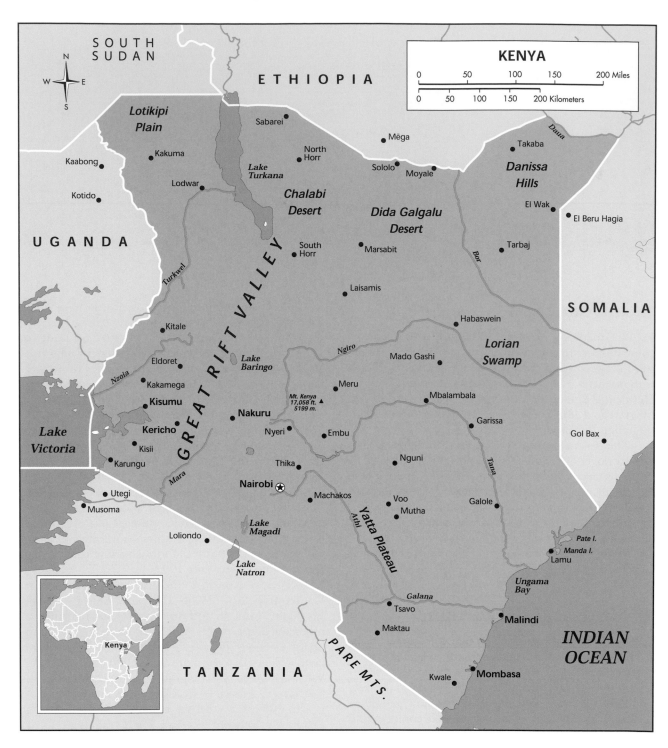

© 2014 Cengage Learning

primary education was established. But Kibaki was criticized by some for failing to fight corruption and poverty. The elite and the middle classes prospered, but even as the economy grew, the majority of Kenyans earned less than $1 a day and were plagued by crime and unemployment. In the campaign for the 2007 election, Raila Odinga gained support as a champion of the poor.

Contested Election

On December 27, 2007, Kenyans lined up to vote in a national election in which incumbent President Kibaki and his Party of National Unity (PNU) faced top contender Raila Odinga and the Orange Democratic Movement (ODM). The previous presidential election in 2002, in which Kibaki had won the presidency from the

Mau Mau terrorist suspects are escorted to cells by Kenyan policemen in Nairobi, Kenya, in 1952.   *© Bert Hardy/Picture Post/Getty Images*

ruling party without violence, had been a milestone in Kenya's history. On December 27, the Western press was already celebrating Kenya's 2007 election as a showcase of African democracy.

After three days of tallying the vote, the Electoral Commission of Kenya announced that the ODM had won the most seats in Parliament, but Kibaki had won the presidential election. Kibaki hastily took the oath of office amid widespread accusations of election-rigging. Raila Odinga denounced Kibaki for stealing the presidency, and suddenly several hotspots in Kenya—the Rift Valley cities of Eldoret and Kisumu, the urban slums

around the capital city of Nairobi, and the coastal city of Mombasa—erupted into violence.

Ethnic Violence

The violence in the Rift Valley quickly evolved into a conflict between ethnic groups. Initially, Odinga supporters attacked members of the Kikuyu ethnic group (presumably supporters of Kibaki, who is Kikuyu) with machetes, iron bars, and bows and arrows. Within days, gangs of young Kikuyu men organized revenge attacks on people of the Luo and Kalenjin ethnic groups, at times dragging people from their homes and hacking them with machetes or clubbing them in the streets. Some attackers told residents to leave their homes or they would be killed. Thousands fled.

The violence eased in the first week of February. By then, an estimated 1,000 people had died and hundreds of thousands were displaced. The United Nations (UN), the African Union (AU), and nations from around the world sent envoys to Kenya to help restore peace.

Long-Held Resentment

Observers attributed the sudden violence in Kenya to a network of historical, political, economic, and ethnic divisions. Some hostilities that surfaced in 2007 had roots in the years prior to Kenya's independence, when the British colonial government reportedly gave members of the Kikuyu ethnic group choice government jobs and lands in the Rift Valley, traditionally the home of the Kalenjin and Luo tribes. Resentment over land issues and other injustices had festered over generations. Many Kenyans believe their government has failed to address the misallocation of land since independence, preserving

outdated colonial systems of title allotment and corruptly transmitting public lands to well-connected political elites. During election campaigns, political aspirants often play on land issues to provoke simmering ethnic and class-based resentments, raising the political temperature and the threat of violence.

It became clear after the 2007 election and ensuing crisis that Kenya needed strong, united leadership, but Kibaki and Odinga refused to meet. Odinga demanded that Kibaki step down or set up a power-sharing government until another vote could be organized. Kibaki insisted that the election had been fair and would not discuss a recount or second election.

Coalition Government

Diplomats and heads of state poured in to Kenya to try to broker a peace agreement. Eventually the two Kenyan leaders were convinced to meet under the mediation of former UN Secretary-General Kofi Annan (1938–). Annan, arriving in mid-January, formed a negotiation committee that included representatives from Kibaki's PNU and from Raila Odinga's ODM under the

A supporter of Kenyan presidential candidate Raila Odinga is beaten by two supporters of Presidential candidate Mwai Kibaki and during a street fight in the Mathare neighborhood of Nairobi, Kenya, on December 29, 2007. Opposition leader Raila Odinga led incumbent Mwai Kibaki in Kenya's tight presidential race Saturday, but delays in the tallying raised suspicions of rigging and sparked nationwide riots. Angry Odinga supporters went on a rampage in Nairobi and across the country, looting, and burning. © *Boniface Mwange/AFP/Getty Images*

guidance of himself and a team of diplomats. Progress was slow and difficult, but after weeks of negotiating, an agreement was reached to create a power-sharing cabinet and create a prime minister position to be filled by Raila Odinga. Putting this into effect took another six weeks of bitter dispute, which came close to breakdown at several points, but in April 2008 Raila Odinga became prime minister and the new cabinet was in place.

Much remained ahead of the new coalition government of Kenya as it tackled the revision of Kenya's constitution. Issues such as land distribution, power, and the wealth gap, which have divided the ethnic groups for many years, were primary. Under Moi, the constitution had given the President extraordinary powers, and in revision, many hoped to create a system of checks and balances. Though the formation of the new cabinet was extremely expensive, Kenya's economy—which had been ravaged by the violence—showed positive signs with each forward move of the government. Observers in Kenya feared breakdowns in the new government, but also expressed optimism for the future should the coalition hold.

⊕ Impacts and Issues

The disputed election of 2007 illustrates the tragedy of modern Sub-Saharan Africa. A country that seemed to have a working democracy and did have a growing economy was torn apart by tribal animosities. The problem has its roots in the colonial period, when the British favored one ethnic group, the Kikuyu, over others. Political corruption also played a role in creating the dissatisfaction that lead to violence. Though major malefactors escaped punishment, the country did not disintegrate into chaos and become a failed state like neighboring Somalia.

Refugees

After the post-election violence in Kenya, an estimated 600,000 refugees were sheltered in 41 temporary camps. In the areas of heavy violence, ethnic communities that had lived together as neighbors for generations had been forced to flee from one another. Seeking safety, ethnic communities had segregated themselves in new areas, redrawing the country's map. On May 5, 2008, Operation Rudi Nyumbani (Return Home) began, in which the Kenyan government promised houses, food, tools, and money to farmers who returned to their farms. Fearful of renewed violence but unhappy with life in the refugee camps, many Kenyans cautiously went home.

Despite occasional flare-ups, the coalition government functioned relatively effectively in 2009. However, signs remained that the tribal tensions ignited by disputed elections had not been soothed. Student union elections on Kenyan university campuses were split

along tribal lines and apparently funded by members of Kenya's parliament. Furthermore, no progress was made on bringing those responsible for the post-election violence to justice.

The International Criminal Court Investigates

In March 2010, the ICC announced an investigation into the post-election violence. The ICC's chief prosecutor, Luis Moreno-Ocampo (1952–), said in May 2010 that he would travel to Kenya to meet with victims of post-election violence and investigate reported crimes. The investigation began as threats of renewed violence emerged. On March 8, 2011, the ICC issued summonses for six Kenyans to appear before the court in The Hague in connection with the post-election violence. The six included Deputy Prime Minister Uhuru Kenyatta, former Higher Education Minister William Ruto, former Minister for Industrialisation Henry Kosgey (1947–), businessman Joshua Arap Sang, and two others; they appeared before the court in April. The purpose of the preliminary hearings was to determine whether cases against the men should be sent to trial. Ruto was suspended from his position as Higher Education Minister in April. He was acquitted of corruption by a Kenyan court that same month, but was fired from his position in August.

Kenyatta, Sang, Ruto, and another defendant, Francis Muthaura (1946–) faced charges of crimes against humanity, including financing death squads. However, while awaiting prosecution, key witnesses withdrew their testimony, often citing concerns for their safety. In March 2013, the ICC dismissed charges against top civil servant Francis Muthaura after the testimony of a key witness was withdrawn.

Sporadic violence continued throughout Kenya, especially in areas with high concentrations of refugees from the 2007 ethnic violence. In late August 2012, 112 people died in a fight between longstanding rival communities, the Orma and Pokomo, in the Tana River County of Kenya. The Orma, semi-nomadic cattle

---

WITNESS

As violence broke out following the disputed 2007 election in Kenya, social media played a key role. Ushahidi.com (*ushahidi* means "witness" or "testimony" in Swahili) is a Web site built during the outbreak. It allowed eyewitnesses to email or text reports of violence that would then be placed on a Google map.

Ushahidi.com has since been used in several disasters, including the 2010 earthquake in Haiti and the tsunami and subsequent nuclear disaster in Japan in 2011. Preliminary studies have indicated that it is valuable in helping first responders identify areas that need assistance.

Graca Machel, the wife of Nelson Mandela, stands with Kofi Annan, former U.N. Secretary-General, Mwai Kibaki, Kenya's president, Raila Odinga, leader of the Orange Democratic Movement and Benjamin Mkapa, former Tanzanian president in Nairobi, Kenya, on Thursday, Jan. 24, 2008. Kibaki and Odinga broke a weeks-long deadlock over forming a coalition government, part of a February peace agreement that ended two months of post-election violence. © *Boniface Mwangi/Bloomberg via Getty Images*

herders, and the Pokomo, historically farmers, have long shed blood over access to the river and the rich land, but weapons from neighboring Somalia have increased the casualties and the violence. These incidents raised the fear that the March 2013 elections would be bloody as politicians capitalized on tribal rivalries, but the elections were mostly peaceful.

The Election of 2013

Both Kenyatta and Ruto announced their candidacy for the forthcoming presidential election. Although the two men had supported opposing sides in the 2007 contest (Kenyatta supported Kibaki, the incumbent, while Ruto backed Odinga and his Orange Democratic Movement), they agreed to join forces in the 2013 polling, with Ruto serving as Kenyatta's running mate in the Jubilee alliance. Both maintained their willingness to cooperate in good faith with the ICC, but opponents accused them

of manipulating and politicizing the legal process by denouncing their indictment as foreign interference in Kenya's internal affairs.

On March 4, 2013, Kenyans went to the polls, in a state of trepidation, for their first general election since the fateful balloting of 2007. On March 9, Kenyatta was declared the winner on the first round, having taken a 50.07 percent majority over Raila Odinga and six other candidates. Odinga challenged the results and refused to concede, yet he urged his supporters to remain calm. He vowed to conduct his protest in the courts instead of in street demonstrations and abide by the court's ruling. This time, fears of new post-election violence did not materialize. On March 30, Kenya's Supreme Court upheld the validity of the vote and let the results stand.

On May 22, 2013, the Truth, Justice and Reconciliation Commission (TJRC) released its official report covering the 2007 election violence. The TRJC, which was formed just after the events, found that President Kenyatta and Vice President Ruto were responsible for "planning incitement and financing violence during the 2007/2008 post-election violence," when the two were running against each other. The committee did not make any recommendations for action to be taken against the two as they both were awaiting charges from the ICC.

⊕ Future Implications

Kenyans have been divided on how to proceed with the ICC charges. In a survey of 2,000 Kenyan adults in June 2013, 39 percent of the respondents told pollsters they wanted Kenyatta's case to stay at The Hague, 32 percent said they wanted the case tried in Kenya, and 29 percent said the charges should be dismissed. The 2013 survey showed a dramatic shift: only 39 percent of Kenyans supported the ICC process, dropping from 59 percent in 2011.

Ruto flew to The Hague to be present for the opening of his trial at the ICC on September 10. On October 12–13, at an African Union (AU) summit meeting in Addis Ababa, Ethiopia, Kenyatta denounced the ICC as "a painfully farcical pantomime, a travesty that adds insult to the injury of victims. It stopped being the home of justice the day it became the toy of declining imperial powers." The AU formally requested the court to postpone Kenyatta's trial and declared that no sitting head of state should have to face charges in any international tribunal. In September, the Kenyan Parliament voted to leave the ICC, however this move would not stop the cases against Kenyatta and Ruto. On October 31, Kenyatta's trial date was pushed back to February 5, 2014, however prosecutors in Kenyatta's trial requested an adjournment until the Kenyan government agreed to turn over financial records and other documents, without which they claim they cannot successfully prosecute. Ruto's trial was ongoing as of early 2014.

SEE ALSO *International Law and Justice*

BIBLIOGRAPHY
Books

Branch, Daniel. *Kenya: Between Hope and Despair, 1963–2011*. New Haven, CT: Yale University Press, 2011.

Hornsby, Charles. *Kenya: A History Since Independence*. New York, NY: I.B. Tauris, 2012.

Njogu, Kimani, ed. *Defining Moments: Reflections on Citizenship, Violence, and the 2007 General Elections in Kenya*. Nairobi, Kenya: Twaweza Communications, 2011.

Periodicals

McGroarty, Patrick, and Gabriele Steinhauser. "Court to Prove Its Case in Africa—Trial of Kenyan Leader on Charges Related to Postelection Violence Is Test of International Tribunal." *Wall Street Journal, Eastern Edition* (May 29, 2013): A.16.

Wanjohi, Kabukuru. "A Triumph for the Nation." *African Business* 396 (April 2013): 68–70.

Web Sites

Associated Press. "Kenyan President Accused of Backing Post-Election Violence That Killed 1,000." *The Guardian*, May 22, 2013. http://www.guardian.co.uk/world/2013/may/22/uhuru-kenyatta-election-violence-report (accessed November 26, 2013).

"In-Depth: Kenya's Post-Election Violence." *IRIN Humanitarian News and Analysis, a service of the UN Office for the Coordination of Humanitarian Affairs*, January 7, 2008. http://www.irinnews.org/in-depth/76116/68/kenya-s-post-election-crisis (accessed November 26, 2013).

"Kenya Profile: A Chronology of Key Events." *BBC News: Africa*. http://www.bbc.co.uk/news/world-africa-13682176 (accessed November 26, 2013).

"Kenyans Divided on Presidential War Crimes." *UPI.com*, July 10, 2013. http://www.upi.com/Top_News/Special/2013/07/10/Kenyans-divided-on-presidential-war-crimes/UPI-12061373470756/ (accessed August 31, 2013).

Korean Conflicts

⊕ Introduction

On March 5, 2013, North Korea announced that it would end its truce with South Korea because of a combination of United Nations (UN) sanctions and South Korean military exercises. The next day, South Korean military general Kim Yong-hyun said that South Korea would react with "resolute retaliations" if "North Korea carries out provocations that threaten the lives and safety of South Koreans." This threat of renewed hostilities was the latest event in a long history of incendiary rhetoric and occasionally violent confrontations interspersed with fleeting movement toward reconciliation and reunification. Though played out on the Korean Peninsula, the ongoing conflict between the two nations was born of political decisions made by world powers—and continues to be influenced by them. On March 27, 2013, North Korea severed its last direct communication link to South Korea when it cut off a military hotline between the two countries. North Korea claimed that war could break out at "any moment."

⊕ Historical Background

Situated on a peninsula between the Yellow Sea and the Sea of Japan, Korea was a unified country until Japan invaded and forcibly annexed it in 1910. Japan's occupation of Korea continued until the end of World War II (1939–45) in August 1945. When the United States and the former Soviet Union accepted Japan's surrender, the Soviet Union handled disarmament of the northern half of Korea, and the United States handled disarmament in the south. With the democratic United States and the communist Soviet Union unable to agree upon the terms of Korea's independence, the north and south were divided. The United States and the Soviet Union helped create separate governments at either end of Korea, and North Korea and South Korea became

distinct countries. North Korea was politically aligned with the Soviet Union, while South Korea was politically aligned with the United States.

The Korean War

On June 25, 1950, with the support of the Soviet Union and China, North Korea invaded South Korea in an attempt to reunite the two countries as one communist nation. In response, the UN, which the Soviet Union was boycotting at the time, asked UN member nations to provide military support to South Korea. The two sides engaged in a military conflict that became known as the Korean War (1950–53). It eventually resulted in the deaths of an estimated 2.5 million people, including soldiers and citizens from North Korea and South Korea, and U.S. and UN forces.

When North Korea invaded South Korea, crossing the 38th parallel—a short strip of land dividing North from South—they had a large, well-equipped army. South Korea's army was smaller and poorly trained. North Korea initially met little resistance and its army was able to reach the outskirts of the South Korean capital of Seoul within 36 hours. The UN, however, quickly agreed to assist South Korea in repelling the attack and driving the North Korean army back across the 38th parallel.

As the UN coalition pushed North Korea back, the People's Republic of China came to the aid of North Korea. The two sides—South Korea and the UN coalition, led by the United States, against North Korea and its ally China—dug in and fought for the next two years. Bloody battles resulted in many deaths, but little territory changed hands.

Negotiations to End the Korean War

Negotiations to end the conflict proceeded in fits and starts for months, with North Korea frequently withdrawing from talks. South Korean president Syngman

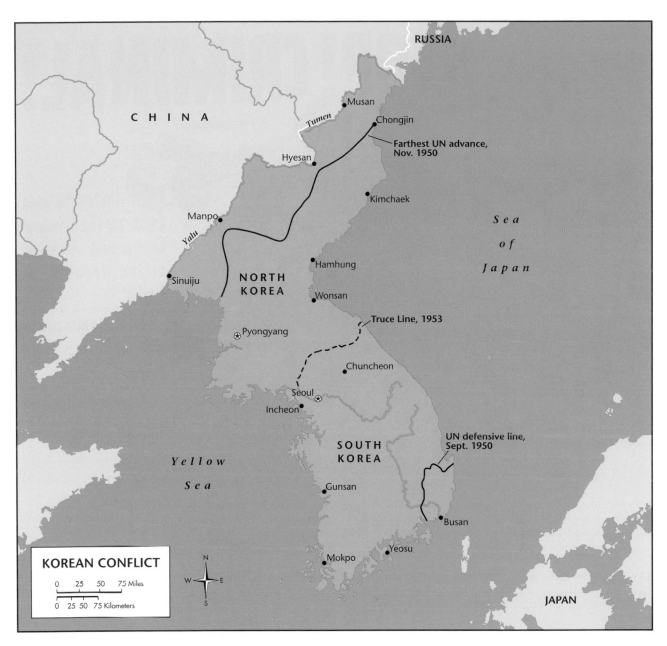

KOREAN CONFLICT

0   25   50   75 Miles

0   25 50 75 Kilometers

© 2014 Cengage Learning

Rhee (1875–1965) wanted negotiations to result in a unified Korea and opposed any solution short of that. In addition, there were significant disagreements over how to handle the repatriation, or homecoming, of prisoners of war (POWs). Even after the armistice was reached and the exchange of prisoners completed, thousands of South Korean soldiers remained imprisoned in North Korea. The status of these POWs, most of whom are now presumed dead, has been an area of continued conflict.

Following a long and complex negotiation process, which began in July of 1951, an armistice was finally signed on July 27, 1953. It called for a truce and withdrawal of each army to about a mile back on either side of the existing battle line, just below the 38th parallel.

⊕ Impacts and Issues

While a cease-fire agreement was made, the war did not officially end. Technically, South and North Korea remained at war 60 years later. As of early 2014 each side continued to police the area below the 38th parallel, known as the demilitarized zone (DMZ), which is fenced off and studded with land mines.

Violence Following the War

Despite the cease-fire agreement, violent incidents have occurred over the years. On January 21, 1968, a unit of 31 commandos from North Korea attempted to assassinate South Korean president Park Chung-hee

A picture taken circa October 1950 during the Korean War shows an anti-communist UN propanganda poster. The Korean War between armies from North Korea and from South Korea lasted from June 25, 1950, to July 27, 1953. The north was helped by the People's Republic of China and the USSR. The south was helped by countries in the United Nations, especially by the United States.   © *AFP/Getty Images*

(1917–1979) in Seoul; all but one of the commandos were killed. Another attempt was made on Park's life on August 15, 1974. This assassin also failed to kill Park, but did kill first lady Yook Young-su (1925–1974). On October 9, 1983, North Korean agents attacked a gathering of South Korean ministers in Rangoon, Burma (Myanmar). Twenty people were killed in the attack, including four of the ministers. Four years later, North Korean agents bombed a Korean Air Lines jet, killing all 115 people aboard the airplane. In April 1996, North Korea renounced the armistice forged 43 years earlier and sent troops into the demilitarized zone separating North and South Korea. The following September, North Korea sent a submarine containing 26 commandos into South Korean waters.

On March 26, 2010, an explosion caused the South Korean warship *Cheonan* to sink off the coast of Baengnyeong Island, near the maritime border between North and South Korea. Forty-six crew members were reported missing and presumed dead. Investigations into the explosion implicated North Korea, and South Korean

investigators claimed to have proof that the *Cheonan* was torpedoed by a North Korean submarine. North Korea dismissed the report and denied responsibility. After the incident, South Korea strengthened its naval power by launching a new missile-firing destroyer and preparing another for launch.

South Korea conducted its largest ever antisubmarine military exercises on August 5, 2010, in the Yellow Sea, near the disputed maritime border with North Korea. Fifty airplanes, 29 ships, and 4,500 service members were involved. The North Korean government characterized the drills as an "invasion." On August 8, North Korea seized a South Korean squidding boat, which may have crossed the maritime border. The vessel had a crew of four South Korean and three Chinese members, who were detained and interrogated before being released a month later.

Several months after the sinking of the *Cheonan*, South Korean marines held military drills along the sea border between the two countries. North Korea responded by launching an artillery attack on the South Korean island

A US soldier from the UN forces displays a portrait of North Korean Prime Minister Kim Il-sung found on June 14, 1952, at Koje prison camp. Chinese and North Korean prisoners of war were detained in Koje Island until they rioted in May 1952 and were moved to other prison facilities. © *AFP/Getty Images*

of Yeonpyeong on November 23, 2010, killing two South Korean marines and two civilians, and injuring more than a dozen people. The United States, which has more than 28,000 troops stationed in South Korea, called on North Korea to "halt its belligerent action."

Following the attack on Yeonpyeong, China faced international pressure to rein in its ally. China sent its highest-ranking diplomat, State Councilor Dai Bingguo, to meet directly with the supreme leader of North Korea, Kim Jong-il (1941–2011), on December 9, 2010. The two leaders reported they had reached a "consensus on bilateral relations and the situation on the Korean peninsula," though details were not given. Meanwhile, Admiral Mike Mullen, Chairman of the Joint Chiefs of Staff, visited South Korea and Japan to aid in preparations for any new aggression by North Korea. To that end, South Korea announced it would hold several live-fire exercises on Yeonpyeong between December 18 and 21. The U.S.-led United Nations command observed the exercises.

North Korea's Journey to Nuclear Power

In the 1950s and 1960s, the Soviet Union assisted North Korea with nuclear research, including construction of a small nuclear research reactor at the Yongbyon nuclear facility. In the 1970s and 1980s, North Korea began designing and testing its own nuclear and ballistic-missile technologies. In 1980 it began construction of a larger plutonium-building nuclear reactor at Yongbyon that would be capable of producing nuclear weapons; the facility became operational in 1986. In 1993 and 1995, North Korea announced it would withdraw from the 1968 Nuclear Non-Proliferation Treaty (NPT), which was designed to limit the spread of nuclear weapons. North Korea then changed its mind about withdrawing from the NPT and was rewarded by a U.S. promise of aid to build nuclear reactors for power generation. From 1998 to early 2001, a "Sunshine Policy" was initiated by South Korea to improve relations with North Korea, with the support of the administration of U.S. president Bill Clinton (1946–). However, relations between the two countries deteriorated after U.S. president George W. Bush (1946–) took office in 2001.

In his State of the Union address on January 29, 2002, Bush announced his intention to respond to the September 11 terrorist attacks by fighting a "war on terror." He claimed that North Korea, along with Iran and Iraq, constituted an "axis of evil" that posed a threat to world security by developing weapons of mass destruction and aiding terrorist groups. He accused the North Korean government of neglecting the welfare of its own people while also seeking to manufacture nuclear weapons in violation of the NPT. North Korean leader Kim Jong-il interpreted Bush's statement as a declaration of war. In 2003, North Korea withdrew from the NPT; in 2005, it announced that it possessed nuclear weapons; and in 2006 it conducted an underground test of a nuclear device. The following year, though, North Korea offered to shut down the nuclear program at Yongbyon in exchange for foreign aid. Negotiations between North Korea, South Korea, the United States, Russia, Japan, and China—so-called "six-party talks"—attempted to ease tensions between North Korea and the rest of the world and convince North Korea to end its nuclear program. However, Kim Jong-il announced in 2009 that North Korea would never return to these talks, and on May 25 of that year North Korea detonated a second nuclear device. In 2010, North Korea revealed that it had a uranium enrichment plant at Yongbyon.

New Leader, Same Policy

Kim Jong-il died in December 2011 and was succeeded by his son Kim Jong-un (1983–). Though international leaders had hoped that the death of Kim Jong-il would lead to a thawing of relations between the two Koreas and a less belligerent foreign policy in North Korea, no such change of policy occurred. In fact, relations between North and South Korea continued to be filled with tension and threats. United States president Barack Obama (1961–) visited the demilitarized zone between North and South Korea on March 25, 2012, just ahead of a nuclear summit in Seoul, in an effort to

ATTEMPTS TO REUNIFY

Both South and North Korea have initiated several attempts to reunify. Though the two sides agreed to peaceful unification on July 4, 1972, nothing came of the agreement. In 1990, South Korean President Roh Tae Woo (1932–) renewed calls for reunification, resulting in a series of eight prime minister-level meetings between the two countries. The talks resulted in the formation of two major agreements—the Agreement on Reconciliation, Nonaggression, Exchanges, and Cooperation; and the Declaration on the Denuclearization of the Korean Peninsula—but the talks faltered when the two sides could not reach an agreement regarding nuclear weapons inspections.

Reunification is important to many Koreans not only for the symbolic or patriotic value of having a single Korea, but because families have been separated by the border, in some cases since the beginning of the Korean War. On June 14, 2000, President Kim Dae-jung (1925–2009) of South Korea and Kim Jong-il of North Korea produced a pact allowing families on either side of the Korean border to reunite. The pact was an attempt to reduce tensions between the two Koreas, and a period of relative civility followed. Representatives of North and South Korea marched together at the 2000 Olympics in Sydney, Australia. The following February, the countries agreed to build a railroad across the border dividing them.

Reunification remains an oft-discussed goal between North and South Korea, though little progress toward that goal has been made. As recently as 2012, North Korea's president Kim Jong-un called for an end to provocations between the nations and enhanced political and economic ties. No formal talks regarding reunification had begun as of early 2014.

---

warm up relations between the two countries. However, by April 13, Obama's plan was in shambles after North Korea proceeded with a planned long-range rocket launch over strong U.S. objections. Although North Korea insisted that the rocket was intended for peaceful space exploration—and the rocket malfunctioned and broke into pieces in less than two minutes—the launch was condemned by most world leaders as a breach of UN Security Council resolutions. The United States responded by canceling its plans to provide food aid to the country.

On February 12, 2013, Kim Jong-un conducted another test of a larger nuclear weapon, which much of the world viewed as a provocative act. The event was confirmed by a Korean government-run news agency just hours after the U.S. Geological Survey detected a 4.9 magnitude earthquake. South Korea immediately spoke out against the test, and an international outcry followed. The UN Security Council "strongly condemned" the test, and the United States' outgoing Pentagon chief called North Korea a "serious threat." A few days later, during a UN conference on North Korean disarmament, North Korean diplomat Jon Yong Ryong threatened South Korea, saying that its "erratic behavior [will] only herald its final destruction." In March 2013 North Korean leaders declared the 1953 armistice agreement invalid and claimed that a state of war existed with South Korea. When the United States and South Korea conducted joint naval maneuvers in October 2013, North Korea threatened "all-out war" against both countries.

⊕ Future Implications

Following Korea's division in 1945, North and South Korea evolved into very different countries with unique cultures. Though grounded in hundreds of years of shared culture and identity, the lives of the people living in each country are now quite distinct. North Korea is one of the most impoverished countries in the world, with hundreds of thousands—perhaps millions—of people dying in a series of famines. South Korea is a wealthy country, experiencing relatively fast economic growth, and considered one of the four "Asian Tigers" of highly developed economies in Asia. South Korea is technologically sophisticated; North Korea remains very isolated. In 2011, the World Bank, which compiles statistics on all the countries of the world, found a telling difference in the life expectancy in the two Koreas. The life expectancy in South Korea is 81 years; that of North Korea is 69 years. In addition, the UN issued a report in early 2014 documenting abuses by the North Korean government against it citizens that included murder, torture, slavery, sexual violence, and mass starvation. The UN stated that it would refer its findings to the International Criminal Court, however China stated it would not allow the charges to proceed.

At least for the immediate future, the differences may be too much to overcome. Each country's government is fiercely protective of its power and highly suspicious of the other, and occasional attempts to move toward more openness, such as allowing family members to visit each other, are quickly curtailed. North Korea continues to threaten South Korea and the United States, including almost daily threats in 2013 to launch pre-emptive nuclear strikes.

The two Koreas also have the added burden of trying to resolve their significant differences with the guidance of the major world powers. Since they were initially divided following World War II, when the Soviet Union and the United States could not agree on how to configure a unified Korea, the countries have often been the stage on which international political posturing has played out. With Russia and China backing their ally North Korea and the United States and other western

North Korean soldiers march during a military parade past Kim Il-Sung Square marking the 60th anniversary of the Korean war armistice in Pyongyang on July 27, 2013. North Korea mounted its largest ever military parade on July 27 to mark the 60th anniversary of the armistice that ended fighting in the Korean War, displaying its long-range missiles at a ceremony presided over by leader Kim Jong-Un.
© *Ed Jones/AFP/Getty Images*

governments backing South Korea, diplomacy between the two nations often has been a microcosm of global politics.

PRIMARY SOURCE

Six-Party Talks—Second-Phase Implementation of the September 2005 Joint Statement

SOURCE *Office of the Spokesman. "Six-Party Talks— Second-Phase Actions for the Implementation of the September 2005 Joint Statement." Press release 2007/842.* U.S. Department of State Archive, *October 3, 2007. http://2001-2009.state.gov/r/pa/prs/ ps/2007/oct/93217.htm (accessed October 14, 2013).*

INTRODUCTION *In 2003 North Korea withdrew from the Nuclear Non-Proliferation Treaty (NPT) that seeks to prevent the spread of nuclear weapons. In response to the withdrawal and the perceived likelihood that North Korea would pursue the development*

of nuclear weapons, a series of talks were held involving both North and South Korea, Japan, the United States, Russia, and the People's Republic of China. Though the talks occasionally appeared to make progress, as in this statement from 2007, in 2009 North Korea announced that it would pull out of the talks and resume its nuclear enrichment program.

The Foreign Ministry of the People's Republic of China released the following joint statement on October 3, 2007:

The Second Session of the Sixth Round of the Six-Party Talks was held in Beijing among the People's Republic of China, the Democratic People's Republic of Korea, Japan, the Republic of Korea, the Russian Federation and the United States of America from 27 to 30 September 2007.

Mr. Wu Dawei, Vice Minister of Foreign Affairs of the PRC, Mr. Kim Gye Gwan, Vice Minister of Foreign Affairs of the DPRK, Mr. Kenichiro Sasae, Director-General for Asian and Oceanian Affairs, Ministry of Foreign Affairs of Japan, Mr. Chun Yung-woo, Special Representative for Korean Peninsula Peace and Security Affairs of the ROK Ministry of Foreign Affairs and Trade, Mr. Alexander Losyukov, Deputy Minister of

Foreign Affairs of the Russian Federation, and Mr. Christopher Hill, Assistant Secretary for East Asian and Pacific Affairs of the Department of State of the United States, attended the talks as heads of their respective delegations.

Vice Foreign Minister Wu Dawei chaired the talks.

The Parties listened to and endorsed the reports of the five Working Groups, confirmed the implementation of the initial actions provided for in the February 13 agreement, agreed to push forward the Six-Party Talks process in accordance with the consensus reached at the meetings of the Working Groups, and reached agreement on second-phase actions for the implementation of the Joint Statement of 19 September 2005, the goal of which is the verifiable denuclearization of the Korean Peninsula in a peaceful manner.

I. ON DENUCLEARIZATION OF THE KOREAN PENINSULA

1. The DPRK agreed to disable all existing nuclear facilities subject to abandonment under the September 2005 Joint Statement and the February 13 agreement.

The disablement of the 5 megawatt Experimental Reactor at Yongbyon, the Reprocessing Plant (Radiochemical Laboratory) at Yongbyon and the Nuclear Fuel Rod Fabrication Facility at Yongbyon will be completed by 31 December 2007. Specific measures recommended by the expert group will be adopted by heads of delegation in line with the principles of being acceptable to all Parties, scientific, safe, verifiable, and consistent with international standards. At the request of the other Parties, the United States will lead disablement activities and provide the initial funding for those activities. As a first step, the US side will lead the expert group to the DPRK within the next two weeks to prepare for disablement.

2. The DPRK agreed to provide a complete and correct declaration of all its nuclear programs in accordance with the February 13 agreement by 31 December 2007.

3. The DPRK reaffirmed its commitment not to transfer nuclear materials, technology, or know-how.

II. ON NORMALIZATION OF RELATIONS BETWEEN RELEVANT COUNTRIES

1. The DPRK and the United States remain committed to improving their bilateral relations and moving towards a full diplomatic relationship. The two sides will increase bilateral exchanges and enhance mutual trust. Recalling the commitments to begin the process of removing the designation of the DPRK as a state sponsor of terrorism and advance the process of terminating the application of the Trading with the Enemy Act with respect to the DPRK, the United States will fulfill its commitments to the DPRK in parallel with the DPRK's actions based on consensus reached at the meetings of the Working Group on Normalization of DPRK-U.S. Relations.

2. The DPRK and Japan will make sincere efforts to normalize their relations expeditiously in accordance with the Pyongyang Declaration, on the basis of the settlement of the unfortunate past and the outstanding issues of concern. The DPRK and Japan committed themselves to taking specific actions toward this end through intensive consultations between them.

III. ON ECONOMIC AND ENERGY ASSISTANCE TO THE DPRK

In accordance with the February 13 agreement, economic, energy and humanitarian assistance up to the equivalent of one million tons of HFO (inclusive of the 100,000 tons of HFO already delivered) will be provided to the DPRK. Specific modalities will be finalized through discussion by the Working Group on Economy and Energy Cooperation.

IV. ON THE SIX-PARTY MINISTERIAL MEETING

The Parties reiterated that the Six-Party Ministerial Meeting will be held in Beijing at an appropriate time. The Parties agreed to hold a heads of delegation meeting prior to the Ministerial Meeting to discuss the agenda for the Meeting.

SEE ALSO *Cold War; Weapons of Mass Destruction; World War II*

BIBLIOGRAPHY

Books

Halberstam, David. *The Coldest Winter.* New York City: Hyperion, 2007.

Jager, Sheila Miyoshi. *Brothers at War: The Unending Conflict in Korea.* New York City: W.W. Norton & Co., 2013.

Oberdorfer, Don. *The Two Koreas: A Contemporary History.* New York City: Basic Books, 2001.

Web Sites

"A History of the Korean Tensions." *The Wall Street Journal,* May 24, 2012. http://online.wsj.com/article/SB10001424052702304879604575582343372934982.html (accessed May 25, 2013).

"North Korea v South Korea in Figures—Interactive." *The Guardian,* April 9, 2013. http://www.guardian.co.uk/world/datablog/interactive/2013/apr/09/north-korea-south-korea-interactive (accessed May 25, 2013).

"Rising Tensions on the Korean Peninsula." *The Wall Street Journal,* April 9, 2013. http://online.wsj.com/article/SB10001424127887324050304578412820255386646.html (accessed May 25, 2013).

"Timeline of North Korea's Nuclear Program." *The New York Times,* April 4, 2013. http://www.nytimes.com/interactive/2013/02/05/world/asia/northkorea-timeline.html?_r=1&#/#time238_7085 (accessed May 25, 2013).

Kosovo's Independence

⊕ Introduction

Kosovo declared itself an independent state in 2008. Before that time, the region had a long history of ethnic conflict among its majority Albanian and minority Serbian population. Kosovo was part of the former Yugoslavia for much of the 20th century, both as a semi-autonomous province and later as part of Serbia. During the course of the violent Yugoslav Wars in the 1990s, ethnic Albanian guerrilla groups, including the Kosovo Liberation Army, attacked Serb targets.

After the break-up of Yugoslavia, Kosovo became part of the Serbian-dominated successor state, the Federal Republic of Yugoslavia. (Some countries referred to this entity as Serbia and Montenegro until those two nations split in 2006.) Interethnic violence erupted into war in Kosovo in 1999. International outcry over alleged human rights crimes and ethnic cleansing prompted the North Atlantic Treaty Organization (NATO) to intervene in the conflict. After the Kosovo War of 1999, the United Nations (UN) administered and oversaw peacekeeping efforts in Kosovo.

⊕ Historical Background

Kosovo was under the rule of the Ottoman Empire from 1389 to 1913, but when the empire dissolved after World War I (1914–18), Kosovo became part of Yugoslavia. At that time Yugoslavia included the territory of present-day Bosnia and Herzegovina, Macedonia, Montenegro, Serbia, Croatia, and Slovenia. From 1945 until 1990, Kosovo enjoyed autonomous status, or informal independence within its own local governmental structures, within the Socialist Republic of Serbia. By 1974, Kosovo's status was equivalent in most respects to that of the six Yugoslav republics, with direct representation in Yugoslav federal bodies and the right to write its own constitution.

The region holds deep emotional and symbolic significance to both Albanians and Serbs. Albanians claim to have lived in Kosovo before the Slavs settled there in the sixth and seventh centuries. However, Serbs claim Kosovo as the cradle of Serbian culture. It was the center of the medieval Serbian state and was long the seat of the Serbian Orthodox Church. So when Kosovo's ethnic Albanian majority began to press for elevation of Kosovo's status to that of a republic within the Yugoslav Federation, the minority Serbs were alarmed. Ethnic Serbs (about 7 percent of the population) complained of oppression by ethnic Albanians. The plight of the Serbs in Kosovo evoked passionate sympathy in Serbia.

Tensions between Serbians and Albanians in Kosovo mounted. In 1985 and 1986, Serbian politician Slobodan Milosevic (1941–2006) campaigned for the Serbian presidency on a nationalistic platform that served to incite and manipulate the growing Serb hostility toward the ethnic Albanians in Kosovo. Milosevic won the 1989 Serbian presidential election and began the process of dismantling Kosovo's autonomy. In fact, the Serbian constitution of 1990 eliminated Kosovo's autonomy.

The Dissolution of Yugoslavia

In late 1991, the Soviet Union, for 50 years a major world power, broke apart into separate countries. Yugoslavia, which had been cobbled together from several entities in 1918 following World War I, began to fracture as well. The various states that comprised Yugoslavia asserted their desire for independence. In 1991, Croatia and Slovenia (and later Bosnia and Herzegovina and Macedonia) seceded from the Yugoslavian federation. That left only Serbia (of which Kosovo was a province) and Montenegro in the federation ruled by President Milosevic.

The newly established administration systematically removed Albanians from positions in the mass media, government, business, and health and educational

© 2014 Cengage Learning

systems. The Albanian language ceased to be taught in the schools. Legislation was passed forbidding the sale of property to Albanians. The repression only increased as the Serbian government fought wars with Croatia and Bosnia to prevent them from leaving the former Yugoslav federation.

Many thousands of Albanians fled Kosovo to escape persecution by the Serbian government. Those who remained boycotted all aspects of official social and political life. The Albanian Kosovars organized a nonviolent parallel political system, led in the early years by the Democratic League of Kosovo (LDK). Contributions from Albanians in Albania and Albanians living abroad provided the funding for the education and health care in the parallel system.

War and Intervention

By 1997, the failure of the LDK to win independence or international recognition led to the emergence of the Kosovo Liberation Army (KLA), which engaged in guerrilla warfare against Serbian forces.

In 1999, international diplomats tried to hammer out a political settlement. The effort failed when the Serbian government refused to sign an agreement that would give Albanians autonomy within Serbia. Fighting between the ethnic Albanians and the Serbs escalated.

In March 1999 NATO forces intervened with a 78-day air campaign called Operation Allied Force, which targeted Serbian military bases and infrastructure. During the NATO campaign, Serbian forces killed an estimated 11,000 Kosovar Albanians and drove almost

a million more out of Kosovo. The bombing ended in June, when the Serbian government agreed to withdraw its forces from Kosovo; NATO, in turn, agreed to a UN administration of Kosovo and pledged that there would be no independence initiative in Kosovo for the next three years.

The UN interim administration established in 1999 was charged with preparing Kosovo for self-government. It was bolstered by a NATO force of 42,000 troops to provide security. Hundreds of thousands of Albanian refugees flooded back into Kosovo. Nevertheless, the region suffered from high unemployment, corruption, power shortages, and lawlessness. Tensions remained high between the majority Kosovar Albanians, who numbered about 2 million, and Kosovo's population of about 120,000 Serbs.

War Crimes

During the war and subsequent NATO bombing, the Serbs engaged in a campaign of ethnic cleansing. While the bombing was still going on, Milosevic became the first serving head of state to be indicted for crimes against humanity by the international war crimes tribunal in The Hague. Milosevic and his colleagues were charged with direct responsibility for the deportation of about 750,000 and the murder of about 600 Kosovo Albanians. In some towns, the men were separated from the women and machine-gunned to death.

Massacres occurred in a number of towns and prisons. In Poklek in April of 1999, people were forced into a room and gunned down; at least 23 children

Ethnic Albanian refugees in Kosovo trudge down a muddy road in a blizzard away from their village, Bukos, as they flee fighting between Kosovo Liberation Army (KLA) fighters and Serb police and army troops. Fighting broke out in Bokus after KLA soldiers killed a Serbian villager. *© David Brauchli/Getty Images*

were killed. On May 2, 1999, as Kosovar Albanian refugees fled the fighting near the town of Vucitrn, Serbian military and paramilitary forces massacred more than 100 men.

Later investigations showed that the Serbs had also been the victims of appallingly brutal revenge attacks. More than 80 Serbs were found in mass graves near Gnjilane. Six Serb teenagers were killed in 1998 outside of the town of Pec in what became known as the Pada Bar massacre. There were also charges that some Serbs were abducted and had their organs stolen and sold on the black market.

Both Milosevic and his colleagues and leaders of the ethnic Albanians have been charged with war crimes. Milosevic's death, partway through his trial, prevented the court from ruling on his guilt.

Kosovo Declares Independence

When Kosovo declared its independence from Serbia on February 17, 2008, the Serb minority, isolated in enclaves in northern Kosovo, expressed outrage and disbelief. The European Union (EU) and the United States supported Kosovo's independence, but Serbia and Russia strongly opposed Kosovo's secession from Serbia. In the Serbian capital of Belgrade, a group of some 2,000 Serbs stormed the U.S. embassy in protest. Security in Kosovo was maintained by 16,000 NATO troops.

Under Kosovo's new constitution, which went into effect on June 15, 2008, the EU was slated to take on an oversight role. Most of the UN mission's former security and government development roles were assumed by the European Union Rule of Law Mission in Kosovo (EULEX) in December 2008. Russia and Serbia claim that the EU lacked the authority to take on that role because it had not been approved by the UN Security Council. Serbia rejected Kosovo's independence and pressed its case with the International Court of Justice (ICJ), claiming that Kosovo's declaration of independence violated international law. The ICJ, however, affirmed the legality of that Kosovo's independence. While other Balkan nations put aside tensions for the sake of EU membership and economic advancement, Serbia and Kosovo remained at loggerheads. Leaders of the two countries were to meet at a pan-Balkan

A relative comforts the mother of two young men killed in the western Kosovo village of Glodjane. The two young ethnic Albanians died while fighting with Serbian police.   © *Joel Robine/AFP/Getty Images*

conference in Slovenia on March 20, 2010; while a representative from Kosovo attended, Serbia boycotted the meeting.

According to a leaked U.S. diplomatic cable dating to 2009, the Serbian government privately told the State Department that the EU government in Kosovo would not be successful in asserting control over the predominantly Serbian northern part of the country. The cable was one of thousands of U.S. State Department documents released by WikiLeaks in November and December 2010. WikiLeaks is an online organization that publishes leaked corporate and government documents. Serbian president Boris Tadic (1958–) has long pushed for the partition of Kosovo, while the United States has worked for more than 10 years against partition.

Disputed Election

Kosovo held its first elections since declaring its independence on December 12, 2010. Many Serbs threatened to boycott the vote. Exit polls showed that incumbent prime minister Hashim Thaci (1968–) had won the election, but opposition leaders claimed the election was marred by vote rigging. International observers noted that there had been irregularities in the voting, but, according to the European Network of Election

Monitoring Organizations, the election "met many international standards." The Central Election Commission called for a partial revote on January 9, 2011.

Because Thaci's Democratic Party of Kosovo (PDK) did not win enough seats to form a government, it formed a power-sharing deal with the New Kosovo Alliance under which its candidate, Behgjet Pacolli (1951–), would become president of Kosovo. He assumed office on February 22, 2011. On March 30, Kosovo's constitutional court ruled that Pacolli's election as president violated the constitution. Pacolli agreed to comply with the court's decision. The elections were also marred by the release of a Council of Europe report accusing Thaci of ties to an organized crime syndicate involved in trafficking drugs, weapons, stolen goods, humans, and human organs.

Tension Along the Serbian Border

In July 2011, Kosovo's new government established customs stations and border controls along the Serbian border, enraging many of the ethnic Serbians in northern Kosovo who still consider themselves Serbian citizens. In retaliation, Serbs set up roadblocks and barricades leading to two border posts with the aim of preventing the Kosovo government from posting troops at

HUMAN TRAFFICKING

In the chaos that followed the disintegration of the Soviet Union and the breakup of Yugoslavia, human trafficking grew quickly. Human trafficking is the illegal transnational and international trade in people for the purposes of servitude. The conflict in Kosovo led to a steep increase in the number of women, men, and children who were trafficked in the war-torn region.

In 2000, the United Nations (UN) published a global standard for the definition of human trafficking titled the "Protocol to Prevent, Suppress and Punish Trafficking in Persons, Especially Women and Children." In part, it defines human trafficking as "…the recruitment, transportation, transfer, harboring or receipt of persons, by means of the threat or use of force or other forms of coercion, of abduction, of fraud, of deception, of the abuse of power or of a position of vulnerability or of the giving or receiving of payments or benefits to achieve the consent of a person having control over another person, for the purpose of exploitation. Exploitation shall include, at a minimum, the exploitation of the prostitution of others or other forms of sexual exploitation, forced labor or services, slavery or practices similar to slavery, servitude or the removal of organs…"

The extent of the global human trafficking problem is vast. According to U.S. State Department estimates, which are considered conservative, each year somewhere between 600,000 and 820,000 men, women, and children are trafficked across international borders. Approximately 70 percent of those trafficked are women and girls—nearly 50 percent are minors. (It is worth noting that nongovernmental organization, or NGO, estimates are generally higher than governmental estimates for the actual numbers trafficked each year.) The State Department contends that most transnational victims are trafficked for the purpose of commercial sexual exploitation. Nevertheless, trafficking for the purposes of bonded and sweatshop labor, forced marriage, domestic servitude, and military service also persists. In 2013, the European Union Rule of Law Mission in Kosovo convicted several suspects of organ harvesting from victims who had been trafficked, a practice believed to have been practiced by the Kosovo Liberation Army during the Kosovo conflict.

In Europe, human trafficking became a phenomenon with the fall of communism in 1991. At that time, border controls eased across the European Union, lessening the risk of detection for human traffickers on transit routes. In the first half of the 1990s, as governments in parts of Eastern Europe lost authority, criminal gangs took hold of entire sectors of their economies, trading with Western partners in drugs, weapons, and women.

According to the European Commission, by 1997 two-thirds of the 500,000 women trafficked annually worldwide for prostitution came from Eastern Europe, mainly Moldova, Ukraine, and Russia, as well as Romania and Serbia. In some countries, trafficking reached epidemic levels: it is estimated that one-tenth of Moldovan women have been trafficked into Europe's sex trade at some time. Many of these women are trafficked into Kosovo, which has been called an "oasis of human trafficking" by the U.S. government. It has ranked 4th or 5th internationally each year in the number of people trafficked into the country.

In 2004 the group Amnesty International issued a report stating that NATO soldiers, UN police, and western aid workers were some of the main exploiters of the women who had been trafficked into the sex trade in Kosovo. In the five years following the start of the UN administration, forced prostitution of Kosovar women and those brought in from other countries became a large-scale industry. The UN admitted that year that its forces had been part of the problem.

these stations. In November 2011, almost two dozen NATO troops were injured in clashes with ethnic Serbs in northern Kosovo. The United States and the EU have accused Serbia of sending clandestine forces into the area and have called on the Serbian government to stop its interference. More clashes between NATO troops and Serbians occurred as NATO-led troops tried to clear some roadblocks in late May 2012. According to some witnesses, NATO troops and Serbs traded fire at a roadblock near Zvecan.

⊕ Impacts and Issues

The Republic of Kosovo declared its independence on February 17, 2008, but the issue of Kosovo's independence is not completely settled in the international community. The country still suffers from strained relationships between its Serbian and Albanian citizens. As of 2013, 106 UN member states recognized Kosovo. However, several large nations such as China, India, Brazil, and Russia, along with numerous other United Nations members, have yet to formally recognize the republic.

After months of strained negotiations, Serbia and Kosovo signed an EU-brokered agreement in late April 2013 to normalize relations. Under the deal, Kosovo will be required to set up a separate police force and appeals court for the Serbs in its northern region. Both countries also agreed not to hinder each other's efforts to join the EU.

⊕ Future Implications

International pressure remains on both Serbia and Kosovo to quell deeply held national, ethnic, and religious animosity in the region. Kosovo continues to struggle with organized crime involved in money laundering, human trafficking, and the international heroin trade.

Kosovo Police face demonstrators in Pristina on June 27, 2013, during a protest against the ratification of an agreement with Serbia. Protesters from a radical nationalist movement attempted to block the entrance to Kosovo's parliament to prevent deputies ratifying an agreement that would normalise ties with Serbia. The Self-Determination movement, a nationalist party that seeks to unify Kosovo with neighbouring Albania, is attempting to block the historic agreement struck on April 19 between Kosovo and Serbia.   © *Armen Nimani/AFP/Getty Images*

The country has also engaged in long-term efforts to rid the region of deadly land mines left over from the 1999 war.

PRIMARY SOURCE

SOURCE *The Independent International Commission on Kosovo. "Final Comments," in* The Kosovo Report: Conflict, International Response, and Lessons Learned. *Oxford: Oxford University Press, 2000, 295–298. Available online at: http://reliefweb.int/ sites/reliefweb.int/files/resources/6D26FF88119644C FC1256989005CD392-thekosovoreport.pdf (accessed December 4, 2013). By permission of Oxford University Press.*

INTRODUCTION *The Independent International Commission on Kosovo was established by the prime minister of Sweden to investigate the events that led to NATO's military intervention in 1999. Among the topics examined were human rights violations; the effects of diplomatic efforts to address the conflict; the refugee crisis caused by the conflict; the role of humanitarian workers, NGOs, and the media; and military intervention on the part of the UN and NATO. The Commission hoped to provide lessons that would help drive decisions on how best to handle such conflicts in the future. One of the conclusions reached by the Commission was that NATO's military intervention was illegal (because it did not receive prior approval from the UN Security Council) but justified.*

FINAL COMMENTS

The Commission takes it for granted that military intervention should always be a strategy of last resort, when all other peaceful means of responding to human rights violations have been exhausted. The Commission also believes that military intervention is a poor second best, and that non-coercive forms of early engagement with societies in the midst of human rights crisis are not only superior to military intervention, but actually might make the resort to force unnecessary. One of the major lessons of Kosovo is that greater early engagement with a region in crisis with a view to preventing conflict is invariably a more effective response than late intervention using force. Early engagement means not only making clear representations to defaulting governments condemning their human rights abuses, but also lending support to democratic and non-violent groups in civil society who are seeking to change government policy in the country concerned. A further lesson of the Kosovo story is that an outside presence—monitors, observers, peace-keeping forces—introduced with the consent of all parties can play an essential role in reducing human rights abuses and in ensuring transparency and assigning responsibility for those that do occur. If the international community had been conscientiously engaged with the developing Kosovo crisis from 1989 onwards, and if the Belgrade government had shown the foresight to internationalize its human rights problems in Kosovo, the whole downward spiral towards a tragic and costly military intervention might have been avoided. This might appear to be a counsel of perfection—and therefore useless—were it not for the fact that governments can now avail themselves of an early warning capability, in the form of human rights monitoring from a host of competent non-governmental organizations (NGOS), who did not exist 25 years ago. If governments were to listen more carefully to the human rights warnings of NGOS and use their political and diplomatic influence on abuser states at an earlier stage, the focus of international intervention could shift towards prevention, with long-term benefits for vulnerable communities everywhere. Yet it must always be remembered that early preventive engagement with countries in the midst of a human rights crisis is only possible when the government in question is prepared to engage. Some regimes, and certainly Serbia is one of them, are much more resistant than others to the internationalization of their problem. In the long run this may have made an eventual coercive intervention unavoidable.

If the intervention was ultimately unavoidable, its legitimacy was and remains questionable in non-Western eyes. In the majority of countries of the world there is a much stronger commitment to the protection of their sovereignty than currently exists in the West.

At a seminar held by the South African Institute of International Affairs and the University of Witwatersrand in cooperation with the Commission on August 25–6, 2000 in Johannesburg, South Africa, former president Nelson Mandela criticized the double standards in humanitarian intervention (his remarks are published at the beginning of this book), giving the examples of Kosovo, where intervention took place, and Sierra Leone, where it did not. However, most African as well as non-African participants emphasized the defense of sovereignty and criticized the new doctrine of humanitarian intervention as a tool of Western powers.

Given the dual history of colonialism and the Cold War, there is widespread concern about Western interventionism. The global power of NATO specifically the United States creates a feeling of vulnerability in other parts of the world, especially in a case such as Kosovo where NATO claimed a right to bypass the UN Security Council.

At the same time, some aspects of the intervention demonstrated unmistakable partiality in the protection of supposedly universal human rights norms. The international community intervened in Kosovo in 1999, but did not intervene in for example Rwanda. The Commission, composed as it was of citizens of many non-European, non-Western societies, is keenly aware that for non-Europeans the intervention was less a demonstration of moral universalism than further proof that European lives and liberties command a more immediate and substantial response from the international community than non-European ones.

All of these facts point to the need for a further strengthening of the United Nations. The inequities support the case for creating a United Nations standing army, with a robust full-time capability to rescue civilian victims of gross human rights abuses. Such a force would help to equalize the currently unequal distribution of military capability in the humanitarian field. But there are enormous political difficulties in the way of creating such a force and vesting its command and control within the UN system. Until these problems can be overcome, humanitarian intervention will be plagued with legitimacy problems which derive essentially from inequalities in military and political capabilities among UN member states.

If, therefore, we stand back from the Kosovo intervention, it becomes clear that it did not so much create a precedent for intervention elsewhere as raise vital questions about the legitimacy and practicability of the use of military force to defend human rights and humanitarian values in the 21st century. It exposed the limitations of the current international law on the balance between the rights of citizens and the rights of states; it demonstrated the difficulties that ensue when even the most sophisticated and professional military forces are deployed to achieve humanitarian goals; it showed, in the UN administration's difficulties in Kosovo, the immense obstacles that lie in the path of creating multi-ethnic cooperation in societies torn apart by ethnic war. Far from opening up a new era of humanitarian intervention, the Kosovo experience seems, to this Commission at least, to teach a valuable lesson of scepticism and caution. Sometimes, and Kosovo is such an instance, the use of military force may become necessary to defend human rights. But the grounds for its use in international law urgently need clarification, and the tactics and rules of engagement for its use need to be improved. Finally, the legitimacy of such use of force will always be controversial, and will remain so, so long as we intervene to protect some people's lives but not others.

SEE ALSO *Bosnian War; European Union; Genocide; International Law and Justice; North Atlantic Treaty Organization (NATO); United Nations; Yugoslav Wars*

BIBLIOGRAPHY

Books

Independent International Commission on Kosovo. *The Kosovo Report: Conflict, International Response, Lessons Learned.* Oxford: Oxford University Press, 2000.

Judah, Tim. *Kosovo: War and Revenge.* New Haven, CT: Yale University Press, 2000.

McShane, Denis. *Why Kosovo Still Matters.* London: Haus Publishing, 2011.

Web Sites

"Kosovo: A Bitter Struggle in a Land of Strife." *The New York Times Learning Network.* http://www. nytimes.com/learning/general/specials/kosovo/ (accessed January 6, 2014).

"Kosovo Declaration of Independence." *Republic of Kosovo Assembly*, February 17, 2008. http://www. assembly-kosova.org/?cid=2,128,1635 (accessed January 6, 2014).

"NATO Force 'Feeds Kosovo Sex Trade.'" *The Guardian*, May 6, 2004. http://www.theguardian.com/ world/2004/may/07/balkans (accessed January 6, 2014).

"NATO's Role in Kosovo." *North Atlantic Treaty Organization.* http://www.nato.int/cps/en/ natolive/topics_48818.htm (accessed January 6, 2014).

Schmidle, Nicholas. "Bring Up the Bodies." *The New Yorker*, May 6, 2013. http://www.newyorker. com/reporting/2013/05/06/130506fa_fact_ schmidle (accessed January 6, 2014).

Kurdish Conflicts

🌐 Introduction

The Kurdish conflict is an ongoing situation revolving around the treatment of Kurds in the Middle East and the proposed creation of a new nation called Kurdistan. If created, Kurdistan would include land controlled in the early 21st century by Turkey, Iraq, Iran, and Syria. With an estimated 30 to 38 million Kurds worldwide, the Kurds are the largest ethnic group in the world without their own country. Despite living for centuries near Turks, Arabs, and Persians, they remain ethnically, culturally, and linguistically distinct. The majority of Kurds are Sunni Muslim, but there are populations of Shia Muslim Kurds and small groups of Christian and Jewish Kurds as well.

Although separated from each other by national borders and different religious faiths, the Kurds maintain a strong sense of ethnic identity. During the 20th century, they formed several nationalist movements to fight for an independent Kurdish country and their right to maintain the Kurdish way of life. In intermittent conflicts beginning in 1918, Turkey, Iran, and Iraq each fought Kurdish attempts to form an independent Kurdish state. Only in Syria have the government and Kurdish population remained largely at peace. The international community does not currently recognize the Kurdish right to independence, and several of the nationalistic groups, most notably the Kurdistan Workers' Party (PKK) in Turkey, are considered terrorist organizations by most nations.

At the end of the Persian Gulf War (1990–91), a section of northern Iraq was made into Iraqi Kurdistan, an autonomous state within Iraq. It was allowed to have its own local government and parliament. The establishment of a no-fly zone over the region, which was enforced by an international coalition, protected the area from attacks by forces under the control of Iraqi President Saddam Hussein (1937–2006). Following the U.S.-led invasion of Iraq in 2003, Iraqi Kurdistan worked closely with U.S. forces and enjoyed a continuation of its autonomous status. The region generally was spared the ravages of the Iraq War (2003–11) and has prospered economically since the U.S. invasion of Iraq.

The Syrian civil war (2011–) appears to have inadvertently created a semiautonomous Kurdish region in western Syria. Syrian troops have ceded control of the region to Kurds in order to focus military resources on more direct rebel threats in eastern Syria. The situation in western Syria, however, remains tenuous at best as the civil war rages on. Kurds in other nations have not experienced such levels of autonomy, and they remain controlled by whatever national government claims their region.

🌐 Historical Background

The Kurds have inhabited an area of rugged mountains and high plains at the headwaters of the Tigris and Euphrates rivers for more than 2,000 years. The territory Kurds regard as Kurdistan (the land of the Kurds) is distributed across the borders of Turkey, Iraq, Iran, and Syria. On a few occasions in the late ancient (235–650 AD) and high medieval (1000–1300) eras, the area was referred to as Kurdistan, but there was never a single nation that was officially known by that name.

During the era of the Ottoman Empire (1301–1922), the Turks controlled large regions of southwestern Asia, northeastern Africa, and southeastern Europe. Kurdish leaders had an arrangement with the empire's rulers that allowed the Kurds to maintain order within their own population. This semiautonomous rule lasted until the end of World War I (1914–18), when the Ottoman Empire crumbled. During the peace negotiations after the war, the Kurds were initially promised their own country, but in the end the more powerful Turks, Persians, and Arabs were awarded the Kurds' land.

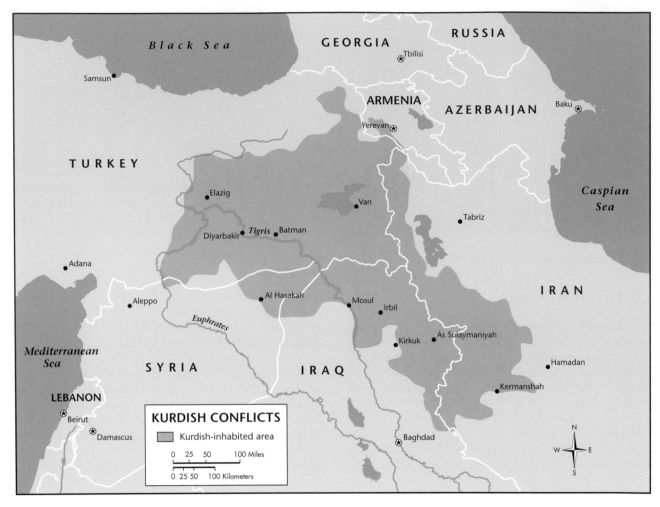

Black Sea

GEORGIA
RUSSIA
⊛Tbilisi

Samsun•

ARMENIA
AZERBAIJAN
Baku⊛

Yerevan⊛

TURKEY

Caspian
Sea

Elazig•
•Van

Tabriz•

Diyarbakir• *Tigris* •Batman

•Adana

IRAN

•Aleppo

•Al Hasakah
Mosul•
Irbil•

Euphrates

Mediterranean
Sea

Kirkuk• As Sulaymaniyah•

Hamadan•

SYRIA
IRAQ

Kermanshah•

LEBANON
Beirut⊛

KURDISH CONFLICTS
Kurdish-inhabited area

Damascus⊛

0 25 50   100 Miles

N
W⊛E
S

0 25 50   100 Kilometers

Baghdad⊛

In the first decade of the 21st century, the Kurdish population in the Middle East was estimated at more than 30 million people, with approximately 15 million in Turkey, 5 to 6 million in Iraq, 2 million in Syria, and 8 million in Iran. Another 500,000 Kurds live in areas of the former Soviet Union and 150,000 reside in Israel. Additional large Kurdish populations inhabit Europe, including about 750,000 in Germany.

⊕ Impacts and Issues

Each Kurdish diaspora community maintains a strong sense of ethnic identity and steady support for the creation of an independent Kurdish state. Kurds have been regularly and systematically persecuted throughout the Middle East—deeds that have only strengthened the Kurdish commitment to independence.

Kurds in Iraq

The Kurdish population in Iraq experienced years of repression and intermittent open conflict with Iraqi governments. By the 1970s, two separate Kurdish groups

had formed to work for independence in Iraq: the Kurdistan Democratic Party (KDP) and the Patriotic Union of Kurdistan (PUK). They united to form the Kurdistan Front in 1987, when Iraqi forces sharply escalated attacks on the Kurds.

In the final years of the Iran-Iraq War (1980–88), Iraqi President Saddam Hussein launched Operation Anfal, a campaign reportedly designed to purge northern Iraq of Kurdish guerrillas, whom he believed had ties to Iran. From February through September 1988, the Iraqi government bombed an estimated 2,000 Kurdish villages, razing many to the ground. Tens of thousands of Kurds who survived the bombings were deported to camps, where many of the men and boys were executed, according to survivors' accounts.

In March 1988, the Iraqi government attacked the Kurdish town of Halabja with chemical weapons, releasing mustard gas and other deadly poison gases. This attack killed an estimated 5,000 Kurds, wounded thousands more, and was responsible for lingering diseases and health complications for years afterward. The extermination campaign waged by Hussein against the Kurds from 1986 to 1989 claimed an estimated

Kurds have fought for their freedom for many years. Here, Mullah Mustapha Barazani, the leader of the Kurdish Democratic Party in Iraq and legendary hero of the Kurds, is pictured with two of his followers in 1960. © *Paul Popper/Popperfoto/Getty Images*

50,000 to 180,000 Kurdish lives and forced tens of thousands of Kurds to become refugees.

Since the Persian Gulf War in the early 1990s, in which a United Nations (UN) coalition stopped Iraqi troops from taking over Kuwait, the Kurds in northern Iraq have enjoyed limited self-government under the Kurdish Regional Government with the protection of Western forces. After 1992, the leaders of the KDP and the PUK stressed that the Kurds in northern Iraq did not demand independence, but rather wanted political autonomy within the state of Iraq. From 1994 to 1998, these two main Kurdish groups fought between themselves over who would control the region, but, by 2002, the Iraqi Kurds began working together to form a functioning regional parliament.

With the forced removal of Saddam Hussein from office by a U.S.-led coalition of troops in 2003, the Kurds experienced another step forward toward independent political power. Kurds won control of 25 percent of the votes in the National Assembly in the Iraqi interim (or temporary) government that replaced Hussein's government. In April 2005, Iraqis elected the country's first Kurdish president, Jalal Talabani (1933–).

In June 2009, the U.S. military began a planned withdrawal of troops from Iraqi urban areas, a cause for celebration for most Iraqis. The Kurds, however,

worried that their progress toward increased political power would be erased once the United States pulled out. To quell such fears, the administration of U.S. president Barack Obama (1961–) announced that vice president Joe Biden (1942–) would oversee policy in Iraq and ensure that the Kurds remained safe. The situation for Iraqi Kurds has been complicated by an ongoing situation between Turkey, its Kurdish population, and Iraqi Kurdistan.

Kurds in Turkey

After World War I, the leaders of Turkey attempted to unify the state under a secular government. In their efforts to revive Turkish cultural pride, Turkey's leaders banned all expressions of non-Turkish culture. Over a period of 10 years, Kurdish schools, organizations, publications, and even the Kurdish language were outlawed. All references to Kurdish regions were wiped from the map. The very name "Kurd" was expunged and Kurdish peoples were officially referred to as "mountain Turks." Almost every administrative and military post in the Kurdish parts of Turkey was staffed by ethnic Turks.

During the 1920s and 1930s, the Kurds in southeastern Turkey attempted to revolt. Each time, the Turkish military brutally defeated the uprisings. Turkey took increasingly harsh measures to suppress Kurdish rebellions, bringing a troubled peace to Turkish Kurdistan for almost half a century. After a military coup in 1980, Turkey's persecution of Kurds increased. The harsh measures were such that over the next 20 years, some 3 million Kurds fled the country.

Kurdistan Workers' Party   Around 1984, Turkey's various Kurdish rebel groups formed the Kurdistan Workers' Party (PKK) to press for the creation of an independent Kurdistan and the protection of Turkey's Kurdish population. Unwilling to assimilate into Turkish culture, the PKK launched a military and terrorism campaign against Turkey. The Turkish military responded with often heavy-handed tactics. The Kurdish-Turkish conflict has claimed approximately 45,000 lives. Although the PKK and its supporters consider the organization "freedom fighters," their cause is not supported by the majority of the international community, and they are generally considered to be terrorists.

The PKK continued to wage guerrilla warfare against the Turkish government into the 21st century. Contending that any Kurdish lands were the homelands of all Kurds, the PKK established military bases inside Iraqi Kurdistan after the removal of Iraqi dictator Saddam Hussein. Turkey's leaders have long feared that Iraq's autonomous Kurdish population, so close to its own borders, would inspire increased fervors of nationalism among Turkey's large population of Kurds.

In October 2007, responding to PKK raids and bombings in southeast Turkey, the Turkish government retaliated with bombing raids in Iraqi Kurdistan. In

A Kurd father and his baby killed by an Iraqi chemical attack on the city of Halabja in northeastern Iraq in March 1988. Saddam Hussein targeted the Kurdish population in Iraq during the Iran-Iraq War, and also used chemical weapons against Iraqi civilians. © *IRNA/AFP/ Getty Images)*

February 2008, Turkey sent thousands of troops across the border for an eight-day ground incursion. Air strikes on PKK targets in northern Iraq continued intermittently throughout 2008.

KURDISH HUNGER STRIKE

In the fall of 2012, thousands of Kurdish activists protested to bring attention to the plight of nearly 700 Kurds imprisoned in Turkey. Most of those inmates were convicted members of the PKK. Seventy prisoners launched a hunger strike on September 12, demanding expanded Kurdish rights and improved conditions for imprisoned PKK leader Abdullah Öcalan. Ultimately 682 prisoners in 67 prisons around the country joined in the strike.

The hunger strike continued for 68 days until Öcalan called for the strike to end. Despite having been in prison for well over a decade, Öcalan still retains a remarkable hold over the Kurdish community. Turkish leaders recognize that any solution to the Kurdish problem will almost certainly require Öcalan's cooperation.

In 2009, Turkey attempted to ally itself with Iraqi Kurdistan against the PKK, but negotiations failed due to a dispute over the Kirkuk territory. Located in an oil-rich region of Iraq, Kirkuk has a large population of Turkmen (an ethnic group related to the Turks). Turkey has vowed to invade northern Iraq to protect the interests of the Turkmen should the Iraqi Kurds attempt to annex Kirkuk. While Turkey and Iraqi Kurdistan argue over this point, the battle between Turkey and the PKK continues unabated.

Elections in Turkey in June 2011 sparked a resurgence in violence by the PKK. The Justice and Development Party of Prime Minister Recep Tayyip Erdogan (1954–) maintained control of the parliament, but the Kurd-supported Peace and Democracy Party won 36 seats—up from 16. Five of the winning candidates are in prison on terrorism charges, and a sixth was barred from taking his seat because he was convicted of being a member of the PKK. The decision by the Turkish High Election Board to bar this candidate from taking his seat resulted in a boycott of the parliament by the Peace and Democracy Party members, and a threat of war by the PKK. Several

Pro-Kurdish politicians Sirri Sureyya Onder (L) and Pelvin Buldan (R) read jailed Kurdish rebel chief Abdullah Öcalan's message on March 21, 2013, in the southern Turkish city of Diyarbakir at a Nowruz (Persian New Year) festival. The festival is celebrated in Turkey, Central Asian republics, Iraq, Iran, and Azerbaijan as well as war-torn Afghanistan and coincides with the astronomical vernal equinox. Jailed Kurdish rebel chief Abdullah Öcalan called on March 21 for a cease-fire, telling militants to lay down their arms and withdraw from Turkish soil, raising hopes for an end to a three-decade conflict with Turkey that has cost tens of thousands of lives. Turkish Prime Minister Recep Tayyip Erdogan responded cautiously to the much-anticipated announcement by saying Turkey would end military operations against Öcalan's outlawed Kurdistan Workers' Party (PKK) if militants halt their attacks.   © STR/AFP/Getty Images

violent skirmishes resulted in deaths on both sides of the conflict.

A series of secret talks from 2012 to 2013 between Turkey, Iraqi Kurdistan, and imprisoned PKK leader Abdullah Öcalan (1948–) led to a new solution, one in which PKK members would be allowed to migrate to Iraqi Kurdistan. Although some regard this as a sign that peace may finally be possible, many Kurds in Turkey worry that without the protection of the PKK, Turkey may once again crack down on Kurds living within Turkey's borders. Observers estimate that between 1,500 and 2,000 PKK fighters reside in Turkey, and the withdrawal process would take place over several months, if not years.

In mid-May 2013, the first groups of heavily armed fighters entered Iraqi Kurdistan after leaving Turkey. Since then the Iraqi government in Baghdad has strongly protested the migration of the PKK but has not otherwise intervened in the affairs of Iraqi Kurdistan. Despite the ceasefire, the PKK stated in October 2013 that its fighters would launch attacks in Turkey if the Turkish government and military did not cease their support of Islamist militants in Syria. The PKK fears that Syrian Islamists will attack Kurds in western Syria if the Islamist forces prevail in the Syrian civil war.

Syria

Kurds constitute the largest ethnic minority in Syria, making up approximately 10 percent of the country's population. As in other countries, Syrian Kurds have faced routine discrimination by the government. At various points, Syrian Kurds have asked for political autonomy of the Kurdish-majority regions of western Syria, hoping for an arrangement similar to Iraqi Kurdistan. Syrian Kurds have also joined in dialogue for an independent Kurdistan.

Late in 1979, Kurdish rebel leader Abdullah Öcalan moved his rebel forces from Turkey to Syria, where for the next 20 years he received the support of the Syrian government. From 1984 until 1999, up to 20 percent of the PKK guerrillas fighting in Turkey were Kurds from Syria. In October 1998, Turkey threatened to invade Syria if it did not evict Öcalan and other PKK fighters. Öcalan was captured and imprisoned in 1999 and the PKK was evicted from Syria.

Since the Syrian civil war broke out in 2011, the Syrian government has been forced to abandon much of western Syria. The Kurds immediately began to fill the political power vacuum in the region and have governed these areas virtually autonomously. However, the Syrian civil war is an ongoing conflict and until it is resolved, the fate of Syrian Kurds remains unknown.

Iran

The Kurds of Iran succeeded in establishing the Kurdish Republic of Mahabad at the end of 1945, though the state lasted less than a month. Nevertheless, the Kurdish Republic of Mahabad has been a symbol of hope for all Kurds who still work and fight for an independent Kurdistan. After the assumption of power by the Islamic Republic of Iran in 1979, warfare between the Iranians and the Kurds persisted until the end of the century, with the Kurdish leaders continuing to seek political autonomy. The situation for Kurds in Iran is currently stable and looks to remain so for the foreseeable future.

⊕ Future Implications

The Kurds may eventually win their independence. The semiautonomous Kurdish regions in Iraq and Syria will likely grow stronger in the coming years. Whether these regions will become fully independent or join together to form an independent Kurdistan remains unknown. Turkey has repeatedly indicated an unwillingness to give up any of its territory for the creation of a Kurdistan nation, and Iran retains a stranglehold on its Kurdish population.

A large part of the resistance to Kurdish independence is attributable to the sizable portions of the Middle East's most prized resources—oil reserves and water sources—that are located in the proposed country of Kurdistan. Although ethnic discrimination is often cited as a reason for the conflicts, the economics of the Kurdish situation feature prominently in the ongoing dispute. Currently, the civilian Kurdish populations are protected and, even in Turkey, there has been a loosening of laws in regard to Kurdish language and cultures. The Kurdish situation remains tenuous, however. Tensions could reignite into open war at any time and the Kurdish situation amid the Syrian civil war remains a source of concern for the Kurds.

SEE ALSO *Iran-Iraq War; Iranian Revolution; Islam: Sunni and Shia Disputes; Syrian Civil War; U.S.-Iraq War*

BIBLIOGRAPHY

Books

King, Diane E. *Kurdistan on the Global Stage: Kinship, Land, and Community in Iraq.* New Brunswick, NJ: Rutgers University Press, 2013.

Lawrence, Quill. *Invisible Nation: How the Kurd's Quest for Statehood Is Shaping Iraq and the Middle East.* Chicago: University of Chicago Press, 2008.

Marcus, Aliza. *Blood and Belief: The PKK and the Kurdish Fight for Independence.* New York: NYU Press, 2009.

McKiernan, Kevin. *The Kurds: A People in Search of Their Homeland.* New York: St. Martin's Press, 2006.

Meiselas, Susan. *Kurdistan: In the Shadow of History.* Chicago: University of Chicago Press, 2008.

Web Sites

"Kurdistan." *Google Maps.* https://maps.google.com/maps/ms?ie=UTF8&t=h&oe=UTF8&msa=0&msid=10164012686043517 0753.00048e850e000496e2f84 (accessed December 27, 2013).

"The Kurds' Story." *Frontline, PBS.* http://www.pbs.org/wgbh/pages/frontline/shows/saddam/kurds/ (accessed December 27, 2013).

"Welcome to Washington Kurdish Institute." *Washington Kurdish Institute.* www.kurd.org (accessed December 27, 2013).

"Who Are the Kurds?" *Washington Post.* http://www.washingtonpost.com/wp-srv/inatl/daily/feb99/kurdprofile.htm (accessed December 27, 2013).

Lebanon: Civil War and Political Instability

⊕ Introduction

The Republic of Lebanon is a country on the eastern Mediterranean Sea bordered by Syria and Israel. The Lebanese population is divided among 18 officially recognized sects of Islam and Christianity. Lebanon's diverse religious communities led to a unique power-sharing political system. Based on the population census of 1932, Lebanon's government requires a Maronite Christian president, a Sunni Muslim prime minister, and a Shia Muslim speaker of the house.

For 40 years this political division of power functioned fairly well and Lebanon was a rare democratic nation in the Middle East. However, since 1975, Lebanon has suffered from extreme political instability. Government systems meant to deter sectarian conflict have instead made it difficult, if not impossible, to maintain peace in Lebanon.

Lebanon is home to the Shia militant group Hezbollah ("Party of God"), which has become an exceedingly powerful force in the region. It emerged during the Lebanese civil war (1975–90) and initially focused on ending Israel's occupation of southern Lebanon. After the civil war, Hezbollah was the only militant group that was allowed to remain armed. During the 21st century Hezbollah has become a major player in Lebanon's domestic and international political relations. The country's government is fairly weak, and Hezbollah is the most organized and well-funded political group in the nation.

⊕ Historical Background

Lebanon's political system is based on the 1932 population census. At that time, Maronite Christians were the majority religious group with approximately 33 percent of the total population, followed by Sunni Muslims

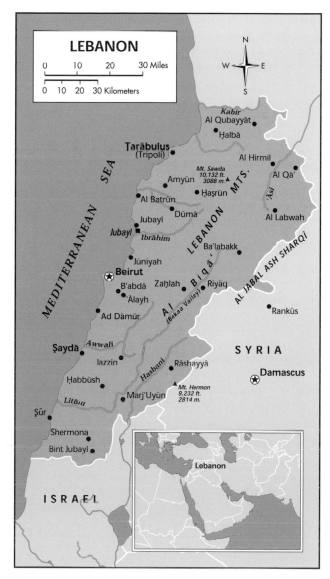

© 2014 Cengage Learning

at 25 percent, and Shia Muslims at 20 percent. The remaining 22 percent was divided among 15 other religious sects, notably adherents to the Eastern Orthodox Church in Lebanon (the second largest Christian denomination after the Maronites) and the Druze, members of a monotheistic faith whose teachings draw on multiple religious and philosophical sources.

Since that time, the population demographics have shifted significantly, partly because the Muslim population is growing at a faster rate than the Christians, and partly as a result of emigration patterns. In the 21st century, the largest religious populations are equally divided between Sunni and Shia at 26–29 percent, followed by Maronites at 21 percent, but the government division remains the same.

The establishment of the state of Israel in 1948 displaced 100,000 Palestine refugees, predominantly Sunnis, who took shelter in southern Lebanon. Although this population has not been granted citizenship in Lebanon, their presence changed the demographics of the country and threatened to upset the balance of power within the government.

In 1970 the Palestine Liberation Organization (PLO) was expelled from Jordan, prompting an arms race among Lebanon's religious sects. The Cold War (1945–91) further polarized Christian and Muslim groups in Lebanon, as Christians tended to favor the United States and Muslims generally sided with the Soviet Union.

Lebanese Civil War

The Lebanese civil war was a multifaceted conflict that resulted in an estimated 120,000 fatalities, 76,000 displaced people, and an exodus of almost one million people, primarily from the upper and middle classes. It began as a fight between the Maronite Christians and the Palestinian forces, and then became more complicated as various Muslim groups allied themselves with the Palestinians. Alliances shifted regularly, and by the end of the war, virtually every group had at one point allied with and betrayed every other party.

Foreign governments—including Iraq, Israel, Libya, and the Soviet Union—funded or supplied arms to the

A katyusha rocket is fired from the back of an army truck into an apartment complex during the Lebanese Civil War, Lebanon, in 1975. The war, which lasted until 1990, was fought between a bewildering array of sectarian, ideological, and foreign armed factions in continuously shifting alliances. Most prominent were the rightist Maronite Christian Phalangists, the secular Palestinian PLO, the Israelis, the Syrians, the Druze, the Shia Amal, and Hezbollah. © *Express/Getty Images*

militias, prompting more alliances and betrayals. Syrian troops entered Lebanon in 1976 ostensibly as a peace-keeping force but remained in the country for nearly 30 years.

Hezbollah was conceived at this time as a more militant answer to the existing Shia organization, Amal. As a Shia militant group, it had immediate allies among the Shia in Lebanon, the Alawis-dominated government in Syria, and the Shia government in Iran. (The Alawis are a small Muslim sect that has some affinities to the Shia.) Unlike the other militant groups, Hezbollah did not spend its time fighting other Lebanese sects. Instead it concentrated its energy on guerrilla warfare against Israel, which had invaded southern Lebanon in 1982.

The Taif Agreement In 1989 the Arab League (formally the League of Arab States, an association of independent countries with mainly Arabic-speaking populations), spearheaded by Saudi Arabia (Taif is a city in Saudi Arabia), helped Lebanese leaders draft the Taif Agreement and end the war. The document pardoned all political crimes, dissolved the militias, and allowed the government to begin slowly rebuilding the nation. According to the Taif Agreement, the Lebanese government would be restructured (at some undefined period in the future) to reflect the changing demographics.

The civil war had destroyed the Lebanese economy and left the capital city, Beirut, in ruins. Syrian armed forces were allowed to remain in the country until peace was fully secured. Hezbollah was also allowed to remain armed since Israeli troops were stationed in a security zone in southern Lebanon.

Lebanon: 1990–2000

In 1990, as sectarian fighting was winding down, the Syrian army pushed into the Christian stronghold of General Michel Aoun (1935–) in eastern Beirut. Newly elected Lebanese president Elias Hrawi (1925–2006), a Maronite Christian, supported the Syrian army's move against a rival Christian sect that denied the legitimacy of his presidency. In May 1991 President Hrawi signed the Treaty of Brotherhood, Cooperation and Coordination with Syria. The treaty stated that Syria, through its military occupation of Lebanon, would ensure Lebanon's independence and sovereignty.

Throughout the 1980s and 1990s, Hezbollah carried out regular suicide attacks against Israeli military and civilian targets in Lebanon and Israel. From humble beginnings, Hezbollah gradually morphed into a well-armed paramilitary organization. As its access to advanced weaponry increased, Hezbollah began launching grenade and missile attacks on Israeli targets. Israeli forces finally withdrew from southern Lebanon in 2000. The Israeli withdrawal boosted the popularity of Hezbollah among Lebanon's Shia population and temporarily earned it the grudging respect of other Muslims.

Problems with Syria

Lebanese tensions with Syria boiled over following the assassination of the former prime minister of Lebanon, Rafic Hariri (1944–2005), in February 2005. Hariri and 21 others were killed in an explosion in front of the St. George Hotel in Beirut. Anti–Syrian political parties in Lebanon accused Syria of sponsoring the assassination of Hariri, who was critical of a Syrian-supported constitutional amendment to allow Lebanon's pro–Syrian president to remain in office. Syria and pro–Syrian political parties in Lebanon blamed the killing on Israel.

The assassination launched the peaceful Cedar Revolution, which demanded the withdrawal of Syrian troops from Lebanon. After two months of nonsectarian demonstrations, Syria withdrew all of its troops from Lebanon. The country's pro–Syrian government was dissolved. The relationship between Lebanon and Syria has remained strained ever since.

Hezbollah in the 21st Century

The role of the pro–Syrian militant group Hezbollah has further complicated the Lebanese-Syrian relationship, particularly following a month-long war between Hezbollah paramilitary forces and Israel in 2006. The fighting began after Hezbollah killed three Israeli soldiers and took two soldiers hostage. After a failed rescue attempt, Israel conducted air strikes and artillery bombing of targets in Lebanon. Israeli ground forces also moved into southern Lebanon in an attempt to neutralize Hezbollah forces. In response Hezbollah fired missiles into towns in northern Israel.

A November 2006 United Nations (UN) report on the conflict estimated that the fighting killed more than 1,000 Lebanese civilians and 500 Hezbollah militants, while 121 Israeli soldiers and 44 Israeli civilians died. The conflict displaced approximately one million Lebanese civilians and between 300,000 and 500,000 Israeli civilians. Following a UN-negotiated cease-fire, Israel withdrew from southern Lebanon, except for a few disputed areas. This was the first time that an Arab group had successfully fought against Israel, and Hezbollah's ranks and reputation soared.

After the Israeli retreat, Hezbollah no longer faced a direct enemy, and it turned its attention to the political instability of Lebanon itself. Beginning in December 2006, Hezbollah and other opposition parties sponsored sit-in demonstrations against the government of Prime Minister Fouad Siniora (1943–). In early May 2008 the Lebanese government responded by shutting down Hezbollah's telecommunications network. Hezbollah militants then seized several neighborhoods in West Beirut. This action was viewed by the Lebanese government as a coup attempt.

The street fighting ended on May 21, 2008, when all parties agreed to the Arab League-negotiated Doha Agreement. Under the terms of the agreement, all sides

A Shia Lebanese family walks past an abandoned Israeli Army armored personnel carrier (APC) in August 2006, decorated with Lebanese and Hezbollah flags, a picture of the Hezbollah leader Sheikh Hassan Nasrallah, and picture of Iranian spiritual leader Ali Khamenei amid the rubble of the former Israeli-run prison of Khiam on the Lebanese-Israeli border. Parts of Khiam were levelled by Israeli bombardment the previous month until a cease-fire, claimed as a victory by both sides, was declared.   *© Patrick Baz/AFP/Getty Images*

approved Michel Suleiman (1948–) as Lebanon's president. The agreement also formed a national unity government that guaranteed the opposition a veto over most government decisions. Rafic Hariri's son, Saad Hariri (1971–), became the majority leader in parliament as leader of the anti–Syrian Future Movement political party.

Hezbollah seemed to enjoy a resurgence of popular support just weeks before the June 2009 elections in Lebanon. Analysts speculated that if Hezbollah became the majority party in parliament, Syria would have renewed influence in Lebanon. Further, efforts by U.S. president Barack Obama (1961–) to negotiate a peaceful solution to the ongoing territorial dispute between the Israelis and Palestinians could be stymied by a resurgent Hezbollah, whose members are against reconciliation with Israel. However, the pro–Western coalition retained its majority after the June 2009 election, which saw heavy voter turnout.

Despite his coalition's victory, Saad Hariri still needed support from other political parties to form a government. Hariri tried for 10 weeks to negotiate with various political leaders to come up with a list of cabinet nominees, but in early September 2009 he abandoned his effort and proposed his own cabinet list. The move outraged the Hezbollah-led opposition and prompted Hariri to step aside as prime minister designate rather than submit a new list. President Suleiman renamed Hariri as prime minister designate a few days later and asked him to try again to form a government. Hariri finally succeeded in forming a working government in November 2009.

The Return of Sectarian Violence

In January 2011 the Lebanese government collapsed after 11 pro-Syrian ministers resigned ahead of indictments being issued in the Rafic Hariri assassination case. A new government headed by a pro–Syrian coalition was formed in June 2011, after months of intense bickering. In the first half of 2011, widespread antigovernment protests in Syria included deadly sectarian clashes along the Lebanese-Syrian border. This in turn led to an increase in sectarian violence in Lebanon. Analysts voiced concern that the fall of the Syrian government could also further destabilize Lebanon and inflame Sunni-Shia tensions.

As protests in Syria continued, Hezbollah leader Sayyed Hassan Nasrallah (1960–) announced the organization's support for embattled Syrian president Bashar al-Assad (1965–). The next day former Lebanese prime minister Saad Hariri announced via Twitter that he and his Future Movement bloc "openly and proudly" supported the uprising of the Syrian people. Nasrallah had accused protesters in Syria of seeking a regime that would "rubber stamp" U.S. and Israeli policies.

On October 19, 2012, Lebanon's head of internal intelligence, Wissam al-Hassan (1965–2012), and eight other people were killed in a massive car bomb attack in central Beirut. Al-Hassan was generally regarded as an adversary of Syria, in part due to his friendship with opposition leader Saad Hariri as well as his role in organizing the arrest of a former minister who supposedly was planning—with the backing of Syria—a bombing campaign in Lebanon. Both the Syrian government and Hezbollah condemned the assault. Attended by thousands, the funeral for al-Hassan ended in a riot, as protesters called for the prime minister of Lebanon, Najib Mikati (1955–), to resign.

In late March 2013 Prime Minister Mikati resigned, partly due to increasing sectarian discord caused by Lebanon's close association with Syria and the tensions caused by the ongoing civil war in Syria. Mikati, a Sunni, initially had the support of the powerful Hezbollah bloc of the government and tried to reconcile the pro–Syria Shia Lebanese and the Sunni Lebanese, most of whom supported the rebels in Syria. However, as the Syrian war continued, the compromise Mikati sought became unreachable as Sunni activists increasingly viewed him as pro–Hezbollah.

⊕ Impacts and Issues

Tensions in Lebanon remain significant. Violence is a common occurrence. Political turmoil with nearby nations fuels the internal conflict. The country still struggles from the impact of the Lebanese civil war. With so much unrest within and outside Lebanon, citizens are concerned that another conflict could erupt, especially with Syria.

In November 2013, the Iranian Embassy in Beirut was bombed, killing at least 23 people. According to various Middle East experts, the incident could indicate that the civil war in Syria was moving into Lebanon. Coupled with a significant increase in violence along the border, the bombing caused concern over the impact that Hezbollah's support of the Syrian government is having on Lebanon.

In most of the Arab world, Hezbollah is considered a resistance group. However, Israel and many Western nations have designated it a terrorist organization due to its alleged high-profile terror attacks. The European Union (EU) added Hezbollah's military wing to its list

A SHIA PERSPECTIVE OF HEZBOLLAH

Hezbollah is viewed by Israel and many Western nations as a terrorist organization due to various actions by its military wing. Yet many Shia view Hezbollah as more than a militia. For them, the organization functions as a political group as well as a provider of social services. Hezbollah, along with Amal, is one of two political parties that represents the Shia population of Lebanon. Hezbollah runs hospitals and medical clinics, news outlets, schools, and agricultural centers, among other services.

In addition, it has set up economic and infrastructure developmental projects throughout southern Lebanon. When the old infrastructure failed, as in 2006 when tens of thousands of people were without clean water, Hezbollah immediately responded to the situation. According to news reports in 2006, Hezbollah stepped in like a government would, helping hospitals, schools, and public utilities.

The organization also provides financial support to the families of "martyrs" killed during the frequent fighting. For many Shia, Hezbollah is the only social service on which they can predictably rely.

A girl holds posters of Hezbollah leader Sayyed Hassan Nasrallah, who is viewed as a hero by some supporters of Hezbollah.
© *Scott Peterson/Getty Images*

of terrorist organizations in mid-2013. Within Lebanon itself Hezbollah's status is contentious.

⊕ Future Implications

The UN estimates that more than 100,000 people have been killed in the Syrian civil war. The situation in Lebanon remains extremely unstable. The possibility of war with Syria is high as is the chance of another Lebanese civil war. Hezbollah could potentially protect Lebanon

The ambassador of the European Union to Lebanon, Angelina Eichhorst, meets with head of Hezbollah's International Relations, Ammar al-Mussawi (L) following the European Union's decision to blacklist Hezbollah's armed wing on July 25, 2013, in the Lebanese capital Beirut. © *AFP/Getty Images*

or cause it to descend into chaos. Hezbollah retains the support of Lebanon's Shia population, but is widely mistrusted by Sunnis and Christians.

In April and June 2013 Syrian helicopters fired rockets into Lebanon. Meanwhile Syrian rebels threatened to move the battle into Lebanon and fired into the eastern region of Hermel in Lebanon. The rebels claimed they were retaliating for previous strikes from Hezbollah, which dominates the region. The Lebanese government warned that any further attacks would be considered an act of war. Hezbollah responded with its own attacks on Syrian rebel forces.

More than 677,000 Syrian refugees, many of them Sunnis of Palestinian descent, have fled into Lebanon to escape the Syrian civil war. If they remain in Lebanon, they will add one more complicated factor to the demographics of this Middle Eastern nation. The Lebanese government has refused to build additional refugee camps, so the Syrian refugee population can be found throughout the country. More than three-quarters of the refugee population are women and children.

SEE ALSO   *Israeli-Palestinian Conflict; Terrorism: State Sponsored; United Nations*

BIBLIOGRAPHY

Books

Blanford, Nicholas. *Warriors of God: Inside Hezbollah's Thirty-Year Struggle Against Israel.* New York: Random House, 2011.

Fisk, Robert. *Pity the Nation: The Abduction of Lebanon.* New York: Nation Books, 2002.

Haugbolle, Sune. *War and Memory in Lebanon.* New York: Cambridge University Press, 2010.

Mackay, Sandra. *Lebanon: A House Divided.* New York: W. W. Norton & Company, 2006.

Rabinovich, Itamar. *The War for Lebanon: 1970–1985.* New York: Cornell University Press, 1985.

Web Sites

Brumfield, Ben. "Record Sum Needed to Handle Burden on Lebanon from Syria's Civil War." *CNN,* December 16, 2013. http://www.cnn.com/2013/12/16/world/meast/syria-civil-war-lebanon/index.html (accessed December 17, 2013).

Gradstein, Linda. "Israel Launches Information War Against Hezbollah." *The Jerusalem Post*, July 14, 2013. http://www.jpost.com/Middle East/Israel-launches-information-war-against-Hezbollah-319786 (accessed December 17, 2013).

"Lebanon Asks the EU Not to Blacklist Hezbollah." *AlJazeera*, July 19, 2013. http://www.aljazeera.com/news/europe/2013/07/20137195158260569.html (accessed December 17, 2013).

"Who Are Hezbollah?" *BBC News*. http://news.bbc.co.uk/2/hi/middle_east/4314423.stm (accessed December 17, 2013).

Liberia's Civil Wars

⊕ Introduction

Beginning in 1980, the African nation of Liberia was wracked by civil war. In that year a non-commissioned officer, Samuel Doe (1951–1990) led a military rebellion that overthrew and murdered the elected president, William R. Tolbert, Jr. (1913–1980). The assassination plunged Liberia into a long period of instability. Between 1989 and 1996, civil war raged throughout the country; an estimated 250,000 Liberian lives were lost. In 1990, rebels led by Prince Johnson and Charles Taylor (1948–) overcame government forces and captured and killed Doe. During the following years, Taylor continued to gain land and power and was elected president in 1997. The corruption of his regime led to another civil war, which began in 1999, and again devastated the county. His rule over Liberia was also marred by his involvement in the Sierra Leone War, which led to Taylor's resignation and arrest in 2003. In 2006 Ellen Johnson Sirleaf (1938–) was elected president; she is the first woman head of state in Africa. She was reelected in 2011.

⊕ Historical Background

Situated on the west coast of Africa, Liberia's southern shores border the Atlantic Ocean. The country is bordered by Sierra Leone to the northwest, Guinea to the due north, and Côte d'Ivoire to the east and northeast. Liberia is comprised of a low-lying coastal plain to the south, with a central rolling plain and a mountainous region in the country's northeast. Liberia was relatively stable until a 1990s civil war ravaged the country, leaving approximately 250,000 people dead and the infrastructure in ruins.

The population of Liberia was estimated at more than almost 4 million in 2013. The nation is home to

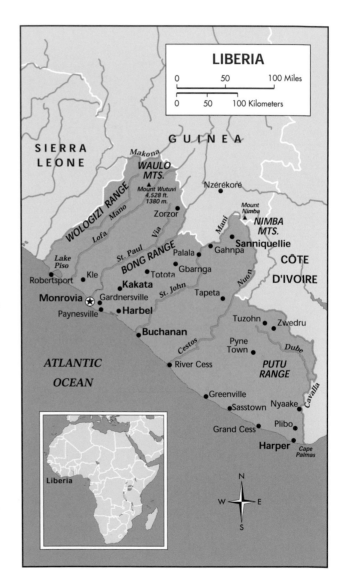

© 2014 Cengage Learning

about 28 different ethnic groups, with most of the population (approximately 95 percent) comprised of indigenous African tribes that can be divided into 3 main groups: the Mande, the Kru, and the Mel. The remaining 5 percent of the population is descended from slaves from the United States and the Caribbean who immigrated to Liberia after gaining their freedom.

"Americo Africans"

The former slaves that immigrated to Liberia ruled the country for many years, wielding extensive power over the other ethnic groups and, in some cases, amassing huge fortunes. The continued tensions between these "Americo Africans," or "Americo Liberians," and the other ethnic groups remains a source of unrest in contemporary Liberia.

Liberia was founded in 1822 as a colony for freed slaves from the United States. In 1847, Liberians declared their nation to be a republic. Though Liberia avoided political domination by any European power during the 19th century, the nation suffered economically through the loss of some of its lands. In the 20th century, under the 27-year tenure (from 1944–1971) of President William Tubman (1895–1971), Liberia thrived economically and united politically. There was a peaceful transition after Tubman's death in 1971, when Tubman's Vice President, William Tolbert (1913–1980), took power. However Tolbert's presidency was ended by a coup led by Doe. Eventually the nation exploded into civil war that lasted for many years, ending in 2003. The country has hosted peaceful democratic elections since then, although the political situation in the country remains fragile and United Nations (UN) peacekeepers maintain a strong presence in the country.

Liberia's First Civil War

In 1980, Doe led a coup that made him the first non-Americo Liberian president of Liberia. During the weeks

Rebels loyal to warlord Charles Taylor of the National Patriotic Front of Liberia (NPFL) beat a civilian in the streets of Monrovia August 15, 1990, during the fighting with the Armed Forces of Liberia (AFL) loyal to president Samuel Doe. In December 1989 an armed insurrection by rebel forces began in the northeastern border region of Nimba County. In early 1990 several hundred deaths ensued in fighting between the AFL and rebels, who claimed to be members of a hitherto unknown opposition group the NPFL, led by a former government official, Charles Taylor. © *Pascal Guyot/AFP/Getty Images*

and years following the coup, Doe and his followers held mass executions, murdering Tolbert's cabinet and supporters. Doe later had many of his political opponents assassinated. Though he had promised a return to civilian government (Doe created a new constitution in 1984 and held elections in 1985), his military-backed regime oppressed dissenters and was widely suspected of running fraudulent elections. Resistance to Doe's regime grew, and a civil war broke out in 1989. Rebels captured Doe in 1990, then tortured and executed him. The civil war, which became known as the First Liberian Civil War, continued. A former member of Doe's administration, who had left following charges of embezzlement, emerged as one of the victors. Following elections marred by allegations of widespread voter intimidation, Taylor was sworn in as president on August 2, 1997.

The Second Liberian Civil War started in 1999 with attacks by several rebel groups. One of the main groups was comprised of people displaced by the first war.

The Organization of Displaced Liberians invaded from their refugee camps in Ghana. Other groups, including Liberian United for Reconciliation and Democracy (LURD) and Movement for Democracy in Liberia, attacked in other regions. By 2003, Taylor's forces controlled only one third of the country. Following the two-month Siege of Monrovia, during which LURD forces battled Taylor's forces in fighting that left more than 1,000 civilians dead, Taylor went into exile. He was stopped trying to cross the border into Cameroon; his car allegedly contained large amounts of cash and heroin.

⊕ Impacts and Issues

The turmoil in Liberia reflects a familiar pattern that can be found in other countries. A soldier (Samuel Doe) takes power in a coup, but the corruption and brutality that follow his usurpation provoke a vicious armed

A Liberian child refugee walks among plastic tents at the Gerihun camp July 18, 2002, near Bo, Sierra Leone. Liberia was in the midst of a decade-long conflict, causing an influx into the camps that once housed internally displaced Sierra Leonians. Liberia's rebels waged an insurgency for three years, but stepped up attacks against President Charles Taylor's government in mid-2002. Taylor, a former warlord who won presidential elections in 1997, said he was being targeted by some of his rivals from the 1989–96 civil war. The heavy toll on civilians in the fighting posed a threat to the stability of other countries in the region, particularly Sierra Leone. In July 2002, there were about 50,000 Liberian refugees in Sierra Leone and 100,000 internally displaced people within Liberia according to the World Food Program. © *Ami Vitale/Getty Images*

resistance that leaves him dead and the nation in ruins. However in the case of Liberia, the pattern was broken. Taylor, another corrupt soldier, seized power and ruled after Doe's death, but he was brought to justice and a free election held, hopefully leading to a lasting peaceful democracy.

The civil wars all but destroyed the Liberian economy. Though the nation is rich in mineral resources, water, arable farm land, and forests, an estimated 85 percent of the country's workforce was unemployed and about 80 percent of the nation's population lived below the poverty line after the wars. All sides were alleged to have committed atrocities. Mutilation of the human body became the calling card of the war. Combatants hacked off limbs, ears, and noses of both their military and political foes and innocent civilians, leaving them to live or die where they lay.

Corruption

In 2012, Taylor was convicted by the Special Court for Sierra Leone of war crimes for his part in aiding and abetting the rebels in Sierra Leone during the 1991–2002 civil war in that country. The Special Court for Sierra

BLOOD DIAMONDS AND THE SUPERMODEL

Blood diamonds, also called "conflict diamonds," are diamonds that are illegally mined and traded by rebel or outlaw groups in war-torn areas to fund military actions against legitimate governments. Blood diamonds are usually associated with violent conflict in the African countries of Liberia, Angola, Sierra Leone, the Democratic Republic of Congo, and Côte d'Ivoire.

Liberia's blood diamond trade was in the media spotlight in August 2010, when celebrity supermodel Naomi Campbell (1970–) was called to testify in the war crimes trial of Charles Taylor. Campbell testified that in 1997 she was given "dirty-looking stones" by two men who appeared outside her room after she attended a charity dinner at which Taylor was present. Campbell says the men told her the stones were "a gift." She says she gave the stones, presumably diamonds, to the manager of a charity founded by former South African president and anti-apartheid activist Nelson Mandela (1918– 2013). The blood diamonds were part of the case that led to Taylor's conviction in April 2012.

Liberian President Ellen Johnson Sirleaf (C) walks to the UN Security Council to brief it on the situation in Liberia on March 17, 2006. Johnson Sirleaf confirmed that she had formally asked Nigeria to hand over her exiled predecessor Charles Taylor. "I asked the African (Union) leadership to bring the Taylor issue to closure," she told reporters shortly before the briefing. Taylor was convicted of war crimes in 2013. © *Nicholas Roberts/AFP/Getty Images*

ELLEN JOHNSON SIRLEAF

Ellen Eugenia Johnson was born in 1938 in the Liberian capital of Monrovia. Her father was the first indigenous African in Liberia's national legislature. She married James Sirleaf when she was 17 and soon became the mother of four children. She accompanied her husband to the United States and earned degrees from the Madison College of Business, the University of Colorado, and the John F. Kennedy School of Government at Harvard University.

In 1972 she went to work in the Finance Department of the Liberian government, becoming Finance Minister in 1979. The following year, Samuel Doe seized control of the government and executed most of the cabinet ministers, sparing Sirleaf's life. She was jailed twice during the years of the Doe dictatorship. After several years working as an Assistant Secretary General of the United Nations, with responsibility for African development, she returned to Liberia and ran in its 1997 presidential election, finishing a distant second to Charles Taylor. She departed the country again, returning in 2003, as the Second Liberian Civil War wound down, and participated in the nation's interim government.

Sirleaf ran as the Unity Party candidate for president in 2005, defeating soccer star George Weah with a 59 percent majority in the second round of voting, and was inaugurated on January 16, 2006, as the first female head of state in modern African history. Among her accomplishments in office were the establishment of a universal right to primary education and negotiating the cancellation of most of the nation's external debt.

Leone was jointly established by the government of Sierra Leone and the United Nations to investigate and prosecute crimes committed during Sierra Leone's civil unrest. Throughout the trial, which began in 2007, Taylor adamantly maintained his innocence, denying any involvement in the atrocities that occurred during the war.

In April 2012, the court convicted Taylor on 11 counts of war crimes and crimes against humanity, including murder, rape, torture, terrorism, and the conscription of child soldiers. Although the court also found Taylor guilty of providing significant support to the rebels and having knowledge of their criminal actions, the judges ruled that he could not be held responsible for ordering the crimes committed by Sierra Leone's rebel forces, stating that the prosecution had not proven beyond a reasonable doubt that he was involved in a joint criminal enterprise.

Taylor's conviction was the first time that an international court had convicted a former head of state since the post–World War II (1939–45) Nuremberg Trials, which prosecuted the Nazi leadership at the end of the war. In a brief submitted to the court, prosecutors, citing the magnitude of Taylor's crimes, pushed for the maximum sentence: 80 years in prison. In his final opportunity to speak before the court before sentencing, Taylor accused the prosecutors of bribing and coercing witnesses against him. He further insisted that he was no threat to society, and appealed to the court to recognize his familial responsibilities as a father, grandfather, and great-grandfather. Nevertheless, Taylor was sentenced to 50 years in prison for his crimes.

Taylor appealed his conviction at a United Nations-backed court in The Hague in January 2013. Taylor's lawyers argued that the trial's verdict was based on "uncorroborated hearsay evidence" and filed more than 40 grounds for appeal. Yet in October 2013 he began to serve the remainder of his 50-year sentence in a prison in the United Kingdom.

Fighting Corruption

Following the end of the Second Liberian Civil War, elections were scheduled. Ellen Johnson Sirleaf became Africa's first female head of state when she took office as president of Liberia in 2006. Making good on a campaign promise to fight corruption, Sirleaf rolled out new measures in December 2009, offering financial compensation and job security to anyone who reported fruitful leads on acts of corruption. The measures were designed to protect and reward individuals who break their silence about corruption. Under the program, 5 percent of any recovered funds were to be given to the whistleblower, and if that person testified against his or her work superior, the government would arrange a job transfer to reduce employee fear.

Sirleaf was a candidate for reelection in 2011. In the first round of voting in October 2011, Sirleaf captured 44 percent of the vote while her rival, Winston Tubman (1941–), came in with 31 percent. Since neither candidate won a majority, a runoff election was held November 8, 2011. Despite pleas by foreign observers, Tubman boycotted the runoff election, claiming that the process was rigged. As a result, Sirleaf was the only candidate on the ballot and won reelection. She pledged reconciliation and a commitment to cooperation, steps seen as necessary both to preserve democracy and navigate a legislature in which her party was the minority.

Sirleaf was awarded the Nobel Peace Prize in October 2011 for her political reforms and for encouraging reconciliation in postwar Liberia. Another Liberian woman, Leymah Gbowee (1972–), shared the award with Sirleaf for her opposition to the civil war and for her advocacy of female participation in the political process.

⊕ Future Implications

In 2014, eleven years after warring parties signed a peace agreement and nine years since the historical elections took place, Liberia was more stable. Still burdened by its history of violence and, especially, a challenging

Colonel "Black Diamond" (C, with glasses) is flanked by her women bodyguards, members of the LURD (Liberians United for Reconciliation and Democracy) on August 9, 2003, as they return from a patrol around the bridge "Newbridge" in Monrovia's rebel held Northern area. Black Diamond began fighting for the rebels' Women's Artillery Commandos (WAC) after her parents were killed and she was gang-raped by President Charles Taylor's troops. Many of the other women fighters have similar stories, taking up arms because they believed it better to fight than to be victimized. Taylor stepped down from power August 11, 2003, and went into exile in Nigeria. He was later convicted of war crimes, including rape and murder, by the international court in the Hague. © *Georges Gobet/AFP/Getty Images*

economy, Liberia is moving toward having a respectable, strong democracy.

However, old problems persist. Sirleaf, once lauded as a leader in fighting corruption, is now occasionally criticized as being corrupt herself. Whether she is or not, the initial joy of newfound peace is giving way to the rigors of a messy, impoverished democracy. Despite its fragility, the nascent democracy continues to take hold: former warlords are talking about fighting for votes in the 2017 elections.

PRIMARY SOURCE

The Prosecutor vs. Charles Ghankay Taylor: Summary of Charges

SOURCE *"The Prosecutor vs. Charles Ghankay Taylor: Summary of Charges."* The Special Court for Sierra Leone, *March 16, 2006. http://www.sc-sl.org*

/LinkClick.aspx?fileticket=Mb00aVVb4Cg=&ta bid=107.html (accessed November 5, 2013).

INTRODUCTION *The trial of former Liberian President Charles Taylor, held at The Hague, commenced in 2007 and ended in his conviction in April 2012 for aiding and abetting war crimes and crimes against humanity. An appeal was overturned and the conviction upheld on September 26, 2013. Taylor's conviction marked the first time since the World War II Nuremberg Trails that a former head of state was convicted by an international court. In October 2013 Taylor was transferred to an unnamed British prison to serve the remainder of his 50 year sentence. The summary of charges shown here was presented by the UN backed Special Court for Sierra Leone.*

The Accused

Charles Ghankay Taylor, the former President of Liberia, was indicted on 7 March 2003 on a 17-count indictment for crimes against humanity, violations of Article 3 common to the Geneva Conventions and of Additional

Protocol II (commonly known as war crimes), and other serious violations of international humanitarian law. The indictment was ordered kept under seal. The Prosecutor unsealed the indictment on 4 June 2003, during Taylor's first trip out of Liberia since the signing of the indictment.

On 16 March 2006 a Judge of the Special Court approved an amended indictment reducing the number of counts to 11.

The Charges

Charles Taylor faces an 11-count indictment for crimes against humanity, violations of Article 3 Common to the Geneva Conventions and of Additional Protocol II, and other serious violations of international humanitarian law.

*1 = Crimes Against Humanity

*2 = Violation of Article 3 Common to the Geneva Conventions and of Additional Protocol II (war crimes)

*3 = Other serious violation of international humanitarian law

Terrorizing the civilian population and collective punishments

1. Acts of terrorism. *2

Unlawful killings

2. Murder *1
3. Violence to life, health and physical or mental well-being of persons, in particular murder *2

Sexual violence

4. Rape *1
5. Sexual slavery and any other form of sexual violence *1
6. Outrages upon personal dignity *2

Physical violence

7. Violence to life, health and physical or mental well-being of persons, in particular cruel treatment *2
8. Other inhumane acts *1

Use of child soldiers

9. Conscripting or enlisting children under the age of 15 years into armed forces or groups, or using them to participate actively in hostilities *3

Abductions and forced labour

10. Enslavement *1

Looting

11. Pillage *2

SEE ALSO *International Law and Justice; Sierra Leone's Civil War*

BIBLIOGRAPHY

Books

Hetherington, Tim. *Long Story Bit by Bit: Liberia Retold*. New York, NY: Umbrage Editions, 2009.

Pham, John-Peter. *Liberia: Portrait of a Failed State*. New York, NY: Reed Press, 2004.

Williams, Gabriel I. H. *Liberia: The Heart of Darkness. Accounts of Liberia's Civil War and Its Destabilizing Effects in West Africa*. Victoria, BC, Canada: Trafford Publishing, 2002.

Periodicals

De Ycaza, Carla. "A Search for Truth: A Critical Analysis of the Liberian Truth and Reconciliation Commission." *Human Rights Review* 14, no. 3 (September 2013): 189–212.

Fulton, R.M. "Charles Taylor and Liberia: Ambition and Atrocity in Africa's Lone Star State." *Choice* 49, no. 10 (June 2012): 1960.

Gbowee, Leymah. "A Dictator, Vanquished: Charles Taylor is Going to Jail. Rebuilding Life in Liberia." *Newsweek* 159, no. 19 (May 7, 2012).

Pajibo, Ezekiel. "Accountability and Justice in Post-Conflict Liberia." *African Identities* 10, no. 3 (August 2012): 301.

Web Sites

Huband, Mark. "Liberia." Crimes of War. http://www.crimesofwar.org/a-z-guide/liberia/ (accessed August 21, 2013).

"Liberia's Uneasy Peace." *PBS: Online NewsHour*. http://www.pbs.org/newshour/bb/africa/liberia/post1980_timeline.html (accessed August 21, 2013).

"Timeline: From Civil War Chaos to Fragile Hope." *Reuters*, November 7, 2011. http://www.reuters.com/article/2011/11/07/us-liberia-election-events-idUSTRE7A62BN20111107 (accessed August 21, 2013).

Libyan Civil Unrest

🌐 Introduction

A civil war that raged in Libya from February to October 2011 left parts of the country in ruins and thousands dead. Fighting was particularly relentless in the eastern city of Benghazi, with government-directed militia fighting rebel groups. Despite hopes that a stable democracy would emerge from the overthrow of long-time dictator Muammar al-Qadhafi (1942–2011), militias of pro-Qadhafi fighters threatened the stability of the country beginning in 2012, and much of the country was still suffering from poverty and violence in 2013.

In the aftermath of the civil war, pro-Qadhafi forces were not the only threat to stability in Libya. Throughout the revolution, dozens of anti-government militia fought against the Qadhafi regime. After the war ended, many of these groups banded together to form the Libya Shield Force—a security unit that the government brought under its command in 2012. However, Libya Shield has proven to be unpopular with Libyans, who increasingly see the group as violent and lawless.

Such concerns were fueled in June 2013 when a group of protesters stormed Libya Shield's Benghazi headquarters demanding that the country's military and police forces take charge of security. The protesters wanted to see such militia groups finally disband—it had been almost two years since the overthrow of the Qadhafi dictatorship. In the fighting that ensued, more than 30 people were killed with another 100 people injured. Libya Shield, in turn, mistrusts the police and military because of those groups's former association with the Qadhafi regime. Shifting alliances and tribal tensions led to violent clashes between Libya Shield and various armed groups throughout 2013.

🌐 Historical Background

Libya is situated on the North African coast of the Mediterranean Sea, between Tunisia and Egypt. Until the Zaltan oil field was discovered in 1959, Libya was one of the world's poorest countries. After that discovery, Libya developed a strong economy based on oil exports.

The population of Libya was estimated at 6 million in 2013. Berbers and Arabs account for 97 percent of the population, with the remaining 3 percent made up of Egyptians, Greeks, Indians, Italians, Maltese, Pakistanis, Tunisians, and Turks. Small tribal groups of African Tuareg and Tebou live as nomads in the south. Islam is the main religion and 97 percent of the population is Sunni Muslim. The country's strong affinity for Islam is depicted by the crescent and star on the Libyan flag.

Although "Berber" is a term widely applied to an ethnic group inhabiting North Africa that shares a common linguistic history, Berber groups differ considerably in culture and tend toward a tribal or clan structure to which they are loyal. Although Arabic is the official language of Libya, genetic studies show that most Libyans

QATAR FLEXES ITS MUSCLES

As anti-Qadhafi protests grew in size and violence, and as civilians died by the hundreds in 2011, world leaders struggled to find an appropriate response. A key player in solidifying Arab support for action against Qadhafi was Qatar, Libya's tiny, but extremely wealthy, neighbor. Qatar not only backed UN-approval of NATO strikes to protect Libyan civilians, it also sent generous shipments of arms, fuel, food, and other aid directly to Libyan rebels. The nation also sent troops to aid in fighting and training.

The outsized role of Qatar in aiding the Libyan rebels was risky—had the rebellion failed, Qatar would have faced a hostile regime at its border and possibly the disapproval of the rest of the Arab world. However, the success of the rebellion gave Qatar broader influence in the region and enormous goodwill within Libya.

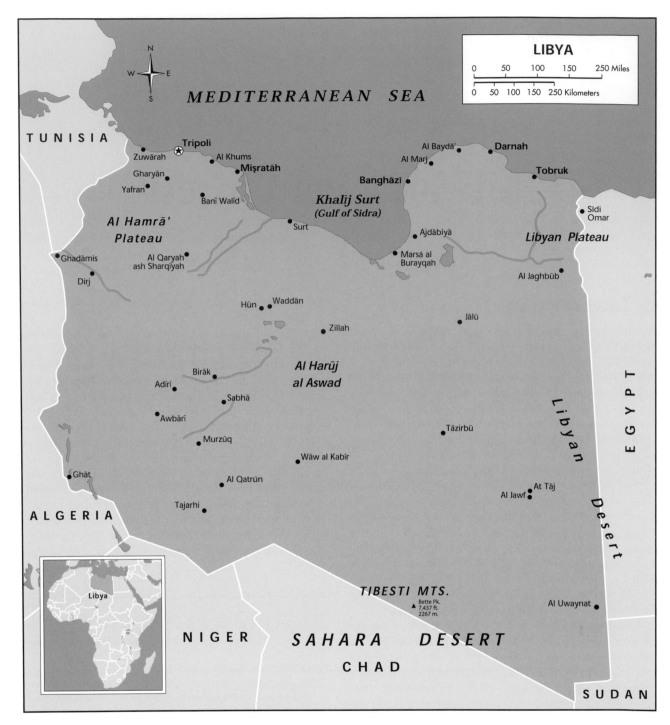

LIBYA

MEDITERRANEAN SEA

TUNISIA

Tripoli

Zuwārah · Al Khums
Misrātāh
Gharyān
Yafran
Banī Walīd
Surt

Al Baydā' · Darnah
Al Marj
Banghāzī · Tobruk

Khalīj Surt
(Gulf of Sidra)

Sīdi Omar

Ajdābiyā

Al Hamrā'
Plateau

Libyan Plateau

Ghadāmis
Al Qaryah ash Sharqīyah
Dirj

Marsá al Burayqah

Al Jaghbūb

Hūn · Waddān
Zillah

Jālū

Al Harūj
al Aswad

Birāk
Adīrī
Sabhā
Awbārī
Murzūq
Wāw al Kabīr

Tāzirbū

Ghāt

Al Qatrūn
Tajarhi

At Tāj
Al Jawf

Al Uwaynat

Libyan Desert

ALGERIA

TIBESTI MTS.
▲ Bette Pk.
7,437 ft.
2267 m.

SAHARA DESERT

NIGER

CHAD

EGYPT

SUDAN

Libya

are in fact of Berber descent, and the Berber language is still widely spoken. There are close to 150 tribal networks in Libya. In turn, tribes are composed of clans, or groups of families descended from a common ancestor. Waves of foreign invasion and interference—by the Arabs, the Spanish, the Ottomans, and the Italians—had a lasting impact on Libya's culture and demographics.

Libya was a colony of Italy from 1912 to 1941. In losing World War II (1939–45), Italy also lost Libya, which came under occupation by the victorious forces of Great Britain and France. Libya achieved independence in 1951 and was, for a time, governed by a monarch named King Idris I (1889–1983). The discovery of the vast oil reserves in 1959 complicated Libyan politics, as the question of who should control the country's oil wealth became contentious. In 1969, Colonel Muammar al-Qadhafi led a coup that ousted the king and, thereafter, he assumed near total control of Libya.

Outside of Libya, Qadhafi gained a reputation as an erratic leader who supported terrorist groups and repressive, ultraviolent regimes in Africa, including that of Ugandan dictator Idi Amin (c. 1925–2003) and Mengistu Haile Mariam (1937–) of Ethiopia. Within Libya, Qadhafi fended off multiple coup attempts by the military and the civilian population. He maintained power through a mixture of calculation and repression. He managed to placate rival tribal groups while also brutally quashing dissent. In Qadhafi's Libya, dissent was, in fact, illegal. Frustration with the Qadhafi regime grew as his dictatorship stretched for more than 40 years.

In December 2010, a wave of protests and revolutions began, first in Tunisia, then in other parts of Africa and the Middle East. Simmering tensions over a lack of human rights, high unemployment, and skyrocketing food prices fueled the rebellions. Called the Arab Spring by Western media, the revolution in Tunisia touched off similar actions throughout portions of the Arab world that brought significant political change, including the toppling of several long-standing dictators, Qadhafi among them. In Libya, after protests against the government were met with strong military force in February 2011, tensions escalated. In the fighting that ensued, the country became divided, with pro-government forces having a foothold over most of western Libya and rebels controlling eastern Libya.

The Revolution Begins

The anti-Qadhafi protests that eventually swelled into a revolution began in late 2010. Activists used the social networking site Facebook to call for peaceful demonstrations in support of reform of the Libyan government that had led the country since the 1969 military coup by Qadhafi. On February 15, 2011, a few hundred demonstrators gathered in the streets of Benghazi, Libya's second largest city. The demonstrators were confronted by police and many were injured. Protests quickly escalated in both size and violence. Foreign journalists were not given access to the areas in which protesters gathered, but eyewitness reports indicated that 200 to 300 demonstrators had been killed by security forces.

Anti-government forces gained momentum in Benghazi, capturing several key military and government installations, essentially taking control of the city. On February 21, protesters were targeted by Libyan air force attack helicopters. Reports of mass defections of army and air force personnel surfaced, with military leaders urging soldiers to join the people in their protests. Several religious and tribal leaders also renounced Qadhafi

Libyan protesters hold up a huge old national flag during a demonstration in the eastern dissident-held Libyan city of Tobruk on February 24, 2011, amid political turmoil and an insurrection against Muammar al-Qadhafi's regime. © *Trevor Snapp/AFP/Getty Images*

and threw their support behind anti-government protesters. Reports emerged that several Libyan ambassadors, including the Libyan ambassadors to the United Nations (UN) and the European Union (EU), resigned their posts to protest Qadhafi's decision to authorize violence to quell the protests. Meanwhile, residents of Tripoli, Libya's capital, began organizing protests of their own.

A Defiant Qadhafi

Rumors that Qadhafi had fled the country were put to rest when the aging, defiant leader appeared on state television on February 22 and delivered an hour-long speech in which he extolled his own achievements, vowed to fight to keep power, and promised to severely punish all those who challenged him. The same day, the UN Security Council issued a statement on Libya in which it "condemned the violence and use of force against civilians, deplored the repression against peaceful demonstrators, and expressed deep regret at the deaths of hundreds of civilians." Protesters in eastern Libya expanded their control over the area near Libya's border with Egypt.

On February 24, Qadhafi gave another address in which he accused the terrorist group al-Qaeda of fomenting unrest in his country and claimed that the protesters were under the influence of drugs and alcohol. Pitched battles between pro- and anti-government forces raged in Misrata and al-Zawiya. Zuara was reportedly controlled by anti-government forces. Thousands of foreigners crowded into the Tripoli airport seeking evacuation as Western nations hurried to send airplanes and ferries to rescue their citizens.

International Response

By March 3, rebels had made significant gains in cities near Tripoli, but Qadhafi maintained full control of the capital city, protected by fiercely loyal militia members and foreign mercenaries. As Libya teetered on the brink of full-blown civil war, the international community struggled to arrive at an appropriate response to the crisis. The EU and United States quickly imposed economic sanctions on Libya but debated whether to establish a no-fly zone over the country to prevent Qadhafi from turning the Libyan air force against rebels.

The International Criminal Court (ICC) began an inquiry into possible crimes against humanity in Libya. In early March, Venezuela's president, Hugo Chávez

National Transitional Council (NTC) fighters flash the V-sign for victory as they prepare to raid a house in search for activists suspected of belonging to a pro-Qadhafi underground group in Tripoli's flashpoint Abu Salim neighborhood on September 6, 2011, as Libya's new authorities launched a fresh bid to stave off a battle in Bani Walid, one of Muammar al-Qadhafi's last bastions south of the capital Tripoli.
© Patrick Baz/AFP/Getty Images

(1954–2013), offered to broker a peace deal between Qadhafi and rebel forces, reportedly submitting a proposal to the Arab League. Analysts were skeptical that Chávez's plan, which contained little detail, would be accepted by rebels.

On March 17, the UN Security Council approved military action to establish a "no-fly" zone over Libya to prevent the Libyan air force from continuing to attack civilians. Within days, U.S., British, and French missile strikes and bombing raids had disabled the Libyan air force. Rebel forces, which had lost ground to Qadhafi's troops, regained lost territory and pushed east toward Tripoli following the UN action in a five-day offensive; however, fighting remained fierce and bloody as government troops entrenched in the eastern city of Ajdabiya refused to give way. By March 30, Qadhafi's forces had pushed rebels out of Ajdabiya, eastward toward Benghazi, reversing the rebels' recent gains.

Qadhafi "Must Go"

On April 15, 2011, U.S. President Barack Obama (1961–), French President Nicolas Sarkozy (1955–), and British Prime Minister David Cameron (1966–) jointly issued an article in which they committed their militaries to the protection of Libyan rebels and asserted that Qadhafi "must go, and go for good." They said they would not remove Qadhafi by force, since they were not authorized to do so under the UN resolution, but that "so long as [Qadhafi] is in power, NATO and its coalition partners must maintain their operations so that civilians remain protected."

One major problem in aiding the rebels, however, was that the rebellion was fractured, with multiple militias opposing the government. Meanwhile, Qadhafi's forces besieged Misrata, the country's third largest city and a major port. To help relieve beleaguered rebels, Obama approved the use of Predator drones over Libya. Announcing the

The president of Libya for 42 years, Muammar al-Qadhafi, arrives for a state visit to the Ukraine on November 4, 2008, in Kyiv, Ukraine, flanked by his elite female bodyguards. He was ousted and killed by rebels three years later in the Libyan Civil War. © *Mark III Photonics/ Shutterstock*

المؤتمر الوطني العام

Members of Libya's National Assembly sort ballots as they choose their president in Tripoli on August 9, 2012. Libya's ruling national assembly picked Mohammed Magarief, leader of the National Front party, as its first elected president after the 42-year rule of Muammar al-Qadhafi, in a vote carried out a day after it took power from the outgoing National Transitional Council.   © *Mahmud Turkia/AFP/GettyImages*

decision on April 21, Secretary of Defense Robert Gates touted the drones as one of the "unique capabilities" of the United States military. On May 1, Libyan media reported that one of Qadhafi's sons and three grandchildren were killed in a NATO air raid the previous day.

As the rebels advanced, media speculation about the whereabouts of Qadhafi intensified. The dictator had not appeared publicly since April 30, the date of the air raid that killed his son, and he was not present at his son's funeral. NATO officials said they had no information about Qadhafi's location; however, a new round of air strikes on May 9 targeted Qadhafi's compound in Tripoli, according to witnesses.

The Dictator Falls

On July 15, the United States and several other countries recognized Libya's main opposition group as the country's legitimate government. U.S. officials met face-to-face with representatives from the Qadhafi regime during the weekend following the decision. The location of the meeting was not disclosed, and U.S. officials stressed it was not a negotiating session, but an effort to underscore that the U.S. government was committed to helping remove Qadhafi from power.

Qadhafi himself remained at large and defiant. Rebel leaders said they believed he had fled south into the desert, where loyalist forces still controlled territory, setting the stage for renewed fighting should Qadhafi refuse to surrender. On September 8, the ICC issued a Red Notice, authorizing Interpol to circulate arrest warrants widely in an effort to locate and extradite Qadhafi.

Qadhafi was found and killed by rebel forces on October 20. Most members of the dictator's family had already fled Libya in the preceding months. The chief prosecutor of the ICC said on December 16 that the manner of Qadhafi's death suggested that a war crime had been committed. Libya's National Transitional Council promised that an investigation into the circumstances of Qadhafi's death would be conducted. On December 21, the ICC announced it had no plans for an independent investigation into Qadhafi's death.

⊕ Impacts and Issues

As the unrest of the revolution in Libya settled, reports of abuses on both sides continued to surface. Amnesty International asserted in January 2012 that Libyan militias had tortured soldiers and others loyal to former dictator Qadhafi. UN officials said that about 6,500 people accused of being loyal to Qadhafi were being held, and possibly tortured by militias, in about 60 centers throughout Libya. Sporadic fighting continued in Libya with various rebel groups—and former supporters of Qadhafi—fighting for power.

Libya struggled to put a stable government in place. On October 14, 2011, the General National Congress appointed Ali Zidan (1950–), a human rights lawyer, as prime minister. He took office on October 31 after the Congress officially approved his proposed cabinet. No sooner had the new government been approved, however, than armed gunmen stormed the parliament to protest the appointment of some cabinet members who had former ties to Qadhafi.

Abdel Hafiz Ghoga, the deputy head of the National Transitional Council, resigned on January 22, 2012, amid protests from Libyan civilians who voiced concern that the new government was likely to be corrupt and interested only in personal profit and power. Mustafa Abdul-Jalil, the head of the council, urged protesters to have more patience.

⊕ Future Implications

Observers hoped that Qadhafi's ousting would signal the birth of a multiparty democratic government, but tensions remained high between the new government, local militias, and rival ethnic groups as of late 2013. Violence continued in Libya, much of it related to Qadhafi and his now-defunct government. The continuing unrest allowed anti-U.S. terrorist groups to gain a foothold in the country.

On September 11, 2012, exactly 11 years after the terrorist group al-Qaeda attacked the United States and left nearly 3,000 people dead, armed terrorists overran a U.S. diplomatic compound in Benghazi, killing the U.S. ambassador to Libya, J. Christopher Stevens (1960–2012), and three members of his staff. The circumstances surrounding the attack were not immediately clear, although later investigations pointed to several problems with the security provided to Stevens and faulty intelligence about militias and terrorist groups in Libya. The violent death of a U.S. ambassador caused an uproar in the United States, and cast further doubt on the possibility that a Qadhafi-free Libya would welcome stronger ties with the West.

U.S. officials have not been the only targets of organized attacks. On April 28, 2013, at least 200 armed men and 20 vehicles carrying anti-aircraft guns surrounded Libya's foreign ministry in Tripoli. The protesters were demanding the removal of anyone who had worked for Qadhafi. Prime Minister Ali Zeidan dismissed their demands, saying that the protesters were trying to destabilize Libya while terrorizing foreigners.

SEE ALSO *Arab Spring; North Atlantic Treaty Organization (NATO); United Nations*

BIBLIOGRAPHY

Books

Chorin, Ethan Daniel. *Exit the Colonel: The Hidden History of the Libyan Revolution.* New York: Public Affairs, 2012.

Hilsum, Lindsey. *Sandstorm: Libya in the Time of Revolution.* New York: Penguin Press, 2012.

McKinney, Cynthia. *The Illegal War on Libya.* Atlanta, GA: Clarity Press, 2012.

Pargeter, Alison. *Libya: The Rise and Fall of Qaddafi.* New Haven, CT: Yale University Press, 2012.

Vandewalle, Dirk J. *A History of Modern Libya.* Cambridge, UK: Cambridge University Press, 2012.

Periodicals

"Is the Tide Turning? Libya's Government and the Militias." *The Economist* 407, vol. 8840 (June 15, 2013): 48–49.

Zinin, Yu. "The War in Libya: Today and Tomorrow." *International Affairs* (Minneapolis) 57, vol. 4 (2011): 85–94.

Web Sites

Fadel, Leila. "After the War, a Bitter Feud Remains in Two Libyan Towns." *National Public Radio,* May 29, 2013. http://www.npr.org/blogs/parallels/2013/05/29/186927435/after-the-war-a-bitter-feud-remains-in-two-libyan-towns (accessed December 18, 2013).

General National Congress of Libya. http://www.temehu.com/gnc.htm (accessed December 18, 2013).

"Guide to Key Libyan Militias and Other Armed Groups." *BBC News Africa,* November 28, 2013. http://www.bbc.co.uk/news/world-middle-east-19744533 (accessed December 18, 2013).

"Libya." *The Guardian.* http://www.theguardian.com/world/libya (accessed December 18, 2013).

"Libya Letter by Obama, Cameron and Sarkozy: Full Text." *BBC News Africa,* April 15, 2011. http://www.bbc.co.uk/news/world-africa-13090646 (accessed December 18, 2013).

"Security Council Press Statement on Libya." *United Nations Security Council,* February 22, 2011. http://www.un.org/News/Press/docs/2011/sc10180.doc.htm (accessed December 18, 2013).

Thorne, John. "In Liberated Libya, Women Struggle to Raise Their Hand." *Christian Science Monitor,* July 14, 2013. http://www.csmonitor.com/World/Middle-East/2013/0714/In-liberated-Libya-women-struggle-to-raise-their-hand (accessed December 18, 2013).

Mexican Revolution

⊕ Introduction

The Mexican Revolution (1910–20) began as a revolt against the Mexican government and transformed into a multisided civil war. The conflict led to the creation of the Mexican Constitution of 1917 and created a more democratic Mexican government. The war had no clear end, as sporadic outbreaks of violence continued well into the 1920s and were in many ways just a continuation of the previous conflict.

One of the defining features of the Mexican Revolution was the presence of numerous rebel leaders who captured the popular imagination. These leaders, including Francisco "Pancho" Villa (1878–1923) and Emiliano Zapata (1879–1919), frequently allied with one another to destroy a common enemy, only to later dissolve their partnerships and form new alliances against whichever leader was currently in power. As a result, peace was almost impossible to create, let alone maintain, despite frequent revolutionary victories. These personal rivalries in large part dictated the course of the conflict. The war officially ended when Villa agreed to let the then-current president rule without further revolutionary dispute.

⊕ Historical Background

Porfirio Díaz (1830–1915) was the president of Mexico from 1876 to 1911, a period known in Mexican history as the Porfiriato era. Like many modern dictators, Díaz held regular elections, but he ensured his own victory by frightening people into voting for him or simply rigging the votes in his own favor. When questioned about his continued rule, Díaz justified his position by claiming that Mexico was not ready to govern itself and that he was the only one who knew what was best for the country. Díaz's presidency promoted industrialization and saw the rise of an urban working class.

Such advances came at the expense of the rural working class, many of whom complained of oppression and exploitation. In 1910 more than 95 percent

PANCHO VILLA AND THE UNITED STATES

Less than a year after their defeat in the Battle of Celaya, Pancho Villa and his Villistas crossed the border into the United States and attacked the small town of Columbus, New Mexico. During the early morning raid on March 9, 1916, 18 U.S. citizens were killed and many buildings in town were set ablaze. U.S. Army troops stationed in the area at Camp Furlong responded to the attack, setting up two machine guns in town. Ultimately, Villa lost about 100 men and fled back to Mexico, pursued by the army. After pushing Villa back across the border, the army troops ran out of ammunition and other supplies.

The United States called on Brigadier General John J. Pershing (1860–1948) to lead a Punitive Expedition of about 5,000 troops into Mexico in an attempt to capture Villa and bring him to justice. Villa intimately knew the inhospitable terrain of the Sonoran Desert and the Sierra Madre mountains. He managed to stay one step ahead of his pursuers, and the epic chase continued throughout Mexico and the United States. After nearly a year of pursuit by ground as well as by air, the U.S. forces returned home empty handed. Pershing was then called by U.S. President Woodrow Wilson to lead the American Expeditionary Forces in World War I.

By the end of the Punitive Expedition, Villa's reputation as a modern-day Robin Hood, a bandit who fought for the rights of the people, had grown enormously. His legend was discussed among the peasants of Mexico and in newspapers and paperback novels in the United States, growing embellished with every retelling. Having successfully escaped the U.S. Army, Pancho Villa continued his fight against Carranza's government. Villa was assassinated on July 20, 1923.

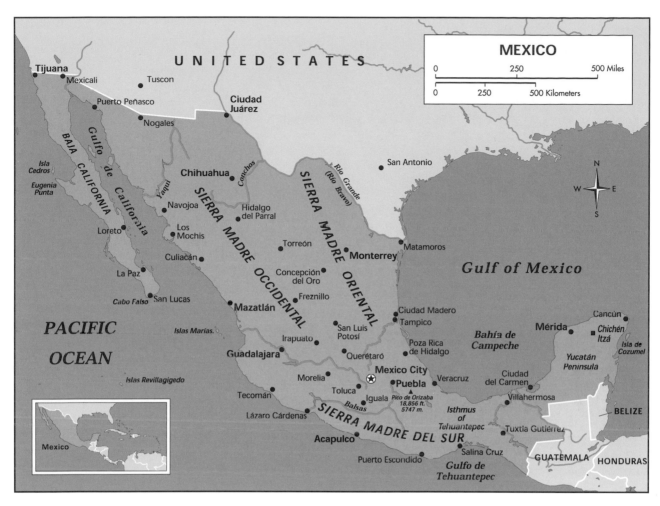

MEXICO

0   250   500 Miles

0   250   500 Kilometers

of Mexico's land was owned by less than 5 percent of the population. Rural workers were often treated little better than slaves, and debt was passed down from generation to generation, ensuring farmers stayed in perpetual debt bondage. An increasingly angry population of small farmers and landless peasants came to realize that only a change in political leadership would offer protection and advancement for themselves and their families.

In 1910 Díaz decided to run for president again, expecting to control the election much as he had the previous seven times. His main competition was Francisco I. Madero (1873–1913), a member of the elite who ideologically was not particularly different from Díaz. However, Díaz disapproved of Madero and had him jailed on election day. Unsurprisingly, Díaz won by a landslide in an obviously rigged election. Madero penned a letter from jail in which he declared Díaz's presidency illegal and called for a revolt. He promised vague agrarian reforms for Mexico if Díaz was removed. Madero's supporters took up arms on November 10, 1910, starting the Mexican Revolution.

Díaz and Madero

The promise of agrarian reforms attracted tens of thousands of peasants throughout Mexico. Several militant revolutionary movements, consisting primarily of working class Mexicans and native populations, were quickly formed. Pascual Orozco (1882–1915) led one such army in northern Mexico and was able to capture Mexicali and Chihuahua City. These victories led to an alliance between Orozco and another rebel leader, Pancho Villa. A southern army, led by Emiliano Zapata, also formed and had similarly successful revolutionary victories. Eventually all of the rebel armies joined into one, under the banner of Madero, dedicated to ousting Díaz.

On May 21, 1911, Madero defeated the Mexican federal army. Díaz abdicated and Madero was elected president later that year. Although some supporters felt that he was weak for not assuming the presidency immediately, Madero insisted on establishing a truly liberal democracy. He was supported in this endeavor by other popular leaders including Orozco, Villa, and Zapata.

Once in power, however, Madero proved an ineffective leader, managing to anger both the more radical

Porfirio Diaz, who was president of Mexico from 1876 to 1880 and from 1884 to 1911, stands with his wife and members of the military, circa 1910.   © *Library of Congress*

revolutionists and the conservative counter-revolutionists. He refused to bring about the promised land reforms, earning him the anger of Zapata and Orozco. The two rebel leaders called for a new rebellion against Madero. The rural working class sided with the two revolutionary heroes and took up arms against Madero.

In 1913 a coup led by General Victoriano Huerta (1850–1916) overthrew Madero. The former president was forced to resign, and a week later he was assassinated. Although Madero had lost much of his support among the larger population, his murder nevertheless captured the passions of the people and he was quickly praised as a martyr of the revolution. Huerta became president of Mexico and was recognized by most foreign governments, with the notable exception of the United States.

Huerta, Carranza, and Villa

Venustiano Carranza (1859–1920) emerged as the leader of the opposition against Huerta. His rebel army, called the Constitutionalists, received covert financial support from the United States. On March 26, 1913,

Carranza issued the Plan de Guadalupe, a document that called for war between all revolutionary rebels and the Huerta government. Villa and Zapata immediately joined Carranza and other rebel leaders in the fight to depose Huerta. In late July, Huerta resigned from office and fled to Europe.

But peace would still prove elusive for Mexico. Villa, Zapata, and other revolutionaries wanted to continue to fight and soon became enemies of Carranza. A gathering of revolutionary leaders met at the Convention of Aguascalientes and voted to destroy Carranza. They then moved to occupy Mexico City. Eventually the more moderate-minded citizens of the city drove the rebel army out. In a series of battles in April 1915, collectively known as the Battle of Celaya, Pancho Villa was defeated by Carranza's army and was forced to flee. Carranza seized power and was soon recognized as the president of Mexico by the United States.

Carranza became president in 1914 by virtue of overthrowing the Huerta government. But his dedication to implementing social and agrarian reform soon earned him the support of the masses. He was officially

Rebel fighters pose for a picture during the Mexican Revolution (1910–1920), including Rodolfo Fierro, standing far right, who stands by as Pancho Villa (in the presidential chair) chats with Emiliano Zapata at Mexico City. Tomas Urbina is seated at far left and Otilio Montano (with his head bandaged) is seated to the far right. *© Universal History Archive/Getty Images*

elected president in 1917 and set about creating a new constitution that included most of the rebel leaders' social demands.

⊕ Impacts and Issues

The Constitution of 1917 was written by young populist professionals. It imposed term limits on politicians and introduced major labor reforms including the eight-hour workday, right to strike, equal pay for equal work, and an end to child labor and company stores. The creation of this constitution and the agreement of Villa to stop fighting against Carranza officially ended the Mexican Revolution.

Carranza was assassinated on May 21, 1920, before he could enforce the new reforms created in the constitution. His political successors continued to support the constitution of 1917 and successfully implemented many of the social and land reforms demanded by the revolutionaries. In 1929 the rise of a new political party, the National Revolutionary Party (later renamed the Institutional Revolutionary Party), came to power, and over the next decade carved out a more stable peace.

It is not easy to determine whether the Mexican Revolution was a revolution, a civil war, or some combination of the two. Although the old system of government was removed and a new one set up in its place, each of the Mexican governments, regardless of origin, operated on similar foundations. The Constitution of 1917 essentially streamlined the federal government. It empowered certain officials, but added term limits. In many ways all the revolution did on the political level

The federal irregular cavalry, a part of the Mexican Army during the Mexican Revolution, prepares to fight. © *Popperfoto/Getty Images*

was make the mechanisms of power less autocratic and more efficient.

The various governments during and after the revolution were revolutionary in name only. They used the rhetoric of the revolution to gain popular support and stability. But many of the political leaders did not personally believe in the populist principles. Although some land reforms did take place, the disparity in wealth and land ownership remains extremely unbalanced in modern Mexico.

⊕ Future Implications

One of the legacies of the Mexican Revolution was the formation of the Institutional Revolutionary Party (PRI), one of the most powerful political parties in modern Mexico. The PRI controlled the presidency of Mexico from 1929 until 2000. During this period the PRI was supposed to bring every political faction and interest group together in a cohesive parliament. In reality, real political power was wielded by a central executive committee that budgeted government projects.

Although the PRI is authoritarian and hierarchical in nature, its purpose is primarily just to keep order. Pragmatism has traditionally won over ideology, and the PRI has played whatever role and used whatever

rhetoric is necessary to keep the peace in Mexico. In 2000 the PRI was briefly replaced by its rival, the Party of the Democratic Revolution. The PRI returned to power in 2012.

SEE ALSO *Mexico's Drug War*

BIBLIOGRAPHY

Books

Easterling, Stuart. *A Short History of the Mexican Revolution: 1910–1940.* New York: Bedford/ St. Martin's Press, 2012.

Gonzales, Michael, J. *The Mexican Revolution: 1910–1940.* Albuquerque: University of New Mexico Press, 2002.

McLynn, Frank. *Villa and Zapata: A History of the Mexican Revolution.* New York: Basic Books, 2002.

Periodicals

Yockelson, Mitchell. "The United States Armed Forces and the Mexican Punitive Expedition: Part 1." *Prologue Magazine* 29, no. 3 (Fall 1997). Available online at: http://www.archives.gov/ publications/prologue/1997/fall/mexican-punitive-expedition-1.html (accessed December 23, 2013).

Web Sites

Hudson, Elizabeth. "Vivid Memories of Pancho Villa: 4 Veterans of the Mexican Revolution Are Reunited." *Los Angeles Times*, November 27, 1988. http://articles.latimes.com/1988-11-27/news/mn-807_1_villa-mexican-revolution (accessed December 23, 2013).

"Mexican Revolution." *History Detectives, PBS*. http://www.pbs.org/opb/historydetectives/feature/mexican-revolution/ (accessed December 23, 2013).

"The Mexican Revolution: November 20th, 1910." *National Endowment for the Humanities*. http://edsitement.neh.gov/feature/mexican-revolution-november-20th-1910 (accessed December 23, 2013).

"The Storm That Swept Mexico: Faces of the Revolution." *PBS*. http://www.pbs.org/itvs/storm-that-swept-mexico/the-revolution/faces-revolution/ (accessed December 23, 2013).

Mexico's Drug War

⊕ Introduction

Mexico has been a major international producer and trafficker of illegal drugs for decades. It is the single largest trafficker of drugs to the United States. The drug trade from Mexico to the United States began during the Prohibition Era (1919–33), when the sale, production, or transportation of alcohol was illegal in the United States. In the decades since, the drug trade has escalated into a major source of tension between the United States and Mexico.

During the 1970s and 1980s, Miguel Ángel Félix Gallardo (1946–), known as the "Godfather," single-handedly controlled Mexico's drug trade through the Guadalajara Cartel. Following Gallardo's arrest in 1989, fiercely competitive cartels fought for control over the thousands of tons of marijuana, methamphetamine, heroin, and cocaine sold in the United States every year. In 2013, it was estimated that annual revenues from the drug trade were $39 billion.

During the 20th century, the Mexican government largely ignored the drug trade. However, starting in 2006, Mexican President Felipe Calderón (1962–) began to crack down on the cartels and their trade. The resulting drug war in Mexico has left more than 60,000 people dead and has threatened to destabilize the entire country.

Mexico's drug war is an ongoing conflict with both domestic and international ramifications. Although the Mexican government has successfully destroyed or weakened some of the cartels, new ones are continually created to take their place. Experts speculate that as long as the demand for drugs remains high in the United States, drug trafficking will remain a problem, and the drug war will continue.

⊕ Historical Background

The border between the United States and Mexico stretches more than 2,000 miles (3,200 kilometers), giving Mexican drug traffickers ample opportunities to smuggle narcotics into the United States. During the Prohibition Era, early Mexican cartels supplied alcohol to gangsters running speakeasies (illegal drinking establishments) in the United States. When Prohibition ended, these Mexican cartels shifted their focus to marijuana and heroin, eventually becoming the leading suppliers for the U.S. drug market.

During the late 1960s, Colombia was the global leader in drug trafficking, particularly cocaine. In order to reach its U.S. markets, the Colombian criminal networks formed partnerships with Mexican drug traffickers. During the 1970s and 1980s, Mexican drug trafficking became an increasingly sophisticated and entrenched business, which the Mexican government largely ignored. U.S. president Richard Nixon (1913–1994; served 1969–1974) declared a "war on drugs" in 1971, largely in response to the Colombian-Mexican drug traffic. Later U.S. presidents continued this battle, with mixed results.

Mexico's "Godfather"

During the 1980s, most of Mexico's drug trafficking was conducted under the watchful eye of the Guadalajara Cartel led by Gallardo, the drug lord known as "the Godfather." Gallardo was the first Mexican drug lord to form an alliance with the Colombian cocaine cartels. He soon was overseeing Mexico's entire drug trafficking industry, protected by politicians who had accepted bribes in order to ignore his activities.

By 1987, Gallardo determined that his empire would be safest if it were divided into five distinct territories. Essentially, this served to drive the trade underground, allowing it to be run by drug lords with low profiles and making it harder for officials to disrupt business. The Godfather intended to act as a linchpin, controlling the nationwide business but no longer concerned with individual shipments.

Gallardo invited each of Mexico's top drug traffickers to a meeting in the coastal city of Acapulco and gave them each a territory to control— Tijuana, Ciudad Juárez, Sonora, Matamoros, Tamaulipas (Gulf Cartel), and Pacific Coast (Sinaloa Cartel). From this meeting arose Mexico's oldest active drug cartels. On April 8, 1989, Gallardo was arrested; his capture left no single figure in control of the cartels. Fierce rivalries over territory and influence led to countless deaths among cartel and gang members, as well as innocents, in Mexico and the United States during the 1990s, a situation that continued into the 21st century.

Rise of the Cartels

The current Mexican drug trade is run by several cartels, or groups of smaller drug rings, all united to control the illegal drug market in a region. These cartels are usually based around a family identity, such as the Beltrán-Leyva Cartel, or a geographic area, such as the Sinaloa Cartel (from whom the Beltrán-Leyva Cartel broke off). Of the original five territories designated by Gallardo, one is extinct (Sonora) and three others have been weakened by a combination of infighting and government crackdowns. In their place, a myriad of other cartels have been organized to take control of the territories and their illegal trade. Of the original five, the Sinaloa Cartel remains the most powerful. It has controlled the Pacific Coast region since 1989, and it is the strongest cartel in western Mexico.

The Sinaloa Cartel's biggest rival is the Los Zetas, formed by ex-commandos from the Mexican army who joined the Gulf Cartel, then broke off from that cartel in 2010. Los Zetas is now Mexico's largest cartel and controls drug trafficking in eastern Mexico. The Los Zetas cartel is the most openly violent of all of Mexico's cartels, a fact that some believe has contributed to its growth, as smaller regional gangs may have been forcibly taken over by Los Zetas. In addition, the threat of extreme violence may keep local leaders firmly under Los Zetas control. By contrast, though occasionally known for displays of ruthless violence, in the past the Sinaloa cartel usually conducted business through bribery and political corruption. That changed in 2008 as factions of the Sinaloa Cartel splintered off from each other. The warring gangs, mainly near the Arizona-Sonora border, began a series of brutal murders to warn off the rival gangs.

These and other cartels are responsible for producing and distributing drugs such as marijuana, methamphetamine, heroin, and cocaine. Some of these drugs are produced within Mexico, while others—such as cocaine—are brought into Mexico from countries in South and Central America as part of their journey to the United States. Various cartels are also involved in trading illegal weapons and even human trafficking.

Since the turn of the 21st century, the Mexican government has actively fought to destroy the drug cartels. During most of the 20th century, Mexico's ruling party was the PRI (Institutional Revolutionary Party), a single party that controlled the presidency for 71 years. During most of this time, the PRI ignored the growing influence and violence of the drug cartels. In 2000, the opposing party finally won an election and President Vincente Fox (1942–) made it clear that the cartels would no longer be tolerated. His successor, President Felipe Calderón, was even less tolerant of the cartels.

A native of the Mexican state of Michoacán, Calderón was concerned with the growing influence of the drug trade in this area. In 2006, a mere 10 days after taking office, he sent military troops to Michoacán in an attempt to shut down illegal drug operations in the state. More than 600 people were killed, with losses on both sides. Operation Michoacán is considered the first major fight against Mexico's organized crime and marks the beginning of Mexico's drug war.

President Calderón continued to fight the cartels throughout his term, eventually using more than 45,000 troops as well as police forces in his anti-drug campaign. In 2010, the president insisted that Mexico's drug war was no longer merely about narcotics but had become a fight to protect Mexico's democracy from cartels that wished to take political control of the county. Speaking at an anti-crime conference in 2010, Calderón warned that Mexican drug cartels were attempting to replace the state and local governments in parts of Mexico. The president revealed that armed gangs were imposing their own laws by force and even collecting tax-like fees. Calderón said the fight against the cartels must continue, despite the spiraling death count. By the end of Calderón's tenure in November 2012, it was estimated that 60,000 people had died and 25,000 had disappeared as a direct result of the drug trade in Mexico. Detailed government statistics released earlier in the year, in January, put the official death toll from Mexico's drug war at 47,500, with more being added on an almost daily basis. Approximately half of the killings have occurred in Chihuahua, Tamaulipas, and Sinaloa.

Drug War Violence

Mexico's drug war has resulted in the arrest of thousands of people believed to be cartel members. Among those arrested were several high-ranking cartel leaders. Many people have been killed as a result of drug-related violence. The aggressive stance of the government has created some unintended consequences. As the leaders of the cartels have been arrested or killed, power struggles within the cartels have become increasingly violent, and the resulting chaos has spread throughout the country.

Mexican drug cartels often have access to sophisticated weapons and protective gear that the police and military do not, with much of this equipment

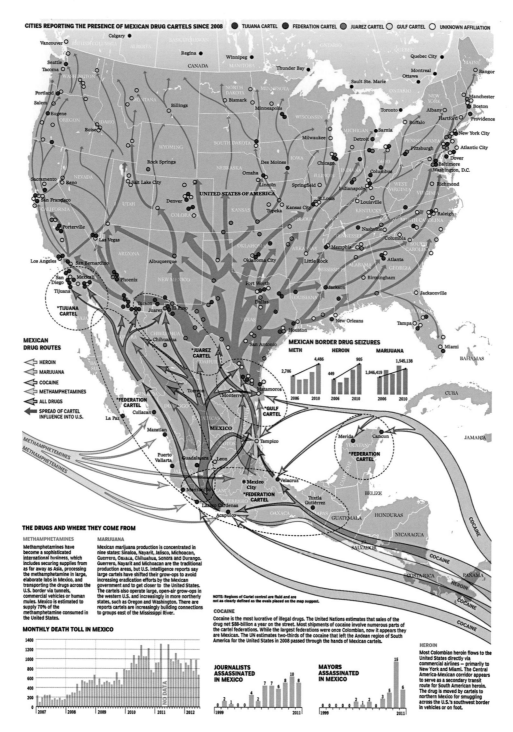

Jonathan Rivait and Richard Johnson, "Graphic: Mexican Drug Cartels' Spreading Influence," *National Post*, July 13, 2012. *Copyright © 2012 National Post. All rights reserved. Republished with permission.*

originating in the United States. As former Secretary of State Hillary Clinton (1947–) has acknowledged, less restrictive gun laws in the United States have led drug cartel members across the border to purchase weapons, which are then smuggled back into Mexico. The cartels have fought directly with government and police forces on several occasions, resulting in hundreds of losses for both sides. Cartel agents have also launched grenade attacks on public areas, have gunned down civilians to intimidate local populations, killed journalists, and have used beheadings of other cartel members and other citizens to terrorize.

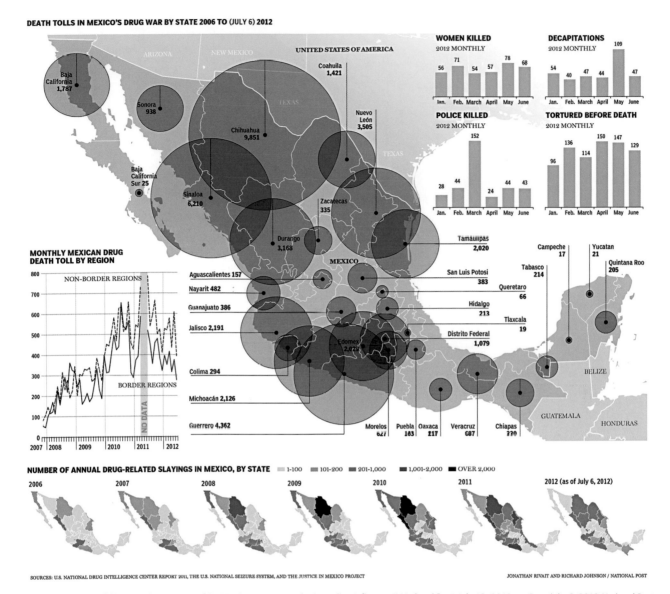

DEATH TOLLS IN MEXICO'S DRUG WAR BY STATE 2006 TO (JULY 6) 2012

Jonathan Rivait and Richard Johnson, "Graphic. Mexican Drug Cartels' Spreading Influence," *National Post*, July 13, 2012.   Copyright © 2012 National Post. All rights reserved. Republished with permission.

Government and Police Corruption

In many cities local police, politicians, and military officials have been accused of working with the drug cartels. In December 2009, the municipality of Tancítaro had its entire police force dismissed due to its failure to curb crime. The officers were replaced by federal personnel. Similar attempts to clean up corrupt or ineffective police forces have taken place throughout Mexico, and high-level officials—including several mayors and a congressman—have faced accusations of working with the drug cartels. Even the acting commissioner of the Federal Police, Victor Gerardo Garay, was arrested on charges of corruption in 2008, as was Noe Ramirez Mandujano, the former head of the country's anti-organized crime agency.

Police and government officials who refuse to help the drug cartels have often suffered even worse fates. Dozens of police chiefs, politicians, and even crime reporters have been murdered by those they sought to expose and arrest. Victims include Édgar Eusebio Millán Gómez, commissioner of the Federal Preventive Police, and Esteban Robles Espinosa, leader of the Investigative Police Force in Mexico City. On June 28, 2010, Rodolfo Torre Cantú, a politician running for governor in the state of Tamaulipas, was gunned down along with several campaign workers just one week before the election.

Mexico and the United States

Drug related violence between rival cartels has threatened security in Mexican cities and towns along the

Mexican Federal Police personnel patrol the streets of Ciudad Juárez during an anti-narcotics operation on March 2, 2009. President Felipe Calderón acknowledged the country's drug war was bloodier and tougher than he thought when he first took office in 2006, but vowed to eradicate the "cancer" consuming Mexico. In 2009, he ordered the deployment of an additional 5,000 military troops and 1,000 police to the drug-ravaged northern border with the United States. © *Ronaldo Schemidt/AFP/Getty Images*

border between the United States and Mexico. Bloodshed increased after Mexican president Calderón committed tens of thousands of military troops and federal police to battle the cartels. The violence escalated to such an alarming degree by 2008 that some U.S. government officials were concerned that fighting could spill across the border into the United States.

The U.S. government has made an effort to help end the drug war, hoping to prevent bloodshed from moving onto American soil. In 2008, Congress signed into law the Merida Initiative, aimed at helping Mexico and various Central American nations fight back against the powerful drug cartels. Through this initiative, the United States has provided equipment such as helicopters and drug-sniffing dogs and has also worked to stop the flow of guns from the United States into Mexico. U.S. forces have also arrested hundreds of cartel workers within the United States through various raids and sting operations since the start of the war.

In April 2009, U.S. President Barack Obama (1961–) announced that the United States shared responsibility for the deteriorating situation in Mexico, since high demand for drugs in the United States drives the Mexican drug cartels. He pledged increased assistance as well as more cooperation with the Mexican government to combat the problem. Obama approved $700 million to beef up security and crime-fighting efforts along the U.S.-Mexico border. The new funds are in addition to the $1.4 billion in anti-drug aid offered to Mexico by the United States in 2007.

The United States also began to arrest Mexican cartel members operating within the United States itself. In October 2009, more than 300 people were arrested by U.S. law enforcement officials in drug raids in 19 U.S. states targeting the Mexican crime organization La Familia, an organization with widespread operations in the United States. U.S. Attorney General Eric Holder (1951–) announced that La Familia's supply chain had been severely disrupted.

In May 2010, President Obama pledged to station an additional 1,200 National Guard troops along the border between the United States and Mexico in an attempt to stem the violence and stop the drug trade. In June 2010, Obama also requested emergency funding from Congress to hire an additional 1,000 Border Patrol agents. That

People rallied against drug war violence in Guadalajara, Mexico, on April 06, 2011. This event, which called for peace, was organized by Javier Sicilia after the murder of a group of seven young men, including his son, in the city of Temixco, Morelos. More than 500 people died in the first four months of 2011 due to the drug war. Similar demonstrations were held in many foreign cities, including Buenos Aires, New York, Barcelona, Paris, Santiago, La Haye, and San Sebastian.   © *Leonardo Suárez Romero/LatinContent/Getty Images*

same month, drug raids in Texas and Oklahoma led to more than 50 arrests, including an alleged high-ranking member of the Sinaloa Cartel. Despite increased funding and more troops, the death toll in Mexico's drug war continued to grow, particularly along the U.S.-Mexico border.

Fighting Back against the Cartels

By September 2011, the situation in Mexico had become so dire that Calderón decided to address the United Nations (UN) General Assembly to apprise them of the situation and ask for assistance. In particular, the president asked the UN to pass an International Convention on Trade in Arms. If passed, this law would potentially make it more difficult for drug traffickers to get high tech weaponry. The president also asked industrial nations to work to continue to reduce drug use domestically.

The Sinaloa Cartel took significant hits in 2012 and 2014. In January 2012 Mexican security forces launched a raid on a Durango ranch occupied by regional leader Luis Alberto Cabrera Sarabia. Cabrera Sarabia was believed to be in control of operations for Durango and Chihuahua states. Eleven other high-ranking cartel members

were arrested in the raid, which also involved the seizure of weapons, armored vehicles, and communications equipment. Sinaloa's highest-ranking drug lord, Joaquin Archivaldo Guzman Loera, long known as "Mexico's Most Wanted Man," was captured in Mazatlán by Mexican Marines on February 22, 2014. "El Chapo" (Shorty) had been on the run for years after escaping prison in 2001.

The Los Zetas also suffered losses. On October 6, 2012, in Coahuila, Mexican marines killed the leader of the Los Zetas drug cartel, Heriberto Lazcano, in a shootout that occurred when Lazcano resisted arrest. Fingerprints confirmed that the body belonged to Lazcano, also known as "The Executioner," who was allegedly responsible for many mass killings. The body was stolen by armed gunmen after being transported to a funeral home; however, the navy had taken photographs and fingerprints before the theft. Nevertheless, in order to quell worries that the man killed in the gun fight was not actually Lazcano, Mexican officials exhumed the body of the drug boss's father over a week later in order to prove the identity of Lazcano through DNA testing. Lazcano is the most powerful cartel leader killed thus far

THE WORLD'S MOST DANGEROUS CITY

One city that has seen extreme violence against its citizens is Ciudad Juárez, located along the border between Mexico and Texas (El Paso). During 2009, U.S. officials reported more than 2,000 murders in Ciudad Juárez, the vast majority related to the drug trade, making this the most violent city in the world outside of actual war zones. The following year, the murders increased to 3,000—10 times the 2007 death toll of only 300.

in Mexico's drug war. The death or capture of several other high-ranking Los Zetas cartel members has proven a boon to the rival Sinaloa Cartel, which seeks to expand its smuggling network into eastern Mexico.

⊕ Impacts and Issues

Mexico's drug war has left more than 60,000 dead victims in its wake in about six years. The brutality of the cartels increased to extreme levels, creating a bloodbath as traffickers sought a larger share of the drug trade while the Mexican military and government tried to supress them. Cities such as Juárez, the border town across from El Paso in the United States, saw the amount of violence skyrocket as more cartel activity moved into the area. The city became so dangerous that thousands of citizens fled to other areas, including the United States. More than 3,000 homicides were recorded in Juárez in 2011, compared to just five in El Paso. Shocking scenes of violence have rocked the city as beheaded bodies are left in the streets to terrorize members of other cartels as well as regular citizens and the police. Public shootouts have occured without warning.

In 2012, as a new president was elected in Mexico, people wondered if a change in leadership would quell the violence. In December, President Enrique Peña Nieto (1966–) was sworn into office. A member of the PRI, he stated that he is committed to continuing the fight against drug trafficking. Nieto seeks to reduce the spike in murder, extortion, and kidnapping cases that occurred under former president Calderón. On April 10, 2013, the Mexican government reported that during the four-month period between December 2012 and March 2013, murders linked to organized crime fell by 14 percent compared to the same period in the previous year. According to the government, there were 4,249 organized crime-related deaths in the winter of 2013.

Mexico's attorney general, Jesús Murillo (1948–) has been very vocal in his criticisms of Calderón's crackdown on drug trafficking. According to Murillo, Mexico's drug war has led to the creation of 60 to 80 new drug cartels. Murillo argued that the targeting of specific cartels

fractured larger gangs, such as the Los Zetas and Sinaloa Cartels. According to the consulting agency Risk Evaluation, there were only 10 cartels operating when Calderón took office in 2006. Murillo also said that Calderón failed to adequately confront the drug violence. He blamed the former president for letting the situation get of control.

Observers have noted that the current policies of the PRI toward the cartels appear to be a continuation of Calderón's policies. The Mexican drug war has not significantly slowed down despite the change in government, although the Nieto administration did score big victories in 2013 and early 2014: Miguel Angel Treviño, reputed boss of Los Zetas, was arrested on July 19, 2013, and Joaquín Guzmán Loera, head of the Sinaloa Cartel, was arrested on February 22, 2014.

⊕ Future Implications

Many sociologists have argued that rather than continuing to fight the cartels, the real solution to Mexico's drug war is to focus on the economic and social issues within Mexico that lead to recruitment of the impoverished into the cartels. In addition, they suggest that fighting the drug war on the American side will consist of curbing the demand for drugs through prevention, treatment, and educational programs. Another way to combat the power of the cartels is to legalize certain drugs in Mexico and the United States, particularly marijuana. They suggest that decriminalizing certain drugs would be in direct opposition to the financial interests of cartels throughout North America.

Since 2009, Mexico has decriminalized the possession of small amounts of certain drugs, including cocaine and heroin. Those caught with traces of these drugs will be referred to government-sponsored treatment programs instead of being sent to prison. Government officials hope that this will allow police officers to focus more of their time on building cases against drug traffickers. In 2012, the states of Washington and Colorado in the United States legalized the recreational use of marijuana, while 18 states have legalized medical marijuana, with more states considering the issue in 2014. Only time will tell whether legalization will help bring an end to Mexico's drug war.

PRIMARY SOURCE

The Merida Initiative: Expanding the U.S./Mexico Partnership

SOURCE *"The Merida Initiative: Expanding the U.S./Mexico Partnership."* U.S. Department of State. Bureau of Western Hemisphere Affairs, *March 29, 2012. http://www.state.gov/p/wha/rls/fs/2012/187119.htm (October 14, 2013).*

INTRODUCTION *The following is a fact sheet released by the U.S. Department of State describing the Merida Initiative, a joint program of the United States and Mexico meant to combat illegal drug trafficking in both countries.*

"And the United States remains committed to helping the Mexican Government go after the cartels and organized crime and the corruption they generate. . . And we will continue, through the Merida Initiative, to provide significant support."

—*Secretary of State Hillary Rodham Clinton*

The Merida Initiative is an unprecedented partnership between the United States and Mexico to fight organized crime and associated violence while furthering respect for human rights and the rule of law. Based on principles of shared responsibility, mutual trust, and respect for sovereign independence, the two countries' efforts have built confidence that is transforming the bilateral relationship.

The Four Pillars of Merida:

1. Disrupt Organized Criminal Groups
2. Strengthen Institutions
3. Build a 21st Century Border
4. Build Strong and Resilient Communities

Enhancing Citizen Safety

Under the Merida Initiative, the United States has forged strong partnerships to improve citizen safety in affected areas to fight drug trafficking, organized crime, corruption, illicit arms trafficking, money-laundering, and demand for drugs on both sides of the border.

Bilateral efforts are being accelerated to support Mexico's institutions, especially police and justice systems at both the federal and state level; to expand our border focus beyond interdiction of contraband to include facilitation of legitimate trade and travel; and to build strong and resilient communities able to withstand the pressures of crime and violence.

Merida Programs and Activities

The U.S. Congress has appropriated $1.6 billion since the Merida Initiative began in Fiscal Year 2008. Under the partnership:

- Mexico's air mobility in counternarcotics and other security operations increased through the delivery of multiple aircraft for law enforcement and military entities;
- The United States is supporting Mexico's implementation of comprehensive justice sector reforms through the training of prosecutors, defenders, investigators, and forensic experts, and through judicial exchanges and partnerships between Mexican and U.S. law schools;

- Merida funding established 12 and strengthened 48 Alternative Justice Centers, which use alternative mechanisms, such as mediation, for minor offenses. This allows cases to proceed more quickly and reduces court congestion, allowing the system to focus on more serious crimes;
- The United States is helping to strengthen Mexican law enforcement institutions through trainings for Accredited State Police units in Mexico's three priority states of Chihuahua, Tamaulipas, and Nuevo Leon;
- The Mexican government, with Merida funds, established a corrections academy to train Mexican federal and state correctional staff in Xalapa, Veracruz;
- The United States provided scanners, x-ray machines, other non-intrusive inspection equipment, and trained canines to enhance Mexican authorities' ability to detect illicit goods at key checkpoints and ports of entry;
- The United States launched a 30-month Crime & Violence Prevention project to strengthen Mexico's capacity to develop and communicate crime prevention policy at the federal, state, and community level. Support to localities will assist with the design and implementation of crime prevention plans, urban and social planning, and community policing;
- Merida funds support Mexican government and civil society efforts to protect journalists and human rights defenders; and
- With Merida support, Mexico launched an Information Technology platform to link more than 300 addiction resource centers in support of a national drug demand reduction program.

SEE ALSO *Mexican Revolution*

BIBLIOGRAPHY

Books

Ainslie, Ricardo C. *The Fight to Save Juárez: Life in the Heart of Mexico's Drug War.* Austin: University of Texas Press, 2013.

Beith, Malcome. *The Last Narco: Inside the Hunt for El Chapo, the World's Most Wanted Drug Lord.* New York: Grove Press, 2010.

Grayson, George W., and Samuel Logan. *The Executioner's Men: Los Zetas, Rogue Soldiers, Criminal Entrepreneurs, and the Shadow State They Created.* New Brunswick, NJ: Transaction Publishers, 2012.

Grillo, Ioan. *El Narco: Inside Mexico's Criminal Insurgency.* New York: Bloomsbury, 2011.

Web Sites

Fantz, Ashley. "The Mexico Drug War: Bodies for Billions." *CNN*, January 20, 2012. http://www.cnn.com/2012/01/15/world/mexico-drug-war-essay/ (accessed December 20, 2013).

"Mexican Drug War: Waves of Violence." *The Economist*, November 22, 2012. http://www.economist.com/blogs/graphicdetail/2012/11/mexican-drug-war (accessed December 20, 2013).

"Mexico Under Siege: The Drug War at Our Doorstep." *Los Angeles Times*, July 3, 2013. http://projects.latimes.com/mexico-drug-war/#/its-a-war (accessed December 20, 2013).

"World Report: Mexico." *Human Rights Watch*. http://www.hrw.org/world-report/2013/country-chapters/mexico?page=2 (accessed December 20, 2013).

Nicaragua

⊕ Introduction

Relations between Nicaragua and the United States have been tense since a Marxist revolution led by the Sandinistas (as the revolutionary group was popularly known) overthrew the U.S.-backed government in Nicaragua in 1979. The United States has supplied military and financial support to anti-Sandinista groups and candidates in Nicaragua since then, succeeding in breaking the Sandinistas' hold on the government in 1990 with the election of Violeta Chamorro (1929–) as president.

However, U.S. efforts to keep the Sandinistas out of power, such as a strict 1985 trade embargo on the country, negatively impacted the Nicaraguan economy, so Chamorro took the helm of a country in financial shambles. The Sandinistas returned to power in 2007, when one of the group's original and most prominent leaders Daniel Ortega (1945–) became president. Nicaragua is the poorest country in Central America.

⊕ Historical Background

The largest country in Central America, Nicaragua, is bordered by Honduras to the north, the Caribbean Sea to the east, Costa Rica to the south, and the Pacific Ocean to the west. Nicaragua consists of large swaths of low-lying coastal plains, which, on the eastern coast of the country, are also home to tropical forests. The interior of the country is largely mountainous, while the southwestern portion of the nation is home to a large lake region. The population of Nicaragua is estimated at 5.79 million as of 2013. Some 69 percent of Nicaragua's population is of mixed Amerindian and European background known as mestizo. About 17 percent is white, 9 percent black, and 5 percent Amerindian.

Spanish is the official language and is spoken by a majority of the population, though some indigenous Amerindian words and phrases are used in everyday dialect. Miskito is spoken by nearly 2 percent of the Amerindian

population. Most Nicaraguans (58 percent) are Roman Catholic. Another 22 percent are Evangelical Christian.

Nicaragua is part of the Mosquito Coast, named after the Miskito Indians. In 1522, Spanish conquistador Gil González Dávila discovered that a chieftain named Cacique Nicarao was governing the area. The Spanish named the region Nicaragua and quickly subdued the natives and took over the land. The country gained independence from Spain as part of the United Provinces of Central America in 1821; it became an independent republic in 1838.

In the 1840s and 1850s, Nicaraguan politics consisted of a rivalry—often devolving to civil war—between the liberal elite who mostly lived in the city of León and the conservative elite who mostly lived in the city of Granada. In 1855 the liberals asked William Walker (1824–1860), a U.S. citizen and adventurer, to help them fight the conservatives. In 1856, Walker declared himself king, betraying the local liberal faction. Various Central American countries helped to push him out. Walker was executed in Honduras in 1860. For several decades thereafter, conservatives ruled Nicaragua.

José Santos Zelaya

In 1909 the country was run by President José Santos Zelaya (1853–1919), who had led a liberal revolt in 1893 that had brought him to power. Although Zelaya was a proponent of liberal values and a supporter of education and commerce, some of his policies troubled the U.S. government. The United States also was concerned that he would ally himself with another superpower and allow that country to build a canal through Nicaragua. The United States was working on a competing canal in Panama, later completed in 1914, and was hoping to monopolize the market. Canal development was not imminent, but the United States found out Zelaya had been discussing a canal with Japan and Germany, thus putting U.S. canal plans at risk.

Zelaya also proved to be a cruel and despotic ruler who assassinated and imprisoned people he suspected of being opponents. In 1909, some 500 revolutionaries

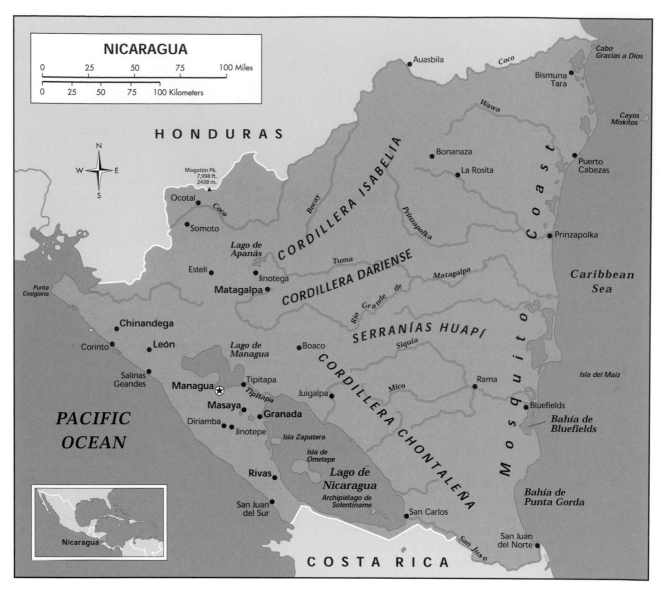

NICARAGUA

0   25   50   75   100 Miles

0   25   50   75   100 Kilometers

HONDURAS

Auasbila

Coco

Cabo
Gracias a Dios

Bismuna
Tara

Mogotón Pk.
7,998 ft.
2438 m.

Wawa

Cayos
Miskitos

Ocotal

Coco

Bocay

CORDILLERA ISABELIA

Bonanaza

La Rosita

C
o
a
s
t

Puerto
Cabezas

Somoto

Prinzapolka

Prinzapolka

Estelí

Lago de
Apanás

Tuma

CORDILLERA DARIENSE

Matagalpa

Caribbean
Sea

Jinotega

Matagalpa

Río Grande de

Punta
Cosigüina

SERRANÍAS HUAPI

Chinandega

Siquia

M
o
s
q
u
i
t
o

Corinto

León

Lago de
Managua

Boaco

CORDILLERA CHONTALEÑA

Isla del Maíz

Salinas
Geandes

Managua

Tipitapa

Tipitapa

Mico

Rama

PACIFIC
OCEAN

Masaya

Diriamba

Granada

Juigalpa

Bluefields

Bahía de
Bluefields

Jinotepe

Isla Zapatera

Rivas

Isla de
Ometepe

Lago de
Nicaragua

Archipiélago de
Solentiname

Bahía de
Punta Gorda

San Juan
del Sur

San Carlos

San Juan

San Juan
del Norte

Nicaragua

COSTA RICA

© 2014 Cengage Learning

were killed on the orders of Zelaya, two of whom were U.S. citizens. The United States sent warships to Nicaragua, and Zelaya resigned later that year.

Zelaya was replaced by a series of acting presidents installed by the United States. In 1911, Adolfo Díaz Recinos (1875–1964) became president. Díaz feared that his secretary of war, General Luis Mena (who had been acting president for three days in 1910), was plotting a coup. He asked Mena to resign, and Mena left to start an insurrection. Díaz asked the United States to intervene, and the U.S. Marines occupied Nicaragua from 1912 to 1933, except for a brief nine-month period in 1925 during a conservative coup.

Sandino's Guerrilla War

From 1927 to 1933, General Augusto César Sandino (1895–1934) led a guerrilla war against the government and the U.S. Marines. His actions made him a hero in Nicaragua, as he fought the United States for control. When the Americans finally left in 1933, they set up and trained a Guardia Nacional (National Guard) designed to be loyal to U.S. interests. For many years thereafter, whoever led the Guardia Nacional controlled the country.

Sandino and the newly elected Juan Batista Sacasa (1887–1946) government reached an agreement by which he would cease his guerrilla activities in exchange for amnesty, a grant of land for an agricultural colony, and retention of a 100–man force for a year. But Sandino's days were numbered. On February 24, 1934, Guardia Nacional leader Anastasio Somoza García (1896–1956) invited him to a meeting in Managua and assassinated him. Hundreds of residents of the agricultural community were executed later.

The Rise of the Somoza Dynasty

Nicaragua was then ruled by a series of military dictatorships. The longest was the 43–year hereditary dictatorship of the Somoza family. Although the Somoza

A Sandinista fighter points a rifle at crouching captives on a street in Nicaragua during the Nicaraguan Revolution that ousted Anastasio Somoza Debayle, the last in a line of Somozas who ruled Nicaragua from 1937 to 1979.   © *Matthew Naythons/Timepix/Time Life Pictures/Getty Images*

family did not always hold the presidency during that period, they were always the de facto power in Nicaragua, at times using puppet governments. Anastasio Somoza García rose through the ranks of the Guardia Nacional and first came to power with help from the United States. He deposed Sacasa, becoming president on January 1, 1937, in a fraudulent election.

Somoza enriched himself throughout his presidency, ending his rule as the largest landowner in Nicaragua. Despite his well-known corruption and brutality toward his own people, he maintained the support of the United States because he was adamantly anti–Communist at a time when anti–Communism was of primary importance to the United States. He was assassinated in 1956 and succeeded by his son, Luis Somoza Debayle (1922–1967). When he died in 1967, Luis was succeeded by his younger brother, Anastasio Somoza Debayle (1925–1980).

The Sandinistas

In 1963, Carlos Fonseca Amador (1936–1976) formed the Sandinista National Liberation Front (FSLN). Inspired by the Cuban Revolution of 1959, in which a Communist insurgency toppled the formerly U.S.-backed government, they hoped to instigate such a revolution in Nicaragua. In 1964, Fonseca was arrested and accused of plotting to assassinate Anastasio Somoza

Debayle, then head of the Guardia Nacional. He fled to Mexico and Costa Rica for most of the mid-1960s. His book, *From Prison: I Accuse the Dictatorship,* claimed that the Somoza Dynasty had committed crimes, including disenfranchising much of the Nicaraguan population.

The Sandinistas, as they came to be called, gained a significant number of new recruits following the 1972 earthquake that devastated the Nicaraguan city of Managua. The earthquake had ruined 90 percent of Managua, leaving the residents in destitution. Anastasio Somoza Debayle ruled Nicaragua from 1967 to 1972 and again from 1974 to 1979. As ruler, he confiscated much of the international aid designated for the victims of the earthquake. Even the elite's support crumbled because of his greed.

Hostage Crisis

In December 1974, the FSLN attempted to kidnap U.S. Ambassador to Nicaragua Turner Shelton during a Christmas party in Managua. However, Turner had already left, so the group kidnapped some other socially prominent guests. The Somoza government agreed to pay the ransom, but later hunted down the perpetrators. Due to high-visibility kidnappings such as this, the FSLN emerged as the internationally recognized opposition to what was known as a corrupt and cruel regime. When Chilean president Salvador Allende (1908–1973)

IRAN–CONTRA AFFAIR

The Iran–Contra affair was a political scandal that emerged in 1986, during U.S. president Ronald Reagan's second term in office. The arrangement was complicated, involving several countries. The scandal began as an operation to free seven American hostages being held in Lebanon by a group with Iranian ties connected to the Army of the Guardians of the Islamic Revolution. It was planned that Israel would ship weapons to Iran, and then the United States would resupply Israel and receive the Iranian payment. The Iranian recipients promised to do everything in their power to achieve the release of the U.S. hostages. In essence, the plan was an arms–for–hostages scheme, in which members of the executive branch of the U.S. government sold weapons to the Iranian government in exchange for help in obtaining the release of the American hostages.

Reagan's campaign promise (which remains the stated policy of the United States) was that the government does not negotiate with terrorists or pay ransom for kidnap victims. Hence, the exchange of weapons and money for the release of hostages was scandal enough. Then it was revealed that a portion of proceeds from the weapons' sales were diverted to fund the Contras, despite the U.S. Congress's prohibition on supporting them. The Boland Amendment of 1982 prohibited "the use of funds 'for the purpose of' overthrowing the government of Nicaragua or provoking a war between Nicaragua and Honduras."

The weapon sales became public knowledge in 1986; the cover–up of the scandal made the incident worse. Large volumes of documents were destroyed, reportedly at the direction of Lt. Col. Oliver North (1943–), a National Security Council member. At the time it was unclear exactly who in the executive branch knew about the plan or authorized it.

In November 1986 Reagan appointed a Special Review Board to investigate the matter. The Tower Commission, named after former Senator John Tower (1925–1991), held hearings and issued a report stating that Reagan did not have knowledge of the funds being redirected to the Contras. The U.S. Congress held hearings on the Iran-Contra affair in 1987.

The Nicaraguan government sued the United States before the International Court of Justice, which ruled that the United States should pay Nicaragua compensation. However, the United States did not comply. Several members of the Reagan administration were indicted in the United States and convicted, although most were subsequently pardoned by Reagan's successor, George H. W. Bush (1924–).

Tendency or Terceristas (Third Way), called for temporary alliances with non–Communists to fight the Somoza regime. The Sandinistas split along these three lines.

Revolution

After a popular editor of the newspaper *La Prensa* was assassinated on January 10, 1978, allegedly by the Somoza regime, riots broke out and the business community demanded Somoza's resignation. Pedro Joaquín Chamorro Cardenal (1924–1978) was an important voice at the only significant opposition newspaper in Nicaragua. While Somoza held onto power in the chaos that followed, the United States suspended military assistance to pressure him to leave.

In August, the Terceristas took the entire Nicaraguan Congress—more than 2,000 people—hostage. Somoza gave into their demands, paying ransom and releasing 60 political prisoners. The FSLN had realized a major victory.

But the riots continued. The FSLN reunified and the armed struggle continued. Nine men formed the National Directorate (of the Sandinistas) in preparation for becoming a provisional government. The FSLN was no longer one of many opposition groups. They were the opposition group—the one that might bring down a brutal dynasty.

On June 4, the Sandinistas called for a general strike until Somoza resigned. On June 16, they formed a provisional Nicaraguan government in exile: Junta of National Reconstruction. On July 17, 1979, Somoza resigned and the Sandinistas junta took over 2 days later. Somoza fled to Paraguay where he was later assassinated.

The Contras

In response to the rise of power of the Sandinistas, various conservative groups banded together to form the Contras. Comprised of the Nicaraguan Democratic Front, among others, the Contras were now the rebels. They called themselves the Nicaraguan Resistance, and operated out of neighboring countries. (Contra is short for *contrarevolucion*, or counter–revolution). The administration of then–U.S. President Ronald Reagan (1911–2004) called them the democratic resistance.

The Contras engaged in economic sabotage and placed mines in Nicaragua's Port of Corinto to impede shipping. They received help—training, supplies, and sometimes manpower—from the U.S. Central Intelligence Agency (CIA) as authorized by President Reagan. They were often brutal to the local population. Edgar Chamorro Coronel (1931–), a former Contra who later became a critic, noted that he received reports of numerous atrocities committed by the Contras. Reported atrocities included torture, rape, kidnapping, and executing civilians, including children. Later it was determined that the Contras employed these tactics as a part of their strategy, designed to demoralize and intimidate.

The CIA's guidance included a manual written especially for the Contras. *Psychological Operations in Guerrilla Warfare* covered everything from selection of an appropriate slogan and the structure of a speech to how to justify killing a civilian trying to leave a town under attack.

died during a military coup, several hundred Chileans joined the Sandinistas, which had come to represent the poor people fighting for their rights and social justice.

The Guardia Nacional struck back, unleashing a repressive campaign of violence. The Sandinistas were divided about the best strategy to pursue. One group supported Guerra Popular Prolongada (Prolonged Popular War, or GPP), a quiet regrouping and rebuilding of peasant support in the mountain region. A second group, which focused on mobilizing urban protests, called themselves the Proletarian Tendency. A third group, known as the Insurrectional

Members of a Contra special forces team carry a comrade wounded by a land mine in Honduras, where some Contras were trained to fight, in 1984. Shortly after leaving the camp, they triggered a mine, which killed three of them. The Contras refer to the loosely organized groups of Nicaraguan rebels (who were at least partially supported by the U.S. government through the Central Intelligence Agency) who militarily opposed the success of the socialist Sandinista political party in Nicaragua in the late 1970s and 1980s. © *Steven Clevenger/Getty Images*

⊕ Impacts and Issues

The Contras and the Sandinistas continued to vie for power. The Sandinistas received military and economic aid from both the Soviet Union and from Cuba. In 1984, Nicaragua held general elections. The Reagan administration had privately encouraged the conservative candidate, Arturo José Cruz Porras (1923–2013), to boycott the election out of concern that his participation would legitimize the voting. When the Sandinistas won, in elections widely considered to be fair, the Reagan administration declared them fraudulent.

In 1990 a coalition of parties from across the political spectrum backed a candidate to run against the Sandinistas. Violeta Chamorro (1929–) won with 55 percent of the vote. The United States had supplied military and financial support to anti-Sandinista groups and candidates in Nicaragua, succeeding in breaking the Sandinistas' hold on the government in 1990 with Chamorro's election. Following the election, a U.S. trade embargo with Nicaragua that had been in place five years was dropped.

The Sandinistas lost again in 1996 and 2001. The Sandinistas returned to power in 2007, when one of the group's original and most prominent leaders, José

Daniel Ortega Saavedra (1945–), became president. Ortega was one of the original leaders of the Junta of National Reconstruction.

Aid to Nicaragua increased with Chamorro's election, but decreased again when the Sandinistas returned to power in 2007. U.S. citizens who lost land and property when the Sandinistas took power continue to advocate for compensation.

⊕ Future Implications

The Nicaraguan government has faced many difficulties in addressing the concerns of the nation's indigenous peoples. For decades the Miskito have accused the established government of political and social marginalization and economic exploitation as the natural resources of indigenous lands have been claimed by outside companies. The Miskito remain especially impoverished. In 2009 the Miskito declared their independence from Nicaragua with the formation of the Community Nation of Miskitia. The Nicaraguan government has ignored their declaration.

Nicaragua has also become a center for drug trafficking, with many former rebels turning to crime. Cartels groups of organized crime members—are growing, and

Nicaraguan President Violeta Chamorro receives an AK-47 assault rifle from a member of the Contra forces to symbolize the end of the war, June 9, 1990, in El Almendro. © *Peter Northall/AFP/Getty Images*

Mexican cartels have expanded their reach into Nicaragua. Trafficking continues to incite violence and encourage crime, especially among the poorest Nicaraguans.

SEE ALSO   *Cuba-U.S. Conflict; Mexico's Drug War*

BIBLIOGRAPHY

Books

Kinzer, Stephen. *Blood of Brothers: Life and War in Nicaragua*. Cambridge, MA: David Rockefeller Center for Latin American Studies, 2007.

Miranda, Roger, and William Ratliff. *The Civil War in Nicaragua: Inside the Sandinistas*. New Brunswick, NJ: Transaction Publishers, 1993.

Morley, Morris H. *Washington, Somoza, and the Sandinistas: State and Regime in U.S. Policy Toward Nicaragua, 1969–1981*. Cambridge, UK: Cambridge University Press, 1994.

Walker, Thomas W., and Christine J. Wade. *Nicaragua: Living in the Shadow of the Eagle*, 5th ed. Boulder, CO: Westview Press, 2011.

Walsh, Lawrence E. *Iran-Contra: The Final Report*. New York: Times Books, 1994.

Periodicals

Brands, Hal. "Reform, Democratization, and Counterinsurgency: Evaluating the U.S. Experience in Cold War-Era Latin America." *Small Wars and Insurgencies* 22, no. 2 (May 2011): 290-321.

Perla, Hector. "Heirs of Sandino: The Nicaraguan Revolution and the U.S.-Nicaragua Solidarity Movement." *Latin American Perspectives* 36. no. 6 (November 2009): 80.

Web Sites

"The Contras, Cocaine, and Covert Operations." *The National Security Archive, George Washington University.* http://www2.gwu.edu/~nsarchiv/NSAEBB/NSAEBB2/nsaebb2.htm (accessed December 22, 2013).

"The Iran-Contra Affair." *American Experience, PBS.* http://www.pbs.org/wgbh/americanexperience/features/general-article/reagan-iran/ (accessed December 22, 2013).

"Understanding the Iran-Contra Affairs." *Brown University.* http://www.brown.edu/Research/Understanding_the_Iran_Contra_Affair/n-sandinistas.php (accessed December 22, 2013).

Nobel Peace Prize

🌐 Introduction

The Nobel Peace Prize is one of five awards established by wealthy Swedish inventor and entrepreneur Alfred Nobel. The first Nobel prizes were given in 1901, and Nobel prizes continue to be awarded in the 21st century. The peace prize is meant to be awarded to a person or group that has "done the most or best work for fraternity between nations, for the abolition or reduction of standing armies and for the holding and promotion of peace congresses." For an award based on peace, however, it has remained perhaps the most controversial of all the Nobel prizes. Its political nature has often led to vocal criticism of the selected winners, as well as accusations of a pro-Western bias against the Norway-based Nobel Committee.

🌐 Historical Background

The Nobel Prize was the brainchild of Alfred Nobel (1833–1896), a Swedish inventor, writer, and social activist. Many considered Nobel's ideas and inventions far ahead of their time and quite radical. By the time of his death, Nobel was a wealthy man, thanks to his invention of dynamite a number of years earlier. Nobel's first efforts in this area ended with an explosion that killed his younger brother and four other scientists. Nobel then worked to create a safer version of the explosive. A pacifist at heart, Nobel was concerned that his reputation would forever be linked to an instrument of death; to prevent this he created an unusual will.

Nobel's will left a large sum of money for a fund that would offer award prizes annually in the areas of literature, chemistry, physics, medicine, and peace. The provisions of Nobel's will were not welcomed by his family or the king of Sweden at the time. Although Nobel died in 1896, a number of years were spent contesting the will before the money was finally available for

Portrait of Alfred Nobel, the Swedish chemist who invented dynamite, and later became a philanthropist who founded the Nobel Prizes. *© Time & Life Pictures/Getty Images*

the Nobel Prize fund; the first prizes were not awarded until five years after his death.

The Peace Prize

The process of selecting Nobel Peace Prize winners is arduous, somewhat secretive, and carried out by the Norwegian Nobel Committee in Oslo, the five members of which are nominated by the Norwegian Parliament. The Nobel Peace Prize is typically given to individuals, but may on occasion go to entire organizations. Invitations to submit nominations are sent to individuals who are qualified to nominate potential winners. This elite group includes members of national assemblies and governments, members of international courts, university rectors, and those who have won or been involved with the Nobel Prize process in the past. The list of candidates in each category is then winnowed down from 200 or more candidates (there were a record-breaking 259 in 2013) to create a group of five to 10 finalists. The peace prizes are awarded at an annual ceremony in Oslo, Norway, on December 10, the anniversary of Nobel's death.

The first Nobel Peace Prize was jointly awarded to Henri Dunant, who founded the International Committee of the Red Cross in 1863, and Frédéric Passy, the founder and president of the International League of Peace in 1867. In 1906 U.S. president Theodore Roosevelt (1858–1918) was the first statesman to receive the Nobel Peace Prize. He was recognized for his role in mediating and ultimately ending the 1905 war between Russia and Japan. However, Roosevelt had fought against Cuba prior to his presidency, and as president he made clear his desire for the United States to become an international power through the use of military force. Critics stated the Nobel Committee violated Alfred Nobel's intentions by presenting the award to Roosevelt. The Nobel Committee argued that they consider prominence when designating awards, and that Roosevelt's role in ending the war between Russia and Japan was more influential than the actions of peace activists.

Sometimes the Nobel Peace Prize is notable for its omissions rather than its recipients. For example, Mohandas Gandhi (1869–1948) was nominated six times in the 1930s and 1940s but never received the prize. Some critics claim the Swedish Nobel Committee did not want to risk offending Great Britain by recognizing Gandhi, but the Nobel Committee refutes this claim. Instead, the official response is that Gandhi did not have the necessary political visibility. Yet Gandhi's actions directly inspired the nonviolent resistance movements led by Martin Luther King Jr. (1929–1968) during the 1960s and Nelson Mandela (1918–2013), who fought to abolish apartheid in South Africa. King was given the Nobel Peace Prize in 1964 for his peaceful leadership during the United States' civil rights era. Mandela received the Nobel Peace Prize in 1993 after serving 27 years in prison and shortly before he became the president of South Africa. Why the Nobel Committee recognized King and Mandela but not Gandhi may never be known.

In 1973 the Nobel Peace Prize was awarded to U.S. secretary of state Henry Kissinger (1923–) and North Vietnamese negotiator Le Duc Tho (1911–1990) for negotiating a cease-fire agreement between U.S. forces and the North Vietnamese. They declined the prize, stating that peace in Vietnam had yet to be achieved. Indeed, the Vietnam War (1954–75) continued for two more years. Similarly, Palestinian leader Yasser Arafat (1929–2004) and Israeli leaders Shimon Peres (1923–) and Yitzhak Rabin (1922–1995) received the prize in 1994 for their peace talks, though actual peace was not reached. Despite the lack of true peace, Arafat, Peres, and Rabin accepted the prize for their efforts.

Burmese human rights and pro-democracy activist Aung San Suu Kyi (1945–) was awarded the Nobel Peace Prize in 1991. She was prevented from accepting the prize at the time, however, by the oppressive military regime in Burma that kept her imprisoned or under house arrest for 15 years over a 21-year period. She was released from house arrest in 2010, and on June 15, 2012, personally accepted her prize in Oslo, Norway, in front of an enthusiastic crowd that twice greeted her with thunderous ovations. In introducing Suu Kyi, the chairman of the Norwegian Nobel Committee stressed her "awe-inspiring tenacity, sacrifice and firmness of principle."

Typically an individual or group of individuals is awarded the Nobel Peace Prize, but on a few occasions the award has gone to an entire organization. In 1999 Médecins San Frontières (Doctors Without Borders) was given the Nobel Peace Prize for its good works. In 2012 the European Union (EU) was awarded the Nobel Peace Prize for transforming the region "from a continent of war to a continent of peace." Europe was the site of the two deadliest wars of the 20th century: World War I (1914–18) and World War II (1939–45). The EU was formed in large part to ensure that further conflict between European nations would be unlikely.

⊕ Impacts and Issues

In many years, the awarding of the peace prize draws controversy, and critics expound publicly on why certain people or organizations should not have been selected. Suu Kyi is just one of many Peace Prize recipients whose pro-Western ideals have led non-Western critics and governments to condemn the prize as biased. Liu Xiaobo (1955–), a Chinese professor and activist, participated in the student protests at Tiananmen Square in 1989, and became an outspoken supporter of Western-style reforms in China. He was arrested several times during the 1990s and 2000s for his criticism of the Chinese government and calls for political reform, and all his writings were banned in China. In 2009, he was sentenced to 11 years in prison for his subversive activities; his arrest drew outrage from around the world, with many countries and human rights organizations calling for his immediate release. The following year Liu received the Nobel Peace Prize, though he was unable to attend the ceremony. China and a number of its allies, including Russia, Pakistan, and Saudi Arabia, criticized the selection of Liu and boycotted the ceremony.

Carl von Ossietzky (1889–1938) was a controversial winner whose story remains relevant to modern issues of diplomacy. Ossietzky, a German pacifist, was a writer and editor who played a key role in exposing Germany's violation of the Treaty of Versailles. The treaty, signed as part of Germany's surrender in World War I, placed strict limits on the number of troops that could be held by Germany. This was an attempt to prevent further war in the future. However, the German government secretly violated these terms and created additional armed forces.

When Ossietzky published an article on this violation in a newspaper he edited in 1929, both he and the author were charged with treason for revealing state secrets. The author fled, but Ossietzky was sent to prison. After his release, he remained an outspoken critic of the German government, and when Hitler became Chancellor of Germany in 1933, Ossietzky was put in police custody. When he received the Nobel Peace Prize in 1935, he was not allowed to leave Germany to accept the award. He remained essentially a prisoner in his own country until his death from tuberculosis in 1938. His selection for the Peace Prize provoked outrage from conservatives around the world, who viewed him as a man who betrayed his own government—despite the fact that his revelations were true and provided an early warning of the aggressive intentions of Nazi Germany.

Sometimes the connection between the winner of the Peace Prize and the issue of peace itself may seem unclear or tenuous. For example, the 2007 Nobel Peace Prize winners were Al Gore and the Intergovernmental Panel on Climate Change (IPCC), an organization dedicated to quantifying the adverse human impact of climate change on global climate systems and to finding ways to reduce greenhouse gas emissions. The fact that Gore and the IPCC were chosen for a peace award was divisive because climate change has yet to lead to armed conflict between nations or factions.

One of the most controversial winners of the Nobel Peace Prize was U.S. president Barack Obama (1961–), who received the award in 2009, his first year in office. The committee claimed to have chosen the president because he successfully promoted "international diplomacy and cooperation between peoples." Some people believe that the award was offered prematurely in the young leader's career. Others stressed that his election had helped the United States' international reputation in numerous ways. Three years later, when the award went to the EU for its work after World War II promoting human rights and peace, many people objected, stating

FEMALE NOBEL PEACE PRIZE LAUREATES

Women's achievements have been recognized with Nobel Prizes in all fields, however the distribution of all the Nobel Prizes is still widely male-dominated. Between 1901, when the Nobel Peace Prize was introduced, and 2013, the Peace Prize was given 94 times, with the prize going to 22 different organizations and 101 individuals. Of these individuals, 15 women have earned the Nobel Peace Prize. These women are:

- Bertha von Suttner, 1905, Austria. An acquaintance of Alfred Nobel and a leading pacifist.
- Jane Addams, 1931, United States. A prominent figure in the women's suffrage movement and founder of Hull House, a community center in Chicago.
- Emily Greene Balch, 1946, United States. An active pacifist who helped found the Women's International League for Peace and Freedom.
- Betty Williams and Mairead Corrigan, 1976, Northern Ireland. Co-winners of the prize, Williams and Corrigan were founders of Community of Peace People, a group whose aim was to end sectarian violence, known as "the Troubles," in Northern Ireland.
- Mother Teresa, 1979, Albania. Founder of Missionaries of Charity, Mother Teresa was a Roman Catholic nun who worked tirelessly for the poor and suffering. She worked primarily in India.
- Alva Myrdal, 1982, Sweden. A vocal supporter of disarmament as a delegate to the United Nations.
- Aung San Suu Kyi, 1991, Burma. A democracy and human rights activist, held under house arrest intermittently for 15 years over a 21-year period by Burma's repressive military regime. She was released in 2010.
- Rigoberta Menchú Tum, 1992, Guatemala. Guatemala's most prominent activist in the cause of protecting the rights of her country's indigenous peoples.
- Jody Williams, 1997, United States. A founder of the International Campaign to Ban Landmines, an organization that coordinated efforts by governments, the United Nations, and the International Red Cross to create an international treaty banning landmines.
- Shirin Ebadi, 2003, Iran. Human rights activist and lawyer, Ebadi has lived in exile in the United Kingdom since 2009, due to threats against her life and the lives of her family members.
- Wangari Maathai, 2004, Kenya. An environmental and women's rights activist. She was the first African woman to receive the Nobel Peace Prize.
- Ellen Johnson Sirleaf, Leymah Gbowee, and Tawakkol Karman, 2011, Liberia and Yemen. Sirleaf and Gbowee (both from Liberia) and Karman (from Yemen) shared the award for their political activism in the cause of women's rights. Sirleaf became the first female president of Liberia in 2006.

The Nobel Peace Prize Winners for 2011, Liberian President Ellen Johnson Sirleaf, Leymah Gbowee of Liberia, and Tawakkol Karman of Yemen, attend the Nobel Peace Prize ceremony at Oslo City Hall on December 10, 2011, in Oslo, Norway.   © *Nigel Waldron/Getty Images*

that there are many people within the boundaries of the EU who continue to suffer, and that the EU has used military power to achieve stability.

Despite the complaints and controversies, interest in the Nobel Peace Prize remains consistently high, and nominations continue to flow in to the committee. In 2013, more than 200 individuals and 50 organizations were nominated, including the youngest nominee, Malala Yousafzai, a 16-year-old who was shot in the head by the Taliban two years earlier for advocating girls' access to education in her native Pakistan. Before the winner was announced in December, many people believed that Yousafzai was favored to win. However, the prize eventually went to the Organisation for the Prohibition of Chemical Weapons (OPCW) for its attempts to combat the use of chemical weapons, particularly in Syria. The exact reasons that one group or individual may be chosen over another will not be known in the near future: the process of selection is sealed by the Nobel Committee for 50 years after each winner is chosen.

⊕ Future Implications

Though controversy has occasionally surrounded the Nobel Peace Prize, many still consider it one of the most prestigious awards in the world. The prize can also be used to spotlight problems or humanitarian crises around the world, bringing worldwide attention to areas and issues about which the public may have limited knowledge. Though the process and politics are at times imperfect, the peace prize has generally rewarded worthy recipients who have worked to create peace or positive change or to secure human rights in the world. It has also, in some cases, succeeded in focusing attention on or putting public pressure on governments for reform, for example when political prisoners such as Suu Kyi and

Liu win the prize. Each year the number of nominees has increased and the funds for the prize continue to be grow, guaranteeing that the prize will be awarded for many years to come despite any criticisms.

SEE ALSO   *Arab-Israeli Conflict; Burma (Myanmar) Uprisings; European Union; Geneva Conventions; Humanitarian Aid; Israeli-Palestinian Conflict; Liberia's Civil Wars; South Africa: Apartheid; United Nations*

BIBLIOGRAPHY

Books

Fieldman, Burton. *The Nobel Prize: A History of Genius, Controversy and Prestige.* New York: Arcade Publishing, 2009.

Nordlinger, Jay. *Peace They Say: A History of the Nobel Peace Prize, the Most Famous and Controversial Prize in the World.* New York: Encounter Books, 2012.

Web Sites

Nobel Peace Center. http://www.nobelpeacecenter.org/en/ (accessed December 8, 2013).

Nobel Peace Prize. http://www.nobelprize.org/nobel_prizes/peace/ (accessed December 8, 2013).

"Nobel Peace Prize Winners: from 1901–2013." *The Telegraph*, October 11, 2013. http://www.telegraph.co.uk/news/worldnews/10370215/Nobel-Peace-Prize-winners-from-1901-2013.html (accessed December 8, 2013).

The North Atlantic Treaty Organization (NATO)

⊕ Introduction

The North Atlantic Treaty Organization (NATO) is a military alliance between the United States, Canada, and Western European countries. It was formed for "collective defense," whereby member states stand together in mutual defense in the event of an attack on another member state. NATO was founded in 1949 and continues to be the foremost military alliance in the world. Although none of the countries included in NATO have been directly attacked by another nation since NATO's creation, the alliance has been used to create an international army of sorts, which has intervened in several international conflicts over the years.

The combined military spending of NATO members constitutes more than 70 percent of the world's total military spending. NATO currently includes 28 countries, with an additional 22 countries participating in NATO's Partnership for Peace program. Fifteen more nations are involved in institutionalized dialogue programs with NATO, including former NATO enemy Russia. The military alliance has been successful in preventing another war in Europe and is evolving into a truly global taskforce. The brunt of its military might is still concentrated on the U.S. armed forces. As the world power dynamics continue to shift, NATO will need to evolve to stay abreast of events so that it can ensure peace and prosperity for each of its member nations and for the world at large.

⊕ Historical Background

NATO was founded in 1949 by 12 original member states: Belgium, Canada, Denmark, France, Ireland, Italy, Luxembourg, Netherlands, Norway, Portugal, the United Kingdom, and the United States. All of these countries had been allies in World War II (1939–45). During the war these Western nations had been aided by the Soviet Union, and together they had successfully defeated the Germans and other Axis powers. After the war ended, however, political and economic differences between the Western nations and the Soviet Union and its eastern bloc (the Warsaw Pact) quickly became a source of contention.

European leaders could not afford another world war and feared the rising power of the Soviet Union. They believed that an alliance with the United States was essential to counter the military power of the Soviet Union and prevent another rise in nationalist militarism in Europe. The original aim of the alliance, according to NATO's first secretary general, Lord Hastings Ismay (1887–1965), was "to keep the Russians out, the Americans in, and the Germans down."

NATO was created during the Cold War era (1947–91), a time of political and military rivalry between the United States and the Soviet Union. For its first few years NATO was essentially a political association between Western Europe and North America. But as the Cold War tensions between the United States and the Soviet Union grew, NATO formed a more formal military structure, controlled by two U.S. supreme commanders.

Over the next four decades the relationship between NATO's European nations and the United States ebbed and flowed. NATO critics doubted the alliance's ability to protect Western Europe in case of a Soviet invasion. France was particularly concerned, and withdrew from NATO in 1966 to form its own independent nuclear deterrent. Despite frequent high tensions, during the entire Cold War era NATO did not directly engage in any military conflicts.

⊕ Impacts and Issues

The issues that NATO has faced in its more than 50 years have changed through the passage of time. The alliance was successful in preventing another major war in

President Harry S. Truman signs the North Atlantic Treaty which marked the beginning of the North Atlantic Treaty Organization (NATO), behind him are (from left) Sir Derrick Hoyes Miller, Henrik de Kauffman, W. D. Matthews, Louis Johnson, Wilhelm Munthe de Morgenstienne, Henry Bonnet, Pedro Theotonio Pereira, Dean Acheson, Jontchess Reuchlin, and Mario Lucienni.   © MPI/Getty Images

Europe, but tensions emerged between treaty members, principally France, over the dominance of the United States. Also after the fall of the Soviet Union and the entrance of former Soviet satellites into the alliance, the Russian government became concerned about NATO encroaching on its sphere of influence. As the threat of a Soviet attack diminished, the expansion of NATO's role to include fighting wars in southern Europe and other parts of the world transformed the institution from a defensive alliance against Russia to a protector of Western interests throughout the world and created tensions between the United States and the other members.

Expansion

NATO's expansion has occurred in five phases since the inauguration of its 12 founding member states. The first three stages took place during the Cold War era. In 1952 Greece and Turkey, each considered strategically vital to the West, were admitted into NATO. Neither of these Mediterranean countries borders the Atlantic Ocean, but their locations were overlooked because they served as a buffer against the spread of Communism. Three years later West Germany was admitted into NATO out of fear that the Communist East might annex it. A nearly three-decade hiatus on new members followed until Spain became a NATO signatory in 1982. Each of these expansions of NATO was directly related to Cold War dynamics. A further 17 years would pass before NATO was extended again, and this time it was because the Cold War had officially ended and the world was suddenly a very different place.

The dissolution of the Soviet Union in 1991 ended the Cold War and changed the dynamics of European politics. Former Soviet client states remained wary of their former colonial master, Russia, after decades of

COLD AND HOT WARS

A so-called cold war is a war in which the two principal parties never actually declare war but instead subtly try to defeat each other. The Cold War between the United States and Soviet Union lasted more than four decades without the two nations ever directly confronting each other militarily. The tension between the two nations did occasionally erupt in full-blown "hot wars," in which the United States (aided by its allies in NATO) and the Soviet Union indirectly fought to reduce each other's international power. The Korean War (1950–53), Vietnam War (1954–75), Yom Kippur War (1973), and the Soviet War in Afghanistan (1979–89) were each hot wars that occurred in conjunction with the larger Cold War.

repression. They simultaneously sought reassurance that they would never again fall under Russian control, while also seeking to become fully integrated with the democratic West.

Political and economic instability within Russia was deemed a grave international threat. Indeed some political analysts likened Russia to Germany after the conclusion of World War I (1914–18): a wounded nation, capable of striking back with terrifying and unpredictable force. In a speech made in 1993, NATO secretary general Manfred Warner (1934–1994) said: "The first and most important area where change must come is in further developing our ability to project stability to the East."

As such, it was at once inevitable and inherently attractive for NATO to expand its membership into the former Soviet bloc. In 1999 the Czech Republic, Hungary, and Poland joined NATO. They were followed by Bulgaria, Estonia, Latvia, Lithuania, Romania, Slovakia, and Slovenia five years later. In 2009 Albania and Croatia joined, bringing the alliance's total number of signatories to 28.

In 2009 France rejoined NATO, and in September 2009 French general Stéphane Abrial (1954–) became head of Allied Command Transformation. The post is one of two supreme command positions in NATO, and Abrial is the first non–American to hold one of these positions. This move, among others, is a clear sign that NATO is no longer controlled by the United States, but is instead becoming a more European-focused alliance.

NATO and Russia

The expansion of NATO into the old Communist East has been the cause of much controversy, particularly from within Russia. The end of the Cold War left NATO without a clearly defined enemy in its sights, but the expansion into former Russian heartlands antagonized its old enemy. The Russian government has signaled its consternation at everything from proposed missile defense systems on its doorstep to NATO forces "encircling" the Russian enclave of Kaliningrad, located on the Baltic coast between Poland and Lithuania.

Some former Soviet colonies have not been invited to join NATO, which has left them vulnerable to Russian interference. For example the Russian invasion of Georgia in August 2008, ostensibly in support of South Ossetian and Abkhazian secessionists, probably would not have happened if Georgia had been a NATO member. Indeed the invasion was seen by some military analysts as a direct challenge to NATO by Russia.

Russia has long objected to the eastward expansion of NATO into former Soviet territory, and has typically viewed the organization with suspicion or outright hostility. A November 2010 NATO summit showed some easing of Russian-NATO tensions. Russian president Dmitry Medvedev (1965–) attended the summit, the first time a Russian representative has attended a NATO meeting since the 2008 conflict in Georgia.

At the meeting Russia agreed to cooperate with NATO in building a missile defense shield for all of Europe and in supplying training and supplies for the war effort in Afghanistan. Little mention was made of the ongoing Russian occupation of parts of Georgia. Analysts argued that NATO's interest in expanding eastward has waned, both because the organization has come to understand that Russia would move aggressively, as it did in Georgia, to protect its territorial interests, and because Russian cooperation in a variety of NATO initiatives would be beneficial.

New Challenges and Strategies

The alliance's expansion has begged questions about NATO's overall strategic direction. Does it remain a defensive alliance, or has it become so large that it can be considered a global military force? Does the now overwhelming European influence mean it is a European Union military force by proxy? NATO's size also means that less consensus is likely to be reached on major issues. For instance NATO refused to back an invasion of Iraq in 2003, even though many of its members joined the U.S.-led invasion independently.

The challenges facing NATO signatories have also changed in the past decade. Rather than simply facing hostile nations, NATO now faces a less predictable threat in the form of terrorism. For most of its existence NATO assumed the format of a regional alliance that concentrated on the reactive defense of the treaty area. Perhaps its most urgent task now is helping to prevent an international crisis and armed conflict sparked by terrorism. Such an event could happen anywhere in the world. NATO believes that its expansion is an essential part of enhancing global security and ensuring stability in the modern era.

Military Operations

During the Cold War era, NATO did not directly engage in open warfare. But since 1994 NATO forces have been engaged in three interventions, one war, and two additional military operations. Although each of these instances was supposedly addressed with an international army, NATO's armed forces relied heavily on the military might of the United States.

NATO Interventions

On three occasions NATO has engaged in a military intervention. In 1994 NATO took its first wartime action by shooting down Bosnian Serb aircraft that illegally entered the no-fly zone in Bosnia and Herzegovina. The no-fly zone had been ordered by the United Nations, which had asked NATO to enforce its order since there was some concern that the Bosnian War (1992–95), if allowed to get out of control, could negatively affect all of Europe. Soon after these first shots were fired, NATO forces actively engaged in a bombing campaign that helped bring the Bosnian War to an end. The UN asked NATO to remain in the area as a peacekeeping force, which it did until 2004.

In 1999 NATO armed forces were sent to protect Albanian citizens in Kosovo, Yugoslavia. NATO's decision to enter the area was prompted by a request from the UN. Soon afterward it was proposed that all future NATO military attacks should be at the command of the UN, but this motion was vigorously opposed by most NATO nations.

In 2011 NATO once again intervened in global affairs. The UN had declared a no-fly zone over Libya, which was embroiled in a civil war. When this no-fly zone was crossed, NATO forces were asked to respond. After five months of conflict, several European nations began to withdraw their troops, and the United States was left to carry the majority of the military burden. This event has caused the United States to begin to openly question whether NATO is still a worthwhile alliance or if it has become a drain on the U.S. armed forces.

The NATO Secretary General Anders Fogh Rasmussen (L) and Hungarian Minister of Defence Csaba Hende (R) review a military honor guard during a ground breaking ceremony for the enlargement of NATO's Strategy Airlift Capability (SAC) base in Papa Airbase about 93 miles (150 kilometers) west of the Hungarian capital Budapest on July 1, 2013. With less than 140 staffed people of the multi-national military aviation safety systems, the SAC's heavy airlift wing (HAW) is operating from the base. Since the delivery of the first aircraft in 2009, the Wing has flown over 10,000 hours, delivered more than 40,000 tons of cargo and moved over 23,000 passengers over 6 continents, including missions to Mali, Haiti, Afghanistan, Pakistan, South Africa, and Europe. © Attila Kisbenedek/AFP/Getty Images

The War in Afghanistan The terrorist attacks on the United States on September 11, 2001, caused the United States to invoke Article 5 of the NATO Charter for the first time in the organization's history. Article 5 states that any attack on a member nation shall be considered a threat on all. The United States asked NATO to lend its forces to help the United States fight the Taliban in Afghanistan and to help prevent the movement of terrorists or weapons of mass destruction.

NATO troops were deployed to Afghanistan on October 1, 2001. Only a year later, however, several NATO nations, notably France and Belgium, began to question the involvement of NATO in the region. The United States asked NATO to join it in invading Iraq in 2003, but NATO refused, although several of its nations independently sent troops to aid the United States. NATO troops have been in Afghanistan since 2001 and are slated to be removed in December 2014.

Additional Military Operations NATO has been involved in two additional military operations. In 2004 the Iraqi Interim Government asked NATO to assist Iraqi security forces in building an effective and sustainable system for maintaining peace within the nation. NATO Training Mission-Iraq began in August 2004 and officially concluded in December 2011.

In 2009 NATO deployed warships in Operation Ocean Shield, meant to protect vital maritime traffic in the Gulf of Aden and the Indian Ocean from attacks by Somali pirates. Most of the warships were from the United States, although several vessels from other NATO nations were included in the fleet. The operation is expected to continue until at least the end of 2014.

⊕ Future Implications

In a speech delivered on June 10, 2011, in Brussels, Belgium, outgoing U.S. secretary of defense Robert Gates (1943–) offered unusually blunt criticism of NATO and its member states. Gates said that NATO members "are apparently willing and eager for American taxpayers to assume the growing security burden left by reductions in European defense budgets." Gates used NATO action in Libya in May and June of that year as examples of what he considered the major failings of NATO. He said, "The mightiest military alliance in history is only 11 weeks into an operation against a poorly armed regime in a sparsely populated country—yet many allies are beginning to run short of munitions, requiring the U.S., once more, to make up the difference." Gates went so far as to warn that future U.S. leaders may not find the alliance worthwhile.

NATO remains the most powerful military alliance in the world. However, as it is currently structured, the alliance remains essentially an agreement between the United States and Europe to provide mutual aid. As long as that alliance is felt to serve both parties, it will almost certainly continue as an important military force into the foreseeable future. If, however, the United States continues to feel that it is carrying the brunt of the burden of the alliance, NATO may be forced to redefine its goals and strategies.

SEE ALSO   *Afghan War; Cold War; Kosovo's Independence; Libyan Civil Unrest; United Nations; USSR: Dissolution; World War II; Yugoslav Wars*

BIBLIOGRAPHY

Books

Kaplan, Lawrence. *NATO Divided, NATO United: The Evolution of an Alliance.* Westport, CT: Praeger, 2004.

Nazemroaya, Mahdi Darius. *The Globalization of NATO.* Atlanta, GA: Clarity Press, 2012.

Sloan, Stanley. *A Permanent Alliance?: NATO and the Transatlantic Bargain from Truman to Obama.* New York: Bloomsbury Academic, 2010.

Web Sites

Masters, Jonathan. "The North Atlantic Treaty Organization (NATO)." *Council on Foreign Relations*, May 17, 2012. www.cfr.org/world/north-atlantic-treaty-organization-nato/p28287 (accessed November 26, 2013).

North Atlantic Treaty Organization. http://www.nato.int (accessed November 26, 2013).

Office of the Historian. "Milestones: 1945–1952: North Atlantic Treaty Organization (NATO), 1949." *U.S. Department of State.* http://history.state.gov/milestones/1945-1952/nato (accessed November 26, 2013).

Northern Ireland: The Troubles

🌐 Introduction

For decades the question of Northern Irish rule was a source of contention and frustration for all parties involved. The Belfast Agreement of 1998, which provided the framework for a power-sharing government in Northern Ireland, was reached only after three decades of violent conflict and two years of intense negotiations. Even when the agreement was reached, there were years of delay before the establishment of the power-sharing government in Northern Ireland could be achieved.

On May 8, 2007, Martin McGuinness (1950–), the Catholic leader of Sinn Féin and former Irish Republican Army (IRA) leader, became Northern Ireland's deputy first minister. McGuinness took the post alongside Protestant unionist leader Ian Paisley (1926–), the new first minister of Ireland. It was a historic occasion, signifying the beginning of a new, more peaceful era in Irish history. But old wounds are not always easily forgotten, and the enmity between Irish and English, Catholic and Protestant, Republicans and Unionists continues to simmer just below the surface.

🌐 Historical Background

Northern Ireland is an administrative division of the United Kingdom, formed by six of the nine counties of historic Ulster, an Irish province. Northern Ireland has long been the site of conflict between the Republicans, also known as the Nationalists, and the Unionists. The Republicans are predominantly Roman Catholic and generally want to join the Republic of Ireland. The Unionists are predominantly Protestant and favor political unity with Great Britain. The tensions between the two groups have been exacerbated by the long-time religious animosity in Northern Ireland between the Catholics, who experienced centuries of discrimination at the hands of the British, and the Protestants.

The kingdoms of Ireland and England have had a long and bloody history in which England has generally emerged the victor. In 1800 the two nations merged into the United Kingdom of Great Britain and Ireland. The two islands were governed by a central parliament and monarchy, both located in England. By the 20th century, many Irish people wanted a parliament of their own.

In the 1920s the southern Catholic portion of Ireland gained its independence from Great Britain. Ulster, the Northern-most province of Ireland, had a Protestant majority and chose to remain part of the union with Britain. The Government of Ireland Act of 1920 partitioned the island of Ireland, separating the six counties of Ulster to form Northern Ireland. The remaining 26 counties of the south and west formed the Irish Free State under the Anglo-Irish Treaty of 1921.

Violence in Northern Ireland

Sustained conflict between the Republicans and the Unionists in Northern Ireland began in the late 1960s. By then Northern Ireland was increasingly polarized between Protestant Unionists and a rising Catholic militancy. The Unionist forces consisted of several paramilitary groups, including the Ulster Volunteer Force and the Ulster Defense Association. The Republican forces included the Provisional Irish Republican Army (PIRA, more commonly known as the IRA), the Official Irish Republican Army, and the Irish National Liberation Army. Acts of violence between the opposing sides escalated. The era beginning in the late 1960s is known in Northern Ireland simply as "the Troubles." In total more than 3,600 people were killed during the Troubles, with many thousands more injured.

In August 1969 a traditional Protestant march in Derry, Ulster, ended in a riot; the violence spread to Belfast, resulting in seven deaths and the destruction of properties mostly occupied by Catholics. Britain sent

---

BOBBY SANDS' HUNGER STRIKE

In 1981 27-year-old Bobby Sands was one of several Republican supporters imprisoned in Her Majesty's Maze Prison in Northern Ireland. Sands was serving a 14-year prison sentence for a bombing and gun battle with police that was linked to the PIRA. Sands and nine other Republicans went on a hunger strike beginning in March because they felt they had been unfairly labeled as criminals rather than what they felt they were: political prisoners or prisoners of war.

During the strike, Sands was elected as a member of Parliament, but he never served. After 66 days on his hunger strike, Sands died of starvation. The nine others died in the following months of 1981, as they had staggered their protests to begin at different times to maximize the length of time of the protests.

Though Sands and the others were regarded as heroes to many Republicans, there were also many critics of the hunger strikers. However, the publicity and international attention focused on the hunger strikers brought attention to the Republican cause, and membership in the various Republican groups and the IRA increased immediately following the deaths of the hunger strikers.

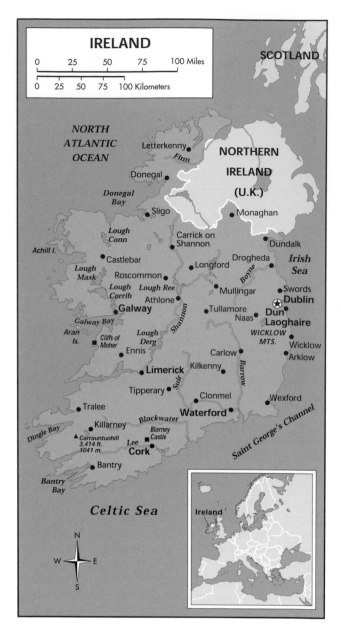

© 2014 Cengage Learning

troops to Ulster to protect the population, but within months the British forces came under attack from the IRA. The British military remained, becoming an occupying force in Northern Ireland.

Bloody Sunday   The violence peaked in the early 1970s. On January 30, 1972, which has come to be known as Bloody Sunday, British forces killed 13 unarmed civil rights protesters in Derry. The anger caused by the shooting in Ireland provided new support, and new recruits, for the IRA. As negotiations for a shared government for Northern Ireland broke down, the IRA ramped up its violence, carrying out bombings and shootings in Northern Ireland and Britain in an attempt to drive the British soldiers out of Ulster. The unionist Ulster Defense Association in turn organized violence against the Catholic community.

Violence Spills into Britain

During the 1970s, the Troubles in Northern Ireland were imported into Britain as the IRA, Real IRA, Provisional IRA, and INLA all launched various attacks in Britain, killing dozens and wounding hundreds. One of the deadliest attacks came on November 21, 1974, when the IRA launched bombing attacks on two London pubs, killing 21 people and injuring almost 200. The British Government responded to the attack with the Prevention of Terrorism Act, giving police emergency power when terrorism was suspected, such as allowing terrorism suspects to be held without charge for up to seven days without official charges being filed. The attacks continued in Britain until the early 2000s.

Moving toward Peace

In the late 1980s Irish nationalist Gerry Adams (1948–), the leader of Sinn Féin, the IRA's political arm, began discussing peace with John Hume (1937–), leader of the Social Democratic and Labour Party, Northern Ireland's mainstream republican party. They in turn held secret peace talks with the British government. In December 1993, after intense, secret discussions,

Bernadette Devlin, a Republican political activist and MP for Mid Ulster, speaks through a megaphone at the barricades in Northern Ireland in 1969.   © *Rolls Press/Popperfoto/Getty Images*

the governments of Ireland and the United Kingdom issued the Downing Street Declaration. The declaration stated that Britain had no economic or strategic interest in Northern Ireland, and that Britain would support Northern Ireland's decision to either join the Republic of Ireland or remain part of the United Kingdom. The declaration called for an end to paramilitary violence in Northern Ireland.

In August 1994 the IRA announced a cease-fire. Two years later the IRA, frustrated by delays, exploded bombs in London and Manchester, England. Further negotiations between Hume, Adams, and IRA leader Martin McGuinness produced another cease-fire in July 1997.

The Belfast Agreement

Throughout late 1997 and early 1998 representatives of most of Northern Ireland's major political parties and the governments of Britain and Ireland met in peace negotiations. United States senator George Mitchell (1933–) chaired the talks. On April 10, 1998, Good Friday, the parties reached a peace agreement. The Belfast Agreement, or Good Friday Agreement, called for an executive power-sharing arrangement between the Unionists and the Republicans. The agreement required all paramilitary groups to decommission their weapons. The agreement also established a Northern Ireland Assembly.

According to the terms of the Belfast Agreement, the new arrangements required approval through referenda (vote) in Northern Ireland and the Republic of Ireland. The Democratic Unionist Party (DUP), led by Ian Paisley, was the only major political party in Northern Ireland that opposed the Belfast Agreement. Turnout for the referendum in Northern Ireland was 81 percent, with 71 percent of the electorate voting in favor of the referendum. Turnout was only 56 percent in the Republic of Ireland, but 94 percent voted in favor of amending

A young girl skips past patrolling British soldiers from the Gloucester Regiment who had become an everyday reality to her, in Belfast, Northern Ireland, 1972. The younger children of the lower Falls Road, the Irish Republican Army (IRA) stronghold, did not understand the potential horror of a high velocity weapon. Many of the older children began to accept violence as a way of life during 1972, the most violent year of the Troubles in Northern Ireland. © *Oliver Morris/Getty Images*

the Irish constitution to reflect the provisions of the Belfast Agreement.

Not all were happy with the peace deal, however. A group of militants opposed to the Belfast Agreement formed a group called the Real Irish Republican Army (Real IRA) in 1997 and vowed to continue fighting. In August 1998 the Real IRA committed the most deadly act of violence in the three decades of unrest in the country—a car bombing in Omagh, Northern Ireland, that left 29 people dead and hundreds injured. Despite the actions of the Real Irish Republican Army, the peace process moved forward.

The Northern Ireland Assembly took office in December 1999. The assembly suspended operations several times over the IRA's reluctance to decommission its weapons. In September 2005 the IRA finally declared that it had decommissioned all of its weapons, in response to a strong request from Adams. Subsequent elections resulted in the rival DUP and Sinn Féin becoming the two largest political parties in Northern Ireland. In May 2007 Ian Paisley of DUP was elected first minister, and Martin McGuinness of Sinn Féin was elected deputy first minister, forcing the two former rivals to share executive power.

⊕ Impacts and Issues

Peace in Northern Ireland held for almost a decade, but it was disrupted again in March 2009, when nationalist militants (former members of the IRA) murdered two British soldiers and, in a separate attack, a police officer. The militants pledged further violence both in Northern Ireland and on the British mainland. The attacks, the worst violence seen in the region since the 1998 peace deal, had many in Great Britain worried that the seeming stability in the region was unraveling. Authorities maintained that the attacks were the actions of a small, increasingly marginalized group of extremists and were not representative of a wider resurgence of nationalist sentiment.

In June 2009 four men accused of involvement in the 1998 Omagh bombing were held liable for their actions in civil court. No criminal convictions were ever reached, but the families of the victims sued five suspected perpetrators for damages. The case against one of the men was dismissed, but a jury ordered the other four men to pay a total of $2.6 million in damages to the families of those killed. The four men appealed the ruling, and in July 2011 the judgment against two of the four men was overturned by an appeals court. They faced a civil retrial, and on March 20, 2013, Colm Murphy and Seamus Daly were again found liable for the attack.

The Saville Report

On June 15, 2010, the long-awaited Saville Report on the 1972 Bloody Sunday killings was published. Lord Mark Saville (1936–) served as chair of the inquiry into the incident. The report found that none of the people injured or killed by British soldiers had been armed with a gun or bomb of any sort, with the possible exception of a man named Gerald Donaghy.

Nail bombs were discovered on Donaghy's body, but the report notes that Donaghy was not attempting to use the bombs and was in fact trying to escape from the soldiers when he was shot. The Saville Report also asserts that the soldiers lost their self-control and fired on the crowd even though the protesters did not pose "a threat of causing death or serious injury."

British prime minister David Cameron (1966–) issued an official apology for the killings, calling the actions of the British army "unjustifiable." In September 2011 Cameron directed the minister of defense to contact attorneys representing families of those killed or injured in the Bloody Sunday massacre and offer to pay compensation.

A hearse containing the body of Northern Irish police Constable Stephen Carroll is driven through Banbridge, Northern Ireland, on March 13, 2009. Northern Ireland grieved for the first policeman killed here for a decade, after his widow called for an end to violence threatening the province's peace process. Hundreds of black-clad mourners turned out for Carroll's funeral. Carroll was shot by Republic dissidents in the second deadly attack in 48 hours.   © *Peter Muhly/AFP/Getty Images*

⊕ Future Implications

A decision in December 2012 to stop the 100-year tradition of flying the British flag from Belfast's city hall every day erupted in several days of rioting in early 2013. Pro–British groups threw gasoline bombs, paint bombs, and fireworks at policemen, who responded by firing a water cannon. About 1,000 people were arrested by January 11, 2013. The riots were some of the most violent since the signing of the Belfast Agreement of 1998 and clearly signified that true peace and unity may still be elusive in Northern Ireland for many years to come.

Most of Northern Ireland remains segregated along Catholic and Protestant lines. Few schools are integrated and huge walls and fences still separate communities. The government has promised to tear the walls down, but many people fear that the decision may be premature. Old rivalries and fears are not easily forgotten.

The legacy of the Troubles continues to haunt the national psyche of Northern Ireland. Each side wishes to honor its fallen heroes in parades and memorials, but one side's heroes are the other side's terrorists, as is often the case during times of revolution and civil warfare. Finding ways to honor each side while remaining respectful toward the other requires a precarious balance. Since many Northern Ireland politicians came of age during the Troubles, an uneasy peace may be all that is possible for the time being. As new generations come into power, an easier peace may be the result.

PRIMARY SOURCE

Easter 1916 Proclamation of an Irish Republic

SOURCE *"Easter 1916 Proclamation of an Irish Republic." http://www.wwnorton.com/college/english/ nael/noa/pdf/27636_20th_U01Anonymous-1-2.pdf (accessed November 23, 2013).*

INTRODUCTION *On April 17, 1916, while World War I was ongoing, seven members of the Irish Republican Brotherhood Military Council approved the proclamation of an Irish republic. The seven who signed the document intended to make up the provisional government should the uprising succeed. The proclamation was read by Patrick Pearse, one of the seven, outside the Dublin general post office on Easter Monday, April 24, 1916, marking the commencement of what came to be known as the Easter Uprising. The uprising failed.*

A HISTORIC VISIT

In June 2012, Queen Elizabeth II of England, during her Diamond Jubilee tour celebrating her 60 years on the throne, visited Northern Ireland with minimal protests. She met and shook hands with Northern Ireland's Deputy First Minister McGuinness, though the event was not photographed. The visit followed the queen's appearance in the Republic of Ireland in 2011, which marked a historic turn in relations between Britain and Ireland as it was the first visit of a British head of state since independence. The visits were hoped to signal an end to the years of turmoil.

Britain's Queen Elizabeth II and Prince Phillip drive in a open top car as they attended a special Diamond Jubilee event in the grounds of the Stormont Estate in Belfast, Northern Ireland, on June 27, 2012. Queen Elizabeth II shook hands with former IRA commander Martin McGuinness on Wednesday in a highly symbolic moment in the Northern Ireland peace process. The initial handshake between the queen and McGuinness, who is now deputy first minister of the British province, took place behind closed doors in a Belfast theatre.
© Peter Muhly/AFP/Getty Images

All seven of the original signatories as well as several others involved in the uprising were tried for treason in a military court and executed. The poorly armed rebels had received little support from the public at the time of the uprising, however after their trial and execution, which was carried out in secret and only announced after the fact, they achieved the status of heroes.

THE PROCLAMATION OF POBLACHT NA H-EIREANN THE PROVISIONAL GOVERNMENT OF THE IRISH REPUBLIC TO THE PEOPLE OF IRELAND

IRISHMEN AND IRISHWOMEN: In the name of God and of the dead generations from which she receives her old tradition of nationhood, Ireland, through us, summons her children to her flag and strikes for her freedom.

Having organised and trained her manhood through her secret revolutionary organisation, the Irish Republican Brotherhood, and through her open military organisations, the Irish Volunteers and the Irish Citizen Army, having patiently perfected her discipline, having resolutely waited for the right moment to reveal itself, she now seizes that moment, and supported by her exiled children in America and by gallant allies in Europe, but relying in the first on her own strength, she strikes in full confidence of victory.

We declare the right of the people of Ireland to the ownership of Ireland and to the unfettered control of Irish destinies, to be sovereign and indefeasible. The long usurpation of that right by a foreign people and government has not extinguished the right, nor can it ever be extinguished except by the destruction of the Irish people. In every generation the Irish people have asserted their right to national freedom and sovereignty; six times during the past three hundred years they have asserted it in arms. Standing on that fundamental right and again asserting it in arms in the face of the world, we hereby proclaim the Irish Republic as a Sovereign Independent State, and we pledge our lives and the lives of our comrades in arms to the cause of its freedom, of its welfare, and of its exaltation among the nations.

The Irish Republic is entitled to, and hereby claims, the allegiance of every Irishman and Irishwoman. The Republic guarantees religious and civil liberty, equal rights and equal opportunities to all its citizens, and declares its resolve to pursue the happiness and prosperity of the whole nation and of all its parts, cherishing all of the children of the nation equally, and oblivious of the differences carefully fostered by an alien Government, which have divided a minority from the majority in the past.

Until our arms have brought the opportune moment for the establishment of a permanent National Government, representative of the whole people of Ireland and elected by the suffrages of all her men and women, the Provisional Government, hereby constituted, will administer the civil and military affairs of the Republic in trust for the people.

We place the cause of the Irish Republic under the protection of the Most High God, Whose blessing we invoke upon our arms, and we pray that no one who serves that cause will dishonour it by cowardice, inhumanity, or rapine. In this supreme hour the Irish nation must, by its valour and discipline, and by the readiness of its children to sacrifice themselves for the common good, prove itself worthy of the august destiny to which it is called.

Signed on behalf of the Provisional Government:

THOMAS J. CLARKE
SEAN Mac DIARMADA
THOMAS MacDONAGH
P. H. PEARSE
EAMONN CEANNT
JAMES CONNOLLY
JOSEPH PLUNKETT

SEE ALSO *Religious Extremism; Terrorism: Large Group*

BIBLIOGRAPHY

Books

Cochrane, Feargal. *Northern Ireland: A Reluctant Peace*. New Haven, CT: Yale University Press, 2013.

Conroy, John. *The Belfast Diary: War as a Way of Life*. Boston: Beacon Press, 1995.

Toolis, Kevin. *Rebel's Hearts: Journeys Within the IRA's Soul*. New York: St. Martin's Griffin, 1997.

Web Sites

"BBC History—The Troubles." *BBC*. http://www.bbc.co.uk/history/troubles (accessed October 24, 2013).

"CAIN Web Service—Conflict and Politics in Northern Ireland." *University of Ulster*. http://cain.ulst.ac.uk (accessed October 24, 2013).

"Special Report: Northern Ireland: A Brief History of The Troubles." *The Guardian*. http://www.theguardian.com/northernireland/page/0,12494,1569841,00.html (accessed October 24, 2013).

Organization of the Petroleum Exporting Countries (OPEC)

⊕ Introduction

The Organization of the Petroleum Exporting Countries (OPEC) is one of the most powerful and controversial global organizations in the world. It is an intergovernmental group consisting of 12 of the top 30 oil-exporting countries, which together hold approximately 42 percent of the world's known oil reserves. The organization's purpose is to coordinate oil prices among the member countries to satisfy producers and to ensure a steady supply of oil on the world market. Although many associate OPEC with the Middle East, the organization also includes countries in Africa and South America.

OPEC is often accused of controlling the price of oil and allowing it to reach record highs. In reality OPEC has often ramped up production of oil to keep prices from spiraling out of control. OPEC also ensures that there is at least a three-month supply of crude oil available at all times so that any dramatic change in oil production can be addressed before it affects the global economy.

⊕ Historical Background

OPEC was created in 1960 by five founding member nations: Saudi Arabia, Iraq, Iran, Kuwait, and Venezuela. Originally based in Geneva, Switzerland, in 1965 the secretariat moved to Vienna, Austria, a neutral location in the midst of the Cold War. At the time, oil production was dominated by multinational companies whose extensive wealth came from buying oil from developing nations and selling it to industrial nations. OPEC was designed as an alliance that would allow developing nations to maintain control over their countries' oil reserves, rather than simply selling off oil rights to the global corporations.

The OPEC alliance also gave member nations a greater control of oil prices through coordinated production. At the time of OPEC's formation, the founding members controlled just over one-fourth of the world's oil supply. By limiting the amount of oil they produced, they could potentially cause the price of oil to increase, thereby increasing their own profits.

Member Nations

OPEC's member nations are located in the Middle East, Africa, and South America. OPEC's founding member nations have welcomed nine additional nations into the oil cartel including: Algeria (1969), Angola (2007), Ecuador (2007), Gabon (1975), Indonesia (1962), Libya (1962), Nigeria (1971), Qatar (1961), and United Arab Emirates (1967). Seven of these nations have remained in OPEC. Ecuador, Gabon, and Indonesia have each left OPEC at some point, although Ecuador has since rejoined.

OPEC MEMBER NATIONS' OIL PRODUCTION

In 2014, OPEC had 12 member nations, including 5 of the top 10 oil-producing nations in the world (Saudi Arabia, Iran, Iraq, United Arab Emirates, and Venezuela). Oil production is monitored by the International Energy Agency (IEA). According to an IEA report published in 2011, there are 115 nations producing oil. Of these, the top 10 nations produce approximately 63 percent of the total global production.

The top position fluctuates between Saudi Arabia and Russia. Together these two nations produce approximately 25 percent of world's oil. The third largest oil-producing nation is the United States, bringing in more than 10 percent of the total global production. More than 2 percent of that oil comes from Texas, while North Dakota, California, and Alaska each produce more oil than either Libya or Ecuador, both members of OPEC. The other top 10 oil-producing nations in 2011 were China (fifth), Canada (sixth), and Mexico (10th).

Gabon Gabon was a member of OPEC from 1975 until 1995. Although it still has sizable oil fields, the country chose to leave OPEC when the organization refused to reduce its annual contributions. Each member of OPEC is expected to contribute $1.79 million annually. With its global position for oil production at 41st, Gabon was the smallest-producing nation of OPEC. The West African nation did not think it was fair that its annual dues were the same as those of the much wealthier nations and so chose to leave the organization.

Indonesia Indonesia was a member of OPEC from 1962 until 2009. Indonesia still produces a huge amount of oil—enough that its global oil production position was 21st. However, Indonesia also has the fourth-largest population in the world and a high population growth rate. The South Asian nation left OPEC because it could no longer fulfill its own nation's oil needs, let alone be a net exporter of oil.

Ecuador Ecuador initially joined OPEC in 1973 but became a non-active member in 1992. The second-smallest oil producing nation after Gabon, Ecuador likewise chafed under the large annual contribution fee. However, Ecuador ultimately chose to allow its membership to become inactive because OPEC refused to let the Central American country raise its production limit. A lower production level meant that the price of oil was raised overall, which was a boon to the richer nations. But for smaller nations like Ecuador, limiting production meant a lower bottom line. Ecuador's own economic needs required that it sell more crude oil than was allowed by OPEC. In 2007 Ecuador chose to rejoin OPEC in a move that reflects its growing national economy. Because it had never officially left, it was allowed to restore its active membership easily.

⊕ Impacts and Issues

As the organization grew in size, OPEC's power as a controlling force in the petroleum industry became clear. In 1973 Arab members of OPEC placed an embargo on oil exports to the United States, partly

U.S. Secretary of State Henry Kissinger meets December 14, 1973, with King Faisal of Saudi Arabia. Kissinger was on a tour of six Arab capitals and Tel Aviv to prepare the ground for the Geneva Middle East Conference. Saudi sources said Kissinger tried, but failed, to get King Faisal to agree to lift the Saudi embargo on oil shipments to the U.S. On March 17, 1974, OPEC ministers announced the lifting of the five month oil embargo that brought about a loss of production to industry in the western world and an "oil crisis" that lead to high gas prices and shortages. © *Bettmann/Corbis/AP Images*

in response to U.S. support of Israel in its territorial dispute against Palestinians and other Arab nations of the Middle East during the Yom Kippur War. OPEC members also sought to cut production and thus raise oil prices for all their exports in an attempt to bolster their generally weak economies. The embargo and production cut had a dramatic impact on oil prices, causing the cost of oil and petroleum-based products such as gasoline to triple almost overnight. The crisis was fairly short-lived, though oil prices remained elevated throughout the 1970s and spiked in 1979 when one of OPEC's key members, Iran, experienced a revolution that derailed the country's oil production for a time.

Oil prices fell throughout the 1980s and stabilized during the 1990s, but they began to soar again at the turn of the century. Between 2003 and 2008 the price of oil quintupled, reaching nearly $150 per barrel. Although OPEC has often been blamed as the main culprit by consumers in the developed world, its member nations as a whole increased production levels between 2003 and 2006 in an attempt to ease the price spike. The group agreed to cut production in 2008

after prices finally began to fall, but Saudi Arabia—by far the largest oil exporter in the organization—vowed to continue its high production levels to satisfy global demand.

At a 2011 meeting OPEC members could not agree on a plan to raise production levels in the face of continued high oil prices. Some members argued that the global supply was adequate and that the high prices were the result of other factors. Indeed, at a time when OPEC production remained fairly steady, oil prices rose and fell dramatically. One possible explanation was the interference of commodities speculators, who had recently been granted greater access to participate in oil markets.

OPEC and the United States

Politicians in the United States have frequently criticized OPEC for allowing politics to play a role in their decisions. Some OPEC nations, such as Venezuela and Iran, have poor relations with the United States; indeed, the United States has maintained sanctions against Iran since the 1979 revolution, made them stricter in 1995, and added to them several times in the period from

Organization of the Petroleum Exporting Countries (OPEC) Secretary General, Libya's Abdalla Salem El-Badri (C), answers journalists during the 163rd meeting of the OPEC conference in Vienna, Austria, on May 31, 2013. At that time, OPEC ministers said they expected to hold oil output levels unchanged despite concern about global demand as they started a crucial meeting. © *Alexander Klein/AFP/Getty Images*

2006 to 2012. When U.S. Special Forces killed terrorist Osama bin Laden (1957–2011) in Pakistan in 2011, Venezuela was the only country to officially condemn the action. In contrast, OPEC's most important oil producer, Saudi Arabia, has maintained close economic relations with the United States. OPEC's dramatic influence on world petroleum markets has led many American politicians to call for energy independence from "foreign oil," by developing alternative energy sources or by attempting to increase drilling production within the United States.

OPEC and the Arab Spring

The Arab Spring was a series of rebellions and revolutions that swept across North Africa and the Middle East starting in December 2010, in which people demonstrated for increased freedom and overthrew entrenched leaders. For a time the Arab Spring seemed to threaten global oil production. Several OPEC member states experienced uprisings, notably Kuwait, Iraq, and Libya. In the former two countries, the protests were quickly put down before they could have a dramatic effect on oil production. In Libya, by contrast, the Arab Spring led to a revolution.

Libya had been controlled by dictator Muammar al-Qadhafi (1942–2011) for 42 years. In 2011, when Libyan citizens began to protest the Qadhafi regime and call for a democratic government, Qadhafi destroyed his own country's largest refineries and essentially shut down its oil industry, presumably to punish foreign nations that relied on its exports. Qadhafi was overthrown and assassinated in late 2011, and the country's new leaders quickly went about the business of once again ramping up oil production.

⊕ Future Implications

Some analysts have argued that OPEC is already operating near peak production, and that as its oil reserves decline, so too will OPEC's influence on the world oil market. The success of other, non-OPEC oil producers, especially Russia and Canada, have also led some to suggest that OPEC's importance as a "swing supplier" is fading. However, as world oil consumption continues to grow each year, and without enough affordable

alternative energy solutions on the horizon, OPEC seems likely to continue to play a key role in the global economy for decades to come. In fact, far from declining, OPEC's crude oil production reached 30,667 million barrels a day in December 2011, its highest level in three years.

Various dates have been given as to when oil production will have (or already has) peaked and when it will cease altogether. The reality is that no one really knows how much oil is left, and that as old oil fields are exhausted new ones may still be discovered. Whether it will be possible to reach those oil fields is debatable. Researchers believe that the remaining large oil fields are either under the ocean or under the Arctic ice; neither of which can be easily reached at this time. However, as Arctic ice melts due to climate change, countries have begun to stake claims on these reserves. Regardless of the amount left, oil remains a nonrenewable resource and eventually it will be gone. Until that point, however, OPEC will likely play a crucial role in the global marketplace.

SEE ALSO *Arab-Israeli Conflict; Arab Spring*

BIBLIOGRAPHY
Books
Al-Chalabi, Fadhil. *Oil Politics, Oil Myths: Analysis and Memoir of an OPEC Insider.* London: I. B. Taurus, 2011.

Marrin, Albert. *Black Oil: The Story of Oil in Our Lives.* New York: Alfred A. Knopf, 2013.

Parra, Francisco. *Oil Politics: A Modern History of Petroleum.* London: I. B. Taurus, 2009.

Web Sites
Carlyle, Ryan. "How Big Are The Currently Known Oil Reserves And What Are The Chances Of Finding New Ones?" *Forbes,* March 27, 2013. http://www.forbes.com/sites/quora/2013/03/27/how-big-are-the-currently-known-oil-reserves-and-what-are-the-chances-of-finding-new-ones (accessed August 29, 2013).

International Energy Association. http://www.iea.org (accessed August 29, 2013).

Organization of the Petroleum Exporting Countries. http://www.opec.org (accessed August 29, 2013).

Pakistan-Afghanistan Conflict

🌐 Introduction

Afghanistan and Pakistan share a border that runs approximately 1,500 miles (2,400 kilometers), primarily through the Hindu Kush mountain range. The border divides the ethnic Pashtun population and their native lands.

WIKILEAKS AND OSAMA BIN LADEN

In July 2010, more than 90,000 classified U.S. military intelligence documents pertaining to the Afghan War were published by a Web site called WikiLeaks. The documents contain a wide range of information. The most serious implications maintain that Pakistan's intelligence agency had collaborated with the Taliban. Pakistan denied the allegations, but tensions between Pakistan and Afghanistan escalated. Shortly after the documents were leaked, Afghani president Hamid Karzai urged allied forces to strike Taliban strongholds within Pakistan, most of which are along the border with Afghanistan. Karzai has frequently charged that Pakistan tacitly supports the Taliban even while hosting NATO equipment and personnel.

On May 1, 2011, U.S. president Barack Obama (1961–) made a televised statement informing the world that Osama bin Laden (1957–2011), leader of the terrorist group al-Qaeda, had been killed in a U.S. military operation in Abbottabad, Pakistan, just 30 miles (50 kilometers) from the capital, Islamabad. The announcement led to jubilation in the United States, but also to many questions for U.S. and Pakistani diplomats.

Intelligence experts had long claimed that bin Laden was hiding in Pakistan, maybe even with the help of the Pakistani military. The fact that he was found so close to the capital, and little more than a half mile (1 kilometer) away from a military training facility, seemed to bolster these suspicions. The Pakistani government, for its part, expressed outrage at the raid, about which they were neither consulted nor informed in advance.

Approximately 29 million Pashtuns live in Pakistan, and 13 million live in Afghanistan. The border between Afghanistan and Pakistan has traditionally been porous, with people moving freely between the two nations. The Pashtuns and other groups in the border region have never recognized the border as an international dividing line. Cross-border tribal alliances have remained stronger than allegiance to country, and the Pashtuns consider the area on both sides of the border to be their land. Pashtun nationalists on both sides of the border desire an independent state of Pashtunistan to be carved out of both Afghanistan and Pakistan.

The governments of Afghanistan and Pakistan have used ethnic and tribal alliances in the border region to meddle in each other's political affairs. Over the past 60 years, both nations have reportedly incited conflict in the border region in efforts to destabilize the other nation. An October 2006 report by the United States Institute of Peace, "Resolving the Pakistan-Afghanistan Stalemate," notes, "The long history of each state offering sanctuary to the other's opponents has built bitterness and mistrust between the two neighbors." Since then, however, the two nations have shifted their focus from tribal disputes to monitoring the actions of independent terrorist groups that threaten both nations. International pressure to resolve their differences and a rise in trading relations have helped calm the area considerably.

🌐 Historical Background

For centuries, the Pashtuns and other groups moved freely throughout the Hindu Kush mountain range. An agreement between the Afghani monarchy and the British government, which controlled the area that became modern Pakistan, created the border between Afghanistan and modern Pakistan in 1893. The modern state of Afghanistan has never recognized the border, which is called the Durand Line after a British colonial administrator. Pakistan recognizes the line, but only

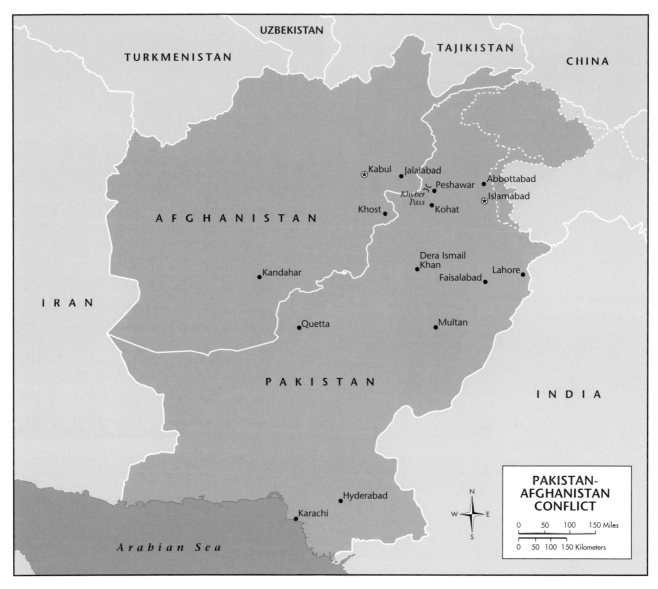

loosely governs it, instead giving considerable autonomy to the Pashtun tribes that live in the Pakistani Federally Administered Tribal Areas (FATA).

Afghanistan and Pakistan have each covertly and blatantly provoked the other along the border since 1949. Both sides have regularly engaged in cross-border shelling along the Durand Line. In 1960, the government of Afghanistan sent troops into northwest Pakistan in an attempt to create instability in that region. Afghanistan, which is more than 40 percent Pashtun, also hoped to push the issue of uniting the Pashtun people. But the militarily superior Pakistani forces easily pushed back the Afghani army. During the 1970s, Afghanistan harbored Balochi nationalists who sought the creation of a Balochi state in Pakistan.(Balochistan is a province in southwestern Pakistan.)

Pakistan and the Taliban

In the 1980s, Pakistan served as a safe haven for the Afghani *mujahideen,* Islamic fighters who opposed the invasion of Afghanistan by the Soviet Union. Throughout the 1980s, the Pakistani military attempted to militarize and destabilize the border region by arming Afghani Islamist organizations and funding radical *madrasas,* or Islamic schools.

During the Afghani civil war, which followed the withdrawal of Soviet troops from Afghanistan in 1989, Pakistan supported the Taliban of Afghanistan, an extremely strict Islamist group, which took control of large parts of the country.

Following the United States-led invasion of Afghanistan in 2001, Islamist militants, including the Taliban, fled to the mountainous region along the Afghanistan-Pakistan

Afghan refugees cross into neighboring Pakistan in February 1980, days after the Soviet Army invaded Afghanistan to prop up the communist government of Babrak Karmal. Millions of Afghans became refugees in Pakistan and Iran after the war intensified, with Western material aid and weaponry pouring in for the mujahideen guerrillas. © *AFP/Getty Images*

border. Pakistan joined the United States in its war on terrorism. This essentially placed Pakistan in the position of capturing or killing the same Islamist militants that it had funded in the 1990s.

Pakistan refused to allow Afghani or American forces to enter Pakistan to track Islamist insurgents. Despite the presence of 80,000 Pakistani troops in the border region, insurgents regularly conducted cross-border raids into Afghanistan. In 2006, Afghanistan's president Hamid Karzai (1957–) accused Pakistan of harboring leaders of the Taliban and other insurgent groups. On several occasions the United States similarly accused Pakistan of harboring terrorists, including members of al-Qaeda. Pakistani president Pervez Musharraf (1943–) denied all allegations.

In May 2007, a brief military skirmish along the Afghanistan-Pakistan border resulted in deaths on both sides. Tensions between the two nations increased markedly after the border clash. The Afghan government continued to accuse Pakistan of doing too little to quell attacks by insurgents living in Pakistan. In June 2008, Afghani president Karzai threatened to send troops into Pakistan to pursue Pakistan's Taliban militants.

Taliban Attacks Near Islamabad In 2008, the Taliban seized control of the Swat Valley (just 81 miles, or 130 kilometers, northwest of Islamabad) in Pakistan and killed hundreds of its political opponents. To quell the violence, Pakistan's president, Asif Ali Zardari (1955–), offered to instate sharia (Islamic law) in the region. After the Taliban continued to press toward Islamabad, Pakistan launched a full-scale military offensive against them.

The move was welcomed by President Obama, who met in May 2009 with President Zardari and President Karzai to express his concern over the seeming lack of progress in subduing the Taliban's resurgence and to stress the need for increased cooperation between Pakistan, Afghanistan, and the United States. After the meeting, the interior ministers of Afghanistan and Pakistan announced a joint action plan to flush out terrorists and address drug trafficking along their mutual border.

⊕ Impacts and Issues

The border region between Afghanistan and Pakistan remains one of the most dangerous and troubled regions in the world. The United Nations Refugee

Pakistan's Foreign Minister, Hina Rabbani Khar, attends a Regional Conference on Afghanistan held on November 2, 2011, in Istanbul, Pakistan. At the conference, Khar stated that Afghanistan's neighboring countries should work with other world countries to play a supporting role in rebuilding Afghanistan after years of war. She also stated that Pakistan would support Afghan sovereignity and Afghan-led solutions.   © Asianet-Pakistan/Shutterstock.com

Agency (UNHCR) established repatriation centers along the Afghanistan-Pakistan border to help Afghan citizens in Pakistan return to their homes. In July 2009, however, a UNHCR employee was shot and killed near Peshawar, a city in northwest Pakistan. In response, the UN briefly suspended operations in the area. In July 2013, Pakistan announced that it would extend its support of UNCHR's efforts and continue to provide protection to over 1.6 million Afghan refugees in the country.

In July 2010, Karzai approved a plan put forth by the leader of U.S. forces in Afghanistan, General David Petraeus (1952–), to use village militias to patrol the border with Pakistan. Karzai had expressed concern that the plan would empower dangerous warlords, but agreed to try it. The agreement called for the United States military to recruit and train the militias. Pakistan already has such a force in its Paktia border province, where the Arbakai tribal militia protects the population from militants.

In 2010, Pakistani major general Tariq Khan countered U.S. and Afghan criticism over Pakistani efforts in the border region, telling BBC journalists that it was unfair for Pakistan to take all the responsibility for securing the border between Afghanistan and Pakistan.

Khan said the North Atlantic Treaty Organization (NATO) must shoulder more of the responsibility for border patrol, and pointed out that Pakistani troops have sustained twice as many casualties as NATO troops in the region.

⊕ Future Implications

Afghanistan and Pakistan are currently working together to find solutions to their border disputes. The nations continue talks about possible defense cooperation and intelligence sharing. The Afghan-Pak Transit Trade Agreement (APTTA) has helped to establish two-way trade between the nations. A proposed railroad in Afghanistan is expected to connect with Pakistan Railways, and visas for truck drivers have been issued. In July 2012, Pakistan and Afghanistan agreed to admit Tajikistan to the APTTA, which will facilitate the creation of a north-south trade corridor among the three countries. In August 2013, Pakistan and Afghanistan signed an agreement to strengthen trade and economic cooperation between the countries. Trade between Afghanistan and Pakistan is expected to reach $5 billion by 2015.

SEE ALSO   *9/11; Afghan War; Al-Qaeda; Pakistan-India Conflict; Terrorism: Large Group*

BIBLIOGRAPHY

Books

Ahmed, Aisha. *Pashtun Tales: From the Pakistani-Afghan Frontier.* London: Saqi Books, 2008.

Khan, Riaz Mohammad. *Afghanistan and Pakistan: Conflict, Extremism, and Resistance to Modernity.* Washington, DC: Woodrow Wilson Center Press, 2011.

Rashid, Ahmed. *Pakistan on the Brink: The Future of America, Pakistan and Afghanistan.* New York: Penguin Books, 2013.

Rashid, Ahmed. *The Taliban: Militant Islam, Oil, and Fundamentalism in Central Asia.* New Haven, CT: Yale University Press, 2010.

Web Sites

Dalrymple, William. "A Deadly Triangle: Afghanistan, Pakistan, & India." *The Brookings Institution*, June 25, 2013. http://www.brookings.edu/research/essays/2013/deadly-triangle-afghanistan-pakistan-india-c# (accessed December 23, 2013).

Elias, Barbara, ed. "Pakistan: The Taliban's Godfather?" *The National Security Archive, George Washington University*, August 14, 2007. http://www2.gwu.edu/~nsarchiv/NSAEBB/NSAEBB227/ (accessed December 23, 2013).

Gannon, Kathy. "Pakistan Militants Prepare for War in Afghanistan" *Associated Press*, September 8, 2013. http://bigstory.ap.org/article/pakistan-militants-prepare-war-afghanistan (accessed December 23, 2013).

"The Troubled Afghan-Pakistan Border." *Council on Foreign Relations*. http://www.cfr.org/pakistan/troubled-afghan-pakistani-border/p14905 (accessed December 23, 2013).

Pakistan-India Conflict

🌐 Introduction

India and Pakistan share historic, cultural, geographic, and economic ties, but international relations between the nations have been strained for decades. The two South Asian countries were created following the partition of British India in 1947, which divided the region along religious lines: Hindu-majority India and Muslim-majority Pakistan. The territory of Kashmir is claimed by both countries, and this disputed region has been the center of several major wars (the Indo-Pakistani Wars of 1947, 1965, and 1999), one undeclared war (the Kargil Conflict of 1999), numerous armed skirmishes, and an ongoing military standoff. Another war, the Indo-Pakistani War of 1971, resulted in the secession of East Pakistan and the creation of the independent nation of Bangladesh. Both India and Pakistan are nuclear-armed nations, so the potential stakes of continued warfare between the nations is a matter of great international concern.

Relationships between the two nations have improved in the 21st century. The newest threat to the fragile peace is not necessarily the national governments, but terrorist attacks. The 2001 India Parliament attack, the 2007 Samjhauta Express bombings, and the 2008 Mumbai attacks each halted the détente between the countries. Long-standing distrust and suspicion between the two populations only serves to deepen the divide and make a lasting peace elusive.

🌐 Historical Background

The troubled relations between India and Pakistan can be traced to the colonial rule of India by the British. In the late 1700s, Britain expanded its empire by subjugating much of South Asia. The period of British rule in that region was termed the British Raj ("Raj" is the Hindi word for "reign" or "rule").

Britain was unable to preserve its empire after World War II (1939–45), as the home country was weakened and nationalist movements took root throughout the world. Britain was also opposed on the Indian subcontinent by a long, nonviolent independence movement led by Indian political and spiritual leader Mohandas (Mahatma) Gandhi (1869–1948) from 1921 onward. British imperial holdings throughout the Middle East and Central Asia were partitioned or divided in the late 1940s.

The partition of the British Empire was often along arbitrary lines deemed by the British to be in their own long-term best interests, or along borders that reflected ethnic or religious divisions. In the case of south-central Asia, the land area that is now Pakistan, Bangladesh, and India was divided into three parts: India itself, with a Hindu plurality, and two Muslim-majority areas on opposite sides of India, politically united as East and West Pakistan, although they were more than 1,000 miles (1,600 kilometers) apart.

The rulers of the almost 700 subdominions or native states (also termed Indian states or princely states) covering most of the subcontinent were allowed to decide which country, Pakistan or India, they wished to join. The ruler of the state of Jammu and Kashmir (a single state, despite the "and" in the name) had not committed to either Pakistan or India at the time of partition. This political decision would have grave ramifications.

Independence and the Kashmir Dispute (1947 and 1965)

Pakistan declared its independence on August 14, 1947, and India followed suit the next day. Violence erupted immediately. Muslims living in the Hindu-majority India and Hindus living in the Muslim-majority Pakistan were attacked by neighbors and gangs. The number of people who died in community violence has been estimated at one million, and tens of millions of refugees streamed from each country into the other.

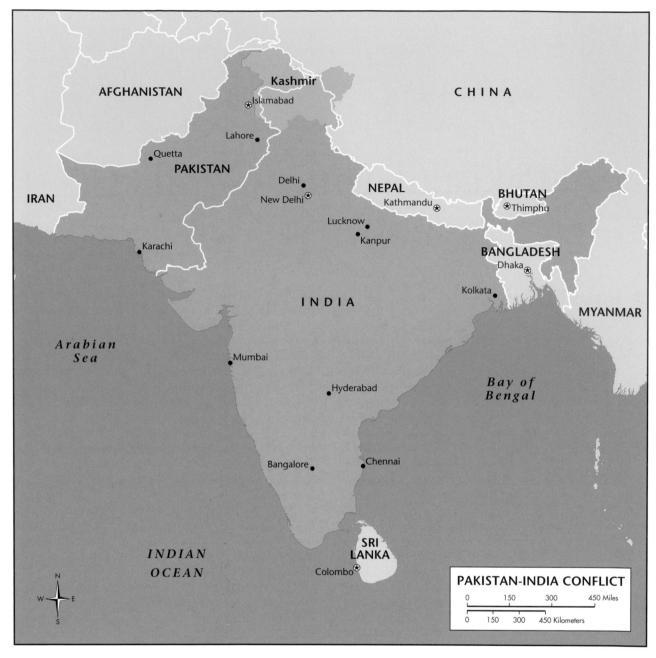

© 2014 Cengage Learning

Both Pakistan and India claimed the state of Jammu and Kashmir. Pakistan backed a Muslim rebellion in the province, and India sent troops to support its Hindu maharaja (prince). A border war, the Indo-Pakistani War of 1947, resulted, ending the following year with the establishment of a cease-fire line (the Line of Control) dividing the province. The United Nations (UN) demanded a democratic vote among the Kashmir people to peacefully determine their political fate. These elections never took place, and the region remains under dispute. About a third of the region is on the Pakistani side. Pakistan considers it a Pakistani state, and India refers to it as "Pakistan-occupied Kashmir."

In 1965, war between India and Pakistan erupted again in Kashmir. The five-week confrontation was fought along the border between the nations and resulted in the deaths of thousands of soldiers and civilians on both sides. The conflict ended with another UN-mandated cease-fire and the issuance of the Tashkent Declaration, which forced the two countries to return to their 1947 borders.

East Pakistan and Bangladesh

In 1971, a secular nationalist movement began a revolt against the Islamist government of East Pakistan. The Bangladesh Liberation War was brief but bloody.

Indian Mukti Bahini guerilla troops prepare to bayonet men who collaborated with the Pakistani Army during East Pakistan's fight to become the independent state of Bangladesh.   © *William Lovelace/Getty Images*

Hundreds of thousands of civilians were killed, and more than 30 million Bengalis were displaced.

Indian troops entered the region on December 3, 1971, to assist the revolutionaries. The Indian army immediately captured 90,000 Pakistani troops. This victory allowed the revolutionaries to declare East Pakistan the independent nation of Bangladesh only four days later. The next week the West Pakistan army fully surrendered, bringing the conflict to an end.

In 1974, Pakistan officially recognized Bangladesh, and the new country joined the United Nations as a member state. Bangladesh is a Muslim-majority state but operates under a secular (nonreligious) political system. There have been no additional military conflicts between Bangladesh and India or Pakistan, nor have India and Pakistan clashed over the issue again.

Nuclear Weapons

In 1974, India exploded its first nuclear weapon. Pakistan commenced its own program to build a nuclear bomb to counter India's. Tensions remained high between the two countries, particularly over the fate of Jammu and Kashmir. In the late 1980s, Muslim separatists organized militant groups in the India-controlled part of the province. India accused Pakistan of giving military aid to the rebels. In 1996 and 1997, the foreign ministers of both countries met, and military officials from both countries attended border meetings. In 1998, in response to a new series of Indian underground nuclear tests, Pakistan conducted its first nuclear test. Both countries also had arsenals of long-range missiles that could reach every city in both countries.

Fears became widespread that a regional nuclear war might arise from the tensions between India and Pakistan. A nuclear war seemed perilously close in 1999 when war broke out yet again in Jammu and Kashmir, with India carrying out air strikes on Pakistani-supported militants on the ground. Fifty thousand refugees fled from both sides of the border area. That year, Pakistani general Pervez Musharraf (1943–) took over Pakistan's government, installing a military dictatorship.

Pakistan and India in the 21st Century

After the September 11, 2001, terrorist attacks on the United States, the U.S. government made common-cause agreements with Musharraf's government. The

CRICKET DIPLOMACY

Cricket is the second most popular and widely played sport in the world, after football (called soccer in the United States). Cricket diplomacy uses the game of cricket as a political tool to enhance the diplomatic relations of two cricket-playing nations. Both India and Pakistan are passionate cricket nations, and cricket diplomacy has helped soothe tensions between the two nations on numerous occasions. When officials attend cricket matches played between Indian and Pakistani teams, their presence indicates a commitment to peace. When political extremists dig up a cricket pitch (playing ground, or field), it can be construed as a serious insult.

Since 2004, cricket tours between India and Pakistan have been encouraged. Both nations have relaxed their strict visa regulations so that thousands of fans can cross the border to attend games. In 2005, General Musharraf, the leader of Pakistan, attended one such match, which adopted the appearance of a peace summit as both countries were encouraged to use the "historic chance to end their dispute over Kashmir."

During the 2001 Cricket World Cup, both India and Pakistan made it to the semifinals. Once again the sporting event was used as an opportunity to strengthen international relationships. The prime ministers of both countries attended the match. India won, and went on to win the entire World Cup; Pakistan gracefully accepted its defeat. When the two teams met again in the semifinals of the 2011 Cricket World Cup in India, Indian Prime Minister Manmohan Singh (1932–) invited Pakistani Prime Minister Yousaf Raza Gillani (1952–) to attend the match. The prime ministers watched together—along with an estimated 1 billion viewers worldwide—as India defeated Pakistan.

Firefighters attempt to extinguish the flames coming out from the Taj Palace hotel in Mumbai, India, during a terrorist attack by Pakistani militants on November 26, 2008. That month, there were 12 coordinated shooting and bombing attacks over a three-day period by members of Lashkar-e-Taiba. The Mumbai attacks killed 164 and injured more than 300. The siege at the Taj hotel lasted three days until commandos raided the hotel and killed the remaining militants. © *Bhaskar Paul/The India Today Group/Getty Images*

agreements enlisted Pakistani aid against Islamic militants associated with the terrorist group al-Qaeda, which claimed responsibility for the September 11 attacks, and the ruling Taliban of Afghanistan. Relations between India and Pakistan improved considerably thereafter. In May 2003, India and Pakistan restored full diplomatic relations and began peace talks. In November 2003, India and Pakistan agreed to a full cease-fire in Kashmir. Pakistan encouraged separatist groups in Kashmir to abide by the cease-fire. India and Pakistan also cooperated on relief efforts following an earthquake in Kashmir in October 2005 that killed 80,000 people.

⊕ Impacts and Issues

Terrorist attacks and continued incidences of violence in border regions threatened India-Pakistan relations in the early decades of the twenty-first century. On November 2008 terrorists in Mumbai conducted 10 bombing and shooting attacks on prominent targets, including popular restaurants, a train station, a Jewish center, and luxury hotels. The attacks resulted in more than 160 deaths and more than 300 injuries.

Terrorist Attack in Mumbai Members of Lashkar-e-Taiba, an Islamist terrorist group operating primarily out of Pakistan, carried out the attacks. Investigators determined that the attackers had planned the attack in Pakistan. India warned that it would strike against Pakistani terrorist camps to protect itself. In June 2009 an Indian court issued arrest warrants for 22 Pakistani citizens in connection with the Mumbai attack and demanded that they be extradited from Pakistan to face trial. Pakistan refused, saying that the suspects could be tried in a Pakistani court. Pakistan arrested seven people in connection with the Mumbai attacks in 2009.

Since the Mumbai attack, the prime ministers of India and Pakistan have met on several occasions and demonstrated a willingness to renew peace talks and cooperation between their countries, especially in combating terrorism. But India's prime minister, Manmohan Singh (1932–), has remained adamant that renewed cooperation between India and Pakistan is dependent on bringing the suspects in the 2008 Mumbai attack to justice. Pakistan officials have stated they welcome a "comprehensive dialog."

Peace talks officially resumed in 2011. New terrorist attacks in India appear to have strengthened the desire for peace. No terrorist group has claimed responsibility for the attacks. In the past India would have almost assuredly blamed Pakistan for the violence, but instead, India has refrained and focused on eradicating terrorism domestically and abroad.

Another positive sign for peace is that the Pakistani government did not voice any objection to a new agreement between India and Afghanistan. The Strategic Partnership Agreement between India and Afghanistan involves Indian army training of Afghan security personnel, an issue that has provoked outrage in Pakistan in the past, as the government worried that India sought to expand its regional influence.

⊕ Future Implications

Violence flared again in early 2013, along the Kashmir Line of Control. Although exchanges of fire along the line are common, they do not usually result in fatalities. During the summer of 2013, a pro–Pakistan separatist demonstration against the Indian prime minister visiting Kashmir turned violent, resulting in more deaths. Police and paramilitary forces had to be deployed to return peace to the area. Until the political fate of Kashmir is fully determined, relations between Pakistan and India will likely remain unstable with the possibility of war a constant threat.

PRIMARY SOURCE

Communal Disturbances

SOURCE *"Report on Developing Partition Situation by British High Commisioner in India, 15 September 1947 (DO 133/59)."* UK National Archives, September 15, 1947. http://www.nationalarchives. gov.uk/education/topics/communal-disturbances.htm (accessed November 23, 2013).

INTRODUCTION *When India gained its independence from the British on August 14, 1947, Pakistan came into existence as part of a two state solution and the mass migration of tens of millions of people began—Muslims to*

Pakistan and Hindus and Sikhs to India. In addition to the hardships caused by the physical movement of so many people so quickly, the rioting and violence that broke out between Muslims and Hindus and Sikhs added to the toll and exacerbated the tragedy. The numbers of victims reported in the September report below were only a fraction of the estimated 18 million displaced and 1 million killed in the following days and months.

OUTWARD TELEGRAM

From the High Commissioner for the United Kingdom
To Commonwealth Relations Officer
15th September 1.30 p.m.
Priority Immediate Secret
My telegram No. 749 dated 13th September.

COMMUNAL DISTURBANCES

1. PUNJAB Following is main information received during last two days regarding situation.

   A. There was continued tension in rural areas of East Punjab but movement of refugees has continued satisfactorily.

   B. In Ambala District situation was reported to have deteriorated greatly and in Rohtak district heavy killing was reported at one place (please treat this para. as confidential)

   C. Mob of 25,000 people attacked village about 30 miles North of Delhi but was beaten off by military force.

   D. Disturbed conditions continue in Jullundur, Hoshiarpur and Kapurthala.

   E. Sikhs attacked Muslim refugee column near Amritsar and inflicted about 60 casualties on raiders (please treat name of communities concerned and number of casualties as confidential).

   F. Sikhs attacked a refugee train between Jullundur and Kapurthala and inflicted about 70 casualties. Raiders also suffered heavy casualties.

   ...

4. CASUALTIES. Nehru at Press Conference on 12th (September) said that the official and non-official sources estimated number of deaths in Delhi disturbances roughly at 1,000. Official verified figures of casualties in disturbances in West and East Punjab were 15,000 killed but he felt these figures were very low and might be doubled or trebled.

5. REFUGEES.

   A. Official figures on view in Government House Map room show that between 17th August and 7th September 325,000 Muslim refugees and 838,000 non-Muslims had crossed over principal frontier posts between Pakistan and

A picture taken in October 1947 shows wagons packed with Muslim refugees fleeing to Pakistan while Hindus flee to India by train in the border city of Amritsar between the two countries at the start of the first Indo-Pakistan War (October 1947–December 1948). The conflict and the hostility between Hindus and Muslims arose over Kashmir's status when Pakistan supported a Muslim insurgency in Kashmir after the Indian subcontinent was partitioned and the two countries became independent of Great Britain.
© AFP/Getty Images

India. Nehru at Press Conference said that by September 12th one and a quarter million persons have come from West Punjab to East Punjab and similar number from East to West. Probably another half a million are waiting to be moved.

B. Delhi refugee figures obtained from Map room show that on 12th September there were 162,000 non-Muslim refugees of which only 12,000 were in refugee camps, the remainder staying with friends or relatives. On same date there were 90,000 Muslim refugees in about six camps and 14,000 more had been cleared from Delhi during the preceding two days. Nehru said nearly quarter of Delhi population now consisted of refugees.

6. EXCHANGE OF POPULATIONS. In his prayer speech on 13th (September) Gandhi said that transfer of population would mean nothing but greater misery and wished that India and Pakistan would unitedly make up their minds against transfer of population. In contrast Nehru said that they had not been thinking of exchange of population but it was forced upon them and they had to carry out their duty.

7. SIKHS. Nehru in press conference said that he found in reports, especially in foreign reports, statements made that blame, if not all a great part of it, lay with Sikhs. That was not fair to Sikhs, who had undoubtedly misbehaved themselves as others had misbehaved but to cast blame on Sikhs was completely wrong.

PRIMARY SOURCE

Mohammed's Story

SOURCE *"Mohammed's Story."* UK National Archives, *2010. http://www.nationalarchives. gov.uk/panjab1947/mohammed.htm (accessed November 22, 2013).*

INTRODUCTION *This interview is one of four similar recordings included in the Panjab 1947 Collection of The United Kingdom National Archives. Each of the four men interviewed for the collection are from different faiths (Hindu, Muslim, Sikh, and Christian); all were affected by the 1947 partition of British India. Mohammed was eight years old at the time of the mass migrations that took place after partition. After spending several months in a refugee camp, Mohammed and his family settled in what is now Faisalbad, just over the Pakistan border. Some 18 million people were displaced and one million died in the post-partition migrations. Mohammed moved to England in 1969.*

Transcript

It was a mixed village; we never realised that somebody was Hindu or Sikh or Muslim. In marriages, the whole village used to join in. If somebody died, the whole village would mourn. Whether it was Hindus or Sikhs, it would not make a difference.

All of a sudden, in the space of a year or so this madness came. I remember people saying slogans; "Pakistan ka matlab kiya", ("What's the meaning of Pakistan?") "La ilaha il Allah" ("there is only one God") People were debating whether to vote for Congress or for the Muslim League. At the time people did not understand what that would mean. There was a lot of propaganda and hate spreading against communities and religions.

India was divided. Nobody knows exactly how many people died, but it was in the millions. Nobody was brought to justice. It was not the people who did it. It was the politicians who did it.

People left their homes because they were afraid for their lives and they were driven into the camps. We were in a camp at Seleempur for two and a half months waiting to move to Pakistan. We never had any problem with our food or our animals' food because it was being brought by people who were not Muslims. They were Sikhs and Hindus—my father's friends, who looked after us while we were in camp. I have seen the children; I have seen the elders living on grass. That's terrible—children suffering and refusing to eat that stuff. But you have to live on something. They were terrible times.

The time came for that camp to move to Pakistan. We were told by the army that was guarding us that this was a temporary arrangement because nobody wanted to go. We moved 12–15 miles a day and then camped again for the night. People were so weak by staying in camp when they didn't have much food as well. . . . It was difficult for them to move and walk.

Amongst us, there were certain people who had lost most of their family, who were murdered. I remember one woman who had two small babies with her. After moving the third time, some 45 miles, her feet were swollen and she had no proper shoes on either but she had two babies to carry. After the third day, she could not carry the babies. One day she left one baby on the roadside because she could only carry one. This happened to many other women and children because they could not walk and their parents were not strong enough to carry them. If you were slow, you were more likely to be killed.

We settled in a village. Eventually, the government allotted us some land which was vacated by Hindus and Sikhs. That happened in 1947. My father died in 1958. He was still waiting to move back to his own house. He said: "this cannot happen that somebody can take away my property, my house, my land, everything".

I was brought up hating Hindus and Sikhs until I was educated and went to the civil service. I was put in charge of India-Pakistan trade, representing Pakistan. The first time I went to Amritsar, it was a completely new world. It was amazing. People greeted me in such a way; Hindus, Sikhs. People wanted to take me to their houses and eat there, spend time with their families. The first day I was completely taken aback. What I was taught in Pakistan had no reality. Hindus, Sikhs loved to see people from Pakistan. I did not see a sign of hate. I have seen similar positions over here. There is no difference between Hindus and Sikhs and Muslims . . . especially Panjabi people together.

"My memories of my childhood are not the sort of memories that one should have." Those experiences have taught me to have a lot of respect for everybody. I live for the people and I hope I will live for the people till I die.

SEE ALSO *Pakistan-Afghanistan Conflict; Terrorism: Small Group and Individual; Weapons of Mass Destruction*

BIBLIOGRAPHY

Books

Ganguly, Sumit. *India, Pakistan and the Bomb: Debating Nuclear Stability in South Asia.* New York: Columbia University Press, 2010.

Khan, Feroz. *Eating Grass: The Making of the Pakistani Bomb.* Stanford, CA: Stanford Security Standards, 2012.

Khan, Yasmin. *The Great Partition: The Making of India and Pakistan.* New Haven, CT: Yale University Press, 2008.

Web Sites

"After Partition: India, Pakistan and Bangladesh." *BBC News,* August 8, 2007. http://news.bbc.co.uk/2/hi/in_depth/629/629/6922293.stm (accessed December 8, 2013).

Dalrymple, William. "A Deadly Triangle: Afghanistan, Pakistan, & India." *The Brookings Institution*, June 25, 2013. http://www.brookings. edu/research/essays/2013/deadly-triangle-afghanistan-pakistan-india-c# (accessed December 23, 2013).

"India and Pakistan: Border Disorder". *The Economist*, August 15, 2013. http://www. economist.com/news/asia/21583654-more-violence-along-line-control-challenges-forces-reconciliation-border-disorder (accessed December 23, 2013).

"India-Pakistan Conflict." *GlobalSecurity.org.* http:// www.globalsecurity.org/military/world/war/indo-pak.htm (accessed December 8, 2013).

"India-Pakistan: Troubled Relations." *BBC News.* http://news.bbc.co.uk/hi/english/static/ in_depth/south_asia/2002/india_pakistan/ timeline/1947.stm (accessed December 8, 2013).

"Milestones: 1961–1968: The India-Pakistan War of 1965." *U.S. State Department. Office of the Historian.* http://history.state.gov/ milestones/1961-1968/india-pakistan-war (accessed December 8, 2013).

Religious Extremism

Introduction

"Fundamentalism" is frequently used to describe strict or literal adherence to the basic principles or text of a traditional religion. The word was coined in the early 20th century in reference to a Protestant movement in the United States. Since then, the term "fundamentalism" has been applied to religions worldwide, though some scholars object to this broad use of the word. "Fundamentalism" and "extremism" are often used interchangeably, however extremism usually implies that the fundamentalist ideologies are then used as a pretext for violence against those who do not espouse the same ideologies. Throughout history, religious fundamentalism has been used to justify numerous conflicts and other atrocities.

Historical Background

As applied to all religions, fundamentalism can be described by some or all of the following characteristics: a view of religion as a complete moral or legal code, providing answers for all of life's questions; a tendency toward literal understanding of scriptures; a belief in a foundational golden age when the principles of the faith were perfectly applied, and a desire to recreate such a period in modern times; suspicion and sometimes renunciation of people of other faiths and supposedly hypocritical adherents of the same faith; and the rejection of many aspects of modern, secular societies.

Christian Origins

One of the first uses of the word "fundamentalism" appeared in an American Baptist magazine in 1920, with the editor's call to "do battle for the Lord." The editor rejected numerous aspects of modern Christian theology, which emphasized the use of human reason to interpret the Bible. Many modern Christian theologians accommodated the theory of evolution and other scientific doctrines. They also considered parts of the Bible, such as the creation story, virgin birth, atonement, and resurrection, as myths that had spiritual meaning but were not necessarily historic realities. To fundamentalists, the Bible's authority was absolute; it presented only literal truths.

A key concept of Christian fundamentalism was the view that the world would end in a cataclysm with the second coming of Christ, a time when nonbelievers would be judged. For many Christian fundamentalists, missionary activity in order to save souls throughout the world in preparation for that time of judgment, was, and still is, a central part of their religious life. Since World War II (1939–45), thousands of fundamentalist Christian missionaries have established congregations, mission agencies, and Bible training centers around the world. For example, Protestant missionaries have established thousands of fundamentalist congregations in Southeast Asia and Africa.

Many fundamentalist Christians in the United States reject the modern concept of pluralism, or the idea that there can be more than one perspective on what is true and valuable. Instead, they contend that the United States was founded as a Christian nation and achieved its preeminent place in the political, military, and economic realms because of the nation's commitment to Bible-based morality. From a Christian fundamentalist view, the United States is currently in a state of moral decline because it has strayed from traditional religion.

The sectarian conflict in Ireland and Northern Ireland in the 20th century is a recent example of armed, Christian extremism. In 1922, British-controlled Ireland was divided into the predominantly Catholic Republic of Ireland, an independent nation, and Northern Ireland, a predominantly Protestant area that remained part of the United Kingdom. Following the partition of Ireland, armed groups, such as the Irish Republican Army (IRA)

Malala Yousafzai, the 16-year-old Pakistani advocate for girls education who was shot in the head by the Taliban as she attempted to attend school with other girls in Pakistan, attends a conversation with the United Nations Secretary General Ban-ki Moon and other youth delegates at the United Nations Youth Assembly on July 12, 2013, in New York City. After being shot and spending months of recovery in a British hospital (it was deemed too dangerous for the then 15-year-old to undergo treatment for her head wound in her home country), Yousafzai was honored by the United Nations, which declared July 12 "Malala Day," when she also celebrates her birthday. *© Andrew Burton/Getty Images*

and, later, the Real IRA and the Provisional IRA, continued to fight for a united Ireland. The fighting, which escalated in the late 1960s through 1998 in a period known as the Troubles, often had sectarian overtones. The Troubles left over 3,600 dead and 45,000 wounded before all parties agreed to a peace accord.

Islamic Fundamentalism

Because the word fundamentalism has Christian origins, many scholars and religious activists reject its use in other religious contexts, particularly regarding Islam. Some argue that terms like "Islamic fundamentalism" are used indiscriminately to describe all Islamic activists, whether they are radicals or moderates, and that the term has become loaded with negative connotations. Despite these objections, "religious fundamentalism" is frequently applied to Islam.

While no single, clearly defined ideology of Islamic fundamentalism exists, to most observers, its most central aspect is the application of sharia (divine law) to all aspects of social and individual life. Fundamentalists

interpret the law themselves through their own reading of the Qur'an and sunna (traditions of Islam based on the teachings of Muhammad). But compared to modernists, the fundamentalist reading of scriptural sources is literal and conservative.

The Muslim fundamentalist worldview is based on the idea that most societies are in a state of ignorance like that which prevailed before the prophet Muhammad brought Islam to the world. In the fundamentalist viewpoint, only a small, committed group of true Muslims discern the corrupted state of Muslim affairs and the proper means to remedy it. The true Muslims must therefore withdraw mentally and even physically, if need be, from this state of ignorance in order to establish truly Islamic values within themselves and their organization. This *hijra,* or "flight," is the first type of jihad (struggle or striving for spiritual perfection) that they must wage. On the instructions of the leader, the Muslim vanguard must transform their inner jihad into an outer jihad aimed at overthrowing the un-Islamic order and correcting societal ills.

Islamic fundamentalism is found today, in varying degrees of strength and popular support, in every Muslim-majority country and in many countries with large Muslim minorities. The modern form of Islamic fundamentalism was first set forth by Muhammad ibn Abd al-Wahhab (1703–1792). The movement started by Wahhab, known as Wahhabism, began as a movement within Sunni Islam to return to the fundamental teachings of the Qur'an and Hadith. Wahhab rejected modern interpretations of the Qur'an. Wahhabism grew in popularity throughout the Muslim world, particulary the Middle East, throughout the 19th century.

In the 20th century, fundamentalist Muslim revivalist movements sprang up in Egypt under the Muslim Brotherhood and in India under Jama'at-e Islami. In 1928, Hassan al-Banna (1906–1949) founded the Muslim Brotherhood with the goal of establishing the Qur'an and sunna as the cornerstones of Islamic families, society, and government. In 1941, Abul-A'la Maududi (1903–1979), founded the Islamic political party Jama'at-e Islami in British-controlled India. Both Jama'at-e Islami and the Muslim Brotherhood formed in an effort to assert Muslim traditions as a counter to the influence of secular or modernist European ideas and institutions.

Both the Muslim Brotherhood and Jama'at-e Islami initially advocated using forceful means to establish an Islamic order. The Muslim Brotherhood officially renounced revolutionary violence against the Egyptian state in 1949 and focused its efforts on political movements. Maududi, meanwhile, focused on the establishment of Pakistan as a democratic, Islamic state governed by sharia following the partition of India and Pakistan in 1947.

In 1979, Iran underwent an Islamic revolution, transforming the state from a monarchy to a fundamentalist Islamic republic. Following the Iranian Revolution, a younger generation of activists began to form some new, and sometimes violent, spin-offs of the fundamentalist groups in other parts of the world. One of these groups, Islamic Jihad, was responsible for the assassination of Egyptian President Anwar Sadat (1918–1981) in October 1981.

Other spin-offs from the original fundamentalist groups took their places at the forefront of violent struggles in such diverse parts of the Muslim world as Algeria, Palestine, Afghanistan, Kashmir, and Indonesia. It should be noted, though, that one of the most widespread and important fundamentalist organizations, the Tablighi Jama'at, is nonviolent in its tactics and generally avoids politics altogether. Many of the new Muslim fundamentalist groups reject the idea of a secular state, as well as concepts like equality between men and women and freedom of religion. The Taliban in Afghanistan is an example of an extremely strict form of Muslim fundamentalism.

One of the most widely publicized examples of fundamentalist religious extremism in modern memory is the infamous *fatwa* (religious decree) pronounced by Iran's Ayatollah Khomeini (1902–1989) against British-Indian author Salman Rushdie (1947–) in 1989. Khomeini demanded Rushdie's execution, accusing him of blasphemy for his depiction of Islam in the 1988 novel *The Satanic Verses*. Numerous death threats by Islamic extremists forced the author into hiding, under police protection, for several years. Although Rushdie gradually resumed public life, as recently as January 2012 he withdrew from India's largest literary festival, citing threats against his life by Muslim clerics in India.

Jewish Fundamentalism

Among a variety of Jewish fundamentalist groups is Gush Emunim (Hebrew for "the bloc of the faithful"). Gush members were among the groups who settled in areas known as the West Bank and Gaza Strip, regions contested between Israel and the Palestinians. Gush Emunim believes these territories belong to the Jewish people and the State of Israel by divine promise. Its members oppose any territorial compromise or Israeli withdrawal from these regions, even as part of a peace agreement between Israel and the Palestinians. Their opposition is based, in part, on the belief that the return of a large Jewish presence to Israel will help bring about the arrival of the Messiah and that the Jews, through divine assistance, will triumph over their non-Jewish adversaries.

Mormon Fundamentalism

In recent years, fundamentalist sects of the Mormon Church in the United States have made headlines because of allegations of polygamy and child sex abuse. In 2008, for example, Texas authorities raided the Yearning for Zion Ranch in Eldorado, Texas, a compound of the Fundamentalist Church of Jesus Christ of Latter-Day Saints. Police chose to enter the compound after receiving calls from juveniles within the facility who claimed they were being abused or forced into marriages with much older men. Almost all the minors in the facility were taken into protective custody. A year later, about two-thirds of the families returned to the ranch, church leaders promised to end underage marriage, and 14 men had been charged with crimes, including assault and bigamy.

The president of the church, Warren Jeffs (1955–), has been in prison since 2007, after being convicted as an accomplice to rape. In July 2010, however, the Utah State Supreme Court threw out the rape convictions and ordered a new trial for Jeffs. In 2011, Jeffs was sentenced to life in prison on two felony counts of sexual assault of a child. Polygamy is illegal in the United States and is not sanctioned by the mainstream Church of Jesus Christ of Latter-day Saints. Polygamy was part of early Mormonism, but the church banned the practice in 1890. However, polygamy continues to be a prominent feature of Mormon fundamentalism.

American-born Israeli settler Yaakov (Jack) Teitel flashes the V for victory sign as he arrives for his trial at the Jerusalem District Court on April 9, 2013. An Israeli court sentenced the extreme right-wing Jewish settler to two life terms in prison for the murder of two Palestinians in 1997. Teitel, 41, was found guilty in January 2013 of murdering a bus driver and a shepherd, as well as two separate attempted murders, illegal possession of weapons, and incitement to violence. © *Ahamd Gharabli/AFP/Getty Images*

⊕ Impacts and Issues

Most multicultural societies still struggle with balancing varying, and sometimes conflicting, interests or standards of different religious communities. For some people, deeply held beliefs require not just that they have the right to personal expression, but that they and their community remain free from all dissenting beliefs. Alternative beliefs are considered both unholy and a threat to social cohesion. Defense of their beliefs requires suppression—sometimes violent—of others' beliefs.

Fundamentalism, Extremism, and Terrorism

Perhaps the best-known Islamic fundamentalist group in the world today is the Taliban, which controlled Afghanistan from 1996 to 2001 and harbored the Islamic terrorist group al-Qaeda, which was responsible for the deadly 9/11 attacks on the United States. The Taliban regime in Afghanistan enforced a strictly-interpreted version of sharia under which women were denied education and careers, were required to wear clothing covering them from head to foot, and were forbidden from leaving their homes unaccompanied by a male family member. Men were required to wear long beards. The Taliban regime was toppled by a U.S.-led invasion of Afghanistan in 2001 but still maintains an active insurgency and, many fear, will eventually regain power after the United States completes its troop withdrawal scheduled in 2014.

Other Islamist groups have sought to establish Islamist controlled states or regions in parts of Africa during the 21st century. Since 2001, a Muslim fundamentalist group called Boko Haram has led an uprising in northeastern Nigeria that has resulted in over 10,000 killed in clashes with security forces and Christian gangs. Boko Haram has called for sharia to be adopted throughout Nigeria. In Somalia, al-Shabab, an Islamist group linked to al-Qaeda, has conducted an insurgency and terrorism campaign against the Somali government and its allies. In 2012, Ansar Dine and other Islamist groups co-opted a rebellion against the government of Mali waged by ethnic Tuaregs. The Islamist groups captured the northern half of Mali and imposed strict Islamic rule in the region. Ansar Dine destroyed many Islamic mosques and other historic monuments that

Buddhist militant leader Wirathu studies inside his room at the Masoeyein monastery on June 30, 2013, in Mandalay, Burma. Wirathu is the leader of the Buddhist extremist movement in Burma known as 969. He was once jailed for anti-Muslim violence and also has called himself the "Burmese bin Laden." Buddhist leader Wirathu resides at the Masoeyein monastery where over 2,800 monks live; it is one of the largest in Mandalay, Burma's second largest city.   © *Paula Bronstein/Getty Images*

they deemed offensive to their interpretation of Islam. The Malian government, aided by troops from France, recaptured most of the Islamist-controlled areas in early 2013, though sporadic fighting continued.

Extremism is not limited to one faith. Terrorism has been committed by religious extremists of all religions. In 2007, train bombings in India killed 68 people; the attacks were linked to Hindu fundamentalists. Buddhists in Myanmar (also called Burma) have been linked to terrorist attacks against the ethnic Rohingya people, who are primarily Muslim. An American-born Israeli physician killed 29 Muslim worshipers and wounded 125 more inside a mosque in Israel in 1994.

Confronting Religious Extremism

Governments have approached religious extremism in various ways. Most Western countries regard religious beliefs as personal, and only seek to keep those beliefs from becoming unlawful actions. Other countries have taken unique measures. In 2011, Tajikistan took an unusual step in its struggle against religious extremism: it banned children and teenagers from worshipping in mosques. The law was unanimously supported by the parliament, but strongly condemned by religious groups. Tajikistan, a largely secular, Muslim-majority state that shares a border with Afghanistan, has accused fundamentalist groups of trying to spread radical forms of Islam in the hope of establishing Islamic rule. Mosques are seen as the main conduit through which radicalization occurs.

In 2013 Nigeria's president, Goodluck Jonathan (1957–), confronted religious extremism in his country by demanding that Boko Haram, the Islamic fundamentalist group, state its demands as a precursor for talks. Boko Haram has claimed responsibility for numerous acts of violence and has explicitly threatened to attack non-Islamic schools. The schools that were attacked were burned during nighttime hours and mostly destroyed, but no children were hurt.

Religious Freedom

For many people, regardless of faith, their religious beliefs are deeply personal. It is those deeply personal beliefs that have led to the modern concept of religious freedom. Religious freedom is a human rights principle or right that guarantees individuals, communities, and group members universal, free expression in matters of religious faith.

Religious freedom infers other rights, including the freedom of conscience, freedom of assembly, and freedom of expression. Religious freedom as a human rights principle advocates the ability of individuals to choose any system of religious belief, change their religious beliefs, or choose not to adopt any religious belief system. It further asserts that individuals have the right to associate with fellow believers, form religious congregations or communities, and assemble to observe religious customs. Individuals and groups should also be able to freely express their religious beliefs, or lack thereof, without fear of oppression or discrimination. Modes of expression comprise voluntary verbal and non-verbal conduct, including speech, teaching and education,

A veiled woman speaks with another woman while waiting at the courthouse in Nanterre, Paris. French lawmakers voted for a bill April 11, 2011, that made it illegal for Muslim women to wear the full-face veils called burqas in public. A U.S. poll has found that while a majority of Europeans back such a ban, Americans reject it. The French overwhelmingly endorse a ban on Muslim face coverings, as do majorities in Britain, Germany, and Spain, a survey conducted by the Washington-based Pew Research Center's Global Attitudes Project found. © Miguel Medina/AFP/Getty Images

customs of dress, religious rites, and holidays so long as such expression does not substantially infringe on the rights of others. Some human rights concepts of religious freedom also advocate freedom from state-sponsored religion.

Balancing Individual and Community

Some nations make laws limiting personal religious symbols, such as the wearing of headscarves, as a way of protecting the community values. These values may be another religion or may be secular, but either way the dominant values are deemed worthy of, and in need of, protection from unfamiliar expression. Other nations make laws requiring personal religious symbols, such as requiring women to cover their heads—or their entire bodies—when in public. Each of these nations is trying to reconcile how personal expression impacts the community and whether the individual or the community should take precedence.

Throughout history, nations have offered varying degrees of protection for religious freedom. However, the modern concept of religious freedom as a universal human right arose in the late 1700s among European and American Enlightenment thinkers. The post-Revolution French Republic adopted guarantees of religious freedom in their 1789 Declaration of the Rights of Man and Citizen, equating religious liberty with freedom of conscience. The Declaration stated, "no one may be questioned about his opinions, including religious opinions, provided that their manifestation does not trouble the public order established by the law."

The fledgling United States of America enshrined religious freedom in the nation's Constitution. The First Amendment to the Constitution of the United States, part of the amendments known as the Bill of Rights, states: "Congress shall make no law respecting an establishment of religion, or prohibiting the free exercise thereof. . . ." The full scope of the amendment guarantees individual freedom of religious belief, expression, and assembly. It also mandates separation of church and state and prohibits state-established religion. Legal protection of religious freedom in the United States has expanded through centuries of Supreme Court decisions interpreting First Amendment rights. In France, a 1905 expansion of the principles expressed in the Declaration of the Rights of Man and of the Citizen added express protections on the free exercise of religion and the separation of government and religion.

The United Nations Universal Declaration of Human Rights, adopted on December 10, 1948, moved human rights-based principles of religious freedom into international law. Article 18 states: "Everyone has the right to freedom of thought, conscience and religion; this right includes freedom to change his religion or belief, and freedom, either alone or in community with others and in public or private, to manifest his religion

THE VEIL: PERSONAL RELIGIOUS EXPRESSION AND THE COMMUNITY

The word *hijab* refers to the head covering worn by many Muslim women, a headscarf that covers the forehead, hair, and often the neck. In a broader sense, hijab refers to modesty and humility, which many Muslims define as covering all but the hands, feet, and face for Muslim women. Other forms of headscarves include the *burqa,* a full-body covering with a thin mesh strip across the eyes, allowing the woman to see through the mesh, and the *niqab,* which shows only the eyes. Opinions on how hijab should be defined vary. Conservative scholars and Muslims generally advocate the burqa and cite verses of the Qur'an to support their views. Liberal scholars and Muslims tend to advocate a broader interpretation that does not require specific covering or veiling, but instead promotes modesty in general, as set out in the Qur'an.

Head covering among Muslims in Western society has, since the 1970s, taken on political as well as religious meaning. For nearly two decades the issue of headscarves worn by female Muslims has been a topic of debate in French society. In France, religion is treated as a private matter; a 1905 law separates church and state. Religious symbols from other religions such as Christianity (the cross) or Judaism (the yarmulke) were tolerated in public schools and by government institutions as long as the display was modest. As the Muslim population increased in France and more young women entered schools wearing headscarves, this highly visible mode of religious expression became a source of debate, culminating in the 2004 French law banning conspicuous religions symbols (including yarmulkes and hijab) from schools and government institutions.

In June 2009, French President Nicolas Sarkozy (1955–) sparked controversy when he endorsed banning the burqa in France, saying, "We cannot accept, in our country, women imprisoned behind a mesh, cut off from society, deprived of all identity. That is not the French republic's idea of women's dignity." As wearing the burqa has become increasingly widespread in France's Muslim community, many in the government have worried publicly that women may not be adopting the burqa voluntarily. Further, they view the burqa as a threat to French secularism. In 2010,

France adopted a ban on face covering in public places, including the burqa and niqab. Critics say that the ban on the burqa and niqab in France further stigmatize Muslims, who already feel marginalized. France is home to 5 million Muslims, the largest Muslim population in Western Europe.

The controversy has enveloped other European nations. Current German law allows for symbols from such religions as Christianity or Judaism; critics characterize a ban on headscarves as a form of discrimination against Muslims. In Germany in 2003, the Federal Constitutional Court in Karlsruhe ruled that banning teachers from wearing headscarves was an issue for legislation, not judicial determination. In the several years following the case, half of Germany's states enacted laws banning the wearing of headscarves by public school teachers and other civil servants. On August 4, 2011, Italy's parliament passed a draft of a law banning the wearing of full Islamic veils in public. Lawmakers behind the bill said they wanted to encourage "integration."

The political and religious issues surrounding headscarves are not limited to Europe. In Singapore, laws ban children from wearing headscarves in school. In 2002, four young Muslim girls, ages six to seven, were banned from school for wearing the "tudung" or head covering.

The country of Turkey faces a different challenge regarding headscarves and politics. Though 99 percent of Turkey's population identifies as Muslim, strict secular laws dating back to the founder of modern Turkey, Mustafa Kemal Ataturk (1881–1938), ban the wearing of headscarves in government institutions. Turkey's law banning headscarves received international attention in 1999 when a newly elected female member of parliament, Merve Kavakçi, attended her swearing-in ceremony wearing a headscarf. She was denied her swearing in and later had her Turkish citizenship revoked, though for reasons unrelated to the headscarf. In 2008, Turkish President Abdullah Gul (1950–) signed legislation removing a ban on wearing headscarves in Turkish universities, claiming the lifting of the ban does not clash with Turkey's secularization laws.

or belief in teaching, practice, worship and observance." Furthermore, all of the other provisions of the Declaration were to be applied to all people, "without distinction of any kind," including discrimination based on religion.

⊕ Future Implications

Some areas of the world seem to be moving toward more secularism. The percentage of American adults that identify themselves as Christian has dropped about 1 percent per year since 1990. An increasing number of Americans (up to 20 percent) claim no religious affiliation. In

the United Kingdom, a third of the adults identify as agnostic or atheist. In an attempt to protest the question regarding religious affiliation on government census surveys, or just in fun, the practice of declaring one's religion to be the Jedi Knights of Star Wars has gained traction in several countries since 2001, including Australia, Canada, Croatia, Czech Republic, New Zealand, and the United Kingdom, where it now is reported to be the most often selected alternative religion. The initial demands for greater democratic freedoms seen during the Arab Spring were largely secular, though vocal religious groups have since emerged.

Many people do not see a desire for democracy as inconsistent with a religious state, or, more specifically, a state government along the lines of their personal religious beliefs. However others believe that religious identity is often interwoven with ethnic and national identity, and perceived threats and alternative religious views are particularly frightening and must be suppressed. This type of thinking shows no signs of slowing, nor does oppression and violence in the name of religion.

SEE ALSO *9/11; Afghan War; Al-Qaeda; Arab-Israeli Conflict; Bosnian War; Burma (Myanmar) Uprisings; Chechnya; Islam: Sunni and Shia Disputes; Islamophobia; Israeli-Palestinian Conflict; Kosovo's Independence; Lebanon: Civil War and Political Instability; Northern Ireland: The Troubles; Pakistan-India Conflict; Somalia; Terrorism: Large Group; Terrorism: Small Group; Terrorism: State Sponsored*

BIBLIOGRAPHY

Books

Hood, Ralph W. *The Psychology of Religious Fundamentalism.* New York, NY: Guilford Press, 2005.

James, Patrick, ed. *Religion, Identity, and Global Governance: Ideas, Evidence, and Practice.* Toronto, ON, Canada: University of Toronto Press, 2011.

Periodicals

Afzal, Saima, Hamid Iqbal, and Mavara Inayay. "Terrorism and Extremism as a Non-Traditional Security Threat Post 9/11: Implications for Pakistan's Security." *International Journal of Business and Social Science* 3, no. 24 (December 2012).

Stevens, David. "Reasons to Be Fearful, One, Two, Three: The 'Preventing Violent Extremism' Agenda." *British Journal of Politics and International Relations* 13, no. 2 (May 2011): 165–188.

Web Sites

Davis, Kenneth C. "American's True History of Religious Tolerance." *The Smithsonian*, October 2010. http://www.smithsonianmag.com/history-archaeology/Americas-True-History-of-Religious-Tolerance.html (accessed December 30, 2013).

"Extremism in America." *The Anti-Defamation League.* http://archive.adl.org/learn/ext_us/ (accessed December 24, 2013).

"What is Religious Fundamentalism?" *The Brookings Institute.* http://www.brookings.edu/events/2012/02/22-religious-fundamentalism (accessed July 24, 2013).

"What Is Religious Militancy and Its Relationship to Terrorism?" *Global Connections: The Middle East.* http://www.pbs.org/wgbh/globalconnections/mideast/questions/militant/ (accessed December 24, 2013).

Wracker, Grant. "The Rise of Fundamentalism." *National Humanities Center.* http://nationalhumanitiescenter.org/tserve/twenty/tkeyinfo/fundam.htm (accessed February 12, 2014).

Russian Revolution and Civil War

🌐 Introduction

The Russian Civil War (1917–22) directly followed the Russian Revolution of 1917 and resulted in the formation of the Soviet Union. During the conflict the main forces were the Bolshevik Red Army and the White Army along with other loosely allied anti-Bolshevik forces. (The Bolsheviks believed in Marxist Communism, which is a political ideology that purports to bring about a workers' utopia in which all people have equal wealth.) The Allied Forces and pro-German armies of World War I (1914–18) also intervened in support of the White Army. The war ended after the Red Army defeated the White armed forces in Ukraine and Siberia in 1919 and Crimea in 1920.

During the Russian Civil War, several territories that had formerly belonged to the Russian Empire formed pro-independence movements. Several of these led to independent sovereign states including Estonia, Finland, Latvia, Lithuania, and Poland. The rest of the territory was consolidated into the Soviet Union. The Russian Civil War later served as an inspiration for the establishment of various Communist regimes around the world.

🌐 Historical Background

At the beginning of the 20th century, Russia was one of the few remaining absolute monarchies in Europe. The Romanov Dynasty had ruled Russia since 1613. But by the early 20th century, numerous economic, political, and military problems resulted in a revolution that overturned the monarchy and threw Russia into a brutal civil war.

Economic, Political, and Military Problems in Russia

At the turn, the 20th century, Russia's traditional land-owning classes, the nobility and wealthy peasants known as boyars, found themselves in massive amounts of debt. To alleviate this debt they began mortgaging land and firing workers. This in turn led to a mass migration to the cities, where newly displaced peasants began to compete with the traditional urban inhabitants for food and jobs. This twofold pressure raised food prices at the same time that the overabundance of labor caused a drop in wages.

In December 1904, factory workers in the capital of St. Petersburg began demanding more pay and shorter working hours. A crowd of more than 80,000 marched on the emperor's palace. They were stopped by the Russian army, which opened fire on the crowd, killing hundreds, in an event known as Bloody Sunday. The massacre served to further alienate Emperor Nicholas II (1868–1918) from the people. Until this event, much of the population viewed the emperor as a "loving father" who had been "misled" by evil advisors. But after Bloody Sunday, the people began to see the emperor as part of their repression.

The discontent of the masses found a voice among the educated, liberal, urban elites who were advocating for a larger voice in government and limits to imperial power through some sort of legislative oversight body. They hoped to see the return of the Duma, a traditional council made up of leading citizens. The role of the Duma was purely advisory, but it provided a way for citizens to petition the government. Following the massacre on Bloody Sunday, the emperor agreed to let the Duma meet again. Before its reestablishment in 1905, the Duma had not met since the time of Peter the Great (1672–1725) in 1721.

The Russo-Japanese War (1904–05) In addition to these domestic pressures, Russian and Japanese imperial ambitions began to clash on the Pacific coast. Russia had been expanding toward the Pacific since the time of Tsar Ivan the Terrible (1530–1584). Much of this expansion had gone unchallenged, but, with the opening of Japan in 1854 and the rapid modernization that followed under the Meiji Restoration (1868–1912), Japan was able to challenge imperial Russia's eastern ambitions.

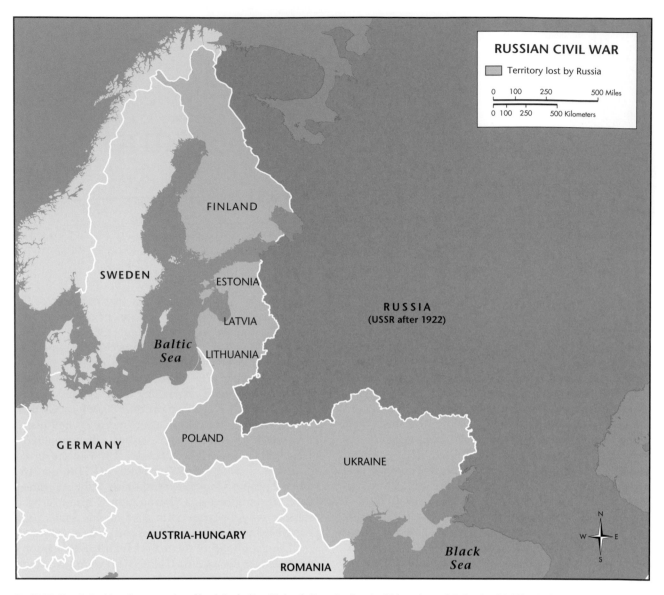

By 1918, Russia had lost large swaths of land, including Finland, Estonia, Latvia, Lithuania, and Poland, with Ukraine's territory in dispute. By 1919, the Western part of Ukraine was absorbed into Poland and most of the remainder became the Ukrainian Soviet Socialist Republic, joining the USSR in 1922. © *2014 Cengage Learning*

The Russo-Japanese War erupted over competing imperial ambitions in Korea and Manchuria. Russia desired a warm-water port on the Pacific, and Japan wanted a foothold on mainland Asia. The war, which most of the world predicted would end with a Russian victory, instead ended with a humiliating Russian defeat. The defeat was a tremendous blow to Russian imperial prestige and caused massive discontent within both the civilian population and the ranks of the military.

Russia in World War I Following the reforms of the 1905 revolution, the Russian Empire experienced a period of relative peace. But in 1914, Russia joined World War I on the Allied side. Nicholas II personally oversaw the Russian army from the front. He left his wife, Alexandra (1872–1918), in charge of Russia.

Alexandra was widely distrusted, with some people even suggesting she was a German spy. Court observers and public rumor held that the royal family was influenced by a manipulative advisor named Grigori Rasputin (1869–1916).

As World War I dragged on, the Russian army was wracked by a series of defeats. As the death toll mounted, tens of thousands of soldiers began to desert. Throughout the Russian Empire, the people clamored for a withdrawal from World War I. When this failed to happen, a revolution erupted that later dissolved into civil war.

February Revolution (1917)

The February Revolution was the result of massive desertions from the front as well as spreading anarchy throughout the countryside. Many soldiers who had formerly supported the government joined local *soviets* and began to plot revolution. The word soviet is a derivative of the Russian word for council.

The soviets were groups of dissidents who began to demand not only an end to World War I but also major reform within Imperial Russia. Their rallying cry became "Peace, land, bread." This cry reflected the desire for an end to Russian involvement in World War I, as well as a call for the redistribution of land from the wealthy land owners to the peasant farmers. The call for bread referred to the famine that had been ongoing since 1916. Bad weather coupled with poor military decisions had left huge segments of the Russian population starving. Much of the country's transportation networks were being used for the war effort and were not available to transport food to urban areas. Additionally, many able-bodied men who normally would have helped with the harvest had been sent to the fronts, so grain was left rotting in the fields.

By February 1917 the protest had grown so severe that Nicholas II was forced to return from the front. Upon arriving in the capital of Petrograd (having changed its name from St. Petersburg in 1914), the emperor was confronted by members of his council who insisted that he abdicate the throne. Nicholas II did this on March 11, 1917, handing power over to a provisional government composed of liberal nobles, led by Alexander Kerensky (1881–1970) and the local Petrograd soviet group.

But the provisional government did not bring about the promised peace, land, and bread, and refused to pull out of World War I. As 1917 progressed and anarchy quickly spread throughout the country, many of the more centrist members of the soviets began to advocate working more closely with the conservative groups. They hoped they might bring order and stability back to Russia.

The Rise of the Bolsheviks

The Bolsheviks were originally just a vocal minority within most soviet groups. Founded in 1905 by Vladimir Lenin (1870–1924), the Bolsheviks believed in Marxist Communism. Communism is a political ideology that purportedly will bring about a workers' utopia in which all people have equal wealth. Such an ideal found many adherents in the Russian population. During 1917, the Bolsheviks consolidated much popular support throughout Russia.

October Revolution

By October 1917, the provisional government was deeply unpopular. A Russian army marched on Petrograd, hoping to overthrow the provisional government. Kerensky panicked and turned to the only people left who had even tacit support for the provisional government: the Bolsheviks.

Kerensky arranged for 40,000 rifles to be distributed to the Bolsheviks, thinking they would protect the government. Instead, the Bolsheviks used the arms

RASPUTIN

Rasputin was a Russian mystic who came from western Siberia. In 1907, he was invited to the palace to heal the young prince, Alexei (1904–1918), who had been born with hemophilia, a genetic disease in which blood does not clot. Although Rasputin was unable to heal the prince, he nevertheless impressed the royal family. He soon became the chief advisor of Alexandra, who believed Rasputin had psychic powers.

By 1916, Rasputin had become a symbol to many of the decadence and excess of the royal family and ruling classes. In the winter of 1916, Russian nobles had Rasputin killed. But his assassination only added to his mystique, with various stories surrounding the events. Rasputin was reportedly first poisoned, then beaten, then shot. When he failed to die, the nobles threw his bleeding body into a freezing river. Autopsies later found bullet wounds in his body, but determined that he died from drowning.

to suppress the Mensheviks, their main rivals within the soviets. By early November, the Bolsheviks felt secure enough to overthrow the provisional government and declare the rise of the soviets. Within ten days, Bolshevik power under the leadership and domination of Lenin had spread as far east as Moscow and Baku, which lies on the shores of the Caspian Sea. As increasing numbers of soviets rose up against the provisional government, the Bolshevik revolutionary coup spread all the way to the Pacific Ocean by December 1917.

Soviet Reforms

Upon ascension to power, the soviets quickly moved to institute reforms. Private bank accounts were seized and the wealth purportedly redistributed to the people. Land formerly owned by the wealthy elite and middle class, as well as land owned by the Orthodox Church, was gathered into communes and given over to peasant farmers. Wages and the cost of bread and other goods were frozen at predetermined rates.

The soviets also signed the Treaty of Brest-Litovsk, which withdrew Russia from World War I. The soviets were willing to lose large swaths of Russian territory because Lenin believed that, once the soviets had consolidated power within Russia, the soviet revolution would quickly spread, and Russia would regain any lost territories.

The nationalization of private land and the concessions in the Brest-Litovsk Treaty gained the soviets the support of the poorest segments of society. But it just as quickly alienated many others and led to the formation of anti-Bolshevik armed groups that extended the civil war for another four years.

Through the course of the civil war and economic reshaping of Russia, some of the groups that had initially supported the Bolsheviks later turned against them.

Vladimir Ilyich Lenin (1870–1924), the Russian revolutionary and communist politician who led the October Revolution of 1917, speaks to a crowd in Red Square. He headed the Soviet state from 1917–1924. © *Popperfoto/Getty Images*

Sailors at the Kronstadt naval garrison had mutinied against their commanders in 1905 and were active in the overthrow of the monarchy in support of the Bolsheviks in 1917. However, many of the same leaders later rose against the Bolshevik government in February 1921. The Kronstadt uprising leaders criticized Bolshevik communism and the growing police state. In March 1921, the army brutally quelled the uprising after the organizers published a list of demands for increased political and economic freedoms in Russia.

The Kronstadt sailors acted on their own, but Lenin blamed the uprising on agents of the White Army and the influence of foreign saboteurs. Hundreds of sailors were later executed or sent to labor camps. Lenin did, however, swiftly introduce his New Economic Policy (NEP) which somewhat liberalized the economy by allowing private small enterprises while still nationalizing large industry. The NEP also ended the on-demand seizure of agricultural products to meet food needs in the cities, but required farmers to give the government a percentage of their harvest as a form of tax.

⊕ Impacts and Issues

Major Conflicts of the Civil War

The Russian civil war developed directly out of unresolved issues that arose during the revolution. Like most civil wars, it was exceedingly bloody. Its outcome profoundly affected the history of the 20th and the 21th centuries. The civil war was fought by many combatants over large areas and was loosely divided between the Reds and the Whites. The Reds were represented by the Bolshevik-controlled soviets. The Whites were a loose assortment of monarchists, nationalists, republicans, and large groups of army deserters who objected to the humiliation imposed by the Treaty of Brest-Litovsk.

Most of the fighting involved autonomous groups supporting one side or the other. Combat deaths in the war are estimated to be around one million. During the Red Terror, a period of terror carried out by the Bolsheviks during September and October 1918, the secret police (Cheka) executed an estimated 250,000 to one million persons. Decossackization, a policy aimed

In an image taken from a collection of propaganda posters issued by the Soviet government between 1918–1921, the White Army is shown burning crops. The poster reads: "Retreating from the Red Army, the Whites are burning crops," blaming those fighting the Red Army for food shortages. © *The British Library/Robana via Getty Images*

to decimate the ethnic minority Cossack population who had attempted to form independent states and fought against the Bolsheviks, resulted in the deaths of 300,000–500,000 Cossacks between 1917 and 1930. In all of Russia, widespread famine and disease during and after the civil war killed as many as 10 million people, with many millions displaced.

Foreign Intervention   In addition to the disorganized fighting among the various Russian factions, an international force also joined the fray. The Allied governments and Central Powers each sent troops into Russia. The Allied powers hoped to keep Russia in World War I by reestablishing either the provisional or imperial government. Pro–German troops hoped to get more land concessions and reparations. Eventually the number of foreign troops participating in the Russian Civil War reached approximately 270,000.

Death of the Imperial Family

In April 1918, the Romanovs, the former Russian ruling family, were moved from the area around Petrograd to a home in a more secure area in Yekaterinburg. They were held by the Red Army, which hoped that the family

would be out of reach of the Russian White forces, who hoped for restoration of the monarchy. On July 16, 1918, news reached Yekaterinburg of the approach of a legion of the pro-imperialist White Russian army.

To prevent any future rescue attempts, the entire Romanov family (Nicholas, Alexandra, and their five children) as well as four family servants, were moved to the basement, ostensibly to wait for transportation to another secure location. Instead they were read an order for their execution. All members of the royal family were shot and buried in a secret location that was not rediscovered until the fall of the Soviet Union nearly 70 years later.

Independence and Consolidation

Imperial Russia had been a sprawling Eurasian empire. During the Russian Civil War, certain western territories located in Eastern Europe broke away and became independent nations. Estonia, Finland, Latvia, Lithuania, and Poland each declared their independence during the Russian Civil War. But the Russian government did not recognize their independence, and years later the Soviet Union reclaimed some of these territories.

Tsar Nicholas II (1868–1918) and Tsarina Alexandra Feodorovna of Russia (1872–1918) with their children Olga, Tatiana, Maria, Anastasia, and Alexei, circa 1914, three years before they were imprisoned and executed during the Russian Revolution.
© *Popperfoto/Getty Images*

Following the victory of the Bolshevik soviets over the Allied expeditionary forces and the various White Russian forces, the Union of Soviet Socialist Republics, or USSR, was created. The USSR was formally declared on December 30, 1922, and was in theory a federation of the Russian Soviet Federative Socialist Republic (SFSR) as well as the Ukraine Soviet Socialist Republic (SSR), Byelorussian SSR, and the Transcaucasus SFSR. The USSR was eventually composed of 15 Soviet Republics until its ultimate collapse in 1991.

⊕ Future Implications

The USSR spent the 1920s and 1930s industrializing. It participated in World War II (1939–45) on the side of the Allies. During the war it regained territory lost in the Treaty of Brest-Litovsk and also gained control over the countries that had declared their independence during the Russian Civil War. After victory in World War II, the Soviet Union postured against its rival superpower, the United States, in an elaborate Cold War that lasted for nearly 50 years.

The Cold War ended in 1991 when the USSR collapsed due to economic and political difficulties. The Russian Federation lost many of its former territories as they splintered off into independent states. The country went through a difficult transition from a communist country to a more democratic government and a capitalist economic system. Russia's relations with the United States and Europe became more open, however tensions remain with some Western countries due to questions about human rights issues. In addition, Russia has taken stances unpopular with some in the West on several issues addressed by the United Nations Security Council, as it kept the USSR's seat as one of the five permanent members after the dissolution. Despite its opposing viewpoints with the United States on some issues, Russia remains a powerful actor on the world stage and has reached out to form alliances with other nations, including China, and continues to wield significant power.

PRIMARY SOURCE

Excerpt from *Ten Days that Shook the World*

SOURCE *Reed, John. "Chapter IX. Victory," from* Ten Days that Shook the World, *New York: Boni & Liveright, 1922; Bartleby.com, 2000. www.bartleby. com/79/9 (accessed December 6, 2013).*

INTRODUCTION *John Silas Reed (1887–1920) was an American revolutionary, poet, and journalist who became a symbol in many American minds of the Communist revolution in Russia. After graduating from Harvard in 1910, he worked for a number of publications, including* Metropolitan Magazine. *Reed, who had covered world events in various hot spots, including Mexico and various European battle fronts during World War I, was in Russia with his wife when the October Revolution began. While there, he developed a friendship with V. I. Lenin and gathered material for his most notable work,* Ten Days that Shook the World. *After returning to America, he formed the Communist Labor party in the United States, was arrested several times for incendiary speeches, and eventually indicted for sedition. He fled to the Soviet Union where he died in 1920 from typhus. He was given a state funeral and buried in the Kremlin.*

. . .Passing under the huge grey stone archway of the Moskovsky Gate, covered with golden hieroglyphics, ponderous Imperial eagles and the names of Tsars, we sped out on the wide straight highway, grey with the first light fall of snow. It was thronged with Red Guards, stumbling along on foot toward the revolutionary front, shouting and singing; and others, grey-faced and muddy, coming back. Most of them seemed to be mere boys. Women with spades, some with rifles and bandoleers, others wearing the Red Cross on their arm-bands—the bowed, toil-worn women of the slums. Squads of soldiers marching out of step, with an affectionate jeer for the Red Guards; sailors, grim-looking; children with bundles of food for their fathers and mothers; all these, coming and going, trudged through the whitened mud that covered the cobbles of the highway inches deep. We passed cannon, jingling southward with their caissons; trucks bound both ways, bristling with armed men; ambulances full of wounded

from the direction of the battle, and once a peasant cart, creaking slowly along, in which sat a white-faced boy bent over his shattered stomach and screaming monotonously. In the fields on either side women and old men were digging trenches and stringing barbed wire entanglements.

Back northward the clouds rolled away dramatically, and the pale sun came out. Across the flat, marshy plain Petrograd glittered. To the right, white and gilded and coloured bulbs and pinnacles; to the left, tall chimneys, some pouring out black smoke; and beyond, a lowering sky over Finland. On each side of us were churches, monasteries. . . . Occasionally a monk was visible, silently watching the pulse of the proletarian army throbbing on the road.

At Pulkovo the road divided, and there we halted in the midst of a great crowd, where the human streams poured from three directions, friends meeting, excited and congratulatory, describing the battle to one another. A row of houses facing the cross-roads was marked with bullets, and the earth was trampled into mud half a mile around. The fighting had been furious here. . . . In the near distance riderless Cossack horses circled hungrily, for the grass of the plain had died long ago. Right in front of us an awkward Red Guard was trying to ride one, falling off again and again, to the childlike delight of a thousand rough men.

The left road, along which the remnants of the Cossacks had retreated, led up a little hill to a hamlet, where there was a glorious view of the immense plain, grey as a windless sea, tumultuous clouds towering over, and the imperial city disgorging its thousands along all the roads. Far over to the left lay the little hill of Kranoye Selo, the parade-ground of the Imperial Guards' summer camp, and the Imperial Dairy. In the middle distance nothing broke the flat monotony but a few walled monasteries and convents, some isolated factories, and several large buildings with unkempt grounds that were asylums and orphanages. . . .

"Here," said the driver, as we went on over a barren hill, "here was where Vera Slutskaya died. Yes, the Bolshevik member of the Duma. It happened early this morning. She was in an automobile, with Zalkind and another man. There was a truce, and they started for the front trenches. They were talking and laughing, when all of a sudden, from the armoured train in which Kerensky himself was riding, somebody saw the automobile and fired a cannon. The shell struck Vera Slutskaya and killed her. . . ."

And so we came into Tsarskoye, all bustling with the swaggering heroes of the proletarian horde. Now the palace where the Soviet had met was a busy place. Red Guards and sailors filled the court-yard, sentries stood at the doors, and a stream of couriers and Commissars pushed in and out. In the Soviet room a samovar had been set up, and fifty or more workers, soldiers, sailors and officers stood around, drinking tea and talking at the top of their voices. In one corner two clumsy-handed workingmen were trying to make a multigraphing machine go. At the centre table, the huge Dybenko bent over a map, marking out positions for the troops with red and blue pencils. In his free hand he carried, as always, the enormous bluesteel revolver. Anon he sat himself down at a typewriter and pounded away with one finger; every little while he would pause, pick up the revolver, and lovingly spin the chamber.

A couch lay along the wall, and on this was stretched a young workman. Two Red Guards were bending over him, but the rest of the company did not pay any attention. In his breast was a hole; through his clothes fresh blood came welling up with every heart-beat. His eyes were closed and his young, bearded face was greenish-white. Faintly and slowly he still breathed, with every breath sighing, "Mir boudit! Mir boudit! (Peace is coming! Peace is coming!)". . .

SEE ALSO *USSR: Dissolution; World War I; World War II*

BIBLIOGRAPHY

Books

Borrero, Mauricio. *Hungry Moscow: Scarcity and Urban Society in the Russian Civil War, 1917–1921.* New York: Peter Lang Press, 2003.

Lih, Lars, T. *Bread and Authority in Russia: 1914–1921.* Berkeley: University of California Press, 1990.

Massie, Robert. *Nicholas and Alexandra.* New York: Ballantine Books, 2000.

Web Sites

"Lenin Internet Archive: Biography: Timeline of V. I. Lenin." *Marxists.org.* http://www.marxists.org/archive/lenin/bio/timeline.htm (accessed September 5, 2013).

"Russian Revolution." *Fordham.edu.* http://www.fordham.edu/halsall/mod/modsbook39.asp (accessed September 5, 2013).

Smele, Jonathan. "War and Revolution in Russia: 1914–1921." *BBC.com,* March 10, 2011. http://www.bbc.co.uk/history/worldwars/wwone/eastern_front_01.shtml (accessed September 5, 2013).

Rwandan Genocide

⊕ Introduction

Over a period of 100 days in April and May of 1994, the ethnic Hutu people of Rwanda, which comprise a majority of the population, slaughtered between 800,000 and one million ethnic Tutsis, as well as tens of thousands of sympathetic Hutus. In all, an estimated 10 percent of the Rwandan population was killed, and an even higher percentage fled the violence by summer. The violence was well organized by the Rwandan government and reported on by the media and United Nations (UN) observers. No one intervened to stop the killing.

⊕ Historical Background

Rwanda, with a total population of nearly 8 million people in 1994, is an area smaller than the U.S. state of Maryland and one of the most crowded nations in Africa. Tension over land ownership in Rwanda can be explosive, and the country lacks enough industries to employ the people living in its cities.

Three African ethnic groups inhabit Rwanda: the Tutsi, the Hutu, and the tiny population of the Twa. These groups coexisted for centuries. Tutsis held the highest social status, but a Hutu could advance to the status of a Tutsi. The general population intermarried and lived in ethnically mixed communities. The two groups fought in the same army and shared the same religion, language, and political culture. Although there is no biological evidence of difference among the races, many Rwandans perceive physical distinctions between the Tutsi and Hutu. According to most scholars, these distinctions are not physically apparent, but they have become cultural perceptions of difference.

German Colonists Separate Ethnic Groups

In 1899, German forces conquered the Tutsi kingdom. The Germans issued ethnic identity cards to separate the

© 2014 Cengage Learning

ethnic groups and advanced Tutsis to leadership positions and better jobs, heightening tensions between the two groups. After World War I (1914–18), Belgium administered Rwanda as a trust territory until independence. Like the Germans, the Belgians instituted a

447

classification system, sorting all native people as either Tutsis or Hutus and granting Tutsi chiefs nearly all of the power. Inequalities persisted until about 1959, when the frustrated Hutus rose up in a series of violent riots against the Tutsis. Belgium gave Rwanda its independence in 1961 and called for democratic elections. Because 85 percent of the population of Rwanda was Hutu, the Tutsis lost power to the Hutu. More than 750,000 Tutsis migrated to Uganda and Tanzania.

HOTEL RWANDA

In 2004, the movie *Hotel Rwanda* was released to critical acclaim. The movie depicted the story of a hero of the Rwandan Genocide. As Tutsis ran for their lives, one man, Paul Rusesabagina (1954–), a Hutu married to a Tutsi, offered them sanctuary in the Hotel des Mille Collines in Kigali, the capital of Rwanda. Saving hundreds of Tutsi, moderate Hutus, and others by keeping them in the hotel, Rusesabagina faced down the Hutu militia. More than 1,200 people were sheltered at the hotel from the genocide happening around them. They survived due to Rusesabagina's business connections with powerful Hutus and bribes and negotiations with the militia and government.

The survivors were there for over three months, living off of smuggled food and eventually drinking pool water when the water supply was cut. Rusesabagina's story of bravery and commitment to human life was inspiring. He was given several awards for his heroism and his continued humanitarian work, including the Congressional Medal of Freedom given to him by U.S. President George W. Bush in 2005 and the Lantos Foundation Award in 2011. Rusesabagina formed the Hotel Rwanda Rusesabagina Foundation to advocate a Rwandan Truth and Reconciliation commission and fight genocide. He gives speeches throughout the world.

Rusesabagina's story was challenged several years after the movie was released. Some survivors and UN observers claimed that he demanded payment from those who were sheltering at the hotel. Furthermore, some stated that the hotel was spared due to the large number of foreign reporters and observers rather than Rusesabagina's influence. In 2010, Rusesabagina was charged by the Rwandan government with helping finance terrorist activities in Rwanda by sending money to Forces Democratiques de Liberation du Rwanda (FDLR), a Hutu rebel group centered in the Democratic Republic of the Congo.

Rusesabagina, who left Rwanda in 1996 and now lives in exile in Brussels with his wife and children, said the charges are false, politically motivated, and part of a smear campaign against him sparked by his continued public criticism of Rwandan president Paul Kagame, a Tutsi who is also the former head of the Rwandan Patriotic Front. Kagame's government has been accused by human rights groups of silencing opposition leaders and tightly controlling the Rwandan media. Though the Belgian government questioned Rusesabagina on the financing of terrorism charges in 2011, as of early 2014, he has never been extradited or convicted of any crime.

In 1973, General Juvenal Habyarimana (1937–1994), a Hutu, overthrew Rwanda's president, beginning a 20-year dictatorship. Habyarimana and his close circle of advisers favored the Hutus, particularly the elite. Habyarimana established rigid ethnic quotas and expelled Tutsis from politics, government, businesses, and schools. Many Tutsis left Rwanda for neighboring countries.

Beginning around 1979, Tutsi exiles in Uganda formed a rebel group called the Rwandan Patriotic Front (RPF). The RPF regularly launched raids into Rwanda in an attempt to destabilize the government. Rwanda's shaky economy deteriorated. By 1990, the RPF had initiated a civil war against the government of Rwanda. In 1993, a multinational attempt to broker peace in Rwanda resulted in the Arusha Agreement, under which Tutsi refugees were granted safe return to Rwanda. Habyarimana and the RPF pledged to form a transitional government and to hold multiparty elections in 1995. The United Nations issued a UN Assistance Mission in Rwanda (UNAMIR)—2,500 troops from several nations—to monitor the peace settlement.

Habyarimana's Death Sparks Rampage

Even while laying the foundations for a coalition government, though, both sides continued to fight. The Rwandan military strongly opposed the Arusha settlement and stepped up its attacks against Tutsis. Opposition also came from Habyarimana's own party and the Committee for the Defense of the Republic (CDR), a Hutu extremist organization. The RPF fought on as well. The tiny UN peacekeeping force was unable to bring about peace. The peacekeepers remained in Rwanda as witnesses of what was to come.

On April 6, 1994, as Habyarimana flew to Dar es Salaam, Tanzania, for a round of peace talks, his plane was shot down. Habyarimana and the president of Burundi were both killed. No one knew who was behind the killing, but the assassination inflamed Rwanda's extremist Hutus, who immediately sent out an order for Rwanda's mayors, militias, and death squads to start killing the Tutsis.

Neighbors Killing Neighbors

The genocide began with the assassination of every Tutsi in the government cabinet. Death lists were established and everyone on them was hunted down and killed. The *Interahamwe* (those who attack together), an unofficial militia group of about 30,000 fighters, was organized. Radios broadcast the command for all Hutus to join the campaign to kill the Tutsis. The speed and level of the violence shocked many. Hutu gangs armed with swords, spears, and machetes attacked Tutsis, hacking, clubbing, or beating them to death.

The Tutsis fled, gathering in central locations, such as hospitals, churches, and stadiums. At first their numbers protected them, but soon the national army,

Wounded refugees from south western Kibeho camp in Rwanda rest as UN soldiers mount guard.   © *Alexander Joe/AFP/Getty Images*

Presidential Guard, and national police arrived bearing rifles, grenades, and machine guns. Hutu militias threw hand grenades into the buildings housing the Tutsis. Anyone who ran out was shot, and Tutsis remaining alive inside were hacked to death. Many who survived the initial killings were raped and mutilated. An estimated 20,000 people died per day during the worst part of the slaughter. Moderate Hutus were often killed to discourage other Hutus from sympathizing with Tutsi victims. Some were forced under threat of death or torture to kill their Tutsi neighbors.

Tutsi's Fight Back

The slaughter convinced the RPF that it had to defeat the Hutu government or face the total extermination of the Tutsis. By late July 1994, just four months after the killing began, the Tutsi rebel group had gained control of essentially all of Rwanda and the war ended. The RPF established a government in accordance with the principles outlined in the Arusha Agreement.

The new government was faced with rebuilding a collapsed nation with little economic or political structure and with a huge percentage of its population living in other countries as refugees. In fact, as the war ended, more than 2 million Hutu refugees crossed the border into Zaire (now the Democratic Republic of the Congo, or DRC), Burundi, and Tanzania, including many of those responsible for orchestrating the Tutsi murders. Some used the Hutu refugee camps as a staging area for guerrilla attacks on Rwanda's new government as it struggled to restore order and peace to the country.

In September 2010, a leaked UN report that accused Rwanda's Tutsi-led army of genocide of Hutus during the 1990s caused an uproar in Rwanda, sparking protests by citizens and threats by the government to pull Rwandans out of UN peace-keeping missions. The leaked report said that after the 1994 genocide the Tutsi-led Rwandan army killed tens of thousands of Hutus in the DRC, its neighbor to the west. The report also accused Congolese troops of participating in the killing of Hutus. The UN high commissioner on human rights announced that the official publication of the report would be delayed to allow for comments from the Rwandan government. The report, released on October 1, 2010, asserted Rwandan, Ugandan, and Burundian fighters committed acts against the Hutus that may constitute genocide. It details 617 incidents, the most serious of which occurred in 1996 and 1997. Rwanda has firmly rejected the report. The UN has promised to launch a full judicial investigation.

A United Nations representative photographs the remains of slain Tutsis on September 16, 1994, at a church in Ntarama, Rwanda. The bodies of 400 Tutsis murdered by Hutu militiamen were found in the church at Ntarama by an Australian-led UN team.
© *Scott Peterson/Hulton Archive/Getty Images*

⊕ Impacts and Issues

The Rwandan genocide reflects the deep tribal animosity that exists in many parts of Africa, but rarely expresses itself in such a brutal way. The reluctance of the international community to become involved in this desperate situation allowed the situation to continue and hundreds of thousands to be killed. The country has struggled to come to terms with the genocide, however in the 20 years following the violence, the country has generally been stable.

Recovery

In the decade following the war, most of Rwanda's refugees returned home, though a small troop of rebels remained in the DRC and continued to attack Rwanda. Rwanda had its first post-genocide national elections in 2003, electing Paul Kagame (1957–), the former leader of the RPF, who had been the de facto president since 2000. The government under Kagame has been repressive in terms of freedom of speech and the right to dissent. Rwanda has been involved in wars in the DRC that threaten its fragile peace. But many observers comment

on the economic and political stability of Rwanda. The country's new leaders have made health and education services a priority. The movement toward reconciliation is complicated but ongoing.

Rwanda's economy proved surprisingly resilient in the face of the global economic downturn of 2008 and 2009. Government figures released in 2009 showed that agricultural production in 2008 leaped by 15 percent and that tourism increased by 30 percent between 2007 and 2008. Overall, Rwanda's economy grew by an impressive 11.2 percent in 2008, even as much of the world plunged into recession. The drastically improved agricultural output in Rwanda has also led to much better nutrition for the country's populace.

War Crimes and Crimes against Humanity

The international community reeled as the details of the genocide in Rwanda became known. But the overall facts of the violence had actually been known to the world as it occurred. UNAMIR and a contingent of journalists had been on hand observing and reporting the violence. The failure of the UN and other countries to stop the genocide in Rwanda remains a bitter issue

Genocide suspect Bernard Munyagishari (C) is escorted by police upon his arrival at Kigali airport in Rwanda on July 24, 2013. Munyagishari was transferred from the International Criminal Tribunal for Rwanda (ICTR) based in Arusha, Tanzania. It is the second time that the UN-backed ICTR has transferred a genocide suspect to Rwanda. *© Stephanie Aglietti/AFP/Getty Images*

of contention many years after the killings. UNAMIR, strengthened after the genocide, maintained a presence in Rwanda until 1996 in an effort to provide stability as the new government established itself. The UN also established an international tribunal in Rwanda to try those accused of genocide.

Former Rwandan army chief Augustin Bizimungu was sentenced to 30 years in prison on May 17, 2011, by the International Criminal Tribunal for Rwanda (ICTR), a court established in Tanzania specifically to try those accused of orchestrating the Rwandan genocide. Bizimungu directly ordered the massacres of Tutsis. Augustin Ndindiliyimana, former head of the paramilitary police force in Rwanda, faced the same charges as Bizimungu and was also found guilty; however, he was released for time served (he had already been in prison for 11 years since being arrested in Belgium) because the judges decided he had exerted only "limited" control of his men. Bernard Munyagishari, a Rwandan militia leader on the run for 17 years, was arrested in the Democratic Republic of Congo on May 26, 2011. Munyagishari is the alleged mastermind of attacks on Tutsis in Gisenyi, a resort city in Rwanda. He faces genocide, murder, and rape charges at the ICTR.

Individual countries have also made some effort to prosecute those implicated in the genocide. In May 2009, a Canadian court found Rwandan Desire Munyaneza (1966–) guilty of genocide, war crimes, and crimes against humanity in connection with the Rwandan genocide. In October 2009, he was sentenced to life in prison. In December 2009, Mozambique announced that it would fully cooperate with Rwandan investigators and hand over all genocide suspects to Rwandan authorities. French president Nicolas Sarkozy (1955–) visited Rwanda in March 2010 and pledged to ensure that any Rwandans living in France who were involved in the genocide would be found and punished. However, most who participated in the killing have not been prosecuted.

⊕ Future Implications

The genocide in Rwanda did not happen in secret. The brutality was widely reported as it was going on, but the international community did not intervene. Rwanda continues to bear the scars—literal and figurative—of the organized massacre of the Tutsis. And the international community continues to discuss how it let genocide happen.

Some critics contend that the UN didn't intervene because the genocide was taking place in an African country—that if the same thing happened in a European country, the West would quickly intercede. The genocide happened about six months after the Battle for Mogadishu in Somalia, where UN peacekeeping forces were brutally attacked, killed, and mutilated. Some defenders claim that the full extent of the killing was not known, nor was it clear what could be done and how to do it. Regardless, the lack of intervention to stop genocide in Rwanda has become a rallying cry to encourage intervention in violent countries around the world.

PRIMARY SOURCE

Testimony of Helen, a Survivor of the Rwandan Genocide

SOURCE *Helen. "Testimony of Helen, a Survivor of the Rwandan Genocide." Part of Testimonies Given on the 15th Anniversary of the Rwandan Genocide, April 7, 2009, from Survivors Fund (SURF).* United Nations Department of Public Information. The Outreach Programme on the Rwanda Genocide and the United Nations. *http://www.un.org/en/ preventgenocide/rwanda/testimonies/pdf/79%20 -%20Helen2009.pdf (accessed October 14, 2013). Copyright © 2009 by Survivors Fund.*

INTRODUCTION *The British nonprofit group Survivors Fund has collected the stories of survivors of the Rwandan genocide. Some of these were read on the 15th anniversary of the genocide at the United Nations Remembrance Ceremony at the Trusteeship Council at UN Headquarters in New York. This is the story of Helen, one of the survivors.*

I was only sixteen when I witnessed the genocide. My entire family was slaughtered in the massacres of 1994. For four months, I managed to survive alone, running from swamp to swamp, hiding in shrubs and abandoned homes, all the time hiding from the killers. Eventually a family friend found me wondering the street. She recognised me and, horrified about my physical and mental deterioration, she helped me.

For sometime before the genocide, feelings against Tutsis were intense. Everyone knew that something terrible was going to happen. When the time finally came, the attackers came running into our houses, screaming and singing songs about how they were going to kill us all. There was this huge noise, like a massive swarm of bees descending on the house. All the children managed to run away. But my energy just left me. I was drained. But I did manage to climb and hide in a nearby mango tree. They didn't see me. They chased the children, then went into the house and killed everyone in there my

mother, my father, my grandmother, all the people hiding there. I didn't see it but I could hear the crying; the moaning; the screaming. Then the screaming stopped, and I knew everyone was dead.

At one point, I saw my mother try to run away. She made it out of the door, but they killed her under the tree with machetes. When the killing was done, they pulled all the bodies out of the house and into the courtyard. I couldn't recognise anyone. They were all cut up. Disfigured. Dismembered. Unrecongisable.

After the people left, I stayed hiding in the tree for many hours. I was numb. I couldn't think. Then the wild dogs arrived. They were moving the bodies around, scavenging for food, eating the people. I couldn't bear to watch, so I climbed down from the tree and ran. From that day on I kept running, joining this group and that, not really knowing where I was going. I just made a conscious decision to keep moving, to never stop. I wouldn't eat for so long, that when I was finally given food I couldn't even open my mouth.

Whilst I was on the run, I found a group of Hutu men who knew me. For a week they kept me and raped me. They used me like everyone else. They would leave every day, then come back at night and boast about how many people they had killed. I thought that I might as well try and escape. I would die anyway. For me, at that time it didn't matter if it was a bullet or a machete that killed me.

My family killers were never caught. Without justice, I don't feel safe. I fear Hutus may come and finish the business they started. I have tried to move on, and have had a few friendships. But they haven't worked out because of me. It's my fault. I make sure it doesn't happen. I just can't cope with the extra responsibility. My big passion is to have a child, somebody to live for. But how can I do that, when my life is just one big nightmare of unanswered questions? Bad times are so bad. People think the genocide is in the past, but I live with it still. Everywhere there is something that reminds me it. I no longer have a sister or mother. I'm not jealous, just so sad. Sometimes all I want is to be with my parents again. I just want to finish it. I want it to stop.

SEE ALSO *African Union; Democratic Republic of the Congo; International Law and Justice; United Nations*

BIBLIOGRAPHY

Books

Gourevitch, Philip. *We Wish to Inform You That Tomorrow We Will Be Killed with Our Families: Stories from Rwanda.* New York: Farrar, Straus, and Giroux, 1998.

Prunier, Gérard. *Africa's World War: Congo, the Rwandan Genocide, and the Making of a Continental Catastrophe.* New York: Oxford University Press, 2009.

Periodicals

Baldauf, Scott. "Legacy of Rwanda's Genocide: More Assertive International Justice." *The Christian Science Monitor* (April 7, 2009).

Kayigamba, Jean Baptiste. "Haunted Mornings, Sleepless Nights: Jean Baptiste Kayigamba Describes How He Survived Genocide in Rwanda." *New Internationalist* (June 2006).

Wallis, Andrew. "Even Now, World Fails Rwanda." *USA Today* (April 28, 2010): 9A.

Web Sites

Genocide Archive Rwanda. http://www.genocidearchiverwanda.org.rw/index.php/Welcome_to_Genocide_Archive_Rwanda (accessed July 10, 2013).

"Rwanda: How the Genocide Happened." *BBC News*, December 18, 2008. http://news.bbc.co.uk/2/hi/1288230.stm (accessed July 10, 2013).

"Timeline." *Frontline*. http://www.pbs.org/wgbh/pages/frontline/shows/ghosts/etc/cron.html (accessed July 10, 2013).

"World Prosecutes Rwanda's Genocide." *Agence France-Presse*, June 21, 2013. http://www.globalpost.com/dispatch/news/afp/130621/the-world-prosecutes-rwandas-genocide (accessed July 10, 2013).

Sierra Leone's Civil War

⊕ Introduction

Sierra Leone suffered through a brutal civil war that saw the deaths of 50,000 people between 1991 and 2002. Rebels went into villages, viciously cutting off the arms or legs of men, women, and children, leaving them as living symbols of the power and ruthlessness of rebel forces. While Sierra Leone does not have the highest amputee rate in the world (that country is Cambodia), what is unusual is that its large number of amputations was caused by axes and machetes, and very often involved the loss of both arms, leaving the victim incapable of using crutches or a wheelchair.

It took United Nations (UN) and British military intervention to finally bring an end to the war. Though its reputation is marred by wartime involvement in illegal diamond mining, in the years after the war the West African nation enjoyed substantial economic growth and a stable, democratically elected government.

⊕ Historical Background

Sierra Leone is located on the west coast of Africa and is bordered by Guinea to the north and east, Liberia to the southeast, and the Atlantic Ocean to the south and west. In addition to the mainland, the country includes the offshore Banana and Turtle islands and Sherbro Island. The population of Sierra Leone is estimated at 5.6 million (as of 2013) and is composed of 90 percent native Africans from some 20 ethnic groups. The largest of these groups are the Temne (35 percent) and the Mende (31 percent). English is the official language, but is used regularly only by the literate minority. The Temne and Mende tongues are spoken widely in the north and south. Sierra Leone's population is 60 percent Muslim, 10 percent Christian, and 30 percent practitioners of indigenous religions.

Sierra Leone was raided for slaves during the Atlantic slave trade from the 16th through the early 19th century, during which time it was settled by the British. It became an independent nation in 1961 but suffered constant political unrest. In 1985, General Joseph Saidu Momoh (1937–2003) became president, leading an administration notorious for its corruption and ineffectiveness. Civil war broke out in Sierra Leone in 1991 when a group of young rebels called the Revolutionary United Front (RUF) rose up against the government, unseating Momoh in 1992. Though initially claiming to fight a corrupt administration, the RUF rebels quickly realized that their most effective route to power and wealth lay in controlling Sierra Leone's diamond mines. By 1994 the RUF had seized large parts of the country, including the mines. The rebels smuggled the diamonds into neighboring Liberia; from there they were sold to world markets. The diamonds funded a gruesome civil war, known especially for its use of child soldiers.

Civil War

As Sierra Leone faced its own escalating civil war, neighboring Liberia, also rich in diamonds, endured a similar conflict that killed more than 200,000 people and left millions homeless. Liberian President Charles Taylor (1948–), himself a rebel before gaining power 1997, threw his support behind the RUF, funding his own war with so-called "blood diamonds" (diamonds forcibly mined under dangerous and often deadly circumstances) from Sierra Leone.

The RUF had support from the special forces of the National Patriotic Front of Liberia as authorized by Liberia's President Taylor. The Sierra Leone Army (SLA) fought the RUF with ferocious brutality. After capturing an area from rebels, they often moved all the civilians to "strategic hamlets." While the SLA claimed the move was designed to keep the civilians safe from

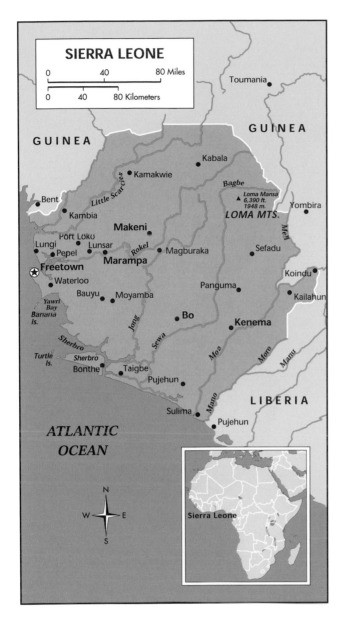

SIERRA LEONE

© 2014 Cengage Learning

the rebels, it allowed the SLA to loot the villages in the civilians' absence.

In 1992 young military officers overthrew President Joseph Momoh (1937–2003), one of many violent changes of power in Sierra Leone. The new leader, Valentine Strasser (1967–) was also overthrown by his own officers in 1996. In that year democratic elections were held, and Ahmad Tejan Kabbah (1932–) was elected president. He tried unsuccessfully to broker a peace between the RUF and the SLA, but the SLA continued to fight the rebels. However, they often had to concede large amounts of territory to them.

The distinctions between the soldiers of the SLA and the rebels and ad hoc militia groups were not always clear. Soldiers were often called "Sobels," which means "soldiers by day, rebels by night." The inability of the local population to distinguish friend from foe and the brutality of both the SLA and the RUF forced the civilians to organize local militias. Kamajors were local groups dedicated to defending specific families and their homes. Primarily of the Mende ethnic group, Kamajors were later used as militia throughout the country on behalf of the SLA.

Private Armies

In 1995, Executive Outcomes, a South African-based private military company, was hired to beat back the RUF. Executive Outcomes was created from former members of the South African Defence Force. As South Africa's wars in Namibia and Angola wound down in 1989, and with budget cuts from the government going into effect, some members of the Defence Force formed a private military that could be hired to provide strategic advice and training or actual military services. Executive Outcomes was not affiliated with any political or religious group and would sell its services to anyone who would pay. In Sierra Leone, they were able to beat back the RUF and reclaim control of the diamond fields, forcing the RUF into a short-lived peace agreement.

The agreement was called the Abidjan Peace Accords. It required that the contract with Executive Outcomes be terminated and that they leave Sierra Leone within 5 weeks of the arrival of international peacekeeping troops. The peacekeeping force proved no match for the RUF, which renewed attacks. Members of the SLA, demoralized and with little faith in the government, freed 600 people from prison, including Johnny Paul Koroma (1960–), who headed the Armed Forces Revolutionary Council (AFRC), a group of Sierra Leone soldiers who fought with the RUF. They staged a coup, forcing President Kabbah into exile, and made Koroma the new president in 1997.

The Economic Community of West African States (ECOWAS) protested the coup, and demanded that the government be reinstated. In 1997, the RUF and ARFC agreed to a preliminary peace plan, the Conakry Peace Plan, though they continued to fight. The Economic Communities of West African States Monitoring Group (ECOMOG) retook the capital, Freetown, and reestablished Kabbah as president in 1998. But in 1999 the RUF and ARFC terrorized Freetown in an mission called "Operation No Living Thing," which resulted in more than 7,000 deaths.

Peace and Disarmament

Finally, in July of 1999, all sides signed the Lome Peace Agreement, in which the RUF agreed to disarm. The RUF agreed to this in exchange for a raft of pardons that prohibited prosecution for treason and other crimes, as well as positions in government. Disarmament was to be monitored by ECOMOG and the UN.

BLOOD DIAMONDS

In Sierra Leone, as in several other African countries, profits from diamond mining enabled rebels to fight for long periods of time. Diamond sales paid for weapons, transportation, food, and other necessities for the rebel troops. Because of their use to fund violence, they have been nicknamed "blood diamonds." Blood diamonds have been around for at least a century, but it was their use in the civil wars in Angola and Sierra Leone in the 1990s that drew international attention. Since then, measures to isolate blood diamonds from the world's legitimate diamond production have been credited with reducing some, but by no means all, diamond-connected violence in Africa.

By the turn of the 21st century, critics began to blame at least part of the devastation caused by blood diamonds on the legitimate international diamond traders who purchased them. At that time, the world's leading diamond enterprise, De Beers Consolidated Mines Ltd. of South Africa, had a large stockpile of diamonds it wished to sell. Anxious to avoid boycotts and bad press, in March 2000 De Beers declared it would guarantee that none of its diamonds came from war zones. The company then informed its trading partners that unless they agreed to do the same, De Beers would no longer do business with them.

In July 2000, the UN Security Council voted to impose a ban on diamonds from Sierra Leone, as it had done the previous year in Angola. In 2001, the Security Council imposed sanctions on diamond exports from Liberia, which had reportedly been supporting the RUF by smuggling its gems and providing arms to the rebels. Around that time, al-Qaeda, the militant organization claiming responsibility for many terrorist attacks, had become a buyer of blood diamonds from rebel groups in Africa, according to numerous sources.

When the Hollywood movie *Blood Diamond,* a Leonardo DiCaprio blockbuster about traffickers of the precious gems, was released in 2006, pressure groups tested a new way to deliver their message through an alliance with Hollywood. Its showing in the United States, where half the world's diamond output is sold, triggered an avalanche of articles on war diamonds and forced the diamond industry to counter attack with a 15-million-dollar public relations campaign.

A diamond prospector filters earth on September 28, 2001, in Koidu, Eastern Sierra Leone, some 155 miles (250 kilometers) east of Freetown. Sierra Leone's infamous blood diamonds still were being mined with impunity despite a government ban on the trade. © *Georges Gobet/AFP/Getty Images*

In October 1999, the United Nations Mission to Sierra Leone (UNAMSIL) was established.

In 2001, the disarmament of the rebels began. Rebels were provided with food and shelter in exchange for turning in their weapons. Former rebels were quarantined for 6 weeks in a DDR (Disarmament, Demobilization, and Reintegration) camp, where they were taught how to live in a peaceful society. In 2002, Sierra Leone's long civil war officially ended. Sierra Leone voted in watershed presidential and parliamentary elections in 2007 that were seen as a test of whether the west African nation had turned a page from its decade-long civil war fuelled by blood diamonds.

⊕ Impacts and Issues

President Kabbah was reelected by a landslide in 2004, and another successful democratic election in 2007 gave the power to Ernest Bai Koroma. Koroma (1953–)

A picture taken on April 7, 2006, shows players of the Sierra Leone civil war amputees football team on a beach in Freetown. Many civilians lost limbs to land mines, bullets, or mutilations by rebel forces to enforce silence or compliance during the West African nation's bloody civil war.   © *Issouf Sanogo/AFP/Getty Images*

was reelected in 2009 and 2012. During these years, attempts were made to stabilize the government and punish some of the worst perpetrators of violence.

UN Special Court of Sierra Leone

Like many other countries plagued by protracted civil violence, Sierra Leone established a Truth and Reconciliation Committee. The Truth and Reconciliation Committee provided a forum for victims to tell their stories and for the perpetrators of violence to confess. In addition, the UN Special Court of Sierra Leone was established in 2004 to oversee the trials of leaders of the pro-government militias, the Civil Defense Force (the Kamajors), and the RUF.

Former Liberian president Charles Taylor, who faced 17 counts of war crimes associated with the support his forces provided to the RUF, was exiled in Nigeria until March 2006, when Nigerian authorities handed him over to the UN. After several delays,

Taylor's trial began at the International Criminal Court in 2007, with UN justices presiding.

Throughout the trial, Taylor adamantly maintained his innocence, denying any involvement in the atrocities that occurred during the Sierra Leone civil war. In April 2012, the court convicted Taylor on 11 counts of war crimes and crimes against humanity, including murder, rape, torture, terrorism, and the conscription of child soldiers. Although the court also found him guilty of providing significant support to the RUF (particularly through the supply of weapons), and having knowledge of the criminal actions of the RUF, the judges ruled that he could not be held responsible for ordering the crimes committed by that group. They stated that the prosecution had not proven its case beyond a reasonable doubt. On 30 May 2012, Taylor, age 64, was sentenced to 50 years in a British prison. Taylor filed an official appeal against the ruling in June 2012. Taylor began serving the remainder of his 50-year sentence in Britain at an undisclosed prison in October 2013.

DISARMAMENT, DEMOBILIZATION, AND REINTEGRATION

Disarmament, demobilization, and reintegration (DDR) programs are part of the process of building peace and reconciliation in many societies that have undergone lengthy conflicts. United Nations agencies have coordinated dozens of such programs in Africa, often in conjunction with peace-keeping operations, national governments, and non-governmental organizations. Typically the DDR process begins with disarmament; ex-combatants register with authorities, turn in their weapons to peacekeepers, receive an identification card and, often, a cash benefit, and are transferred to cantonments where they may remain for several weeks. The demobilized ex-combatants, their armed units disbanded, receive civic education, job training, and psychological counseling. Former child soldiers are a focus of special concern and are sometimes reconnected with their families or with foster parents. Reintegration into civil society is often the most difficult phase. Ideally, those who complete the program are eligible for employment and may receive an additional stipend; however, finding legitimate employment in post-conflict societies can be a nearly impossible task.

Following the conclusion of the Lome Peace Agreement in 1999, according to figures from Sierra Leone's national DDR commission, roughly 24,000 adults and children had been demobilized by 2000, and over 70,000 three years later. However, significant problems marred the DDR program. A number of those who passed through the program may not have been combatants but civilians simply seeking to obtain benefits. Only a small number of the child soldiers who took part in the conflict entered DDR. Former militia commanders, who played a key role in the process on the ground, appear to have been responsible for a great deal of petty corruption. Commanders were tasked with providing lists of ex-combatants to program administrators, but some inserted the names of friends and family members, denying the real ex-combatants a place—or demanding kickbacks from their cash stipends. Some others, particularly Kamajors, were unable to access DDR programs because they did not possess weapons of their own to turn in.

⊕ Future Implications

As in many other wars, the civil war in Sierra Leone was especially hard on the children. Entire generations have grown up without knowing peace. Youth illiteracy and unemployment remain very high. In April 2009, Save the Children revealed in a report that "children often make up the majority of victims of rape and sexual abuse in many of the world's war zones." According to the children's rights group, 70 percent of the sexual violence cases in Sierra Leone since 2012 involved girls under age 18, with more than a fifth of those cases involving girls under age 11. Creating an environment where the affected children (some of whom are now

adults) can heal and become productive citizens is a major challenge for Sierra Leone.

Sierra Leone is further hampered by pervasive corruption. While still rich in natural resources, the majority of the country's population remains impoverished. About 70 percent of the young people in Sierra Leone live on less than $2 a day. In 2013, Sierra Leone's diamond exports were up 43 percent.

Prosecution of the perpetrators of the violence has dwindled. Some of the worst offenders emerged from hiding, but Sierra Leone's government has chosen, in most cases, not to prosecute them, but to deport them instead. In August 2013, Ibrahim Bah (also known as Ibrahim Baldeh) an ally of Taylor's accused of aiding the RUF rebels, surfaced. He was to stand trial in Sierra Leone on charges of kidnapping and wounding with intent, but was deported instead.

PRIMARY SOURCE

Bai Koroma's Presidential Address

SOURCE *Bai Koroma, Ernest. "Presidential Address Delivered by His Excellency the President Ernest Bai Koroma on the Occasion of the State Opening of the Third Parliament of Sierra Leone." Sierra Leone Web, October 5, 2007. http://www.sierra-leone.org/ Speeches/koroma-100507.html (accessed November 5, 2013).*

INTRODUCTION *Ernest Bai Koroma, business leader and former secondary school teacher, stepped into the international spotlight in 2002, when he first ran for president in Sierra Leone, which was emerging from more than a decade of brutal civil war. Though he lost that race, he maintained a leadership position in the All People's Congress (APC), one of the country's strongest parties, and in 2007 he ran again, this time successfully. His victory marked the first time since independence in 1961 that power had passed peacefully from one party to another in Sierra Leone. Upon taking office, Koroma faced many serious challenges, including poverty, corruption, mismanagement of natural resources, and serious deficiencies in the nation's infrastructure, caused in part by the long civil war. Koroma won a second term as president in 2012 with more than 58 percent of the vote.*

Sierra Leone Government

Presidential Address Delivered by His Excellency the President Ernest Bai Koroma

President of the Republic and Commander-in-Chief of the Republic of Sierra Leone Armed Forces

On the Occasion of the State Opening of the Third Parliament of the Second Republic of Sierra Leone

Employees of a polling station watch voters during the first round of presidential elections August 11, 2007, in Freetown. © *Issouf Sanogo/ AFP/Getty Images*

In the Chamber of Parliament Building Tower Hill, Freetown

On Friday, 5th October; 2007 at 10:00 a.m.

Mr. Speaker,
Honourable Vice-President,
My Lord Chief Justice,
His Worship the Mayor of Freetown
Honourable Members of Parliament,
Excellencies, Members of the Diplomatic Corps
Distinguished Guests,
Ladies and Gentlemen:

1. It is the will of God and the consent of the people of this great nation of ours, that I address you here today as President on the occasion of the state opening of the Third Parliament of the Second Republic of Sierra Leone.

2. I must take this opportunity to thank all Sierra Leoneans who reposed their confidence in me, by electing me President of this great nation. I am grateful for your commitment to the democratic process and I will execute the duties of my office in the best possible manner, by the grace of God.

3. I call on all of you to join hands with me in a public reconciliation to affirm our nation purpose of unity, freedom and justice.

4. Never again shall we turn against each other to spill the precious blood of our brothers, our sisters or our children. We must continue to keep the peace and build upon it for our time and for posterity.

5. A new dawn has broken on the horizon of our nation, bringing forth a new Sierra Leone, a new era of peace, security, stability and socio-economic progress in our country. A new Sierra Leone, where there are no ethnic or regional boundaries. A new Sierra Leone where we work harder than we did before. A new Sierra Leone where our children learn better in school. A new Sierra Leone where market women and men prosper in their traders. A new Sierra Leone where the youth train and work to live productive lives.

6. Mr. Speaker, Honourable Members, I envisage a new Sierra Leone where women stand side by side with their men folk, in the workplace and in business. A new Sierra Leone where the dark days are brightened again by electricity and water flows

Sierra Leone's local chiefs arrive to watch the broadcast of Liberian ex-leader Charles Taylor's trial taking place in the Hague, at the Special Court, in Freetown on April 26, 2012. Liberian ex-leader Charles Taylor was convicted of arming rebels during Sierra Leone's civil war in return for blood diamonds, in an historic verdict for international justice. © *Issouf Sanogo/AFP/Getty Images*

freely once more for drinking, cooking and cleansing a new Sierra Leone where farmers make more profit from their cash crops and grow enough to feed ourselves and to spare.

7. In this new era of our renewed commitment to self-reliance, freedom, independence, and prosperity, we must develop anew those values of honesty and hard work that once made this nation, the envy of our neighbours in the sub-region. Our new values must include a devotion to law and order and respect for the rule of law, human rights, good governance, and a commitment to make a positive difference to the lives and welfare of our people. Mr. Speaker that is why I am in politics. To make a difference.

8. Mr. Speaker, Honourable Members, in this new age of devotion to national service, I appeal to all Sierra Leoneans at home and abroad to join me in making this difference. To those in the diaspora, come home and serve your country if you can, or find other ways to contribute from afar. Home is where your heart is. As true patriots, you must contribute to the development of your country and your people.

9. Mr. Speaker, on this historic occasion, at the commencement of my administration as President of the Republic of Sierra Leone, I am humbled and deeply moved by the transformation of my Party, and All Peoples Congress (APC), from a minority party to the Government benches in this noble House.

10. This dramatic change, through the will of the people of our great nation, clearly illustrates the advantages and pitfalls of democracy. This underpins the fact that when a government fails in its principal duties of good governance, reneges on it promises to effectively serve the people, and neglects to provide for the basic needs of its people, that government is destined to be rejected by the people. This ominous prospect, my government will avoid by working hard to fulfill our campaign promises to develop our nation.

11. Mr. Speaker, Honourable members, the centre piece of my government, will be anchored on

acceptable democratic practice. I will ensure that all state institutions created by statutes and conventions, for the promotion of democracy, function independently.

12. Mr. Speaker, Honourable Members, democracy goes well beyond the electoral process. The separation of powers between the executive, parliament and the judiciary creates a system of checks and balances that enhances transparency and accountability. It therefore pleases me to thank the Members of Parliament, including those from the PMDC and the SLPP, for their commitment to the democratic process and to emphasize that we hope to enjoy a constructive working relationship between my administration and this parliament. Having served as the minority leader in the previous Parliament, I am well aware of the need for us all to work together, to secure a more promising future for our country.

13. Mr. Speaker, with this guiding sense of purpose to provide effective leadership for our country, I shall now give a broad outline of the priorities in the plan of action of my government to move this country forward. In this plan, my Government, intends to:

   a. keep the hard won peace and maintain national security;

   b. maintain respect for human rights, the rule of law and an independent judiciary;

   c. instill discipline in the conduct of Ministries of Government, public servants and the general citizenry;

   d. introduce performance target for all government functionaries and parastatal managers and employees;

   e. institute emergency measures to restore the supply of electricity while accelerating the completion of the Bumbuna Dam Power Generation Project. To this end, a Presidential Energy Emergency Task Force will be set up shortly;

   f. improve the delivery of healthcare services especially the reduction of infant and maternal mortality and reduce the incidence of HIV/AIDS, and malaria, by providing pro-poor medical programmes while holding health administrators accountable to the public at all times;

   g. provide affordable medical care for children, nursing mothers, pregnant women and the aged;

   h. ensure compulsory and free basic education for all children of school going age while improving access to affordable tertiary education;

   i. deliver clean potable water, enhance public health and introduce compulsory sanitary practices;

   j. modernize petty trading practices by providing purpose-built markets for our hardworking traders;

   k. initiate development programmes to improve our economy through accessible baking, agricultural extension services, judicious marine resources exploitation and development of the tourism industry;

   l. regulate the mineral resources industry and minimize the incidence of smuggling while increasing annual exports;

   m. maintain our traditional relations with our international development partners;

   n. Maintain and strengthen our existing membership of the Mano River Union, ECOWAS and the African Union.

   o. strengthen Local Government performance through enhanced decentralization and rural development;

   p. gradually work towards bridging the gender gap in all spheres of our society, especially in education, the workplace, government and the marketplace, thereby ensuring equal opportunities for women;

   q. heal the wounds of war victims, secure national and international attention and aid to the war affected.

SEE ALSO *International Law and Justice; Liberia's Civil Wars; United Nations*

BIBLIOGRAPHY

Books

Mustafa, Marda, and Joseph J. Banqura. *Sierra Leone Beyond the Lome Peace Accord.* New York: Palgrave Macmillan, 2010.

Zack-Williams, Tunde. *When the State Fails: Studies on Intervention in the Sierra Leone Civil War.* London: Pluto Press, 2012.

Periodicals

Cohen, Dara Kay. "Female Combatants and the Perpetration of Violence: Wartime Rape in the Sierra Leone Civil War." *World Politics* 65, no. 3 (July 2013): 383–415.

Faia, Tiago. "Sierra Leone: From Swords into Ploughshares." *Foreign Policy in Focus* (June 5, 2013).

McGovern, Mike, and Danny Hoffman. "The War Machines: Young Men and Violence in Sierra Leone and Liberia." *American Ethnologist* 40, no. 2 (May 2013): 407–408.

Web Sites

"Post-Conflict Care in Sierra Leone." *British Red Cross*. http://www.redcross.org.uk/What-we-do/Health-and-social-care/Health-issues/ Conflict-and-postconflict-care/Postconflict-care-in-Sierra-Leone (accessed November 26, 2013).

"Sierra Leone Profile." *BBC News*. http://www.bbc.co.uk/news/world-africa-14094419 (accessed November 26, 2013).

"United Nations Mission in Sierra Leone Background." *United Nations*. http://www.un.org/en/peacekeeping/missions/past/unamsil/background.html (accessed November 26, 2013).

Somalia

⊕ Introduction

Somalia has experienced substantial political turmoil and violence since the formation of the republic in the 1960s. The country has had difficulty establishing and maintaining a functioning central government since the previous socialist government was overthrown in 1991. Ongoing civil conflict and clan warfare have negatively impacted the nation's economy, agriculture, and living conditions. As of early 2014, even the south and central sections of the country under government control remained dangerous and at risk of assassinations, bombings, and other armed attacks by militants.

Peacekeeping troops supplied by the African Union (AU), with United Nations (UN) approval, have tried to establish stability and support the fragile Somali government in battling al-Shabab, an ultra Islamist militant group with ties to the al-Qaeda terrorist network, since 2007. However, violence escalated, especially in the nation's capital of Mogadishu. Consequently, the number of AU troops in Somalia was increased from about 4,000 troops in 2007 to nearly 18,000 in 2012.

Over one million Somalis are internally displaced people, forced from their homes by violence or starvation to take refuge in camps mostly located near urban centers. Another million are refugees in neighboring countries. Numerous health issues affect the population, which, as of 2013, had the ninth highest estimated death rate in the world and a life expectancy of about 51 years. (Worldwide life expectancy averaged 71 years in 2013.) Access to clean water and sanitary facilities is available to only a small fraction of the population, especially in rural areas. The country has a high risk of infectious diseases such as hepatitis, typhoid, dengue fever, and malaria; health care facilities and providers are scarce in all areas of the country.

At least four million Somalis were believed to have been affected by the drought and famine of 2011, which was noted as the worst drought in decades in the Horn of Africa. Al-Shabab hindered international efforts to mitigate the effects of the drought by expelling foreign organizations and preventing starving people from leaving al-Shabab–controlled territory.

The poor economic and living conditions, combined with the lack of a strong central government, also contributed to an increase in the number of young Somali men engaged in piracy in the Indian Ocean, the Gulf of Aden, and other waters. Although the number of attacks dropped substantially between 2011 and 2012, such waters were still considered areas of significant risk for such activities.

⊕ Historical Background

Nearly 60 percent of Somalis are nomadic or semi-nomadic pastoralists raising camels, sheep, goats, and cattle. Another 20 percent of the population are settled farmers, primarily living along the coastal districts and in the Juba and Shabelle River valleys. The banana plantations in the south provide the main cash crop, comprising nearly 50 percent of export earnings.

Northern Somalia is the world's largest source of incense and myrrh. There is also a small fishing industry for tuna and shark. Although Somalia has substantial natural resources, including petroleum, uranium, and natural gas, the development of the mining industry has been at a standstill due to civil conflict and political instability. Remittances from family members living and working abroad have become increasingly important to many citizens.

In ancient Egyptian times, Somalia was most probably the land of Punt, legendary source of gold, frankincense, ivory, and other products. During the Middle Ages, most of the Somali people converted to Islam and were ruled by several independent sultanates. In the 19th century, Somalia fell under the colonial domination of Great Britain, which ruled the northern part of the

SOMALIA

| 0 | 75 | 150 | 225 | 300 Miles |

| 0 | 75 | 150 | 225 | 300 Kilometers |

Gulf of Aden

Caluula

Seylac

Bender Cassim

Bargaal

DJIBOUTI

Shimbiris 7,926 ft. 2416 m. ▲ **Erigavo**

Xaafuun

Berbera

SOMALILAND

Qardho

Bandarbeyla

Hargeysa

Burao

Dooxo Nugaaleed

Togoch'ale

Deruksi

LaaCaanood

Garoowe

ETHIOPIA

Eyl

Ogaden

Galadi

Webi Shabeelle

Dila

Shilabo

Galcaio

Dusa Marreb

Dimtu

Hobyo

Dawa

Genale

Beledweyne

Oddur

Luuq

Mereeg

INDIAN OCEAN

Baidoa

El Wak

El Beru Hagia

Giohar

Cadale

Baardheere

Jubba

Webi Shabeelle

☆ **Mogadishu**

Merca

KENYA

Baraawe

Jilib

Hagadera

Jamaame

Chisimayu

Kolbio

Buur Gaabo

N W E S

Somalia

© 2014 Cengage Learning

country and called it British Somaliland. Italy controlled Italian Somaliland in the south. The British gained control of the entire country during World War II (1939–45) and maintained a protectorate over the northern part after the war. The southern part became a UN protectorate. In 1960 the two regions were united to form the Somali Republic. In 1969 Mohamed Siad Barre (1919–1995) seized power and then ruled the country as a dictator for the next 22 years.

Warring Clans

Somalia experienced more than a decade of violent turmoil beginning in 1991, when Barre was ousted from power and warring factions prevented a new central government from forming. The UN, led by the United States, sent troops to Somalia to establish a central authority and prevent mass starvation in 1992, but such efforts were ineffective. In 1993, 18 U.S. soldiers were killed and 75 were wounded by Somali militia in

Hard-line Islamist fighters exchange gunfire with government forces in Mogadishu on July 3, 2009, after Somali government forces tried to retake positions previously lost to insurgent fighters of the Al-Shabab Islamist movement and Hezbul Islam. Nearly 250 people, including senior Somali government officials, were killed and more than 200,000 Mogadishu residents were displaced in two months of intense confrontations.   © Mohamed Dahir/AFP/Getty Images

what is called the First Battle of Mogadishu. The negative reaction to these losses in the United States led to the removal of all U.S. forces from Somalia in 1994. No significant change had been achieved.

In 2004, a transitional government, the Transitional Federal Government (TFG) of Somalia, was formed, but had little power. In 2006 the Somali Council of Islamic Courts gained control over much of south and central Somalia for six months. The TFG regained power but remained very weak.

Because the factions that had overthrown Barre could not agree on how to form a new government, no central government held power. One group established an independent Republic of Somaliland in the north. In 1998, another faction took control in the autonomous state of Puntland in the east. Meanwhile, the UN-backed faction in the southern capital of Mogadishu led the struggle to end the internal conflict among warring clans, while holding onto the hope of eventual reunification and reconciliation of the country—a hope that remained unfulfilled as of early 2014.

Rise of Militant Islamists

With the global rise of militant Islamic extremism in the 21st century, a number of groups deemed terrorist organizations by the international community have joined the fight in Somalia, increasing global fears that the nation has become a prime training ground for terrorists. At the heart of the political conflict is the interpretation of Islamic law and its role in the government. Sunni Islam is the dominant religion in the nation. Although most adherents practice a moderate form of Islam, fundamentalists believe in a literal interpretation of the Qur'an and an adherence to Sharia (Islamic law) in both the social and political arenas.

Splintering off from the Islamic Courts Union, an orthodox organization that views itself as an alternative to the TFG, was al-Shabab, which has become a militant terrorist organization within Somalia. Led by a multiethnic group of Islamists, al-Shabab has taken credit for numerous attacks against government officials and peacekeeping troops. While primarily fighting within Somalia, al-Shabab also claimed responsibility for the 2010 twin bombing attacks that killed 74 people who had gathered

Mogadishu residents flee from southern Mogadishu on October 13, 2011, where African Union forces and Somalia's TFG troops launched an offensive against the final pockets of an al-Shabab militia group. Hundreds of residents in the war-torn Somali capital fled before the AU-led assault, which followed a Shabab suicide bomb attack the previous week in Mogadishu that killed at least 82 people and demonstrated they were still able to wreak havoc deep inside the city.   © *Abdurashid Abdulle/AFP/Getty Images*

to watch a televised transmission of a World Cup game in a restaurant and a club in Kampala, Uganda.

In February 2012, leaders from al-Shabab and al-Qaeda released a joint video announcing a formal merger of the two groups. Although al-Qaeda members have worked alongside al-Shabab militants for quite some time, the formal merger fueled fears that the coordinated, combined efforts of both groups would change the direction of the fight within Somalia and lead to a renewal of al-Qaeda attacks in other nations. In 2013, al-Shabab claimed responsibility for an attack on a mall, which killed at least 67 people in Nairobi, Kenya.

Attempts to Restore Central Government

From 1991 to 2004, officials in Mogadishu held 14 national reconciliation conferences, trying to restore the central government. The Transitional Federal Government (TFG) was finally established in 2004 with a five-year mandate to lead the process of establishing a new government and drafting a new constitution. This process was hindered by continuing violence and the rise of al-Shabab in 2006. Over the next several years, al-Shabab militants seized control of much of the southern and central portions of the nation and imposed a strict version of sharia.

In January 2009, the TFG mandate was extended for another two years, and Parliament elected Sheikh Sharif Sheikh Ahmed (1964–) as Somalia's new president. Ahmed is an Islamist cleric, with moderate views, who focused on reaching a peaceful accord among the factions. Though Ahmed introduced some moderate applications of Islamic law, the militant Islamist factions were not appeased. Violent conflict continued into June 2009, when the president called a state of emergency and issued a plea for foreign military intervention.

Peacekeeping Mission

Amid a renewed surge of violence in mid-2010, East Africa's Intergovernmental Authority on Development (IGAD) agreed to send 2,000 troops to serve within the existing AU peacekeeping mission, the African Union Mission in Somalia (AMISOM). By October 2010, the pro-Somali allied forces had successfully regained control of part of Mogadishu and the border town of Bulo Hawo.

In October 2011, AU officials announced that all members of al-Shabab had been driven out of the capital in a final gun battle that left one AU soldier and eight civilians dead. By November 2011, AU forces totaled nearly 10,000, with the goal of an eventual force of 20,000. The governments of Burundi, Uganda, and Kenya offered additional military support to increase troop levels. At the end of December 2011, a force of more than 3,000 Ethiopian troops assisted in the successful capture of the strategic town of Beledweyne, forcing al-Shabab to retreat from the town into surrounding regions. The town is a main stop on the road to Mogadishu. A spokesperson for al-Shabab claimed that the retreat was merely a planned withdrawal. Some 20 deaths were reported as a result of the capture.

The Garowe Agreement

In 2011, Somali leaders extended the TFG's mandate. Sheikh Ahmed remained president and Abdiweli Mohamed Ali was appointed prime minister. The TFG's mandate, already extended several times, was scheduled to expire in August 2012. In anticipation of the August expiration, government officials met in Garowe in February to design what would become the Federal Government of Somalia. The Garowe Agreement called for a bicameral parliament based in Mogadishu. The agreement won immediate support from members of the international community, who met at a London conference a few days later to consider a larger plan for ending the crisis in Somalia. In September, a new parliament elected a new president, Hassan Sheikh Mohamud (1955–), thus establishing the first central government Somalia had in almost 20 years.

The Benefits of Piracy

The bleak economic situation and the absence of a central government authority have given rise to other damaging economic enterprises, including a rise in the number of young Somali men who engage in piracy in the Gulf of Aden to the north and in the Indian Ocean to the east and south. Somali pirates frequently seize foreign ships in these waters in order to secure ransom payments for later releasing the ships and their passengers. In total, Somali pirates receive an estimated $70 million per year in ransom.

A 2012 study from the British think tank Chatham House indicated that much of these funds were used to support significant economic growth and development in the primary pirate base of Puntland. Evidence showed that the Puntland capital city of Garowe nearly doubled in area from 2002 through 2009, with the addition of several new housing, industrial, and commercial developments. The report also noted that the standard of living increased in the town, based on improvement in housing standards and a higher percentage of vehicle ownership.

In the provinces of Nugal and Muduq, where many of the pirates are based, there was an increase in daily wages from 2005 to 2011, from about $1.60 per day to about $4.80 per day. This increase has been attributed to greater employment opportunities sparked by investments in local businesses, which were likely funded by money acquired through piracy. The report further indicated that governmental and international efforts to stop the pirates led to an increase in violent attacks beginning in mid-2010. The Chatham House report suggested that further attempts to end piracy must focus on a "land-based" solution involving alternative resources to provide the same, if not greater, economic benefits to remove the economic incentives to commit piracy. The report also warned that pirates might join forces with the Islamist militants, thereby providing additional funding for terrorism and increasing political instability.

The number of Somali pirate attacks dropped to its lowest level in years in 2012. Also, according to the International Maritime Bureau (IMB) of the International Chamber of Commerce, vessels traveling in waters around Somalia experienced fewer incidents in the first nine months of 2013 than they did in the first nine months of 2012. Reported Somali-related attacks totaled 10 in January to September of 2013 compared to 70 during the same timeframe in 2012.

The Costs of Piracy

For many people, the word "pirate" calls up romanticized images of peg-legged sailors, buried treasure, and swashbuckling heroes of the early 19th century. In reality, however, piracy has always been a dangerous, violent business, and a serious threat to marine commerce. Although never completely eradicated, piracy made a dramatic resurgence in the second half of the 20th century. Global commerce has increased tremendously in the last quarter century; about 80 percent of international freight is shipped by sea. Worldwide, piracy at sea costs an estimated $13 to $16 billion annually.

In 2008, Somalia had the highest number of incidents of piracy in the world, with 111 attacks (a 200 percent increase over 2007). Somalia's 1,880-mile (3,000-kilometer) coast is a vital international trade route near the connection of the Red Sea with the Indian Ocean via the Gulf of Aden. Piracy has made shipping and tourism in the region risky. The piracy has also presented an obstacle to the delivery of humanitarian aid to the estimated 2 to 3 million hungry people in Somalia. However, Somali-initiated piracy declined as a percentage of worldwide piracy in 2012 and 2013.

⊕ Impacts and Issues

Somalia is a classic example of a failed state, a country where the central government is unable to rule the entire nation. In some regions of the country, warlords and clans provide the people with what government there is. The situation has allowed terrorists, pirates, and other criminals to flourish in relative safety, since there is no one to hold them to account. The situation not only puts the local population in dire straits, but the violence impacts the international community as well.

The continued political conflict has created one of the world's worst humanitarian crises. Estimates from various organizations place the total number of deaths from the 2010 to 2012 famine alone at 260,000. A more exact number is hard to determine due to numerous unrecorded deaths from war, famine, and disease, and due to the large number of people who are internally displaced or have fled the country.

On March 26, 2013, Human Rights Watch released a report detailing the widespread abuse and rape of internally displaced people in Somalia. The report claimed that

A HOSTAGE OF THE PIRATES

On April 8, 2009, a U.S.-flagged container ship, the *Maersk Alabama,* was en route to Kenya with a shipment of food aid when it was attacked and boarded by Somali pirates 350 miles (563 kilometers) off the coast of Somalia. The ship's captain, Richard Phillips (1955–), offered himself as a hostage in order to safeguard his ship and crew. He was taken aboard a lifeboat by four pirates armed with automatic weapons, and the *Maersk Alabama* continued to Kenya under the command of its first mate. The U.S.S. *Bainbridge* arrived on the scene the next morning, followed thereafter by two more U.S. Navy warships. Captain Phillips was rescued on April 12 after Navy snipers killed three of the pirates holding him hostage. Phillips was recovered unharmed. The *Maersk Alabama* incident prompted President Barack Obama (1961–) to call for further international cooperation to combat piracy off the coast of Somalia. The event was depicted in a 2013 movie titled *Captain Phillips,* starring Tom Hanks in the lead role.

A Somali woman reacts on March 18, 2013, near the site of a car bomb in central Mogadishu, Somalia. At least eight people were killed in one of the bloodiest attacks in the war-ravaged capital in the first months of 2013, police said.   *© Mohamed Abdiwahab/AFP/Getty Images*

managers of refugee camps, called "the gatekeepers," also siphon off the international aid given to the camps. Because running a camp is so lucrative, the report states, the gatekeepers often prevent people from leaving.

⊕ Future Implications

Despite continued sporadic violence, including bombings and gun battles, the 2012 election of a national government seems to indicate progress toward stability and unity. International organizations are cautiously optimistic. In March 2013, the UN Security Council voted to partially lift its embargo on selling weapons to Somalia for one year. Imposed since 1992, the ban was the oldest in the world. The measure allows for the Somali government to buy small weapons but keeps the restrictions on heavy weapons in place.

Somalia remains a dangerous place, with violence fed by ethnic, religious, and economic disparities. On November 7, 2012, an explosion disrupted the capital city of Mogadishu, killing one person. The explosion, believed to be a car bomb, was set off close to parliament and was one of many in a string of attacks in the city in 2012 and 2013. During the first week of June 2013, 18 people died in gun battles in the port city of Kismayo. The clashes began when gunmen from one of the

country's rival groups, the Ras Kamboni, tried to arrest a member of an opposing group. An assault on a UN office in Mogadishu left 15 people dead on June 19. Al-Shabab claimed responsibility for the attack, which was carried out by a suicide car bomber and four gunmen.

The violence has even spread to neighboring Kenya. In September 2013 al-Shabab terrorists attacked the upscale Westgate shopping mall in Nairobi, Kenya. The incident, which lasted for 48 hours, left at least 67 people dead and over 200 wounded. Reportedly, the attack was in retaliation for the help that the Kenyan army provided to the Somali military in its fight against al-Shabab. The violence has not dissuaded the Kenyans, who, in October 2013, launched air strikes against the al-Shabab camp in southern Somali where the attackers of the mall were trained.

The desolation emerging from the warfare since 1991 has left Somalia poor and with little of the infrastructure required to create a safe and secure country. Despite occasional signs of progress, in August 2013 the humanitarian relief organization Doctors Without Borders/Médecins Sans Frontières announced that it was closing its operations in Somalia. The country had become too dangerous for its staff. Many observers believe that al-Shabab, in particular, seems positioned to continue disruption of Somalia for the foreseeable future.

PRIMARY SOURCE

The Federal Republic of Somalia Provisional Constitution: Chapter 2: Fundamental Rights and the Duties of the Citizen

SOURCE *"Chapter 2: Fundamental Rights and the Duties of the Citizen."* The Federal Republic of Somalia Provisional Constitution, *August 1, 2012. Available online at: http://unpos.unmissions.org/ LinkClick.aspx?fileticket=RkJTOSpoMME%3d &tubid=11451&mid=14705&language=en-US (November 15, 2013).*

INTRODUCTION *The constitution from which the section below was taken was adopted by the Somali Transitional Federal Government (TFG) on August 1, 2012. The TFG was created in 2004 after more than a dozen failed attempts since 1991 to establish a functional government in the war-torn country. For the first several years, due to security and safety concerns, the government was located in Kenya. It was first convened in Somalia in 2006.*

Chapter 2: Fundamental Rights and the Duties of the Citizen

Title One: General Principles of Human Rights

Article 10. Human Dignity

(1) Human dignity is given by God to every human being, and this is the basis for all human rights.

(2) Human dignity is inviolable and must be protected by all.

(3) State power must not be exercised in a manner that violates human dignity.

Article 11. Equality

(1) All citizens, regardless of sex, religion, social or economic status, political opinion, clan, disability, occupation, birth or dialect shall have equal rights and duties before the law.

(2) Discrimination is deemed to occur if the effect of an action impairs or restricts a person's rights, even if the actor did not intend this effect.

(3) The State must not discriminate against any person on the basis of age, race, colour, tribe, ethnicity, culture, dialect, gender, birth, disability, religion, political opinion, occupation, or wealth.

(4) All State programs, such as laws, or political and administrative actions that are designed to achieve full equality for individuals or groups who are disadvantaged, or who have suffered from discrimination in the past, shall not be deemed to be discriminatory.

Article 12. Application of the Fundamental Rights

(1) The fundamental rights and freedoms recognized in this Chapter shall always be respected in the making and application of the law. Likewise, they must be respected by all individuals and private organisations, as well as by every state institution and state official as they carry out their official functions.

(2) It is the responsibility of the state not only to ensure it does not violate rights through its actions, but also to take reasonable steps to protect the rights of the people from abuse by others.

(3) The rights recognized in this Chapter may be limited only by a law as provided for in Article 38.

SEE ALSO *African Union; Al-Qaeda; Religious Extremism*

BIBLIOGRAPHY

Books

Bahadur, Jay. *Deadly Waters: Inside the Hidden World of Somalia's Pirates.* London: Profile Books, 2011.

Fergusson, James. *The World's Most Dangerous Place.* Boston: Da Capo Press, 2013.

Hansen, Stig Jarle. *Al-Shabaab in Somalia: The History and Ideology of a Militant Islamist Group, 2005–2012.* New York: Oxford University Press, 2013.

Harper, Mary. *Getting Somalia Wrong?: Faith and War in a Shattered State.* New York: Zed Books, 2012.

Periodicals

Balthasar, Dominik. "Somaliland's Best Kept Secret: Shrewd Politics and War Projects as Means of State-Making." *Journal of Eastern African Studies* 7, no. 2 (May 2013): 218–238.

Little, Peter D., Markus Hoehne, and Virginia Luling. "Milk and Peace, Drought and War: Somalia Culture, Society, and Politics." *International Journal of African Historical Studies* 45, no. 1 (January 2012): 123–125.

Web Sites

Gardner, Frank. "Q&A: Who Are Somalia's al-Shabab?" *BBC News Africa*, September 24, 2013. http://www.bbc.co.uk/news/world-africa-15336689 (accessed December 4, 2013).

Hogg, Annabel Lee. "Timeline: Somalia, 1991–2008." *The Atlantic*, December 22, 2008. http://www.theatlantic.com/magazine/archive/2008/12/timeline-somalia-1991-2008/307190/ (accessed December 4, 2013).

Stewart, Christopher S. "Frontier Capitalism: A Bet on Peace for War-Torn Somalia." *Wall Street Journal*, April 27, 2013. http://online.wsj.com/news/articles/SB10001424127887323820304578410573747048086 (accessed January 21, 2014).

South Africa: Apartheid

⊕ Introduction

Apartheid, from the Afrikaans for "state of being apart," refers to the government policy of segregation according to race or ethnicity such as occurred in South Africa from 1948 to 1994. Though South Africa was already highly segregated, the official policies instituted by apartheid in 1948 were designed to ensure maximum racial segregation, white supremacy, and Afrikaner minority rule. Proponents of apartheid sought to reinforce racial inequality and limit the urbanization of non-whites.

Apartheid deprived blacks, coloreds (people of mixed ancestry), and Asian citizens of South Africa from exercising many basic rights. Under the laws of apartheid, the majority of citizens could not own property or vote and were restricted in their movements and activities. Many black South Africans living in urban areas were moved to townships where they were expected to develop self-governing societies, while those living in rural areas were confined to "homelands" or "reserves." These reserves consisted of poor quality lands with insufficient resources, leaving residents in extreme poverty.

After decades of struggle, in 1994, the African National Congress (ANC) took over the government of South Africa, officially ending apartheid. The ANC instituted nationwide reforms to promote equality, civil rights, and economic prosperity for all South Africans, and in the years that followed many advances were made. The legacy of racism, though, remains firmly entrenched in the nation's economy. In the first decade of the 21st century, the majority of black South Africans were as poor, or poorer, than they had been under apartheid policies.

⊕ Historical Background

The origins of apartheid in South Africa date back to the colonial period. Racial segregation and inequality were a simple fact of life under Dutch rule (1652–1806) and British rule (1806–1934). White European explorers and colonists settled in South Africa, gradually growing in number and extending their political power and economic dominance over the region. During the latter part of the 19th century and early 20th century, the first major segregation laws were passed. These laws dealt

COLONIAL SEGREGATION LAWS

Beginning in 1892, the white minority who held political power in South Africa began to restrict the rights of black and Asian residents of South Africa by passing a series of laws that began the formal government policy of apartheid. These laws included the following:

- *Franchise and Ballot Act* (1892) limited the black (native) vote by placing requirements on black citizens to meet certain financial and educational conditions.
- *Natal Legislative Assembly Bill* (1894) deprived Indians (Asians) from voting.
- *General Pass Regulations Bill* (1905) denied blacks the vote altogether and restricted their movements.
- *Asiatic Registration Act* (1906) required all Indians to carry passes.
- *South Africa Act* (1910) gave white citizens complete political control over all other races.
- *Native Land Act* (1913) prevented blacks from buying land outside of reserves.
- *Natives in Urban Areas Act* (1918) moved blacks living in "white areas" to new residential areas.
- *Urban Areas Act* (1923) institutionalized residential segregation between the races and provided cheap unskilled labor for white industries.
- *Colored Bar Act* (1926) prevented blacks from practicing skilled trades.

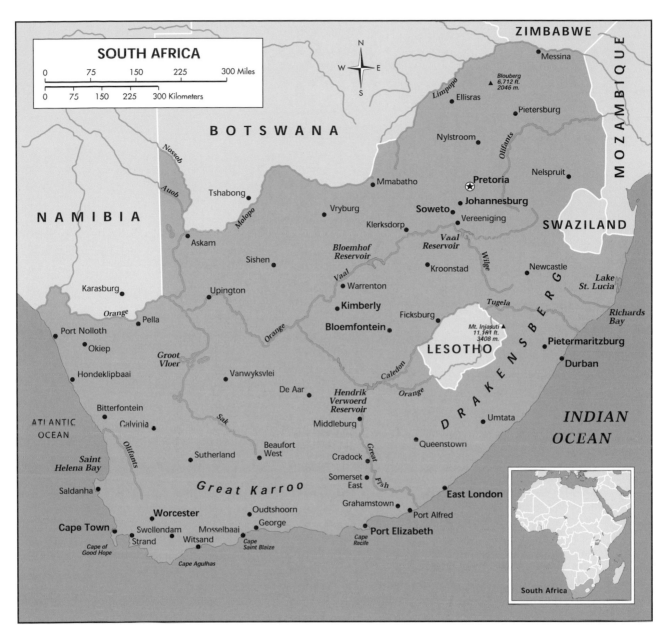

SOUTH AFRICA

ZIMBABWE

MOZAMBIQUE

BOTSWANA

NAMIBIA

SWAZILAND

LESOTHO

DRAKENSBERG

ATLANTIC
OCEAN

INDIAN
OCEAN

Great Karroo

*Cape of
Good Hope*

Cape Agulhas

South Africa

© 2014 Cengage Learning

primarily with voting and property rights and instituted a pass system for racial identification and travel restrictions.

Disenfranchising the majority of the population left them without a political voice. But the Native Land Act and Colored Bar Act were far more devastating than much other legislation because they institutionalized the economics of segregation. Without access to viable land and education, poverty was inevitable and not easily reversible.

The Native Land Act was a cornerstone of the apartheid system. Under the act the black population was forced to live on only 13 percent of the land in South Africa. The land available for purchase was restricted to special reserves, which supposedly made up the "original homelands" of the black tribes. These reserves were expected to be self-governing and quasi-independent, similar to the Native American Reservations in North America. As in North America, the reserves were purposefully located in the poorest regions where farming was extremely difficult and few natural resources were available. The remaining 87 percent of white-owned land included all of the most productive land in South Africa.

The Colored Bar Act restricted the educational opportunities of the black population and barred them from skilled trades. Without education, the black population was forcibly reduced to a large pool of unskilled laborers who worked on the white-owned farms and in the mines. This allowed the white population to grow richer while the black population grew poorer.

A black woman sits in the wagon reserved for white people to protest against Daniel Francois Malan's government and his regime of apartheid, in South Africa on September 2, 1952. Having come to power in 1948, Malan and his national party systematized racial segregation in South Africa. © *Keystone-France/Gamma-Keystone via Getty Images*

In 1934, South Africa became an independent nation. The United Party ruled South Africa from 1934 to 1948 and drew its support from a combination of white and colored populations. The United Party left in place the racist policies of the colonial period and created new segregation legislation. In 1948, the National Party (NP) took control of the South African government and made apartheid an official policy.

Apartheid: Classifications and Racial Segregation

Apartheid classified South African inhabitants into four racial groups: "native" (black), "white," "colored" (people of mixed ancestry), and "Asian" (typically from India). Starting at the age of 18, every individual was expected to carry an identification card that specified their race. Intermarriage was outlawed and any physical contact between the races strictly frowned upon. A law passed in 1950 made sexual relations between races a criminal offense.

Residential areas were fully segregated, by forced removal if necessary. Education, medical care, public services, and public lands were also segregated, with white

services being significantly superior to those available to other races. Almost every year a new law was passed that expanded racial inequality.

In 1970, black political representation was completely abolished. Native people were deprived of South African citizenship, which was replaced with membership in one of ten tribes called *bantustans*. South Africa treated the bantustans as quasi-independent nations, even going so far as to build South African embassies on the tribal lands.

Ending Apartheid

It took decades and a concentrated rebel response as well as international cooperation to end apartheid. The South African Native National Congress (SANNC) founded in 1912 specifically fought to increase the rights of the black South African population. In 1923, it was reorganized as the African National Congress (ANC). The National Party government banned the ANC and jailed its leaders. For more than two decades the ANC was largely ineffective and inactive.

During the mid-1940s, the ANC was remodeled as a mass movement, rather than a political party, and began

Two black youths kneel in front of the police, holding their hands in the air to show the peace sign, in Soweto, South Africa, 1976.
© Jan Hamman/Gallo Images/Alamy

gaining traction. During the 1950s, the NP accused the ANC of being a communist party and once again jailed its leaders. The ANC responded by calling for strikes, boycotts, and other acts of resistance to apartheid. Anti-apartheid protests became increasingly frequent. While these protests typically started peacefully, violence all too often erupted.

In 1960, peaceful protesters in Sharpeville, South Africa, were fired upon by the police. Sixty-nine people were killed in the Sharpeville massacre. The massacre prompted the ANC to create the *Umkhonto we Sizwe* (Spear of the Nation, abbreviated MK), a military wing of the ANC, which used violence to fight apartheid. The MK was responsible for killing members of the military and civilians during its fight against apartheid.

On June 16, 1976, high-school students in Soweto protested for better education. Police fired teargas and live bullets into the marching crowd, killing innocent people and igniting what is known as "The Soweto Uprising," a bloody episode of riots between police and protesters in which at least 176 were killed, many of

them children. News and images of the uprising focused international attention on the situation in South Africa.

Nelson Mandela

One of the founders of the MK was Nelson Mandela (1918–2013), a long-time opponent of apartheid. In 1962, the ANC sent Mandela abroad as a representative. When he returned to South Africa he was jailed for inciting strikes and leaving the country without permission. Mandela was put on trial and convicted of treason in 1964 and sentenced to life in prison. His trial was publicized internationally, and he quickly became a symbol of the struggle against apartheid.

What the NP could never have anticipated is that Mandela would be able to do more for the ANC while in prison than he could do on the outside. For the next 27 years, Mandela would communicate with the outside world through letters as he served his prison sentence. He became the face of the resistance, a single individual who represented the suffering experienced by all people

Police with dogs intimidate pedestrians while raiding Khotso House, the office of the anti-apartheid United Democratic Front and South African Council of Churches during a delcared State of Emergency. The house was bombed in 1988 by the government for harboring anti-apartheid activists. © *Selwyn Tait/Time Life Pictures/Getty Images*

under apartheid. As his fame spread, the outcry for his release escalated, including a demand from the United Nations (UN) that he be freed. For decades, the South African government ignored these requests.

International Response to Apartheid

The UN had officially condemned apartheid since 1962 and imposed economic sanctions against South Africa. The United States, the United Kingdom, and 23 other nations all imposed their own sanctions against South Africa. In 1973, the UN formally qualified apartheid as a "Crime Against Humanity" and threatened to bring its enforcers before an international court for criminal prosecution. The African Union (AU) refused to allow South Africa membership as long as the apartheid laws existed and offered to help apartheid resisters in their fight for equality.

Resisters also found support from the Catholic Church. Pope John Paul II (1920–2005) was an outspoken opponent of apartheid and lent his voice to the international condemnation. He refused to visit South Africa and called on neighboring nations to impose economic sanctions. He urged peaceful resolution, as opposed to armed conflict. Since the majority of Catholics in South Africa belonged to the white population, the Vatican's

condemnation of apartheid was applied directly where it might do the most good.

International sanctions had a brutal effect on the South African economy. During the 1960s, its economic growth was second in the world, directly after Japan. Trade with the United States, Europe, and Asia ensured a bustling economy. By 1987, South Africa's economic growth was one of the lowest in the world. International pressure to end apartheid was not merely rhetoric; it had clear ramifications that the South African government could not ignore. However, violence against anti-apartheid activists and discrimination against blacks by the government still continued.

F.W. De Klerk and the End of Apartheid

By the late 1980s, it was finally becoming clear that apartheid was an antiquated system that must be demolished so that South Africa could have a viable future. F.W. de Klerk (1936–) was the final NP President, serving from 1989 to 1994. Although he had supported segregation for much of his political career, upon becoming president he immediately called for an end to apartheid. In an historic speech on February 2, 1990, de Klerk announced the lifting of the ban on the ANC and other organizations, the release of Nelson Mandela and

On December 9, 1993 in Oslo, Norway, Nelson Mandela, President of South African political group African National Congress (C) and South African President Frederik de Klerk (R) display their Nobel Prizes after being awarded jointly for their work to end apartheid peacefully. They shared the prize for their efforts in securing a peaceful transition from apartheid rule. De Klerk resigned as leader of the South African National Party in 1997, having served as Mandela's second deputy President until 1996.　*© Gerard Julien/AFP/Getty Images*

other anti-apartheid leaders from prison, and his intention of negotiating a democratic constitution. His presidency was dominated by negotiations between his own NP government and Mandela's ANC. In 1992, a whites-only referendum overwhelmingly supported de Klerk's efforts to end apartheid.

In 1993, de Klerk and Mandela were jointly awarded the Nobel Peace Prize for their work to end apartheid. The next year, the first universal elections were held in South Africa, and Nelson Mandela was elected president, serving from 1994 to 1999, when he voluntarily retired from public life. De Klerk became the deputy president, a position he held until 1996. The two statesmen worked toward a peaceful transition in South Africa.

Truth and Reconciliation Commission

As part of the *Promotion of National Unity and Reconciliation Act*, the government established the Truth and Reconciliation Commission (TRC). The TRC's Human Rights Violations Committee was charged with investigating human rights abuses that occurred in Africa between 1960 and the fall of apartheid in 1994. The TRC's Reparation and Rehabilitation Committee allowed victims to give testimony about crimes committed against them and perpetrators to account for their crimes. The Amnesty Committee heard applications for amnesty from perpetrators who had cooperated with TRC investigations and hearings. Under the direction of chairman Archbishop Desmond Tutu (1931–), hearings began in 1996. The goals of the full commission were to provide a record of human rights crimes committed during the apartheid era, have perpetrators regognize and account for their role in apartheid atrocities, adjudicate reparations, and promote peace, reconciliation, and healing within the nation.

⊕ Impacts and Issues

The ANC has controlled South Africa since 1994 and still enjoys widespread support as of early 2014. At the centennial celebration of the organization's founding, South African President Jacob Zuma (1942–) praised the movement for its diverse membership and announced that the organization had reached the goal (established in 1942) of having one million members by its centennial year, with official

DESMOND TUTU (1931–)

Desmond Mpilo Tutu was born in Klerksdorp, Transvaal, South Africa and, like most other black South Africans at that time, raised in relative poverty and under the harsh conditions imposed by segregation and apartheid. While in high school, he met an English parish priest, Father Trevor Huddleston, who became his role model. Huddleston encouraged his parishioners to stand against oppression. When Tutu was confined to his home while recovering from tuberculosis, Huddleston visited weekly, providing encouragement, schoolbooks, and an introduction to a daily prayer routine. Tutu would have liked to attend medical school, but could not afford the tuition. He earned his degree from the Bantu Teachers' Training college in 1954 with plans to teach high school literature.

In 1955 new government policies were introduced that limited what black teachers could teach. The scaled-back curriculum was designed to fit the government's plans to produce more manual laborers for the mines and factories. Teacher salaries were also reduced. Many black teachers resigned in protest, including Tutu, who quit in 1958. Tutu entered St. Peter's Theological College in Johannesburg and was ordained in 1960. He obtained his master's degree in London, returning to South Africa where he lectured in Botswana, Lesotho, and Swaziland and was consecrated bishop of Lesotho in 1976. He became an international spokesperson for the fight against apartheid and was awarded the Nobel Peace Prize in 1984. He retired as archbishop of Cape Town in June of 1996 and in January was appointed chair of the Commission on Truth and Reconciliation by President Mandela.

membership noted at 1,027,389. Zuma also announced that the party expected to revitalize its efforts to improve and encourage education and skills development, to discourage factionalism, and to promote political discipline. These pledges may have been made in answer to ANC opponents, who have accused the party of elitism, political infighting, and a lack of attention to the plight of the poor.

While the end of apartheid legally instituted equality among South African citizens, the stark reality of economics tells a very different story. Despite advances, the nation remains essentially divided into two societies, one wealthy and mostly white and the other poor and mostly black. Change rarely occurs overnight, sometimes not even with decades of effort, and redistributing the wealth of South Africa looks to be a long process.

Most of the nation's wealth and property remains in the possession of the white population. (In 2001, whites represented approximately 10 percent of South Africa's population.) In an attempt to compensate people who had been forced from their homelands during apartheid, the ANC promised to carry out a policy of land redistribution that would eventually give some white-owned lands to black South Africans. Fearing racial conflict, though, the ANC decided not to seize land forcibly from whites, vowing to appropriate it only through negotiation. Almost no land redistribution has occurred under this policy. According to the Southern African Regional Poverty Network, 96 percent of South Africa's farmland was still owned by whites as of 2007. In urban areas the situation is similar. Because few South African blacks can afford to live in them, wealthy suburbs remained mostly white as of 2008, and many poor blacks continued to live in black townships.

Analyses at the end of 2007 showed South Africa's unemployment rate at 40 percent. In the ever-widening gap between the poor and the wealthy, the wealthiest 20 percent of South Africans earned approximately 65 percent of the nation's total income, while the poorest 20 percent earned only about 3 percent. More than half of South African households lived in poverty in 2008 and the overwhelming majority of the poor were black. The rate of poverty was actually worse than it had been under apartheid.

Economics is typically closely entwined with access to education. Education was strictly segregated during apartheid, with spending on white students 10 times higher than for black students. When apartheid ended, whites, with more training and education than blacks, continued to dominate in the post-apartheid business world. Inferior education is a huge factor in the chronic unemployment experienced among poor blacks in the post-apartheid era, despite South Africa's economic growth.

⊕ Future Implications

By the early 21st century, many of South Africa's universities had enrolled black majorities for the first time—a hopeful sign for the future. While this increased access to education will almost certainly affect the economic distribution across South Africa, it will likely take a generation, if not more, to truly transition into a more equitable society. As of 2014, some university living quarters remained segregated for the protection of black students. Black students have been the victims of racist threats and ostracism in several highly publicized incidents.

PRIMARY SOURCE

The Freedom Charter

SOURCE *"The Freedom Charter."* African National Congress, *June 26, 1955. http://www.anc.org.za/ show.php?id=72 (accessed December 12, 2013).*

INTRODUCTION *The Freedom Charter was drafted in 1955 by delegates to the Congress of the People, an alliance of existing organizations dedicated to ending apartheid in South Africa, including the African National Congress (ANC), the South African Indian Congress, the South African Coloured People's Congress, the South African Congress of Democrats, and the*

South African Congress of Trade Unions (SACTU). More than 3,000 delegates gathered outside Johannesburg on June 25, 1955, to formulize the alliance and draft the Charter, which was adopted the next day. In response to the adoption, 156 people were arrested, 91 of whom were later tried for treason. The ANC responded with boycotts and strikes. All of the defendants were found not guilty by the time the trial ended in 1961.

As adopted at the Congress of the People, Kliptown, on 26 June 1955

We, the People of South Africa, declare for all our country and the world to know:

that South Africa belongs to all who live in it, black and white, and that no government can justly claim authority unless it is based on the will of all the people;

that our people have been robbed of their birthright to land, liberty and peace by a form of government founded on injustice and inequality;

that our country will never be prosperous or free until all our people live in brotherhood, enjoying equal rights and opportunities;

that only a democratic state, based on the will of all the people, can secure to all their birthright without distinction of colour, race, sex or belief;

And therefore, we, the people of South Africa, black and white together equals, countrymen and brothers adopt this Freedom Charter;

And we pledge ourselves to strive together, sparing neither strength nor courage, until the democratic changes here set out have been won.

The People Shall Govern!

Every man and woman shall have the right to vote for and to stand as a candidate for all bodies which make laws;

All people shall be entitled to take part in the administration of the country;

The rights of the people shall be the same, regardless of race, colour or sex;

All bodies of minority rule, advisory boards, councils and authorities shall be replaced by democratic organs of self-government.

All National Groups Shall have Equal Rights!

There shall be equal status in the bodies of state, in the courts and in the schools for all national groups and races;

All people shall have equal right to use their own languages, and to develop their own folk culture and customs;

All national groups shall be protected by law against insults to their race and national pride;

The preaching and practice of national, race or colour discrimination and contempt shall be a punishable crime;

All apartheid laws and practices shall be set aside.

The People Shall Share in the Country's Wealth!

The national wealth of our country, the heritage of South Africans, shall be restored to the people;

The mineral wealth beneath the soil, the Banks and monopoly industry shall be transferred to the ownership of the people as a whole;

All other industry and trade shall be controlled to assist the wellbeing of the people;

All people shall have equal rights to trade where they choose, to manufacture and to enter all trades, crafts and professions.

The Land Shall be Shared Among Those Who Work It!

Restrictions of land ownership on a racial basis shall be ended, and all the land re-divided amongst those who work it to banish famine and land hunger;

The state shall help the peasants with implements, seed, tractors and dams to save the soil and assist the tillers;

Freedom of movement shall be guaranteed to all who work on the land;

All shall have the right to occupy land wherever they choose;

People shall not be robbed of their cattle, and forced labour and farm prisons shall be abolished.

All Shall be Equal Before the Law!

No-one shall be imprisoned, deported or restricted without a fair trial; No-one shall be condemned by the order of any Government official;

The courts shall be representative of all the people;

Imprisonment shall be only for serious crimes against the people, and shall aim at re-education, not vengeance;

The police force and army shall be open to all on an equal basis and shall be the helpers and protectors of the people;

All laws which discriminate on grounds of race, colour or belief shall be repealed.

All Shall Enjoy Equal Human Rights!

The law shall guarantee to all their right to speak, to organise, to meet together, to publish, to preach, to worship and to educate their children;

The privacy of the house from police raids shall be protected by law;

All shall be free to travel without restriction from countryside to town, from province to province, and from South Africa abroad,

Pass Laws, permits and all other laws restricting these freedoms shall be abolished.

There Shall be Work and Security!

All who work shall be free to form trade unions, to elect their officers and to make wage agreements with their employers;

The state shall recognise the right and duty of all to work, and to draw full unemployment benefits;

Men and women of all races shall receive equal pay for equal work;

There shall be a forty-hour working week, a national minimum wage, paid annual leave, and sick leave for all workers, and maternity leave on full pay for all working mothers;

Miners, domestic workers, farm workers and civil servants shall have the same rights as all others who work;

Child labour, compound labour, the tot system and contract labour shall be abolished.

The Doors of Learning and Culture Shall be Opened!

The government shall discover, develop and encourage national talent for the enhancement of our cultural life;

All the cultural treasures of mankind shall be open to all, by free exchange of books, ideas and contact with other lands;

The aim of education shall be to teach the youth to love their people and their culture, to honour human brotherhood, liberty and peace;

Education shall be free, compulsory, universal and equal for all children; Higher education and technical training shall be opened to all by means of state allowances and scholarships awarded on the basis of merit;

Adult illiteracy shall be ended by a mass state education plan;

Teachers shall have all the rights of other citizens;

The colour bar in cultural life, in sport and in education shall be abolished.

There Shall be Houses, Security and Comfort!

All people shall have the right to live where they choose, be decently housed, and to bring up their families in comfort and security;

Unused housing space to be made available to the people;

Rent and prices shall be lowered, food plentiful and no-one shall go hungry;

A preventive health scheme shall be run by the state;

Free medical care and hospitalisation shall be provided for all, with special care for mothers and young children;

Slums shall be demolished, and new suburbs built where all have transport, roads, lighting, playing fields, creches and social centres;

The aged, the orphans, the disabled and the sick shall be cared for by the state;

Rest, leisure and recreation shall be the right of all:

Fenced locations and ghettoes shall be abolished, and laws which break up families shall be repealed.

There Shall be Peace and Friendship!

South Africa shall be a fully independent state which respects the rights and sovereignty of all nations;

South Africa shall strive to maintain world peace and the settlement of all international disputes by negotiation—not war;

Peace and friendship amongst all our people shall be secured by upholding the equal rights, opportunities and status of all;

The people of the protectorates Basutoland, Bechuanaland and Swaziland shall be free to decide for themselves their own future;

The right of all peoples of Africa to independence and self-government shall be recognised, and shall be the basis of close co-operation.

Let all people who love their people and their country now say, as we say here:

THESE FREEDOMS WE WILL FIGHT FOR, SIDE BY SIDE, THROUGHOUT OUR LIVES, UNTIL WE HAVE WON OUR LIBERTY

PRIMARY SOURCE

Nelson Mandela's Address to a Rally in Cape Town on His Release from Prison

SOURCE Mandela, Nelson. "Address to a Rally in Cape Town on His Release from Prison." South African History Online, February 11, 1990. http://www.sahistory.org.za/archive/nelson-mandelas-address-rally-cape-town-his-release-prison-11-february-1990 (accessed January 8, 2014).

INTRODUCTION *Nelson Mandela, one of the world's most respected and beloved political figures, spent his life fighting for the rights of oppressed black South Africans and an end to apartheid. His courage and determination through nearly 27 years of political imprisonment inspired South African blacks as well as opponents of apartheid and racial discrimination throughout the world. After his release from prison in 1990, Mandela reclaimed his leadership role in the once-banned African National Congress (ANC) and fought tirelessly for democratic reform. In this speech, given on the occasion of his release from prison and heard around the world, Mandela called for an end to government-mandated discrimination and full democratization for South Africa. Mandela became South Africa's president four years later. When his term in office ended in 1999, Mandela decided to step down and continue to work for causes of racial equality, justice, and peace as a private citizen.*

. . .Today the majority of South Africans, black and white, recognise that apartheid has no future. It has to be ended by our own decisive mass action in order to build peace and security. The mass campaign of defiance and other actions of our organisation and people can only culminate in the establishment of democracy. The destruction caused by apartheid on our sub-continent is incalculable. The fabric of family life of millions of my people has been shattered. Millions are homeless and unemployed. Our economy lies in ruins and our people are embroiled in political strife. Our resort to the armed struggle in 1960 with the formation of the military wing of the ANC, Umkhonto we Sizwe, was a purely defensive action against the violence of apartheid. The factors which necessitated the armed struggle still exist today. We have no option but to continue. We express the hope that a climate conducive to a negotiated settlement will be created soon so that there may no longer be the need for the armed struggle.

I am a loyal and disciplined member of the African National Congress. I am therefore in full agreement with all of its objectives, strategies and tactics.

The need to unite the people of our country is as important a task now as it always has been. No individual leader is able to take on this enormous task on his own. It is our task as leaders to place our views before our organisation and to allow the democratic structures to decide. On the question of democratic practice, I feel duty bound to make the point that a leader of the movement is a person who has been democratically elected at a national conference. This is a principle which must be upheld without any exceptions.

Today, I wish to report to you that my talks with the government have been aimed at normalising the political situation in the country. We have not as yet begun discussing the basic demands of the struggle. I wish to stress that I myself have at no time entered into negotiations about the future of our country except to insist on a meeting between the ANC and the government.

Mr De Klerk has gone further than any other Nationalist president in taking real steps to normalise the situation. However, there are further steps as outlined in the Harare Declaration that have to be met before negotiations on the basic demands of our people can begin. I reiterate our call for, inter alia, the immediate ending of the State of Emergency and the freeing of all, and not only some, political prisoners. Only such a normalised situation, which allows for free political activity, can allow us to consult our people in order to obtain a mandate.

The people need to be consulted on who will negotiate and on the content of such negotiations. Negotiations cannot take place above the heads or behind the backs of our people. It is our belief that the future of our country can only be determined by a body which is democratically elected on a non-racial basis. Negotiations on the dismantling of apartheid will have to address the overwhelming demand of our people for a democratic, non-racial and unitary South Africa. There must be an end to white monopoly on political power and a fundamental restructuring of our political and economic systems to ensure that the inequalities of apartheid are addressed and our society thoroughly democratised.

It must be added that Mr De Klerk himself is a man of integrity who is acutely aware of the dangers of a public figure not honouring his undertakings. But as an organisation we base our policy and strategy on the harsh reality we are faced with. And this reality is that we are still suffering under the policy of the Nationalist government.

Our struggle has reached a decisive moment. We call on our people to seize this moment so that the process towards democracy is rapid and uninterrupted. We have waited too long for our freedom. We can no longer wait. Now is the time to intensify the struggle on all fronts. To relax our efforts now would be a mistake which generations to come will not be able to forgive. The sight of freedom looming on the horizon should encourage us to redouble our efforts.

It is only through disciplined mass action that our victory can be assured. We call on our white compatriots to join us in the shaping of a new South Africa. The freedom movement is a political home for you too. We call on the international community to continue the campaign to isolate the apartheid regime. To lift sanctions now would be to run the risk of aborting the process towards the complete eradication of apartheid.

Our march to freedom is irreversible. We must not allow fear to stand in our way. Universal suffrage on a common voters' role in a united democratic and non-racial South Africa is the only way to peace and racial harmony.

In conclusion I wish to quote my own words during my trial in 1964. They are true today as they were then:

I have fought against white domination and I have fought against black domination. I have cherished the ideal of a democratic and free society in which all persons live together in harmony and with equal opportunities. It is an ideal which I hope to live for and to achieve. But if needs be, it is an ideal for which I am prepared to die.

SEE ALSO *African Union; Economic Sanctions; Nobel Peace Prize*

BIBLIOGRAPHY
Books

Clark, Nancy. *South Africa: The Rise and Fall of Apartheid*. Bloomington, MN: Pearson, 2011.

Mandela, Nelson. *The Long Walk to Freedom: The Autobiography of Nelson Mandela*. New York: Bay Back Books, 1995.

Ross, Robert. *A Concise History of South Africa*. Cambridge, MA: Cambridge University Press, 2009.

Web Sites

"African National Congress." http://www.anc.org.za/ (accessed December 27, 2013).

Drew, Allison. "South African Politics: An Introduction Using Internet Resources." *Department of Politics, University of York*. http://www-users.york.ac.uk/~ad15/SApolitics.htm (accessed December 27, 2013).

"Nelson Mandela Centre of Memory." http://www.nelsonmandela.org. (accessed December 27, 2013).

"South Africa: Overcoming Apartheid, Building Democracy." http://overcomingapartheid.msu.edu/ (accessed December 27, 2013).

Spanish Civil War

⊕ Introduction

On July 17, 1936, the Spanish Civil War began, initiated by an uprising of right-wing Spanish military officers stationed in Spanish Morocco who disapproved of Spain's increasingly liberal government of the Second Spanish Republic. The insurrection spread to the Spanish mainland, leading to a vicious and bloody conflict that lasted nearly three years.

The conflict pitted those who supported the Spanish Republic (the Republicans) against those who saw themselves as Nationalists. The head of the rebel Nationalists was General Francisco Franco (1892–1975). The war was a battle between political philosophies: a liberal democracy that leaned toward socialism and anticlericalism versus fascism (authoritarian ultra-nationalism). The Republicans embraced the former; the Nationalists supported the latter. It was also a war of economic class. In the decades leading up to the civil war, Spain had become a deeply divided nation. One side included the military, wealthy landowners, businessmen, and the nation's Roman Catholic Church. The other side comprised urban workers, agricultural laborers, and an educated middle class.

The Spanish Civil War has often been described as a preview of, or a prelude to, World War II (1939–45), as Spanish Nationalists were bolstered by aid from Nazi Germany and Fascist Italy, while the Republicans, also called Loyalists, received help from the Communist Soviet Union, as well as volunteers from the United States, Europe, and other countries. Ultimately, the Nationalists were victorious. The outcome had a significant impact on the power balance in Europe, and it proved to be a testing ground for the military power of Germany and Italy, which would come into play during World War II. After the Spanish Civil War, Francisco Franco ruled Spain until he died in 1975.

⊕ Historical Background

In 1931, Spanish King Alfonso XIII (1886–1941) allowed an election that would determine how Spain would be governed. The majority voted for a more liberalized republic. This development compelled Alfonso to seek exile.

The newly proclaimed Second Spanish Republic came into power, with middle-class liberals and socialist moderates dominating political life. The first two years of this new republic were characterized by liberal reform policies, such as the enfranchisement of women, the legalization of divorce, and the establishment of freedom of speech. These changes, however, were strongly opposed by the country's conservatives and elites: the land-owning aristocrats, the Catholic Church, and a sizeable portion of the military.

In November 1933, in another election, the right-wing element reclaimed governmental control. Sympathizers with the old administration instigated an uprising in the Asturias mining districts. Meanwhile, an oppositional response was staged in Barcelona. The activity, termed the October Revolution, was quashed by General Franco. The conservative faction gained a victory. Subsequently, Franco was appointed the army's chief of staff. But in February 1936 yet another election enabled the leftist Popular Front to regain political power. As a result, Franco, an authoritarian monarchist, was assigned to a remote and minor command in the Canary Islands, a Spanish archipelago just off the coast of Africa's mainland.

Right-leaning Spanish military officers feared that a liberal-leaning government was the first step toward a Marxist revolution. They conspired to retake political power, and they convinced a hesitant Franco to take part in the conspiracy.

The civil war, originally caused by internal tensions within Spain, became enmeshed in international

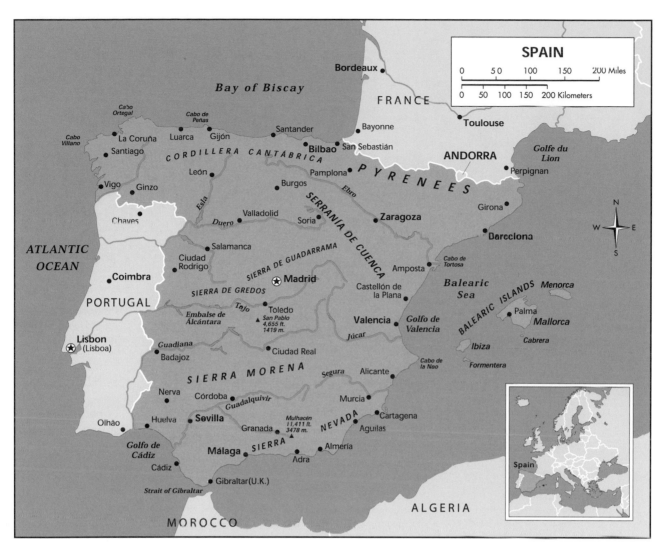

© 2014 Cengage Learning

politics that ultimately involved Nazi Germany, Fascist Italy, and Communist Russia. In the eyes of many, the issue was bigger than Spanish politics and concerned the direction in which the world, poised on the brink of a world war, was to go. Would it head toward democracy, communism, or fascism? The victory of the fascist forces was greeted with foreboding by many supporters of democracy.

The Civil War Begins

The conservative Spanish military elite planned a coup to start in the early morning of July 18, 1936. However, the plans were discovered, and this forced the right-wing rebels into swift action. Their hasty measures proved effective. The Nationalists took control of Seville. They were assisted by conservative Moroccan troops who also objected to Spain's emerging left leaning leadership. As the Republican government delayed a response, the

uprising quickly spread farther into Spain. On July 20, General Franco assumed control of the insurgent armies.

The situation led to a divided Spain, and outside forces were ready to seize portions. The Franco-led Nationalists received aid (weaponry and soldiers) from the leading Fascist countries: Nazi Germany and Italy. The Republicans initially received aid from the Soviet Union and Mexico.

Spanish battalions rose up quickly, but they lacked sufficient weaponry to fight the Nationalists effectively. In the months that followed, Nationalists wrested control of areas in central and northern Spain. By November the Nationalists besieged the capital, Madrid.

The Republican faction successfully quelled uprisings in Madrid and several other areas. In this highly emotional conflict, both sides executed thousands of political opponents. General Franco's military units were better able to carry out organized eliminations, but both sides committed atrocities.

General Francisco Franco was invested as "head of the government of the Spanish state" in Burgos on October 2, 1936, following the decree of September 29, 1936, by which Franco obtained from his peers complete military and political power. He was also named Generalissimo of the ground, naval, and air forces. © *Keystone-France/Gamma-Keystone via Getty Images*

The Conflict Progresses

In 1937 Franco benefited from a united Nationalist force and continued aid from Germany and Italy. Communists and leftists in the United States, France, and the Soviet Union contributed to Spain's Republican cause by establishing the International Brigades, military units composed of volunteers from several different countries. These entities contributed to a successful defense of Madrid, which lasted until the end of the civil strife.

As the conflict progressed, the Nationalists broke out of well-held territories in the south and west and soon dominated Spain's northern coastline in 1937. In 1938 they cut a divisional course that reached the Mediterranean Sea and halved the Republican territory. That same year, Franco's army launched a major offensive move in Catalonia. This resulted in the January 1939 seizure of Barcelona.

The Republicans faced a harsh fact: Their cause was lost. This realization compelled them to assume a conciliatory stance. But Franco had no interest in negotiation.

In February 1939, some 250,000 Republican soldiers and an equal number of civilians fled to France. On March 5 the Republican government fled to exile in France. Two days later, battles broke out in Madrid between Communist and anti–Communist factions. The end of the civil war came on March 28, 1939, with the surrender of Madrid by the Republicans. The Republican army fell apart and surrendered. The Nationalist army seized control of the city. Franco announced the official end to the war on April 1, 1939.

Franco Establishes His Power

A key factor in Franco's victory was the Soviet Union's decision to abandon Spain's Republicans in 1938. This enabled Franco's armies to end what might once have seemed to be an endless standoff.

Following the victory, Franco's authoritarian government was recognized by Western democratic nations. But in Great Britain, France, and the United States, controversy continued. Within these nations some

Spanish militia fighters on the march at the beginning of the Spanish Civil War. © *Keystone/Getty Images*

viewed Franco and his followers as crusaders against Communism. Others considered the Republican struggle a battle for democracy against reactionary and tyrannical forces. But neither side could claim to have clean hands. In the beginning of the conflict, the Republicans killed priests and nuns. Nationalist slaughter was even greater. About 600,000 people were killed, and Franco placed about a million people in prisons and concentration camps.

⊕ Impacts and Issues

The Spanish Civil War amounted to class warfare, with the rich overcoming the poor. Yet the Republican side appeared to have more popular support, which helps explain why the war dragged on for three years, despite German and Italian help for the Nationalists' cause.

In the end Franco's victory signaled a significant defeat for democratic values in Europe. Democratic powerbrokers overseas and in Europe had been hesitant and inconsistent in their support of the Spanish Republicans. The Fascist powers, however, demonstrated a united front in their support of Franco.

Franco's rule was marked by violent repression of all opposition. This included murder and the indefinite imprisonment in concentration camps of anyone he considered an enemy of his regime. When Franco died in 1975, Juan Carlos, the grandson of Alfonso XIII, ascended to the Spanish throne, but quickly initiated a transition to democracy in Spain. Juan Carlos also granted a large degree of autonomy to Catalonia and the Basque Country, two regions of Spain with distinctive, non-Spanish languages and cultures that experienced especially extreme repression under Franco.

An ongoing controversy in Spain concerns how to deal with the countless human rights abuses conducted by Franco's government. In other nations, such as South Africa, governments have chosen to address wrongs committed by past governments by allowing victims to come forward and have their stories heard and validated– a so-called "truth and reconciliation" approach. Spain's government chose the opposite path, going so far as to institute a "Pact of Forgetting" in 1977, an agreement by left-wing and right-wing factions simply to ignore the atrocities committed under Franco.

A socialist government in Spain reversed course in 2004 with the Historical Memory Law, which condemned Franco and offered assistance to victims of

Picture taken during the Spanish Civil War in the late 1930s of Dolores Ibarruri, nicknamed "La Pasionaria," general secretary of the Spanish Communist Party, delivering a speech to support the Republic. © *STF/AFP/Getty Images*

repression under Franco, or their families, in finding information about the whereabouts of those missing or dead. When a center-right government came into power in 2011, the new law was not repealed, but the office of the Historical Memory Law was closed that year. However, because the Pact of Forgetting was never repealed, Spain has two conflicting positions on how to handle Franco's legacy.

⊕ Future Implications

In the wake of the global economic crisis that began in 2008, Spain's economy was devastated and unemployment skyrocketed, especially among the young. Those overwhelmingly affected were the working and middle classes, who became increasingly outraged by what they believed was irresponsible and reckless behaviors of bankers and other elites, whom they hold responsible for the downfall of the economy. This recent crisis has reopened old wounds from the Spanish Civil War and

left unhealed by the Franco regime and its successors. Anti-government protests erupted across Spain in 2011 and continued sporadically through 2013.

In July 2013, the protests regained urgency after allegations of corruption emerged centering on Prime Minister Mariano Rajoy, a member of Spain's conservative party. Protesters waved chorizo sausages above their heads to symbolize their discontent—"chorizo" is slang for thief. Although many Spaniards have typically turned a blind eye to political corruption, a rash of scandals, involving politicians and elites who appear to be enriching themselves while the general populace suffers, has changed that.

Large groups of unemployed young people who believe their government has betrayed them can quickly become revolutionaries—a situation that was repeatedly demonstrated by the successful revolutions that swept through the Middle East and North Africa during the Arab Spring of 2011 and 2012. As protests continued over government corruption and a dismal economy in Spain, concern grew that the country was fracturing along regional lines. In September 2013, hundreds of thousands of Catalonians took to the streets to demand complete independence from Spain. It remains to be seen whether the Spanish government can satisfy the pressing demands of millions of discontented Spaniards—or what will happen if it fails to do so.

SEE ALSO *Arab Spring; World War II*

BIBLIOGRAPHY

Books

Beevor, Antony. *The Battle for Spain: The Spanish Civil War, 1936–1939.* New York: Penguin Books, 2006.

Buckley, Henry. *The Life and Death of the Spanish Republic: A Witness to the Spanish Civil War.* New York: I. B. Tauris, 2013.

Hughes, Stuart H. *Contemporary Europe: A History.* Englewood Cliffs, NJ: Prentice-Hall, 1971.

Payne, Stanley G. *The Spanish Civil War.* New York: Cambridge University Press, 2012.

Preston, Paul. *The Spanish Holocaust: Inquisition and Extermination in Twentieth Century Spain.* London: Harper Press, 2012.

Web Sites

Alpert, Michael. "Uncivil War: The Military Struggle." *History Today,* March 1989. http://www.historytoday.com/michael-alpert/uncivil-war-military-struggle (accessed December 4, 2013).

"Church Beatifies 522 'Martyrs' of Spanish Civil War." *The Telegraph,* October 13, 2013. http://www.telegraph.co.uk/news/worldnews/europe/spain/10376516/Church-beatifies-522-martyrs-of-Spanish-Civil-War.html (accessed December 4, 2013).

"Francisco Franco." *Biography.com.* http://www.biography.com/people/francisco-franco-9300766 (accessed December 4, 2013).

"Guernica: Testimony of War." *Public Broadcasting Service (PBS).* http://www.pbs.org/treasuresoftheworld/a_nav/guernica_nav/main_guerfrm.html (accessed December 4, 2013).

Nebehay, Stephanie. "Spain Must Probe Civil War Disappearances, U.N. Watchdog Says." *Thomson Reuters,* November 15, 2013. http://uk.reuters.com/article/2013/11/15/uk-un-rights-spain-idUKBRE9AE0YH20131115 (accessed December 4, 2013).

THE WAR THROUGH THE EYES OF ARTISTS

The ferocity of the Spanish Civil War was described by many famous writers of the time. Many writers and artists were personally familiar with the progress of the war, often because they volunteered for service among the Republicans or because they covered the war as reporters. For example, American author Ernest Hemingway's famous novel *For Whom the Bell Tolls* (1940) was based on his experience reporting on the war for the North American Newspaper Alliance. British author George Orwell also wrote movingly about the war in *Homage to Catalonia* (1938).

Spanish painter Pablo Picasso created one of his most famous works, *Guernica* (1937), during the war. It was inspired by the bombing of the city of Guernica by German and Italian warplanes, sent on their mission by the Nationalists. The black-and-white painting shows a scene of chaos and horror, with the dead and dying citizens of Guernica strewn across the ground.

Sri Lanka's Civil War

⊕ Introduction

Sri Lanka is an island nation of 20 million people in the Indian Ocean, located less than 20 miles (31 kilometers) off the southeastern coast of India. The Sri Lankan Civil War was a long-running conflict between ethnic Tamil separatists and the Sri Lankan military that began in 1983 and ended in 2009. The Tamil separatists, led by the Liberation Tigers of Tamil Eelam (LTTE), also known as the Tamil Tigers, desire an independent Tamil state in the northern and eastern parts of Sri Lanka. The United Nations (UN) estimates that between 80,000 and 100,000 people died in intermittent fighting during the Sri Lankan Civil War, particularly in the last several months of fighting before the end of the war in 2009.

⊕ Historical Background

Britain controlled Sri Lanka, referred to as Ceylon during the colonial period, until the island gained independence in 1948. The majority ethnic Sinhalese population quickly asserted itself politically in the new nation's government. In 1956, the Sri Lankan parliament angered the Tamil minority community with the passage of the Sinhala Only Act, which declared Sinhala the official language of Sri Lanka. Political confrontations between the Sinhalese and Tamil communities increased throughout the 1960s and 1970s, and the Tamil United Liberation Front (TULF), a political party advocating for a separate state, formed in 1976. At the same time, the LTTE, led by Velupillai Prabhakaran (1954–), formed in support of violent action to create a new state, and it quickly became the most prominent Tamil militant group.

Eelam War I

On July 23, 1983, the LTTE killed 15 Sri Lankan soldiers in an ambush in northern Sri Lanka. In response, Sinhalese citizens in Colombo, the Sri Lankan capital, formed mobs and began attacking Tamils in the city. The riots spread to other Sri Lankan cities over the next several days. The series of riots, called "Black July," resulted in the deaths of between 1,000 and 3,000 Tamils, and injuries were sustained by an additional 1,000 Tamils. Sinhalese rioters also burned approximately 18,000 Tamil-owned homes and businesses. The events of Black July forced hundreds of thousands of Tamils to flee Sri Lanka for India, Canada, Australia, and Europe. Black July marked the beginning of the Sri Lankan Civil War.

Fighting continued between Sri Lankan and LTTE forces during the first phase of the Sri Lankan Civil War—often referred to as the Eelam War I—until a brief break in 1985, during which the two sides engaged in peace talks in Bhutan. After the peace talks failed, fighting resumed, and the Sri Lankan military made significant gains against the LTTE. By 1987, Sri Lankan troops had pushed LTTE forces into a small northern corner of the island. Under threat of an Indian ground invasion, the Sri Lankan government signed the Indo-Sri Lankan Accord in July 1987. Under this agreement, Sri Lankan forces withdrew from the northern part of Sri Lanka, and Indian peacekeeping forces moved in to prevent future clashes there.

Eelam War II

By 1989, new governments in both India and Sri Lanka desired a withdrawal of the Indian Peace Keeping Forces (IPKF). By March 1990 India completed the withdrawal of its peacekeeping forces, which had numbered 100,000 troops. The ceasefire lasted for several months while the Sri Lankan government and the LTTE solidified their power bases. The second stage of the Sri Lankan Civil War, known as Eelam War II, began in June 1990 when the LTTE killed more than 100 Sinhalese and Muslim policemen. Indian sympathies for the LTTE evaporated in May 1991 when an LTTE suicide bomber killed former Indian Prime Minister Rajiv Gandhi (1944–1991).

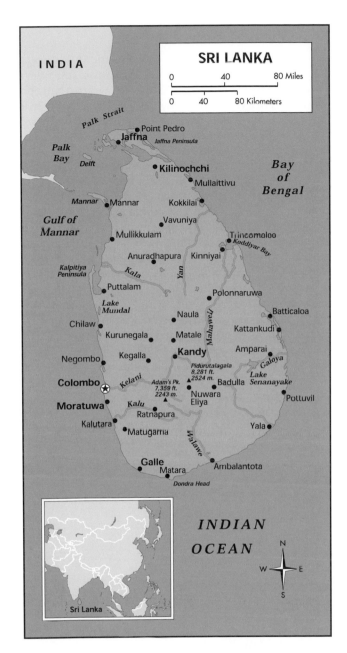

SRI LANKA

INDIA

Palk Strait

Point Pedro
Jaffna Jaffna Peninsula

Palk
Bay
Delft

Kilinochchi
Mullaittivu

Mannar Mannar
Kokkilai

Gulf of
Mannar
Vavuniya
Mullikkulam
Trincomaloo
Koddiyar Bay

Kalpitiya
Peninsula
Kala
Anuradhapura Kinniyai
Puttalam
Yan
Polonnaruwa
Lake
Mundal
Naula
Batticaloa
Chilaw
Matale
Kattankudi
Kurunegala
Mahaweli
Negombo Kegalla
Kandy
Amparai
Galoya
Pidurutalagala
8,281 ft.
2524 m.
Lake
Senanayake
Colombo
Kelani
Adam's Pk.
7,359 ft.
2243 m.
Badulla
Pottuvil
Moratuwa
Kalu
Nuwara
Eliya
Kalutara
Ratnapura
Yala
Matugama
Walawe
Galle
Matara
Ambalantota
Dondra Head

Bay
of
Bengal

INDIAN
OCEAN

INDIAN OCEAN / Sri Lanka inset

© 2014 Cengage Learning

The LTTE had feared that Gandhi would redeploy Indian troops to Sri Lanka if his party won the 1991 elections.

Eelam War III

The pro-peace People's Alliance party won the Sri Lankan parliamentary elections of 1994. The LTTE and the new Sri Lankan government agreed to a cease fire in January 1995, but peace talks collapsed in April 1995 and led to the third stage of the Sri Lankan Civil War, or Eelam War III. The Sri Lankan military made rapid progress against the LTTE's northern strongholds

and captured the city of Jaffna, forcing thousands of LTTE soldiers and hundreds of thousands of civilians to go inland for safety. The LTTE, failing on the military front, began carrying out terrorist bombings of civilian targets in Colombo and other cities. These attacks aided the Sri Lankan government's efforts to enlist other nations to declare the LTTE a terrorist organization, in order to limit LTTE funding. As of 2009, 32 nations, including the United States, Canada, India, and all European Union nations, listed the LTTE as a terrorist organization.

Eelam War IV

By the late 1990s, more than one million Sri Lankans had been displaced by the war, leading to increased calls for peace talks. Following the terrorist attacks by al-Qaeda on New York on September 11, 2001, the LTTE, fearing that the United States and other nations would lend greater support to the Sri Lankan government, agreed to a cease-fire. Peace negotiations dragged on for several years with the leadership of the LTTE and the Sri Lankan government divided over the best path to peace.

The fourth stage of the Sri Lankan Civil War, or Eelam War IV, started in December 2005 when LTTE forces increased attacks on Sri Lankan troops. Although LTTE and Sri Lankan forces resumed fighting, both sides remained in peace negotiations until the LTTE formally withdrew from peace talks in April 2006.

The Sri Lankan army responded to the renewal of hostilities by launching a military offensive in July 2006 that rapidly pushed LTTE forces out of eastern Sri Lanka and back to LTTE strongholds in northern Sri Lanka. The LTTE again began carrying out terrorist attacks on civilian targets. On January 2, 2008, the Sri Lankan government officially withdrew from the 2002 cease-fire and increased its offensive in northern Sri Lanka. The Sri Lankan army made significant gains throughout the autumn of 2008.

In November 2008, the Sri Lankan army launched an attack on Kilinochchi, the de facto administrative capital of the Tamils. Kilinochchi fell on January 2, 2009. LTTE forces quickly abandoned their positions throughout the Jaffna peninsula and withdrew to Mullaitivu, the location of the last remaining LTTE base. On January 25, 2009, the Sri Lankan army captured Mullaitivu, and on February 5, 2009, the army captured the last LTTE naval base, effectively cutting off supplies to the LTTE. With these victories, the Sri Lankan army had forced the remaining LTTE troops into a section of jungle comprised of less than 78 square miles (200 square kilometers). In May 2009, after a bloody offensive, the Sri Lankan military defeated the remaining LTTE holdouts and declared victory in the 26-year war.

LAND MINES IN SRI LANKA

One of the tragic legacies of war is the death and destruction caused by land mines that are left behind to kill an estimated 15,000 to 20,000 victims each year, many of them children. Many more are injured and maimed by these weapons. Found in nearly 80 countries, including Sri Lanka, the humanitarian impact of land mine deaths and injuries began receiving worldwide attention in the 1980s and continues to generate calls for abolishing their use as well as efforts to find and remove or destroy those already in place.

In Sri Lanka, land mines were used by both government and opposition forces, with government troops laying well-defined "belts" as they advanced on the LTTE (Liberation Tigers of Tamil Eelam) positions. The LTTE laid their mines randomly, frequently near homes in densely populated areas and on agricultural lands.

While government and aid groups have joined in ongoing efforts to locate, mark, and remove or destroy mines, hundreds of thousands remain, hampering efforts to restore farmland and resettle internal refugees in their former homes.

Humans have not been the only casualties of land mines. Animals have also been affected, including the already endangered Asian elephant, some 20 of which are killed by land mines each year.

⊕ Impacts and Issues

After the declaration of victory, President Mahinda Rajapaksa (1945–) called for reconciliation and tolerance between the country's Sinhalese majority and the Tamil minority. By mid-June 2009, there were still nearly 300,000 Tamils who remained displaced and were forced to live in refugee camps. United Nations officials decried conditions in the overcrowded camps and warned that new conflicts might erupt if the displaced civilians were not allowed to return home quickly.

As part of its effort to achieve national reconciliation, the Sri Lankan army announced in July 2009 that it would form an ethnic Tamil regiment in the Sri Lankan army and welcome members of the militias it had recently considered enemies. In January 2010, voting began in war-scarred Sri Lanka's presidential election, which pitted incumbent Rajapakse against his former army chief in a tense contest hit by pre-dawn bomb blasts. Rajapaksa was declared the winner, with an estimated 57 percent of the vote.

In June 2010, two senior U.S. foreign policy advisors arrived in Sri Lanka for meetings with Sri Lankan government officials. The United States and other countries have urged Sri Lanka to undertake a vigorous program of reconciliation to heal the rifts caused by the country's long civil war. The June visit was a

Sri Lankan security personnel attempt to move a car from beside burning vehicles in the convoy of Defence Ministry Secretary Gotabaya Rajapakse after a suicide bomb attack in Colombo, December 1, 2006. A suspected Tamil suicide bomber attacked a defence ministry convoy carrying the president's brother, killing at least one soldier, police said. Gotabaye Rajapakse, secretary to the defence ministry and brother of President Mahinda Rajapakse, was unhurt after the blast in the heart of the Sri Lankan capital. *© Lakruwan Wanniarachchi/AFP/ Getty Images*

Sri Lankan war displaced ethnic Tamils show their inked fingers after voting outside the Tamil Madhya Maha Vidayalaya polling station in Vavuniya, some 180 miles (290 kilometers) north of capital Colombo, on January 26, 2010. © *Indranil Mukherjee/AFP/Getty Images*

continuation of talks begun by U.S. Secretary of State Hillary Clinton (1947–) and Sri Lankan external affairs minister G. L. Peiris in May 2010.

War Crimes Investigation

On June 22, 2010, UN Secretary General Ban Ki-moon (1944–) appointed a panel to investigate alleged war crimes committed during the final months of the Sri Lankan civil war. Sri Lankan President Rajapaksa strongly objected and said Sri Lanka has its own commission investigating human rights abuses during the war, and that the UN interference is unwelcome. On July 8, Ban recalled the UN envoy to Sri Lanka and closed a Colombo office after unruly protests outside the office disrupted the work of UN employees. The Sri Lanka housing minister, Wimal Weerawansa, announced he was beginning a hunger strike to put further pressure on the UN to stop its war crimes investigation.

Sri Lanka came under renewed pressure to cooperate with the UN war crimes investigation in December after the authentication by the UN of a May 2009 video showing the gruesome murders of bound captives by Sri Lankan soldiers. Sri Lanka's military spokesman, Ubaya Medawala, claimed the video was altered and maintained the position that no UN inquiry is necessary because Sri Lanka is conducting its own war crimes investigation.

However, a UN special investigator announced on May 31, 2011, that after conducting a thorough analysis of the footage, he was convinced it was authentic.

The Sri Lankan government has repeatedly resisted efforts by the UN to conduct an inquiry into possible war crimes committed during the country's protracted civil war, saying that it would rely on its own internal investigative commission, the Lessons Learnt and Reconciliation Commission (LLRC). In September 2011, however, Amnesty International issued a report strongly criticizing the Sri Lankan commission as "flawed at every level," saying the LLRC failed "to appropriately investigate credible allegations of systematic violations by both sides to the conflict." The Sri Lankan government rejected the Amnesty International report.

Sri Lanka's army, under diplomatic pressure from the United States, agreed on February 14, 2012, to launch a war crimes probe into possible offenses against civilians committed by Sri Lankan soldiers during the final months of the civil war. The United States warned Sri Lanka that failure to agree to an investigation would result in censure at the UN Human Rights Council meeting in Geneva in March 2012. The UN's civil rights body voted on March 22 to approve a resolution calling for an investigation into possible Sri Lankan war crimes.

Internally displaced Sri Lankan people during a visit by UN Secretary General Ban Ki-moon at Menik Farm refugee camp in Cheddikulam on May 23, 2009. Ban came face-to-face with the despair of Sri Lanka's war-hit civilians as he toured the nation's largest refugee complex. Just days after Colombo declared victory over the Tamil Tigers, Ban toured the sprawling Menik Farm camp, 155 miles (250 kilometers) north of Colombo, which was jammed with civilians who had fled the war zone. © *Joe Klamar/AFP/Getty Images*

The Missing and Detained

In mid-June 2011, Sri Lankan police forces announced they would give family members details about thousands of people, mostly Tamils, held in detention since the end of the civil war two years earlier. However, when hundreds of people arrived in Vavuniya seeking information on their family members, no information was available. Few have had any luck finding news of their relatives, despite the announcement by police that families were free to make inquiries.

Families of some of those who had disappeared during the country's civil war participated in a peaceful protest in early March. The protesters asked for a UN-backed investigation of human rights abuses that allegedly took place during the 26-year-long fight. The government had previously rejected the demand, dismissing the claims and stating that it was not responsible for the disappearances.

Closing the Last Refugee Camp

In late September of 2012, Sri Lanka finally shut down what was once one of the largest refugee camps in the world. Menik Farm, which was opened as a refugee camp

during the final stages of the civil war, at one time held up to 300,000 mostly Tamil internally displaced persons (IDPs). It was rumored by some diplomats to be more of a military-run internment camp than a refugee camp for those fleeing the fighting. Conditions in the camp were overcrowded, and many suffered from communicable diseases, as well as a lack of water, food, and medical supplies. On September 25, 2012, the government moved the last of Manik Farm's inhabitants back to their lands in the Mullaitivu district. After the camp was shut down, more than three years after the civil war officially ended, the government stated that there were no more IDPs in the country. However, some of the families who had moved out of Manik Farm to return to their home district were unable to move back into their own homes because they still were occupied by the military.

⊕ Future Implications

Ethnic tensions continue in Sri Lanka. International leaders continue to pressure the government to protect minority rights. In addition to the Tamils, there is a large Muslim minority that faces discrimination and sometimes violence. Various countries, including India and Saudi Arabia, have advocated on behalf of specific groups to which they are sympathetic. Furthermore, the dispossession of refugees and the missing from the war, as well as the investigation into war crimes, remain challenges to fully integrating the community.

Thousands of people, primarily Tamils, are missing, and acts of ethnic violence take place frequently. The ethnic Sinhalese population remains in control of most aspects of the government and military, and there have been charges that an extremist Sinhalese terrorist group has formed. A particular hurdle to change appears to be the government, which is controlled by the president and his two brothers. The brothers control a large portion of the Sri Lankan budget, and they have shown little interest in reaching out to marginalized and displaced populations.

SEE ALSO *Humanitarian Aid; United Nations*

BIBLIOGRAPHY

Books

Clarance, William. *Ethnic Warfare in Sri Lanka and the UN Crisis.* London, England: Pluto Press, 2007.

Holt, John Clifford. *The Sri Lanka Reader: History, Culture, Politics.* Durham, NC: Duke University Press, 2011.

Kingsbury, Damien. *Sri Lanka and the Responsibility to Protect: Politics, Ethnicity and Genocide.* New York, NY: Routledge, 2012.

Web Sites

Doucet, Lyse. "UN 'Failed Sri Lankan Civilians' Says Internal Probe." *BBC News,* November 13, 2012. http://www.bbc.co.uk/news/world-asia-20308610 (accessed January 6, 2014).

International Crisis Group. "Sri Lanka's Authoritarian Turn: The Need for International Action." *Asia Report No. 243,* February 20, 2013. http://www.crisisgroup.org/en/regions/asia/south-asia/sri-lanka/243-sri-lankas-authoritarian-turn-the-need-for-international-action.aspx (accessed January 6, 2014).

"Q & A: Post-war Sri Lanka." *BBC News,* September 20, 2013. http://www.bbc.co.uk/news/world-south-asia-11393458 (accessed January 6, 2014).

"Sri Lanka Shuts Manik Farm IDP Camp." *The Hindu,* September 25, 2012. http://www.thehindu.com/news/sri-lanka-shuts-manik-farm-idp-camp/article3935374.ece (accessed January 6, 2014).

Williams, Rachel, and Matthew Weaver. "Timeline: Sri Lanka Conflict: Key Events in the 25-year Civil War between the Government and the Tamil Tigers." *The Guardian,* May 18, 2009. http://www.guardian.co.uk/world/2009/may/18/sri-lanka-conflict (accessed June 28, 2013).

Sudan and South Sudan

⊕ Introduction

The bloody military conflict between northern and southern Sudan has lasted for more than 50 years. It

has led to many atrocities, some of which have involved heads of state. On March 4, 2009, the International Criminal Court (ICC) issued an arrest warrant for Sudan's President, Omar Hassan al-Bashir (1944–), on charges of war crimes and crimes against humanity. In July 2010, the ICC amended the charges to include genocide. With the indictment, Bashir became the first sitting head of state to be indicted by the ICC. Bashir led Sudan during years of civil conflict that have created a humanitarian crisis for the people of Sudan, particularly in the western Darfur region. More than four million people have been displaced by conflict and many more have suffered from famine and disease.

In a 2011 referendum that won nearly 99 percent approval by voters in the south, the new independent nation of South Sudan was born as it split from Sudan. Although Bashir agreed to abide by the results of the referendum, relations between the two nations have been tense, with accusations from both sides of military interference by the other. Further complicating relations is the fact that South Sudan has vast oil reserves but, as a landlocked country, it can only market its oil via the pipelines and port controlled by Sudan.

⊕ Historical Background

The Republic of the Sudan was emancipated from decades of Anglo-Egyptian rule in 1956. Since then, Sudan has been a hotspot of civil war, caused by rebel groups, militant Islamic policies, and on-and-off rule by the military. By the 1990s, tensions had arisen between Sudan and its neighbors, from which Sudan became increasingly isolated.

Sudan, situated in northeast Africa, had a population estimated at 45 million in 2011, before the secession of South Sudan. Indigenous Africans constituted 52 percent of the population and Arabs accounted for

SUDAN

| 0 | 125 | 250 | 375 Miles |
| 0 | 125 | 250 | 375 Kilometers |

EGYPT

LIBYA

Libyan Desert

Nubian Desert

Halā'ib Ras Hadarba

Wādi Ḥalfā'

Red Sea

Port Sudan

Suakin

Dunqulah

'Aquiq

'Aṭbarah

'Aṭbarah

CHAD

Iriba

Howar

Nile

Malik

Nile

Omdurman Khartoum

Blue

Sebderat

Kassalā ERITREA

Jebel Teljo 6,411 ft. 1954 m.

Adré

Al Fāshir

Wad Madani

Al Qaḍārif

Al Junaynah

JEBEL MARRA

Al Ubayyid

Kūstī

Sannār

Nile

Nyala

An Nuhūd

NUBA MTS.

Kāduqli

Ad Damazin

Lake Tana

Haraze

Birao

'Arab

indefinite

Abyei Area

Ghazāl

indefinite

White Nile

ETHIOPIA

Malakāl

Nhar Subāt

South Sudan–Sudan Boundary
Represents the January 1, 1956 alignment; final alignment pending negotiations and demarcations.

Lol

Sudan

Waw

SOUTH SUDAN

Sue

Jabal

Akobo Wenz

Kangen

Hosa'ina

CENTRAL AFRICAN REPUBLIC

Māji

Yambio

Juba

Kapoeta

Kinyeti 10,456 ft. 3187 m.

DEMOCRATIC REPUBLIC OF THE CONGO

UGANDA

KENYA

© 2014 Cengage Learning

39 percent. At that time, the single largest African ethnic group in Sudan was the Dinka, with an estimated population of four million people. After the country split, the Dinka were located primarily in South Sudan.

After the split, Sudan's population decreased to about 35 million. Arabic is the official language, but Nubian, Ta Bedawie, and English are also widely spoken. Islam (Sunni) is the state religion. Some residents practice Indigenous beliefs, while a small percentage are Christian. In South Sudan, the population numbered more than 11 million in 2013. Arabic and English serve as the official languages, although regional languages,

such as Dinka, Bari, Nuer, Shilluk, and Zande, are also spoken. The majority of South Sudanese are Christian with some observing indigenous religious practices.

Located south of Egypt, Sudan has been claimed as territory of both Middle Eastern and European empires. In the 1820s, the ruler of Egypt took control of northern Sudan and claimed it as part of his own nation. It remained under his control for several decades, until Sudanese rebels pushed both Egypt and its British occupiers back to the north. However, Great Britain once again assumed control in 1899, effectively making Sudan a British colony. During this colonial period, British

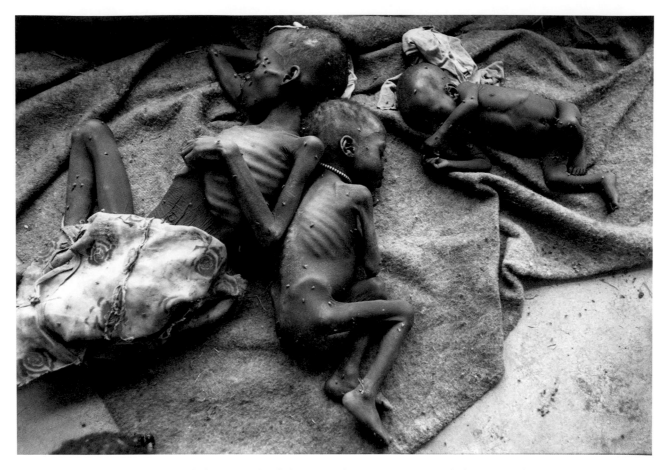

In addition to war, the Sudanese have had to contend with devastating famine. Here, victims of a famine in Sudan sleep in July 1998 at a hospital in Wau, southern Sudan. The Sudanese government and the Sudan People's Liberation Army (SPLA) agreed to a three-month cease-fire to facilitate the sending of food to the region, devastated by civil war since 1983. In 1998, the SPLA had been fighting government troops for 15 years in a bid to end the domination of the Islamic north over the largely Christian and animist south. The conflict was not resolved until South Sudan became independent in 2011. © *Eric Feferberg/AFP/Getty Images*

officials intensified the gap between northerners and southerners by not allowing Sudanese citizens to travel freely between the two regions. Great Britain ultimately granted Sudan its independence in 1956.

Sudan had long been dominated by those in its northern region, which led to ethnic and religious conflict. Many southern Sudanese are Christian and tribal, while northerners are mostly Muslim. The southerners wanted more autonomy and the right to control their own affairs. The religious and cultural differences have been exacerbated by discovery of oil in the poorer and militarily weaker south. Yet not even the 2011 partition of the country has been able to end the hostilities between the two regions.

Civil War

The northern part of Sudan and the southern part of Sudan fought what became known as the First Sudanese Civil War from 1955 to 1972, resulting in half a million deaths. In 1972, the south was granted some level of autonomy. But conflicts rose anew in the 1980s when

the northern government attempted to introduce sharia (Islamic law) throughout the country. These religious laws restricted southern Sudanese also, even though they were primarily non-Muslim. Shared oil revenues also became an issue of conflict as new oil fields were discovered in the south. The southerners fought back against the Islamic rule of northern Sudan by forming the Sudan People's Liberation Army (SPLA) in 1983. This marked the beginning of the Second Sudanese Civil War.

The second civil war had a devastating impact on various people from the Dinka and Nuer ethnic groups. Thousands of children, especially boys, were separated from their families when their villages in southern Sudan were raided and many residents were assaulted and killed. Because boys were responsible for tending the family's cattle, they were not home during the day when their villages were attacked. As such, they returned to find their homes destroyed; many found themselves orphaned. Since Sudanese girls traditionally performed domestic work at home, the majority of the girls in the

Pro-government Arab paramilitary groups called "Janjaweed" are responsible for helping the government in the raid of African villages that left 1.6 million Africans in the Darfur region of Sudan homeless and tens of thousands dead in Kabkabiya, Sudan, on November 21, 2004. © *Jahi Chikwendiu/The Washington Post via Getty Images*

targeted villages were either killed or kidnapped by the attackers and few escaped.

Displaced with few resources available to them, many ran away, walking for months, even years, on a dangerous journey across Africa until they reached refugee camps in Ethiopia and Kenya. During their long and difficult trek, thousands died from various causes, including dehydration, starvation, or disease. Some lost their lives when attacked by enemy soldiers or wild animals in the forest. The children came to be called "The Lost Boys of Sudan"—a name given to them by relief agency workers in reference to the fictional character Peter Pan and his group of orphans. Numbering more than 20,000, the young refugees and their plight were the subject of the 2004 documentary film *The Lost Boys of Sudan*, which garnered worldwide attention. A few thousand boys were sponsored by refugee organizations for immigration to the United States.

Fighting continued between rebels and government forces in southern Sudan for decades, making the conflict one of the longest-running wars in modern history. Nearly two million Sudanese were killed during the conflict. Meanwhile, the government of Sudan was weak and ineffectual, and in 1989 military leader Omar al-Bashir seized control of Sudan, suspending political parties and instituting Islamic law even more strictly than previous rulers. In the 1990s, the Sudan

government invited Osama bin Laden (1957–2011), leader of the terrorist group al-Qaeda, to Sudan, resulting in Sudan being labeled a state sponsor of terrorism. In response to ever-more brutal imposition of Islamic law, rebels in the south, including the region of Darfur, took up arms against the state. The War in Darfur was notorious for a high level of cruelty and destruction, garnering international charges of genocide.

Darfur

One of the most volatile crises began in 2003, as fighting broke out in the Darfur region between government forces and two militant groups, the Sudan Liberation Movement/Army (SLM/A) and the Justice and Equality Movement (JEM). At the heart of the conflict is an ethnic rivalry between indigenous African groups—including the Fur, Massaleet, and Zaghawa—and Arab nomads of the region. The Africans accused the government of persecution and marginalization against them in favor of the Arabs. The SLM/A and JEM, representing the indigenous Africans, launched their first attacks against government targets in March 2003. The government responded by sending what it described as self-defense militias, but reports soon surfaced that a militia group known as Janjaweed began attacking Fur civilians. The Janjaweed raids on villages initiated one of the world's worst humanitarian crises. Some reports indicate

Sudanese President Omar al-Bashir (R) and his South Sudan counterpart Salva Kiir hold a joint press conference in Khartoum on October 9, 2011, as Sudan set deadlines to resolve outstanding disputes with South Sudan at the end of the first top-level southern delegation's visit to Khartoum since independence. South Sudan proclaimed independence from the north on July 9, after years of devastating civil war, in which some two million people died.   © *Ashraf Shazly/AFP/Getty Images*

that up to 300,000 people were murdered between 2003 and 2009. Several million people were displaced from their homes.

Although the Sudanese government claims to have no control over or affiliation with the Janjaweed, many international groups have called the Darfur conflict a government-sponsored genocide. The government claims that reports concerning the conflict have been grossly exaggerated, placing the number of deaths at about 10,000. The situation has been difficult to assess, particularly since the Sudanese government has been known to close borders to humanitarian agencies, whose services are much needed. Omar al-Bashir (1994–), the President of Sudan, is the world's only sitting president to be indicted by the International Criminal Court. He is accused of genocide and war crimes connected with unrest in Sudan's Darfur region.

Peace Agreement

In response to the continuing warfare, neighboring countries attempted to broker peace talks. The Intergovernmental Authority on Development, of which

Sudan is a member, encouraged a settlement. An initial cease-fire between the government of Sudan and the Sudan People's Liberation Movement (SPLM) in the south was set in January 2002. This was followed by the 2005 Comprehensive Peace Agreement that established the Government of National Unity (dominated by the National Congress Party, or NCL) and the interim Government of Southern Sudan (dominated by the SPLM) and outlined steps toward the sharing of wealth, power, and security between the two parties. A major point in the agreement called for a 2011 referendum for independence in the south, as many southern residents supported a secessionist movement since Sudan gained independence.

⊕ Impacts and Issues

After more than a year of debates and delays, the referendum for independence in the south took place on January 9, 2011. By late January, it was clear that about 99 percent of the votes were cast in favor of secession. As a result, South Sudan became an independent country on July 9, 2011. The population of the new country,

South Sudan, was estimated at more than 11 million in 2013. The population is young, with more than half under the age of 18 and 72 percent under the age of 30. About 83 percent of the population lives in rural areas. Christianity is the predominant religion.

"Sudan's Jerusalem"

Nevertheless, violence between ethnic and political factions has continued along the border between the two nations, and the governments of Sudan and South Sudan have been unable to agree on the proper demarcation of the new border between the nations. Fighting in this region continued after South Sudan's official independence date as some southern rebels found themselves still part of the north, and as officials from South Sudan continued to negotiate with the government for measures that would ensure the rights of all former southern rebels remaining in the north.

Conflict was particularly intense regarding the Abyei region, which has been referred to as "Sudan's Jerusalem," since it is claimed by both northern and southern Sudan and has been in dispute for years. In April 2011, fighting between South Sudan's army and rebel groups broke out in two states in the region, resulting in an estimated 180 deaths. Two separate incidents of fighting occurred in the states of Unity and Upper Nile, both parts of South Sudan. In both cases, clashes occurred between rebel groups and the South Sudanese army, although the first involved the Sudan People's Liberation Army, based in South Sudan, and the second was led by a former northern army commander. South Sudan was eventually able to get the situation under control, but observers inside and outside the country worried that the new state army would not be able to hold South Sudan together after independence.

In June 2011, Sudan's government and representatives from South Sudan signed an agreement to govern the controversial border states together. Even though the agreement was made, UN troops from Ethiopia were sent into the Abyei region in an attempt to diffuse the tensions that were building in the area. Although the deal did not implement an immediate cease-fire, negotiations were begun, and both northern and southern Sudan reached a compromise over the states of Blue Nile and South Kordofan. Control over Abyei was still a source of conflict between South Sudan and Sudan, hence Sudanese of the area are considered citizens of both countries.

Border Conflicts

As in Abyei, a primary issue concerning these states is the fate of the pro-southern rebels who have been left living on the wrong side of the newly drawn border. In South Kordofan, a surge in violence began as early as June 2011 as the Sudanese government attempted to disarm the pro-southern ethnic Nuban rebels, who were fighting in favor of South Sudan independence. The government was initially accused of staging an attack of ethnic cleansing against the Nubans, an allegation that was immediately denied. Fighting in this region continued after the South Sudan's official independence date as these southern rebels found themselves still part of the north, and as officials from South Sudan continued to negotiate with the government for measures that would ensure the rights of all former southern rebels remaining in the north.

On August 23, 2011, the Sudanese government issued a two-week cease-fire in South Kordofan to allow a break for more peaceful negotiations and for safe shipments of humanitarian aid. It was estimated that nearly 200,000 people had been displaced from their homes from June through August. At the time the cease-fire was called, the Sudanese government named the Sudanese Red Crescent organization as the only group allowed to deliver aid shipments to the region.

Continuing Conflict

In early 2012, general peace talks between South Sudan and Sudan showed signs of success. Representatives from each government met in Ethiopia and signed a nonaggression pact on February 11, 2012. The pact brought both sides under an agreement to respect the sovereignty and territorial integrity of each other. It also included a pledge to refrain from physical attacks in settling disputes. Nonetheless, violence erupted again between the two nations in March 2012 over the Heglig oil field, which lies near the border. Although the international community recognizes the field as Sudanese territory, South Sudan continues to claim the field as its own. Military clashes in the region escalated in April 2012. The South Sudanese military seized the town of Heglig, claiming that the action was necessary to prevent Sudanese forces from launching their own attacks from the territory. The UN Security Council called for an immediate end to all violence. South Sudan said that it withdrew its troops from Heglig, but Sudan claimed that it drove the troops out of the region.

On April 16, 2012, the parliament of Sudan voted unanimously to name the government of South Sudan as an enemy of the state. Although this action fell short of an official declaration of war, Sudan pledged to use all means necessary to recapture Heglig. Sudan bombed a border town in late April, prompting the UN Security Council to issue a demand that the two countries cease all violent conflict.

Under pressure from the UN, Sudan withdrew its troops from the disputed region of Abyei in May 2012, just as peace talks were set to begin again in Ethiopia. Although the withdrawal of military troops was confirmed by the UN, some reports indicated that the number of Sudanese police officers in the area increased. This stoked concerns that some soldiers may simply have changed uniforms in order to maintain a strong presence in the area.

⊕ Future Implications

Despite the negotiations, agreements, and the creation of South Sudan, conflict in the region continues. The clashes, which are founded in long-standing ethnic and religious animosity, are exacerbated by economic tensions. In July 2013, South Sudan's president Salva Kiir (1951–) dismissed his entire cabinet, including Vice President Riek Machar (1953–), in an effort to appease the Sudanese government. At the crux of this disagreement was an economic crisis caused by Sudan's refusal to let South Sudan export oil. Both countries remain poor, and the populations are young. Most of the people who live in the region today have never known a time without war. On December 15, 2013, fighting broke out in South Sudan when rebels loyal to former vice president Machar allegedly attempted a coup. Violence between government and rebel forces resulted in some 1,000 deaths and the displacement of some 200,000, which has taxed the resources already engaged in helping refugees from earlier conflicts. The violence continued into the new year as both sides entered negotiations in an attempt to find a peaceful resolution.

The genocide in Darfur persists, and Sudan also continues to limit the presence of humanitarian aid workers to deflect documentation of the abuses. Almost 1.5 million people displaced by the violence live in camps and rely on food donations. Rebel groups continue to fight the government, and the Janjaweed continue to terrorize villages. Promised power-sharing arrangements have yet to be implemented and seem unlikely to occur soon.

In July 2013, Sudanese president al-Bashir made a brief appearance at an African Union meeting in Nigeria, but disappeared after human rights activists demanded that Nigeria arrest him and remand him to the ICC for trial. Sudan is unlikely to extradite al-Bashir to face trial. The president continues to detain those with opposing voices in Sudan, including journalists who raise questions about his rule. His travel is limited, however. In August 2013, his plane was prevented from entering Saudi Arabian airspace. It remains uncertain when or if he will be put on trial at the Hague.

SEE ALSO *African Union; Genocide; Religious Extremism; Uganda; United Nations*

BIBLIOGRAPHY

Books

Brosche, Johan, and Daniel Rothbart. *Violent Conflict and Peacebuilding: The Continuing Crisis in Darfur.* New York: Routledge, 2013.

Dau, John Bul, with Michael S. Sweeney. *God Grew Tired of Us.* Washington, DC: National Geographic, 2007.

Deng, Alephonsion. *They Poured Fire on Us from the Sky: The True Story of Three Lost Boys from Sudan.* New York: PublicAffairs, 2005.

Hastrip, Anders. *The War in Darfur: Reclaiming Sudanese History.* New York: Routledge, 2013.

Johnson, Douglas H. *The Root Causes of Sudan's Civil Wars: Peace or Truce,* Rev. ed. Suffolk, UK: James Currey, 2011.

LeRiche, Matthew, and Matthew Arnold. *South Sudan: From Revolution to Independence.* New York: Oxford University Press, 2013.

Periodicals

Moon, Claire. "The Crime of Crimes and the Crime of Criminology: Genocide, Criminology and Darfur." *British Journal of Sociology* 62, no. 1 (March 2011): 49–55.

Pflanz, Mike. "Is West Now Looking Past Darfur Genocide to Engage Sudan?" *The Christian Science Monitor* (June 12, 2013): 4.

"South Sudan Says It Will 'Embarrass' Sudan Over Support to Rebel Groups." *McClatchy-Tribune Business News* (July 23, 2013).

Travis, Hannibal. "On the Original Understanding of the Crime of Genocide." *Genocide Studies and Prevention* 7, no. 1 (April 2012): 30–55.

Walle, Nicolas van de, and David Cockett. "Sudan: Darfur and the Failure of an African State." *Foreign Affairs* 90, no. 3 (May 2011).

Web Sites

Epatko, Larisa. "South Sudan's Independence Gets a 'Rocky' Start." *PBS NewsHour,* July 9, 2012. http://www.pbs.org/newshour/rundown/2012/07/south-sudans-independence.html (accessed December 5, 2013).

Nwazota, Kristina. "Origins of the Darfur Crisis." *PBS Newshour,* July 3, 2008. http://www.pbs.org/newshour/updates/africa-july-dec08-origins_07-03/ (accessed January 21, 2014).

"South Sudan Profile." *BBC News.* July 24, 2013. http://www.bbc.co.uk/news/world-africa-14069082 (accessed December 5, 2013).

"Sudan Profile." *BBC News.* October 26, 2013. http://www.bbc.co.uk/news/world-africa-14094995 (accessed December 5, 2013).

"The UN Responds to the Crisis in Darfur: A Timeline." *United Nations.* http://www.un.org/news/dh/dev/scripts/darfur_formatted.htm (accessed December 5, 2013).

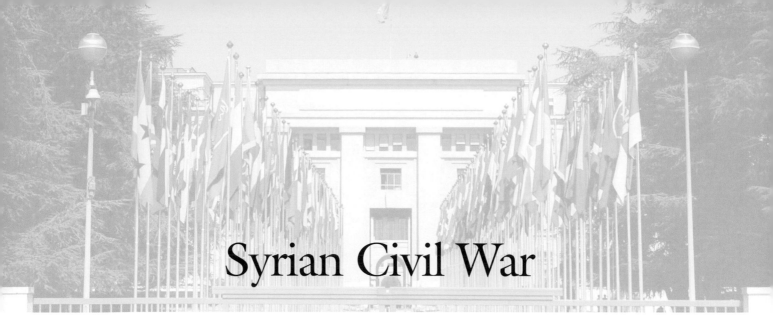

Syrian Civil War

⊕ Introduction

A wave of anti-government protests and revolutions swept through the Middle East and North Africa beginning in December 2010. This so-called "Arab Spring" began, tragically, with the self-immolation of a Tunisian man who had been trying to sell fruit in a public square when his wares were confiscated by the police. His injury and subsequent death incited anti-government rioting that spread through the country with incredible speed. Less than a month after protests began, Zine El Abidine Ben Ali, longtime dictator of Tunisia, fled the country.

Encouraged by the success of the Tunisian protestors, citizens of Egypt, Libya, Yemen, Bahrain, Jordan, and multiple other countries also rose up in large numbers to protest poor economic conditions and lack of human rights. The protests successfully toppled dictators in Egypt and Yemen. The government of Libya also fell after a violent civil war and foreign intervention. Protests in other nations continued sporadically through 2013, but were quelled through a combination of placation, compromise, and force.

Such was not the case in Syria. Popular protests that began in March and April 2011 focused on the resignation of President Bashar al-Assad (1965–). The Assad regime and the opposition are from different ethnic groups: Assad and his supporters are primarily Alawite, a Shia Islamic sect, while the majority of the country is Sunni. Syria also has significant communities of Druze (a variant Islamic sect) and Christians, as well as Kurds (who are Sunnis but not Arab). The Alawites had long been persecuted for their beliefs before Hafez al-Assad took power in 1970. While the ruling Assads were relatively secular, their regime favored Alawites. Some analysts are concerned that if either group were to attain complete control there would be no checks to protect the other.

When protests began in Syria, instead of fleeing or stepping down, Assad responded with military force. After several months, the protests evolved into an armed

rebellion, and then into a full-fledged civil war. By early 2014, more than 120,000 people had been killed in the conflict, most at the hands of Syrian military and security forces, and more than 2.4 million had fled the country. With political divisions hindering the international community from intervening, the crisis threatened to engulf the Middle East in a still more devastating war.

⊕ Historical Background

Syria is located in a region of the Middle East often viewed as unstable due to conflicts between religious and ethnic groups. It rests between Turkey, Iraq, Jordan, and Lebanon, and shares a small portion of its border with Israel. Syria was established after independence from France as a republic in 1946, but any attempts at democracy were short-lived: the country's first elected president removed the one-term limit specified in the Syrian constitution so he could be re-elected, and he was overthrown by a military coup in 1949. Control of the Syrian government changed hands no less than 18 times over the next 22 years, with some leaders taking control on two or even three separate occasions.

In 1970, former military leader Hafez al-Assad (1930–2000) assumed control of the country. Assad successfully achieved stability in the Syrian government, but only by crushing members of the opposition and maintaining strict control over the civil liberties of Syrian citizens. In June 2000, Assad died after 30 years of rule. One month later, his son, Bashar, was elected president in an election in which he ran without an opposition candidate. Bashar al-Assad continued the suppression of pro-democracy activists just as his father had done.

Democracy and Dissent

When the Arab Spring erupted in early 2011, Syrian pro-democracy protesters resurfaced and joined in with their own demonstrations. Throughout the uprising,

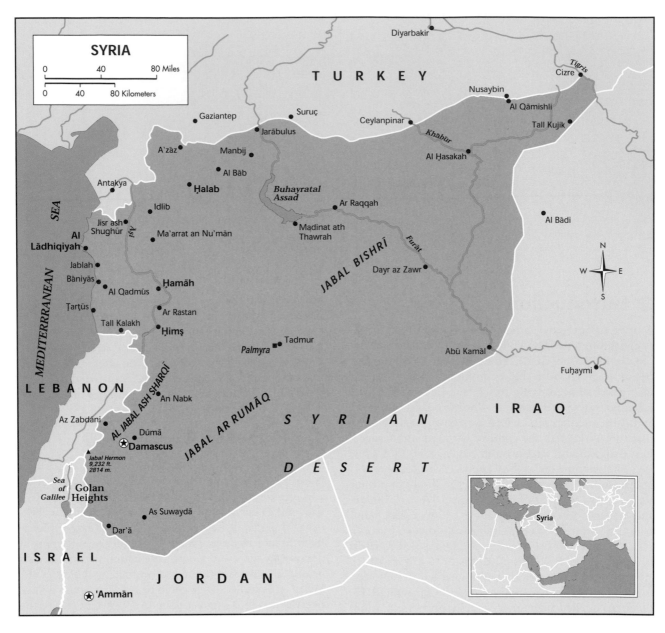

Assad made numerous promises and some concessions to institute reforms within his ruling regime. On March 29, 2011, the existing cabinet resigned in an unsuccessful attempt to quell the unrest. On April 21, Assad issued a decree ending the state of emergency under which Syrian citizens had lived for nearly five decades; however, protests continued and the government's violence against protesters increased.

As reports of protesters killed by police circulated around the world, the demonstrations grew even larger in size. These led to pro-government counter-demonstrations and further violence, especially in the southwestern city of Daraa, where protesters tore down and destroyed a statue of Hafez al-Assad. On April 25, 2011, military forces with tanks moved into Daraa to seize control and subdue the protesters. For more than a week, troops occupied the city; on April 30, they opened fire on a mosque where demonstrators had gathered, killing six. The incident drew international condemnation, and members of Assad's ruling party resigned their posts to protest the violent attacks on Syrian citizens.

The Syrian army moved on to several other cities in an attempt to stop the growing protest movement, occupying Homs, Baniyas, Tafas, and Talkalakh. By the end of May, it was estimated that more than 1,000 civilians had been killed by Syrian police and military forces. Government troops continued to occupy cities

Rebels of the Free Syrian Army show off their Molotov cocktails as they prepare to attack government tanks that advanced into Saraquib city on April 9, 2012, in Syria. Continuing violence in northern Syria between government forces and rebels put any plans for a UN-brokered Syria cease-fire in jeopardy. © *John Cantlie/Getty Images*

where demonstrations broke out, but the ever-growing list of dead and injured served only to strengthen the anti-government movement. By mid-July, more than 1 million protesters had joined in the demonstrations across the country, with the largest number in the city of Hama. On July 31 army tanks and troops launched an assault on protesters in Hama that left more than 100 dead.

Following the assault on Hama, representatives from governments around the world openly called for Assad to resign. Some of the protesters formed their own military, known as the Free Syrian Army, composed mainly of army officers and troops who chose to side with the opposition after refusing to use violence against civilians. Although estimated to number more than 10,000, the Free Syrian Army faced a much larger military force armed with tanks and helicopters. Syrian opposition was hampered by divisions among dozens of opposition groups, some of whom had little in common save their antipathy to the Assad regime. Alongside secular groups and political bodies such as the Syrian National Council were Sunni Islamic militant groups such as the al-Nusra Front, which is affiliated with the al-Qaeda terrorist network.

⊕ Impacts and Issues

Both protests and government violence against protesters escalated in 2012, as hundreds of thousands of Syrians repeatedly took to the streets in cities throughout the country and faced deadly responses from security forces. Pressure on Syria continued to mount as a group called "Friends of Syria," including the United States and European governments, planned a meeting for February 24, 2012, in Tunisia. A draft of an ultimatum to Assad was prepared by high-level diplomats gathered in London in the days before the meeting. Officials familiar with negotiations said that at least 70 countries, including Turkey and Syria's Arab neighbors, were prepared to demand that Assad halt violence against civilians within 72 hours or face unspecified punishment. All calls for Assad to end the violence went unheeded.

The Arab League, an organization of 22 Arab countries, proposed a peace plan. President Assad appeared ready to accept the Arab League–brokered peace deal in November 2012, but a violent clash the next day between security forces and protesters in Homs appeared to doom the plan. Witnesses said Syrian tanks fired on the crowd, killing from 10 to 20 people. The

CHEMICAL WEAPONS

The use of chemical weapons dates back centuries, when early combatants learned that smoke from burning sulfur caused discomfort when it drifted into enemy fortifications. The dawn of modern chemical warfare occurred during World War I (1914–18). On April 15, 1915, German forces released about 160 tons of chlorine gas into the wind near the Belgian village of Ypres. The clouds of the gas drifted into Allied forces, killing some 5,000 soldiers. Two days later, another chlorine attack at the same village killed 5,000 more soldiers. During the remainder of World War I, German, French, and British forces used chlorine gas and such chemicals as mustard gas and phosgene with increasing frequency. An estimated 113,000 tons of chemical weapons were used from 1915 to 1918, killing some 92,000 people and injuring over one million people.

The horrors of chemical warfare during World War I prompted the drafting of the Geneva Protocol of 1925, which banned chemical and biological weapons of warfare. The Chemical Weapons Convention (CWC), a treaty banning the use, production, acquisition, and stockpiling of chemical agents for use in warfare, became international law in 1997. All but a handful of nations have signed and ratified the CWC.

For many years, Syria was one of these holdouts, stockpiling unknown amounts of chemical weapons. In 2013 video of what were reported to be chemical weapons attacks on Syrian citizens surfaced, showing the dead and those suffering symptoms typical of a sarin gas attacks, including children. This lead to an international debate about whether military action should be taken against Syria's government, however the UN could not go forward with sanctions or military action due to objections from Russia and China, who stated that the chemical attacks could have been perpetrated by opposition groups.

After international pressure by other nations and the threat of force by the United States, Russia helped negotiate a deal with Syria to destroy its chemical weapons. Syria acceded to the CWC treaty on September 14, 2013, and destruction of its weapons began in October. An investigation by the United Nations lead to a report in December that UN investigators found evidence that sarin gas, a chemical weapon, had been used in at least five instances on civilians between the months of March and August, killing at least 1,400 in one incident in the region of Ghouta, near Damascus. The UN report did not note who had perpetrated the attacks.

Not all countries, even the 190 who have been state parties to the CWC for many years, have managed to comply with all of its requirements. Although the provisions of the CWC called for disposal of all chemical weapons by all signatories by 2012, many countries, including the United States, have requested extended deadlines. The U.S. Defense Department announced in May 2012 that it would be possible to eliminate only about 90 percent of the

U.S. declared stockpile of chemical weapons by the treaty deadline. The United States goal was to be rid of the remaining weapons by 2021. In June 2013, the Organization for the Prohibition of Chemical Weapons (OPCW), which provides oversight for the treaty, reported that worldwide almost 81 percent of Category 1 chemical weapons (toxic chemicals or precursors with no commercial applications), 52 percent of Category 2 weapons (some commercial applications but high potential for weapons use), and all Category 3 weapons (mainly commercial use chemicals with some potential for weapons use) have been destroyed.

Syrian women hold portraits of Syria's President Bashar al-Assad as pro-regime supporters parade their cars in Damascus to celebrate Assad's 48th birthday on September 11, 2013. The Syrian President marks his birthday as the threat of U.S.-led strikes against his regime in response to an alleged chemical weapons attack appears to have waned while a Russian proposal that Syria hand over its chemical weapons is discussed.   © *Anwar Amro/AFP/Getty Images*

peace plan had called for military withdrawal from Syrian cities, the release of all detainees, and opening a dialogue with the opposition. On November 16, the Arab League issued an ultimatum to the Syrian government: stop the bloodshed within three days, or be suspended. On

November 27 the Arab League followed through on its threat of suspending Syria and approved sweeping economic sanctions. On November 30, the Turkish government also approved tough sanctions on Syria, including a freeze of Syrian government assets in Turkey. Turkey's

Russian Foreign minister Sergey Lavrov, United Nations-Arab League special envoy for Syria Lakhdar Brahimi, and U.S. Secretary of State John Kerry arrive at the UN headquarters in Geneva on September 13, 2013, to resume high-stakes talks on Syria's chemical weapons. The United Nations stated on September 16 that chemical weapons had been used to kill hundreds of Syrians, but the United States and Russia disagreed about whether the government or rebel forces had used them. On September 13, Russia and the United States were set to huddle for a second day of key talks on how to secure Syria's chemical weapons amid reports Damascus was scattering the stockpile to frustrate efforts to track the deadly arsenal. *© Larry Downing/AFP/Getty Images*

Prime Minister, Tayyip Erdogan, intensified his pressure on Assad in his public comments, calling on the world to "hear the screams" of the Syrian people. As the month of November ended, the United Nations (UN) termed the ongoing violence a "civil war."

Assad had two important allies, however, in Russia and Iran. Iran was providing financial and military aid to the Syrian government as well as backing Hezbollah, the Shia paramilitary group based in Lebanon, which was increasingly involved in the conflict on both sides of the Syria-Lebanon border. Meanwhile, Russia provided the Syrian leader crucial diplomatic support. Between October 2011 and July 2012, Russia (along with China) vetoed three separate UN Security Council resolutions that would have condemned and imposed sanctions on the Assad government. The Russian government also made several efforts to facilitate negotiations leading toward a cease-fire, with little success.

Refugees Flee

In November 2012, international charity group Save the Children warned that 200,000 Syrian refugee children were in danger of freezing as sub-zero temperatures and rain moved into the Middle East. Although many families had already fled to neighboring countries, many others were without adequate shelter and clothing as winter approached.

By September 2013, the UN High Commissioner for Refugees (UNHCR) announced that the number of Syrian refugees had surpassed 2 million, including roughly 1 million children. An estimated 4 million people were also displaced within Syria due to the civil unrest. Syria's neighbors, especially Lebanon and Jordan, were overwhelmed by the influx of Syrian refugees within their borders and appealed to the international community to help provide both emergency aid and long-term development assistance. UN officials said the Syrian civil war had become the world's most pressing humanitarian emergency. In late 2013, the UN estimated that by the end of 2014, there would be more than 4 million Syrian refugees.

Chemical Weapons Use Sparks U.S. Threat

An attack on Aleppo that appeared to involve chemical weapons left 16 people dead on March 19, 2013. Both the Syrian army and opposition army placed the blame on the other and demanded an official inquiry be made into the event. The use of chemical and biological weapons can be difficult to prove, however in December 2013, the UN confirmed that chemical weapons had been used in Syria between March and August 2013 in at least five separate incidents.

After months of weighing the decision, the White House announced on June 14, 2013, that Syrian rebels would be supplied with direct lethal military aid. The Obama administration made the decision after it decided that Assad's forces had used nerve gas. UK Foreign Secretary William Hague stated that the UK approved of the decision. The Syrian government claimed that the White House "relied on fabricated information" and that its statement was "full of lies."

The U.S. faced mounting pressure to intervene in order to halt the Syrian civil war. The U.S. and European allies had given military assistance to the Libyan opposition in its fight against dictator Muammar al-Qadhafi (1942–2011) in 2011. However, Western governments hesitated to commit resources to another volatile Middle Eastern conflict, particularly without UN Security Council approval. Nevertheless, U.S. President Barack Obama (1961–) told reporters in August 2012 that repeated use of chemical weapons would transgress a "red line" and "would change my calculus" on the question of intervention.

The president's words appeared to be put to the test after an incident in the outskirts of Damascus on August 21, 2013, in which as many as 1,400 people were reportedly killed in a sarin gas attack. Obama responded by putting the U.S. military on alert for possible cruise missile strikes on Syria. The president said he was willing to launch attacks without UN backing and without a vote in Congress. He later backtracked and asked Congress to vote on authorizing the use of force. At a press conference on September 9, Secretary of State John Kerry (1943–) suggested that Assad could stave off U.S. bombing by voluntarily turning over his chemical weapon stockpile to international control.

The next day, Russian diplomats surprised the world by turning Kerry's apparently offhand remark into a formal disarmament proposal, approved by the Syrian government. Syria subsequently signed on to the Chemical Weapons Convention and allowed UN weapons inspectors into the country to oversee the dismantling of its chemical arsenal. On September 27, the UN Security Council unanimously approved a resolution endorsing the plan.

⊕ Future Implications

On October 6, 2013, Syria began destroying its chemical weapons facilities under the oversight of the Organisation for the Prohibition of Chemical Weapons. The program was hailed by some as progress because the Assad regime could no longer utilize chemical weapons. However, the move was seen by others as a last ditch effort by Assad to stay in power. Critics of the regime stated that Assad would never give up his complete stockpile of chemical weapons. They stated that some of the locations of the weapons were secret and some of the weapons were merely being moved to sympathetic countries such as Iraq. In addition, some saw allowing the program to go forward with Assad in remaining control of the country as legitimizing his regime and allowing him to continue in power without any real consequences. By early 2014, critics of the plan felt their views had been confirmed, as a deadline to remove all chemical weapons components (including sarin, mustard and VX gases) by December 31 was not met, nor was one on February 5, 2014. At that time it was reported that only 4 percent of the weapons components had been delivered for destruction. Russia stated that Syria would work towards a revised schedule and that despite the delays, a final deadline of June 30, 2014, would be met.

As the controversy surrounding the chemical weapons issue continued into early 2014, factions fighting the Assad government remained at odds, with hardline Islamist fighters The Islamic Front pitted against the more secular Free Syrian Army. The divisions in the opposition against Assad seemed to indicate that an immediate resolution to Syria's civil war was unrealistic.

PRIMARY SOURCE

Six-Point Proposal of the Joint Special Envoy of the United Nations and the League of Arab States

SOURCE *"Six-Point Proposal of the Joint Special Envoy of the United Nations and the League of Arab States."* United Nations, *April 14, 2012. https://www. un.org/en/peacekeeping/documents/six_point_ proposal.pdf (accessed December 4, 2013). Copyright © 2012 by the United Nations. All rights reserved. Reproduced by permission.*

INTRODUCTION *On February 2, 2012, in response to the increasing violence in Syria, Former UN Secretary General Kofi Annan was appointed Joint Special Envoy for the UN and League of Arab States in an effort to help end the crisis. Earlier attempts by an Arab League peace mission had failed to achieve a peaceful resolution. Annan's Six-Point Proposal was presented to the UN in mid-March 2012. The Syrian government accepted it on March 27 and the cease-fire commenced on April 12, but collapsed in early June.*

Six-Point Proposal of the Joint Special Envoy of the United Nations and the League of Arab States

(1) commit to work with the Envoy in an inclusive Syrian-led political process to address the legitimate aspirations and concerns of the Syrian people, and, to this end, commit to appoint an empowered interlocutor when invited to do so by the Envoy;

(2) commit to stop the fighting and achieve urgently an effective United Nations supervised cessation of armed violence in all its forms by all parties to protect civilians and stabilize the country;

To this end, the Syrian government should immediately cease troop movements towards, and end the use of heavy weapons in, population centres, and begin pull-back of military concentrations in and around population centres;

As these actions are being taken on the ground, the Syrian government should work with the Envoy to bring about a sustained cessation of armed violence in all its forms by all parties with an effective United Nations supervision mechanism.

Similar commitments would be sought by the Envoy from the opposition and all relevant elements to stop the fighting and work with him to bring about a sustained cessation of armed violence in all its forms by all parties with an effective United Nations supervision mechanism;

(3) ensure timely provision of humanitarian assistance to all areas affected by the fighting, and to this end, as immediate steps, to accept and implement a daily two hour humanitarian pause and to coordinate exact time and modalities of the daily pause through an efficient mechanism, including at local level;

(4) intensify the pace and scale of release of arbitrarily detained persons, including especially vulnerable categories of persons, and persons involved in peaceful political activities, provide without delay through appropriate channels a list of all places in which such persons are being detained, immediately begin organizing access to such locations and through appropriate channels respond promptly to all written requests for information, access or release regarding such persons;

(5) ensure freedom of movement throughout the country for journalists and a non-discriminatory visa policy for them;

(6) respect freedom of association and the right to demonstrate peacefully as legally guaranteed.

SEE ALSO *Arab Spring; Egyptian Revolution; Lebanon: Civil War and Political Instability; United Nations; Weapons of Mass Destruction*

BIBLIOGRAPHY

Books

Ajami, Fouad. *The Syrian Rebellion.* Stanford, CA: Hoover Institution Press, Stanford University, 2012.

Lesch, David W. *Syria: The Fall of the House of Assad.* New Haven, CT: Yale University Press, 2012.

Lynch, Marc. *The Arab Uprising: The Unfinished Revolutions of the New Middle East.* New York, NY: PublicAffairs, 2012.

Periodicals

Robinson, Glenn E. "Syria's Long Civil War." *Current History* 111, no. 749 (December 2012): 331–336.

Web Sites

Cafiero, Giorgio. "The Somaliazation of Syria." *Foreign Policy in Focus,* March 26, 2013. http://fpif.org/the_somaliazation_of_syria/ (accessed December 17, 2013).

Engel, Richard, Jim Miklaszewski, and Robert Windrem. "Syria's Chemical Weapons Arsenal Remains a Menacing Mystery." *NBC News.* http://news.ca.msn.com/top-stories/syrias-chemical-weapons-arsenal-remains-a-menacing-mystery (accessed December 17, 2013).

"Executive Council Receives Destruction Plan for Syrian Chemicals." *Organisation for the Prohibition of Chemical Weapons,* December 18, 2013. http://www.opcw.org/news/article/executive-council-receives-destruction-plan-for-syrian-chemicals/ (accessed December 17, 2013).

"Organization for the Prohibition of Chemical Weapons (OPCW)." *Nuclear Threat Initiative.* http://www.nti.org/treaties-and-regimes/organization-for-the-prohibition-of-chemical-weapons/ (accessed December 17, 2013).

Stack, Liam, ed. "Watching Syria's War." *New York Times.* http://projects.nytimes.com/watching-syrias-war?ref=syria (accessed December 17, 2013).

"Syria Profile." *BBC.* http://www.bbc.co.uk/news/world-middle-east-14703856 (accessed December 17, 2013).

Taiwan: Conflicts With China

⊕ Introduction

The 22 islands of Taiwan lie approximately 100 miles (161 kilometers) off the southeast coast of China. In December 1949, at the end of the Communist revolution in China, Chinese nationalist forces retreated to the islands with about two million refugees. Since then, Taiwan has essentially been an independent country and has adopted a tradition of capitalism and orientation to the West. The Chinese mainland, known as the People's Republic of China (PRC), remains the largest Communist nation in the world and claims the islands of Taiwan are a part of the PRC.

From 1950 to 1990 the Taiwanese government insisted that it was the legitimate Chinese government. In 1991 Taiwan renounced its claim to mainland China and has instead pushed for international recognition as an independent nation. More than 20 nations have diplomatic ties with Taiwan, but the island nation is not officially recognized by the United Nations (UN).

The PRC has always maintained that Taiwan is a Chinese province and must be reunited with the mainland. Before 1978 the official policy was to use military force to achieve that goal. Then, in 1978, the PRC resolved to seek peaceful reunification. In 1984 Chinese leader Deng Xiaoping (1904–1997) proposed a "one country, two systems" program that recognized Taiwan's separate political and economic concerns. The "one country, two systems" plan has continued to be China's official policy since that time. However, since 2008, a thawing in Taiwanese-Chinese relations may indicate a forthcoming change in the PRC policy.

⊕ Historical Background

Taiwan was settled by the Dutch in the early 1600s, and during the same period the first major influx of immigrants from mainland China arrived. In 1664 the island chain was claimed as a territory by mainland China. More than two centuries later, in 1885, the islands became an official Chinese province. By then native Taiwanese were far outnumbered by people from mainland China or their descendants.

In 1895 the Taiwanese islands were ceded to the Japanese at the conclusion of the first Sino-Japanese War (1895). For the next 50 years Taiwan was a Japanese colony, although it remained predominately ethnically and culturally Chinese. After Japan's defeat at the end of World War II (1939–45), Taiwan was "restored" to to the Republic of China (ROC) even though the ROC had only been created 16 years after Taiwan was ceded to Japan (and therefore had never previously been under its governance).

At that time the ROC was ruled by the Kuomintang Party under the leadership of Chiang Kai-shek (1887–1975). Most Taiwanese initially welcomed the Kuomintang, but tensions began to develop soon after, due to Kuomintang mismanagement and corruption, eventually leading to popular protests that culminated in what became known as the February 28 incident. On February 28, 1947, the accidental shooting of a civilian sparked riots, which were quelled by reinforcements sent from mainland China. Thousands of Taiwanese were massacred, including many of the educated and elite citizens who had been in the forefront of negotiations and maintaining order.

In the meantime, civil war in China had erupted in 1945, pitting the Communist forces led by Mao Zedong (1893–1976) against Chiang Kai-shek's ROC government. Chiang was defeated, and Mao established the People's Republic of China in Beijing in 1949. Chiang fled to Taiwan with more than two million mainlanders, reestablishing the ROC government there in 1950, with the city of Taipei acting as the provisional capital. Martial law was declared on Taiwan in January of 1950 and remained in effect until 1987.

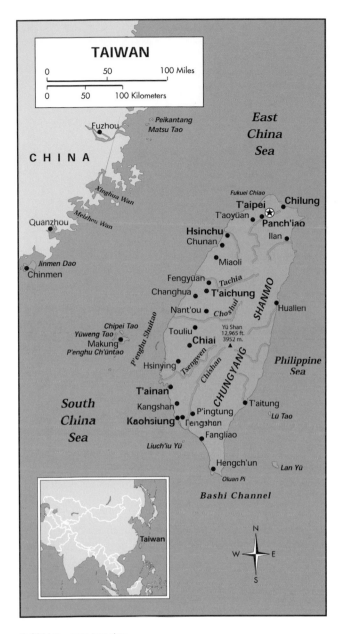

TAIWAN

0 50 100 Miles

0 50 100 Kilometers

© 2014 Cengage Learning

Taiwan and China: 1950–1988

During his 25 years of rule, Chiang focused on preventing the spread of the Chinese Communists' power to Taiwan. He was not in favor of an independent Taiwan but rather considered the islands as a base from which to fight communism and recover the mainland. His fight against the spread of communism found him an ally in the United States throughout the first half of the Cold War (1945–91).

By late 1949, few expected the Kuomintang regime would survive, but Chiang's government on Taiwan received unexpected protection against Mao's forces during the Korean War (1950–53). Fearing the spread of communism across Asia, the United States sent its

Seventh Fleet to defend Taiwan from mainland China and established an official advisory group in Taiwan to train Chiang's troops. By 1954 Taiwan had received a total of $4.2 billion in military aid and $1.7 billion in economic aid from the United States. These assistance programs, plus a 1954 defense treaty with the United States, helped Chiang build Taiwan from an impoverished and threatened group of islands into a strong modern state.

The ROC was one of the founding members of the UN in 1945. When the Communist Party established the People's Republic of China on the mainland in 1949, Chiang's exiled ROC government continued to represent China in the UN. The ROC also enjoyed a permanent seat on the UN's Security Council for 26 years. In 1971 the international political climate had sufficiently changed that the ROC lost its UN recognition. The UN recognized the PRC as the sole legitimate government of China, and the PRC replaced the ROC on the Security Council.

Despite this turn of events, Chiang continued to maintain that the Taiwanese government was the Chinese government-in-exile and that one day it would reclaim its control over the Chinese mainland. After Chiang's death in 1975, power fell to his son, Chiang Ching-kuo (1910–1988). Like his father, he opposed independence for Taiwan, and hoped that the Kuomintang Party would one day regain control of mainland China.

Taiwan and China: 1988–2008

Upon the death of Chiang Ching-kuo in 1988, native-born Taiwanese Lee Teng-hui (1923–) became president. Under his leadership Taiwan became a more democratic society. In addition to the Kuomintang Party, the Democratic Progressive Party (DPP) gained support among voters, transforming Taiwan into a multiparty democracy.

In 1991 Taiwan renounced its claims to the Chinese mainland and asked the international community to recognize it as an independent nation. As of early 2014, the PRC has not yet officially shifted its stance toward Taiwan and has made it clear that any nation that recognizes Taiwanese independence will lose all international relationships with mainland China. Considering the size and power of the Chinese economy and military, the threat is taken seriously. Although 23 nations and the Holy See have diplomatic ties to Taiwan, it is not officially recognized as an independent nation. Taiwan has unsuccessfully applied and reapplied for UN membership under various versions of the name "Republic of China (Taiwan)." Since the PRC so strongly opposes the recognition of Taiwan as a state, the situation is currently at a stalemate.

In 1995 Lee became the first high-ranking Taiwanese representative to visit the United States since 1979. China, fearing Lee's visit might lead to international recognition of Taiwan as a state, made a great show of its

In the UN assemby hall, results of the vote concerning the admission of People's Republic of China to the United Nations are posted during the 26th general assembly. Admission was granted by 76 votes against 35. At the rostrum, from left to right: Burmese General Secretary U Thant, the Indonesian President of the Assembly Adam Malik and the Greek General under-secretary for General Assembly Affairs Constantin A. Stavropoulos. © *Keystone-France/Gamma-Keystone via Getty Images*

military power by conducting military exercises involving 400,000 troops across the Taiwan Strait and firing Chinese missiles near the islands. In response, the United States dispatched two nuclear-armed aircraft carrier groups to the area. China concluded its military exercises, but left about 160 missiles directed at Taiwan.

In 2000 Taiwanese voters elected pro-independence DPP candidate Chen Shui-bian (1951–) president. Chen accused China of planning an invasion of the islands. China accused him of planning constitutional changes that would destroy the possibility of eventual reunification. According to observers, during Chen's presidency China added to its missiles, so that by 2011 there were about 2,000 short- and medium-range missiles aimed at Taiwan from the mainland.

Taiwan and China: Since 2008

In 2008 Kuomintang Party candidate Ma Ying-jeou (1950–) was elected president of Taiwan after campaigning to improve relations with China. Ma quickly established more direct flights and promoted mutual tourism between Taiwan and China. He also unveiled plans to advance the economic and political bonds between the two governments.

In March 2009 China's prime minister, Wen Jiabao (1942–), announced that relations between the former foes were on a track of peaceful development. Moreover, China was ready to begin formal talks with Taiwan to end the state of war that has technically existed between the two countries since 1945. In a further sign of warming between the countries, China has begun refusing the requests of countries seeking to switch their diplomatic ties from Taiwan to China, apparently out of deference to Taiwan.

Responding with a diplomatic gesture of its own, Taiwan announced in September 2009 that it would not allow exiled Uyghur leader Rebiya Kadeer (1947–), head of the World Uyghur Congress, to enter the country for a series of planned speeches in December 2009. The Uyghurs are a Turkic ethnic group that lives mainly in the Xinjiang region of China. The Chinese government has clashed with Uyghur Muslim and separatist groups, which it calls terrorists, for several years. Kadeer had been invited by an anti-China political group to speak in Taiwan, but the Taiwanese government decided that it would not be appropriate to host Kadeer considering the thawing political relationship between Taiwan and the PRC.

Taiwan's President Ma Ying-jeou speaks at the headquarters of the island's quasi-official Straits Exchange Foundation in Taipei on April 29, 2013. Ma renewed the "one China" policy of his government as Taiwan marked the 20th anniversary of the first high-level talks between Taiwan and the Chinese mainland since their split in 1949 at the end of a civil war. © *Mandy Cheng/AFP/Getty Images*

In June 2010 China and Taiwan announced a major trade agreement called the Economic Cooperation Framework Agreement (ECFA), which analysts say could significantly boost trade between the countries. The agreement lifts tariffs on hundreds of products. The deal appears to benefit Taiwan more, as about $14 billion worth of Taiwanese goods exported to China will no longer have tariffs imposed on them. Critics worry that the deal will make Taiwan economically dependent on China. The Taiwanese government agreed to a number of economic deals, but officials were not ready to commit to a promise of political reunification based on the "One China" principle still favored by the mainland.

Since 2008 efforts toward greater cooperation have been handled in part through negotiations between the mainland-based Association for Relations Across the Taiwan Strait (ARATS) and the Taiwan-based Straits Exchange Foundation (SEF). The groups have met several times since 2008. At the 2010 meeting negotiators signed a medical and health care cooperation agreement designed to enhance cooperation in pharmaceutical research and safety management, while strengthening prevention and emergency measures aimed at combating the spread of infectious diseases. The agreement also calls for the establishment of quality guarantees

and enhanced research for traditional Chinese medicine. About 90 percent of the traditional medicines used in Taiwan come from the mainland.

⊕ Impacts and Issues

For decades, Taiwan's political goal of retaking mainland China and the PRC's "One China" policy placed the two nations on the brink of war. Closer economic

CONFUCIUS PEACE PRIZE

On December 9, 2010, China unveiled the Confucius Peace Prize, a counter to what it considers the Western-biased Nobel Peace Prize. The Chinese government was outraged by the Nobel Committee's decision to award its 2010 peace prize to jailed Chinese dissident Liu Xiaobo (1955–). The first Confucius Peace Prize was awarded to the former vice president of Taiwan, Lien Chan (1936–). In a statement from prize officials announcing the award, Lien was praised for building a "bridge of peace between Taiwan and the [Chinese] mainland."

An U.S.-made Hawk missile is launched from the Chiupeng missile base in southern Pingtung county during a live fire drill on January 18, 2011. Taiwan showed its force during a live fire missile exercise, highlighting China's perceived military threat despite warming between the two former acrimonious rivals. *© Sam Yeh/AFP/Getty Images*

and cultural ties between Taiwan and China since 2008, however, have lessened the immediate likelihood of armed conflict. The potential for conflict and concerns over reunification continue to dominate the political landscape in Taiwan and greatly influence domestic and foreign policy and the PRC.

The ballistic missiles aimed at Taiwan by China continue to be a source of conflict between the nations and their allies. Between 2000 and 2010, China increased the number of ballistic missiles aimed at Taiwan from a couple hundred to over 2,000. In January 2010, U.S. President Barack Obama (1961–) announced the sale of over $6 billion of anti-missile systems to Taiwan. In response, China discontinued direct military contacts with the United States and warned of the potential for deterioration in U.S.-China relations.

Despite lingering military issues following decades of tense relations, the 2008 election of Taiwanese President Ma has produced the most significant thaw in China-Taiwan relations in history. Ma's conciliatory rhetoric and actions were welcomed by China following the staunch pro-Taiwanese independence administration of President Chen.

⊕ Future Implications

On October 18, 2011, Taiwan's prime minister, Ma Ying-jeou (1950–), suggested at a press conference that China and Taiwan might sign a formal peace treaty within the next 10 years. He qualified the statement in the following days, saying that a peace treaty with China would require a referendum. Although the time frame for peace is currently unknown, it seems likely that a peaceful coexistence between Taiwan and the PRC will become a reality.

PRC president Xi Jinping (1953–), who was sworn into office in 2013, has vowed to find "peaceful means" to improve China's relationship with Taiwan. Eighteen agreements have been signed with Taiwan between 2011 and 2013; however, Xi asserts that "core issues" still need to be resolved. In the meantime a strengthening of economic and cultural ties seems capable of subtly influencing the political stalemate, likely moving toward a two-state solution that will benefit both governments.

PRIMARY SOURCE

2758 (XXVI). Restoration of the Lawful Rights of the People's Republic of China in the United Nations

SOURCE *"Resolution 2758: Restoration of the Lawful Rights of the People's Republic of China in the United Nations."* United Nations, *October 25, 1971. http://www.un.org/en/ga/search/view doc. asp?symbol=A/RES/2758(XXVI)&Lang=E&Area=RESOLUTION (accessed December 6, 2013). Copyright © 1971 by the United Nations. All rights reserved. Reproduced by permission.*

INTRODUCTION *The People's Republic of China (PRC) fully supported the establishment of the UN and joined the Republic of China (ROC) delegation in signing the UN Charter in 1945. By 1965 however, unhappy with the repeated refusal of the UN to recognize the PRC as the organization's official representative, PRC leaders became increasingly critical of the organization and called for it to be replaced. It was not until 1971 that the UN, through Resolution 2758, recognized the PRC as the sole representative of China, expelling the ROC in both the General Assembly and the Security Council.*

The General Assembly,

Recalling the principles of the Charter of the United Nations,

Considering that the restoration of the lawful rights of the People's Republic of China is essential both for the protection of the Charter of the United Nations and for the cause that the United Nations must serve under the Charter,

Recognizing that the representatives of the Government of the People's Republic of China are the only lawful representatives of China to the United Nations and that the People's Republic of China is one of the five permanent members of the Security Council,

Decides to restore all its rights to the People's Republic of China and to recognize the representatives of its Government as the only legitimate representatives of China to the United Nations, and to expel forthwith the representatives of Chiang Kai-shek from the place which they unlawfully occupy at the United Nations and in all the organizations related to it.

1976th plenary meeting,
25 October 1971

SEE ALSO *Chinese Revolution; Korean War; United Nations; World War II*

BIBLIOGRAPHY

Books

Bush, Richard. *Uncharted Strait: The Future of China-Taiwan Relations.* Washington, DC: Brookings International Press, 2013.

Ching, Ching. *Taiwan after China: Our Stories Since 1948.* Indianapolis, IN: Dog Ear Publishing, 2012.

Wasserstrom, Jeffery. *China in the Twenty-First Century: What Everyone Needs to Know.* Oxford: Oxford University Press, 2010.

Web Sites

"China-Taiwan History." *PBS Online NewsHour*, March 7, 2000. http://www.pbs.org/newshour/bb/asia/china/china-taiwan.html (accessed January 6, 2014).

Roberge, Michal, and Youkyung Lee. "China-Taiwan Relations." *Council on Foreign Relations.* http://www.cfr.org/china/china-taiwan-relations/p9223 (accessed January 6, 2014).

"Taiwan: History." *Lonely Planet.* http://www.lonelyplanet.com/taiwan/history#161958 (accessed January 6, 2014).

"Taiwan's Ma Says Ending China Standoff a Must for the Economy." *Reuters*, January 2, 2014. http://www.reuters.com/article/2014/01/02/us-taiwan-china-idUSBREA0107C20140102 (accessed January 6, 2014).

"U.S. Relations with Taiwan." *U.S. Department of State*, February 25, 2013. http://www.state.gov/r/pa/ei/bgn/35855.htm (accessed January 6, 2014).

Terrorism: Large Group

⊕ Introduction

Terrorism is the attempt to achieve a goal through violent or destructive acts intended to induce change by instilling fear among a group of people. Large-scale terrorism is conducted on a national or international scale, but is not state sponsored or the work of a single individual or small group. Modern terrorist groups may be divided into religious or politically based groups, although the lines may at times be blurred. The most famous large-scale terrorist group of the early 21st century is al-Qaeda, an Islamist extremist group that has conducted brutal terrorist attacks throughout the world.

International law does not provide a single definition of terrorism, but the United Nations Security Council Resolution 1566 (2004) contains the best attempt by the United Nations at specifying one. Resolution 1566 states that terrorism refers to "criminal acts, including against civilians, committed with the intent to cause death or serious bodily injury, or taking of hostages, with the purpose to provoke a state of terror in the general public or in a group of persons or particular persons, intimidate a population or compel a government or an international organization to do or to abstain from doing any act."

Despite efforts to provide a universal definition of terrorism, whether a group considers an act to be a terrorist act is often a matter of interpretation. Events that constitute terrorism are often contentious and heavily tied to cultural perspective. One society may label a suicide bomber a terrorist, while another society may refer to the bomber as a martyr, freedom fighter, revolutionary, or separatist. Such distinctions even exist in news reports that are designed for more politically sympathetic audiences. Most large-scale terrorist groups, including al-Qaeda, state in propaganda material that their primary purpose is protection and/or the advancement of specific ideals, and that, while violence is sanctioned, it is not the driving force behind the organization.

⊕ Historical Background

A variety of motives underlies terrorist acts, including religious, social, economic, and political motivations. Typically, large-scale terrorist groups either promote extreme religious views or champion a particular separatist group or nationalist government. In general, terrorists are unwilling to negotiate with their perceived enemies, or are prevented from doing so by political, social, or economic circumstances. Although terrorist groups may specifically target a national government, terrorists typically have little regard for innocent noncombatants. Terrorist attacks increased greatly in the 20th and early 21st centuries due in part to the development of more powerful and easily obtained explosives.

Political Terrorists: 20th- and 21st-Century Separatist Movements

Numerous separatist movements of the 20th century, including the Irish, Kurdish, and Palestinian independence movements, have used terrorism as a means of achieving their political goals. In each case, these separatists movements have had ethnic or religious elements, but the primary purpose of each group is to gain political sovereignty for their people.

Irish Republican Army   The Irish Republican Army (IRA) fought for northern Irish independence from the United Kingdom during the 20th century. After the signing of the Anglo-Irish Treaty in 1921, Ireland was divided into the independent Republic of Ireland and British-controlled Northern Ireland. Successor organizations of the IRA, including the Provisional IRA and Real IRA, continued to wage a terrorist campaign for independence for Northern Ireland. An escalation of fighting from 1968 to 1998, a period known as the Troubles, involved attacks on citizens in Ireland, Northern Ireland, and England. More than 3,500 people died as a result of the conflict during the Troubles. The terrorist

IRA women wear stockings over their faces to mask their identities while being trained in use of firearms in a secret camp in Ireland.   © *John Reader/Time & Life Pictures/Getty Images*

campaign waged by the IRA, along with its predecessors and successors, was the longest sustained terrorist campaign of the 20th century.

During the 21st century the IRA decommissioned all of its weapons and its leaders took over many of the top political offices in Northern Ireland. Most former IRA members are now dedicated to a peaceful Northern Ireland. However, IRA splinter groups engaged in new terrorist attacks starting in 2009. Unlike the former attacks, these terrorist attacks were fairly small-scale in nature.

Kurdistan Workers's Party   Around 1984, Turkey's various Kurdish rebel groups formed the Kurdistan Workers' Party (PKK) to press for the creation of an independent Kurdish state, known as Kurdistan, and the protection of Turkey's Kurdish population. Kurdish separatists envision Kurdistan incorporating the predominantly Kurdish portions of Turkey, Iraq, Iran, and Syria. The establishment of Kurdistan would allow the Kurds, an ethnically and linguistically unique people, to have their own nation. Of the various Kurdish

separatist groups that have been created, the PKK has been the largest.

Unwilling to assimilate into Turkish culture, the PKK fought with the Turkish government from 1984 to 1999 in battles that claimed nearly 30,000 lives. Although the PKK and its supporters consider the PKK an organization of freedom fighters, their cause is not supported by the majority of the international community, and they are generally considered to be terrorists.

During the 21st century, the PKK continued to wage guerrilla warfare against the Turkish government. Contending that any Kurdish lands were the homelands of all Kurds, the PKK established military bases inside Iraqi Kurdistan after the removal of Iraqi dictator Saddam Hussein (1937–2006). In 2012 the PKK began openly migrating to Iraqi Kurdistan. In March 2013, however, the PKK and Turkey announced a ceasefire. Under the terms of the ceasefire, the PKK agreed to withdraw its troops and arms from Turkey.

The Palestinian Liberation Organization   The Palestinian Liberation Organization (PLO) was founded in 1964 with the purpose of creating an independent Palestinian state. In 1945, the United Nations had intended to divide the British-controlled Palestine into two distinct countries: Jewish Israel and Arab/Muslim Palestine. While Zionists agreed to the partition, the Palestinians rejected it, and a civil war erupted. During the conflict Israel declared its independence. The next day, Egypt, Iraq, Jordan, and Syria attacked Israel. After a series of wars in the mid-20th century in which Israel gained territory, many Arabs lived in Israeli-controlled areas where they had little political voice.

The PLO and other Palestinian groups employed terrorist tactics to advance their political agenda for a free Palestine. The most notable terrorist attacks were suicide bombings, which often targeted Israeli citizens. Most terrorist attacks occurred during the First Intifada, a period of Palestinian uprising from 1987 to 1993, and during the Second Intifada, which began in 2000. Approximately 5,500 Palestinians and over 1,200 Israelis have died in the Palestinian-Israeli conflict since 1987.

For many years, the international community considered the PLO to be a terrorist organization. In 1974, however, the United Nations (UN) recognized the PLO as the "representative of the Palestinian people," and granted the PLO observer status at the UN. Both Israel and the United States denounced this decision, and both countries continued to consider the PLO a terrorist organization. In 1993, Yassar Arafat (1929–2004), the PLO leader, helped broker a peace agreement with Israeli prime minister Yatzhak Rabin (1922–1995) that temporarily eased the Israeli-Palestinian conflict. They also set the groundwork for the Palestinian National Authority, a self-governing body over the contested West Bank and Gaza Strip, which can speak for the Palestinian people.

The PLO enjoyed observer status at the UN from 1974 until 2012. Since 2012, the Palestinian National Authority has represented the Palestinian people at the UN. This decision was met with dismay by both Israel and the United States, but was widely supported worldwide. The PLO continues to work toward an independent Palestinian state, and it seems likely that their aim may someday be realized.

Religious Terrorists: 20th- and 21st-Century Extremism

Numerous religious extremist groups emerged in the 20th century, particularly in poverty-stricken Islamic countries. Islam is a religion that advocates tolerance and compassion, but many groups have perverted the tenets of Islam to suit their political and economic goals. Like other historical religious extremist groups, these modern organizations spew hate-based propaganda that preaches the dominance of one religious sect over all others. The primary purpose of these groups is to exert their own religious beliefs over a region and to injure or kill anyone who represents a different way of life. Numerous religious extremists groups exist; the largest and most well-known is al-Qaeda.

Al-Qaeda   Al-Qaeda is the name adopted by a radical Islamist group closely associated with acts of global terrorism throughout the Western world, North Africa, Central Asia, and the Middle East. The name al-Qaeda can be translated as "the base," or "the foundation," and refers to the original training camp established to train Islamic resistance fighters who repelled invading Soviet troops in Afghanistan during the 1980s. Osama bin Laden (1957–2011), al-Qaeda's founder and longtime leader, was a key supporter of this resistance movement. After the Soviets withdrew from Afghanistan in 1989, bin Laden became a well-known figure among radical Islamists. Bin Laden also become the most despised terrorist in a generation after the September 11, 2001, attacks on the United States.

The members of al-Qaeda support a return to what they view as the basic tenets of Islam, which they aim to spread across the globe. In their view Muslims must

This still photo handout, taken from footage released by al-Qaeda's media wing as-Sahab and provided by the SITE Intelligence Group September 7, 2007, shows al-Qaeda chief Osama bin Laden delivering a speech at an unidentified time and place. Bin Laden appeared on the video in his first public showing in three years, mocking the "weakness" of the United States. U.S. services monitoring Islamic militant web sites announced that bin Laden was to appear in a recording to mark the following week's anniversary of the September 11, 2001, attacks.   *© AFP/Getty Images*

follow sharia, a detailed set of rules and traditions governing human behavior as outlined in the holy literature of Islam. This includes, among many other things, restrictions on gambling and the consumption of pork, harsh penalties (including stoning and mutilation) for crimes such as theft or adultery, and dress codes that are especially strict with regard to women. Many of these rules involve subjective interpretation of ancient holy texts. Fundamentalists often enforce their views against more moderate Muslims through violent means. Al-Qaeda followers view the Western world as immoral, sexually permissive, and financially exploitative. They also believe that it is their holy duty to eliminate this immorality from the world by any means necessary.

Although many radical Islamist groups differ in their beliefs and goals, throughout the 1990s and early 21st centuries, bin Laden successfully called for these groups to unite against their common enemies. The two targets most frequently cited are Israel, a country that was established in a region that many Muslims view as their own rightful lands, and the United States, which helped fund Israel and has maintained a military presence in the Middle East since the beginning of the Gulf War in 1990.

Because of this cooperation between otherwise distinct terrorist groups, al-Qaeda's direct role in acts of global terrorism is often difficult to discern. Even some terrorist leaders associated with al-Qaeda, such as Abu Musab al-Zarqawi (1966–2006), were not originally part of the al-Qaeda organization. Zarqawi, for example, did not pledge allegiance to al-Qaeda until 2004, although he had engaged in terrorist activities for many years and had operated with funds provided by bin Laden. Some organizations in other areas of the world claim to be part of al-Qaeda, and although some clearly are affiliated (including al-Qaeda in Iraq and Abu Sayyaf in the Philippines), most analysts agree that many act independently and merely attempt to attach themselves to al-Qaeda.

Al-Qaeda has claimed credit for several notable terror attacks against the United States. The attacks on the World Trade Center in 1993 and again in 2001 were both claimed by al-Qaeda, as were the 1998 bombings of U.S. embassies in Kenya and Tanzania, and the 2000 attack on the U.S.S. *Cole.* Members of al-Qaeda are believed to have been involved in several other bombings and attacks, although the organization's leaders generally have a history of denying involvement rather than attempting to claim credit for specific terrorist activities.

Following the September 2001 terror attacks, the United States led a military force into Afghanistan that destroyed al-Qaeda's established training camps. Observers estimate that more than three-fourths of the members of al-Qaeda present in Afghanistan were killed during the military operation. Even as al-Qaeda has encountered significant setbacks—including a decrease in support from Muslims worldwide—the group has

continued to partner with Islamist radicals in places such as Yemen, Pakistan, and Somalia, to pursue its goals.

⊕ Impacts and Issues

In addition to the destruction wrought by acts of terrorism, efforts to bring terrorists to justice and prevent future attacks can have far-reaching effects. The September 2001 terrorist attacks against the United States triggered the largest restructuring of the U.S. government in more than 50 years when 22 agencies were reorganized to fall under the newly created Department of Homeland Security (DHS). Employing nearly 200,000 people, the DHS through its various divisions is responsible for increasing border and transportation security, controlling the flow of immigrants, protecting potentially vulnerable infrastructure and buildings, and gathering intelligence. Security procedures implemented in U.S. airports underwent dramatic changes post 9/11, including the now common and still controversial full-body scanners. Some of the increased security procedures were borrowed from other countries such as Israel, where measures had been in effect for many decades due to ongoing terrorist threats.

Even more controversial than airport security measures, is the U.S. Patriot Act of 2001, which gives the government broad powers to fight terrorism at the expense, many contend, of personal freedoms. Other U.S. policies intended to combat terrorism such as extraordinary rendition have drawn sharp criticism within and outside the United States. Extraordinary rendition,

---

TERRORISTS AND MODERN TECHNOLOGY

Many terrorists attack using only basic weaponry, including homemade bombs and box cutters, but other terrorists use very sophisticated technology. During the November 2008 terrorist attacks in Mumbai, India, the attackers, members of an Islamist terrorist group known as Lashkar-e-Taiba, managed highly coordinated attacks using satellite-based GPS navigation equipment, satellite imagery, and Internet-based communications networks.

The Mumbai attackers also used real-time intelligence gathered by online news services to help coordinate their efforts and prolong the battle waged by Indian authorities to regain control. It took three days for Indian military and police to retake the two hotels filled with Western tourists and a Jewish center seized by the Pakistani-based terrorists. The attack took the lives of over 160 people and injured more than 600 others. Lashkar-e-Taiba is a Muslim extremist group based in Pakistan that has often targeted Hindu groups in India.

enacted in 1995, is the U.S. Central Intelligence Agency's (CIA's) practice of forcible detention of prisoners suspected of being terrorists both within the United States and in other countries without the legal rights usually afforded U.S. citizens. Critics claim that the extralegal detention and kidnapping conducted under this policy is illegal under international law. For similar reasons, the continued detainment of suspected terrorists at the U.S. Guantánamo Bay Naval Base remains a point of contention within and outside the United States.

International organizations such as the United Nations (UN) have also adopted strategies to fight terrorism. For example, on September 8, 2006, the UN adopted a Global Counter-Terrorism Strategy that reaffirms previous commitments to fight terrorism and that seeks to "promote comprehensive, coordinated and consistent responses, at national, regional and international levels, to counter terrorism, which also takes into account the conditions conducive to the spread of terrorism." The UN places a strong emphasis on fighting terrorism through improving the conditions that often lead to successful recruitment by terrorist groups and the willingness of terrorists to sacrifice their own lives in the act of terrorism. By fostering peaceful resolutions to ongoing conflicts and addressing human rights violations and discrimination as well as lack of economic stability it is hoped that the conditions that lead to the spread of terrorism can be improved.

As the number of attacks carried out by Muslim terrorist groups has increased, so has Islamophobia and acts of discrimination and hostility fueled by fear of those of the Islamic faith. Muslim communities in the United States and European countries where Muslims are a minority slice of the population have experienced an increased incidence of prejudice-fueled acts, including discrimination and racial profiling, verbal abuse, physical violence, and damage to mosques and other property. In some instances, some of these events have sparked retaliatory violence by Muslims, which has reinforced negative anti-Muslim stereotypes among those already inclined toward Islamophobia.

⊕ Future Implications

Large-scale terrorism is an undeniable feature of the 21st century. Large-scale, long-term terrorist organizations are born out of religious fundamentalism and despair caused by socioeconomic factors.

In 2001 the United States called upon the North Atlantic Treaty Organization (NATO) to join it in a global campaign to eliminate terrorist organizations,

particularly al-Qaeda. The War on Terror has successfully hunted down many al-Qaeda leaders, including bin Laden. But splinter groups have replaced the larger organization. Numerous old and new religious extremist groups have risen around the world, particularly in areas with large Muslim populations. It is not enough to merely destroy one organization if the root cause of the anger that inspired that organization is not addressed and resolved. Until the socioeconomic problems of the Islamic world are solved, it is likely that religious extremist terrorist groups will continue to exist and evolve.

By contrast, political terrorist groups may be evolving away from terror and toward more peaceful discussions. The international sympathy for separatist movements appears to be growing as it becomes increasingly obvious that some national borders do not accurately reflect population demographics. The United Nations has heard petitions by numerous separatist groups and helped to broker peace in several occasions. But once again, unless the actual socioeconomic and political concerns of the people are addressed, a return to terrorism is possible.

SEE ALSO *9/11; Afghan War; Arab-Israeli Conflict; Guantánamo Bay Detention Center; Islamophobia; Religious Extremism; Terrorism: Small Group and Individual; Terrorism: State Sponsored*

BIBLIOGRAPHY

Books

Chaliand, Gerard. *A History of Terrorism: From Antiquity to Al-Qaeda.* Berkeley: University of California Press, 2007.

Hoffman, Bruce. *Inside Terrorism.* New York: Columbia University Press, 2006.

Sageman, Marc. *Leaderless Jihad: Terror Networks in the Twenty-First Century.* Philadelphia: University of Pennsylvania Press, 2008.

Web Sites

"General Assembly Actions to Counter Terrorism." *United Nations.* http://www.un.org/en/terrorism/ga.shtml (accessed September 6, 2013).

"Terrorism." *FBI.* http://www.fbi.gov/about-us/investigate/terrorism (accessed February 11, 2014).

Yousafzai, Sami. "Inside Al-Qaeda." *Newsweek,* September 4, 2010. http://www.newsweek.com/inside-al-qaeda-72049 (accessed February 11, 2014).

Terrorism: Small Group and Individual

⊕ Introduction

Terrorism is the attempt to achieve a goal through violent or destructive acts designed to instill fear in a group of people. Small-group and individual terrorism is conducted by angry, alienated, or socially disturbed people who act independently without the support of an organized party or command structure. Generally small-group and individual terrorists use small arms or homemade bombs to incite terror.

Small group and individual terrorists often leave rambling manifestos or written statements documenting their reasons and justifications for their violent acts. The manifestos may list social, political, or economic diatribes, which often focus on a religion or ethnic group. Such writings generally appear to be the product of a disturbed mind, although the terrorists themselves may claim to be fully sane. Small group and individual terrorist attacks are becoming increasingly common worldwide due to the relatively easy access to automatic rifles and the free circulation of blueprints for homemade bombs on the Internet.

⊕ Historical Background

The terms *terrorism* and *terrorist* entered the lexicon in the 1790s when British journalists, historians, and politicians used those words to refer to the Jacobins (radical republicans) and other violent rebels of the French Revolution (1789–99). The roots of modern terrorism can be traced back nearly 200 years before the French Revolution, however, to the unrealized November 5, 1605, Gunpowder Plot of Guy Fawkes (1570–1606), who planned to blow up the British Parliament and kill King James I (1566–1625).

Even with the availability of explosives in the 17th and 18th centuries, acts of terrorism remained rare until the rise of anarchism (revolution) in the mid-19th century. Anarchists, though united in rejecting the concept of a compulsory government, remained a splintered political movement. Some groups maintained individual ideologies, and others associated themselves with the emerging fascist or communist movements.

International law does not provide a single definition of terrorism, but the United Nations Security Council Resolution 1566 (2004) contains the best attempt by the United Nations at specifying one. Resolution 1566 states that terrorism refers to "criminal acts, including against civilians, committed with the intent to cause death or serious bodily injury, or taking of

---

LONE WOLF

A "lone wolf" is a term sometimes used to describe individual terrorists. Although they may share some ideological agreement with other terrorist groups, their actions are committed wholly independently. U.S. law enforcement agencies and the U.S. media are most likely to use this term for suspected individual terrorists.

One of the most infamous lone wolf terrorists was the Unabomber, Ted Kaczynski (1942–). A brilliant yet disturbed man, Kaczynski built 16 bombs between 1978 and 1995, which he then mailed or delivered to various individuals, ultimately killing three people and wounding 22 others. On April 24, 1995, Kaczynski sent a letter to the *New York Times* promising "to desist from terrorism" if the *Times* or the *Washington Post* would publish his manifesto in which he argued that his bombs were meant to draw attention to the erosion of human freedom by modern civilization. Out of concern for human life, both newspapers printed the manifesto. Based on a tip from Kaczynski's brother following the publication of the manifesto, the FBI captured Kaczynski, who was found guilty of murder and building bombs.

hostages, with the purpose to provoke a state of terror in the general public or in a group of persons or particular persons, intimidate a population or compel a government or an international organization to do or to abstain from doing any act."

Despite efforts to provide a universal definition of terrorism, whether an individual or a member of a small group is considered to be a terrorist or simply a murderer is often a matter of interpretation. Events that constitute terrorism are often contentious and heavily tied to cultural perspective. One society may label a suicide bomber a terrorist, but another society may refer to the bomber as a martyr, freedom fighter, revolutionary, or separatist. Such distinctions even exist in news reports that are designed for more politically sympathetic audiences. Sometimes small group or individual terrorists will claim brotherhood with large or state-sponsored terrorist groups. In such cases it is easier to label them terrorists. At other times they work completely independently, and how they are labeled may depend heavily on the current political atmosphere and the media coverage.

⊕ Impacts and Issues

A variety of motives underlies terrorist acts, including religious, social, economic, and political motivations. In general, terrorists are unwilling to negotiate with their perceived enemies, or are prevented from doing so by political, social, or economic circumstances. Terrorists may specifically target a national government, but they are just as likely to target peaceful civilians.

Because of their size, small-group and individual terrorists are generally hunted down by the national government where their crimes were committed. If captured alive they are then subject to the laws and punishments of that land. Often other nations issue official condolences to countries that have suffered from particularly vicious terrorist attacks. When two nations or groups are at odds, however, politicians, religious leaders, or other public figures may make public remarks in support of the terrorists and their actions. Considering that the violence is almost always directed at innocent noncombatants, such remarks in support of terrorists are overtly political.

Security officials remove a handgun from the grip of former Northern Ireland Protestant paramilitant Michael Stone (C) at Stormont Parliament buildings, in Belfast, Northern Ireland, in November 2006. Northern Ireland's first session to discuss power-sharing plans was suspended days earlier after the well-known former paramilitary killer threw a smoking device in the entrance of the building, witnesses said. In 1988 he was also responsible for a "lone wolf" attack with hand grenades and two pistols on an IRA funeral in Belfast that left three people dead and many wounded. He was sentenced to life in prison for that crime and several other murders and attempted murders of Catholics, but was released in 2000 due to the 1998 Good Friday Peace Agreement and became an artist. At his trial for the 2006 attempted attack, Stone claimed it was performance art.   © *Peter Muhly/AFP/Getty Images*

Suicide Bombs

A suicide bomber is an individual who carries out an attack in which he or she has little or no chance of surviving. Typically a suicide bombing is a low-tech operation, carried out using a mixture of homemade explosives and household implements such as nails and bolts. These are contained in a so-called suicide belt, or carried in a backpack or carrying bag. The bombs are deadly because of their compactness and because a suicide bomber can move virtually anywhere undetected: to a marketplace, subway station, or religious building. Worldwide, suicide bombings comprise less than 5 percent of terrorist attacks but account for about 33 percent of terrorism related deaths.

Suicide attacks are usually simple to plan and carry out and require only rudimentary technology. A bomber can work alone and no escape route or safe house is required, nor is there danger that accomplices may be betrayed in the event of capture. Suicide bombings are significantly more effective in causing casualties than shooting or conventional bombing attacks. Moreover, as a psychological attack, suicide bombs impart the ultimate message of mercilessness to an enemy or victimized population—that the bomber's cause is worth dying for.

Suicide bombings have been used by state-sponsored and large-group terrorist organizations as well as by small-group and individual terrorists. Suicide bombings have particularly risen to notoriety over the past several decades, and are typically associated with Islamist terrorism, though other groups have used them. In the early 1980s, fewer than 10 suicide attacks occurred globally each year on average. By 2005, the number of suicide attacks had risen to over 450 in that year alone.

Since the beginning of the 21st century, suicide bombings have been widely deployed in terrorist attacks, in such diverse areas as the United States, Iraq, Israel, Indonesia, Afghanistan, Pakistan, the United Kingdom, Spain, Turkey, and Russia. In total, suicide bombings have occurred in over 30 different countries.

A wounded man is carried away following a suicide bombing close to the home of MP Imad Yohana in the northern city of Kirkuk, Iraq, in September 2013. Some 47 people were wounded, including the Christian MP. The violence came a day after some 73 people were killed in bombings in the capital of Baghdad. The city of Kirkuk has a mixed population of Arabs, Kurds, Muslims, and Christians. © *Marwan Ibrahim/AFP/Getty Images*

Suicide Bombs in Iraq Since the United States invaded Iraq in 2003, well over 1,000 suicide bombing attacks have taken place in that country, resulting in at least 13,000 deaths and injuring more than 30,000 others. This is an unprecedented level of such attacks. Many of them have been organized by large terrorist groups such as al-Qaeda, and others are thought to have been the work of small groups or individuals.

Homemade Bombs

Terrorists may also build homemade bombs that they leave in a public spot, attach to a car, or put in the mail where they later explode, causing death and destruction, but leaving the terrorist unharmed. Typically, homemade bombs are low-tech operations. Blueprints and instructions can be found online and the materials may often be easy to purchase. The bombs created by small groups or individuals are usually small enough that they can be carried by one person. Such terrorist attacks are fairly simple to plan and carry out, but can cause widespread damage. Even worse is their psychological power—that no place is safe and that terror may occur anywhere.

Boston Marathon Attack Homemade bombs are made and deployed around the world, but terrorist attacks on the United States receive the widest news coverage domestically. For example, on April 15, 2013, two homemade bombs made from pressure cookers exploded at the Boston Marathon, killing three people and wounding at least 180 others. Authorities were quickly able to determine that the bombs were carried to a location near the race's finish line in black nylon bags. Because the Boston Marathon was heavily photographed and recorded, law enforcement agents had access to hundreds of hours of footage, which they examined for clues leading to the perpetrators. The day after the bombing, during a press conference at the White House, President Barack Obama (1961–) stated that "any time bombs are used to target innocent civilians, it is an act of terror."

Only three days after the marathon, the FBI released video and still photos of two suspects and asked for help from the public in identifying them. Within 24 hours one suspect had been killed in a shootout with the police. The other was captured and

Defense lawyers Geir Lippestad (L) and Tord Jordet (R) stand next to self-confessed mass murderer Anders Behring Breivik (C) as he places a clenched fist on his heart while leaving court after being sentenced to 21 years in prison, at Oslo District Court on August 24, 2012. An Oslo court found Breivik guilty of "acts of terror" and sentenced him to 21 years in prison for his killing spree in 2011 that left 77 people dead. Breivik dismissed his sentence of 21 years in jail by declaring the Oslo court "illegitimate," but also said he would not appeal the sentence. © Heiko Junge/AFP/GettyImages

charged with using a weapon of mass destruction. The two suspects in the Boston Marathon attack did not belong to any larger terrorist group, but instead were working essentially independently. Militant, pro-Islamic statements were found among their belongings, indicating they were at least influenced by Islamic terrorist groups.

Shooting Sprees

Small groups or individuals may also use semiautomatic or automatic rifles to commit mass murder. Such shootings occur with alarming regularity in the United States, often in schools. To date, all school shootings in the United States have been the work of individuals or small groups. U.S. gun control policy makes it fairly easy for terrorists, who may be referred to as mass murderers, to obtain relatively heavy weaponry. In other countries, particularly in Western Europe, it is much more difficult to get weapons, and mass shootings are more rare.

The 2011 Norway Attacks   On July 22, 2011, Norway was struck by two sequential terrorist attacks. The first was a car bomb that exploded outside a government office in the capital, Oslo. The apparent target, Prime Minister Jens Stoltenberg (1959–), was not harmed, but eight people were killed and several others injured. About an hour later, Anders Behring Breivik (1979–) traveled to the island of Utoya, where the Labour Party (Stoltenberg's political party) was holding a youth camp. Breivik, disguised as a policeman, opened fire on the campers, most of them teenagers, killing 69 before police arrived, when he then surrendered peacefully. Breivik was also the perpetrator of the Oslo bombing.

Breivik was described as a right-wing extremist. On the day of the attacks, he posted a manifesto online, expressing strong support for the eradication of Islam and multiculturalism in order to save Christian Europe. Breivik confessed to the charges, which include committing "acts of terror." At a court hearing Breivik said that he had hoped to kill everyone on the island, more than 500 people in all.

Breivik's defense hinged on a determination of criminal insanity. Two psychiatrists came to conflicting opinions on Breivik's mental condition. One judged him insane, and therefore not culpable; the other judged him sane. Breivik himself insisted that he is sane and acted for rational reasons. Breivik's stance is not unusual; many other individual terrorists have been accused of mental instability but insist that they are sane. In August 2012, a Norwegian court determined that Breivik was sane and convicted him on 77 counts of murder.

⊕ Future Implications

Small-group and individual terrorism is an undeniable feature of the 21st century. Large-scale terrorist attacks are typically born out of a despair caused by socioeconomic factors. By contrast, small-scale terrorist attacks are more often the product of individuals with mental disorders acting out against some perceived injustice, inequality, or unjust institution or group. Access to proper psychiatric care remains limited in most countries worldwide. Even in countries where mental care is available, the social stigma against seeking psychiatric attention can be difficult to surmount.

Equally difficult is the ability of most police and intelligence agencies to track individual or small-group terrorists until after they have at least attempted an attack. Countries that monitor the actions and communications of their citizens may be able to better discover potential terrorist threats in some instances. Freedom of speech and freedom of information advocates decry such internal "spying" on citizens. Instances of individual and small-group terrorism will likely continue on a large scale until socioeconomic factors are addressed, religious and ethnic divides healed, and mental health issues taken seriously.

SEE ALSO   *Religious Extremism; Terrorism: Large Group; Terrorism: State Sponsored*

BIBLIOGRAPHY

Books

Chaliand, Gerard. *A History of Terrorism: From Antiquity to Al-Qaeda.* Berkeley: University of California Press, 2007.

Hoffman, Bruce. *Inside Terrorism.* New York: Columbia University Press, 2006.

Pape, Robert. *Dying to Win: The Strategic Logic of Suicide Terrorism.* New York: Random House Trade, 2006.

Web Sites

"Lone Wolf Terrorism" *Transnational Terrorism, Security, and the Rule of Law*, June 7, 2007. http://www.transnationalterrorism.eu/tekst/publications/Lone-Wolf%20Terrorism.pdf (accessed December 24, 2013).

Thompson, Nick. "Armies of One: Are Lone Wolf Attacks the Future of Terrorism?" *CNN*, May 23, 2013. http://www.cnn.com/2013/05/23/world/europe/london-attack-lone wolf fears (accessed December 7, 2013).

"United Nations Action to Counter Terrorism." http://www.un.org/en/terrorism/ (accessed December 24, 2013).

Terrorism: State Sponsored

⊕ Introduction

Terrorism is the attempt to achieve a goal through violent or destructive acts intended to induce change by instilling fear among a group of people. State-sponsored terrorism is terrorism that is funded or otherwise supported by a national government. State-sponsored terrorism is not to be confused with state terrorism, which is terrorism that is actively perpetrated by the national government as, for example, Nazi Germany and the Holocaust or the Taliban in Afghanistan.

Viewed objectively, numerous examples of state-sponsored terrorism in the 20th and 21st centuries are identifiable. Since no single definition of what constitutes terrorism exists, however, the list of countries accused of sponsoring terrorism is long. Although some nations actively admit to funding various organizations, governments rarely, if ever, refer to the organizations as "terrorists." Instead, governments sponsoring violent organizations often refer to such groups as "freedom fighters" or other similar terms.

⊕ Historical Background

Numerous instances in which governments have directly or indirectly supported paramilitary groups that engage in terrorist activities exist. However, because terrorism itself does not have a single agreed-upon meaning, there is often some political dispute that can be cited as a factor in state-sponsored terrorism. International law does not provide a definition of terrorism, but the United Nations (UN) Security Council Resolution 1566 (2004) contains the best attempt by the UN at specifying a definition. Resolution 1566 states that terrorism refers to "criminal acts, including against civilians, committed with the intent to cause death or serious bodily injury, or taking of hostages, with the purpose to provoke a state of terror in the general public or in a group of persons or particular persons, intimidate a population or compel a government or an international organization to do or to abstain from doing any act."

Despite efforts to provide a universal definition of terrorism, whether an act is considered a terrorist act is often a matter of interpretation. Events that constitute terrorism are often contentious and heavily tied to cultural perspective. One society may label a suicide bomber a terrorist, while another society may refer to the bomber as a martyr, freedom fighter, revolutionary, or separatist. Such distinctions even exist in news reports that are designed for more politically sympathetic audiences. Even in cases of state-sponsored terrorism there can be notable global disagreement about whether or not an organization is in fact a terrorist group.

For example, during the 1950s and 1960s the National Liberation Front of Southern Vietnam (often referred to in the United States as the Viet Cong) was one of the primary military forces during the Second Indochinese War, more commonly known in the English-speaking world as the Vietnam War (1954–75). Because some of its actions were terrorist in nature, the Viet Cong could have potentially been termed a large-scale terrorist organization. However, the Viet Cong received direct financial support from North Vietnam, and could also be considered a state-sponsored terrorist organization. The Viet Cong and North Vietnam both considered the National Liberation Front to be a resistance movement, which fought against imperial invaders.

⊕ Impacts and Issues

A variety of motives underlies terrorist acts, including religious, social, economic, and political motivations. State-sponsored terrorist groups may be directed against their nation's own citizens, against another nation, or even have a global ideology that could potentially affect the entire world.

One of the more infamous acts of terrorism in the late 20th century occurred in 1985 when a TWA airplane was hijacked by Lebanese gunmen. Here, TWA Boeing 727 Captain John L. Testrake from Richmond, Missouri, is seen in the cockpit of his hijacked airliner at the Beirut airport. He talks to newsmen while a Shia terrorist (background) holds him at gunpoint. Lebanese gunmen from Amal and Hezbollah (the Party of God) hijacked the TWA jetliner on June 14, 1985, with 153 people on board, after taking off from Athens to Rome. After twice flying to Beirut and Algiers, and releasing more than 100 hostages, the hijackers landed for the third time in Beirut. They demanded the release of more than 700 prisoners, mostly Shias, from Israeli jails and the withdrawal of Israeli troops from southern Lebanon. The hijackers killed young U.S. Navy Seabee Robert Stetham on June 15, then freed all but 39 passengers who were held hostage in Lebanon and not released until June 30. Americans were then driven in a Red Cross convoy to Damascus before flying to a U.S. base in West Germany. Iran has been accused of funding Hezbollah.   © *Nabil Ismail/AFP/Getty Images*

In general, state-sponsored terrorists are unwilling to negotiate with their perceived enemies. Terrorist groups may specifically target a national government, but terrorists typically have little regard for innocent noncombatants. The scale of state-sponsored terrorist attacks increased greatly in the 20th and the early 21st centuries, due to the development of more powerful and more easily concealed technologies capable of killing hundreds or thousands of people.

State-Sponsored Terrorism in the 21st Century

Numerous countries have been accused of sponsoring terrorism during the 21st century including India, Iran, Libya, Pakistan, Qatar, Saudi Arabia, the United Kingdom, and the United States.

India   Pakistan has accused the Republic of India of supporting various insurgent groups in Pakistan and for perpetuating human rights violations against the Kashmiri people. India has also been accused of supporting the Liberation Tigers of Tamil Eelam (LTTE, or Tamil Tigers), a separatist militant group in Sri Lanka. The Tamil Tigers were founded in 1976 and waged a nationalist campaign to create an independent state for the Tamil people. This campaign evolved into the Sri Lankan civil war (1983–2009). India admitted to supporting the LTTE during the 1980s, but has since denied all accusations of state-sponsored terrorism. The Sri Lankan military final defeated the LTTE in 2009.

Iran   Iran has been accused by the United States, United Kingdom, Yemen, and Israel of sponsoring terrorism either in or against their respective countries. Western nations have also accused Iran of sponsoring Shia terrorist organizations throughout the Middle East. Former U.S. president George W. Bush (1946–) went so far as to call Iran the "world's primary state sponsor of terror." The vast majority of international observers and governments acknowledge that Iran offers financial, tactical, and moral support to Shia militant groups throughout the Middle East. In 2006, Hezbollah, a Shia organization operating out of southern Lebanon, successfully fought a guerrilla war against Israel, almost certainly with financial and military support from Iran.

Libya   For decades Libya was accused by the United States and many other Western nations of state-sponsored terrorism. The Libyan government under Muammar al-Qadhafi (1942–2011) openly supported a vast array of paramilitary groups. The government provided weapons, financial aid, and even training camps to various left- and right-wing organizations. Leftist groups included the Provisional Irish Republic Army, the Basque Fatherland and Liberty, the Umkhonto We Sizwe (operating in South Africa), the Polisario Front (operating in the Western Sahara), the Palestinian Liberation Organization, and the Popular Front for the Liberation of Palestine. Far-right organizations sponsored by Libya included the Moro National Liberation Front (operating out of the Philippians).

Libya openly admitted to supporting the organizations, which it referred to as freedom fighters rather than terrorist organizations. In 2006, Libya stopped supporting foreign militant organizations. In 2011, a revolution in Libya resulted in the assassination of Qadhafi and the creation of a new government.

Pakistan   Pakistan has been accused by Afghanistan, Canada, France, India, Israel, Poland, the United Kingdom, and the United States of sponsoring terrorism in Afghanistan, India, and Kashmir. In July 2009, Pakistani president Asif Ali Zardari (1955–) admitted that the Pakistani government had "created and nurtured" a variety of terrorist groups to achieve its short-term foreign policy agendas. Among the terrorist organizations funded by Pakistan are the Jammu Kashmir Liberation Front, the Taliban in Afghanistan, and Lashkar-e-Taiba in India.

Qatar   Qatar has been accused by France and the United States of sponsoring various Islamic terrorist groups throughout the Middle East. Between 2011 and 2012, various U.S. newspapers reported that Qatar was sponsoring U.S.-designated terrorist groups including

An Afghan mujahideen fighter carries a U.S.-made shoulder-fired Stinger missile during the 1989 Jalalabad offensive in eastern Afghanistan. The weapon is capable of shooting down fast-moving aircraft by locking on to the heat signal generated by the engines. The missiles were supplied to guerillas fighting the Soviet-backed Afghan government in the 1980s and were credited with helping the resistance to drive the Soviet army from Afghanistan. When the United States invaded Afghanistan in 2001, many of those weapons were unaccounted for, and many U.S. policy makers believed the Stingers might be in the hands of terrorists willing to use them on commercial aircraft or U.S. forces.   © *Larry C. Price/The Denver Post via Getty Images*

the Libyan Islamic Fighting Group and Al-Nusra Front (operating out of Syria), Hamas (operating out of the West Bank and Gaza Strip), various Islamist groups in Mali, and the Muslim Brotherhood (operating in Egypt and throughout the Middle East). Qatar has neither denied nor confirmed these accusations.

Saudi Arabia Saudia Arabia has been accused by the United States and numerous other Western powers of funding terrorist organizations such as al-Qaeda, the Taliban, and Lashkar-e-Taiba. Observers believe that Saudi Arabia is also the largest donor to other Sunni militant groups throughout the world. Although Saudi Arabia openly acknowledges its support of Sunni Muslims, it is also an ally of the United States and the U.S.-led War on Terror.

United Kingdom In 2006, the United Kingdom was accused by Iran of supporting Arab separatist terrorists in the city of Ahwaz. After a series of bombings shook the city, the Iranian government speculated that "British spies" or "British soldiers" had a hand in the attack. The United Kingdom has denied the accusation.

United States The United States has been accused of sponsoring terrorism on numerous occasions throughout the 20th and early 21st centuries. The U.S. Central Intelligence Agency (CIA) has been directly responsible or influential in perpetrating regime changes in countries all over the world and helping create some of the terrorist organizations, including al-Qaeda, which it now must fight against.

During the 21st century, the United States has helped nationalist groups overthrow or fight against governments in Afghanistan, the Gaza Strip, Libya, Iran, Iraq, and Syria. The United States admits to helping these groups, but it denies funding terrorist groups. Instead, the United States maintains that its efforts are to expand democracy and freedom worldwide.

⊕ Future Implications

State-sponsored terrorism is an undeniable feature of the 21st century. Terrorist organizations are born out of radical ideologies and despair caused by socioeconomic factors. Until such factors are adequately addressed, fear and hatred can grow until it inspires acts of violence. National governments can help or hinder terrorist groups. Many nations loudly proclaim their opposition to terrorist groups, but political or economic advantages can cause nations to quietly or openly support organizations perpetrating acts of terror.

Modern international dialogue is rife with examples of nations charging rivals with sponsoring terrorism. Very rarely are these allegations accepted by the accused nation, despite evidence to the contrary. Only the most brazen of authoritarian rulers—for example, Qadhafi of Libya—dare to openly flout international

---

THE UNITED STATES AND AL-QAEDA

During the 1970s, the United States helped to fund the *mujahideen* (Islamic fighters) in Afghanistan. At the time, the United States and the Soviet Union were in the midst of the Cold War (1945–91) and regions around the world were affected by the ambitions of the two superpowers. The Soviet Union occupied Afghanistan from 1979 to 1989, and the United States funded the groups that fought against the invading superpower. In a twist of fate, the same mujahideen fighters in Afghanistan would eventually transform into the Taliban and al-Qaeda, the terrorist groups that later launched attacks on the United States during the 21st century.

---

regard and admit to supporting militant groups. Until all nations agree to support peaceful resolution rather than armed conflict, state-sponsored terrorism will likely continue.

SEE ALSO *Islam: Sunni and Shia Disputes; Lebanon: Civil War and Political Instability; Libyan Civil Unrest; Pakistan-India Conflict; Religious Extremism; Syrian Civil War; Terrorism: Small Scale and Individual; Terrorism: Large Group*

BIBLIOGRAPHY

Books

Chaliand, Gerard. *A History of Terrorism: From Antiquity to Al-Qaeda.* Berkeley, CA: University of California Press, 2007.

Gareau, Frederick. *State Terrorism and the United States: From Counterinsurgency to the War on Terror.* Atlanta, GA: Clarity Press, 2010.

Hoffman, Bruce. *Inside Terrorism.* New York: Columbia University Press, 2006.

Web Sites

Bruno, Greg. "State Sponsors: Iran." *Council on Foreign Relations*, October 13, 2011. http://www.cfr.org/iran/state-sponsors-iran/p9362 (accessed December 22, 2013).

"State Sponsors of Terrorism." *U.S. Department of State.* http://www.state.gov/j/ct/list/c14151.htm (accessed December 22, 2013).

"Syria: State Sponsored Terrorism." *GlobalSecurity.org.* http://www.globalsecurity.org/intell/world/syria/terrorism.htm (accessed December 22, 2013).

United Nations Action to Counter Terrorism. http://www.un.org/en/terrorism/ (accessed December 22, 2013).

Tibet

⊕ Introduction

Tibet is a plateau region in central Asia that the People's Republic of China (mainland China) declares is part of China. For many Tibetans, however, it is an independent country occupied by China. The United Nations (UN) has declined to accuse China of occupying an independent country but, along with human rights organizations, has formally expressed concern over many Chinese practices in the region. In particular, China has been accused of human rights violations during its crackdowns on dissent and for systematically transferring large numbers of Han (Chinese majority) immigrants into Tibet as part of what has been called a "cultural genocide."

A Tibetan government-in-exile, the Central Tibetan Administration, is headed by the 14th Dalai Lama, Tenzin Gyatso (1935–). Although the Central Tibetan Administration considers Tibet to be illegally occupied and colonized by China, in a speech on October 14, 2001, given to the European Parliament in Strasbourg, France, the Dalai Lama stated that he is willing to compromise for a "middle way." Moreover, the Dalai Lama is willing to accept the Strasbourg Proposal, which "envisions that Tibet enjoy genuine autonomy within the framework of the People's Republic of China." The Chinese government, however, refuses to engage in any negotiations about the legal status of Tibet and insists it is a Chinese province.

Tibet also has been claimed by the Republic of China, also known as Taiwan, which considers itself the legitimate government of China. Taiwan itself is also claimed by the People's Republic of China (PRC). Taiwan's claim on Tibet is purely formal, as it has limited influence in the region.

⊕ Historical Background

Tibet and China have had a complex relationship for more than 1,000 years. In its official claim on Tibet, the PRC makes reference to their shared ancient history, arguing that Tibet has been part of China since the 1200's. In fact Chinese rule has been intermittent in Tibet. Tibet achieved its most recent independence in 1912 after the fall of the Chinese Qing Dynasty (1644–1912). Upon gaining independence, Tibet deliberately closed itself off from the outside world, limiting access by foreigners.

The Dalai Lama

For centuries Tibet had been ruled as a feudal theocracy, a form of government in which political and spiritual rule are combined in a single figure. Tibet is a Buddhist nation whose leader is known as the Dalai Lama, a title signifying the highest teacher of Dharma, or spiritual law. Since 1578 there have been 14 Dalai Lamas, each a monk dedicated to a celibate life of study and reflection.

There is no family bloodline linking the various Dalai Lamas. Instead, after the death of the Dalai Lama, other monks begin to search for his reincarnated spirit. According to Buddhist belief, after death every soul is reincarnated into new and different forms. Within a few months or years of the previous Dalai Lama's death, a young boy is found who passes all the necessary tests and is recognized as the new Dalai Lama, or rather the "return" of the Dalai Lama. The current Dalai Lama, Tenzin Gyatso, was found in 1937 when he was only two years old. He was raised in a gentle and loving environment and began his training as a Buddhist monk and political leader when he was six years old.

In October 1950 China invaded Tibet. The next month Tenzin Gyatso, only 15 years old, was officially enthroned as the 14th Dalai Lama. A peace-loving young man, the Dalai Lama recognized that his country could not defend itself against the Chinese army. Instead, as one of his first actions as the Tibetan ruler, he sent a delegation to China to sign a peace treaty. The Seventeen-Point Agreement for the Peaceful Liberation

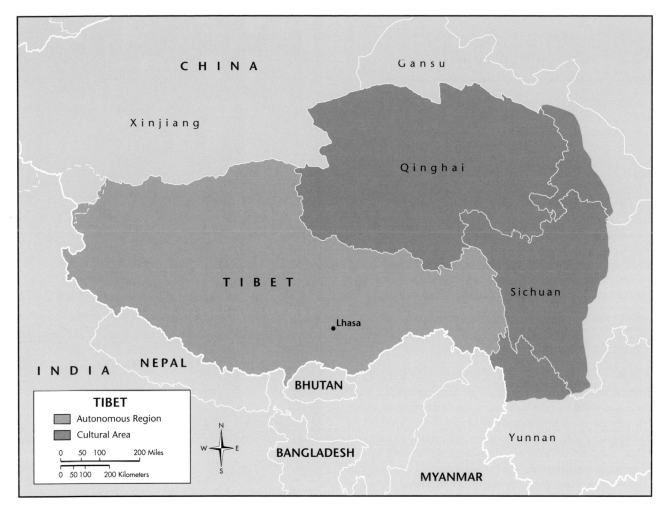

TIBET
- Autonomous Region
- Cultural Area

0 50 100   200 Miles

0 50 100   200 Kilometers

© 2014 Cengage Learning

of Tibet formalized Chinese sovereignty over Tibet. But, according to the Dalai Lama,

> By that agreement the Chinese government recognized the distinctiveness and the autonomy of Tibet and pledged not to impose their system on Tibet against our wishes. However, in breach of this agreement, the Chinese authorities forced upon Tibetans their rigid and alien ideology and showed scant respect for the unique culture, religion and way of life of the Tibetan people.

For almost a decade the Dalai Lama attempted to preserve the Tibetan way of life and coexist with Communist rule. But in 1959, fearing for his life, he fled across the border to India. Once there he gained permanent asylum in India and set up a government-in-exile. For more than 50 years the Dalai Lama has continued to preach nonviolent resistance to Chinese occupation and called for peaceful coexistence between all peoples. In 1989 he was awarded the Nobel Peace Prize in acknowledgment of his efforts. The Dalai Lama is recognized worldwide as a man of deep integrity and wisdom.

Nevertheless the government of the People's Republic of China considers the Dalai Lama a criminal and has sought to undermine his political and spiritual authority.

From Theocracy to Democracy   In 1950 Tibet was a feudal theocracy; the government-in-exile has since shifted into a democracy. The Dalai Lama began the process of democratizing the Tibetan government early in his reign, having recognized that Tibet needed to be modernized. In 1960 the Dalai Lama outlined his plan for a democratic government, including a parliament that would have representatives from each of the Tibetan provinces and Buddhist schools of thought. The next year he revealed a constitution, and the first elections occurred soon afterward. The constitution has evolved regularly since then to reflect new ideas.

⊕ Impacts and Issues

Since 1950 the Chinese government has been accused of numerous human rights violations in Tibet. The Tibetan

TIBET'S CHANGING DEMOGRAPHICS

Since the end of the 1990s, ethnic Tibetans have become a minority in their own nation. As of 2010 there were an estimated 6 million ethnic Tibetans and 7.5 million non–Tibetans in Greater Tibet. The center of Tibetan culture, an area called the Tibet Autonomous Region, remains predominately ethnically and culturally Tibetan.

The Tibetan diaspora refers to the communities of Tibetan people in exile. There have been three waves of emigration from Tibet. The first was in 1959, occurring in tandem with the self-exile of the Dalai Lama. Another wave occurred in the 1980s when the People's Republic of China opened Tibet to trade and tourism. A third wave began in 1996 and continues into the 21st century. According to a 2009 census, there are up to 150,000 registered Tibetans in exile, most living in India, Nepal, and Bhutan.

In this 1956 picture, the two spiritual leaders of Tibet, the rival Panchen (L) and Dalai Lama (R), are shown flanking their "protector," Mao Zedong, chairman of the People's Republic of China, in Beijing. Communist China announced in March 1959 that it had deposed the Dalai Lama and set up a new government in rebellious Tibet under the Panchen Lama. The Panchen Lama (1938–1989), a spiritual leader and teacher in Tibetan Buddhism (second in importance to the Dalai Lama), was said to be the reincarnation of the Buddha Amitabha. He became the ward of the Chinese in his childhood, and some Tibetans disputed his status. Dalai Lama or Tenzin Gyatso, born in 1935, is the traditional religious and temporal head of Tibet's Buddhist clergy. In March 1959, there was an unsuccessful armed uprising by Tibetans against Chinese rule. As a result, the Dalai Lama fled with some 100,000 supporters to northern India, where a government-in-exile was established. The Chinese ended the former dominance of the lamas (Buddhist monks) and destroyed many monasteries. Tibet (Xizang), occupied in 1950 by Chinese Communist forces, became an "Autonomous Region" of China in September 1965, but the majority of Tibetans have continued to regard the Dalai Lama as their leader and to resent the Chinese presence, leading to intermittent unrest. © *AFP/Getty Images*

people are denied freedom of religion and freedom of the press. Arbitrary arrests for dissenting voices, maltreatment and torture in custody, and the death sentence have been used for political prisoners and prisoners of conscience. The Chinese government has also imposed strict population control programs, including forced abortions, sterilization, and infanticide.

For the most part Tibetans have followed the guidance of the Dalai Lama and not attempted to violently resist Chinese policies. During the 1950s and 1960s the Chinese government destroyed more than 6,000 Tibetan Buddhist monasteries and killed, tortured, or imprisoned thousands of Buddhist monks and nuns. Only a small handful of religiously or culturally important monasteries remain intact today.

During the 1970s and 1980s the Chinese government briefly relaxed its attacks on Tibetan culture. However, during the late 1980s civil unrest in Tibet had reached a critical mass, and monks in the Drepung and Sera monasteries began loudly calling for Tibetan independence. In response, the Chinese government began encouraging a huge influx of Han Chinese people to immigrate to Tibet, offering financial bonuses, improved jobs, and better living conditions. The purpose of this migration was to assimilate Tibetan culture with the rest of China. Numerous human rights groups have referred to the migration as a policy of "cultural genocide."

Tibet and the Beijing Summer Olympics

In 2001 the International Olympic Committee awarded the 2008 Summer Olympics to the PRC. The Chinese government invested billions of dollars in preparing facilities for the games and even closed down polluting industries in a wide radius around the site of the games in Beijing to assure relatively clean air for international visitors. However, the games became a global flashpoint of controversy, in large part because of China's conflict with Tibet.

On March 10, 2008, hundreds of Buddhist monks from monasteries in and near Lhasa, the capital of

Tibet, marched to commemorate the anniversary of an uprising against China 49 years earlier. The march also protested the continued imprisonment of monks arrested in 2007 for protesting. Violence erupted during the March 2008 protests, with police attacking protesters, and several deaths were reported. In response, Tibetan rebels attacked ethnic Chinese Han neighborhoods. The PRC accused the Dalai Lama of orchestrating the violence. The Dalai Lama denied the accusation and stated that the violence was a sign of the discontent felt by the Tibetan people. He reminded his people that nonviolence is the pathway to peace.

The March 2008 protests were the strongest challenge to Chinese rule that Tibet has mounted in 20 years. Despite efforts to block press coverage of the protests, China was portrayed as an oppressor and human rights violator in much of the world media only months before the Olympics. In China and elsewhere in the world, some concerned Chinese people protested what they considered to be unfair media coverage of their country.

In April 2008 the hand-carried Olympic Torch made a global journey to China, a traditional ritual in the months leading up to the Olympics. China routed the torch through 21 countries, including the United States, on a tour named the Journey of Harmony. However, due to pro–Tibet protesters, the route was repeatedly changed, gatherings to welcome the torch were canceled, and a heavy guard had to be mounted around it. In Paris, the torch was briefly extinguished and a security detail moved it aboard a bus to guard it from angry crowds.

Violence within Tibet caused China to restrict tourism there, resulting in marked economic hardship in the tourism-dependent region. Official data showed that tourism dropped nearly 50 percent in Tibet in 2008 as compared to 2007. The government later eased restrictions and even offered tourism incentives. All restrictions on travel to Tibet were lifted in April 2009.

Future Implications

In November 2010 it was announced that the Dalai Lama would renounce his position as the head of the Tibetan government-in-exile at the next meeting of the exiled government's parliament. The Dalai Lama would retain his role as the spiritual leader of Tibet.

Tibetans in exile take part in a candlelight vigil in Kathmandu, Nepal, on February 13, 2013, following the self-immolation attempt by a monk earlier in the day in protest against Chinese rule in Tibet. The Tibetan exile turned himself into a ball of fire in front of a Buddhist monument, the 100th self-immolation attempt since 2009 in a wave of protests against Chinese rule. © Prakash Mathema/AFP/Getty Images

A spokesman explained that it was the leader's hope to make the Tibetan movement less centered on the Dalai Lama and thus less vulnerable to Chinese pressure. On March 10, 2011, the Dalai Lama announced that he would indeed relinquish his role as head of the government, ceding his position to the winner of the elections held on March 14.

Instead, the parliament unanimously agreed to ask the Dalai Lama to remain the political leader of Tibet. The aging monk refused and explained that he wanted to see Tibet fully democratized during his lifetime, while he could offer advice and counsel. He reminded his people that he was already 76 years old and that when he died, the Tibetan people would need a political leader who could speak for them when he was gone. On April 27, 2011, Dr. Lobsang Sangay (1968–) was announced as the chief of the cabinet of the Central Tibetan Administration, making him the new political leader of the Tibetan government-in-exile. His term is expected to last until 2016, at which point new elections will take place.

The Chinese government has declared it plans to be deeply involved in choosing a 15th Dalai Lama when the time comes. In response, the current Dalai Lama has said that his successor will be born in exile and may choose to break with tradition and come in a different form. The future 15th Dalai Lama, if the position continues, will be the spiritual leader of the Tibetan people. The current Dalai Lama has stated that he will reveal the plans for his reincarnation in 2025 when he is 90 years old.

SEE ALSO *Chinese Revolution; Taiwan: Conflicts with China*

BIBLIOGRAPHY

Books

Dalai Lama. *Freedom in Exile: The Autobiography of the Dalai Lama.* New York: Harper Perennial, 2008.

Smith, Warren. *China's Tibet?: Autonomy or Assimilation.* Lanham, MD: Rowman and Littlefield Publishers, 2009.

Van Schaik, Sam. *Tibet: A History.* New Haven, CT: Yale University Press, 2011.

Web Sites

Central Tibetan Administration. http://www.tibet.net (accessed December 22, 2013).

His Holiness the 14th Dalai Lama of Tibet. http://www.dalailama.com (accessed December 22, 2013).

"Q&A: Tibet and China." *BBC News,* August 15, 2011. http://www.bbc.co.uk/news/world-asia-pacific-14533879 (accessed December 22, 2013).

"Tibet." *GlobalSecurity.org.* http://www.globalsecurity.org/military/world/war/tibet.htm (accessed December 22, 2013).

"Tibet: Its Ownership and Human Rights Situation." *Information Office of the State Council of The People's Republic of China,* September 1992. http://www.china.org.cn/e-white/tibet/ (accessed December 22, 2013).

Uganda

⊕ Introduction

Uganda has experienced very little peace or stability since 1971, when brutal dictator Idi Amin (1925–2003) seized power in a coup and proceeded to order the killings of hundreds of thousands of Ugandans in order to maintain his rule. Amin led the country into war with Tanzania in 1978. His defeat and exile led to the ascendency of Apollo Milton Obote (1925–2005) as president, followed by Yoweri Kaguta Museveni (1944–). Museveni seized power in 1986 and continued to hold that office as of early 2014.

Museveni's long term in office has been marred since the beginning by the rebellion of the Lord's Resistance Army (LRA), a violent group of armed rebels who operated in the country between 1986 and 2006. This rebellion forced more than 1.6 million Ugandans to flee to crowded refugee camps. Those who escaped were considered the lucky ones. An estimated 100,000 others were brutally killed. Unable to fill its ranks with adults, the LRA forced tens of thousands of children, some as young as eight, to serve as child soldiers or sex slaves. According to reports, some of the children were forced to torture and kill relatives, including parents and siblings. The LRA and its child soldiers terrorized Uganda and neighboring countries. Its leader, Joseph Kony, had the LRA withdraw from Uganda only to continue its activities in other African nations.

⊕ Historical Background

Located north and northwest of Lake Victoria, the landlocked east-central African country of Uganda is bordered by South Sudan to the north, Kenya to the east, Tanzania and Rwanda to the south, and the Democratic Republic of the Congo (DRC) to

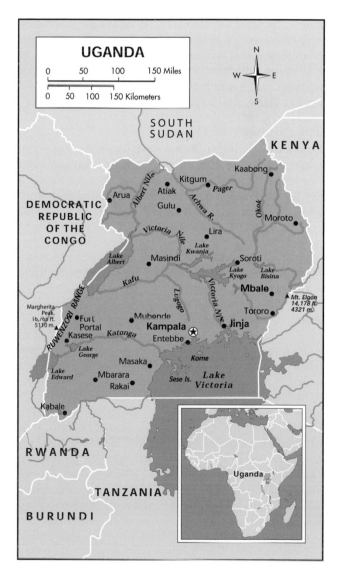

© 2014 Cengage Learning

531

the west. Uganda has a population estimated at 34.8 million (as of 2013). African communities make up 70 percent of the population, most of which belong to one of three main ethnic groups—Bantu, Nilotic, and Nilo-Hamitic. These three groups are further divided into dozens of subgroups. The single largest group, the Baganda (16.9 percent), are Bantu. The non-indigenous population includes a mixture of nationalities, with Asians predominant.

English is the official national language of Uganda. In addition to its use in courts of law, English is taught to schoolchildren. Many of the country's newspapers are written in English. Luganda (or Ganda) is the most widely spoken Bantu language, but Kiswahili (Swahili) and Arabic are also commonly used. Some 85 percent of the population is Christian, with membership split between Roman Catholicism as the largest denomination (42 percent) and Anglicanism (36 percent). Just over 12 percent are Muslim. It is estimated that nearly 16 percent of Ugandans live in urban areas; the capital of Kampala is the most populated city, with around 1.5 million inhabitants (2009). Life expectancy is about 54 years; the country ranks about eighth highest in the world in HIV/AIDS deaths.

The "Butcher of Uganda"

For centuries, the land that now forms the nation of Uganda was ruled by the kingdoms of Buganda and Bunyoro. Buganda unwillingly became a protectorate of the British Empire in 1894 and remained as such until 1962. Uganda became a unified republic in 1967, but political upheaval continued. In 1971, Idi Amin formed the Second Republic of Uganda, naming himself as president. Under Amin's administration, Uganda endured a reign of terror that claimed the lives of some 50,000–300,000 people.

Amin was known as being highly charismatic, erratic, and brutal. Initial hopes for a progressive democracy that protected western interests were dashed as Amin targeted for death both foreigners and Ugandans from tribes other than his own. Under the president's orders, squads of militia tortured and killed both ordinary Ugandans and political opponents. Executions were often public, and victims were sometimes forced to beat each other to death. Amin awarded himself many titles and honors; his official title was "His Excellency President for Life, Field Marshal Alhaji Dr. Idi Amin Dada, VC (Victoria Cross), DSO (Distinguished Service Order), MC (Military Cross), CBE (Conqueror of the British Empire)." He also claimed to be the uncrowned King of Scotland.

Amin, known as "The Butcher of Uganda," fled the country in 1979, following the Uganda-Tanzania War. He died in exile in Saudi Arabia in 2003. He left Uganda in economic ruin.

Ugandan military dictator Idi Amin gives a speech on April 3, 1975. © *Hulton Archive/Getty Images*

Museveni

Even after the overthrow of Amin's government in 1979, Uganda was passed from one provisional leader to another until Obote, Uganda's exiled president, was reelected the next year. Obote was deposed in a military coup in 1985 and replaced by Tito Okello (1914–1996), who was in turn deposed in 1986 as rebels from the National Resistance Army installed Museveni as president. Museveni was officially elected to the office in 1996 and reelected in 2001, 2006, and 2011. Although Museveni has been credited with initiating some democratic reforms and improving the human rights record of the nation, Uganda continues to fight for peace among its own people and neighboring states.

When Museveni was reelected to a new term in 2011, he won 68 percent of the vote. Kizza Besigye (1956–), the runner-up, deemed the election fraudulent and called for peaceful protests. Museveni threatened to jail any protesters, especially after some Ugandans threatened to mimic the demonstrations that erupted in Egypt during the early 2011 overthrow of longtime dictator Hosni Mubarak (1928–).

Ugandan soldiers shoot at demonstrators, who pelt them with rocks from apartment buildings, during riots in Kampala on April 29, 2011, a day after Uganda's opposition leader Kizza Besigye was arrested for the fourth time that month. Rioters setting tires alight in Kampala clashed with police firing tear gas, leaving one dead and dozens in hospital. On April 28, opposition leader Besigye was arrested by police who smashed his car windows with guns and hammers before bundling him into the back of a pick-up truck. Besigye and other opposition leaders earlier in April started walking to work twice a week as a symbolic protest against rising fuel costs but the demonstrations met with a tough response from the police.   © *Marc Hofer/AFP/Getty Images*

Besigye went on to organize Action for Change, a walk-to-work movement to protest government corruption and the rising cost of living. Although protesters insisted that the case was a civil rather than political matter, the government began blocking the marches, even deploying tear gas to disperse crowds. The United Nations (UN) and other international organizations condemned the actions of the Ugandan government. In April 2012, the government officially declared Action for Change to be an illegal group, stating that members had organized rallies and processions without consulting the police in advance.

⊕ Impacts and Issues

The civil war in Uganda was precipitated by the military coup that brought Museveni to power. Although Museveni legitimized his takeover by winning elections, government corruption and the lack of a democratic tradition made his government susceptible to a counter-coup and allowed the brutal and eccentric warlord Joseph Kony (1961–) to mount a serious threat to the central government.

Lord's Resistance Army

Since 1986, the Lord's Resistance Army (LRA), led by warlord Joseph Kony, has terrorized civilians in the border regions of northern Uganda, Sudan, the Central African Republic (CAR), and the DRC. The rebel force initially formed with the goal of initiating a system of government in Uganda based on the biblical Ten Commandments. The LRA tactics have included the abduction, torture, and murder of tens of thousands of civilians. The United Nations estimated in May 2013 that 2.5 million people have been displaced since the LRA rebellion began, and between 60,000 to 100,000 children have been abducted, with girls forced into service as sex slaves and boys initiated as soldiers in the LRA.

Although the governments of all four border nations have worked to end the conflict through both

KONY 2012

When an Internet video about the ruthless Ugandan insurgency leader became tremendously popular in March 2012, many Americans heard the name Joseph Kony for the first time. The short film *Kony 2012,* produced by a non-governmental organization (NGO) called Invisible Children, urged Americans to raise awareness about the conflict in central Africa and to advocate for the capture of the rebel leader. As details about Kony's organization, the ongoing conflict, and the role of the U.S. military and NGOs in Uganda emerged, however, the message of *Kony 2012* turned into larger discussions about the ethics of Western intervention in Africa and the limitations of social media in enacting political change.

Kony's brutal tactics and bizarre behavior (he often wears wigs and costumes while seemingly possessed by spirits) left him few international allies, with the notable exception of Sudan. The Sudanese government, which was fighting rebels in South Sudan (the region became a sovereign nation in 2011), backed Kony's group, which terrorized not only Uganda, but the Central African Republic and the Democratic Republic of the Congo. After September 11, 2001, the U.S. government labeled Kony a terrorist. The International Criminal Court issued an indictment against him in May 2005 for crimes against humanity, including sexual enslavement, rape, and torture.

The conflict between the LRA and the African nations where the group remains active became a major topic of conversation in March 2012, when *Kony 2012* went viral and was viewed by more than 100 million people in little over a month. The video tells the story of a young Ugandan boy named Jacob who had been abducted by the LRA. It describes the kidnapping of thousands of children by Kony's group and shows scenes of the faces of children who have been maimed and disfigured by the LRA. The video concludes with a call to action called Cover the Night, which was planned for April 20, 2012. The event would consist of acts of community service promoting visual displays of the Kony 2012 campaign. Only a few dozen people actually showed up for activities in major cities, leading some media critics to point to the shortcomings of Internet-based activism. Cover the Night occurred in the wake of a public nervous breakdown by Jason Russell, Invisible Children's spokesperson and the narrator of *Kony 2012,* in the streets of San Diego.

In the weeks following the release of the video, a number of activists and policymakers started to question Russell's motives and his proposed solutions to the problem. The criticisms generally revolved around a few core issues. First, the video did not explain that Kony had withdrawn from Uganda, although he continued his activities in other African nations. Second, the human rights violations by the Ugandan military as well as the failed U.S.-backed plans to capture Kony were not discussed in the documentary. Third, much of the video centered on Russell and his son Gavin, not on the plight of Africans, many of whom want to put the Kony and LRA issues behind them. Finally, and perhaps most controversially, the video advocates a solution based on U.S. military intervention. Critics worried that increased militarization would be counterproductive.

UN-assisted negotiations and military force, the LRA has consistently disregarded cease-fire agreements and has responded to military attacks by killing more civilians. The UN estimated in May 2013 that nearly 100,000 people have been killed by the LRA in the 25 years it has been active, with tens of thousands more abducted. The International Criminal Court has an outstanding arrest warrant against Kony for crimes against humanity.

Repercussions of Colonialism

The roots of the current conflict between Kony's Lord's Resistance Army and the African countries where his group operates are to be found in the relatively recent formation of Africa's modern states. The country known today as Uganda was formed only after the end of British colonialism in 1962. Like many war-torn countries in Africa, Uganda has borders that encompass the traditional lands of several ethnic groups and tribes who had uneasy relationships with one another. During the British reign, certain ethnic groups fulfilled certain roles in society; some were marginalized, while others were fully integrated into the governing administrative system.

The Acholi ethnic group, which resides in the north of the country, near the border of South Sudan, played an important role in the development of the modern Ugandan military, even though the region was not favored for economic development by the British. Kony is a member of the Acholi group, and his initial following came from fellow Acholi who felt persecuted by the regime of Museveni.

As resistance to Museveni took shape in the north of the country, a group called the Holy Spirit Movement became prominent. The movement, headed by Alice Auma, was based on mystical beliefs that drew from the region's Christian, Islamic, and spiritualist teachings. Followers of the movement believed they could channel dead spirits and be protected from live bullets by covering themselves in an oil sanctified by a priest. Kony stepped into this milieu and began directing a military resistance to the Ugandan government while also following some of Auma's teachings.

Brutality and Intimidation

Kony's own insurgency group, the LRA, achieved some early victories against the Ugandan military in the late

A picture taken September 2, 2006, shows a former abductee of the Lord's Resistance Army. She was taken in 2005 when she was 17, and bears the scars of her encounter with the rebels who cut off her lips, nose, and ears before she was able to escape back to her family. The rebel group brought terror to Northern Uganda for almost 20 years, fighting the Ugandan government. The victims of the LRA are usually children, who are abducted and used as child soldiers and sex slaves.   © *Tugela Ridley/AFP/Getty Images*

1980s, but lost much of its initial civilian support due to its brutal methods of intimidation, which included the rape, torture, and kidnapping of some of the very same people he claimed to protect. Kony saw himself as carrying out the Ten Commandments and believed himself to be possessed by spirits.

After the ICC indictment of 2005, with increasing military pressure against him, Kony and a few hundred remaining followers withdrew to the jungles of the CAR and the DRC, where his attacks on villages diminished in size, if not in brutality. In 2008, the U.S. military aided a Ugandan plan to crush the LRA, but the attack did not succeed. LRA fighters escaped into the jungle and carried out a violent reprisal attack, raping, torturing, and murdering hundreds of people. The nonprofit group Invisible Children (the group behind the *Kony 2012* documentary) pushed the U.S. Congress to pass the Lord's Resistance Army Disarmament and Northern Uganda Recovery Act in 2010, which led the way for more U.S. intervention.

The Ugandan government announced in early April 2013 that it was suspending its search for Kony in the CAR, where he and his army were suspected of residing.

Officials were encountering "hostility" from the CAR's new government, which had recently deposed its old one. In response, the United States announced it would offer a $5 million reward for information leading to the capture of Kony.

⊕ Future Implications

Uganda's democracy is tenuous at best. On May 20, 2013, police raided the offices of the *Daily Monitor*, an independent Ugandan newspaper, after it published a letter written by a top general to the internal security service. The letter requested a probe into allegations that President Museveni intended to have his son succeed him and to assassinate opponents of this purported succession plan. The printing press at the newspaper was disabled by police, and the managing editor and two reporters were detained and interrogated.

Despite impressive growth, Uganda remains one of the poorest countries in the world. The nation is still sharply divided along ethnic lines, and the animosity between groups does not appear to be abating. Uganda has been active in supporting rebels in some neighboring countries, causing regional dissent.

The pervasive poverty and ethnic hostility do not bode well for the country's future stability. It seems likely that groups will continue to use extra-electoral means to battle for control of the country—and the riches that come with it.

SEE ALSO *African Union; Democratic Republic of the Congo; Sudan and South Sudan*

BIBLIOGRAPHY

Books

Branch, Adam. *Displacing Human Rights: War and Intervention in Northern Uganda.* New York: Oxford University Press, 2011.

Cook, Kathy. *Stolen Angels: The Kidnapped Girls of Uganda.* Toronto: Penguin Canada, 2007.

Eichstaedt, Peter. *First Kill Your Family: Child Soldiers of Uganda and the Lord's Resistance Army.* Chicago: Lawrence Hill Books, 2009.

Jagielski, Wojciech. *The Night Wanderers: Uganda's Children and the Lord's Resistance Army,* translated by Antonia Lloyd-Jones. New York: Seven Stories Press, 2012.

Rice, Andrew. *The Teeth May Smile But the Heart Does Not Forget: Murder and Memory in Uganda.* New York: Metropolitan Books/Henry Holt, 2009.

Web Sites

Akumu, Patience. "Uganda: Rigged Elections and Mysterious Killings. . . It's the Mugabe Script with a Different Cast." *The Guardian,* August 17, 2013. http://www.theguardian.com/world/2013/aug/18/uganda-yoweri-museveni (accessed December 5, 2013).

"A Country Study: Uganda." *Library of Congress.* http://lcweb2.loc.gov/frd/cs/ugtoc.html (accessed December 5, 2013).

Gettleman, Jeffrey. "In Vast Jungle, U.S. Troops Aid in Search for Kony." *The New York Times,* April 29, 2012. http://www.nytimes.com/2012/04/30/world/africa/kony-tracked-by-us-forces-in-central-africa.html?ref=lordsresistancearmy&_r=0 (accessed December 5, 2013).

Invisible Children. http://invisiblechildren.com/ (accessed December 5, 2013).

Kaufman, Michael T. "Idi Amin, Murderous and Erratic Ruler in the 70's, Dies in Exile." *The New York Times,* August 17, 2003. http://www.nytimes.com/2003/08/17/world/idi-amin-murderous-and-erratic-ruler-of-uganda-in-the-70-s-dies-in-exile.html?pagewanted=all&src=pm (accessed December 5, 2013).

Moses, Kara. "Lord's Resistance Army Funded by Elephant Poaching, Report Finds: Eyewitness Accounts Say Warlord Joseph Kony Traded Ivory from Elephants Killed in Central Africa for Arms and Supplies." *The Guardian,* June 4, 2013. http://www.theguardian.com/environment/2013/jun/04/lords-resistance-army-funded-elephant-poaching (accessed December 5, 2013).

Pflanz, Mike. "Joseph Kony 2012: Growing Outrage in Uganda Over Film." *The Telegraph,* March 8, 2012. http://www.telegraph.co.uk/news/worldnews/africaandindianocean/uganda/9131469/Joseph-Kony-2012-growing-outrage-in-Uganda-over-film.html (accessed December 5, 2013).

"Uganda." *Lonely Planet.* http://www.lonelyplanet.com/uganda/history#44681 (accessed December 5, 2013).

"Uganda." *World Health Organization (WHO).* http://www.who.int/countries/uga/en/ (accessed December 5, 2013).

"Uganda Profile." *BBC News Africa,* November 25, 2013. http://www.bbc.co.uk/news/world-africa-14112446 (accessed December 5, 2013).

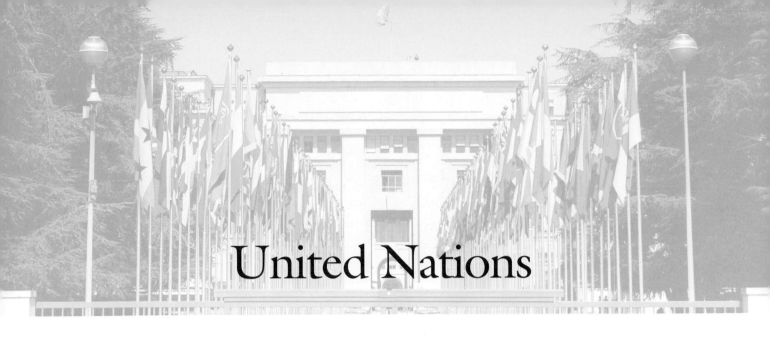

United Nations

⊕ Introduction

The United Nations (UN) is an international government organization dedicated to peace and humanitarian causes. It provides national governments with a forum in which to discuss and hopefully settle global problems. The first of its two most notable organs is the permanent five-seat Security Council that includes the People's Republic of China, France, the Russian Federation, the United Kingdom, and the United States. The second is the General Assembly, which includes 193 member nations and two non-member states as well as numerous observers who gather together to discuss the appropriate international response to the many global issues affecting the modern world.

The UN's special agencies pool international resources and funds for humanity's greater good. While the UN does not have an army, peacekeeping troops made up of soldiers from member nations are frequently deployed in its name. The UN addresses a broad range of issues around the world, including disaster relief, counterterrorism, international health concerns, human rights, gender equality, and world hunger.

⊕ Historical Background

The UN was founded in 1945 at the end of World War II (1939–45). Its predecessor, the League of Nations, was the first truly global international peacekeeping organization. The League of Nations was founded at the end of World War 1 (1914–18) as a means to ensure that such a horribly destructive war could never happen again. However, just a generation later, a new and more terrible world war broke out, and the League of Nations was helpless to stop it.

U.S. President Franklin D. Roosevelt (1882–1945; president 1933–45), first coined the term "United Nations" in the 1942 Declaration of United Nations, which formalized the partnership of the 26 Allied nations of World War II. Even before World War II officially ended, 50 nations and non-government organizations gathered together on April 25, 1945, to begin drafting the United Nations Charter.

Only two weeks later, Germany, the aggressor nation in the European theater of the war, surrendered. Japan, Germany's ally and the aggressor in the Pacific theater of the war, continued to fight for three more months.

World War II ended after the first, and thus far only, nuclear weapons were deployed in open warfare by the United States, which dropped atomic bombs on the Japanese cities Hiroshima and Nagasaki in August 1945. The death toll and destructive power of these new weapons astonished the world. The end of World War II thus also marked the beginning of the nuclear age and the possibility of total world destruction. With this possibility in mind, the international community strengthened its dedication to maintain world peace. The United Nations was born from this motivation.

On October 24, 1945, the UN charter was ratified by the five permanent members of the Security Council as well as the majority of the 46 nations who sent representatives. The permanent member states of the Security Council are the principle Allied nations that fought together in World War II: the People's Republic of China (China was represented until 1971 by the Republic of China's government-in-exile based in Taiwan), France, the Russian Federation (formerly the Soviet Union or USSR) the United Kingdom, and the United States. Ten other nations are non-permanent members of the Security Council. All participating nations are members of the General Assembly, whose first meeting took place in London on January 6, 1946, and included 51 member nations. The Security Council's main purpose is to maintain international peace through sanctions and military actions.

Overall view looking down on the first meeting of the United Nations Organization's General Assembly in January 1946, in the Methodist Church's Central Hall with Clement Attlee speaking from the podium. © *David E. Scherman/Time Life Pictures/Getty Images*

⊕ Impacts and Issues

The ultimate goal of the UN has not changed much since its creation. The UN is still dedicated to making the world a safe and peaceful place for today's population as well as future generations. According to the UN website, the UN has four main functions: to keep peace throughout the world; to help nations work together to improve the lives of the poor, including conquering hunger, disease, and illiteracy; to encourage respect for each other's rights and freedoms; and to be a center for harmonizing the actions of nations to achieve these goals.

Organization

Membership in the UN is open to all peace-loving states that accept the terms and conditions of the United Nations Charter. The General Assembly decides which states are admitted based upon recommendations from the Security Council. The UN is a truly international organization and is meant to include the voices of all

nations, even those that are bitter enemies. The UN headquarters, which house the Security Council and the General Assembly, is in New York City. Regional headquarters are located in Geneva, Switzerland; Vienna, Austria; and Nairobi, Kenya. The major UN agencies are all located elsewhere, such as the Food and Agriculture Organization (FAO; Rome, Italy); the International Monetary Fund (IMF; Washington, D.C.); the Education, Scientific and Cultural Organization (UNESCO; Paris, France); and the World Health Organization (WHO; Geneva, Switzerland). The UN's official languages are Arabic, Chinese, English, French, Russian, and Spanish. Its most visible post is that of Secretary-General, who acts as the organization's spokesperson and head diplomat. This person is recommended by the Security Council and then appointed by the General Assembly for a term of five years, which can be renewed.

New states and governments are granted UN recognition by existing member states. A new member state must submit an application to the Secretary-General of the UN along with a letter stating that it accepts the terms of the Charter. The Security Council then reviews the application and puts it up to a vote. If the application receives affirmative votes from at least nine of the 15 Council members, with five of those votes signifying unanimous agreement from the permanent members— the Russian Federation, China, France, the United Kingdom, and the United States—then the Council will present the application to the General Assembly for a vote. If the new state receives a two-thirds majority vote in the General Assembly, it becomes a member of the UN with all rights and responsibilities.

The UN has several departments, or organs, including the General Assembly, the Security Council, the Economic and Social Council, the Trusteeship Council, the International Court of Justice, and the Secretariat. Each of these bodies has several subsidiaries, including organizations such as the WHO. The decisions of these organs are documented in the Repertory of Practice of United Nations Organs, a legal document that is used as a reference guide and authority for interpreting UN practices.

The General Assembly and Non-Member States

The General Assembly is the main deliberative organ of the United Nations. It meets every year from September to December as well as other times in the year as circumstances dictate. Many of the decisions and actions of the United Nations begin with this body, and each session is typically dominated by a handful of key issues. For example, in 2012 the General Assembly agenda was principally concerned with improving Israel-Palestine relations, halting Syria's violent civil war, ending the U.S. embargo against Cuba, and establishing a nuclear-weapon-free zone in the Middle East.

The General Assembly currently includes member representatives from 193 of the world's 196 nations. Only the Vatican, Kosovo, and Taiwan lack official UN representation. The State of Palestine is not yet considered a nation since it remains entangled in a bitter territory conflict with Israel. Nevertheless, since the rights of the Palestinians are recognized by the majority of the international community, in 2012 it was given a non-member observer status within the UN, similar to that of the Vatican, by a 138–9 vote of the General Assembly.

The Holy See

The Vatican, or Holy See, is recognized by the international community as the world's smallest independent nation. The tiny nation comprises only 110 acres and has a population of less than 1,000. Its sovereign ruler is the Pope, the religious leader for millions of Catholics throughout the world. The Vatican expressed interest in joining the UN at the end of World War II, but was declined since at the time the UN was composed of

military allies. Instead, the Vatican was allowed to act as an unofficial observer and an unofficial participant and/ or adviser during private negotiations between nations. In 2004, the Holy See asked for and was granted permanent observer status. This allows the Vatican to actively participate in all discussions and to make proposals and counterproposals. However, the Holy See does not have a vote in the Assembly. If in the future, the Vatican wants to become a full member, that option is open. However, the Holy See currently prefers its status as a non-voting observer since this allows it to act as an adviser while remaining impartial.

Kosovo Controversy and South Sudan

Kosovo, by contrast, has not yet been granted full recognition by the international community despite having declared its independence from Serbia in 2008. The United States, the United Kingdom, France, and approximately half of the world's nations have recognized the new state. The Russian Federation and China, as well as the remaining half of the world's nations, do not recognize Kosovo. If Kosovo is finally recognized by each member of the Security Council then it will almost certainly gain the necessary votes in the General Assembly and become a member of the UN. The newest member of the UN, as of June 2013, is South Sudan, which declared its independence in 2011 and was recognized by virtually the entire international community only days later. For Kosovo, full international recognition remained stalled as of early 2014.

Taiwan

Taiwan remains a source of international tension because both the Taiwanese government (officially the Republic of China) and the government of the mainland People's Republic of China claim full sovereignty over the island. The history of this dispute is intimately tied to the UN. In 1945, the Republic of China (ROC) was one of the founding members of the UN and had a permanent spot on the Security Council. At that time, the ROC government headquarters was located in Taiwan, an island off the coast of the Chinese mainland. Following World War II, a bitter civil war broke out in China between the ROC and the Communist Party. In 1949, the Communist Party took control of the Chinese mainland and declared it the People's Republic of China (PRC). The ROC in Taiwan continued to assert that it was still the legitimate Chinese government.

For more than two decades the international community was divided over which government truly represented the Chinese people. During this period Taiwan continued to hold its seat in the UN and on the Security Council. In 1971, the PRC was officially recognized internationally as "China" and replaced Taiwan in all of its roles in the United Nations. Taiwan has attempted to regain its seat several times, but the PRC and other permanent members of the Security Council have consistently voted against it. Today the PRC insists that Taiwan is a Chinese province, while the ROC officially still claims to be the legitimate Chinese government. However, the ROC has not made any attempt to regain control over the Chinese mainland since 1991. The majority of the Taiwanese population now wants to be recognized as an independent nation, a move the PRC flatly refuses to consider. In 2008, Taiwan made another attempt to join the UN as an independent nation, but the application failed due to division in the Security Council and low voter participation.

Palestine

In 2011, Palestinian representatives moved to circumvent a longstanding impasse in its negotiations with Israel over establishing an independent Palestinian state by pressing the UN for official membership. The so-called "Palestinian Question" was in some ways a creation of the UN. One of the UN's first major acts after its formation was to try to make reparations to the European Jews for the genocide perpetrated on them by the Nazi government of Germany during World War II by providing them with their own country. The problem, however, was the land being offered to the Jews was already populated, mostly by Arabs who identified themselves culturally as Palestinians.

In 1947, the UN suggested a plan for an Arab state of Palestine and a Jewish state of Israel, a plan that would have resulted in two separate countries. This plan was rejected by the Palestinians. A few months later, Israel declared its independence and established borders that encompassed a part of what would have been an independent Palestinian state. Fearing violence from Israelis, hundreds of thousands of Palestinians fled. The United States and other nations quickly recognized Israel, and the country joined the UN the following year without any mention of Palestine or its refugee population. Since then, the question of a Palestinian state has sparked several wars, countless skirmishes, and decades of mostly failed peace negotiations. The Palestinians' repeated requests for recognition by the UN have failed to gain adequate support for more than 60 years.

In October 2011, the State of Palestine was granted membership in UNESCO. On November 30, 2012, the UN General Assembly voted to recognize the State of Palestine as a non-member observer state. While 138 members, including Russia, China, India, Brazil, and many Eurozone countries, voted for the resolution, nine countries, including Israel, the United States, and Canada, voted against the measure. Forty-one nations, including the United Kingdom and Germany, abstained from voting. This makes Palestine the only other permanent observer at the UN besides the Holy See.

For Palestine to be granted full membership in the UN, the United States will have to support the formation of an independent Palestinian nation. The United States and Israel are close allies, and while U.S. leaders have often supported a so-called "two-state" solution to the Palestinian problem, with an independent Palestine and an independent Israel, negotiations toward that end remained stalled as of early 2014.

Security Council

The Security Council has 15 member states. Five are permanent members who were the main victors of World War II—the Russian Federation, China, France, the United Kingdom, and the United States. These nations hold veto power, and a single negative vote by one of these nations effectively prevents any measure from being adopted. The other 10 non-permanent member states are elected five at a time, every two years. The non-primary members vote on measures and help make decisions, but do not have any veto power. In 2013, the non-primary members were Argentina, Azerbaijan, Australia, Guatemala, Luxemburg, Morocco, Pakistan, Republic of Korea (South Korea), Rwanda, and Togo. The primary responsibility of the Security Council is to maintain international peace and security.

The Security Council has several broadly defined powers. It investigates any situation threatening international peace and makes recommendations for peaceful resolutions. The Security Council may also call upon member nations to completely or partially place an economic embargo or sever diplomatic relations with a nation or region that is threatening international peace. Such sanctions are meant to enforce peace without resorting to armed force. While the Security Council may deploy peacekeeping troops to stabilize an area, the main purpose of the Council is to avoid conflict and instead focus on international cooperation.

The Economic and Social Council

The Economic and Social Council has 54 members and coordinates the economic and social programs of the UN. It meets annually in April and July to discuss the activities of 14 specialized agencies that fall under its jurisdiction. Several of the agencies focus on human rights, such as the UN Commission on Human Rights, the UN Commission on the Status of Women, and the UN Children's Fund (UNICEF). The mission of the UN's Food and Agriculture Organization (FAO) is to eliminate hunger worldwide and improve global food security by promoting sustainable agricultural practices. The World Food Programme (WFP) carries out humanitarian aid by providing food to over 50 million people each year. The UN Environment Programme (UNEP) helps developing nations institute sustainable practices that limit air and water pollution and help conserve natural resources. Along with the UN's World Meteorological Organization, it formed the Intergovernmental Panel on Climate Change in 1988, which has called for a global decrease in greenhouse gas emissions. The World Health Organization (WHO) addresses global public health issues, such as malaria and HIV/AIDS. Numerous other UN agencies are devoted to international justice, maritime law, social and economic development, telecommunications, the rights of indigenous peoples, atomic energy, aviation, and labor issues. These special agencies are assisted by numerous international nongovernmental organizations (NGOs) committed to social activism for the greater good.

Many of these special agencies have made markedly positive global changes. For example, in 1967 WHO declared its intention to eradicate smallpox through an intensive immunization program. Only 13 years later, the WHO announced that smallpox had been totally eliminated by human effort—the first such achievement in history. More recently, in 2003, the WHO's quick response to the Severe Acute Respiratory Syndrome (SARS) pandemic quickly and effectively halted the spread of the disease. UNESCO has successfully helped countries increase literacy rates, especially among women, worldwide. As of 2011, UNESCO declared that an estimated 80 percent of all women worldwide were literate, compared to 70 percent in 1990 and only 20 percent in 1950.

International Court of Justice, the Secretariat, and the Trusteeship Council

The remaining three organs of the UN are the International Court of Justice (ICJ), the Secretariat, and the Trusteeship Council. The ICJ is the principal judicial organ of the UN and is based in the Netherlands. Its purpose is to settle legal disputes between the member states. Its 15 judges serve nine year terms in both a decision-making and advisory capacity. The ICJ deals with disputes between nations who participate voluntarily rather than with individuals. It is distinct from the International Criminal Court (ICC), which is an independent, international body of justice set up to prosecute individuals accused of crimes with an international impact such as genocide and war crimes. Prior to the establishment of the ICC in 2002, the UN tried some governmental leaders and other individuals accused of genocide, war crimes, and crimes against humanity from the former Yugoslavia and Rwanda, however these individuals were tried via separate ad hoc tribunals set up by the UN rather than through the ICJ.

The Secretariat is the organizational and administrative body of the UN. It provides administrative support to the other organs, including preparing studies on human rights issues and surveying social and economic

THE UNITED NATIONS, HAITI, AND CRITICISM

On January 12, 2010, the small Caribbean nation of Haiti was rocked by a magnitude 7.0 earthquake that was centered in a suburb of the nation's capital, Port-au-Prince. At least 100,000 people died and 250,000 houses were destroyed. Already one of the world's poorest nations, Haiti was plunged into chaos and humanitarian aid groups responded en masse with medical assistance, water, food, and other provisions.

In October 2010 cholera was reported in Haiti for the first time in more than 50 years. Haitian health minister Alex Larsen confirmed that cholera type O1 was responsible for the outbreak. In this outbreak, cholera first was identified in Artibonite, a poor, rural valley region about 60 miles north of Haiti's capital city of Port-au-Prince. Thousands of refugees had flooded into the region after the earthquake. The Artibonite River served as a source of water for bathing, washing, drinking, and sewage disposal by the community's swollen population, and initial investigations pointed to contamination in the river as the source of the cholera outbreak.

In the midst of the long-term recovery process, the cholera epidemic broke out due to improper sanitation and lack of clean water. By the end of 2010, well over 3,000 people had died from the disease, and by the middle of 2013 the death total had risen to over 8,000 and an additional 600,000 had become ill.

The disease, common during humanitarian crises, is thought to have been introduced by UN peacekeepers from Nepal who improperly disposed of raw sewage into a tributary of the Artibonite River, which people downstream drank. While cholera is not endemic in Haiti, it is common in Nepal. UN officials steadfastly denied that their base was the source of the outbreak, even though the U.S. Centers for Disease Control conducted genetic studies on the local cholera bacteria and found that the strain was indigenous to South Asia. The UN's World Health Organization countered that it had little interest in determining the origin of the outbreak, only in controlling it. The United Nations was careful not to blame the peacekeepers for the epidemic but stressed that a confluence of conditions, including, most importantly, a widespread lack of sanitation, contributed to the cholera outbreak in Haiti.

While this incident generated much bad publicity for the UN, which resulted in anti-UN demonstrations in Haiti, it underscores the fact that the organization is not immune to criticism. One of the most common criticisms of the UN is its moral relativism, as evidenced by the fact that although its primary goal is peace and freedom for all people, less than half of its member states are free democracies. Throughout its history it has sometimes turned a blind eye to dictators, terrorism, and genocide, according to author Dore Gold in his book *Tower of Babble: How the United Nations Has Fueled Global Chaos*. Others criticize the veto power of the five permanent members of the Security Council, all of which have nuclear capabilities. The most frequent criticism, however, is the fact that since the organization's founding in 1945 wars and conflicts are as common as ever.

trends. The Secretariat is responsible for maintaining the *Repertory of Practice of United Nations Organs*, a legal publication that records and archives comprehensive summaries of decisions of the principal organs.

The Trusteeship Council was created to provide international supervision for 11 Trust Territories under the supervision of seven member states. Its purpose was to prepare the territories for self-governance and independence. Having achieved that goal in 1994 with the final territory of Palau achieving independence, the Trusteeship Council now meets only as needed. Former UN Secretary-General Kofi Annan proposed that the Trusteeship Council be eliminated during a future revision of the UN charter.

⊕ Future Implications

The UN will continue to be the premier international organization for the foreseeable future. Some critics refer to it as a "paper tiger" in that it appears threatening, but

is actually powerless, since its rulings are only as strong as the nations that follow them. The UN's effectiveness has often been halted by issues of national pride and national economic concerns, while cultural diversity has often made international communication and organization difficult.

While most governments make frequent pledges to focus on social and economic justice at home and abroad, national defense is often cited as a priority, and human rights abuses are still regrettably common. For example, of the 193 UN member nations, only 30 have consistently good records for human rights. In 2009, the Annual International Human Rights Data Project revealed that the nations with the best human rights records are Norway, San Marino, and Canada, which each scored 28 out of a possible 30 points. The nations with the worst human rights records were Zimbabwe, China, Myanmar, and Iran, each of which had a mere 2 points out of 30. The United States was given 25 points.

The UN's ability to effect positive change is hampered when promises do not match actions. This has

Among the initiatives of the UN are the Millennium Development Goals (MDGs), which aim to reduce poverty as well as the spread of HIV/AIDS by 2015. Eight in all, the MDGs also address universal primary education, child mortality, gender equality, and sustainability. Here, Justine Greening (L), British Secretary of State for International Development, Indonesian President Susilo Bambang Yudhoyono (2nd L), United Nations Secretary General Ban Ki-moon (2nd R), and Florence Chenoweth, Liberia's Minister of Agriculture prepare to meet about the high-level panel report on Post-2015 MDGs in May 2013 at UN headquarters in New York.
© Stan Honda/AFP/Getty Images

been the greatest problem of the UN since its creation. For example, the Kyoto Protocol was signed in 1997 and entered into force in 2005. The protocol calls for developed countries to reduce their greenhouse gas emissions, but at the end of the first phase of reduction in 2012 many countries had missed their targets significantly, including Canada, Australia, Spain, and Japan.

The UN will face many complex challenges in the years ahead. Considering the economic implications of working toward curbing greenhouse gases and other pollution, it will be a huge challenge to get both industrial nations and developing nations to each agree and maintain any global environmental standards. Likewise, the continued development of nuclear weapons by countries like North Korea threatens to undo the UN's efforts in disarmament and could potentially lead to a new arms race. The organization's focus on peace and security, economic development, human rights, humanitarian aid, and international law means that its reach is far and wide. While it remains committed to its missions, the United Nations will be only as successful as its member nations allow.

PRIMARY SOURCE

Charter of the United Nations Preamble

SOURCE *"United Nations Charter Preamble."* The United Nations, *June 26, 1945. http://www.un.org/ en/documents/charter/preamble.shtml (accessed December 4, 2013). Copyright © 1945 by the United Nations. All rights reserved. Reproduced by permission.*

INTRODUCTION *In the wake of World War II, President Franklin D. Roosevelt, along with other Allied leaders, was determined to establish a protocol for dealing with future threats to peace. The UN was not the first international organization formed for this purpose. Its precursor was the League of Nations, formed in the aftermath of World War I. Although the idea of the League was inspired by U.S. President Woodrow Wilson, it failed in part because the United States refused to join. At that time and through the early 1940s, a majority of Americans supported isolationist policies. As the scale of Nazi crimes became known after the end of World War II, Ameican public opinion shifted toward involvement in world affairs as a defensive measure to prevent future wars and to protect U.S. interests. The charter for the new United Nations Organization was signed on June 26 and approved by the U.S. Senate one month later.*

PREAMBLE

WE THE PEOPLES OF THE UNITED NATIONS DETERMINED

- to save succeeding generations from the scourge of war, which twice in our lifetime has brought untold sorrow to mankind, and
- to reaffirm faith in fundamental human rights, in the dignity and worth of the human person, in the equal rights of men and women and of nations large and small, and
- to establish conditions under which justice and respect for the obligations arising from treaties and other sources of international law can be maintained, and
- to promote social progress and better standards of life in larger freedom,

AND FOR THESE ENDS

- to practice tolerance and live together in peace with one another as good neighbours, and
- to unite our strength to maintain international peace and security, and
- to ensure, by the acceptance of principles and the institution of methods, that armed force shall not be used, save in the common interest, and
- to employ international machinery for the promotion of the economic and social advancement of all peoples,

HAVE RESOLVED TO COMBINE OUR EFFORTS TO ACCOMPLISH THESE AIMS

Accordingly, our respective Governments, through representatives assembled in the city of San Francisco, who have exhibited their full powers found to be in good and due form, have agreed to the present Charter of the United Nations and do hereby establish an international organization to be known as the United Nations.

PRIMARY SOURCE

Universal Declaration of Human Rights Preamble

SOURCE *"The Universal Declaration of Human Rights Preamble."* The United Nations, *December 10, 1948. http://www.un.org/en/documents/udhr/index. shtml#atop (accessed December 4, 2013). Copyright © 1948 by the United Nations. All rights reserved. Reproduced by permission.*

INTRODUCTION *The UN Commission on Human Rights, author of the Declaration of Human Rights, was founded to help prevent and address future violations of human rights and atrocities such as those committed during World War II. The Declaration was the first document created by the Commission to establish basic principles and define the scope of rights to be protected. It was adopted on December 10, 1948, one day after the UN General Assembly adopted the Convention on the Prevention and Punishment of the Crime of Genocide. Two additional international covenants addressing civil and political rights as well as economic, social, and cultural rights were adopted in 1966.*

PREAMBLE

Whereas recognition of the inherent dignity and of the equal and inalienable rights of all members of the human family is the foundation of freedom, justice and peace in the world,

Whereas disregard and contempt for human rights have resulted in barbarous acts which have outraged the conscience of mankind, and the advent of a world in which human beings shall enjoy freedom of speech and belief and freedom from fear and want has been proclaimed as the highest aspiration of the common people,

Whereas it is essential, if man is not to be compelled to have recourse, as a last resort, to rebellion against tyranny and oppression, that human rights should be protected by the rule of law,

Whereas it is essential to promote the development of friendly relations between nations,

Whereas the peoples of the United Nations have in the Charter reaffirmed their faith in fundamental human rights, in the dignity and worth of the human person and in the equal rights of men and women and have determined to promote social progress and better standards of life in larger freedom,

Whereas Member States have pledged themselves to achieve, in co-operation with the United Nations, the promotion of universal respect for and observance of human rights and fundamental freedoms,

Whereas a common understanding of these rights and freedoms is of the greatest importance for the full realization of this pledge,

Now, Therefore THE GENERAL ASSEMBLY proclaims THIS UNIVERSAL DECLARATION OF HUMAN RIGHTS as a common standard of achievement for all peoples and all nations, to the end that every individual and every organ of society, keeping this Declaration constantly in mind, shall strive by teaching and education to promote respect for these rights and freedoms and by progressive measures, national and international, to secure their universal and effective recognition and observance, both among the peoples of Member States themselves and among the peoples of territories under their jurisdiction.

SEE ALSO *Genocide; Global Environmental Treaties; International Law and Justice; Rwandan Genocide; Water Rights; World War I; World War II; Yugoslav Wars*

BIBLIOGRAPHY

Books

Gold, Dore. *Tower of Babel: How the United Nations Has Fueled Global Chaos.* New York, NY: Crown, 2004.

Meisler, Stanley. *The United Nations: A History*, Rev. and updated ed. New York, NY: Grove Press, 2011.

Roosevelt, Eleanor, et al. *The Universal Declaration of Human Rights.* Bedford, MA: Applewood Books, 2001.

United Nations. *United Nations at a Glance.* New York, NY: United Nations, 2012.

Web Sites

Katz, Jonathan M. "Experts Ask: Did UN Troops Infect Haiti?" *Associated Press*, November 3, 2010. http://web.archive.org/web/20101107120818/ http://www.msnbc.msn.com/id/39996103/ns/ health-infectious_diseases (accessed October 23, 2013).

Townshend, Charles. "The League of Nations and the United Nations." *BBC History*, February 17, 2011. http://www.bbc.co.uk/history/worldwars/ wwone/league_nations_01.shtml (accessed June 10, 2013).

Townshend, Charles. "United Nations Founded." *BBC History*, February 17, 2011. http://www. bbc.co.uk/history/worldwars/wwone/league_ nations_01.shtml (accessed June 10, 2013).

United Nations. http://www.un.org/en/ (accessed May 31, 2013).

United Nations Economic, Scientific and Cultural Organization (UNESCO). http://www.unesco. org/new/en/ (accessed May 31, 2013).

U.S.-Iraq War

⊕ Introduction

The Iraq War (2003–11), also known as Operation Iraqi Freedom, was a conflict between a coalition of nations led by the United States and a number of opponents in Iraq. The first stated opponent of the coalition was the government of Iraq under President Saddam Hussein (1937–2006).

After that government's downfall in April 2003, a number of nationalist resistance groups rose up in opposition to the continued U.S. occupation of Iraq. These groups, aided by a relatively small number of foreign combatants, are collectively referred to as the insurgency. The fighting between the U.S.-led coalition and the insurgency lasted for approximately seven years, during which time the coalition helped Iraq set up a new democratic government.

⊕ Historical Background

The United States provided some support to Saddam Hussein during Iraq's 1980–88 war with Iran in order to prevent an Iranian victory. At the time the United States was more concerned by Iranian power in the region, especially after the 1979 revolution in Iran toppled a pro-U.S. leader and established a strict theocracy. However, in 1990 Iraq invaded its neighbor Kuwait. A coalition consisting primarily of U.S. forces attacked Iraqi forces with approval from the United Nations (UN) Security Council, and Iraq was defeated rapidly in what came to be called the Persian Gulf War or First Gulf War (1991; confusingly the Iran-Iraq War had also been known earlier as the Persian Gulf War). U.S. president George H. W. Bush (1924–) decided against deposing Saddam and occupying Iraq, fearing U.S. entanglement in a drawn-out occupation.

American Air Force F-15 C fighters fly over a Kuwaiti oilfield torched by retreating Iraqi troops during the Gulf War in 1991. © MPI/ Getty Images

Weapons of Mass Destruction

During the 1990s, international bans on trade with Iraq weakened its economy. The Iraqi military could not recover its pre-Gulf War strength. Under Saddam's direction, Iraq did attempt a new nuclear program but, lacking both the necessary radioactive metals and technical know-how, the program did not evolve very far. By the end of 1998, investigators believed, Iraq had destroyed its last remaining chemical and biological weapons under the supervision of UN inspectors. But many observers were skeptical of Iraq's claims to have dismantled all its weapons of mass destruction (as chemical and nuclear weapons are sometimes called). Moreover, Saddam played a continuing cat-and-mouse game with UN inspectors in an effort to make his regional neighbors think he still possessed weapons of mass destruction.

After the terrorist attacks on the United States of September 11, 2001, the administration of U.S. president George W. Bush (1946–) and its allies argued that Iraq posed a deadly threat to the United States because it might give chemical or nuclear weapons to terrorists for use against the United States. On September 24, 2002, British prime minister Tony Blair (1953–) stated that Iraq could strike the United Kingdom with chemical or biological weapons on "45 minutes' notice" and might obtain a nuclear weapon in fewer than five years.

On October 7, 2002, Bush stated in a speech that the United States could not wait to find the "smoking gun," and warned that the first evidence of Iraq's weapons of mass destruction might come in the form of a "mushroom cloud," or a nuclear attack. Four days later, on October 11, 2002, the U.S. House of Representatives followed the U.S. Senate in approving the use of force against Iraq. The United States did not declare war on Iraq; rather, Congress passed a resolution that authorized the president to use the U.S. Armed Forces "as he determines to be necessary and appropriate . . . to defend the national security of the United States."

In November 2002 United Nations weapons inspectors returned to Iraq to search for chemical, biological, or nuclear weapons, or weapons programs. In a March 7, 2003, speech to the UN Security Council, chief UN weapons inspector Hans Blix stated that after a thorough inspection, no evidence of weapons of mass destruction had been found. However, the United States and other coalition governments insisted that they had conclusive secret evidence of such weapons. Opinion within and between Western intelligence agencies was divided. Subsequently, other Western intelligence agencies, including the French intelligence agency, confirmed that their own assessments indicated that Saddam did possess chemical and biological weapons. On the other hand, a September 2002 U.S. Defense Intelligence

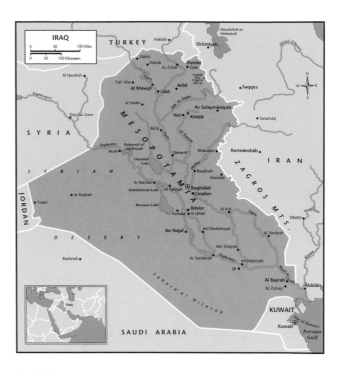

© 2014 Cengage Learning

Agency report stated, "There is no reliable information on whether Iraq is producing and stockpiling chemical weapons, or whether Iraq has—or will—establish its chemical warfare agent production facilities."

In the first three months of 2003, as the United States sought unsuccessfully to obtain UN approval to invade Iraq, more than 30 million people worldwide participated in protests against the impending invasion. On February 15, 2003, alone, somewhere between 6 and 30 million people in the United States, Europe, and elsewhere marched to protest the war. It was the first time in history that there had been significant global activism against a war before it had begun. Protestors worldwide cited the lack of proof that Iraq possessed weapons of mass destruction.

Operation Iraqi Freedom

The United States was unable to garner the support of the UN for the invasion, but it proceeded with its plans anyway, mustering a coalition of forces, mainly American and British, with support from Australia, Denmark, and Poland, and lesser contributions by other countries. By March 2003 there were 125,000 U.S. troops and 45,000 UK troops in Kuwait, ready to invade. The coalition was prepared to carry out a "shock and awe" attack—an intense bombing raid accompanied by a ground invasion. On March 19, 2003, coalition forces began bombarding targets in the capital city of Baghdad and other large cities. Hussein and his followers fled within three weeks, and the coalition forces took over Baghdad.

⊕ Impacts and Issues

On May 1, 2003, President Bush, standing on the deck of an aircraft carrier that had just returned to U.S. waters from its mission in the Persian Gulf, declared that major combat operations in Iraq were over and that it was "mission accomplished." In reality it was just the start of the conflict. The vast majority of soldiers and civilians killed in the Iraq War died after this speech was given.

The Occupation of Iraq

A violent and expensive occupation followed the successful invasion. Groups rebelling against the coalition quickly formed. Saddam and his Baath Party had been members of the Arab Sunni minority in Iraq, ruling over the Shia majority. After the invasion, conflicts between Sunnis and Shias mounted. There had been little sign of the presence of al-Qaeda, an international terrorist organization, in Iraq before the invasion. But by 2004 Arab terrorist groups, notably al-Qaeda in Iraq, had moved into the country and were carrying out high-profile kidnappings and televised beheadings of Westerners.

These groups recruited Iraqis into antigovernment and anti–U.S. campaigns, providing training and funding for acts of violence. They also bred conflict between the Sunnis and Shias and caused great misery among civilians with suicide and car bombs. In this state of chaos, in 2005 the Iraqis held a democratic election and approved a constitution, but the coalition forces remained as a safety precaution for the new government.

In 2007 the United States added 30,000 more troops to its efforts in Iraq, in a move called the "surge." At the same time large segments of the Sunni insurgents turned against the foreign groups such as al-Qaeda. The level of violence in the Iraq War dropped significantly, but the fighting continued.

Throughout 2008 the Iraqi and U.S. governments negotiated a new Status of Forces Agreement (SOFA) to replace the SOFA that expired at the end of 2008. A SOFA is an agreement between two nations regarding the stationing of one nation's troops in the other nation. On November 16, 2008, the Iraqi Cabinet approved a SOFA that called for the withdrawal of U.S. troops from Iraqi cities by the end of 2009 and a total withdrawal in 2011.

Perspectives on the Iraq War and Occupation

Supporters of the war argue that it improved U.S. and regional security, deposed a brutal dictator who had used chemical weapons on his own people, and has improved the lives of Iraqi citizens. Although the coalition did not uncover weapons of mass destruction, for years many U.S. politicians continued to argue that they existed, and that the perceived threat to U.S. security warranted the subsequent invasion. Lacking the smoking gun to justify the war, coalition leaders focused instead on stressing the importance of bringing democracy and freedom to the region.

An Iraqi woman carries a child as she walks past British tanks at a checkpoint on the outskirts of the southern Iraqi city of Basra on March 29, 2003. Hundreds of men were seen going into the city to collect family members and take them out to safety. The British were part of a U.S.-led coalition of troops from several nations who invaded Iraq. *© Roberto Schmidt/AFP/Getty Images*

However, an area of major controversy concerning the war was the use—or misuse—of intelligence reports prior to the invasion. A 2008 U.S. Senate Intelligence Committee report indicated that the administration of President Bush had misused intelligence and misrepresented the threat posed by Iraq to the American people. In June 2009 the United Kingdom, a partner in the war in Iraq, announced the launch of a long-awaited inquiry into the war for similar reasons.

Some opponents of the war continue to declare that the Iraq War was well intentioned but badly mismanaged. Other opponents call the invasion an unwarranted act of aggression that took valuable resources away from a more direct war on terror in Afghanistan and lowered America's moral authority and support globally. Antiwar protests continued throughout the Iraq operation in the United States, Great Britain, and in many other nations across the globe. President Barack Obama (1961–) made clear in a June 2009 speech in Cairo, Egypt, the distinction he saw between U.S. military action in Afghanistan

BLACKWATER

There were many controversies surrounding the run-up to the war in Iraq, its management once begun, and its aftermath. One major area of controversy was the use of private, commercial security forces by the United States.

The largest private security force employed by the U.S. government is Academi, though during most of the Iraq War the company was called Blackwater. Though many of its employees served in security teams devoted to protecting civilian U.S. officials, others operated as what amounted to mercenary forces that were not part of the U.S. military command structure. Iraqi officials in the post-Saddam government repeatedly pointed to excessive use of force by Blackwater employees. In one notorious incident in 2007, Blackwater employees fired on Iraqi civilians in a square in Baghdad, killing 17 people. The details of the incident were disputed, but the U.S. brought manslaughter and other charges against five Blackwater employees. Ultimately, all charges were dropped, sparking outrage in Iraq.

The United Nations concluded in a 2007 report that Blackwater was, in essence, a mercenary force and thus use of Blackwater was illegal under 1989 UN Mercenary Convention. However, the United States is not a signatory to that convention.

and Iraq, calling the former a "war of necessity" and the latter a "war of choice."

A Fragile Democracy

Violence surged in Iraq as the June 30, 2009, deadline neared for withdrawal of American troops from Iraqi cities. Many questioned the prudence of pulling U.S. forces out of the country and leaving security duties to the Iraqis. After attacks continued through July and August 2009, General Charles Jacoby, the second highest-ranking U.S. officer in Iraq, told reporters that al-Qaeda was behind the unrest and that its motives were to reignite sectarian violence and shake public faith in the government. On December 9, 2009, a series of coordinated bombings targeting both government buildings and civilian areas in Baghdad killed 127 people and injured hundreds more. The attacks appeared to be the work of insurgents seeking to destabilize the government and undermine Iraqi confidence in the value of democratic elections. The bombings occurred soon after the announcement that parliamentary elections would be held in March 2010.

Early elections in Iraq began amid controversy and violence. Bombings near polling stations killed 12 people and wounded dozens more. Security officials in Sunni-dominated areas noted that the names of thousands of military and police personnel were missing from polling documents, leading to complaints of fraud. Election officials quickly announced that those whose names were missing would be allowed to cast provisional ballots.

The general parliamentary election took place as scheduled on March 7, 2010. Early results showed that the parliamentary political bloc led by Prime Minister Nouri al-Maliki (1950–), who had been re-elected to a second term in 2010, had significant public support, but allegations of fraud during ballot counting were widespread. Voter turnout was estimated at 62 percent, down from 73 percent in 2005. With 90 percent of the votes counted, al-Maliki's party's lead evaporated and the party of his main rival, Iyad Allawi (1945–), led by 8,000 votes. In the end, Iyad Allawi's Iraqiyya bloc edged out al-Maliki's State of Law alliance party by just two seats. Although both the UN and the United States declared the elections credible, al-Maliki announced he intended to launch a legal challenge of the results. Two months later, an electoral commission upheld the original election results. Since Allawi's party did not have enough seats to form a government of its own, it was forced to seek a broad coalition with other parties.

A period of calm following the election was soon interrupted by more deadly bombings in Baghdad and the surrounding countryside. Both civilians and soldiers were killed in the attacks, although the targets were typically either the Shias or foreigners. Iraq still had no coalition government throughout the fall of 2010. This political disarray left the country more vulnerable to renewed attacks by insurgents, and the suicide bombings increased. On December 22, 2010, Iraq finally established a broad coalition government involving all main parties and ethnic groups.

Withdrawal of Combat Troops

In July 2010, in a sign that the U.S. withdrawal was proceeding despite an uptick in violence in recent months, the United States military handed over control of its last remaining prison in Iraq, Camp Cropper, to Iraqi authorities. Iraq assumed control of 1,600 of the prisoners, but asked the U.S. military to hold about 200 prisoners suspected of being members of al-Qaeda. Several members of the regime of Saddam Hussein were among those 200 prisoners. In August, 50,000 U.S. troops were scheduled to be withdrawn from Iraq.

At a defense conference in Baghdad on August 12, 2010, however, Lieutenant General Babaker Zebari, Iraq's top army official, said the U.S. withdrawal was premature and that Iraq's army would not be capable of securing the country until 2020. Nevertheless, U.S. combat troops were withdrawn on schedule on August 19. The following week, a wave of suicide bombings across Iraq targeting Iraqi police forces killed 50 people. Despite numerous other violent bombings, the withdrawal continued on schedule. In a modest ceremony in Baghdad on December 15, 2011, U.S. secretary of defense Leon Panetta declared the mission in Iraq officially over. The last American soldiers left Iraq three days later. Following the withdrawal (as of early 2014), the United States continued to maintain two bases in Iraq with approximately 4,000 troops total.

The Violence Continues

In late 2012 a new series of protests began, led by Sunni Arabs who feel marginalized by Iraq's Shia-dominated government. About 90 percent of the world's Muslims are Sunnis, but in Iraq roughly 60 percent are Shias. Under the regime of Saddam Hussein, a Sunni, the majority Shia population was repressed and political power was held by the Sunni minority.

After Saddam's regime fell, some powerful Shia leaders emerged. Chief among them, though he holds no political office, is Muqtada al-Sadr (1973–). Al-Sadr organized a political and military movement with the stated goals of establishing an Islamic democracy and ending U.S. occupation. Despite the fact that it had been U.S. and allied forces that toppled al-Sadr's long-time foe, Saddam Hussein, al-Sadr insisted the presence of U.S. forces in Iraq posed a greater threat to the country than Saddam had.

Prime Minister al-Maliki is also a Shia who spent years in exile criticizing Saddam's regime. Critics charged al-Maliki with favoring Shias over Sunnis in government. This perceived anti-Sunni turn in Iraq gave an opening to al-Qaeda, a Sunni terrorist group, which successfully established a foothold in Iraq following the U.S. invasion. Al-Qaeda gradually gathered support among some Sunni Iraqis, and has either claimed responsibility for or been accused of multiple violent attacks and suicide bombings in largely Shia areas.

Though al-Maliki and al-Sadr formed a loose alliance in 2011, with al-Sadr using his influence to prop up al-Maliki's government, al-Sadr became increasingly vocal in his criticism of al-Maliki in 2012 and 2013, accusing him of fanning the flames of sectarian discords and urging him to treat minority Sunnis fairly and bring peace to the country.

⊕ Future Implications

Since the withdrawal of the U.S. troops, the Iraqi government has maintained its precarious control over the country. The "Arab Spring" anti-government protests that erupted throughout the Middle East in 2011 briefly spread to Iraq, but were soon contained.

Peace remained elusive as of early 2014. Suicide bombings, car bombings, and other attacks on Shia targets grew in frequency and deadliness throughout the summer and into the fall. It is clear that if stability in Iraq is to be achieved, old grudges must be put aside and equality achieved for minority and majority alike.

SEE ALSO *Al-Qaeda; Arab Spring; Iran-Iraq War; Islam: Sunni and Shia Disputes; Weapons of Mass Destruction*

BIBLIOGRAPHY
Books

Gordon, Michael. *The Endgame: The Inside Story of the Struggle for Iraq, From George W. Bush to Barack Obama.* New York: Vintage, 2013.

Isikoff, Michael. *Hubris: The Inside Story of Spin, Scandal and the Selling of the Iraq War.* New York: Broadway Books, 2007.

Smithson, Ryan. *Ghosts of War: The True Story of a Nineteen Year Old GI.* New York: HarperTeen, 2010.

Web Sites

Cutler, David. "Timeline: Invasion, Surge, Withdrawal; U.S. Forces in Iraq." *Reuters*, December 18, 2011. http://www.reuters.com/article/2011/12/18/us-iraq-usa-pullout-idUSTRE7BH08E20111218 (accessed December 20, 2013).

Dale, Catherine. "Operation Iraqi Freedom: Strategies, Approaches, Results and Issues for Congress." *Congressional Research Service*, April 2, 2009. http://www.fas.org/sgp/crs/natsec/RL34387.pdf (accessed August 24, 2013).

"Last U.S. Troops Leave Iraq, Ending War." *USA Today*, December 17, 2011. http://usatoday30.usatoday.com/news/world/story/2011-12-17/iraq-us-troops/52032854/1?csp=ip (accessed December 20, 2013).

Sastry, Anjuli, and Alisa Wiersema. "10 Year Iraq War Timeline." *ABC News*, March 19, 2013. http://abcnews.go.com/Politics/TheNote/10-year-iraq-war-timeline/story?id=18758663 (accessed August 24, 2013).

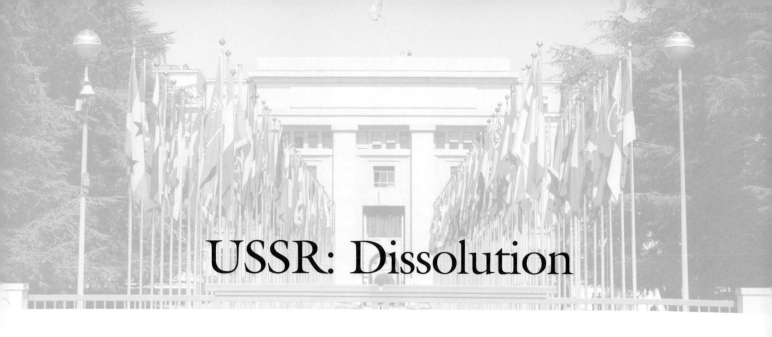

USSR: Dissolution

⊕ Introduction

On Christmas Day in 1991, Soviet president Mikhail Gorbachev (1931–) resigned from office and handed the Soviet nuclear missile launching codes to Russian president Boris Yeltsin (1931–2007). The Soviet flag was lowered from the Kremlin and the Russian flag rose in its place. The next day, the Union of Soviet Socialist Republics (USSR) was formally dissolved and replaced by 15 independent republics. The dissolution of the USSR ended the Cold War (1945–91) and dramatically changed the political balance of the world.

The 12 post–Soviet republics as well as the nations that had been under the Soviet-controlled Eastern Bloc have had very different experiences charting a new independent course. Some nations have successfully embraced democracy and closer ties with the West.

Other nations have fallen under the power of local authoritarian rulers. The remaining nations have an uneasy political mixture, neither completely one form nor the other.

The most powerful post–Soviet nation is the Russian Federation, a semi-democratic nation that is considered a "great power" and a potential "superpower." The USSR was an undeniable superpower, capable of exerting its dominance on a global scale. But since the dissolution of the USSR, Russia can no longer claim to be a full superpower. As a "great power," however, Russia is capable of exerting its influence on a massive scale and has shown particular interest in the affairs of former Soviet nations.

⊕ Historical Background

The USSR was a Eurasian socialist state that existed between 1922 and 1991. Its roots were deeply entrenched in the Russian Revolution of 1917. The USSR gradually grew to include 12 distinct ethnically based Soviet republics. The economy and government of each republic was completely subordinate to the highly centralized Communist government of the Soviet Union located in Moscow, Russia.

Mikhail Gorbachev and Liberal Reforms

The USSR's economy had slowed down considerably during the 1980s, partly as a result of the Soviet War in Afghanistan as well as a dramatic drop in the price of oil in 1985 and 1986. In 1985 Gorbachev became the general secretary of the Communist Party of the Soviet Union, the de facto ruler of the USSR. Gorbachev was the first Soviet leader born after the Russian Revolution and had a more modern view of the world and the Soviet Union's place in it.

Hoping to save the USSR as a political and economic entity, he attempted to reform the Communist

---

THE BALTIC CHAIN

On August 23, 1989, the Baltic Chain was formed when the Popular Front movements of Estonia, Latvia, and Lithuania organized approximately two million people to hold hands in a single chain spanning the three countries. The date was chosen to commemorate the 50th anniversary of the Molotov-Ribbentrop Pact. The original pact had been between the Soviet Union and Nazi Germany and divided Europe into "spheres of influence." Although Germany had lost the war, the Molotov-Ribbentrop Pact had been essentially honored by the Allies when Europe was divided into Western and Eastern blocs. As a result of this pact, the Baltic states lost their independence and were absorbed into the USSR. The Popular Front movements protested the pact and its conclusion. The Baltic Chain remains one of the largest peaceful political demonstrations in world history.

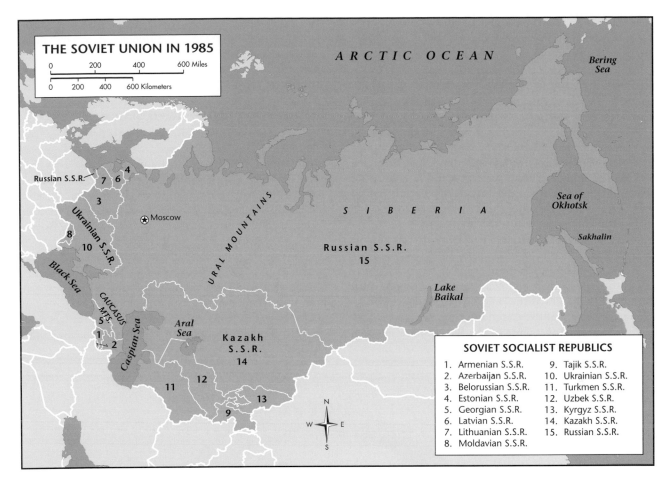

THE SOVIET UNION IN 1985

ARCTIC OCEAN

Bering Sea

Russian S.S.R.

Moscow

SIBERIA

URAL MOUNTAINS

Russian S.S.R.
15

Sea of Okhotsk

Sakhalin

Lake Baikal

Black Sea

CAUCASUS MTS.

Caspian Sea

Aral Sea

Kazakh S.S.R.
14

SOVIET SOCIALIST REPUBLICS

1. Armenian S.S.R.	9. Tajik S.S.R.
2. Azerbaijan S.S.R.	10. Ukrainian S.S.R.
3. Belorussian S.S.R.	11. Turkmen S.S.R.
4. Estonian S.S.R.	12. Uzbek S.S.R.
5. Georgian S.S.R.	13. Kyrgyz S.S.R.
6. Latvian S.S.R.	14. Kazakh S.S.R.
7. Lithuanian S.S.R.	15. Russian S.S.R.
8. Moldavian S.S.R.	

© 2014 Cengage Learning

Party state economy. In 1986 he began introducing numerous liberal measures based on *demokratizatsiya* (democratization), *glasnost* (openness), *perestroika* (restructuring), and *uskoreniye* (acceleration of economic development). What this meant on a practical level was greater political and social freedoms to the USSR constituent republics as well as Soviet territories of the Eastern Bloc.

The policies were meant to stimulate the USSR's economy. Instead, these new freedoms created an atmosphere of open criticism of the Communist regime and the rise of strong nationalist and separatist movements. From 1986 to 1988, mostly peaceful demonstrators in Soviet republics and Soviet satellite states openly challenged Soviet supreme power. These protests were closely watched by the Soviet police forces but not interrupted except to keep the peace.

Once the states that comprised the Soviet Union had a glimpse of freedom, the central government struggled to contain the situation. Some Soviet states took measures toward independence, chipping away at Soviet authority. Ultimately, various factors played a role in the dissolution of the USSR, including nationalism and religion.

Protests in the Caucasus

On February 20, 1988, the city of Stepanakert, Azerbaijan (whose majority population was ethnically Armenian) voted to succeed from Azerbaijan and join Armenia. Although both Armenia and Azerbaijan were Soviet states, the decision stunned the world. It was an unprecedented move for a tiny region to dare to have an independent local vote and attempt to rewrite the territorial boundaries of the USSR.

Two days later, two Azerbaijanis were killed in clashes with Armenians in an event referred to as the Askeran Clash. When the deaths were announced over the radio, the event sparked four days of violent anti–Armenian rioting in the nearby city of Sumgait. The authorities were forced to occupy the city with tanks, and almost the entire Armenian population of 14,000 fled in terror. When increasingly large nationalist protests erupted, the Soviet army was forced to impose a curfew on the area.

Armenia closely watched the events unfolding in Azerbaijan. Previously, Armenia had been among the most loyal of Soviet republics. But in 1988 a new liberal Armenian leader, Suren Harutyunyan, influenced by the nationalist fervor, chose to fly the independent

Armenian flag. Huge nationalist protests immediately erupted, and Soviet military forces were sent into Armenia to keep the peace.

Revolutions in the Baltic States

In 1988 a series of revolutions toppled the Communist regime in the Baltic states of Estonia, Latvia, and Lithuania. Each formed Popular Front organizations between April and June of 1988, which pressured newly appointed liberal presidents to declare independence from the USSR. The Popular Fronts were peaceful organizations that practiced nonviolent resistance. The organizations were highly visible presences in their respective states and included members from every level of Baltic society.

In October and November of 1989, the presidents of each Baltic country bowed to pressure from the Popular Fronts. Their first actions were to legalize the flying of the independent national flags and replace Russian with local languages as the official state languages. In so doing they essentially declared their independence. The Popular Front Movements of the Baltic states inspired

Soviet nationalists across the USSR. Variations of the Popular Front movement were organized in Azerbaijan, Moldova, and Belarus. Other nationalist organizations sprang up in every other Soviet republic and Soviet satellite state.

Pressure from the Western States

The Western states of Belarus, Moldova, and the Ukraine were highly influenced by the nationalist movements of the Caucasus and Baltic states. Belarus and Moldova each had Popular Front organizations that showed support for nationalist movements throughout the USSR. Most of the protests in Belarus and Moldova were peaceful, but occasional conflicts with the Soviet police force occurred throughout 1988 and 1989.

In the Ukraine the nationalist movement was led by the church. In 1988 Ukraine celebrated 1,000 years of Christianity in the region. At first the celebration was held in secret locations, but as the year wore on, the affair became increasingly public. Ukrainian leaders then began to openly discuss human rights violations in the

Two young Lithuanians display a hammer and sickle, the Communist emblem, which was removed from a facade of a building September 3, 1991, in Vilnius as the process of the independence of the Baltic republics culminated with the recognition of the Baltic states by the United States, September 2, 1991. Lithuania unilaterally declared its independence from the Union of Soviet Socialist Republics (USSR) on March 11, 1990. © *Virgis Usinavicius/AFP/Getty Images*

Soviet Union. On January 22, 1989, Ukrainians celebrated Ukrainian Independence Day, commemorating Ukrainian independence from the Russian Federation in 1917. The holiday had not been celebrated for decades, since Ukraine had been incorporated into the USSR in 1922. Throughout the rest of the year, massive, mostly peaceful, protests were organized to decry Soviet policies and urge Ukrainian independence.

Competitive Elections in 1990

In 1989 Mikhail Gorbachev encouraged the Communist Party of the Soviet Union to introduce limited elections to a new central legislature, the Congress of the People. At first only members of the Communist Party could run for office, but the ban on other political parties was soon lifted. Gorbachev hoped that by allowing free elections, the people would feel a greater connection to the USSR and make political decisions that would support the greater good.

On February 7, 1990, the Soviet government allowed each republic to have its own competitive elections. During the election of 1990, nationalists and

reformers won seats in each republic government. In six republics—Lithuania, Moldova, Estonia, Latvia, Armenia, and Georgia—the Communist Party was replaced by nationalist candidates as the majority party.

⊕ Impacts and Issues

Within a few weeks, the republics began to showcase their national sovereignty from the USSR, even going so far as to actively declare their independence. In each state a "war of laws" soon resulted in which the governments of the republics passed laws that were in direct opposition to those of the Moscow central government. Local laws were given precedence, and each republic began to assert control over their local economies and refuse to pay taxes to Moscow. As Soviet supply lines broke down, the Soviet economy plummeted.

The Final Year of the USSR

As the political unrest grew, the authoritarian establishment of the Soviet military and the Communist Party attempted to oust Gorbachev and reestablish a strong

People hold a huge Russian flag and flash victory signs on August 22, 1991, on Red Square in Moscow as they celebrate the failure of a hardline communist-led coup which nearly toppled Soviet President Mikhail Gorbachev. The coup, begun August 19, was headed by the members of the self-styled "committee for the state of emergency" or the "gang of eight," including Soviet Vice President Gennady Yanayev and KGB chief Vladimir Kryuchkov. The same day, thousands in Moscow, Leningrad, and other cities answered Russian Republic President Boris Yeltsin's call to raise barricades against tanks and troops. The collapse of the coup was signaled in the afternoon of August 21, when the defense ministry ordered all troops to withdraw from Moscow. © Anatoly Sapronyenko/AFP/Getty Images

central regime. The coup was foiled, but the event heightened fears that Gorbachev's reforms would be reversed. Nationalist sentiment increased throughout the Soviet Union.

On December 8, 1991, the Soviet presidents of Russia, Ukraine, and Belarus secretly met and signed the Belavezha Accords, agreeing to dissolve the USSR and replace it with a looser union, the Commonwealth of Independent States (CIS). Two weeks later eight of the remaining nine republics signed the Alma-Ata Protocol, which established the CIS and essentially destroyed the USSR.

On December 25, 1991, Gorbachev resigned and dissolved the Soviet Union. In its place 15 constituent republics emerged: Armenia, Azerbaijan, Belarus, Estonia, Georgia, Kazakhstan, Kyrgyzstan, Latvia, Lithuania, Moldova, Russia, Tajikistan, Turkmenistan, Ukraine, and Uzbekistan. The Baltic states (Estonia, Latvia, and Lithuania) had already granted themselves independence and were not part of the CIS.

⊕ Future Implications

The political outcomes of the dissolution ranged widely. The Baltic states of Estonia, Latvia, and Lithuania successfully established fully democratic systems of government. Azerbaijan, Belarus, and the Central Asian republics each passed into the hands of authoritarian rulers. Armenia, Georgia, and Ukraine maintained some democratic freedoms, but still struggle with widespread political corruption.

The Russian Federation assumed the Soviet Union's rights and obligations and was recognized in international law as the successor state of the Soviet Union. Russia underwent a period of political instability and economic decline for several years following the dissolution of the USSR. It eventually reverted to authoritarianism under the presidency of Vladimir Putin (1952–) beginning in 2000. As Russia's global influence has grown, it seems increasingly possible that it may emerge as a new superpower.

Many former Soviet republics have retained close ties with Russia in the framework of multilateral

Russian President Dmitry Medvedev (C) walks near World War II veterans at a wreath-laying ceremony not far from Moscow in Dubosekovo on May 7, 2010, during a visit to a memorial to soldiers of commander Panfilov who died here in defense of Moscow during the war. In an interview with the *Izvestia* newspaper, published two days before Russia marked the 65th anniversary of victory in World War II, Medvedev slammed the Soviet Union as a totalitarian regime that suppressed rights, in the most damning assessment of the USSR by a Russian leader in recent years. Medvedev added that the crimes of wartime dictator Joseph Stalin can never be forgiven. However, some in the country are haunted by regret that the powerful Soviet Union broke up and their country faces an uncertain future.   © *Dmitry Astakhov/ AFP/Getty Images*

organizations such as the Eurasian Economic Community; the Union States; the Customs Union of Belarus, Kazakhstan, and Russia; and the Eurasian Union. Each of these organizations is designed to enhance economic and security cooperation. As these multilateral organizations continue to develop, they may be able to affect the global economy in unique ways. Whether these organizations will be effective on anything more than a local scale, however, remains unknown.

SEE ALSO *Cold War; Georgia-Russia Conflict; Russian Revolution and Civil War; USSR: Invasion of Afghanistan; World War I; World War II*

BIBLIOGRAPHY

Books

Brown, Archie, and Lilia Shevtsova, eds. *Gorbachev, Yeltsin, and Putin: Political Leadership in Russia's Transition.* Washington, DC: Carnegie Endowment for International Peace, 2001.

Bushkovitch, Paul. *A Concise History of Russia.* New York: Cambridge University Press, 2012.

Remnick, David. *Lenin's Tomb: The Last Days of the Soviet Union.* New York: Vintage, 1994.

Roxburgh, Angus. *The Strongman: Vladimir Putin and the Struggle for Russia,* revised ed. New York: I. B. Tauris, 2013.

Strayer, Robert. *Why did the Soviet Union Collapse? Understanding Historical Change.* Armonk, NY: M. E. Sharpe Inc., 1998.

Walker, Edward. *Dissolution: Sovereignty and Breakup of the Soviet Union.* Lanham, MD: Rowman and Littlefield Publishers, 2003.

Web Sites

Brown, Archie. "Reform, Coup and Collapse: The End of the Soviet State." *BBC History.* http://www.bbc.co.uk/history/worldwars/coldwar/soviet_end_01.shtml (accessed December 9, 2013).

"Fall of the Soviet Union." *The Cold War Museum.* http://www.coldwar.org/articles/90s/fall_of_the_soviet_union.asp (accessed December 9, 2013).

"Fall of the Soviet Union." *History.com.* http://www.history.com/topics/fall-of-soviet-union (accessed December 9, 2013).

"A New Russia." *PBS NewsHour,* August 22, 2001. http://www.pbs.org/newshour/extra/features/july-dec01/russia_coup.html (accessed December 9, 2013).

"Perestroika and Glasnost." *History.com.* http://www.history.com/topics/perestroika-and-glasnost (accessed December 9, 2013).

USSR: Invasion of Afghanistan

🌐 Introduction

Afghanistan is a landlocked Muslim nation in south-central Asia that is bordered to the west by Iran, to the south and east by Pakistan, and to the north by several ex-Soviet republics. During the Cold War (1945–91), the Afghan government was closely allied with the Soviet Union, on which it relied for military and economic support.

In the late 1970s the Afghan government attempted to modernize the country and discard Islamic civil laws. When conservative Muslim citizens resisted, they were swiftly and violently punished. Seeing their traditional way of life under attack, the people in the Afghan countryside soon rebelled. The rebels, calling themselves *mujahideen*, a term for Muslim warriors engaged in *jihad*, or holy war, relied on guerrilla warfare tactics. The Afghan government, unable to put down the rebellion, asked Soviet troops to enter the country and help the Afghan army fight against the mujahideen.

The Soviets invaded Afghanistan in 1979. Six months before the Soviet invasion, the United States, under President Jimmy Carter (1924–), had begun a massive funding of the Afghan resistance, including hundreds of millions of dollars of cash and tens of thousands of tons of weapons and supplies. The cause soon recruited mujahideen from Muslim countries around the world. The Soviet invasion quickly evolved into a brutal and prolonged entanglement. The war ended with a Soviet retreat, the old Afghan government disposed, a country in ruins, and a political vacuum that would be filled by the victorious mujahideen, and later, the Taliban.

🌐 Historical Background

For centuries the modern state of Afghanistan was ruled by various empires centered in India and Persia. In 1709 the largest Afghan ethnic group, known as the Pashtun, successfully won its independence. The new nation was variously known as the Hotaki Empire (1709–38), the Durrani Empire (1747–1823), the Emirate of Afghanistan (1823–1926), and the Kingdom of Afghanistan (1926–73). Throughout most of this time, Afghanistan had peaceful relations with its northern neighbors, including Russia.

During the 20th century the kings of Afghanistan hoped to change their country's traditional isolation from the rest of the world. They established diplomatic relations with most major countries and joined the United Nations (UN). The kings introduced numerous reforms meant to modernize the country, including educational reforms and reforms aimed at increasing gender equality. But the opening of coeducational schools and the abolition of the traditional Muslim veil for women alienated many tribal and religious leaders. Political unrest resulted in frequent changeovers in high-ranking offices, including the abdication and assassination of various Afghan kings.

During the 1950s Afghanistan began to form a closer relationship with its northern neighbor, the Soviet Union. Then in the 1960s Afghanistan experimented with a series of democratic elections, an unintended result of which was the rise of several extremist political groups, including the Communist People's Democratic Party of Afghanistan (PDPA), which had close ties with the Soviet Union.

In 1973 a bloodless coup led by former prime minister Mohammad Sardar Daoud Khan (1909–1978) abolished the monarchy and created the Republic of Afghanistan. Daoud attempted to carry out social and economic reforms, but met with limited success. On April 27, 1978, the PDPA led a bloody coup, assassinating Daoud and his entire family, a deed known as the Saur Revolution. A new government was established and the country was renamed the Democratic Republic of Afghanistan. The PDPA regime would last, in some form or another, until April 1992.

The Democratic Republic of Afghanistan

The newly created Democratic Republic of Afghanistan immediately initiated a series of liberal and Marxist-Leninist laws. Traditional Islamic clothing and beards were forbidden and the mosques closed. The PDPA introduced laws meant to promote gender equality, increase education, and improve access to health care. Socialist land reforms and an attempt at promoting state atheism were also initiated. The PDPA invited the Soviet Union to assist in modernizing the economic and military infrastructure of Afghanistan. The Soviet Union agreed, and promised monetary aid of at least $1.2 billion.

The urban population either approved or was ambivalent about the new policies, but the majority of the population, residing in rural regions, fiercely opposed the reforms. When the Afghani people resisted, the government responded violently by arresting, torturing, and murdering village leaders, intellectuals, and members of the religious establishment. Observers estimate that between 10,000 and 27,000 people were killed and a further 14,000 to 20,000 more were imprisoned by the government in 1978 alone. Those who could afford to fled the country. In December 1978 the Soviet Union promised to provide military support for the PDPA if it was needed.

By spring of 1979 most of Afghanistan was in open revolt, with 24 out of 28 Afghan providences experiencing some form of rebellion. Many members of the Afghan army sympathized with the rebels, with more than half eventually either deserting the Afghan army or openly joining the insurrection. Because the PDPA's policies directly attacked traditional Islam, religion quickly became a unifying force, forging together the tribally and ethnically divided populations of Afghanistan. For many Muslims an attempt to replace traditional Islamic laws with modern reforms was an attack on Islam itself and so justified the call of jihad.

With large parts of the country in rebellion, the PDPA looked to the Soviet Union for help. The request was neither surprising nor unwelcomed by the Soviet Union. But what neither government could have predicted was the war that followed. It would prove to be an interminable war in which poorly equipped mujahideen guerrilla soldiers would successfully resist the full military might of one of the world's great superpowers. The insurgents received covert aid, in the form of weapons and training, from many other countries, including the United States.

The Soviet War in Afghanistan

On December 24, 1979, a Soviet army more than 100,000 soldiers strong entered Afghanistan. They joined forces with another 100,000 soldiers in the Afghan army. However, as the war dragged on, increasing numbers of the Afghan soldiers deserted the army

and joined forces with the mujahideen. For most of the war, the Soviet forces controlled urban areas while the mujahideen controlled the countryside. When the two forces met openly, the Soviets quickly defeated the rebels. But whenever the mujahideen used guerrilla war tactics they were much more successful. For the majority of the war, more than 80 percent of Afghanistan was beyond government or Soviet control.

Although the Afghani government had invited the Soviet forces, many countries termed the conflict an "invasion" and increased their financial and military support of the mujahideen. Thirty-four Islamic nations condemned the Soviet intervention, demanding "the immediate, urgent and unconditional withdrawal" of Soviet troops from Afghanistan. The United Nations (UN) General Assembly, agreeing with the Islamic nations, passed a resolution protesting the intervention by a vote of 104 to 10.

Many countries, including China, Egypt, Iran, Israel, Pakistan, Saudi Arabia, Turkey, the United Kingdom, and the United States, helped funnel military supplies to the mujahideen. Early reports suggested that between $6 billion and $20 billion were spent to aid the Afghani rebels by the United States and Saudi Arabia alone. More recent reports indicate it may have been as high as $40 billion in financial and military support, smuggled into Afghanistan through the Pakistani border.

During the 10-year occupation, between 850,000 and 1.5 million Afghan citizens were killed. An additional 6 million fled as refugees to Pakistan and Iran. The

UNDERSTANDING JIHAD

The term *jihad* is usually understood to mean an Islamic holy war. The term entered the popular English lexicon in the 21st century, after the September 11, 2001, attacks on the World Trade Center in New York City and the subsequent U.S.-led wars in Afghanistan and Iraq. But few non-Muslims, and even some Muslims, understand the complexities of jihad.

There are two forms of jihad: the Greater Jihad and the Lesser Jihad. The Greater Jihad is the spiritual struggle every person must engage in during the course of their life. For example, a person who struggles to remain positive while faced with a physical or mental illness or who attempts to remain honest and compassionate when faced with other personal problems may be said to be engaged in the Greater Jihad. It is a holy war between the desire for personal improvement and more base desires, a war in which Allah (God) is the only ally. The Lesser Jihad, by contrast, is a physical war. It can only be declared when an Islamic population is under true threat, and follows numerous rules meant to moderate the loss of life and damage to property. Very few military engagements have ever been remotely close to a true jihad.

Afghan anti-Soviet resistance fighters walk carrying the barrel of an anti-aircraft gun, in the mountainous Khunar area near Pakistani border in Afghanistan, on February 28, 1980. The Afghans repulsed the Red Army invasion (which lasted from 1979–89) with a huge human cost and with the material aid of the western world, above all, the United States. It is estimated that up to 1.5 million Afghans died during the conflict. *© AFP/Getty Images*

Afghan refugee population in Pakistan is considered to be the largest refugee population in the world. Afghan refugees eventually settled in countries all over the world, including 38,000 who immigrated to the United States and perhaps double that to European countries.

Faced with mounting political pressure abroad and economic pressures internally, the Soviet Union fully withdrew from Afghanistan on February 15, 1989. The retreat was deemed a psychological victory for the United States in the Cold War. But the USSR, and later the Russian Federation, continued to support the Communist Afghan government until its collapse in 1992.

⊕ Impacts and Issues

The Russian invasion of Afghanistan posed problems for the Russians that military force alone could not solve. Russian might was counterbalanced by the dedication of the mujahideen, who knew the terrain and received help from the international community. Marxist philosophy had little appeal to a tribal society with a strong devotion to Islam. However the eventual collapse of the Afghan government was in part a result of the refusal of the

Soviet Union to sell oil products in Afghanistan because of its own oil shortages. Grain shortages from drought and warfare and a destroyed infrastructure after more than a decade of war also contributed to the collapse and resulting civil war in Afghanistan.

International Response after the War

In 1989, after the Soviet retreat, a variety of Islamists and Afghan warlords took over Afghanistan. They were not a united group, however, and could not forge a stable government. Civil war continued to wreck the countryside. Perceiving the ruling mujahideen and local warlords as corrupt, a group of extreme Islamic purists known as the Taliban began a new rebellion and took power in 1996. They ruled Afghanistan according to one of the strictest interpretations of Muslim law ever known, violently enforcing public dress codes requiring total covering of women's bodies and forbidding women's education, public applause at sporting events, and many other behaviors.

With the Soviet army gone, U.S. interest in Afghanistan decreased too. Although it continued to send humanitarian assistance, the United States did not

Soviet troops prepare to leave Kabul, Afghanistan, on April 25, 1988. In May 1988 Afghanistan, Pakistan, the USSR, and the United States signed agreements providing for an end to foreign intervention in Afghanistan, and the USSR began withdrawing its forces. *© Robert Nickelsberg/Getty Images*

help with the reconstruction of the country. Prior to the war, Afghanistan was already considered one of the world's poorest nations. After the war, it was all but devastated.

Saudi Arabia and Pakistan, by contrast, attempted to help the nation rebuild. Saudi Arabia's ultra conservative government found an easy ally in the extremist mujahideen's interpretation of Islam. Saudi Arabia encouraged the rebels and Afghan warlords, through a combination of financial and ideological support, to institute *sharia,* or Islamic law, in Afghanistan. Pakistan viewed the war-torn country with a decidedly more pragmatic view. The Pakistani government forged relations with the Afghan warlords and then the Taliban in order to secure favorable trade interests and control over crucial trade routes.

The Soviet Union continued to offer support to Afghanistan until its own collapse in 1991. The Russian Federation assumed the USSR's agreements and debts. A report published in 2004 revealed that Afghanistan had more than $8 billion in debt, most of it owed to Russia. In 2007, however, the Russian Federation agreed

to cancel most of this debt since Afghanistan remains among the poorest nations on the globe.

The U.S. War in Afghanistan

On September 11, 2001, terrorists destroyed the World Trade Center in New York City. An Islamist terrorist organization called al-Qaeda took credit for the attack. Al-Qaeda's chief base of operation was in Afghanistan, where it was sponsored by the Taliban. None of the 9/11 attackers were Afghani, and the Taliban had not personally arranged the attack. Nevertheless, the United States called upon its North Atlantic Treaty Organization (NATO) allies to attack Afghanistan, remove the Taliban, and destroy al-Qaeda.

The United States' war in Afghanistan (2001–) is an ongoing conflict. Despite its vastly superior military power, the United States, like the Soviet Union before it, has found it difficult to subjugate and control Afghanistan. The Russian Federation has provided public support to the Afghan Northern Alliance, an army that has been fighting the Taliban since 1996. But, in an interesting twist, the Russian Federation may have also helped fund the Taliban during the 21st century. According to Taliban officials in June 2013, the Russian Federation secretly funded the Taliban against the U.S.-led coalition, providing financial and military support. The Russian embassy has neither confirmed nor denied these reports.

⊕ Future Implications

International relations between Afghanistan and Russia remain complex. The Russian Federation continues to offer humanitarian aid to Afghanistan and has forgiven the poorer country of the majority of its financial debts. Unresolved issues concerning Soviet prisoners of war and soldiers missing in action continue to be a source of conflict between the two nations.

Afghanistan has been at war for more than three decades and remains politically unstable and economically devastated. How the Afghan people will eventually restore peace to their land, whether through modern democracy, a return to Islamic fundamentalism, or some combination of the two, remains to be seen. Until a clear direction is chosen, however, international relationships with the Russian Federation will remain complex.

SEE ALSO *Afghan War; USSR: Dissolution*

BIBLIOGRAPHY

Books

Barfield, Thomas. *Afghanistan: A Cultural and Political History.* Princeton, NJ: Princeton University Press, 2010.

Brathwaite, Rodric. *Afgantsy: The Russians in Afghanistan 1978–1989.* New York: Oxford University Press, 2011.

Tomsen, Peter. *The Afghanistan Wars: Messianic Terrorism, Tribal Conflict, and the Failures of the Great Powers.* New York: PublicAffairs, 2011.

Web Sites

"The Soviet Occupation of Afghanistan." *PBS NewsHour.* http://www.pbs.org/newshour/updates/asia/july-dec06/soviet_10-10.html (accessed September 4, 2013).

"Timeline: Soviet War in Afghanistan." *BBC News.* http://news.bbc.co.uk/2/hi/7883532.stm (accessed September 4, 2013).

Trenin, Dmitri, and Malashenko, Alexei. "Afghanistan: A View From Moscow." *Carnegie Endowment,* 2010. http://carnegieendowment.org/files/trenin_afghan_final.pdf (accessed September 4, 2013).

Vietnam War

⊕ Introduction

The Vietnam War (1954–75) was the final chapter in a long struggle for Vietnamese unity and independence. For centuries the region had been politically divided by warring rival dynasties. In the late 1800s it became part of the French colony of Indochina. During the 20th century, the Communist Party of Vietnam led Vietnam's independence movement and succeeded in overthrowing French colonial rule in 1954 at the end of the First Indochina War (1946–54). The United States, in the midst of an intense Cold War rivalry with the Soviet Union, intervened to prevent the Communists from gaining control over all of Vietnam. Leaders in the United States at the time believed in the "domino theory"—the idea that if communism were allowed to take hold in any given nation, it would spread quickly throughout the region and shift the balance of world power toward the Soviets. This threat prompted the United States to pursue a policy of "containment" of communism. The peace agreement that ended the First Indochina War divided Vietnam into two countries: Communist-led North Vietnam and U.S.-supported South Vietnam. In 1965, the first American troops were sent to fight the Vietnamese Communist forces and defend the U.S.-supported government of South Vietnam.

For the next decade, the United States was entangled in a brutal war in Vietnam. This conflict is called the "Vietnam War" in the United States, the "American War" in Vietnam, and the "Second Indochina War" by much of the rest of the world. Despite superior military forces, the United States was drawn into a bloody stalemate against the North Vietnamese Army and its Communist allies in South Vietnam—guerrilla fighters known as Viet Cong. As the death toll mounted and antiwar sentiment increased, President Richard Nixon (1913–1994) withdrew U.S. troops from Vietnam in 1973. Two years later, North Vietnamese forces took over South Vietnam,

and Vietnam became unified as a single nation under Communist rule. Centuries of colonialism followed by decades of warfare left Vietnam with a shattered economy, a shell-shocked population, and a devastated environment. Almost 40 years later, modern Vietnam is still recovering and finding its place in the global community.

⊕ Historical Background

The origins of the Vietnam War are intimately tied to French colonialism in Southeast Asia. For the Vietnamese, the so-called "Vietnam War" was the final chapter in a decades-long fight to overthrow foreign colonial influence.

French Colonialism in Vietnam

France first became involved in Vietnamese affairs in the early 17th century. French Catholic missionaries were driven out of Japan and chose to resettle along what is now coastal Vietnam. Warring rival dynastic houses in central Vietnam and in the Red River Valley in northern Vietnam largely ignored the French missionaries, who soon succeeded in converting thousands of Vietnamese to Catholicism. French merchants flocked to the Vietnamese ports, and over time French political, economic, and religious stakes in the region increased.

During the late 18th century, the political struggles of Vietnam's rival dynasties became increasingly chaotic. A true peasant rebellion, the Tay Son Rebellion (1778–1802), toppled and virtually exterminated the Nguyen dynasty in southern Vietnam and the Trinh dynasty in northern Vietnam. The French head of the Vietnam Catholic mission chose to support Nguyen Anh (1762–1820), the one surviving prince of the Nguyen dynasty. With French support, Nguyen Anh soon reclaimed southern Vietnam and invaded the North. In 1802, he became the first ruler of a unified Vietnam and proclaimed himself Gia Long, Emperor of Vietnam. He

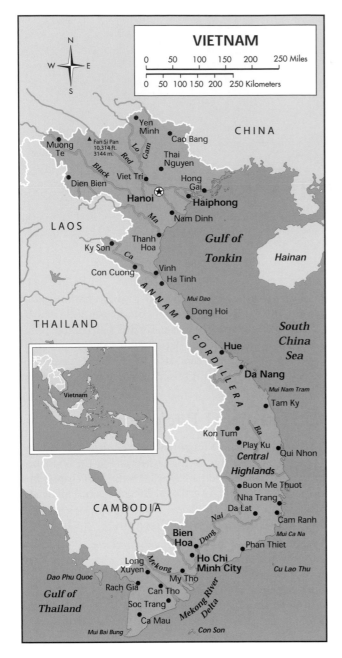

VIETNAM

© 2014 Cengage Learning

rewarded the French missionaries with a special place at his court and gave French merchants greater access to Vietnamese ports.

Gia Long and his successors were traditionalists committed to strengthening Confucianism—a political and philosophical system that originated in China—in Vietnam. This position was deeply disappointing to the French. Gia Long's successor, Minh Mang (1791–1841), saw French influence in general and Catholics in particular as a danger to his dynasty. When he persecuted Christian missionaries, France responded by increasing its political and military intervention in Vietnam. By the

1890s, all of Vietnam was under French control, and the Nguyen dynasty was little more than a puppet government. In the decades that followed, the French exploited the region, taking Vietnamese land and resources and giving the Vietnamese people little in return. French taxes and landownership policies led to extreme poverty and near starvation for the peasant population of Vietnam. The suffering people eventually came to despise the French colonial government, the puppet Nguyen dynasty, and the Confucian bureaucracy.

During the late 19th and early 20th centuries, a western-educated upper and middle class was formed in Vietnam. Their children were sent to French schools abroad and typically returned to Vietnam to work as colonial administrators or in other professional fields. But some chose instead to join nationalist organizations that protested French rule and discrimination. During the 1920s, the nationalist struggle was centered in the Vietnamese Nationalist Party, but they were brutally put down by the French. Their place was soon filled by the Communist Party of Vietnam.

Viet Minh: The Communist Party of Vietnam

The Viet Minh, or League for the Independence of Vietnam, had been founded in the early 1920s. Its leader was a charismatic young man, Nguyen Ai Quoc, later known as Ho Chi Minh (1890–1969). The son of a middle-class family, he had traveled widely as a seaman and had lived in Great Britain, France, China, the United States, and the Soviet Union. Ho embraced Marxism, a form of communism, in France and then became part of the Communist party in the Soviet Union. He soon became dedicated to the idea of Vietnamese independence. During the 1930s, the French colonial authorities tried to destroy the Viet Minh and succeeded in driving its leaders into exile in China. When Japan invaded French Indochina in 1940, an action that was part of World War II (1939–45), the Viet Minh's leaders were quick to take advantage of the chaos and continue their struggle for Vietnamese independence.

During World War II, the Viet Minh successfully wrested northern Vietnam from French rule. In August 1945, the Viet Minh took control over the city of Hanoi, which Ho Chi Minh declared the seat of a new free Democratic Republic of Vietnam. Ho downplayed his Communist philosophy and emphasized his patriotism and nationalism, which had greater resonance among the Vietnamese people. When a massive famine struck, the Viet Minh provided food for starving peasants, which helped increase their popularity and consolidate their power base in northern Vietnam.

First Indochina War

Determined to restore its international standing and reclaim its colonial holdings, France refused to accept North Vietnam's independence. For the next decade,

President of the People's Republic of China Liu Shaoqi (R) with his North Vietnamese counterpart Ho Chi Minh (L), in August 1959 during a lunch in Beijing, China.   © *AFP/Getty Images*

France and the Viet Minh fought for control over Vietnam in the First Indochina War. Under the leadership of General Vo Nguyen Giap (1911–2013), the Viet Minh used guerrilla tactics to fight the French Army and gradually took control of the countryside. In 1954, the Viet Minh captured the giant French fortress at Dien Bien Phu, and France surrendered to end the war.

The 1954 Geneva Peace Accords recognized independent North Vietnam as the Democratic Republic of Vietnam, but divided it from non-Communist South Vietnam at the 17th parallel. The treaty promised that the division was only temporary, and that free elections would be held within two years to decide which political party would control the North and the still politically fragmented South Vietnam. In preparation for the elections, Ho sought to eliminate political opposition and solidify his position. He also instituted a "land reform" campaign that was intended to redistribute land from wealthy private owners to peasants. This campaign turned vicious, however, as Communist officials used it as an excuse to punish people whose views differed from their own. Tens of thousands of Vietnamese who had cooperated with the French colonial authorities or

who were viewed as unfriendly to communism were sent to prison camps or executed. Fear of Communist reprisals, fed by rumors and propaganda circulated by anti-Communists in the South, convinced up to one million Vietnamese to migrate from North Vietnam to South Vietnam under the Geneva Accords in 1954. The elections promised under the treaty never materialized, however, due to the intervention of another foreign power: the United States.

United States Cold War Politics and Vietnam

Like other parts of the post-World War II world, Vietnam became entangled in the Cold War maneuvers of the United States and the Soviet Union. The Viet Minh had allied with the United States against Japan during World War II, but were dismayed to see the United States support France against them during the First Indochina War. When the Democratic Republic of Vietnam won its independence, it did so at a pivotal moment in the Cold War. The Soviet and American governments had antithetical political and economic systems, and each worried that the spread of the other's systems posed an imminent danger. The U.S. government thus considered it unacceptable for South Vietnam to adopt a Communist form of government and grew determined to prevent it at virtually any price.

The anti-Communist sentiment of the United States during the 1950s fed perceptions that South Vietnam, like South Korea before it, must be protected from takeover by Communist factions. Rather than allow free elections, which might result in Communist rule, the United States installed its own candidate, Ngo Dinh Diem (1901–1963), as president of South Vietnam (1955–1963). He was chosen by the United States because he was a Catholic and had been educated in the United States. However, these same traits, and his close ties to the U.S. government, quickly alienated the new president from most of the Vietnamese population. Moreover, Diem's government proved to be corrupt and repressive.

Diem established South Vietnam as a separate country formally known as the Republic of Vietnam. He tried to legitimize his rule by rigging elections and eliminating his rivals, particularly the leaders of the Communist party in South Vietnam. The South Vietnamese Communists soon formed a resistance group, the National Liberation Front, also referred to as the Viet Cong. The Viet Cong were determined to overthrow Diem and end American

influence in South Vietnam. Equally determined to preserve his rule, Diem built up the South Vietnamese military and set out to destroy the Viet Cong. In response, Communists in North Vietnam began to send aid to the Viet Cong.

As guerrilla warfare spread throughout southern Vietnam, and Diem's military response expanded, both the United States and North Vietnam escalated their own involvement. U.S. President John F. Kennedy (1917–1963) recognized that Diem's government was corrupt and unpopular. However, he also feared that a Communist victory in Vietnam would encourage more Communist movements in Southeast Asia and alter the Cold War balance of power. Kennedy increased the number of American military advisers in Vietnam, but Diem proved unable to stabilize his country. In April 1963, the U.S. Central Intelligence Agency (CIA) authorized Vietnamese generals to overthrow Diem in a military coup, a deed which swiftly led to the president's execution.

South Vietnam was plunged into extreme political instability as one military regime after another came into power. Each new government was weaker than the last, and each was viewed as a puppet government of the

South Vietnamese soldiers with a captured Viet Cong guerilla they had flushed from the bush in May 1964. © *Rolls Press/Popperfoto/ Getty Images*

United States. Since these short-lived governments also failed to stop the rising power and popularity of the Viet Cong, the U.S. government decided it was time to commit U.S. military troops to the conflict. American political and military leaders thought that the U.S. troops would achieve a swift victory in Vietnam, but the Viet Cong and the Vietnamese desire for self-determination would prove much stronger than the United States anticipated.

U.S. Military in Vietnam

In November 1963, U.S. President Lyndon Johnson (1908–1973) gained congressional support for an unlimited military deployment to Vietnam. As had been the case during the Korean War (1950–53), the United States did not formally declare war, an action that requires a formal resolution from Congress. Instead, Vietnam was deemed a "police action." The U.S. government drafted tens of thousands of young men to fight in an "undeclared war." In total, more than 500,000 American soldiers fought in Vietnam, approximately one-third of whom were drafted (rather than volunteering), over the course of the decade-long conflict.

The U.S. military strategy for Vietnam was dominated by massive bombing campaigns over both North and South Vietnam. In terms of scale, more bombs were dropped on Vietnam than in all the theaters of World

American napalm bombs explode in fields south of Saigon during the Vietnam War. Napalm kills by asphyxiation and burning, and was first used by the United States against Japan in World War II. © *Hulton Archive/Getty Images*

MY LAI MASSACRE

One of the terrible atrocities of the Vietnam War was the massacre of Vietnamese civilians at the villages of My Lai and My Khein Son My. U.S. soldiers of the "Charlie" Company, which had suffered significant losses in Viet Cong sneak attacks, had been told that the villages were a Viet Cong stronghold. On March 16, 1968, the Charlie Company attacked the villages and killed between 347 and 504 unarmed civilians, including women, children, infants, and the elderly. The soldiers also raped village women and committed other atrocities. Only three American soldiers, from a passing helicopter crew, tried to stop the massacre and protect the wounded. As word of the massacre became public knowledge, it prompted global outrage and fed the flames of the U.S. antiwar movement.

U.S. military officials managed to cover up the violent incident for several months. Eventually, 26 of the soldiers involved in the atrocities were charged with criminal offenses for their actions at My Lai, but only the platoon leader, Second Lieutenant William Calley, was convicted. Although he was found guilty of killing 22 villagers, Calley served only three and a half years under house arrest. The three men who tried to stop the killings (Hugh Thompson Jr., Lawrence Colburn, and Glenn Andreotta) were initially decried as "traitors" by military officials, but they were later vindicated and decorated by the Army for their actions. The My Lai massacre contributed to the characterization of U.S. soldiers in Vietnam as "baby killers," which became a rallying cry for the antiwar movement in the United States. Despite growing public dissatisfaction with the prosecution of the war, however, U.S. involvement would continue for another five years.

War II. The United States also used chemical weapons, mainly the concentrated herbicide Agent Orange, to defoliate the jungles of South Vietnam and destroy food crops in North Vietnam. The Viet Cong, by contrast, relied on guerrilla tactics—including booby traps, sneak attacks, and blending in with the civilian population—to lock the U.S. troops in a war of attrition. Despite the superior military power of the United States, it achieved only a stalemate against the North Vietnamese Army and Viet Cong forces.

Because the Viet Cong was a guerrilla army, they did not fight the Americans in open combat nor did they wear distinctive uniforms. Instead, they attacked from the relative safety of the jungle and blended in with the civilian population. This caused the U.S. troops to mistrust the entire Vietnamese population, since it was difficult to distinguish friends from enemies. Civilians throughout Vietnam were killed, both accidentally and deliberately, by U.S. troops. For the great majority of the Vietnamese population, the war with the United States was a brutally traumatic experience in which their country was all but destroyed by firebombs and foreign troops. Some South Vietnamese civilians viewed the Americans as foreign aggressors and quietly supported the Viet Cong, while others feared a Communist takeover and sought U.S. protection. Most people felt caught in the middle and only wanted an end to the destructive war.

The Tet Offensive

Throughout the conflict, U.S. leaders insisted that the war was nearly over and that it would end in an American victory. These predictions were repeatedly proven to be wishful thinking. On January 31, 1968, the Viet Cong and North Vietnamese Army troops attacked over 100 cities throughout Vietnam as well as a Marine combat base and the U.S. military headquarters and the U.S. Embassy in Saigon. The coordinated attack was launched during Tet (Lunar New Year), a holiday which had traditionally acted as a brief cease-fire in the war. The scale of the attack shocked the U.S. and South Vietnamese forces, but they soon retaliated with massive firepower. Approximately 50,000 people died during the Tet Offensive, the majority of them civilians or North Vietnamese and Viet Cong soldiers. Although the U.S. military technically prevailed, the massive scale and impressive coordination of the Tet Offensive shocked U.S. leaders and the American people, giving North Vietnam a significant public relations victory.

Although the United States had many battleground successes, it failed to gain a comprehensive victory. As the war dragged on and American casualties mounted, the U.S. and global antiwar movements gained in strength. Antiwar protestors borrowed heavily from the nonviolent tactics of the U.S. civil rights movement. Protesters demanded the withdrawal of American troops and a peaceful resolution to the conflict, arguing that the U.S. government and military were acting like brutes rather than protectors of freedom.

The U.S. Retreat

Although he was eligible for re-election, President Johnson chose not to run in the 1968 presidential race. Republican candidate Richard Nixon recognized the mounting public distaste for the war and promised to end it if elected president. Once he won the presidency, Nixon announced a policy called "Vietnamization," which involved gradually withdrawing U.S. troops while preparing South Vietnamese military forces to assume responsibility for defending the country against a Communist takeover. At the same time, though, he made several controversial decisions to escalate the war in hopes of achieving a quick victory. In 1969, Nixon came under criticism for expanding the conflict into Cambodia. He also intensified the bombing of North Vietnam and opened diplomatic channels with the Soviet Union and China, hoping to get them to pressure North Vietnam into ending the war. As the war dragged on, Nixon slowly withdrew U.S. military forces and tried to negotiate an end to the conflict that would let the United States achieve "peace with honor."

In January 1973, the U.S. military phase of the war officially ended with the signing of the Paris Peace Accords. It was a complex agreement signed by Britain, France, the Soviet Union, the United States, North Vietnam, the Viet Cong, and South Vietnam. Some American troops remained in South Vietnam to keep the peace, but the bombing campaigns were halted. The treaty promised that free elections would be held within two years and that South Vietnam would be allowed full political self-determination. The peace treaty did not end the conflict, however, and in April 1975, North Vietnamese troops stormed the capital city of Saigon in South Vietnam. The last remaining American troops were helicoptered out as the city fell. Saigon was renamed Ho Chi Minh City, and Vietnam was reunified as a single nation under Communist rule.

⊕ Impacts and Issues

The end of the war unfortunately did not mean an immediate end to suffering for most of Vietnam's population. The Communist government quickly began a process of collectivizing farms, resulting in an economic collapse and dramatic inflation. Hundreds of thousands of South Vietnamese people were left as war refugees without any significant national or international aid to help them start new lives. More than one million Vietnamese, mostly from the South, were sent to "re-education camps" where they were forced to perform hard labor and sometimes permanently imprisoned or tortured. Murder, or "political disappearance," was rampant on all levels of society for several decades. Today, Vietnam still faces many social and economic problems that are direct results of decades of war and tyranny.

More than one million Vietnamese and 58,000 Americans died during the Vietnam War. The South Asian country was left with a shattered economy, devastated environment, and traumatized people. Vietnam's revolutionary leaders attempted to push hardline Marxist-Leninist (even Stalinist) political and economic

South Vietnamese refugees in boats approach a U.S. warship to seek refuge from the invading force from the North in April 1975 in the South China Sea near Saigon. American involvement in the Vietnam War came to an end when troops from communist North Vietnam invaded Saigon, the capital of the Republic of Vietnam in the South. © Dirck Halstead/Getty Images

THE CHILDREN OF THE WAR

One of the saddest chapters of the Vietnam War was that it created a huge population of interracial children who were never fully accepted by either Vietnam or the United States. Sexual relationships between American soldiers and Vietnamese women were common during the war. In some cases, couples formed romantic relationships and married. In other cases, Vietnamese women served as prostitutes for American servicemen or were victims of rape. The children that resulted were considered "half-breeds" or even "the dust of life." Interracial children were often considered the children of prostitutes, regardless of their origins. Most of these children, and their mothers, were treated as virtual pariahs in their homeland.

Some American soldiers sought to bring their Vietnamese wives and children back to the United States. Those who were successful faced their own challenges in helping their Vietnamese wives integrate into American society and in raising interracial children. In 1988, the Amerasian Homecoming Act attempted to address this lingering issue by allowing approximately 23,000 interracial children and young adults to immigrate to the United States.

agendas throughout the country. These policies stifled growth and left the people almost as impoverished as they had been during colonial times.

By the late 1980s, the obvious failures of the system, along with the collapse of Communist regimes in Eastern Europe, promoted measures that attempted to liberalize and expand the Vietnamese market. In 1986, Vietnam's government instituted a number of political and economic reforms and began encouraging private ownership within both the agricultural and industrial sectors. Vietnam also opened its markets to foreign investment and received an encouraging response from European and Japanese corporations, and eventually American firms. The combination of these policy changes stimulated massive economic growth. Today, Vietnam has one of the fastest-growing economies in the world. Unfortunately, many Vietnamese workers toil in sweatshop conditions, and social and gender inequality is marked throughout the country. The free education system and other public services have largely disappeared.

⊕ Future Implications

As of 2014, Vietnam remained one of the last few remaining single-party Communist countries. It has close diplomatic and economic ties with the Communist People's Republic of China, as well as most other countries in Southeast Asia. Since the end of the Cold War, Vietnam has significantly expanded its economic ties to the Western world. Since 1995, Vietnam has enjoyed normal diplomatic relations with both France and the United States. The return of U.S. soldiers who were missing-in-action (MIAs) helped to heal relations between the two nations. Beginning in the 1980s, both nations worked together to answer questions surrounding MIAs, and the remains of hundreds of missing soldiers have been repatriated to the United States. In 1995, the United States flag was raised over a new U.S. embassy, and the administration of President Bill Clinton worked with the Vietnamese on a bilateral trade agreement that was signed in 2000.

SEE ALSO *Cambodia; Cold War*

BIBLIOGRAPHY

Books

Caputo, Philip. *A Rumor of War.* New York: Holt Paperbacks, 1996.

Lawrence, Mark Atwood. *The Vietnam War: A Concise International History.* Oxford: Oxford University Press, 2010.

Logeval, Fredrik. *Embers of War: The Fall of an Empire and the Making of America's Vietnam.* New York: Random House, 2012.

Weist, Andrew. *Vietnam: A View from the Front Lines.* Oxford: Osprey, 2013.

Web Sites

Brigham, Robert K. "Battlefield Vietnam: A Brief History." *PBS.* http://www.pbs.org/battlefieldvietnam/history/index.html (accessed May 31, 2013).

"In Pictures: The Vietnam War." *BBC News.* http://news.bbc.co.uk/2/shared/spl/hi/picture_gallery/05/in_pictures_the_vietnam_war/html/1.stm (accessed May 31, 2013).

"The United States Of America Vietnam War Commemoration: Interactive Timeline." *U.S. Department of Defense.* http://www.vietnamwar50th.com/timeline/ (accessed May 31, 2013).

"Vietnam War." *History.com.* http://www.history.com/topics/vietnam-war (accessed May 31, 2013).

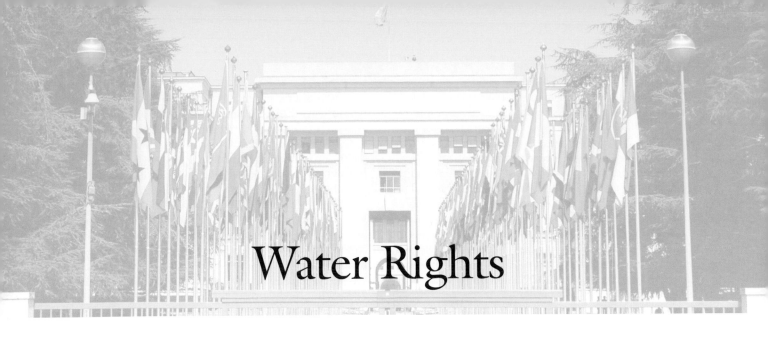

Water Rights

⊕ Introduction

Water is necessary for life in addition to its many household, agricultural, and industrial uses. While 70 percent of the planet is covered in water, only 2.5 percent of that amount is freshwater, and far less than 1 percent is easily accessible for human use. This makes it a very precious and highly prized resource.

Hundreds of millions of people lack ready access to clean water for drinking and cooking, and the consumption of contaminated water proves deadly for millions each year. The surge of the global population and the corresponding emergence of water-intensive industries, pollution, urbanization, and climate change all contribute to steadily increasing scarcity and vulnerability of sustainable water supplies.

In addition, access to navigable waterways (rivers, lakes, and oceans) is a major economic driver for countries' economies, not only because of trade made possible through shipping traffic but because of the tourism industry that often thrives around waterways and seashores.

⊕ Historical Background

Access to water—especially to freshwater—causes significant conflict, and the right to water resources is a crucial issue in diplomatic efforts to resolve longstanding conflicts in the Middle East, North Africa, South Asia, and many other parts of the world. The areas with the least amount of water per capita frequently experience conflict, both legal and military, over scarce water supplies. Secretary General of the United Nations Ban Ki-moon (1944–), in a 2007 column in the *Washington Post*, stated that water shortages and corresponding food shortages were a cause of violent conflicts in Darfur, Somalia, Côte d'Ivoire, and Burkina Faso. He blamed the water shortage in Darfur on drier weather patterns suffered by the region in recent years, a phenomenon at least partly attributable to global climate change.

Water rights also can include the rights to the commodities in the water, such as fish, oil, and natural gas. Many people rely on fish as their primary food source, but the right to fish in specific waters can be contentious. The Atlantic cod, which sustained much of northeastern North America for hundreds of years, became severely depleted by the 1990s due to overfishing. The cod population in the Atlantic Ocean has dropped by more than 99 percent since the 18th century. The Canadian government was forced to close its cod fisheries, causing devastating economic consequences throughout Newfoundland, where it had been a major industry for hundreds of years.

"SMART" PUMPS

Whereas the industrialized world increasingly relies on expensive aqueducts, canals, dams, pipelines, and pumping systems to address localized freshwater shortages, such "concrete and steel" solutions often remain beyond the reach of a large percentage of the developing world's population. Tens of millions of people in rural areas of Africa rely on hand pumps for their primary water supply. However, an estimated one-third of all such pumps are broken at any given time.

Broken pumps deny rural residents a ready source of freshwater, putting them at risk of water shortages and waterborne diseases from less clean secondary sources. A June 2012 report in the *Journal of Hydroinformatics* introduced a project in rural Africa to outfit hand-operated water pumps with text message-capable data transmitters. Theses "smart" pumps, deployed in 60 Kenyan villages as of the middle of 2013, use mobile phone networks to send text messages about water flow or breakdowns in an effort to provide real-time information on well water supplies and expedite needed repairs.

Nations have fought many wars to secure access to harbors. Having a port, especially one that can accommodate deep-hulled ships, is critical to many types of trade and industrial development. Having access to a warm-water port that does not freeze over in the winter allows countries to provide a naval defense. Russia, for example, is a vast country, but is largely landlocked because all its ports are in northern latitudes that freeze in the winter. Among the great powers in world history, only Russia has lacked reliable naval access. Russia has fought many wars over hundreds of years, against enemies ranging from Sweden and Poland to Turkey, Mongolia, and Japan, in its quest to secure access to warm-water ports on the Pacific Ocean and the Baltic, Black, and Caspian Seas. While the invention of long-range ballistic missiles reduced the necessity of having a warm-water port for military purposes, even today, some analysts speculate that Russia's reluctance to censor allies in the Middle East, particularly Syria, comes from a desire to protect access to ports. (Russia maintains a naval facility in the Syrian port of Tartus, on the Mediterranean.)

Ethiopia, one of the poorest countries in the world, was landlocked until it federated with its neighbor Eritrea in 1962. Eritrea was attractive because it had two ports along the Red Sea. However, the province of Eritrea voted to secede and form its own country, which would leave Ethiopia landlocked once again. The two countries fought a lengthy war before Eritrea gained its independence in 1993. One of the primary diplomatic priorities for Ethiopia is making and maintaining relationships that will allow it reliable access to nearby ports.

Access to Freshwater

While the world's oceans seem vast, only 2.5 percent of the world's water is freshwater suitable for human and animal consumption and for agriculture. According to 2013 estimates by the World Health Organization (WHO) and the United Nations Children's Fund (UNICEF), approximately 783 million people worldwide do not have access to an improved source of drinking water. Lack of access to clean water also corresponds to inadequate sanitation facilities for 2.5 billion people. As a consequence, an estimated 5 million people die every year from waterborne diseases. Over the last several decades, the efforts of the WHO, UNICEF, and other organizations have decreased the number of people who lack an improved water source. These organizations have conducted most of their water improvement work in Africa and Asia, the two continents that will see the greatest stress placed on water resources over the next 20 years due to economic development and rapid population increases.

Water pollution occurs in many different ways, ranging from bacteria and other pathogens to litter and other objects left in the water. As shown here, people are looking through debris in the Yamuna River in New Delhi for coins and other valuable items that were among various religious offerings left in the water. Considered one of the holiest rivers in India, the Yamuna River has been dying a slow death from pollution for decades despite the investment of millions of dollars to preserve its ecosystem. According to the Central Pollution Control Board (CPCB), which monitors the water quality of the Yamuna in Delhi, 70 percent of the pollution in the river is from untreated sewage while the remaining 30 percent is from industrial sources, agricultural run-off, and domestic garbage. © Prakash Singh/AFP/Getty Images

In many parts of the world, water pollution and poor sanitation are major contributors to the contamination of drinking water. High levels of bacteria and other pathogens result in epidemic levels of waterborne diseases. According to a 2004 report on water safety by the WHO, diarrheal diseases alone kill 1.8 million people per year. The WHO attributes 88 percent of these deaths to unsafe drinking water. Proper sanitation and access to an improved water source are important to preventing illness and death from waterborne diseases.

In 2010 a study published in the science journal *Nature* estimated that 80 percent of the world's population is vulnerable to freshwater supply shortages. These threats include scarcity, pollution, improper management, and political instability. The study concluded that safeguarding watersheds, wetlands, and floodplains is essential to preserving freshwater resources.

⊕ Impacts and Issues

The planet's warming climate carries a multitude of threats to the sustainability of global freshwater systems. Climate change causes the shrinking or disappearance of mountain glaciers and snow packs that are the source of many of the world's major rivers and increases the frequency and severity of droughts as well as destructive hurricanes and tsunamis. These long-range trends point towards the drying up of mountain- or rain-fed water systems, disrupting the natural balances on which living ecosystems rely and exacerbating the vulnerability of human settlements and agriculture.

Water Rights and Political Conflict

Contested claims to land are the most common cause of tension and armed conflict between groups of people, but these disputes often have an underlying component of competition for limited water supplies. Features of geography or imbalances of political and military power can lead to the perception of inequity in the allocation of shared water resources.

For example, water rights are a crucial but often overlooked dimension of the Israeli–Palestinian conflict. Control over the Jordan River, according to numerous historians as well as former Israeli officials, was a major factor leading to the 1967 Six-Day War, in which Israel defeated its Arab neighbors. The Israelis have continued

Palestinian boys and girls hold plastic containers as they wait to fill-up with fresh water from the desalination station in Deir al-Balah refugee camp in the center of the Gaza Strip on March 26, 2013. Amnesty International has accused Israel of denying Palestinians adequate access to water while allowing Jewish settlers in the occupied West Bank almost unlimited supplies. Israel, the human rights group said, restricts availability of water in the Palestinian territories "by maintaining total control over the shared resources and pursuing discriminatory policies." © Mahmud Hams/AFP/Getty Images

to occupy much of the territory they gained in this war, including the West Bank, the Gaza Strip, and the Golan Heights, giving them control over the Sea of Galilee and the West Bank mountain headwaters. Israel has exerted its authority to allocate the lion's share of waters from the West Bank aquifer to Israel and to Jewish settlers in the Palestinian territory. Israel appropriates 90 percent of available water supplies from the Jordan River, an imbalance enshrined in the Oslo Accords and maintained by military force. Water rights are therefore an underlying complication in Middle East peace negotiations and the challenge of reaching a viable two-state solution.

Tensions over water also contribute to the contentious relations between India and Pakistan. The Indus Waters Treaty, ratified in 1960, is widely considered a diplomatic success. The treaty guarantees Pakistan the use of the majority of water from the Indus River, although the river's sources are located in India. Pakistan subsequently constructed one of the world's largest irrigation systems for agricultural purposes. The agreement has come under strain in the early 21st century due to India's ambition

to build a series of hydroelectric dams, using the waters of the Indus system to provide power for its growing economy. The International Court of Arbitration in The Hague ruled in February 2013, in a case brought by Pakistan, that India can divert only a minimum of water for a planned electric plant on the Kishanganga River.

The Nile, the world's longest river and source of Egypt's ancient glory, flows through 10 countries on its way to its delta in northern Egypt. Formal agreements in place since the colonial era grant Egypt the right to the vast majority of Nile waters. However, the other riparian states (those that abut the river) and scientific experts have long called for joint use and management of its water resources. In 2010 a cooperative framework for the Nile basin, known as the Entebbe Agreement, was approved by representatives of Burundi, Democratic Republic of the Congo, Ethiopia, Kenya, Rwanda, Tanzania, and Uganda. The pact called for the formation of a Nile River Commission to resolve disputes over water sharing. However, Egypt and Sudan, the downstream states, rejected the document. Egypt continued

A picture taken on May 28, 2013, shows the Blue Nile in Guba, Ethiopia, during its diversion ceremony. Ethiopia has begun diverting the Blue Nile as part of a giant dam project, officials said on May 29, 2013, risking potential unease from downstream nations Sudan and Egypt. The $4.2 billion (3.2 billion euro) Grand Renaissance Dam hydroelectric project had to divert a short section of the river—one of two major tributaries to the main Nile—to allow the main dam wall to be built. "To build the dam, the natural course must be dry," said Addis Tadele, spokesman for the Ethiopian Electric Power Corporation (EEPCo), a day after a formal ceremony at the construction site. © *William Lloyd-George/AFP/Getty Images*

to raise objections in 2013 to Ethiopia's Renaissance Dam project on the Blue Nile, which when completed would be the largest hydroelectric dam in Africa.

Location of Water Is a Challenge

Less than 1 percent of the world's water is freshwater available for human use, but the location of some of these resources is a major concern. Much of the world's available freshwater is not located near growing population centers. The context of the distribution problem ranges from population centers developing in areas with scarce water resources to a lack of development in areas with abundant freshwater. For example, the Amazon River Basin contains approximately 15 percent of Earth's freshwater but supplies water to less than 1 percent of the world's population.

Water is so valuable that between 15 and 20 percent of Earth's freshwater is exported from one place to another. When a geographic area appears to have an overabundance of freshwater, they can sell it to their less water-rich neighbors. Water rights are often privately held by the person whose property it is on. The property owner can sell the water (and rights to the water) separately from the land itself. In the case of a river, that can mean that an upstream land owner may be able to divert and sell the water, leaving his downstream neighbors with none. Pakistan has accused India of diverting water, thereby causing Pakistani farms to dry up.

Lack of water has led to some unusual economic configurations. In some parts of California, farmers are paid not to plant and grow crops so that they will not use the water that growing crops require. The water that they are not using—the water "saved"—is then available for people living in cities such as Los Angeles and San Diego.

Management and Mismanagement

In Central Asia the Aral Sea continues to suffer from Soviet-era diversion and mismanagement of water. Once considered the world's fourth largest lake, much of the area once covered by the Aral Sea is now classified as dry salt flats. In just over 50 years, the area of land covered by the lake has shrunk by an estimated 70 percent. Cities and towns that once drew water from the Aral Sea now face chronic water shortages. So dramatic was the loss of water that in 1990, the sea actually divided into two sections and has since shrunk even more and divided into smaller sections. After touring the area in April 2010, Ban Ki-moon promised regional leaders that agencies of the UN would provide assistance and expertise if leaders could agree on a multinational recovery plan.

A picture taken August 4, 2005, shows camels passing by rusty shipwrecks at the place called "Sheeps cemetery" in Dzhambul settlement, some 39 miles (64 kilometers) from the town of Aralsk. The Aral Sea, once the world's fourth largest lake, had been drying up for decades, and in 2007, the salted lake had shrunk to 10 percent of its original size and had split into four unequal parts, all highly polluted, destroying once flourishing fishing industries and local economies. It also caused changes in the local climate with the loss of moisture. It has been called one of the world's worst ecological disasters. © Vyacheslav Oseledko/AFP/Getty Images

In addition to population migration and urbanization, tourism also affects water needs. Local populations, preservationists, and tourism interests have fought over scarce water resources in Botswana's Kalahari Desert region. Tourism interests and animal conservationists had won rights to drill water wells, but local tribes (sometimes collectively referred to as bushmen) had been denied similar rights by the courts. In January 2011 the higher courts granted the Kalahari bushmen rights to access some existing wells and to drill new water wells in the desert conservation area.

⊕ Future Implications

The right to drill and extract oil and natural gas is also an issue impacting water rights. Several high-profile drilling accidents have caused major water and coastline pollution and raised concerns about who financially benefits from deep-water exploration and who bears the costs of cleanup. The long-term implications of accidents such as explosion of the 2010 *Deepwater Horizon* oil rig that killed 11 workers and created an oil spill in the Gulf of Mexico—during which nearly 5 million barrels of oil spewed into the sea, killing marine life, destroying marine ecosystems, and devastating fishing and tourism industries along the gulf—are unknown. Environmentalists in the United States and other countries are fighting to prevent the oil and gas industry from extracting gas from shale rock formations through hydraulic fracturing, an unconventional technology that requires use of several million gallons of freshwater for each wellhead.

The deepest parts of the oceans are still largely unexplored, and scientists are optimistic about finding new and interesting (and potentially valuable) life forms and mineral deposits. Already countries are raising concerns about who owns the discoveries and products created from these resources. For example, compounds derived from non-deep-sea marine species have already shown promise in treating Alzheimer's disease, a progressive and debilitating condition affecting the brain.

However access to safe freshwater is the most pressing water rights' issue. Some analysts predict that water will be the primary resource causing war in the future. Without freshwater people cannot survive, and as the population of the world continues to grow there is more pressure on the water supply. A 2012 report from the U.S. Director of National Intelligence predicted that by the year 2030, global water demand will exceed sustainable supplies by 40 percent. There is also little consensus over who owns the water and what that means. There is even less consensus over how to manage water and the benefits derived from water now and for the future.

Despite this lack of consensus, there is a growing sense that the human right to water is under increasing strain worldwide and the crisis needs to be addressed. The UN General Assembly designated 2013 as the UN International Year of Water Cooperation. The importance of safe drinking water and the limited nature of the resource will require that nations devise solutions, through diplomacy or conflict, for sharing frequently scarce freshwater supplies. Increasing world population and global climate change will make water rights issues more prominent in the coming decades.

SEE ALSO *Arctic and Antarctic Ownership; Global Environmental Treaties; United Nations*

BIBLIOGRAPHY

Books

Grinlinton, David, and Prue Taylor, eds. *Property Rights and Sustainability: The Evolution of Property Rights to Meet Ecological Challenges.* Boston: Martinus Nikhoff Publishers, 2011.

Hi, Desheng. *Water Rights: An International and Comparative Study.* Seattle: IWA, 2006.

Vajpeyi, Dhirendra K. *Water Resource Conflicts and International Security: A Global Perspective.* Lanham, MD: Lexington Books, 2012.

Zeitoun, Mark. *Power and Water in the Middle East: The Hidden Politics of the Palestinian-Israeli Water Conflict.* London: I.B. Tauris and Co., 2008.

Periodicals

Brochmann, M., and Nils Petter Gleditsch. "Shared Rivers and Conflict: A Reconsideration." *Political Geography* 31, no. 8 (November 2012): 519–527.

Nevin, Tom. "End in Sight for River Water Wars?" *African Business* 395 (March 2013): 76–77.

Peterson, Scott. "Why a Dam in Afghanistan Might Set Back Peace." *Christian Science Monitor* (July 30, 2013).

Vorosmarty, C. J., et al. "Global Threats to Human Water Security and River Biodiversity" *Nature* 467 (September 2010): 555–61.

Web Sites

International Water Law Project. http://www.internationalwaterlaw.org (accessed July 31, 2013).

Thomson, Patrick, Rob Hope, and Tim Foster. "GSM-Enabled Remote Monitoring of Rural Handpumps: A Proof-of-Concept Study." *Journal of Hydroinformatics.* http://www.iwaponline.com/jh/up/jh2012183.htm (accessed November 12, 2013).

United Nations. *UN-Water.* http://www.unwater.org/index.html (accessed July 31, 2013).

World Water Council. http://www.worldwatercouncil.org/index.php?id=1 (accessed July 31, 2013).

Weapons of Mass Destruction

⊕ Introduction

The term weapons of mass destruction (WMD) most commonly refers to nuclear, biological, or chemical weapons. A WMD is a political and legal term for large-scale weaponry that can kill many people and/or cause significant damage to an area.

According to U.S. law, the term "weapon of mass destruction" is defined as "any explosive; incendiary or poison gas bomb; grenade; rocket having a propellant charge of more than four ounces; missile having an explosive or incendiary charge of more than one-quarter ounce; mine;" or similar device, "designed or intended to cause death or serious bodily injury through the release, dissemination, or impact of toxic or poisonous chemicals, or their precursors;" using or "involving a biological agent, toxin, or vector;" or "any weapon that is designed to release radiation or radioactivity at a level dangerous to human life."

WMDs may include chemical, biological, radiological, and nuclear weapons. The term was first coined in 1937 by the archbishop of Canterbury in reference to the aerial bombing of Guernica during the Spanish Civil War (1936–39) and the eruption of the Sino-Japanese War (1937–45). After the atomic bombing of Hiroshima and Nagasaki, Japan, in 1945 and throughout the Cold War (1945–91), the term WMD was also used to refer to nuclear and radiological weapons.

The phrase gained popular current use prior to the U.S. invasion of Iraq in 2003. The U.S. and other governments justified the invasion by alleging that Iraq had WMDs, in particular nuclear and chemical weapons, which were a threat to the United States and its allies. The term WMDs is now so broadly applied that devices from homemade bombs to semiautomatic rifles may be referred to as WMDs.

⊕ Historical Background

The first known usage of the term weapon of mass destruction was by Cosmo Gordon Lang, archbishop of Canterbury (1864–1945). The archbishop had lived through World War I (1914–18), in which chemical warfare had been widely used with devastating effect. Lang was distressed to learn of new wars in Spain and China. The London *Times* quoted him in December 1937, saying,

> Who can think of this present time without a sickening of the heart of the appalling slaughter, the suffering, the manifold misery brought by war to Spain and to China? Who can think without horror of what another widespread war would mean, waged as it would be with all the new weapons of mass destruction?

The archbishop rightly feared that another world war would encourage the development and usage of new and increasingly sophisticated weaponry.

During World War II (1939–45) the United States and its Western allies feverishly raced Nazi Germany to develop nuclear weapons while Japan did extensive research on offensive biological weapons. Chemical warfare was also used during World War II, although not to the degree employed during World War I.

However, on August 6, 1945, the first nuclear weapon, nicknamed Little Boy, was dropped by the United States on the city of Hiroshima, Japan. Three days later another nuclear bomb, Fat Man, was dropped on Nagasaki, Japan. The bombs killed approximately 200,000 people, mostly civilians, and resulted in Japan's surrender. While the morality of use of atomic weapons remains a subject of passionate debate, many military historians estimate that compelling Japan's surrender as it was preparing for a population-wide "to the death" defense against an Allied invasion, saved more lives than

Headline from the Chicago Daily News proclaiming the bombing of Japan with atomic bombs, Chicago, 1945. Though it was argued the bombs shortened the length of World War II by causing the Japanese to surrender, the controversial use of atomic bombs caused long-lasting devastation to Hiroshima and Nagasaki, Japan, and ultimately led to the arms buildup of weapons of mass destruction that characterized the Cold War. © *Chicago History Museum/Getty Images*

were lost in the bombings. Regardless, the results of the blasts were horrific, and the bombings of Hiroshima and Nagasaki remain the first and only time that nuclear weapons have been used in warfare.

Nuclear Arms Race

For four years the United States was the only country in the world that possessed nuclear weapons. But on August 29, 1949, the Soviet Union (officially the Union of Soviet Socialist Republics, or USSR) made headlines when it successfully tested its first fully functional nuclear weapon. The United States and the USSR were already in the early stages of the Cold War, and both nations feared that the other would unleash their nuclear weapons. An arms race erupted in which each nation built more nuclear weapons and stockpiled other weapons of mass destruction, hoping to intimidate the other into submission or at the least maintain an uneasy peace.

As the arms race escalated, it soon became apparent that any use of nuclear weapons by the United States or the USSR might result in mutual destruction, not only of the two nations in question, but perhaps the entire world. In fact this became a deterrent policy known as M.A.D. (Mutual Assured Destruction). No country with nuclear weapons would strike another because there was no advantage in the action. Any first strike would result in the ultimate destruction of all parties in the conflict. M.A.D. policy prevented the two world powers from going to war.

Key to M.A.D. policies was maintaining nuclear weapons parity so that one superpower would not have a first strike or survivability advantage over the other. Other nations joined the arms race, developing their own nuclear weapons or borrowing them from the U.S. or USSR.

⊕ Impacts and Issues

More than 30 nations are currently known to openly or secretly possess at least one form of WMDs. Governments also fear that terrorist or extra-governmental organizations may eventually gain control of WMDs.

Chemical WMDs Chemical weapons are devices that use chemicals to inflict death or harm to humans. Variations of chemical warfare have been used since the advent of war, including poison spears and arrows. The first recorded use of gas warfare was noxious fumes used by the Spartans against an Athenian city during the Peloponnesian War (431–401 BC). Numerous other instances of chemical warfare can be found throughout history, worldwide.

Modern chemical weapons can be dispersed in gas, liquid, and solid forms. Nerve gas, mustard gas, and tear gas are all forms of chemical weapons. Chemical weapons were widely used in the trench warfare of World War I.

As of 2012 only four nations—North Korea, Russia, Syria, and the United States—confirmed possession of chemical weapon stockpiles.

Signing of strategic arms limitation talks treaty (SALT 1) in the Kremlin, Moscow, USSR, on May 26th, 1972. The principle signatories were Richard Nixon (L), president of the United States, and Leonid Brezhnev (R), general secretary of the Central Committee of the Communist Party of the Soviet Union (CPSU). SALT was an attempt at armament control during the Cold War. © Sovfoto/UIG via Getty Images

Biological WMDs Biological weapons are devices that use infectious agents to cause death or disease to humans, animals, or plants. Also known as germ warfare, biological weapons have been used in some form since ancient times. The most successful use of biological warfare was in 1346, when Mongol warriors of the Golden Hoard threw bubonic plague-infested bodies over the city walls of the besieged city of Kaffa. The disease-ridden bodies carried the Black Death, a disease spreading across Europe, eventually killing somewhere between one-third and two-thirds of the entire European population.

Disease-ridden corpses, blankets, and other items have been purposefully used to cause lethal or debilitating diseases in targeted populations.

Anthrax is probably the most well-known modern biological weapon. As a naturally occurring disease, anthrax infections are most common in livestock, especially cattle. Natural anthrax remains hyperendemic (coexists with its host population at a high rate) or epidemic (episodically occurs at a high rate) in about 14 countries today. Human case rates are highest today in central and southern Asia, the Middle East, and Africa. The bacteria causing anthrax can also be used a biological weapon. The U.S. National Academy of Science estimated in 2003 that 1 kilogram (2.2 pounds) of anthrax spores sprayed aerially over a large city could kill over 100,000 people. Anthrax spores could also render hundreds of square miles uninhabitable for many decades by lodging in the soil, causing immense economic damage.

During World War II, anthrax was developed as a major weapon by several countries. A biological warfare unit, Unit 731, was formed in the Japanese Imperial Army, which carried out experiments on thousands of Chinese prisoners of war in the 1930s. In one facility, about 4,000 prisoners were killed by biological agents, mostly anthrax.

In the United States, a major offensive biological warfare program was established in 1942 at Camp Detrick, Maryland, where anthrax and a number of other agents were developed as weapons. A plant for developing biological weapons was constructed near Terre Haute, Indiana; thousands of anthrax bombs were produced, but none were used during the war. The British government, which was cooperating with the United States and Canada in developing anthrax as a weapon, contaminated the Scottish island of Gruinard with anthrax spores in 1942. Due to the long-lived nature of the spores, the island was off-limits for 48 years afterward, when it was finally decontaminated.

The Soviet Union also instituted a biological warfare program during World War II, focusing on anthrax and other agents. The Soviet program continued for decades after the war, as did the U.S. program. In response to a 1969 decision by President Richard Nixon (1913–94), the U.S. army destroyed all of its antipersonnel biological warfare stocks, including anthrax, in 1971 and 1972.

As of 2012 six nations—Iraq, Japan, South Africa, Russia, the United Kingdom, and the United States—have confirmed biological weapon stockpiles.

Radiological WMDs A radiological weapon is a device that can spread radioactive material into an area to kill or seriously damage people, animals, and plants, and contaminate the soil, water, and air. No radiological weapons have ever been built, let alone deployed in warfare, although several have been designed. A so-called dirty bomb, if ever created and used, would release fuels from nuclear power plants or other forms of radioactive waste. A dirty bomb would not have the same explosive power as a nuclear bomb, but it would have many of the same long-term effects. Another potential radiological weapon is a "salted bomb," which would be a kind of nuclear weapon that would produce much larger amounts of nuclear fallout than occur with a regular nuclear bomb. No country has a confirmed radiological weapon.

Nuclear WMDs The term weapons of mass destruction was used in official documents several times throughout the Cold War. In almost all cases, WMDs referred specifically to nuclear weapons. Modern nuclear weapons, many times more powerful than earlier generations of weapons, have given rise to a unique complex of international fears, threats, treaties, secrets, and monitoring activities.

A nuclear weapon is an explosive device whose destructive power comes from nuclear reactions, either fission (atomic bomb) or a combination of fission and fusion (hydrogen bomb). Both reactions create enormous quantities of energy from small amounts of matter. The first nuclear weapon ever tested left the equivalent damage of approximately 10 million tons of trinitrotoluene (TNT).

The United States and the Threat of WMDs in Iraq

During the early 21st century, the term weapons of mass destruction came into common usage during the buildup to the United States' invasion of Iraq in 2003. After the terrorist attacks of September 11, 2001, the administration of U.S. President George W. Bush (1946–) and its allies argued that Iraq posed a deadly threat to the United States because it might give chemical or nuclear weapons, or WMD technology, to terrorists for use against the United States.

On October 7, 2002, Bush stated in a speech that the United States could not wait to find the "smoking gun" and warned that the first evidence of Iraq's weapons of mass destruction might come in the form of a "mushroom cloud," or a nuclear attack. Four days later, on October 11, 2002, the U.S. House of Representatives followed the U.S. Senate in approving the use of force against Iraq. The United States did not declare war on Iraq; rather, Congress passed a resolution that authorized the president to use the U.S. armed forces "as he determines to be necessary and appropriate . . . to defend the national security of the United States."

In November 2002 UN weapons inspectors returned to Iraq to search for chemical, biological, or nuclear weapons, or weapons programs. No evidence of weapons was found, but Iraq also delayed and failed to fully comply with inspections.

The United States, United Kingdom, France, and other intelligence agencies insisted that they had conclusive secret evidence that Iraq was both stockpiling and attempting to develop new WMDs. But opinion within and between Western intelligence agencies was also divided. For example, a September 2002 U.S. Defense Intelligence Agency report stated, "There is no reliable information on whether Iraq is producing and stockpiling chemical weapons, or whether Iraq has—or will—establish its chemical warfare agent production facilities."

For the duration of the Iraq War (2003–11) no recently produced weapons of mass destruction were found in Iraq. Weapons were found, but were inoperative or severely degraded and thought to date to the Iran-Iraq War (1980–88).

Amerithrax: Biological Weapons Attacks within the United States

The potential of even a small quantity of anthrax to disrupt a society and drain its resources was shown in 2001, when attacks were carried out through the U.S. mail using anthrax spores. The attacks began on September 18, a week after the terrorist attacks on the World Trade Center in New York City and the Pentagon in Washington, D.C. Letters containing anthrax spores in powder form were mailed from a public mailbox in Princeton, New Jersey, and received by several TV networks, the *New York Post* newspaper, and the offices of two senators. Although neither of the senators was infected, five people were killed by the anthrax and 17 others were hospitalized. The attacks briefly closed the U.S. Senate office building and several postal centers. Intense media coverage helped create a public frenzy to purchase the antibiotic Cipro used to treat anthrax infections. Government and law enforcement officials expressed fears of a wider scale bioterrorist attack using anthrax.

After years of intense investigation that initially focused on a scientist who was later exonerated, the U.S. Federal Bureau of Investigation (FBI) concluded that Bruce Ivins, an anthrax researcher and vaccine developer at the U.S. Army Medical Research Institute of Infectious Diseases (USAMRIID), was the sole mailer of the anthrax spores. In August 2008, Ivins committed suicide before being arrested or formally charged.

Although genetic tests linked the mailed anthrax to that grown in the USAMRIID researcher's laboratory, some experts argued that the researcher did not have the

NATIONS WITH NUCLEAR WEAPONS

A handful of nations currently possess nuclear weapons, the most feared weapons of mass destruction. The list that follows includes nations that have developed and continue to possess their own nuclear weapons as of early 2014. Although Israel has never formally declared itself to be a nuclear power, a number of Western intelligence services and leaders assume Israel has a significant nuclear arsenal as estimated below.

The main international legal instrument for preventing proliferation is the Nuclear Non–Proliferation Treaty (NPT or NNPT) of 1968. The NPT allows current nuclear powers to keep their weapons as long as they promise to eliminate them at a still-unspecified future date. In the meantime the five original nuclear powers—the United States, Russia, Britain, France, and China—promise to provide aid to the rest of the world for the development of civilian nuclear power. The treaty is the basis for international monitoring and inspections conducted by the United Nations International Atomic Energy Agency.

- United States (1945). 2,150 active, 7,700 total.
- Russia (1949). 1,800 active, 8,500 total.
- United Kingdom (1952). 160 active, 225 total.
- France (1960). 290 active, 300 total.
- China (1964). n.a. active, 250 total.
- India (1974). n.a. active, 90–110 total.
- Israel (1979?). n.a. active, 80 total.
- Pakistan (1998). n.a. active, 100–120 total.
- North Korea (2006). n.a. active, 10+ total.

After the fall of the Soviet Union in 1991, three former Soviet Union countries—Belarus, Kazakhstan, and Ukraine—inherited a nuclear arsenal of more than 6,480 weapons. These Eastern European nations chose to voluntarily return the weapons to Russia in 1995 and 1996.

South Africa occupies a unique place in the history of nuclear weaponry. It independently developed nuclear weapons during the 1980s but then chose to disarm them in the early 1990s.

capacity to produce a compound laced with the percentage of silicon that matched the deadly anthrax mailed in 2001. These experts contend that a key unresolved question involves the abnormally high percentage of silicon found in the anthrax powder. The silicon was a component of weaponization that helped the mailed anthrax disperse in the air as the letters were opened. In February 2010, the FBI officially closed its investigation, making public a 92-page report that served as its summary of the case against Ivins.

The FBI's final summary of what the Bureau codenamed the Amerithrax investigation asserted that both "direct evidence that anthrax spores under [Ivin's] sole and exclusive control were the parent material to the anthrax spores used in the attack and compelling circumstantial evidence" supported the FBI's conclusions that Ivins, acting alone, perpetrated the 2001 attacks. In February 2011, the National Academy of Sciences (NAS) National Research Council (NRC) report cast doubt on certain assertions of scientific facts that were central to the FBI's conclusions that Ivins was the lone culprit.

Chemical Weapon Use in Syria

In 2012 Syrian officials admitted resuming the manufacture of chemical weapons. In early 2013, several news agencies reported the use of chemical weapons in the Syrian Civil War. Most early reports claimed that the Syrian government initially deployed chemical weapons against opposition forces in civilian populated areas. Syrian government officials continued to deny that they used such weapons and asserted that rebel forces had themselves used gas agents.

In August 2013, officials in the United States and France announced that they had garnered credible evidence that Syrian government forces had used chemical weapons against opposition forces and Syrian civilians. A UN report released in September 2013 confirmed the use of sarin gas in an attack near Damascus in the rebel-held town of Ghouta.

On September 14, 2013, the United States, Russia, and Syria consented to an arrangement that would avoid retaliatory and debilitating military strikes by the United States on Syrian targets. Under the terms of the pact, Syria agreed to disclose the extent of its chemical weapons program and place them under international control by mid-2014. The Organization for the Prohibition of Chemical Weapons (OPCW) stated that Syria met its October 31, 2013, deadline for destroying all chemical weapons mixing and production facilities, however an interim deadline to remove all chemical weapons by December 31 was not met, nor was one on February 5, 2014. At that time it was reported that only 4 percent of the weapons had been delivered. Syria stated that despite the delays, a final deadline of June 30, 2014, would be met.

⊕ Future Implications

The term weapons of mass destruction or WMDs has been extended far past its original use. For example, in April 2013, the surviving accused suspect in the Boston Marathon bombings was charged with using a WMD

United Nations Secretary-General Ban Ki-moon prepares to speak to the media about the conclusion of the UN inspectors' report on chemical weapons use in Syria after a Security Council meeting at UN headquarters on September 16, 2013, in New York City. The report, which concluded that chemical weapons were used in an attack near Damascus on August 21 in which hundreds died, was handed in by the head of the mission, Professor Ake Sellstrom, to the Secretary-General at his residence in New York. *© Spencer Platt/Getty Images*

to kill three people and injure 264 more. In the Boston case, the two WMDs in question were homemade bombs made out of pressure cookers. The devices, allegedly constructed and altered to cause death and to maim spectators and participants, met current U.S. legal definitions of WMDs.

Many experts have openly speculated that overuse of the term WMDs has diluted it to the point that it masks the threats posed by weapons that can kill hundreds of thousands.

Although many nations, including the United States and Russia, have called for disarmament of all existing weapons of mass destruction, the reality is far from promising. For disarmament to occur, demilitarization would also have to happen, a change that would have extreme economic, political, social, and technical consequences. Some historians have referred to human history as "one long war with brief outbreaks of peace." From this perspective it would take a profound psychological shift for humans to disarm. In the meantime, as recent use in Syria proves, weapons of mass destruction remain a continuing and evolving threat.

PRIMARY SOURCE

The Russell-Einstein Manifesto

SOURCE *Einstein, Albert, and Bertrand Russell. "The Russell-Einstein Manifesto."* Pugwash Conferences on Science and World Affairs, *July 9, 1955. http://www.pugwash.org/about/manifesto.htm (accessed November 5, 2013).*

INTRODUCTION *The Russell-Einstein Manifesto, released in London on July 9, 1955, was a warning to the world against nuclear war. All 11 of the signatories already were or would become Nobel Prize recipients. In the 1950s, as the world continued to recover from the destruction of World War II, the nuclear arms race had already begun. In 1949, only four years after the United States used atomic bombs on Japan to force surrender, the Soviets conducted their first nuclear test. The United States escalated the race in 1952 when it tested a new and more powerful hydrogen bomb, which the Soviet Union answered by testing its version the following year. The threat to humanity from the use of nuclear weapons was horribly clear to many scientists, including those who had helped to create the bombs dropped with devastating results on Hiroshima and Nagasaki. Theoretical physicist Albert Einstein (1879–1955), who had been a pacifist prior to World War II, spent the last decade of his life advocating against the use of nuclear weapons. He signed the manifesto shortly before his death on April 18, 1955. Mathematician, philosopher, and author Bertrand Russell (1872–1970), was largely responsible for writing the Manifesto.*

In the tragic situation which confronts humanity, we feel that scientists should assemble in conference to appraise the perils that have arisen as a result of the development of weapons of mass destruction, and to discuss a resolution in the spirit of the appended draft.

We are speaking on this occasion, not as members of this or that nation, continent, or creed, but as human beings, members of the species Man, whose continued existence is in doubt. The world is full of conflicts; and, overshadowing all minor conflicts, the titanic struggle between Communism and anti-Communism.

Almost everybody who is politically conscious has strong feelings about one or more of these issues; but we want you, if you can, to set aside such feelings and consider yourselves only as members of a biological species which has had a remarkable history, and whose disappearance none of us can desire.

We shall try to say no single word which should appeal to one group rather than to another. All, equally, are in peril, and, if the peril is understood, there is hope that they may collectively avert it.

We have to learn to think in a new way. We have to learn to ask ourselves, not what steps can be taken to give military victory to whatever group we prefer, for there no longer are such steps; the question we have to ask ourselves is: what steps can be taken to prevent a military contest of which the issue must be disastrous to all parties?

The general public, and even many men in positions of authority, have not realized what would be involved in a war with nuclear bombs. The general public still thinks in terms of the obliteration of cities. It is understood that the new bombs are more powerful than the old, and that, while one A-bomb could obliterate Hiroshima, one H-bomb could obliterate the largest cities, such as London, New York, and Moscow.

No doubt in an H-bomb war great cities would be obliterated. But this is one of the minor disasters that would have to be faced. If everybody in London, New York, and Moscow were exterminated, the world might, in the course of a few centuries, recover from the blow. But we now know, especially since the Bikini test, that nuclear bombs can gradually spread destruction over a very much wider area than had been supposed.

It is stated on very good authority that a bomb can now be manufactured which will be 2,500 times as powerful as that which destroyed Hiroshima. Such a bomb, if exploded near the ground or under water, sends radioactive particles into the upper air. They sink gradually and reach the surface of the earth in the form of a deadly dust or rain. It was this dust which infected the Japanese fishermen and their catch of fish. No one knows how widely such lethal radio-active particles might be diffused, but the best authorities are unanimous in saying that a war with H-bombs might possibly put an end to the human race. It is feared that if many H-bombs are used there will be universal death, sudden only for a minority, but for the majority a slow torture of disease and disintegration.

Many warnings have been uttered by eminent men of science and by authorities in military strategy. None of them will say that the worst results are certain. What they do say is that these results are possible, and no one can be sure that they will not be realized. We have not yet found that the views of experts on this question depend in any degree upon their politics or prejudices. They depend only, so far as our researches have revealed, upon the extent of the particular expert's knowledge. We have found that the men who know most are the most gloomy.

Here, then, is the problem which we present to you, stark and dreadful and inescapable: Shall we put an end to the human race; or shall mankind renounce war? People will not face this alternative because it is so difficult to abolish war.

The abolition of war will demand distasteful limitations of national sovereignty. But what perhaps impedes understanding of the situation more than anything else is that the term "mankind" feels vague and abstract. People scarcely realize in imagination that the danger is to themselves and their children and their grandchildren, and not only to a dimly apprehended humanity. They can scarcely bring themselves to grasp that they, individually, and those whom they love are in imminent danger of perishing agonizingly. And so they hope that perhaps war may be allowed to continue provided modern weapons are prohibited.

This hope is illusory. Whatever agreements not to use H-bombs had been reached in time of peace, they would no longer be considered binding in time of war, and both sides would set to work to manufacture H-bombs as soon as war broke out, for, if one side manufactured the bombs and the other did not, the side that manufactured them would inevitably be victorious.

Although an agreement to renounce nuclear weapons as part of a general reduction of armaments would not afford an ultimate solution, it would serve certain important purposes. First, any agreement between East and West is to the good in so far as it tends to diminish tension. Second, the abolition of thermo-nuclear weapons, if each side believed that the other had carried it out sincerely, would lessen the fear of a sudden attack in the style of Pearl Harbour, which at present keeps both sides in a state of nervous apprehension. We should, therefore, welcome such an agreement though only as a first step.

Most of us are not neutral in feeling, but, as human beings, we have to remember that, if the issues between East and West are to be decided in any manner that can give any possible satisfaction to anybody, whether Communist or anti-Communist, whether Asian or European or American, whether White or Black, then these issues must not be decided by war. We should wish this to be understood, both in the East and in the West.

There lies before us, if we choose, continual progress in happiness, knowledge, and wisdom. Shall we, instead, choose death, because we cannot forget our quarrels? We appeal as human beings to human beings: Remember your humanity, and forget the rest. If you can do so, the way lies open to a new Paradise; if you cannot, there lies before you the risk of universal death.

Resolution:

We invite this Congress, and through it the scientists of the world and the general public, to subscribe to the following resolution:

"In view of the fact that in any future world war nuclear weapons will certainly be employed, and that such weapons threaten the continued existence of mankind, we urge the governments of the world to realize, and to acknowledge publicly, that their purpose cannot be furthered by a world war, and we urge them, consequently, to find peaceful means for the settlement of all matters of dispute between them."

Max Born

Percy W. Bridgman

Albert Einstein

Leopold Infeld

Frederic Joliot-Curie

Herman J. Muller

Linus Pauling

Cecil F. Powell

Joseph Rotblat

Bertrand Russell

Hideki Yukawa

SEE ALSO *Iran-Iraq War; Syrian Civil War; World War I; World War II*

BIBLIOGRAPHY

Books

Archer, Christon. *World History of Warfare.* Lincoln: University of Nebraska Press, 2008.

Bernstein, Jeremy. *Nuclear Weapons: What You Need to Know.* Cambridge: Cambridge University Press, 2008.

Bowman, Katherine. *Trends in Science and Technology Relevant to the Biological and Toxin Weapons Convention Summary of an International Workshop: October 31 to November 3, 2010, Beijing, China.* Washington, D.C.: National Academies Press, 2011.

Busch, Nathan. *Combating Weapons of Mass Destruction: The Future of Nonproliferation Policy.* Athens: University of Georgia Press, 2009.

Mayor, Adrienne. *Greek Fire, Poison Arrows, and Scorpion Bombs: Weapons of Mass Destruction in the Ancient World.* New York: Overlook Press, 2008.

Web Sites

"Chemical Weapons Elimination." *Centers for Disease Control and Prevention (CDC).* http://www.cdc.gov/nceh/demil/ (accessed January 6, 2014).

"Chemical Weapons Information." *Federation of American Scientists.* http://www.fas.org/programs/bio/chemweapons/index.html (accessed January 6, 2014).

Counterproliferation Program Review Committee. "Report on Activities and Programs for Countering Proliferation and NBC Terrorism, Volume I, Executive Summary." *Federation of American Scientists,* May 2011. http://www.fas.org/irp/threat/nbcterror2011.pdf (accessed January 6, 2014).

Potter, William, et al. "The CW Revolution will be Tweeted." *Center for Nonproliferation Studies,* September 12, 2013. http://cns.miis.edu/stories/130912_cw_revolution_tweeted.htm (accessed January 6, 2014).

Reed, Laura. "Weapons of Mass Destruction." *Hampshire College.* http://www.hampshire.edu/academics/22169.htm (accessed January 6, 2014).

Shea, Dana A. "Chemical Weapons: A Summary Report of Characteristics and Effects." *Congressional Research Service,* September 13, 2013. http://www.fas.org/sgp/crs/nuke/R42862.pdf (accessed January 6, 2014).

"Weapons of Mass Destruction." *Federal Bureau of Investigation.* http://www.fbi.gov/about-us/investigate/terrorism/wmd (accessed August 29, 2013).

World War I

⊕ Introduction

World War I (1914–18) pitted the Central Powers—mainly Germany and the powerful Austro-Hungarian Empire—against the Allied Powers, which included France, Great Britain, Italy, Russia, and eventually the United States. It was a prolonged war, lasting from July 1914 to November 1918. New types of weapons and new fighting tactics made World War I especially horrific and deadly. Opposing armies fought each other from damp trenches in the ground, battling for months over yards of territory. Armored tanks and modern machine guns made killing from a distance quick and effective. Weaponized chemical agents, such as mustard gas, blistered, burned, and blinded victims. An estimated 16 million people died in the war, including more than 6 million civilians, while 21 million more people were wounded.

The unprecedented level of destruction and death caused by the war earned it the label "the war to end all wars," because the people of Europe could not imagine taking up arms again after suffering so much loss. But their hopes for a peaceful future were soon dashed, as old resentments continued to fester following the conclusion of hostilities. Just 20 years after the formal end of World War I, a new and even more destructive war erupted in Europe, quickly engulfing most of the globe: World War II (1939–45).

⊕ Historical Background

Historians have typically labeled Germany and Austria-Hungary (the Central Powers) as the aggressors in World War I. Under Kaiser Wilhelm II (1859–1941), Germany assumed a belligerent political and military posture that threw off a long-standing balance of power in Europe. Before Wilhelm II assumed the throne, Germany's foreign policy was overseen by its powerful chancellor, Otto von Bismarck (1815–1898). Bismarck sought to maintain stability in notoriously volatile parts of Eastern Europe (such as the Balkans). He also tried to keep Germany safe from the threat of an unfavorable alliance between France and Russia by aligning Germany with Austria-Hungary and Russia. Wilhelm dismissed Bismarck and declined to renew Germany's treaty of alliance with Russia in 1890. As Bismarck had feared, this decision drove Russia into an alliance with France, as both sought mutual protection against a possible military threat from Germany.

Trouble from the Balkans

Throughout the 1890s, Germany focused on modernizing and expanding its navy, setting off an arms race with the world's leading naval power at the time, Great Britain. The rush to develop weaponry spread across Europe. By the first decade of the 20th century, power in Europe resided in two opposing camps: the Triple Alliance (Germany, Austria-Hungary, and Italy) and the Triple Entente (Great Britain, France, and Russia). As Bismarck might have predicted, the spark that ignited this powder keg emerged in the Balkans, a region plagued for centuries by sectarian and ethnic violence. At the turn of the 20th century, the Balkans were at the center of power struggles between Russia, Austria-Hungary, and the Ottoman Empire.

On June 28, 1914, a radical Serb named Gavrilo Princip assassinated Archduke Franz Ferdinand (1863–1914), heir to the throne of Austria-Hungary, on the streets of Sarajevo. The murder set off a chain reaction of events that quickly drew the major powers of Europe into war due to their tangled system of alliances.

The opening round of fire came from Austria-Hungary, which threatened to launch an invasion of Serbia in retaliation for the archduke's murder. Russia, whose people shared ethnic bonds with Serbia, soon mobilized troops to defend its neighbor.

EUROPE IN 1914

Germany responded by mobilizing its own military forces, which prompted France to declare its intention to support Russia. France's decision was made easier by lingering grudges against Germany over territorial losses France had sustained in the Franco-Prussian War of 1870–71. When Kaiser Wilhelm's armies invaded the neutral countries of Belgium and Luxembourg on their way to France, Great Britain was forced to support its ally by declaring war against Germany. The British felt that war was the only option to prevent Germany and its powerful navy from posing an unacceptable threat.

As the conflict engulfed Europe, it spread to the colonies and foreign territories of the warring European nations as well. Germany suffered a quick loss of almost all its Pacific holdings as New Zealand and Australia moved quickly to invade and secure these areas. Raids and battles between colonial forces in Africa and the Middle East continued throughout the war. However, the bulk of the fighting occurred in Europe on two fronts: the Eastern Front, where the Central Powers faced off against Russia; and the Western Front, where Germany fought against France and Great Britain.

Stalemate in the Trenches

Many nations entered the fray between 1914 and 1916. The Ottoman Empire and Bulgaria helped bolster the Central Powers, while Romania and Italy joined the Allied Powers. However, the additional support did little to change the course of the war, which had become a virtual stalemate by 1915.

The Archduke of Austria Franz Ferdinand (1863–1914) and his wife, Sophie, in Sarajevo moments before their assassination. The Archduke's assassination was the immediate cause of World War I.   © *Mansell/Time Life Pictures/Getty Images*

On the Eastern Front, Russian forces endured severe losses at the hands of Germany and Austria. By the end of 1915 the Russians had been forced out of both Poland and Galicia, which they had captured early in the conflict, and the bloodshed had significantly reduced public support for the war. Nevertheless, Russia managed to mount a surprise offensive in 1916 that crippled the Austro-Hungarian Army and shook the confidence of Germany, which was forced to divert manpower away from the Western Front.

Although the Brusilov Offensive, a campaign led from June 4 to late September 1916 by Russian commander Aleksei Brusilov, dealt a blow to the Central Powers, supply shortages caused it to lose momentum in the fall of 1916. By this time Russia's involvement in the conflict had resulted in more than six million casualties, including 1.7 million dead soldiers. It had also thrown the nation into an economic crisis, displaced millions of civilians, and created severe shortages of food and fuel. These problems contributed to the political upheaval that rocked the country in 1917.

Meanwhile, on the Western Front, armies were literally entrenched across France and Belgium. In the tactic of trench warfare, soldiers lived in muddy, rat-infested trenches, exposed to the elements, for weeks on end, occasionally launching offensives or coming under enemy attack. In the famous Battle of Verdun, German and French armies clashed from their trenches for nearly 10 months in 1916. The battle began when the Germans tried to take the French city of Verdun. The French grimly defended the city against an onslaught of German weaponry, including the newly developed flamethrower and corrosive chemical weapons. In the end, the French managed to force a German retreat, but only at the cost of more than 300,000 soldiers' lives. The dearly bought French victory was a morale booster, but the course of the war remained unchanged.

The Battle of the Somme spanned almost five months in 1916, pitting British and French soldiers against German soldiers on opposite sides of the River Somme. Tanks and military aircraft made their first appearances in this battle, which killed more than one million soldiers and resulted in the gain of only about six miles of territory by British and French troops.

The Tide Turns in 1917

After more than two years of useless slaughter, 1917 brought some unexpected changes. Due in part to the staggering economic and human cost of fighting the war on the Eastern Front, Russia's tsarist government fell in March 1917, leading to the Communist revolution in November. This development was a blow to the Allies, as Russia's subsequent withdrawal from the conflict allowed Germany to concentrate all of its efforts on the Western Front. In addition, the new communist

German soldiers march through Brussels, Belgium, shortly after invading the country in 1914, at the start of World War I. © *Underwood Archives/Getty Images*

government ceded vast amounts of territory to invading Germans.

In April 1917, however, the United States formally entered the war on the side of Great Britain and France. Unlike its allies, the United States had not felt a pressing national security threat from Germany, nor did it have any old scores to settle. In fact, citing a lack of public support for intervention, U.S. President Woodrow Wilson (1856–1924) had maintained a neutral stance. Germany, however, forced Wilson's hand. In 1915, the German navy sank the *Lusitania*, a British ocean liner. Nearly 1,200 people, including 128 Americans, died when the ship went down.

German submarines also harassed U.S. commercial maritime traffic, despite repeated assurances by the Germans that U.S. ships would be left in peace. Finally, in January 1917, the United States government received the so-called Zimmerman Telegram. This secret message from the German foreign secretary promised aid to the Mexican government and the return of former Mexican territories (such as Texas, New Mexico, and Arizona) in exchange for Mexican support in the war. The British government intercepted the telegram and shared it with the United States government.

The telegram gave Wilson the impetus he needed to gain Congressional support for a declaration of war. It took the United States, which had a small standing army at the time, several months to conscript a force of useful size, but in the end, two million Americans were deployed in World War I. When the United States brought its wealth, manpower, natural resources, and industrial capacity to bear in the conflict, it helped shift the momentum to the side of the Allied Powers.

The Germans launched an unsuccessful offensive against France in the spring of 1918. That summer, British, French, American, and other allied troops responded with a successful counteroffensive against the Germans. By November 1918, Germany and its allies were defeated.

World War I, French soldiers in a trench, observing the enemy with periscopes, 1914.   © Neurdein/Roger Viollet/Getty Images

⊕ Impacts and Issues

At the end of the war, two major imperial powers, the Austro-Hungarian and Ottoman Empires, no longer existed. The European map was significantly changed, and Russia was transformed by the Communist revolution of 1917.

During the 1919 Paris peace conference, the victorious leaders made clear their intention to safeguard the world against another large-scale and destructive conflict. The Versailles Treaty was signed on June 28, 1919, but ultimately, it did not achieve the intended aims. Punitive components of the treaty, including demands for war reparations and the demilitarization of Germany, humiliated the Germans and crippled their economy. This demoralization, in the opinion of many historians, set the stage for a resurgence of German nationalism in the 1930s, and ultimately the rise of the Nazi party and the outbreak of World War II. Indeed, the "war to end all wars" turned out to be a prelude to a second, and more devastating, world war.

The downfall of dynasties brings unforeseen results. The German and Austro-Hungarian Empires were relatively young—less than a century old—but the Ottoman Empire had been a major force in world politics for hundreds of years. The Russian Empire was similarly well-established, and its overthrow by revolutionaries with a radical new political philosophy had ripple effects through the 20th century.

⊕ Future Implications

For good or ill, empires draw disparate groups of people together under one banner. When an empire falls, those groups splinter. Old grudges resurface—often with tragic results. Such has been the case in the Balkans. The area was long part of a power struggle between the Ottoman and Austro-Hungarian Empires. After those empires fell, the Soviet Union developed into a major world power, extending its influence across the Balkans, including Bulgaria and what was then called Yugoslavia.

When the Soviet Union collapsed in 1991, the long-simmering ethnic and religious conflicts in the Balkans reemerged. In the 1990s, Serbians, Croats, and Bosnians, formerly all Yugoslavians, clashed with each other in the bloodiest European struggle since World War II. The fighting was marked by massive crimes against humanity and genocide, and United Nations intervention was required to stop the violence. In the end, several new nations emerged, including Croatia, Kosovo (although its independence is disputed), Macedonia, Serbia, and Slovenia.

But diplomatic struggles in the Balkans continued as of late 2013, as did trials of various war criminals

An American aircraft carrier is shown in 1914, several years before the United States officially entered in World War I—the first conflict to use airplanes on a wide scale. © *MPI/Getty Images*

GALLIPOLI

While World War I is most remembered for the trench warfare that occurred in Europe, various bloody and tragic battles occurred in other parts of the world. Another famous battle of World War I was fought in what is now Turkey.

In 1915, Great Britain and France launched an ill-conceived assault on the Dardanelles, a strategically important waterway between the Aegean Sea and the Black Sea, near the city of Gallipoli. Securing Gallipoli would offer a sea route across the Black Sea straight to Istanbul, the capital of the Ottoman Empire. Interestingly enough, it was British First Lord of the Admiralty Winston Churchill (1874–1965) who proposed the plan. Churchill would later become the British prime minister during World War II.

The assault began in April 1915, and the battle continued until January 1916. A large number of the troops fighting for the Allies were from Australia and New Zealand. On the Ottoman side was another man who would go on to lasting fame: Mustafa Kemal Atatürk (1881–1938), an able military commander who founded the Republic of Turkey after the fall of the Ottoman Empire.

In the end, the Ottomans repelled the invaders, but casualties were heavy, and relatively equal, on both sides. Estimates vary, but between 50,000 and 60,000 men were lost by each force.

Interestingly, the battle forged a strong bond between the Turks, the Australians, and the New Zealanders. All have come to see the battle as a turning point in their nations' histories, a point at which they saw their potential as independent nations. The date of the initial landing, April 25, is still commemorated as ANZAC (Australia and New Zealand) Day, and tourists from Australia and New Zealand frequent the cemetery where the fallen of Gallipoli lie. A memorial at the site of the landing, erected in 1985, features an inscription of comments first given by Atatürk, then president of Turkey, upon the first arrival of Australian and New Zealanders to visit Gallipoli in 1934:

"Those heroes that shed their blood and lost their lives   You are now lying in the soil of a friendly country. Therefore rest in peace. There is no difference between the Johnnies and the Mehmets to us where they lie side by side now here in this country of ours . . . you, the mothers, who sent their sons from faraway countries, wipe away your tears; your sons are now lying in our bosom and are in peace. After having lost their lives on this land they have become our sons as well."

EUROPE AFTER WWI

- Territory lost by Germany
- Territory lost by Russia
- Territory lost by Bulgaria
- Territory lost by Austria-Hungary

© 2014 Cengage Learning

involved the Balkan Wars of the 1990s. Kosovo broke away from Serbia and declared its independence in 2008. While Kosovo is recognized as an independent nation by the majority of United Nations member states, Serbia does not recognize Kosovo as independent, and, perhaps more significantly, neither does Russia. Skirmishes within Kosovo between ethnic Serbs and the majority population of ethnic Albanians continued into 2014. War crimes trials of Serbian commanders involved in the Balkan Wars of the 1990s also continued into 2014.

SEE ALSO *World War II; Yugoslav Wars*

BIBLIOGRAPHY

Books

Hart, Peter. *The Great War: A Combat History of the First World War.* New York: Oxford University Press, 2013.

Macmillan, Margaret. *The War that Ended Peace: The Road to 1914.* New York: Random House, 2013.

Tuchman, Barbara Wertheim. *The Guns of August: The Outbreak of World War.* New York: Macmillan, 1962.

Web Sites

"1914–1918: The Great War and the Shaping of the 20th Century." *PBS.* http://www.pbs.org/greatwar/ (accessed October 31, 2013).

BBC History: World War I. http://www.bbc.co.uk/history/worldwars/wwone/ (accessed October 31, 2013).

Duffy, Michael. *FirstWorldWar.com.* http://firstworldwar.com/index.htm (accessed October 31, 2013).

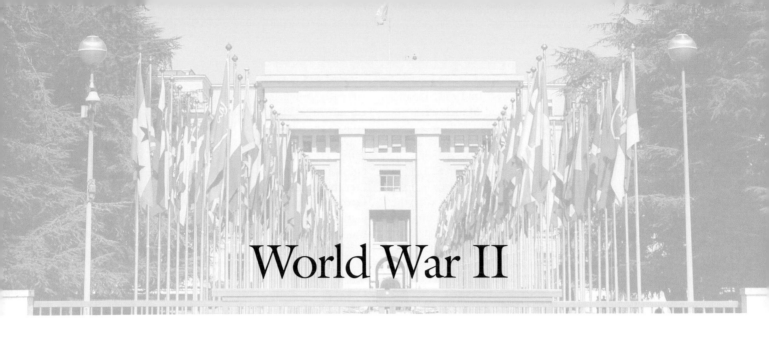

🌐 World War II

🌐 Introduction

The Second World War was the largest armed conflict in history, a cataclysm costing at least 60 million human lives. The war, which lasted from 1939 to 1945, involved dozens of nations, including all the world's great powers. Two armed camps, the Axis powers (primarily Germany, Italy, and Japan) and the Allies (including the United Kingdom, France, the Soviet Union, the United States, and the Republic of China), squared off on many different fronts. The war's major theaters included Eastern, Western, and Southern Europe, North Africa and the Mediterranean Sea, East and Southeast Asia, the Pacific, and the Atlantic.

In World War II, the belligerent states engaged in "total war," a maximum mobilization with nearly the entirety of each nation's industrial resources devoted to the war effort. Innovative forms of destructive power were unleashed, including jet aircraft, ballistic missiles, the destruction of cities by incendiary bombs dropped from the air, the systematic extermination of European Jews and other populations (the Holocaust), and the invention and use of atomic weapons. The defining event of the 20th century, World War II reorganized the balance of world power. A new global order emerged in the war's aftermath, the basic contours of which have held in place for many subsequent decades.

🌐 Historical Background

The roots of World War II can be found in the outcome of World War I (1914–18), which had also redrawn the world's political map. The Austro-Hungarian and Ottoman Empires were dissolved following their defeats in what was also called "the Great War." Russia's devastating losses had brought about the fall of the monarchy and a Communist revolution. Germany had lost significant territory as well as all its overseas possessions.

In the Treaty of Versailles that formally ended the war, Germany was forced to claim sole responsibility for the conflict and pay large sums in war reparations to the victorious Allies. These humiliations and financial burdens made an increasing number of Germans sympathetic to the militant right-wing nationalism of the National Socialist (Nazi) party, especially when Germany entered a lengthy economic and political crisis.

That crisis deepened in the early 1930s, with several coalition governments falling in quick succession until Adolf Hitler (1889–1945), the Nazi party leader, was appointed chancellor in January 1933. Soon afterward, a suspicious fire broke out in the Reichstag, the seat of the German parliament. Hitler immediately proclaimed emergency powers that would remain in place for 12 years and built a powerful dictatorial police state based on propaganda and violence. The Nazi regime, which adopted the designation "Third Reich," launched a rapid rearmament of Germany, in violation of the Versailles Treaty.

Hitler's political model was Benito Mussolini (1883–1945), a dictator who had seized power in Italy in 1922. Mussolini and his Black Shirt followers named their political movement fascism, a militarized nationalism based on a close alliance with industry, disdain for liberal democracy, and violent repression toward Communists and labor activists. To these elements Hitler added a racially motivated theory of history, which valorized the Aryan "master race" and blamed the nation's troubles on the Jewish people and other groups they deemed racially inferior, such as the Roma. In October 1936, Hitler and Mussolini signed a friendship accord and declared that a Rome-Berlin axis would henceforth hold the balance of power in Europe. One month later, Germany and the empire of Japan signed the Anti-Comintern Pact to jointly oppose the Soviet Union.

The Japanese also had a militaristic and authoritarian government with expansive ambitions. With limited land and a rapidly expanding population, Japan sought new territories rich with natural resources. In 1931, Japan's army went on the offensive and seized Manchuria from China, forming a puppet state called Manchukuo. Enlisting Germany's support against a potential Soviet attack provided insurance against Japan's most feared enemy. In 1937, Japan withdrew from a treaty with Great Britain and the United States that had limited the size of its navy and began rapidly building up its fleet. Later that year, the Japanese attacked eastern China, quickly conquering the cities of Beijing, Shanghai, and Nanking, the capital. Japanese soldiers massacred hundreds of thousands of Chinese troops and civilians in Nanking. The Chinese put up fierce resistance in many regions, particularly in areas of the northwest where Communist rebels were based.

The League of Nations, which had been established after World War I to help preserve the peace, proved virtually powerless to respond to crises such as the Italian invasion of Ethiopia in 1935, the Japanese attacks on China, and Hitler's increasingly aggressive moves, such as the annexation of Austria in March 1938. When Hitler then staked a claim to the Sudetenland, a German-speaking region of Czechoslovakia, British and French leaders called a diplomatic conference in Munich, Germany. There, in September 1938, they yielded to the German dictator's territorial demands, hoping to avoid war through a strategy of appeasement. Several months later, Germany seized the rest of Czechoslovakia.

The Axis Rising, 1939–1941

On May 22, 1939, Italy and the German Reich entered a formal military alliance, which Mussolini termed the Pact of Steel. Japan opted not to join the pact, since it

© 2014 Cengage Learning

was drafted to reflect a likely war against the Western powers rather than against Japan's more feared enemy, the Soviet Union. As a new war in Europe became increasingly likely, it remained a mystery what sort of political alignment the Soviet Union might choose. Joseph Stalin (1878–1953), Russia's feared and powerful autocratic leader, began negotiations with Britain and France regarding an alliance against Germany. When the talks temporarily stalled, Stalin's diplomats secretly entered talks with the Germans, hoping the German government might offer better terms.

Hitler had formed the clear intention to invade Poland, well aware that France and Britain would react by declaring war. Stalin had his own designs on Poland, as well as the Baltic states (Lithuania, Latvia, and Estonia) and other territories. Seeking to neutralize a potentially powerful enemy to its east, Germany offered the Soviet government the right to claim much of the territory it wanted. The two countries signed the Molotov-Ribbentrop Pact, a non-aggression agreement, on August 23, 1939.

The Nazi-Soviet Pact included a secret protocol segregating much of Eastern Europe, pending its conquest, into German and Russian spheres of influence. Eight days later, on September 1, German forces invaded Poland—the event historians typically use to mark commencement of World War II. Britain and France declared war on Germany two days later, but neither came to Poland's aid. The country quickly fell, after Russia had entered the fray from the east.

Shortly afterward, the Soviet and Nazi partners followed through on their partition plan. In the German-occupied parts of Poland, the Nazis rounded up Jews and other minorities, placing them into ghettoes and concentration camps. Such camps had existed within Germany since the early days of Hitler's rule for political prisoners and others considered enemies of the regime. The Soviet Red Army attacked Finland in November 1939. The Germans delayed their next offensive through the winter as all sides mobilized and deployed. Germany attacked Denmark and Norway in April 1940. On May 10 came the expected *blitzkrieg* ("lightning war"): coordinated attacks, all successful, against Belgium, the Netherlands, Luxembourg, and France.

The Germans quickly pierced the French defenses. Territory that had been the theater of years of trench warfare during World War I was overrun within weeks. British forces and a few French divisions were evacuated across the English Channel from the French port of Dunkirk. German troops marched on Paris on June 14. Marshal Philippe Pétain (1856–1951), a senior figure in the French military, became head of a new, collaborationist French government, based in Vichy.

After the blitzkrieg, most of Europe was now under German control; only the British Isles remained unvanquished and able to stand up to Hitler. The German Luftwaffe and the Royal Air Force vied for control of the skies over the English Channel throughout the summer of 1940, while Germany carried out nighttime bombing raids—the Blitz—on London and other British cities. The long flight paths between German air bases and their targets, the British use of radar to provide early warning, and the determination of the British people and their Prime Minister, Winston Churchill (1874–1965), prevented the Nazis from forcing a British surrender. Unable to achieve air superiority, Hitler cancelled the planned invasion of Britain in September.

Across the Atlantic, the United States remained out of the conflict, with much of the public unwilling to become involved in another war in Europe that seemed to pose no immediate threat to American interests. After the fall of France, however, the administration of President Franklin D. Roosevelt (1882–1945) began a major military buildup. The popular Roosevelt broke from U.S. political tradition by running for and winning a third term in office in the 1940 election. In September the government instituted a peacetime draft and made a deal with Britain to exchange dozens of naval destroyers for the right to establish military bases in Britain's Caribbean possessions. Six months later, Congress passed the Lend-Lease Act to deliver material support to Great

German Chancellor and Nazi dictator Adolf Hitler, right, with the Italian fascist leader Benito Mussolini in Munich, Germany, June 18, 1940. © Bob Thomas/Popperfoto/Getty Images

Britain. This legislation put an end to all semblance of U.S. neutrality.

Once American industry began supplying the British war effort, U.S. merchant ships became vulnerable to attack by German U-boat submarines and aircraft in the Atlantic. The Germans had fought since the beginning of the war to break through an Allied naval blockade and to disrupt passage of the merchant vessels on which Britain depended for supplies. Even before the United States formally entered the conflict, U.S. warships were involved in ocean escort and engaged U-boats in skirmishes. The Allies maintained control over sea lanes in the North Atlantic, but the U-boats sank thousands of merchant vessels.

On September 27, 1940, Japan formally joined what were known as the Axis powers by signing the Tripartite Pact with Germany and Italy. The three nations recognized each other's spheres of influence and promised assistance in case of an attack, although the agreement specifically exempted Japan from an obligation to fight the Soviet Union. The Soviets were in favor of signing on to the pact, but Germany neglected to reply to the Soviets' diplomatic proposal. Hitler, it soon became apparent, had plans to betray the Soviets.

Italy had been militarily unprepared to join the war at its outset, but by mid-1940 Mussolini had come to believe an Axis victory was imminent and Italy should rush its forces into battle. The Italians launched an offensive in North Africa and, in October 1940, invaded Greece. Neither attack yielded a clear victory, and in the early months of 1941 Germany sent forces to both theaters to assist its struggling ally. The Germans conquered Greece as well as Yugoslavia in April.

The Turn of the War and the Holocaust

As Hitler and the other Nazi leaders saw it, all their victories to this point were preliminary to the central goal of defeating and conquering the Soviets. Operation Barbarossa, the code name for Germany's invasion of the Soviet Union, got underway June 22, 1941. It was the largest invasion by land in the history of warfare.

Germany committed the major portion of its forces to the eastern front, where they would remain for the duration of the war. With several decisive victories at the outset, the German army swept through western Russia. Hitler, who increasingly took sole responsibility for directing the war effort, did not intend to shy away from this fight as he had in the Battle of Britain.

The Soviets defended themselves from Hitler's advance as the Russian Empire had from Napoleon's a century earlier: by retreating northward and preparing to allow the harsh winter to weaken its attackers. The German troops made it to the suburbs of Moscow by December, but they were inadequately equipped for winter combat and forced to retreat. Then they took heavy losses in the Soviet counteroffensive.

Russian women seal and label some of the thousands of flasks of blood donated by citizens of Moscow in 1941 to help with the war effort during World War II. Women in many countries who fought in the war played important roles both in combat and on the homefront. © *Universal History Archive/Getty Images*

The "Final Solution"

Having gained control over a huge swath of Eastern Europe by the end of 1941, the Third Reich unleashed its campaign of genocide on the Jewish population, the so-called "Final Solution." The Holocaust, also referred to by the Hebrew word *Shoah*, meaning catastrophe, refers to the genocide of more than 6 million European Jews, and many millions of non-Jews, by the Nazi German state during World War II.

Hitler had never concealed his vitriolic hatred of the Jewish people; anti-Semitism was a prominent theme in Hitler's manifesto, *Mein Kampf* (1925). The Nazi regime passed progressively more discriminatory laws against German Jews starting in 1934. The Third Reich also soon established forced-labor concentration camps, at first meant principally for political opponents of the regime. By 1939, the Nazis had begun the systematic deportation, ghettoization, and incarceration of Jews within Germany and in the Polish territories it occupied. German leaders clearly foresaw that many of those housed in concentration camps would be worked or starved to death. Nazi policy on the "Jewish question" soon escalated to one of extermination—the ultimate meaning of the commonly used phrase "the Final Solution."

By 1941, such camps as Auschwitz and Treblinka were explicitly designed not as prison camps but for the purposes of extermination, where those targeted were to be killed in gas chambers. At first carbon monoxide was used in the chambers, but later in the war the German chemical company IG Farben furnished the regime with large quantities of a concoction called Zyklon B. Only after the conclusion of the war did the full extent of the crimes of the Holocaust become widely known outside the territories where it took place.

Japan Attacks the United States

In another theater of the war, Japanese leaders aspired to widen their conquests beyond the Chinese mainland into the colonial territories of Southeast Asia. In September 1940, not long after the fall of France, the Imperial Japanese Army occupied French Indochina, gaining a launching site for further ventures in the region. Yet they moved cautiously, largely for fear of provoking the United States, which controlled the Philippines. Imperial leaders eventually formulated plans to initiate a wider Pacific war with sudden, multiple attacks. They carried out these attacks on December 7–8, 1941 (on both sides of the International Date Line). On that day, the forces of Japan invaded Thailand, Malaya, Hong Kong, and the Philippines, and simultaneously attacked the U.S. Pacific Fleet at Pearl Harbor, Hawaii, as well as the U.S.-held islands of Wake and Guam. Operations targeting Burma and the Dutch East Indies (Indonesia) followed in January.

The Japanese planners had gambled that a devastating preemptive strike on the U.S. naval fleet would leave the Americans demoralized and too weak to fight back. Unfortunately for the Japanese, the attack on Pearl Harbor did not, in fact, cripple the U.S. Pacific Fleet.

Nazi soldiers question Jews after the Warsaw Ghetto Uprising. In October 1940, the Nazis began to concentrate Poland's population of over 3 million Jews into overcrowded ghettos. In the largest of these, the Warsaw Ghetto, thousands of Jews died due to rampant disease and starvation, even before the Nazis began their massive deportations from the ghetto to the Treblinka extermination camp. In 1943 the Warsaw Ghetto was the scene of the Warsaw Ghetto Uprising, the first urban mass rebellion against the Nazi occupation of Europe, which took place from April 19 until May 16, 1943, and began after German troops and police entered the ghetto to deport its surviving inhabitants. It ended when the poorly armed and supplied resistance was crushed by German troops under the command of SS Gruppenführer Jürgen Stroop. © OFF/AFP/Getty Images

None of the U.S. aircraft carriers was at Pearl Harbor at the time of the attack, and the U.S. Navy was able to raise and repair 5 of the 8 battleships that had been sunk. Perhaps more important was the reaction of the American people to the attack. Pearl Harbor was at the time the single deadliest attack on U.S. soil, with 2,403 people killed. The shock and anger the American public felt after the Japanese attack overcame their isolationist sentiments and produced a determined commitment to victory. Riding on this wave of patriotic fervor, Roosevelt convinced Congress to declare war against Japan.

After the United States declared war on Japan, Germany and Italy in turn declared war on the United States, drawing America fully into the conflict. A few weeks later, on January 1, 1942, the Allies laid out their war aims in the "Declaration by United Nations." Signed by 26 Allied governments, including the United States, Britain, the Republic of China, and the Soviet Union (whose loyalties had naturally shifted after the German invasion), this document later formed the basis of the United Nations. It presented the conflict as a war against tyranny and stated that the only acceptable outcome was complete victory.

In the Pacific and Southeast Asia, Japan made rapid advances in early 1942, capturing Singapore, Bali, and Java, striking at Ceylon (Sri Lanka), and bombing the Australian city of Darwin. With control over an extensive area of the Western Pacific, the Japanese navy hatched a complicated plan to trap and destroy U.S. aircraft carriers on the island of Midway, but the Americans obtained advance knowledge of the coming attack and scored a stunning victory in June 1942. Two months later, the Allies took the offensive at Guadalcanal, in the Solomon Islands chain, where the Japanese had built an airstrip. In combat over several months, the Allies retook and held Guadalcanal. This conquest marked a turning

The battleship U.S.S. *West Virginia* is in flames after it is hit by Japanese bombs and torpedoes. On December 7, 1941, the Japanese attacked the U.S. naval base at Pearl Harbor, Hawaii, an act of provocation that led the United States to enter World War II.   © *History Archive/Getty Images*

WORLDMARK MODERN CONFLICT AND DIPLOMACY

point, as Japan never regained the strategic advantage in the island-hopping battles of the Pacific War.

A Turning Point, 1942

Meanwhile, on the eastern front in Europe, Germany advanced deep into southern Russia in the summer of 1942, intending to capture the city of Stalingrad and blockade the Volga River en route to the oil reserves near the Caspian Sea. A huge and decisive battle took place in Stalingrad and on the Volga. In November, the Soviets directed a counterattack against the flanks of the Axis forces, leaving the German Sixth Army surrounded inside the city as the winter set in. Hitler, who had publicly announced that his armies would never vacate the city named after the Soviet dictator, attempted to keep his encircled troops supplied by means of an "air bridge," but starvation slowly took its toll.

By January, the Soviet Red Army was closing in. Hitler refused to let his troops surrender but was eventually forced to acknowledge defeat. Casualty figures for the Volga campaign neared 800,000 for the Axis side and over 1 million for the Soviets. Many military historians describe Stalingrad as the distinctive turning point of World War II because it changed the momentum of the war in the east: the Germans were humiliated, and their eastward advance was halted. After their victory at Stalingrad, Soviet forces steadily pushed the Germans westward, back into their own territory.

Also in late 1942, U.S. troops joined British forces in North Africa, where the Germans held positions in Egypt and Tunisia. The Soviets had been pleading for the United States and Great Britian to open a new front in Europe by landing troops, but Allied planners believed it wiser to clear the way for an attack from the south

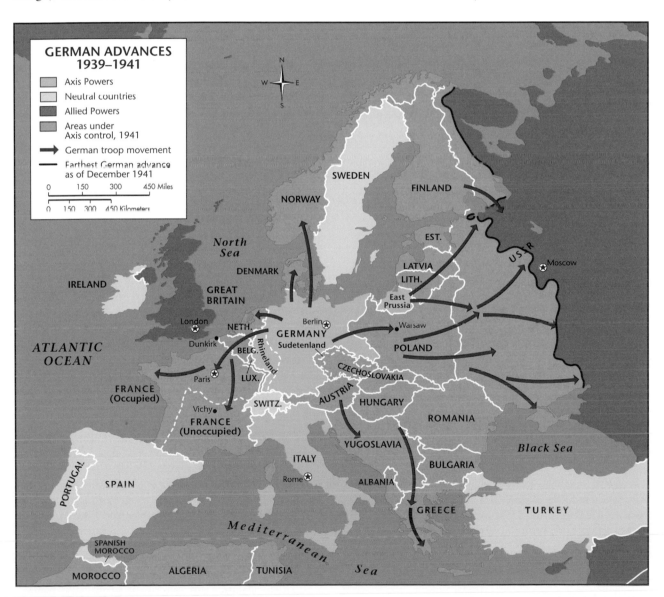

© 2014 Cengage Learning

by first securing the Mediterranean. The arrival of the American forces altered the strategic balance and gave the Allies the upper hand in the Mediterranean theater.

By May 1943, the Allies had achieved victory in their African campaign, forcing the Germans and Italians to surrender in Tunisia. While the fighting was still

LIBERATION OF GERMAN CONCENTRATION CAMPS

As the Allies advanced on Germany, they liberated the internees at multiple Nazi concentration and extermination camps. It was not until early 1945 that the true horror and magnitude of the Nazi genocide became undeniably apparent to the Allies. The racist policies of the German government were well known, and rumors of death camps had circulated, but few were prepared to believe stories of the inhuman atrocities committed in the concentration and extermination camps. But as Allied troops discovered and liberated the camps by the dozens, the truth was revealed. In January 1945, the Soviets liberated Auschwitz, the largest extermination camp, where more than one million prisoners died. Soon after, American troops liberated Dachau and Buchenwald, while the British liberated Bergen-Belsen. Dozens of other camps were also located, and their prisoners freed.

Soliders and reporters who later spoke and wrote of the sights, sounds, and smells of the camps painted nightmarish scenes—of piles of dead, emaciated bodies stacked in ditches; of prisoners so far advanced in starvation or illness that even the medical assistance of the Allies could not save them; of gas chambers where prisoners were executed by the hundreds of thousands.

The Germans had been able to operate the camps with relative secrecy; however, they kept extensive internal records, many of which were seized by Allied troops as they opened the camps. These records later helped establish the scope of the Holocaust, the conditions under which prisoners were kept, and the extraordinary sorts of torture and pseudo-scientific medical experiments to which many were subject.

Still, even more extensive records were held in relative secrecy for decades after the war by the International Tracing Center (ITC), an arm of the International Red Cross. Though the existence of the archives, held at Bad Arolsen, Germany, was known, researchers and Holocaust victims and their families did not have open access to the documents. They had to make formal requests for information and often had to wait years for answers.

The ITS maintained that respect for the victims' privacy necessitated the policy of strict control of access to the documents. It was not until 2006 that the ITS, with the consent of the German government and other nations responsible for overseeing the ITS, agreed to open its extensive archive of some 50 million Holocaust-related documents to the public. The archives, which hold documents related to the fates of 17.5 million people, were officially opened in 2008.

underway in North Africa, Roosevelt, Churchill, and the Free French leader Charles de Gaulle (1890–1970) met in Casablanca, in the French territory of Morocco. Their strategic planning included a public commitment to demand no less than "unconditional surrender" from the Axis powers. Some historians claim that in making this declaration, which critics claimed would prolong the war, Roosevelt intended to warn Stalin not to consider making a separate peace with Germany.

The Path to Allied Victory, 1943–1945

On July 10, 1943, Allied forces under the command of General Dwight D. Eisenhower (1890–1969) landed in Sicily, the large island at the southern tip of the Italian peninsula. Only days into the fighting, with Allied bombers striking at Rome, it became clear that the Italian public and even leading members of the government had turned against Mussolini. "Il Duce," as he was known, was ousted from office by King Victor Emmanuel III (1869–1947) and arrested on July 24.

The new Italian government capitulated to the Allies, but the German military marched in to disarm the Italian army and engage the U.S. and British troops (assisted by French, Polish, and Canadian units) fighting their way northward up the peninsula. The Germans rescued Mussolini and installed him in the town of Salò, in Lombardy, as head of a puppet state called the Italian Social Republic. The Germans repulsed multiple offensives over many months of heavy fighting before the Allies broke through their defensive lines and captured Rome, which the Germans had declared an undefended "open city," on June 4, 1944.

Only two days later came one of the most dramatic battles of the war: the D-Day landing of Allied forces at Normandy in northwestern France, code named Operation Overlord. The operation was the largest amphibious assault ever undertaken. It was also the first time in centuries that an invading army managed to land forces on the French side of the English Channel in the face of resistance. Though the Germans anticipated an Allied landing in France, a sophisticated campaign of deception and misdirection on the part of the Allies kept the Germans confused as to when and where the landing would take place. The subterfuge was so successful that even after D-Day, Germany was slow to commit reinforcements to the Normandy area, concerned that another major incursion was imminent at Calais.

Despite massive casualties, the Allies were able to open a Western European front. Within a month, a million Allied troops had reached the French shores. These divisions, aided by the French Resistance, soon broke out from their beachhead, encircled the counterattacking German troops, and marched on Paris, liberating it from Nazi control on August 25.

In the Pacific, the Americans progressed toward Japan by way of the Gilbert Islands and Marshall Islands.

In June 1944, U.S. forces landed on Saipan, in the Mariana Islands. A major battle took place to control this island, which was within flight range of Tokyo for U.S. bombers. The victory at Saipan gave the Americans a decisive strategic advantage and made Japan's supply lines to Southeast Asia more vulnerable to attack. In October, U.S. and Australian forces reached the eastern Philippine Islands and triumphed in the Battle of Leyte Gulf, the largest naval battle of the war. The Allied forces under General Douglas MacArthur (1880–1964) proceeded to liberate the Philippines.

By 1944 the Germans had lost the initiative on the eastern front. Their defeat the prior July in the massive tank battle at Kursk, near the Ukrainian border, opened the way for a Red Army summer offensive that retook much of the territory the Germans had previously captured. In the summer of 1944, massive Soviet attacks retook Belarus, Ukraine, and Romania.

With the Soviets pressing from the east, Germany shifted its emphasis toward achieving a quick victory on the western front by forcing American and British forces to surrender. The German offensive in the Ardennes forest of France and Belgium in December 1944 was intended to divide the Allied forces at a weak link and dispatch the Americans and British from the field so Hitler could concentrate his forces on the eastern front. The ensuing battle, nicknamed the Battle of the Bulge, was the costliest of the war in terms of U.S. casualties, but it was a decisive Allied victory and the last German offensive on the western front.

With German manpower diverted to the west, the Soviets advanced across Poland and stormed into German territory in January 1945. The Allies were now positioned close enough to launch bombing raids on German cities such as Dresden, which was virtually destroyed after waves of U.S. and British airplanes bombed the city, causing a massive firestorm. German forces were caught between Allied advances toward the German capital, Berlin, from both east and west, and defeat was imminent.

In early February 1945, Churchill, Stalin, and Roosevelt met at Yalta, on the Black Sea, to make provisions for the final stages of the war and the architecture of the peace. The western Allies advanced through German territory and across the Rhine River. On April 25, the U.S. and Soviet armies met at the Elbe River in eastern Germany. Five days later, Hitler committed suicide in his underground bunker. Germany's unconditional surrender and the end of Nazi rule followed on May 8, Victory in Europe (V-E) Day.

Forcing the Surrender of Japan

The Pacific War was nearing its end as well. Allied forces successfully retook Burma in early 1945, and in February the U.S. Marines captured the tiny island of Iwo Jima, located midway between Saipan and Tokyo. Although capturing the heavily fortified island came at the cost of 26,000 American and 19,000 Japanese casualties, this strategic conquest put the Japanese home islands in even closer bombing range. The U.S. Strategic Air Force under General Curtis LeMay (1906–1990) oversaw the firebombing of Japanese cities, including the capital of Tokyo on March 9–10, 1945. The Allies invaded Okinawa in April, precipitating a ferocious three-month battle in which Japanese aviators made increasing use of *kamikaze* suicide attacks. It became clear that the Allies would eventually prevail, but the Japanese refused to negotiate surrender terms. U.S. war planners began preparations for a land invasion of Japan itself, which they predicted would come at the cost of one million Allied casualties.

U.S. President Harry S. Truman (1884–1972), who had taken over after Roosevelt's death on April 12, was reluctant to order an invasion of Japan. He had another option, a secret weapon the Americans had been developing: the atomic bomb. A huge, covert

THE UNITED NATIONS

The origins of the United Nations have a great deal to do with Franklin D. Roosevelt. Even before the United States entered World War II, he expressed concern that victory in the global conflict should advance the principles of human rights and political freedom. These aspirations were reflected in the words of the Atlantic Charter issued by U.S. and British leaders in August 1941 and the January 1942 Declaration by United Nations. In October 1944—when the prospect of an Allied military triumph was beginning to appear more certain—diplomats from the United States, Britain, China, and the Soviet Union met at the Dumbarton Oaks estate in Washington, D.C., to work out a blueprint for a successor organization to the League of Nations. The diplomats conceived a Security Council empowered to use armed force, a General Assembly of all member states, and an International Court of Justice to arbitrate international disputes. The sensitive issue of how the Security Council would make decisions—including permanent and non-permanent members and veto power—was hashed out at the Yalta Conference in February 1945.

Representatives from 50 countries attended the founding conference of the United Nations (UN) in San Francisco in April 1945. Roosevelt had died in the days before the meeting convened, and news of the deaths of both Mussolini and Hitler, as well as the European victory, reached the conference in its first days. On June 25, the assembled diplomats unanimously approved the Charter they had drafted. The official date used for the inauguration of the UN is October 24, 1945, when the General Assembly convened for its first session. The first resolution approved by the Assembly called for nuclear weapons to be eliminated from the arsenals of all nations and placed under international control.

scientific crash program, codenamed the Manhattan Project, had succeeded after three years in splitting the atom and unleashing the nearly infinite power of atomic forces to create an explosive device capable of obliterating a city. When the Japanese leadership refused one last demand to surrender, Truman and his advisors decided to drop the bomb on a Japanese city without warning.

On August 6, 1945, Hiroshima became the first city attacked by a nuclear weapon. Three days later, a second device was dropped on Nagasaki. The two bombs together killed approximately 250,000 people; about half of these died instantly, while the rest succumbed to radiation poisoning over the following weeks and months. In between the two atomic bombings, the Soviet Union launched a huge attack on Manchuria. (Stalin had agreed at Yalta to enter the Pacific conflict within three months of Germany's defeat.) Within days, the Russians crushed the Japanese forces on the Asian mainland, advancing to the northern part of the Korean peninsula. The combined shocks of these

calamities finally compelled the Japanese to offer surrender terms. Victory in Japan, or V-J Day, was proclaimed on August 9, 1945.

⊕ Impacts and Issues

The defeat of the Axis powers brought about a profound restructuring of the international order. One central aspect of the new order was the preeminence of the United States of America. It was the only great power whose infrastructure escaped incalculable damage in World War II. Furthermore, wartime production decisively reversed the effects of the Great Depression on the U.S. economy. At the end of the war, the United States produced nearly 50 percent of global economic output, an unprecedented figure. Its military contribution on both of the war's fronts had been indispensable, and it possessed the most powerful weapon of mass destruction ever created. There could be no doubt that the United States had become a superpower.

The Japanese delegation, including Mamoru Shigemitsu (top hat, cane) and Gen. Yoshijiro Umezu (immediately L of Shigemitsu), faces U.S. Gen. Douglas MacArthur (at mic) and Allied officers during the official, unconditional surrender of Japan, held aboard the battleship U.S.S. *Missouri* in Tokyo Bay. Allies on the front row include, from left to right: Chester A. Nimitz, Chinese Gen. Hsu Yung-Chang, British Adm. Bruce Fraser, Russian Lt. Gen. Kuzma N. Derevyanko, Australian Gen. Thomas Blamey, Canadian Col. L. Moore Cosgrave, French Gen. Jacques LeClerc, Dutch Adm. Conrad Helfrich, New Zealand Vice Marshal L.M. Isitt, Lt. Gen. R.K. Sutherland, and Gen. Jonathan Wainwright. © *J. R. Eyerman/Time Life Pictures/Getty Images*

The "Hot" War Turns Cold

Even though the Axis powers were vanquished, the United States had a potent adversary—its wartime ally, the Soviet Union. Wartime diplomacy had revealed the strains between the eastern and western powers, and the postwar peace soon gave way to a tense, ideologically motivated rivalry known as the Cold War. Although the principal players—the United States and the Soviet Union—did not enter into direct military conflict, they came close on several occasions as they competed to spread their political philosophies and expand their spheres of influence around the world.

Occupied Germany was partitioned into British, French, American, and Soviet zones. The northeastern zone, including Berlin, became a Communist state under Soviet influence. Other Soviet-aligned Communist governments were established across Eastern Europe. Churchill famously stated, in a 1946 address at a small college in Missouri, that an "Iron Curtain" had fallen across Europe dividing the Communist East from the democratic West.

The perils of the new balance of power became starker after the Soviet Union conducted its first nuclear weapons test explosion in 1949. That year, the North Atlantic Treaty Organization (NATO) formed as a military alliance between the United States and European countries. The NATO alliance included the standing threat of U.S. nuclear retaliation in the event of a conventional Soviet attack on Western Europe. Nuclear deterrence thus became a fundamental aspect of international relations, as all parties recognized that a third world war could bring

EUROPE AFTER WWII

- Territory gained by Poland
- Territory gained by USSR
- Territory gained by Czechoslovakia
- Germany, 1939

0   250   500 Miles
0   250   500 Kilometers

about the demise of human civilization and, indeed, of all life on Earth.

Another key American act of humanitarianism and political calculation was the enactment of the Marshall Plan, named after its chief architect, Secretary of State George Marshall. Under the Marshall Plan, which commenced in 1948 and continued for four years, the United States committed over a billion dollars to help rebuild and modernize war-torn Western Europe and restore its economic stability.

In arguing for his plan, Marshall stressed the humanitarian crisis in Europe, including hunger and widespread poverty. But it was also clear that among the major diplomatic goals of the plan were to restore political stability in Western Europe, secure a strong political alignment between Western Europe and the United States, and, as a result, prevent the spread of Soviet communism. Europe did indeed experience a remarkable economic recovery in the early 1950s, though historians dispute the extent to which the Marshall Plan contributed to this boom. However, what is indisputable is that the United States did secure strong alliances with Western European nations, and that the Marshall Plan was viewed positively by the Europeans who benefitted from it.

Yet another keystone of the postwar order was the United Nations, which arose in 1945 to replace the League of Nations as the world's premier multilateral forum tasked with maintaining international peace and security. The World Bank and International Monetary Fund were also established in 1945 to oversee reconstruction, development, and integration of the world economy. With substantial financial aid from the United States, both Western Europe (including West Germany) and Japan swiftly recovered their industrial bases. The former Axis powers were forbidden from rearming for offensive military capability.

The UN also oversaw the gradual dissolution of the colonial empires, as former colonies and protectorates asserted their rights to self-determination and political independence. In addition it oversaw the partition of former British holdings in Palestine, which created the State of Israel as a homeland for the world's Jews. Three decades after its founding, the UN had swelled in membership from 51 to 144 states.

Technology, intelligence, and espionage had played an enormously influential role in shaping the course of World War II. With the advent of the nuclear age in the immediate postwar era, each of the world's leading governments made a concerted effort to augment its capabilities in the intelligence field. In the United States, the National Security Act of 1947 established the National Security Council and the Central Intelligence Agency (CIA), the latter of which replaced the wartime spy branch, called the Office of Strategic Services (OSS). The CIA's functions vastly exceed those of traditional intelligence gathering and analysis; since the 1950s, the

agency has frequently served as a covert and extra-legal arm of U.S. foreign policy.

⊕ Future Implications

Many of the institutions and geopolitical arrangements put in place at the close of World War II have endured well into the 21st century as essential hallmarks of global politics. Indeed, the multilateral diplomatic and financial bodies of the UN system, and even the NATO alliance, have outlasted the Cold War and the Soviet Union, and the five Allied powers remained the only permanent members of the UN Security Council as of 2014. Some international relations scholars argue that the end of the Cold War permitted the Security Council to demonstrate more fully its value in conflict prevention, with examples including the Council's role in the 1990–91 Persian Gulf crisis and the conflicts in the Balkans during the 1990s. The values and international norms for which the Allies went to war against the Axis powers have, arguably, become the prevailing influences on international diplomacy.

Though the power of the United States was unquestionable in the years after the war, and the military protection and financial assistance it provided to its European allies were welcome, America's dominance began to provoke a backlash, especially after the fall of the Soviet Union in 1991 left the United States alone as the world's remaining superpower. Its extensive military presence in Europe, once seen as a necessary check against Soviet aggression, increasingly became viewed as a Cold War leftover (though one that offered economic benefits to the communities surrounding U.S. military bases). European leaders became increasingly open in criticizing U.S. foreign policy, especially as the 21st century dawned. Still, though there have been regional conflicts in Europe since World War II, the post–World War II peace has held and seems likely to continuing holding, even absent major financial or military contributions by the United States.

PRIMARY SOURCE

Obersalzberg Speech

SOURCE *Hitler, Adolf. "The Obersalzberg Speech," August 22, 1939. From* Documents on British Foreign Policy. 1919–1939. *eds. E. L. Woodward and Rohan Riftlep; 3rd series. London: HMSO, 1954, pp. 7:258–260. As found on The Internet Modern History Sourcebook at Fordham University. http://www.fordham.edu/halsall/mod/hitler-obersalzberg.asp (accessed November 5, 2013).*

INTRODUCTION *On August 22, 1939, Adolf Hitler gave the following speech outlining his intentions regarding Poland, which Nazi Germany invaded less than two weeks later. The day following this speech, Germany and the Soviet Union signed a 10-year non-aggression treaty (the Nazi Soviet Pact or Molotov-Ribbentrap Pact). This agreement allowed Hitler to move ahead with plans to invade Poland without worrying about also being at war with the Soviets, even though he apparently had little intention of being bound by the agreement. On December 18, 1940, Hitler violated the treaty when he signed the first operational order for the invasion of the Soviet Union, which took place on June 22, 1941, less than two years after the Nazi Soviet Pact was signed.*

The decision to attack Poland was arrived at last spring. Originally, I feared that the political constellation would compel me to strike simultaneously at England, Russia, France, and Poland. Even this risk would have had to be taken.

Ever since the autumn of 1938, and because I realized that Japan would not join us unconditionally and that Mussolini is threatened by that nit-wit of a king and the treasonable scoundrel of a crown prince, I decided to go with Stalin.

In the last analysis, there are only three great statesmen in the world, Stalin, I, and Mussolini. Mussolini is the weakest, for he has been unable to break the power of either the crown or the church. Stalin and I are the only ones who envisage the future and nothing but the future. Accordingly, I shall in a few weeks stretch out my hand to Stalin at the common German-Russian frontier and undertake the redistribution of the world with him.

Our strength consists in our speed and in our brutality. Genghis Khan led millions of women and children to slaughter—with premeditation and a happy heart. History sees in him solely the founder of a state. It's a matter of indifference to me what a weak western European civilization will say about me.

I have issued the command—and I'll have anybody who utters but one word of criticism executed by a firing squad—that our war aim does not consist in reaching certain lines, but in the physical destruction of the enemy. Accordingly, I have placed my death-head formations in readiness—for the present only in the East—with orders to them to send to death mercilessly and without compassion, men, women, and children of Polish derivation and language. Only thus shall we gain the living space (Lebensraum) which we need. Who, after all, speaks today of the annihilation of the Armenians?

Colonel-General von Brauchitsch has promised me to bring the war against Poland to a close within a few weeks. Had he reported to me that he needs two years or even only one year, I should not have given the command to march and should have allied myself temporarily with England instead of Russia for we cannot conduct a long war. To be sure a new situation has arisen.

I experienced those poor worms Daladier and Chamberlain in Munich. They will be too cowardly to attack. They won't go beyond a blockade. Against that we have our autarchy and the Russian raw materials.

Poland will be depopulated and settled with Germans. My pact with the Poles was merely conceived of as a gaining of time. As for the rest, gentlemen, the fate of Russia will be exactly the same as I am now going through with in the case of Poland. After Stalin's death—he is a very sick man—we will break the Soviet Union. Then there will begin the dawn of the German rule of the earth.

The little States cannot scare me. After Kemal's [i.e. Ataturk] death Turkey is governed by cretins and half idiots. Carol of Roumania is through and through the corrupt slave of his sexual instincts. The King of Belgium and the Nordic kings are soft jumping jacks who are dependent upon the good digestions of their over-eating and tired peoples.

We shall have to take into the bargain the defection of Japan. I save Japan a full year's time. The Emperor is a counterpart to the last Czar—weak, cowardly, undecided. May he become a victim of the revolution. My going together with Japan never was popular. We shall continue to create disturbances in the Far East and in Arabia. Let us think as "gentlemen" and let us see in these peoples at best lacquered half maniacs who are anxious to experience the whip.

The opportunity is as favourable as never before. I have but one worry, namely that Chamberlain or some other such pig of a fellow (Saukerl) will come at the last moment with proposals or with ratting (Umfall). He will fly down the stairs, even if I shall personally have to trample on his belly in the eyes of the photographers.

No, it is too late for this. The attack upon and the destruction of Poland begins Saturday early. I shall let a few companies in Polish uniform attack in Upper Silesia or in the Protectorate. Whether the world believes it is quite indifferent (scheissegal). The world believes only in success.

For you, gentlemen, fame and honour are beginning as they have not since centuries. Be hard, be without mercy, act more quickly and brutally than the others. The citizens of Western Europe must tremble with horror. That is the most human way of conducting a war. For it scares the others off.

The new method of conducting war corresponds to the new drawing of the frontiers. A war extending from Reval, Lublin, Kaschau to the mouth of the Danube. The rest will be given to the Russians. Ribbentrop has orders to make every offer and to accept every demand. In the West I reserve to myself the right to determine the strategically best line. Here one will be able to work with Protectorate regions, such as Holland, Belgium and French Lorraine.

And now, on to the enemy, in Warsaw we will celebrate our reunion.

PRIMARY SOURCE

A Date Which Will Live in Infamy

SOURCE *Roosevelt, Franklin D. "Transcript of Joint Address to Congress Leading to a Declaration of War Against Japan (1941) (A Date Which Will Live in Infamy Speech)."* U.S. National Archives, December 8, 1941. http://www.ourdocuments. gov/doc.php?flash=true&doc=73&page=transcript (accessed November 5, 2013).

INTRODUCTION *On December 8, 1941, the day after the surprise Japanese attack on Pearl Harbor destroyed or damaged more than a dozen U.S. warships, hundreds of airplanes, and killed approximately 2,500 military personnel and civilians, President Franklin D. Roosevelt addressed the U.S. Congress and requested a declaration of war. Roosevelt's powerful and now iconic speech succeeded in gaining the strong support of the population and of Congress, which immediately declared war on Japan. Three days later Germany and Italy declared war on the United States.*

Mr. Vice President, and Mr. Speaker, and Members of the Senate and House of Representatives:

Yesterday, December 7, 1941—a date which will live in infamy—the United States of America was suddenly and deliberately attacked by naval and air forces of the Empire of Japan.

The United States was at peace with that Nation and, at the solicitation of Japan, was still in conversation with its Government and its Emperor looking toward the maintenance of peace in the Pacific. Indeed, one hour after Japanese air squadrons had commenced bombing in the American Island of Oahu, the Japanese Ambassador to the United States and his colleague delivered to our Secretary of State a formal reply to a recent American message. And while this reply stated that it seemed useless to continue the existing diplomatic negotiations, it contained no threat or hint of war or of armed attack.

It will be recorded that the distance of Hawaii from Japan makes it obvious that the attack was deliberately planned many days or even weeks ago. During the intervening time the Japanese Government has deliberately sought to deceive the United States by false statements and expressions of hope for continued peace.

The attack yesterday on the Hawaiian Islands has caused severe damage to American naval and military forces. I regret to tell you that very many American lives have been lost. In addition American ships have been reported torpedoed on the high seas between San Francisco and Honolulu.

Yesterday the Japanese Government also launched an attack against Malaya.
Last night Japanese forces attacked Hong Kong.
Last night Japanese forces attacked Guam.
Last night Japanese forces attacked the Philippine Islands.
Last night the Japanese attacked Wake Island. And this morning the Japanese attacked Midway Island.

Japan has, therefore, undertaken a surprise offensive extending throughout the Pacific area. The facts of yesterday and today speak for themselves. The people of the United States have already formed their opinions and well understand the implications to the very life and safety of our Nation.

As Commander in Chief of the Army and Navy I have directed that all measures be taken for our defense.

But always will our whole Nation remember the character of the onslaught against us.

No matter how long it may take us to overcome this premeditated invasion, the American people in their righteous might will win through to absolute victory. I believe that I interpret the will of the Congress and of the people when I assert that we will not only defend ourselves to the uttermost but will make it very certain that this form of treachery shall never again endanger us.

Hostilities exist. There is no blinking at the fact that our people, our territory, and our interests are in grave danger.

With confidence in our armed forces—with the unbounding determination of our people—we will gain the inevitable triumph—so help us God.

I ask that the Congress declare that since the unprovoked and dastardly attack by Japan on Sunday, December 7, 1941, a state of war has existed between the United States and the Japanese Empire.

SEE ALSO *Cold War; Holocaust; North Atlantic Treaty Organization (NATO); United Nations; Weapons of Mass Destruction; World War I*

BIBLIOGRAPHY

Books

Brokaw, Tom. *The Greatest Generation.* New York: Random House Trade, 2001.

Churchill, Winston. *The Second World War.* 6 volumes. London: Cassell and Co., 1948–1954.

Gilbert, Martin. *The Second World War: A Complete History.* New York: Holt Paperbacks, 2004.

Shirer, William L. *The Rise and Fall of the Third Reich.* New York: Simon and Schuster, 1960.

Weinberg, Gerhard L. *A World At Arms: A Global History of World War II.* New York: Cambridge University Press, 1994.

Web Sites

"World War II." *BBC History.* http://www.bbc. co.uk/history/worldwars/wwtwo/ (accessed December 7, 2013).

"World War II." *The National Archives (UK).* http:// www.nationalarchives.gov.uk/education/ worldwar2/ (accessed December 7, 2013).

"World War II: Documents." *Yale Law School Lillian Goldman Law Library.* http://avalon.law.yale.edu/subject_ menus/wwii.asp (accessed December 7, 2013).

"World War II Timeline." *United States Holocaust Memorial Museum.* http://www.ushmm.org/wlc/ en/article.php?ModuleId=10007306 (accessed September 7, 2013).

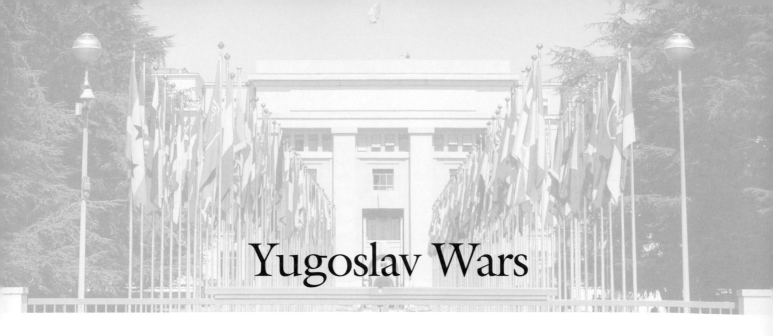

Yugoslav Wars

🌐 Introduction

The Yugoslav Wars were a series of wars fought in southeastern Europe in the 1990s and early years of the 21st century. The Balkans has a long history of conflict due to the large number of ethnic groups in the region that have different religions, languages, and cultures. However, throughout most of the 20th century, the various ethnic groups of the Balkans lived with little conflict under the totalitarian, Communist regime of Yugoslavia.

This changed following the demise of the Communist Party of Yugoslavia in the early 1990s, when the Yugoslav republics broke away from the Serbian-controlled Yugoslav government. Ultimately, seven nations formed from the former Yugoslav state: Bosnia and Herzegovina, Croatia, the Republic of Macedonia, Montenegro, Serbia, Slovenia, and Kosovo. The transition was violent. Over 140,000 people were killed in the wars involved in the breakup of Yugoslavia. The conflicts were the deadliest in Europe since World War II (1939–45).

🌐 Historical Background

Conflict in the Balkans was nothing new. In the late 19th and early 20th centuries, war roiled the region. In 1912 the First Balkan War began as four countries on the Balkan Peninsula (Greece, Bulgaria, Serbia, and Montenegro) formed the Balkan League to fight against the Ottoman Empire, which had been weakened during the late 19th century. By the end of the war, the Ottoman Empire had been driven out of the region, losing most of its territory in Europe, including Macedonia and Albania. During the Second Balkan War, Bulgaria attacked its former allies Greece and Serbia to add more territory to what it had gained in the first war. However, Romania and the Ottoman Empire also entered the war against

Bulgaria, and it was defeated, losing territory to each of the other participants. Tensions regarding disputed territory, as well as religious and ethnic divisions, continued to affect the Balkans for over a century afterward.

In fact, the 1914 assassination of Austro-Hungarian Archduke Franz Ferdinand (1863–1914) by a member of a Serbian militant group sparked World War I (1914–18). In 1918, following the defeat of the Central Powers in World War I, the victorious Entente Powers (also known as the Allied Powers: Britain, France, and Russia) took a large part of the defeated Austro-Hungarian Empire and combined the land with the existing kingdoms of Serbia and Montenegro.

This new Slavic nation was called the Kingdom of Serbs, Croats, and Slovenes, but the name was changed to Yugoslavia in 1946. Under the totalitarian Communist leadership of Josip Tito (1892–1980) from 1946 to 1980, Yugoslavia managed to keep the historic rivalries of the nation's various ethnic groups in check. Following the death of Tito, Slovenia, Croatia, and Kosovo began to demand greater independence from the Serbian-controlled government of Yugoslavia.

War in the Wake of Yugoslavia's Disintegration

From 1989 to 1991, the Communist government of Yugoslavia weakened and eventually collapsed. Uprisings began in Bosnia, Croatia, and Slovenia. In June 1991, Croatia and Slovenia declared their independence from Yugoslavia. Yugoslav forces engaged in a brief 10-day war in Slovenia, known as the Slovenian Independence War or Ten-Day War, before retreating under a cease-fire. The Croatian War of Independence lasted from 1991 to 1995 and resulted in 20,000 dead and 37,000 wounded. In September 1991, the Republic of Macedonia declared its independence from Yugoslavia, becoming the only republic to do so without military opposition from Yugoslavia.

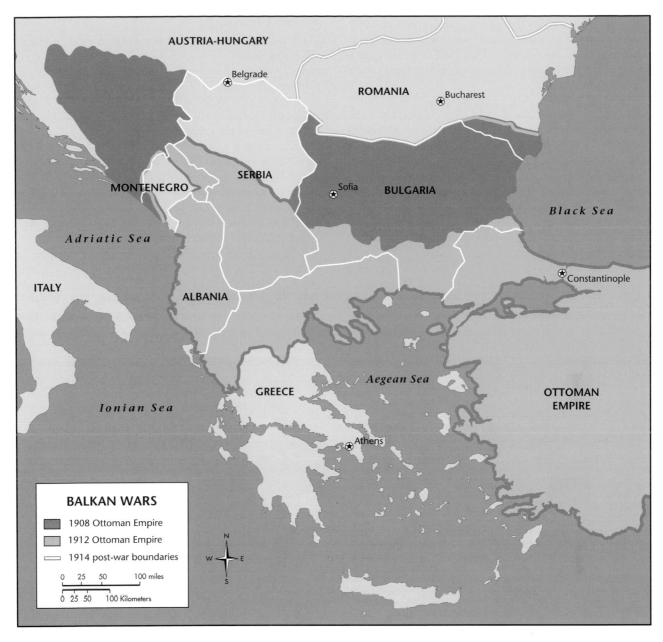

BALKAN WARS

- 1908 Ottoman Empire
- 1912 Ottoman Empire
- 1914 post-war boundaries

0 25 50   100 miles

0 25 50   100 Kilometers

Bosnia declared its independence on April 5, 1992. The minority Bosnian Serb population then declared independence from the newly formed Bosniak-controlled Bosnia (Bosniaks are a Bosnian group, often referred to as Bosnian Muslims, though not all of them are Muslims). The Bosnian War that followed lasted from 1992 to 1995 and consisted of Bosnian Serb, Yugoslav, and Croatian-supported forces against Bosniak forces. The North Atlantic Treaty Organization (NATO) intervened in 1995 and provided air support for Bosniak forces. Casualty estimates from the Bosnian War vary, but most estimates include approximately 100,000 dead, including over 35,000 civilians, and well

over one million civilians displaced. The Bosnian War officially ended with the signing of the Dayton Agreement in December 1995.

The Kosovo War began in 1996 when the Kosovo Liberation Army (KLA), a relatively unknown paramilitary group of ethnic Albanians, attacked Yugoslav police and civilian targets. Fighting between KLA and Yugoslav forces intensified in 1998 and 1999. Western nations generally considered KLA to be a terrorist organization and therefore refused to intervene in the Kosovo War as NATO had done in Bosnia.

Western opinion changed after the Racāk Massacre in 1999, in which Yugoslav forces killed 40 to 50

Kosovo Albanians. In the spring and summer of 1999, NATO carried out an aircraft bombing campaign to push out Yugoslav forces so that NATO peacekeepers could enter and stabilize Kosovo. Yugoslav forces withdrew in June 1999.

United Nations (UN) peacekeeping forces administered Kosovo until Kosovo officially declared its independence from Serbia in February 2008. Although the new nation has been officially recognized by over 100 other countries, Serbia does not recognize Kosovo's independence. Serbia filed a lawsuit with the International Court of Justice, arguing that the Kosovar declaration of independence was a violation of international law. In July 2010, the court concluded that Kosovo's declaration of independence did not violate general international law.

Meanwhile, Montenegro, the only country that had remained with Serbia (with Serbia and Montenegro being what was left of the former Yugoslavia), declared its independence from Serbia in 2006.

Ethnic Cleansing

During the Balkan Wars, there were charges of ethnic cleansing. Ethnic cleansing is the practice of removing another ethnic, national, or religious group by expulsion or extermination. Ethnic cleansing is not the same as genocide (the systematic extermination of an ethnic, religious, or national group), although genocide may occur as part of the ethnic cleansing process.

The term is a literal translation of the Serbo-Croat expression *etničko čiš ćenje*, and first gained common usage during Yugoslavia's civil wars in the 1990s. In that conflict, Croatian, Bosnian-Muslim, Kosovar-Albanian, and, in particular, Serb populations sought to assert ethnic claims on enclaves of the former Yugoslavia so as to create ethnically distinct nation-states.

But while these various campaigns to "cleanse" a territory of another ethnic group were gruesome and tragic, historically they were neither new nor remarkable. Indeed, the Yugoslav civil wars were often a reprise of similar conflicts that took place in the Balkans

Serb residents leave Kosovo to the boos of ethnic Albanian Kosovars on June 17, 1999, in Mitrovica. After a bombing campaign to rid Kosovo of Yugoslav forces, the NATO-led peacekeeping force in Kosovo stepped up its efforts to stop Serb civilians fleeing the province by showing its readiness to disarm KLA guerrillas and by taking a reassuring message to five key towns. Many Serbs continued to leave the area despite NATO efforts. © Jean-Philippe Ksiazek/AFP/Getty Images

HISTORY OF ETHNIC CLEANSING

The history of ethnic cleansing can be traced back at least as far as the Neo-Assyrian empire (911–612 BC), where the tactic of forced deportation of restless minorities was frequently used. The Greeks, Romans, and Byzantines each variously used ethnic cleansing to secure parts of their empires. Through the Middle Ages, Jews were frequently massacred or banished from various European countries. This included, in 1290, the forcible expulsion of English Jews, and in 1396, the expulsion of 100,000 Jews from France.

As modern notions of nationhood and nationality increased through the 19th and early 20th century, so incidence of ethnic cleansing increased. Sometimes, this has been the subject of fierce debate: at what point does ethnic cleansing become genocide, such as that of the Holocaust during World War II, when Nazi Germany systematically murdered most of Europe's Jewish population?

On a narrower basis, ethnic cleansing has been used to describe forcible segregation in various urban districts outside what could be considered conflict zones—for example, between Protestants and Catholics in some parts of Belfast, Northern Ireland; or between French, West African, and Arab populations in Paris's *banlieue* ("outskirts") districts.

One of the most potent debates that still inflames passions to this day is that of the Armenian massacres (1915–17) when the Armenian population of the Ottoman Empire was systematically destroyed through murders and forced deportations by the Ottoman government (part of which is now Turkey). A majority of

Western historians say that this is a simple case of genocide. But others contend that calling it genocide is an exaggeration and that at worst the Armenian massacres can be described as partial ethnic cleansing or a diaspora (dispersion of people from their homeland). The debate has been further inflamed by Turkish law. Under the Turkish penal code, even saying that the Armenian killings were genocide is viewed as an insult against the Turkish identity, which is a crime.

Although ethnic cleansing lacks a formal legal definition, under international law its process—the forcible expulsion or deportation of a population—is considered a crime against humanity. These are the charges that former Yugoslav President Slobodan Milošević (1941–2006), a Bosnian Serb and the most notorious modern exponent of ethnic cleansing, was answering when he died during his trial for war crimes at the Hague in 2006.

One example of the ethnic cleansing that occurred during Milošević's presidency took place in Omarska, a small mining village in what is now Bosnia and Herzegovina. For several months in 1992, Bosnian Serb forces detained more than 7,000 Bosniaks and Bosnian Croats at what was called the Omarska camp, which was later compared to a Nazi death camp. The detainees were victims of the ethnic cleansing of the nearby city of Prijedor. In the five months of its existence, hundreds of detainees died of starvation, beatings, and executions. More than 100 mass graves were subsequently found near the camp, along with hundreds of individual graves. Several of the guards at the camp were later indicted for atrocities including rape, torture, murder, and genocide.

during and immediately after World War II, before Yugoslavia was instituted as an uneasy federation of these republics.

⊕ Impacts and Issues

Although the fighting in the Balkans ended in 2001 following minor engagements in Macedonia and southern Serbia, the effects of the Balkan conflicts linger. Yugoslavia changed its name to the State Union of Serbia and Montenegro in 2003 to placate a growing separatist movement in Montenegro. Even this last vestige of the former Yugoslavia was short lived, however, as Montenegro declared its independence in June 2006.

The wars redrew many of the boundaries in the region, and the countries of Slovenia, Macedonia, Montenegro, Croatia, Serbia, Bosnia-Herzegovina, and Montenegro emerged as independent nations, all moving towards greater political and economic integration with the rest of Europe. In 2004, Slovenia became the first former Yugoslav state to join the European Union (EU). Croatia joined the EU in 2013. Serbia and the Republic of Macedonia are official candidates for accession to

the EU. Montenegro is currently negotiating candidacy with the EU. Bosnia and Herzegovina and Kosovo have not officially applied for accession to the EU, but the EU considers these states to be potential candidates.

War Crimes

Charges of war crimes—especially genocide and torture—were made throughout the Balkan conflicts. The UN formed a special court for prosecuting war crimes that occurred during the Balkan wars, known as the International Criminal Tribunal for the former Yugoslavia (ICTY). On July 20, 2011, the last of 161 suspects wanted by the UN for war crime charges associated with the Balkan conflict was arrested in Serbia. Of the 161 individuals indicted for war crimes by the ICTY, the court had resolved over 100 cases.

The ICTY's most notable trial involved the war crimes prosecution of Milošević, the former president of Yugoslavia. Milošević died in his cell of a heart attack just months before the ICTY rendered a verdict in his case. On July 18, 2008, Radovan Karadžić (1945–), the former president of the Republika Srpska (Bosnian Serb Republic), was arrested under indictments issued by the ICTY for the war crimes of genocide and mass murder, including ordering the massacre of over 8,000 Bosniak men and boys in the Bosnian town of Srebrenica in July 1995.

Prosecution of war crimes has often been successful. ICTY upheld the convictions of two Bosnian Serb commanders, Milan Lukic (1967–) and his cousin Sredoje Lukic (1961–), in early December 2012. In 2009, the two men were convicted of crimes against humanity and war crimes for the events in Visgrad during the 1992–95 conflict. Milan Lukic's life sentence stood unchanged, while the court reduced Sredoje Lukic's sentence slightly from 30 years to 27 years.

In late March 2013, a war crimes tribunal at The Hague convicted two former top Bosnian Serb officials and sentenced them to 22 years in jail. Stojan Zupljanin (1951–) and Mico Stanisic (1954–) were found guilty of crimes against humanity such as murder, torture, and unlawful detention perpetrated in 1992 in various parts of Bosnia. A UN tribunal in The Hague convicted six Bosnian Croats for persecuting and murdering Bosniaks during the Balkan Wars. The former leaders received sentences from 10 to 25 years in prison for war crimes and crimes against humanity.

⊕ Future Implications

Despite the high-profile prosecutions by war crimes tribunals, much is still unresolved regarding the Balkan Wars. Many of the presumed dead are still missing, and their families remain committed to finding their remains and bringing their killers to justice. Some identified killers remain free due to lack of evidence.

The ethnic cleansing was perpetrated by neighbors on neighbors, and so the return to peace is fragile. The various countries emerging out of the former Yugoslavia are somewhat more segregated following the wars. For decades under Communist rule, the various ethnic groups worked and lived side-by-side, sometimes intermarried, and barely differentiated themselves by their

A forensic archaeologist of the International Commission on Missing Persons (ICMP) works on an excavation at the Budak mass grave in the Srebrenica Municipality on July 12, 2005, in Bosnia Herzegovina. The site is a secondary grave site—600 victims were killed and buried in a primary location and later 100 of them were transferred to this secondary grave. The mortal remains at this site were allegedly moved to be buried here from sites at Glogova with heavy machinery, and ballistic and blast damage caused by grenades was observed on many of the remains. The team makes an electronic survey of all items found and maps and records the grave formation. Records of the recovered remains are transferred with the remains to the ICMP mortuary facility as an aid to identification. Some 8,000 Muslims, mostly boys and men, were slaughtered at Srebrenica in July 1995 by Bosnian Serb soldiers. © Marco Di Lauro/Getty Images

ethnic group. Persecution based on ethnicity during the Balkan Wars has strengthened ethnic affiliations.

In addition, there are significant economic disparities among the countries resulting from the breakup of Yugoslavia. Disproportionate wealth and industry made the per capita income of Slovakia and Croatia more than twice that of Bosnia and Herzegovina. Uneven wealth distribution and economic insecurity exacerbate the already tense ethnic divisions.

SEE ALSO *Armenian Genocide; Bosnian War; Genocide; Kosovo's Independence; United Nations*

BIBLIOGRAPHY

Books

Becker, Sally. *Sunflowers and Snipers: Saving Children in the Balkan War.* Stroud, Gloucestershire, UK: History Press, 2012.

French, Laurence. *War Trauma and Its Aftermath: An International Perspective on the Balkans and Gulf Wars.* Lanham, MD: University Press of America, 2012.

Mojzes, Paul. *Balkan Genocides: Holocaust and Ethnic Cleansing in the Twentieth Century.* Lanham, MD: Rowman & Littlefield, 2011.

Periodicals

"2nd-Generation Balkan War Victims Struggle with Violence, Substance Abuse." *U.S. Federal News Service, Including U.S. State News* (March 5, 2013).

Michail, Eugene. "Western Attitudes to War in the Balkans and the Shifting Meanings of Violence, 2012–91. *Journal of Contemporary History* 47, no. 2 (April 2012): 219.

"Winding Down With a Whimper: Balkan War-Crimes." *The Economist* 407, no. 8839 (June 8, 2013): 5B.

Web Sites

"The Balkan Crisis: A Brief History." *CNN*, 1997. http://www.cnn.com/SPECIALS/1997/bosnia/history/ (accessed November 30, 2013).

"Balkans 1940s to 1999." *Washington Post Online.* http://www.washingtonpost.com/wp-srv/inatl/longterm/balkans/timeline.htm (accessed November 30, 2013).

Judah, Tim. "Why Are Balkan War-Crimes Convictions Getting Overturned?" *Bloomberg*, June 6, 2013. http://www.bloomberg.com/news/2013-06-06/why-are-balkan-war-crimes-convictions-getting-overturned (accessed November 30, 2013).

Osborn, Andrew. "Five Serbs Guilty of Omarska Camp Atrocities." *The Guardian*, November 3, 2011. http://www.theguardian.com/world/2001/nov/03/warcrimes.balkans (accessed November 30, 2013).

United Nations International Criminal Tribunal for the Former Yugoslavia. http://www.icty.org/ (accessed November 30, 2013).

Organizations

ABUELAS DE PLAZA DE MAYO

Abuelas de Plaza de Mayo (Grandmothers of the Plaza de Mayo) is a human rights organization formed in 1977 to find more than 500 children of victims of the government who "disappeared" during Argentina's Dirty War from 1976 to 1983. They have used genetic testing to find children who were taken from victims of the military junta and adopted out to other families.

Corrientes 3284, 4 Piso – Dto. H
Virrey Cevallos 592 PB Dpto 1
Buenos Aires, Argentina
1193
Phone: (54)11-4384-0983
abuelas@abuelas.org.ar
http://www.abuelas.org.ar/english/history.htm

AFRICAN UNION

The African Union (AU), founded in 1999, was established to promote unity among African states and rid the continent of vestiges of colonialism. The AU has intervened in several conflicts in Africa, including the crisis in Darfur, the Democratic Republic of Congo, and Somalia.

P.O. Box 3243, Roosevelt St.
Addis Abba, Ethiopia
W21K19
Phone: 251 11 551 77 00
webmaster@africa-union.org
http://www.au.int/en/

AMNESTY INTERNATIONAL USA

Amnesty International is a worldwide campaigning movement that works to promote the human rights enshrined in the Universal Declaration of Human Rights and other international standards. It campaigns to free all prisoners of conscience; ensure fair and prompt trials for political prisoners; abolish the death penalty, torture and other cruel treatment of prisoners; end political killings and "disappearances"; and oppose human rights abuses by opposition groups.

Five Penn Plaza
New York, NY
10001
Phone: (212) 807-8400
Fax: (212) 627-1451
aimember@aiusa.org
http://www.amnestyusa.org/

ARAB LEAGUE

The League of Arab States, or Arab League, is comprised of countries that are primarily Arab speaking. Increased in size from six founding members in 1945, it now has 22 members, which include Palestine. The League works to strengthen ties and influence the political and economic situation in the region.

Tahrir Square 1
Cairo, Egypt
11642
Phone: 20 2 5750511
Fax: 20 2 5740331
info.sect@las.int
http://www.lasportal.org/wps/portal/las_en/
home_page

ARCTIC COUNCIL

The Arctic Council is an intergovernmental forum that comprises the Artic states (Canada, Denmark—including Greenland and the Faroe Islands—Finland, Iceland, Norway, the Russian Federation, Sweden, and the United States), the Arctic indigenous communities, and other Arctic inhabitants. It is focused on sustainable development and environmental issues that affect the Arctic.

Fram Centre
Tromso, Norway
N-9296
Phone: 47 77 75 01 40
acs@arctic-council.org
http://www.arctic-council.org/index.php/en

ASSOCIATION OF SOUTHEAST ASIAN NATIONS (ASEAN)

Established in 1967, ASEAN works to promote growth and prosperity throughout the region of Southeast Asia, as well as the peaceful resolution of conflict and adherence to human rights.

70A Jl. Sisingamangaraja
Jakarta, Indonesia
12110
Phone: (6221) 7262991, 7243372
Fax: (6221) 7398234, 7243504
http://www.asean.org

BOLIVARIAN ALLIANCE FOR THE AMERICAS (ALBA)

ALBA is an organization of nine member countries in central and south America, including Venezuela and a number of island nations. It is named after the 19th century independence leader Simon Bolivar (1783–1830). Founded by the late, charismatic Venezuelan president Hugo Chavez (1954–2013), ALBA seeks to integrate the economies of its members to further the social welfare of the region.

Av. Francisco Solano, sq. Calle San
Gerónimo, Edif. Los Llanos, Piso 8. Sabana
Grande, Parroquia El Recreo.
Caracas, Venezuela
Phone: 58 (212) 905 93 55
Fax. 58 (212) 761 13 64
sejecutiva.alba@gmail.com
http://www.alba-tcp.org/en

CARE

CARE is a not-for-profit organization that works in more than 80 countries around the world, including Syria, India, Mali, and the region of Darfur in the Sudan. It is often on the frontlines of treating people in areas challenged by conflict and violence.

151 Ellis St., NE
Atlanta, GA
39393
Phone: (404) 681-2552
info@care.org
http://www.care.org

CARNEGIE ENDOWMENT FOR INTERNATIONAL PEACE

The Carnegie Endowment for International Peace is a private, nonprofit organization dedicated to promoting peace by advancing cooperation between nations. Founded by Andrew Carnegie in 1910, it now has policy research centers in Russia, China, Europe, the Middle East, and the United States and seeks to advance peace through promoting interactions between government, businesses, and civil society.

1779 Massachusetts Avenue NW
Washington, DC
20036-2103
Phone: (202) 483-7600
Fax: (202) 483-1840
http://carnegieendowment.org/

CARTER CENTER

The non-profit Carter Center strives to relieve the suffering caused by war, disease, famine, and poverty by advancing peace and health in neighborhoods and nations around the world. The Center, in partnership with Emory University, is committed to promoting human rights, waging peace by bringing warring parties to the negotiating table, monitoring elections, safeguarding human rights, and building strong democracies through economic development.

One Copenhill
453 Freedom Parkway
Atlanta, GA
30307
Phone: (404) 420-5100
http://www.cartercenter.org/default.asp

CENTER FOR NONPROLIFERATION STUDIES

The James Martin Center for Nonproliferation Studies (CNS) was established in 1989 by Dr. William Potter and seeks to prevent the spread of weapons of mass destruction by training nonproliferation specialists and distributing timely information and analysis in online and print formats. CNS members also serve as advisors to policymakers and educate high school and college students, as well as the general public, on nonproliferation issues.

460 Pierce Street
Monterey, CA
93940
Phone: (831) 647-4154
Fax: (831) 647-3519
cns@miis.edu
http://cns.miis.edu

CENTRAL INTELLIGENCE AGENCY (CIA)

The CIA is a U.S. government agency responsible for providing national security intelligence. At various times the CIA has intervened in the internal affairs of other countries in order to secure a particular outcome that they believed was in the interests of the United States.

Office of Public Affairs
Washington, DC
20505
Phone: (703) 482-0623
Fax: (571) 204-3800
https://www.cia.gov

CENTERS FOR DISEASE CONTROL AND PREVENTION—EMERGENCY PREPAREDNESS AND RESPONSE (BIOTERRORISM)

The bioterrorism section of the U.S. Centers for Disease Control and Prevention (CDC) Emergency Preparedness and Response program provides information to the public on potential bioterrorism agents and proper preparations for a bioterrorism attack.

1600 Clifton Rd.
Atlanta, GA
30333
Phone: (404) 639-3534
Phone: (888) 246-2675
cdcresponse@ashastd.org
http://www.bt.cdc.gov

COMPREHENSIVE NUCLEAR-TEST-BAN TREATY ORGANIZATION (CTBTO) PREPARATORY COMMISSION

The CTBTO is an organization chartered to prepare for the effective implementation and enforcement of the Nuclear-Test-Ban Treaty, negotiated between 1994 and 1996, signed by 183 countries, and ratified by 159 as of 2013. The treaty "bans nuclear explosions by everyone, everywhere: on the Earth's surface, in the atmosphere, underwater and underground" in order to limit the development of new or more powerful nuclear weapons. Because the treaty has not been ratified by all parties and has not been signed by India, North Korea, and Pakistan, the organization is named the Preparatory Commission for CTBTO.

Vienna International Centre, P.O. Box 1200
1400 Vienna, Austria
Phone: 43 1 26030 ext. 6200
Fax: 43 1 26030 5823
info@ctbto.org
http://www.ctbto.org/

COUNCIL ON FOREIGN RELATIONS

The Council on Foreign Relations is an independent think tank with the mission of providing resources to political and business leaders to help them understand and make better choices regarding issues facing the United States and other countries.

The Harold Pratt House
58 East 68th Street
New York, NY
10065
Phone: (212) 434-9400
Fax: (212) 434-9800

1777 F St., NW
Washington, DC
20006
Phone: (202) 509-8400
Fax: (202) 509-8490
communications@cfr.org
http://www.cfr.org

EUROPEAN UNION (EU)

The EU had its beginnings in the aftermath of World War II as the European Economic Community, an economic partnership between six countries. It became the EU in 1993 and is now an economic and political partnership between 28 European countries based on a series of treaties.

Rue de la Loi / Wetstraat, 175
Brussels, Belgium
B-1048
Phone: 00800 67 89 10 11
http://europa.eu/index_en.htm

FEDERAL BUREAU OF INVESTIGATION (FBI)

The FBI serves the United States by providing both intelligence and law enforcement. Their mission includes protecting the United States from terrorist attacks and espionage.

935 Pennsylvania Ave., NW
Washington, DC
20535-0001
Phone: (202) 324-3000
http://www.fbi.gov

FEDERATION OF AMERICAN SCIENTISTS (FAS)

FAS is a non-profit organization composed of scientists, including those in the fields of biology, biochemistry, chemistry, environmental science, nuclear engineering, physics, and political science, that provides policy recommendations on national and international security issues based on an objective analysis of available scientific data. It was founded in 1945 by several of the scientists who worked on the Manhattan Project and works to prevent "catastrophic threats to national and international security" due to conventional, chemical, and biological weapons.

> 1725 DeSales Street NW, Suite 600
> Washington, DC
> 20036-4413
> Phone: (202) 546-3300
> Fax: (202) 675-1010
> fas@fas.org
> http://www.fas.org

GENOCIDE WATCH

Genocide Watch (GW) was organized in 1998 as the Washington, D.C.-based Coordinator of the International Alliance to End Genocide, which is a coalition of 50 human rights, legal, religious, and civil society organizations from around the world. GW is dedicated to five objectives: educating people about genocide and raising awareness of high-risk situations worldwide, and predicting, preventing, stopping, and punishing genocide and other forms of mass murder. It publishes annual reports on countries at risk.

> P.O. Box 809
> Washington, DC
> 20044
> Phone: (202) 643-1405
> communications@genocidewatch.org
> http://www.genocidewatch.org

GLOBAL POLICY FORUM (GPF)

GPF is a nongovernmental organization created in 1993 to monitor the work of the United Nations, where it has consultative status, and to influence international policymaking. GPF's mission is to promote accountability for global decisions, educate and mobilize for global citizen participation, and advocate on international peace and justice issues. Toward this goal, GPF conducts research and uses its Web site, as well as published reports and newsletters, to disseminate information to policymakers and the general public.

> P.O. Box 3283
> New York, NY
> 10163
> Phone: (212) 557-3161
> gpf@globalpolicy.org
> http://www.globalpolicy.org/home.html

HUMAN RIGHTS WATCH (HRW)

HRW investigates human rights abuses throughout the world, publishing its findings in books and reports every year. HRW was founded in 1978 in Helsinki (now HRW/Europe) and is an independent, nongovernmental organization with branches worldwide. By employing lawyers, journalists, academics, and country experts of many nationalities and diverse backgrounds, sending fact-finding teams into countries where there have been allegations of serious human rights abuses, and publishing their findings, HRW seeks to educate the public, encourage governments and corporations to uphold civil and political rights, and hold violators accountable.

> 350 Fifth Avenue, 34th Floor
> New York, NY
> 10118-3299
> Phone: (212) 290-4700
> Fax: (212) 736-1300
> http://www.hrw.org

INTERNATIONAL ATOMIC ENERGY AGENCY (IAEA)

The IAEA is an independent, intergovernmental organization that encourages nuclear cooperation. The IAEA develops nuclear safety standards and verifies compliance with the Non-Proliferation Treaty and other agreements to use nuclear material only for peaceful purposes.

> P.O. Box 100, Vienna International Centre
> Vienna, Austria
> A-1400
> Phone: 431 2600-0
> Fax: 431 2600-7
> Official.Mail@iaea.org
> http://www.iaea.org

INTERNATIONAL COMMITTEE OF THE RED CROSS (ICRC)

The Red Cross is an international organization dedicated to helping victims of violence and war. The organization is noted for going into places of conflict and disaster and providing food, shelter, and health care, as well as monitoring adherence to the Geneva Conventions for prisoners of war.

> 19 Avenue de la Paix
> Geneva, Switzerland
> CH 1202
> Phone: 41 22 734 60 01
> Fax: 41 22 733 20 57
> http://www.icrc.org/eng/

INTERNATIONAL CRIMINAL COURT (ICC)

The ICC is the primary judicial body of the UN. It was established in 1945 and sits at the Peace Palace in The Hague (Netherlands). It includes a tribunal to prosecute individuals for genocide, crimes against humanity, and war crimes. It is currently investigating crimes in Darfur, Sudan, the Democratic Republic of the Congo, and Uganda, among others.

> P.O. Box 19519
> The Hague, The Netherlands
> 2500 CM
> Phone: 31 (0)70 515 8515
> otp.informationdesk@icc-cpi.int
> http://www.icc-cpi.int

INTERNATIONAL CRISIS GROUP (ICG)

Founded in 1995 and headquartered in Brussels, Belgium, ICG is an independent, nongovernmental organization committed to preventing and resolving deadly conflict by strengthening the ability of the international community to understand and respond to impending crises. The organization, which focuses on field research and advocacy, works closely with governments and the media to bring important issues to the forefront and to provoke discussion of possible policy responses.

> 149 Avenue Louise
> Level 14
> Brussels, Belgium
> B-1050
> Phone: 32 2 502 90 38
> Fax: 32 2 502 50 38
> brussels@crisisgroup.org
>
> 708 3rd Avenue, Suite 1705
> New York, NY
> 10017
> Phone: (212) 813-0820
> Fax: (212) 813 0825
> newyork@crisisgroup.org
> http://www.crisisgroup.org/

INTERNATIONAL ENERGY ASSOCIATION (IEA)

The IEA is a group of 28 nations that was founded in response to the oil crisis of 1973–74 to address disruptions in the international oil supply. It now works in four fields: energy security, economic development, environmental awareness, and engagement worldwide with nonmember nations.

> 9, rue de la Fédération
> 75739 Paris Cedex 15, France
> Phone: 33 1 40 57 65 00
> Fax: 33 1 40 57 65 09
> info@iea.org
> http://www.iea.org/

INTERNATIONAL RESCUE COMMITTEE (IRC)

The IRC is a humanitarian aid organization that responds to emergencies and provides relief and development assistance to refugees and people affected by conflict, persecution, or disasters. The IRC was founded in New York in 1933 at the request of physicist Albert Einstein to aid people affected by crisis in Nazi Germany. It now assists people in more than 40 countries worldwide and 22 cities in the United States.

> 122 East 42nd Street
> New York, NY
> 10168
> Phone: (212) 551 3000
> Fax: (212) 551 3179
> http://www.rescue.org

MÉDECINS SANS FRONTIÈRES (DOCTORS WITHOUT BORDERS)

Méecins Sans Frontières (MSF), also known by its English name, Doctors Without Borders, is dedicated to providing medical aid to those who need it most, regardless of race, religion, or political affiliation. They frequently serve in conflict zones.

> 333 7th Ave.
> New York, NY
> 10001
> Phone: (212) 679-6800
> Fax: (212) 679-7016
> http://www.doctorswithoutborders.org

MIDDLE EAST INSTITUTE

The Middle East Institute is an independent, non-partisan organization providing information and analysis on the Middle East. Promoting education on each country in the region, the organization sponsors presentations and classes conducted by leading scholars in the field.

> 1761 N Street NW
> Washington, DC
> 20036
> Phone: (202) 785-1141
> information@mei.edu
> http://www.mei.edu/

NELSON MANDELA FOUNDATION

The Nelson Mandela Foundation is focused on researching, documenting, and educating people about the memory and legacy of Nelson Mandela, as well promoting the continuing dialogue about social justice and unity that Mandela advocated.

> Private Bag X70000
> Houghton, South Africa
> 2041
> Phone: 27 (0)11 547 5600
> http://www.nelsonmandela.org

NOBEL PRIZE FOUNDATION

The Nobel Prize Foundation, founded in 1900, presents awards annually for groundbreaking work in the sciences and arts, as well as in diplomatic or humanitarian efforts in the form of the Nobel Peace Prize. The Nobel Peace Prize has been awarded to social worker Jane Addams (1860–1935), apartheid fighter and first democratically elected president of South Africa Nelson Mandela (1918–), and civil rights leader Martin Luther King, Jr. (1929–1968), among many others.

> Sturegatan 14, Box 5232
> Stockholm, Sweden
> SE-102 45
> Phone: 46 8 663 17 22
> info@nobelmedia.org
> http://www.nobelprize.org/

NORTH ATLANTIC TREATY ORGANIZATION (NATO)

NATO works to promote the security of its member nations, through diplomatic and military cooperation. They have engaged in military activities in a number of areas of the world, including Afghanistan, Kosovo, and the Middle East.

> Boulevard Leopold III
> Brussels, Belgium
> 1110
> Phone: 49 (0) 6221-398-5216
> pao@fchd.nato.int
> http://www.nato.int/

ORGANIZATION FOR ECONOMIC CO-OPERATION AND DEVELOPMENT (OECD)

The OECD works to promote economic and social progress around the world by providing analysis and recommendations.

> 2, rue Andre Pascal
> Paris, Cedex 16, France
> 75775
> Phone: 33 1 45 24 82 00
> http://www.oecd.org

ORGANISATION FOR THE PROHIBITION OF CHEMICAL WEAPONS (OPCW)

The OPCW is the implementing body of the Chemical Weapons Convention. With 189 Member States, the OPCW works to prevent chemistry from being used for warfare. The OPCW works to investigate, monitor, and destroy existing chemical weapons.

> Johan de Wittlan 32
> The Hague, The Netherlands
> 2517 JR
> Phone: 31 70 416 3300
> media@opcw.org
> http://www.opcw.org/

ORGANIZATION FOR PETROLEUM EXPORTING COUNTRIES (OPEC)

OPEC works to coordinate the petroleum policies of member countries to ensure the stabilization of oil markets. Its members are primarily countries in the Middle East, South America, and Africa.

> Helferstorferstrasse 17
> Vienna, Austria
> A-1010
> Phone: 43-1 21112-3302
> http://www.opec.org/opec_web/en/

SIMON WIESENTHAL CENTER

Founded in 1977, the Simon Wiesenthal Center is an international Jewish human rights organization. Its stated goals are to combat anti-Semitism through teaching tolerance in communities worldwide, to defend Jews worldwide from hate and terrorism perpetrated by extremist groups, to provide educational tools to teach about religious tolerance and the Holocaust, and to stand with Israel.

> International Headquarters
> 1399 South Roxbury Drive
> Los Angeles, CA
> 90035
> Phone: (310) 553-9036
> Phone: (800) 900-9036
> Fax: (310) 553-4521
> http://www.wiesenthal.com

SOUTHERN POVERTY LAW CENTER (SPLC)

The SPLC is an internationally known nonprofit organization founded in 1971 and based in Montgomery, Alabama, that files class action lawsuits to fight discrimination and unequal treatment. It also tracks hate groups and runs the "Teach Tolerance" program to educate Americans about racism, anti-Semitism, and other forms of intolerance.

> 400 Washington Ave.
> Montgomery, Alabama
> 36104
> Phone: (334) 956-8200
> http://www.splcenter.org/

UNITED NATIONS (UN)

The UN, founded following World War II (1939–45), is dedicated to maintaining peace and security and developing peaceful resolution to conflict worldwide. It also protects human rights and promotes better living standards.

> 777 44th St.
> New York, NY
> 10017
> Phone: (212) 963-4440
> unitg@un.org
> http://www.un.org/en/

THE UNITED NATIONS CHILDREN'S FUND (UNICEF)

UNICEF works worldwide to help children by providing health care, food, education, and emergency relief.

125 Maiden Lane, 11th Floor
New York, NY
10038
Phone: (212) 686-5522
http://www.unicef.org/

UNITED NATIONS DEVELOPMENT PROGRAMME (UNDP)

The UNDP is the part of the United Nations dedicated to global development and capacity building.

One United Nations Plaza
New York, NY
10017
Phone: (212) 906-5000
Fax: (212) 906-5001
http://www.undp.org

THE UNITED NATIONS HIGH COMMISSIONER FOR REFUGEES (UNHCR)

The UNHCR was established to coordinate and re-solve refugee problems worldwide and to protect the rights of refugees. Refugee crises can be found throughout the world but are frequently located in places of violence or in regions hit by environmental catastrophes, such as earthquakes and typhoons.

Case Postale 2500
Geneva, 2 Depot, Switzerland
CH-1211
Phone: 41 22 739 8111
http://www.unhcr.org/cgi-bin/texis/vtx/home

THE WORLD BANK

The World Bank was established in 1944 to end extreme poverty and promote prosperity. The bank offers low interest loans and grants to developing countries to fund a variety of projects, including those in areas related to education, the environment, agriculture, finance, health care, and infra-structure.

1818 H St., NW
Washington, DC
20433
Phone: (202) 473-1000
Fax: (202) 477-6391
http://www.worldbank.org/

WORLD HEALTH ORGANIZATION (WHO)

The WHO is charged with leading the world on global health matters, especially those impact-ing public health. In addition to other activities, the WHO monitors the outbreak of diseases and epidemics and develops programs to address the spread of disease.

Avenue Appia 20
Geneva, Switzerland
1211 Geneva 27
Phone: 41 (0)22 791 21 11
http://www.who.int/en/

WORLD TRADE ORGANISATION (WTO)

The WTO is dedicated to globalizing and liberalizing trade and resolving conflicts that inhibit trade. It was established in 1995 after a series of negotiations between international governments to establish and maintain global rules of trade. In 2014, it comprised 159 member nations.

Centre William Rappard, Rue de Lausanne 154
Geneva, Switzerland
CH-1211 Geneva 21
Phone: 41 (0)22 739 51 11

enquiries@wto.org
http://www.wto.org/

WORLD WATER COUNCIL (WWC)

The WWC is an international council established in 1996 in response to increasing international concern about world water issues. Its mission is to promote awareness, build political commitment, and initiate action on critical water issues to facili-tate the efficient management and use of water on an environmentally sustainable basis.

Espace Gaymard
2-4 place d'Arvieux
Marseille, France
13002
Phone: 33 4 91 99 41 00
Fax: 33 4 91 99 41 01
wwc@worldwatercouncil.org
http://www.worldwatercouncil.org

YAD VASHEM

Established in 1963, Yad Vashem is Israel's and the Jewish people's national Holocaust memo-rial institution. It is dedicated to commemorating the victims of the Holocaust and to researching, documenting, publishing materials, and educat-ing future generations about the six million Jews who died under Nazi rule.

The Holocaust Martyrs' and Heroes'
Remembrance Authority
P.O.B. 3477
Jerusalem, Israel
9103401
Phone: 972-2-6443574
Fax: 972-2-6443569
general.information@yadvashem.org.il
http://www.yadvashem.org

General Resources

BOOKS

Al-Chalabi, Fadhil. *Oil Politics, Oil Myths: Analysis and Memoir of an OPEC Insider.* London: I. B. Taurus, 2011.

Ambrose, Stephen E., and Douglas Brinkley. *Rise to Globalism: American Foreign Policy Since 1938.* New York: Penguin Books, 1997.

Archer, Christon. *World History of Warfare.* Lincoln: University of Nebraska Press, 2008.

Armstrong, Karen. *Islam: A Short History.* New York: Modern Library, 2002.

Brokaw, Tom. *The Greatest Generation.* New York: Random House Trade, 2001.

Chaliand, Gerard. *A History of Terrorism: From Antiquity to Al-Qaeda.* Berkeley: University of California Press, 2007.

Clarke, Richard, and Robert K. Knake. *Cyber War: The Next Threat to National Security and What to Do About It.* New York: HarperCollins 2010.

Council on Foreign Relations/Foreign Affairs. *The New Arab Revolt: What Happened, What It Means, and What Comes Next.* New York: Council on Foreign Relations, 2011.

De Rouen Jr., Karl R., and Uk Heo, eds. *Civil Wars of the World: Major Conflicts since World War II,* Vols. I and II. Santa Barbara, CA: ABC-CLIO Inc., 2007.

Diamond, Jared. *Guns, Germs and Steel: The Fate of Human Societies.* New York: Norton, 1997.

Dillon, Michael. *Deconstructing International Politics.* New York, NY: Routledge, 2013.

Fearon, James D. *Economic Development, Insurgency, and Civil War.* Stanford, CA: Department of Political Science, Stanford University, 2007.

Fels, Enrico, Jan-Frederik Kremer, and Kathatina Kronenberg, eds. *Power in the 21st Century.* New York, NY: Springer, 2012.

Fichtelberg, Aaron. *Crimes Without Borders: An Introduction to International Criminal Justice.* Harlow, UK: Prentice Hall, 2007.

Fieldman, Burton. *The Nobel Prize: A History of Genius, Controversy and Prestige.* New York: Arcade Publishing, 2009.

Ganguly, Sumit. *India, Pakistan and the Bomb: Debating Nuclear Stability in South Asia.* New York: Columbia University Press, 2010.

Gilbert, Martin. *The Second World War: A Complete History.* New York: Holt Paperbacks, 2004.

Gonzalez, Nathan. *The Sunni-Shiite Conflict: Understanding Sectarian Violence in the Middle East.* New York: Nortia Press, 2009.

Gurr, Ted Robert, J. Joseph Hewitt, and Jonathan Wilkenfeld, eds. *Peace and Conflict 2012.* Boulder, CO: Paradigm Publishers, 2011.

Hayden, Craig. *The Rhetoric of Soft Power: Public Diplomacy in Global Context.* Lanham, MD: Lexington Books, 2012.

Hazelton, Lindsay. *After the Prophet: The Epic Story of the Shia-Sunni Split in Islam.* New York: Anchor, 2010.

Henderson, Conway. *Understanding International Law.* Malden, MA: Wiley-Blackwell, 2010.

Hiro, Dilip. *The Longest War: The Iran-Iraq Military Conflict.* New York: Routledge, 1990.

Hirst, David. *Beware of Small States: Lebanon, Battleground of the Middle East.* New York: Nation, 2010.

Hogan, Tori. *Beyond Good Intentions: A Journey Into the Reality of International Aid.* Berkeley, CA: Seal Press, 2012.

Hughes, Stuart H. *Contemporary Europe: A History.* Englewood Cliffs, NJ: Prentice-Hall, 1971.

Human Security Report Project. *Human Security Report 2012.* Vancouver: Human Security Press, 2012. Available online at http://www.hsrgroup.org/human-security-reports/2012/text.aspx (accessed January 21, 2014).

MacFarquhar, Roderick, and John K. Fairbank. *The Cambridge History of China*, vols. 1–14. Cambridge: Cambridge University Press, 1986-7.

Marrin, Albert. *Black Gold: The Story of Oil in Our Lives.* New York: Alfred A. Knopf, 2013.

Mayor, Adrienne. *Greek Fire, Poison Arrows, and Scorpion Bombs: Weapons of Mass Destruction in the Ancient World.* New York: Overlook Press, 2008.

Owen, Roger. *The Rise and Fall of Arab Presidents for Life.* Cambridge, MA: Harvard University Press, 2012.

Pinker, Stephen. *The Better Angels of Our Nature.* New York: Viking, 2011.

Rashid, Ahmed. *Pakistan on the Brink: The Future of America, Pakistan and Afghanistan.* New York: Penguin Books, 2013.

Roeder, Larry Winter. *Diplomacy and Negotiation for Humanitarian NGOs.* New York: Springer, 2013.

Sageman, Marc. *Leaderless Jihad: Terror Networks in the Twenty-First Century.* Philadelphia: University of Pennsylvania Press, 2008.

Stafford, Terry. *Deadly Dictators: Masterminds of 20th Century Genocides.* Lexington, KY: Create Space, 2010.

Wright, Robin. *Dreams and Shadows: The Future of the Middle East.* New York: Penguin, 2008.

PERIODICALS

Brookhiser, Richard. "Domestic Terrorism: The Killers Next Door." *American History* 48, no. 4 (October 2013): 17.

Cortright, David. "Winning Without War: Non-military Strategies for Overcoming Violent Extremism." *Transnational Law & Contemporary Problems* 21, no. 1 (Spring 2012): 197.

De Rouen Jr., Karl R., and Jacob Bercovitch. "Enduring Internal Rivalries: A New Framework for the Study of Civil War." *Journal of Peace Research* 45, no. 1 (2008): 55–74.

Handleman, Sapir. "Two Complementary Settings of Peace-Making Diplomacy: Political-Elite Diplomacy and Public Diplomacy." *Diplomacy & Statecraft* 23, no. 1 (2012): 162.

Regnier, Philippe. "The Emerging Concept of Humanitarian Diplomacy: Identification of a Community of Practice and Prospects for International Recognition." *International Review of the Red Cross* 93, no. 884 (December 2011): 1211–1238.

Ryan, Maria. "'War in Countries We Are Not at War With': The 'War on Terror' on the Periphery From Bush to Obama." *International Politics* 48, no. 203 (March 2011): 364–389.

Savoysky, A. "Economic Diplomacy as a Phenomenon of International Life." *International Affairs (Minneapolis)* 59, no. 2 (2013): 132–141.

Sylvester, Christine. "War Experiences/War Practices/War Theory." *Millennium: Journal of International Studies* 40, no. 3 (June 2012): 483–503.

WEB SITES

"The 9/11 Commission Report." *National Commission on Terrorist Attacks Upon the United States.* http://www.9-11commission.gov/report/911Report_Exec.htm (accessed November 30, 2011).

"20th Century Documents." *The Avalon Project: Documents in Law, History, and Diplomacy.* http://avalon.law.yale.edu/subject_menus/20th.asp (accessed January 17, 2014).

"21st Century Documents." *The Avalon Project: Documents in Law, History, and Diplomacy.* http://avalon.law.yale.edu/subject_menus/21st.asp (accessed January 17, 2014).

"The 100 Deadliest Civil Wars and Armed Conflicts Since the Second World War." *The Economist.* http://www.economist.com/content/inner-turmoil (accessed November 11, 2013).

"Afghanistan/Pakistan." *PBS Frontline.* http://www.pbs.org/wgbh/pages/frontline/afghanistan-pakistan/ (accessed February 19, 2014).

"Africa's Conflict Zones." *Council on Foreign Relations.* http://www.cfr.org/world/africas-conflict-zones/p14543 (accessed January 16, 2014).

African National Congress. http://www.anc.org.za/index.php# (accessed January 16, 2014).

"African Union in a Nutshell." *African Union.* http://www.africa-union.org/root/au/AboutAu/au_in_a_nutshell_en.htm (accessed February 18, 2014).

"Algerian National Liberation (1954–1962)." *GlobalSecurity.org.* http://www.globalsecurity.org/military/world/war/algeria.htm (accessed February 17, 2014).

Anderson, Lisa. "Demystifying the Arab Spring: Parsing the Differences Between Tunisia, Egypt, and Libya." *Foreign Affairs*, May/June 2011. http://www.foreignaffairs.com/articles/67693/lisa-anderson/demystifying-the-arab-spring (accessed February 17, 2014).

"Apartheid." *History.com*. http://www.history.com/topics/apartheid (accessed February 19, 2014).

"Arab Spring: A Research & Study Guide." *The Cornell University Library*. http://guides.library.cornell.edu/content.php?pid=259276&sid=2139371 (accessed January 17, 2014).

"Armenian Genocide." *History.com*. http://www.history.com/topics/armenian-genocide (accessed February 17, 2014).

Bates, Crispin. "The Hidden Story of Partition and its Legacies." *BBC*, March 3, 2011. http://www.bbc.co.uk/history/british/modern/partition1947_01.shtml (accessed February 19, 2014).

"The Bay of Pigs." *John F. Kennedy Library and Museum*. http://www.jfklibrary.org/JFK/JFK-in-History/The-Bay-of-Pigs.aspx (accessed February 19, 2014).

"Bay of Pigs Invasion." *History.com*. http://www.history.com/topics/cold-war/bay-of-pigs-invasion (accessed February 19, 2014).

Bilefsky, Dan. "Kosovo Declares Its Independence." *The New York Times*, February 18, 2008. http://www.nytimes.com/2008/02/18/world/europe/18kosovo.html?pagewanted=all&_r=0 (accessed February 19, 2014).

Bolivarian Alliance for the Peoples of Our America – Peoples' Trade Treaty (ALBA–TCP). http://www.alba-tcp.org/en (accessed January 16, 2014).

"Bosnian Genocide." *History.com*. http://www.history.com/topics/bosnian-genocide (accessed February 17, 2014).

Bowden, Mark. "Black Hawk Down: A Story of Modern War." *Philly.com*. http://inquirer.philly.com/packages/somalia/ (accessed February 19, 2014).

The Brookings Institution. http://www.brookings.edu (accessed January 16, 2014).

"Bureau of African Affairs." *U.S. Department of State*. http://www.state.gov/p/af/index.htm (accessed January 16, 2014).

"Bureau of Near Eastern Affairs." *U.S. Department of State*. http://www.state.gov/p/nea/index.htm (accessed January 16, 2014).

Cambodia Tribunal Monitor. http://www.cambodiatribunal.org/ (accessed February 19, 2014).

Carnegie Endowment for International Peace. http://carnegieendowment.org (accessed January 16, 2014).

Center for Basque Studies, University of Nevada, Reno. http://basque.unr.edu (accessed January 16, 2014).

Center for International Development and Conflict Management. http://www.cidcm.umd.edu/ (accessed January 16, 2014).

"Chemical Weapons Elimination." *Centers for Disease Control and Prevention (CDC)*. http://www.cdc.gov/nceh/demil/ (accessed January 16, 2014).

"China and Japan: Seven Decades of Bitterness." *BBC News*, February 13, 2014. http://www.bbc.co.uk/news/magazine-25411700 (accessed February 19, 2014).

"Cold War." *BBC History*. http://www.bbc.co.uk/history/worldwars/coldwar/ (accessed January 16, 2014).

The Cold War Museum. http://coldwar.org/ (accessed January 16, 2014).

Council on Foreign Relations. http://www.cfr.org/ (accessed January 16, 2014).

"Crisis in Syria." *New York Times World*. http://topics.nytimes.com/top/news/international/countriesandterritories/syria/index.html (accessed February 19, 2014).

Crittenden, Stephen. "The Clash within Civilisations: How the Sunni-Shiite Divide Cleaves the Middle East." *The Global Mail*, August 22, 2012. http://www.theglobalmail.org/feature/the-clash-within-civilisations-how-the-sunni-shiite-divide-cleaves-the-middle-east/349/ (accessed January 16, 2014).

"Cuban Missile Crisis." *John F. Kennedy Library and Museum*. http://www.jfklibrary.org/JFK/JFK-in-History/Cuban-Missile-Crisis.aspx (accessed February 19, 2014).

Duva, Anjali Ditter. "Indonesia: A Military Timeline." *PBS Frontline: World*. http://www.pbs.org/frontlineworld/stories/indonesia605/timeline.html (accessed February 18, 2014).

"East Timor Revisited." *The National Security Archive*. http://www2.gwu.edu/~nsarchiv/NSAEBB/NSAEBB62/ (accessed February 19, 2014).

"Egypt News—Revolution and Aftermath." *The New York Times*. http://topics.nytimes.com/top/news/international/countriesandterritories/egypt/index.html (accessed February 19, 2014).

"Enemies of War: El Salvador." *PBS.* http://www.pbs.org/itvs/enemiesofwar/elsalvador.html (accessed February 19, 2014).

European Union. http://europa.eu/index_en.htm (accessed January 21, 2014).

Fadel, Leila. "Looking Back On Libya: 'We Were Naïve' About The Challenges." *NPR Parallels,* February 18, 2008. http://www.npr.org/blogs/parallels/2014/02/16/277982828/looking-back-on-libya-we-were-naive-of-the-challenges (accessed February 19, 2014).

Fredriksson, Lynn. "East Timor." *Foreign Policy in Focus,* October 11, 2005. http://fpif.org/east_timor/ (accessed February 19, 2014).

Friedman, Uri. "The Syrian Civil War: Even Its Most Uplifting Moment Is Controversial." *The Atlantic,* February 19, 2014. http://www.theatlantic.com/international/archive/2014/02/the-syrian-civil-war-even-its-most-uplifting-moment-is-controversial/283929/ (accessed February 19, 2014).

"The Geneva Conventions of 1949 and Their Additional Protocols." *GlobalSecurity.org.* http://www.icrc.org/eng/war-and-law/treaties-customary-law/geneva-conventions/index.jsp (accessed January 16, 2014).

Genocide Archive Rwanda. http://www.genocidearchiverwanda.org.rw/index.php/Welcome_to_Genocide_Archive_Rwanda (accessed February 19, 2014).

"Global Peace Index." *Vision of Humanity.* http://europa.eu/index_en.htm (accessed November 11, 2013).

"The Global Proliferation Status Map, 2009." *The Carnegie Endowment.* http://carnegieendowment.org/files/2009-global-prolif6.pdf (accessed November 11, 2013).

GlobalSecurity.org. http://www.globalsecurity.org/ (accessed January 16, 2014).

Gross, Michael Joseph. "The Changing and Terrifying Nature of the New Cyber-Warfare." *Vanity Fair,* July 2013. http://www.vanityfair.com/culture/2013/07/new-cyberwar-victims-american-business (accessed February 20, 2014).

Hensinger, Shane. "The History of the Cyprus Conflict." *The Daily Kos,* February 20, 2010. http://www.dailykos.com/story/2010/02/20/839037/-The-History-of-the-Cyprus-Conflict-A-Background-w-Peacebuilding-Strategies# (accessed February 19, 2014).

Hirst, Joel D. "A Guide to ALBA." *Americas Quarterly.* http://www.americasquarterly.org/HIRST/ARTICLE (accessed February 19, 2014).

His Holiness the 14th Dalai Lama of Tibet. http://www.dalailama.com/ (accessed February 19, 2014).

Hitchens, Christopher. "A Chronology of the Algerian War of Independence." *The Atlantic,* November 1, 2006. http://www.theatlantic.com/magazine/archive/2006/11/a-chronology-of-the-algerian-war-of-independence/305277/ (accessed January 16, 2014).

The Hive: A Knowledge Platform on Fragility, Conflict and Violence. https://worldbankhive.logicaladvantage.com/_layouts/WBHive/Buzz.aspx (accessed January 16, 2014).

Holocaust Survivors. www.holocaustsurvivors.org (accessed January 16, 2014).

"How Does Cyber Warfare Work?" *Forbes,* July 18, 2013. http://www.forbes.com/sites/quora/2013/07/18/how-does-cyber-warfare-work/ (accessed November 7, 2013).

Human Security Report Project. http://www.hsrgroup.org/ (accessed January 21, 2014).

Intergovernmental Panel on Climate Change (IPCC). http://www.ipcc.ch/ (accessed January 16, 2014).

International Court of Justice. http://www.icj-cij.org (accessed January 16, 2014).

International Criminal Court. http://www.icc-cpi.int (accessed January 16, 2014).

International Monetary Fund. http://www.imf.org/external/index.htm (accessed January 16, 2014).

"International Religious Freedom." *U.S. Department of State.* http://www.state.gov/j/drl/rls/irf/ (accessed January 16, 2014).

"Iraq: 10 Years On." *BBC News,* July 29, 2013. http://www.bbc.co.uk/news/special_reports/struggle_for_iraq/ (accessed January 16, 2014).

Islamophobia.org. http://islamophobia.org (accessed January 16, 2014).

John F. Kennedy Presidential Library and Museum. http://www.jfklibrary.org (accessed January 16, 2014).

Johnson, Carrie. "What Happens To Guantanamo After The War In Afghanistan Ends?" *Morning Edition,* November 13, 2013. http://www.npr.org/2013/11/13/244947838/what-does-end-of-forever-war-mean-for-guantanamo (accessed January 17, 2014).

"Kissinger to Argentines on Dirty War: 'The Quicker You Succeed the Better'" *The National Security Archive: The George Washington University.* http://www2.gwu.edu/~nsarchiv/NSAEBB/NSAEBB104/index.htm (accessed February 19, 2014).

Knefel, John. "Guantanamo Bay: Stories From Inside the World's Most Infamous Jail" *Rolling Stone*, June 17, 2013. http://www.rollingstone.com/politics/news/guantanamo-bay-stories-from-inside-the-worlds-most-infamous-jail-20130617 (accessed February 19, 2014).

"The Korean War." *Dwight D. Eisenhower Presidential Library, Museum, and Boyhood Home.* http://www.eisenhower.archives.gov/research/online_documents/korean_war.html (accessed February 19, 2014).

"Korean War." *History.com.* http://www.history.com/topics/korean-war (accessed February 19, 2014).

Kornbluh, Peter. "Chile and the United States: Declassified Documents Relating to the Military Coup, September 11, 1973." *The National Security Archive: The George Washington University.* http://www2.gwu.edu/~nsarchiv/NSAEBB/NSAEBB8/nsaebb8i.htm (accessed February 19, 2014).

"Kurdistan: Kurdish Conflict." *GlobalSecurity.org.* http://www.globalsecurity.org/military/world/war/kurdistan.htm (accessed February 19, 2014).

"Lebanon: Civil War (1975–1991)." *GlobalSecurity.org.* http://www.globalsecurity.org/military/world/war/lebanon.htm (accessed February 19, 2014).

"Liberia Profile." *BBC News*, October 11, 2013. http://www.bbc.co.uk/news/world-africa-13729504 (accessed February 19, 2014).

"Libya Civil War Fast Facts." *CNN.com*, September 25, 2013. http://www.cnn.com/2013/09/20/world/libya-civil-war-fast-facts/index.html (accessed February 19, 2014).

Locker, Ray, Kevin McCoy, and Gregg Zoroya. "Russia's Chechnya Has Long Terrorist Connections" *USA Today*, April 20, 2013. http://www.usatoday.com/story/news/world/2013/04/19/russia-chechnya-terror-caucasus/2095995/ (accessed February 19, 2014).

Longmire, Sylvia. "Terrorism in Latin America 101: What Is the FARC?" *The Examiner*, November 5, 2009. http://www.examiner.com/article/terrorism-latin-america-101-what-is-the-farc (accessed February 19, 2014).

"Middle East & North Africa." *International Crisis Group.* http://www.crisisgroup.org/en/regions/middle-east-north-africa.aspx (accessed January 17, 2014).

"Milestones 1945–1952: The Chinese Revolution of 1949." *Frontline World.* http://www.pbs.org/frontlineworld/stories/lebanon/history.html (accessed January 17, 2014).

"Milestones of Perestroika: The Dissolution of the USSR." *Spiegel Online International.* http://www.spiegel.de/international/milestones-of-perestroika-the-dissolution-of-the-ussr-a-449404.html (accessed February 17, 2014).

Miller, Talea. "Timeline: Guatemala's Brutal Civil War." *PBS Newshour*, March 7, 2011. http://www.pbs.org/newshour/updates/latin_america-jan-june11-timeline_03-07/ (accessed February 19, 2014).

Montero, David. "Bullets to Ballet Box: A History of Hezbollah." *PBS Frontline World.* http://www.pbs.org/frontlineworld/stories/lebanon/history.html (accessed January 17, 2014).

Muasher, Marwan. "Year Four of the Arab Awakening." *Carnegie Endowment for International Peace*, December 12, 2013. http://carnegieendowment.org/2013/12/12/year-four-of-arab-awakening/gw1m (accessed January 17, 2014).

Murphy, Jarrett. "Remembering the Killing Fields." *CBS News*, April 15, 2000. http://www.cbsnews.com/news/remembering-the-killing-fields/ (accessed February 17, 2014).

The National Archives (UK). http://www.nationalarchives.gov.uk/education (accessed January 16, 2014).

The National Security Archive, George Washington University. http://www2.gwu.edu (accessed January 16, 2014).

National Snow and Ice Data Center. http://nsidc.org/ (accessed January 16, 2014).

"Nicaragua History." *Lonely Planet.* http://www.lonelyplanet.com/nicaragua/history (accessed February 19, 2014).

North Atlantic Treaty Organiztion (NATO). http://www.nato.int/ (accessed January 16, 2014).

Office of the High Representative in Bosnia and Herzegovina. http://www.ohr.int/ohr-info/gen-info/default.asp?content_id=38519 (accessed January 16, 2014).

"Office to Monitor and Combat Trafficking in Persons." *U.S. Department of State.* http://www.state.gov/j/tip/index.htm (accessed January 16, 2014).

Organization of the Petroleum Exporting Countries (OPEC). http://www.opec.org/opec_web/en/ (accessed January 16, 2014).

"Partition of India." *Postcolonial Studies @ Emory.* http://postcolonialstudies.emory.edu/partition-of-india/ (accessed February 19, 2014).

Pizzi, Michael. "Poll: Most in Ex-Soviet States Say USSR Breakup Harmful." *Al Jazeera America*, December 19, 2013. http://america.aljazeera.com/articles/2013/12/19/most-residents-ofexsovietstatessayussrbreakupharmful.html (accessed February 19, 2014).

Preparatory Commission for the Comprehensive Nuclear-Test-Ban Treaty Organization. "CTBTO World Map." *CTBTO.org.* http://www.ctbto.org/map/ (accessed January 16, 2014).

Preparatory Commission for the Comprehensive Nuclear-Test-Ban Treaty Organization. "History: Summary." *CTBTO.org.* http://www.ctbto.org/the-treaty/history-summary/ (accessed January 16, 2014).

Rawlins, Aimee. "Mexico's Drug War." *Council on Foreign Relations*, January 11, 2013. http://www.cfr.org/mexico/mexicos-drug-war/p13689 (accessed February 18, 2014).

"Religious Hostilities Reach Six-Year High." *Pew Research Center*, January 14, 2014. http://www.pewforum.org/2014/01/14/religious-hostilities-reach-six-year-high/ (accessed January 29, 2014).

"Rise of the Drones." *NOVA*, January 23, 2013. http://www.pbs.org/wgbh/nova/military/rise-of-the-drones.html (accessed February 19, 2014).

Roberge, Michal, and Youkyung Lee. "China-Taiwan Relations." *Council on Foreign Relations*, April 11, 2009. http://www.cfr.org/china/china-taiwan-relations/p9223 (accessed February 18, 2014).

"Russia-Georgia Conflict: Why Both Sides Have Valid Points." *The Christian Science Monitor*, August 19, 2008. http://www.csmonitor.com/World/Europe/2008/0819/p12s01-woeu.html/(page)/2 (accessed February 19, 2014).

"Russian Revolution." *History.com.* http://www.history.com/topics/russian-revolution (accessed February 19, 2014).

Sastry, Anjuli, and Alisa Wiersema. "10-Year Iraq War Timeline." *ABC News*, March 19, 2013. http://abcnews.go.com/Politics/TheNote/10-yeariraqwar-timeline/story?id=18758663 (accessed February 17, 2014).

Savranskaya, Svetlana. "The Soviet Experience in Afghanistan: Russian Documents and Memoirs." *The National Security Archive.* http://www2.gwu.edu/~nsarchiv/NSAEBB/NSAEBB57/soviet.html (accessed February 19, 2014).

"Sierra Leone." *Global Policy.* http://www.globalpolicy.org/security-council/index-of-countries-on-the-security-council-agenda/sierra-leone.html (accessed February 19, 2014).

"South Africa: Overcoming Apartheid." *Michigan State University.* http://www.overcomingapartheid.msu.edu/ (accessed February 19, 2014).

South African History Online. http://www.sahistory.org.za/ (accessed February 19, 2014).

"Spanish Civil War." *The George Washington University.* http://www.gwu.edu/~erpapers/teachinger/glossary/spanish-civil-war.cfm (accessed February 19, 2014).

"Sri Lanka Civil War." *Channel4News.* http://www.channel4.com/news/sri-lanka-civil-war (accessed February 19, 2014).

"The Story of the Revolution." *BBC Persian.* http://www.bbc.co.uk/persian/revolution/ (accessed February 19, 2014).

"Sudan Country Profile." *BBC News Africa*, October 26, 2013. http://www.bbc.co.uk/news/world-africa-14094995 (accessed February 19, 2014).

Taylor, Alan. "20 Years Since the Bosnian War." *The Atlantic: In Focus*, April 13, 2012. http://www.theatlantic.com/infocus/2012/04/20-years-since-the-bosnian-war/100278/ (accessed February 18, 2014).

Taylor, Alan. "20 Years Since the Fall of the Soviet Union." *The Atlantic: In Focus*, December 23, 2011. http://www.theatlantic.com/infocus/2011/12/20-years-since-the-fall-of-the-soviet-union/100214/ (accessed February 18, 2014).

Taylor, Alan. "World War II in Photos: A Retrospective in 20 Parts." *The Atlantic: In Focus*, October 11, 2011. http://www.theatlantic.com/infocus/pages/ww2/ (accessed February 18, 2014).

"Terrorist Organizations and Networks." *Council on Foreign Relations.* http://www.cfr.org/issue/terrorist-organizations-and-networks/ri159 (accessed January 17, 2014).

Thompson, Nick. "Armies of One: Are Lone Wolf Attacks the Future of Terrorism?" *CNN*, May 29, 2013. http://www.cnn.com/2013/05/23/world/europe/london-attack-lone-wolf-fears (accessed November 11, 2013).

"Timeline: Break-up of Yugoslavia." *BBC News*, May 22, 2006. http://news.bbc.co.uk/2/hi/europe/4997380.stm (accessed February 18, 2014).

"Timeline: Ivory Coast." *Al Jazeera English*, November 30, 2011. http://www.aljazeera.com/news/africa/2010/12/2010121971745317811.html (accessed February 18, 2014).

"Timeline: Key Events in History of Basque Separatists ETA." *Reuters*, October 20, 2011. http://www.reuters.com/article/2011/10/20/us-spain-eta-events-idUSTRE79J78T20111020 (accessed February 17, 2014).

"Tolerance and Tension: Islam and Christianity in Sub-Saharan Africa." *Pew Research Center*, April 15, 2010. http://www.pewforum.org/2010/04/15/executive-summary-islam-and-christianity-in-sub-saharan-africa/ (accessed January 29, 2014).

"The Triumph of Evil: How the West Ignored Warnings about the 1994 Rwanda Genocide and Turned Its Back on the Victims." *PBS Frontline*. http://www.pbs.org/wgbh/pages/frontline/shows/evil/ (accessed February 19, 2014).

"The Troubles." *BBC History*. http://www.bbc.co.uk/history/troubles (accessed January 16, 2014).

Truth and Reconciliation Commission of Liberia. http://trcofliberia.org/ (accessed February 19, 2014).

"Uganda: Conflict Timeline." *Peace Direct: Insight on Conflict*. http://www.insightonconflict.org/conflicts/uganda/conflict-profile/conflict-timeline/ (accessed February 16, 2014).

UNICEF. http://www.unicef.org/ (accessed January 16, 2014).

United Nations. http://www.un.org/en (accessed January 21, 2014).

"United Nations Action to Counter Terrorism." *United Nations*. http://www.un.org/en/terrorism/ (accessed November 7, 2013).

United Nations Information System on the Question of Palestine (UNISPAL). http://unispal.un.org/unispal.nsf/home (accessed January 16, 2014).

United Nations International Criminal Tribunal for the Former Yugoslavia. http://www.icty.org/ (accessed January 16, 2014).

United Nations Millennium Development Goals. http://www.un.org/millenniumgoals/ (accessed January 16, 2014).

United Nations News Centre. http://www.un.org/News//home (accessed January 16, 2014).

United Nations Peacekeeping Force in Cyprus (UNFICYP). http://www.un.org/en/peacekeeping/missions/unficyp (accessed January 16, 2014).

United Nations Security Council Sanctions Committees. http://www.un.org/sc/committees/ (accessed January 16, 2014).

U.S. Antarctic Program. http://www.usap.gov/ (accessed January 16, 2014).

U.S. Department of State. Office of the Historian. http://history.state.gov/ (accessed January 16, 2014).

U.S. Drug Enforcement Agency. http://www.justice.gov/dea/index.shtml (accessed January 16, 2014).

"U.S. War in Afghanistan." *Council on Foreign Relations*. http://www.cfr.org/afghanistan/us-war-afghanistan/p20018 (accessed February 16, 2014).

United States Holocaust Memorial Museum. http://www.ushmm.org/ (accessed January 16, 2014).

"Vietnam Online." *PBS American Experience*. http://www.pbs.org/wgbh/amex/vietnam/ (accessed February 16, 2014).

"Weapons of Mass Destruction." *Federal Bureau of Investigation*. http://www.fbi.gov/about-us/investigate/terrorism/wmd (accessed November 11, 2013).

Williams, Paul D. "Horn of Africa: Webs of Conflict & Pathways to Peace." *The Wilson Center*, August 2011. http://www.wilsoncenter.org/sites/default/files/Horn%20of%20Africa%20Conflict%20Mapping%20Doc-%20FINAL.pdf (accessed November 11, 2013).

"The World Factbook." *Central Intelligence Agency (CIA)*. https://www.cia.gov/library/publications/the-world-factbook/ (accessed January 16, 2014).

Woodrow Wilson International Center for Scholars. http://www.wilsoncenter.org (accessed January 16, 2014).

"World War One." *BBC History*. http://www.bbc.co.uk/history/worldwars/wwone/ (accessed January 16, 2014).

"World War Two." *BBC History*. http://www.bbc.co.uk/history/worldwars/wwtwo/ (accessed January 16, 2014).

"Yugoslav Wars of Dissolution." *Global Security*. http://www.globalsecurity.org/military/world/war/yugoslavia.htm (accessed January 16, 2014).

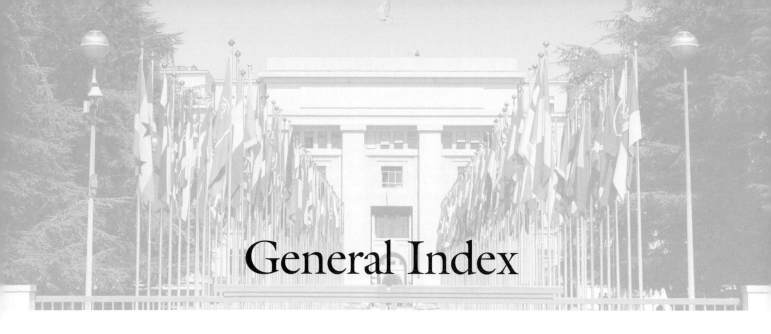

General Index

Page numbers in **boldface** indicate the main essay for a topic, and primary source page numbers are in ***boldface and italics***. An *italicized* page number indicates a photo, illustration, chart, or other graphic.

Biological weapons, 2:578, 579–580

Birkett, Norman, 1:*281*

Birmingham, Alabama, church bombing, 1:2

Bismarck, Otto von, 2:584

Bizimungu, Augustin, 2:451

Black Death, 2:578

Black Diamond (Liberian fighter), 2:*367*

Black Friday (Iran), 1:294

Black hat hackers, 1:157

Black Hat USA security conference, 1:*158*

Black July (Sri Lanka), 2:486–488

Black widows (Chechen suicide bombers), 1:110

Blackwater security agency, 2:548

Blair, Tony, 2:546

Blamey, Thomas, 2:*600*

Blanco, Luis Carrero, 1:76

Ble Goude, Charles, 1:146

Blitz of London (1940), 2:593

Blitzkrieg (1939), 2:593

Blood Diamond (film), 2:456

Blood diamonds
  Democratic Republic of the Congo, 1:170
  Liberia, 2:365, 453
  Sierra Leone, 2:453, 456, *456*

Bloody Sunday (Northern Ireland), 2:408, 410

Bloody Sunday (Russia), 2:439

Bloomberg, Michael, 1:304

Boko Haram, 2:434, 435

Boland Amendment, 2:394

Bolivarian Alliance for the Americas (ALBA), 1:*81*, **81–85**, *83, 84, 85*

Bolivia
  ALBA participation, 1:81, 83
  Operation Condor, 1:114

Bonnet, Henry, 2:*403*

Born, Max, 2:582

Bosnia and Herzegovina
  EU candidacy, 1:213, 2:609
  history, 1:86
  independence, 2:609
  map, 1:*87*

Bosniaks, 1:87, 88–89, 2:607, 609

Bosnian War (1992–1995), 1:**86–92**
  Dayton Peace Accords, 1:89, *89,* 2:607
  genocide, 1:225, *226*
  NATO involvement, 1:89, 2:405, 607
  overview, 1:86, 2:607
  peacekeeping forces, 1:*90*
  soldiers, 1:*88*
  war crimes, 2:609–610
  World War I influence, 2:588, 590

Boston Marathon attack (2013), 2:520–521, 580–581

Bouazizi, Mohamed, 1:38, 50, *51*

Boumedine v. Bush (2008), 1:245

Boxer Rebellion (1897–1901), 1:120

Boyd, Belle, 1:205

BP Deepwater Horizon oil rig explosion (2010), 1:154, 2:574

Brahimi, Lakhdar, 2:*503*

Bratusek, Alenka, 1:*215*

Brazil
  economic sanctions, 1:190
  Mercosur, 1:82
  Operation Condor, 1:114

Breivik, Anders Behring, 2:*520,* 521

Brezhnev, Leonid, 1:130, 2:*577*

Briceño, Jorge, 1:137, 138

Bridgman, Percy W., 2:582

Britain. *See* United Kingdom

British Mandate of Palestine, 1:309, *310*

British Raj, 2:423

Brundtland, Gro Harlem, 1:239

Brundtland Report, 1:239

Brusilov, Aleksei, 2:586

Brusilov Offensive, 2:586

Bryant, Robert, 1:207

Buchenwald concentration camp, 2:598

Budak mass grave, 2:*610*

Buddhism
  Burma (Myanmar), 1:94, *95,* 97, 99–100
  Tibet, 2:526, 528–529

Buldan, Pelvin, 2:*353*

Bulgaria
  EU membership, 1:211, 212
  NATO membership, 2:404
  World War I participation, 2:585

Bulge, Battle of the (1944), 2:599

Bulwer-Lytton, V.A.G.R., 2:323

Burma (Myanmar)
  economic sanctions, 1:188, 190
  humanitarian aid refusal, 1:269
  map, 1:*94*

Burma (Myanmar) uprisings, 1:**93–100**, *97*

Burqas, 1:303, 2:*436,* 437

Burundi
  Africa's World War, 1:167
  Nile basin water rights concerns, 2:572

Bush, Boumedine v. (2008), 1:245

Bush, George H. W., 1:132, *132,* 2:394, 545

Bush, George W.
  9/11 response, 1:*7,* 27
  cyber security strategy, 1:159

Georgia-Russia conflict, 1:233
  Israel relations, 1:44
  Mitchell Report, 1:47
  North Korea relations, 2:337
  Rusesabagina, Paul medal, 2:448
  speech in response to 9/11 attacks, 1:*7*
  U.S.-Iraq War, 2:546, 547, 578
  War on Terror, 1:106, 243, 245, 2:523–524

Bush, Rasul v. (2004), 1:245

C

Cabrera Sarabia, Luis Alberto, 2:387

Café Wars (Algerian War of Independence), 1:37

CAIR (Council on American-Islamic Relations), 1:306

Calderón, Felipe, 2:382, 383, 386, 387, 388

Calley, William, 2:566

Calmy-Rey, Micheline, 1:*72*

Cambodia, 1:**101–105**
  genocide, 1:101, 103, *103,* 104–105, 222, 223, 225
  history, 1:101–102
  map, 1:*102*

Cameron, David, 2:372, 410

Camp David Accords (1978), 1:43, 44

Camp David summit (2000), 1:44

Camp Iguana (Guantánamo Bay detention center), 1:243, 244

Camp X-Ray (Guantánamo Bay detention center), 1:243–244

Campbell, Naomi, 2:365

Canada
  Arctic region ownership claims, 1:57, 60, 62
  Atlantic cod overfishing, 2:569
  Colombia trade agreements, 1:138
  ECHELON participation, 1:159
  human rights score, 2:542
  Kyoto Protocol, 1:240, 2:543
  NATO formation, 2:402
  oil industry, 2:414, 417

Cano, Alfonso, 1:136, 137

Caravan of Death (Chile), 1:114–115

CARE International, 1:269

Carnation Revolution (1974), 1:275

Carranza, Venustiano, 2:378–379

Carroll, Stephen, 2:411

Carson, Rachel, 1:236

Cartagena Protocol on Biosafety, 1:238

Carter, Jimmy
  Afghan resistance funding, 1:10, 2:556
  Cold War diplomacy, 1:130

First Liberian Civil War, 2:363–364

First Persian Gulf War. *See* Iran-Iraq War (1980–1988)

First Sino-Japanese War (1894–1895), 2:321

Five Pillars of Islam, 1:298

Flame (malware), 1:160, 208

FLN (National Liberation Front) (Algeria), 1:35–36

Flores, Carol Patricia, 1:225, 254

FMLN (Frente Farabundo Martí para la Liberación Nacional), 1:200, 201, 202

Foley, Tracey Lee Ann, 1:209

Fonseca Amador, Carlos, 2:393

Food for Peace, 1:268

Ford, Gerald R., 1:182–183

Ford, John A., 1:183

Fourth Geneva Convention (1949), 1:219–220

Framework Convention on Climate Change (UNFCCC), 1:238, 240

France
    Algeria colonization and independence, 1:34–39
    Armenian Genocide denial as crime, 1:223
    Basque nationalism, 1:75, 76, 77, 79
    Côte d'Ivoire colonization, 1:141
    drone program, 1:175
    EEC formation, 1:211
    environmental movement, 1:237
    headscarves ban, 2:436, 437
    NATO membership, 2:402, 404
    nuclear weapons, 2:579
    Paris Peace Accords, 2:567
    religious freedom, 2:436, 437
    United Nations membership, 2:537
    U.S.-Iraq War, 2:579
    Vietnam colonization, 1:130, 2:561–563
    war crimes court, 1:284
    World War I participation, 2:584–589, 588
    World War II participation, 2:591

Franchise and Ballot Act (1892) (South Africa), 2:470

Francis (Pope), 1:64, 201

Franco, Francisco, 1:75, 76, 2:480, 481–484, 482

Franco-Austrian War, 1:217

Frankfurter, Felix, 1:264

Franz Ferdinand (archduke of Austria), 2:584, 586, 606

Fraser, Bruce, 2:600

Free Aceh Movement, 1:274, 276

Free speech, 1:225

freedom of the press, 1:184, 185
    Holocaust denial, 1:223

Free Syrian Army, 2:501, 501

Free trade agreements, 1:81, 82, 138–139
    See also specific agreements

Free Trade Area of the Americas (FTAA), 1:82

Freedom Charter (African National Congress), 2:476–478

Frei, Eduardo, 1:115

French School (counterinsurgency tactics), 1:36, 38–39

Frente Farabundo Martí para la Liberación Nacional (FMLN), 1:200, 201, 202

Frente Revolucionária de Timor-Leste Independente (FRETILIN), 1:182, 183, 275–276

Fried, Daniel, 1:232

FSLN (Sandinista National Liberation Front), 2:393–394

FTAA (Free Trade Area of the Americas), 1:82

Fuerzas Armadas Revolucionarias de Colombia (FARC), 1:134–138, 136, 139, 139

Fundamentalism, 2:431
    See also Religious extremism

Funes, Mauricio, 1:202

G

Gabon, OPEC membership, 2:414, 415

Gallardo, Miguel Ángel Félix, 2:382–383

Gallipoli, Battle of (1915), 2:589

Galtieri, Leopoldo, 1:65

GAM (Gerakan Aceh Merdeka), 1:274, 276

Gandhi, Mohandas, 2:398, 423

Gandhi, Rajiv, 2:486

Gang of Four, 1:124, 125

Garay, Victor Gerardo, 2:385

Garowe Agreement, 2:466

Garzón, Baltasar, 1:114

Gates, Robert, 1:216, 2:374, 406

Gaulle, Charles de, 1:37, 37, 2:598

Gaza-Jericho Agreement—Letters of Arafat and Rabin, 1:314–318

Gaza Strip
    changing control, 1:41
    disputed control, 1:45
    Hamas and, 1:312–313
    raid of humanitarian aid flotilla, 1:45
    resettlement plan, 1:311–312, 316

Gbagbo, Laurent, 1:20, 141, 142–144, 145, 145, 147, 283

Gbagbo, Simone (arrest warrant), 1:146, 147–149

Gbowee, Leymah, 2:366, 399, 400

General Atomics drones, 1:174–175, 175

General Pass Regulations Bill (1905) (South Africa), 2:470

Geneva Conventions, 1:217–221, 218, 220, 243, 245, 267

Geneva Peace Accords (1954), 2:563

Geneva Protocols, 1:220–221, 2:502

Genocide, 1:222–229
    Armenian, 1:68–74, 69, 70, 223, 225, 2:609
    Cambodia, 1:101, 103, 103–104
    Chechnya, 1:107
    ethnic cleansing *vs.*, 2:608, 609
    Guatemala, 1:225–226, 254
    Kurdish people, 1:287, 288
    Rwanda, 1:223–224, 224, 225, 2:447–453, 449, 450, 451
    Srebrenica massacre, 1:88–89, 90, 91, 224, 225, 226, 2:610
    Sudan and South Sudan, 2:492, 495–496, 498
    as term, 1:70, 71
    See also Ethnic cleansing; Holocaust

Georgia (country)
    history, 1:230
    map, 1:231
    USSR dissolution, 2:554

Georgia-Russia conflict, 1:158, 230–235, 232, 233, 2:404

Gerakan Aceh Merdeka (GAM), 1:274, 276

Germ warfare, 2:578

Germany
    drone program, 1:174, 175
    European debt crisis and, 1:214
    headscarves ban, 2:437
    Holocaust denial as crime, 1:223
    Italy relations, 2:591
    Rwanda colonization, 2:447
    Sherbini, Marwa al- stabbing, 1:306
    Spain relations, 2:482, 483
    Treaty of Versailles violation, 2:399
    World War I participation, 2:584–589, 587, 591
    World War II participation, 1:127–128, 2:591–603

Ghailani, Ahmed, 1:246

GHG (greenhouse gas) emissions, 1:240, 241

Ghoga, Abdel Hafiz, 2:375

GIA (Armed Islamic Group), 1:37

Gia Long, 2:561–562

Somalia colonization, 2:464
Spain relations, 2:482, 483
World War I participation, 2:585
World War II participation, 2:591, 594, 598
ITS (International Tracing Service), 2:598
It's Nice to Be Deaf (book excerpt), 1:*110–111*
Ivanishvili, Bidzina, 1:234
Ivins, Bruce, 2:579–580
IWC (International Whaling Commission), 1:237–238
Izetbegovic, Alija, 1:*89*

J

Jacoby, Charles, 2:548
Jama'at-e Islami, 2:433
Jammu and Kashmir conflict, 2:423, 424, 425
Janjaweed (paramilitary group), 2:*495*, 495–496, 498
Japan
  biological weapons, 2:578
  China relations, 1:120, 121–122
  environmental movement, 1:237
  Geneva Conventions, 1:219–220
  history, 2:321–322
  human rights abuses, 1:225, 2:323–325
  Indonesia relations, 1:273
  Kyoto Protocol, 1:240, 2:543
  map, 2:*322*
  purchasing power parity, 1:190
  Russo-Japanese War, 2:321, 439–440
  Taiwan colonization, 2:506
  whaling case, 1:283
  World War II participation, 2:591–605
Japanese invasion of China, 2:**321–326**, *324, 325, 326*, 575, 592
Jawad, Mohammed, 1:247
Jeffs, Warren, 2:433
JEM (Justice and Equality Movement) (Sudan), 2:495
Jemaah Islamiyah (JI), 1:*29*, 277
Jewish fundamentalism, 2:433
Jewish people. *See* Anti-Semitism; Holocaust; Israel
JI (Jemaah Islamiya), 1:*29*, 277
Jiang Qing, 1:124, *125*
Jihad, 2:557
Jihad Against Jews and Crusaders (bin Laden), 1:*5–6*
Jimemez-Naranjo, Carlos Mario, 1:137
John Paul II (pope), 1:114, *183*, 2:474

Johnson, Louis, 2:*403*
Johnson, Lyndon B., 1:184, 2:565
Johnson, Prince, 2:362
Johnson Sirleaf, Ellen
  Liberia presidency, 2:362, *365, 366, 367*
  Nobel Peace Prize, 2:366, 399, *400*
Jojoy, Mono, 1:138
Joliot-Curie, Frederic, 2:582
Jon Yong Ryong, 2:338
Jonathan, Goodluck, 2:435
Jones, Terry, 1:305
Jordan
  Arab-Israeli conflict, 1:41, 42, 309, 2:513
  Palestinian refugees, 1:40
  PLO and, 1:311
  Syrian refugees, 2:504
Jordet, Tord, 2:*520*
Juan Carlos (king of Spain), 1:76, 2:483
Justice, international. *See* International law and justice
Justice and Equality Movement (JEM) (Sudan), 2:495

K

Kabbah, Ahmad Tejan, 2:454, 456
Kabila, Joseph, 1:167
Kabila, Laurent, 1:167, 169
Kaczynski, Ted, 2:517
Kadeer, Rebiya, 2:508
Kadyrov, Akhmad, 1:108–109
Kadyrov, Ramzan, 1:109, *109*, 110
Kagame, Paul, 1:173, 2:448, 450
Kang Kek Iew, 1:104, 105, 225
Karachi, Pakistan, mosque bombing, 1:298
Karadzic, Radovan, 1:91, 225, 2:609–610
Kargil Conflict (1999), 2:423
Karmal, Babrak, 2:420
Karman, Tawakkol, 2:399, *400*
Karzai, Hamid, 1:12, 13–14, 2:418, 420, 421
Kashmir conflict, 2:423, 426, 427
Kaspersky Lab, 1:160
Kauffman, Henrik de, 2:*403*
Kavakçi, Merve, 2:437
Kazakhstan
  nuclear weapons handover, 2:579
  USSR dissolution, 2:554
Keating, Kenneth, 1:154
Keenan, George F., 1:128
Kem Sokha, 1:105

Kennedy, John F., 1:*153*
  Cuba relations, 1:151
  Cuban Missile Crisis, 1:129–130, 154
  USAID founding, 1:268
  Vietnam relations, 2:564
Kenya, 2:**327–333**
  history, 2:327
  map, 2:*328*
  Mau Mau terrorist suspects, 2:*329*
  peace agreement, 2:*332*
  refugee camps, 1:271
  street fight, 2:*330*
  U.S. embassy bombing, 1:3, 26, 2:515
  water access concerns, 2:569, 572
Kenyatta, Jomo, 2:327
Kenyatta, Uhuru, 2:327, 331, 332–333
Kerensky, Alexander, 2:441
Kerry, John, 1:47, 314, *317*, 2:*503*, 504
Khamenei, Ali, 1:295, 296
Khan, Imran, 1:177
Khan, Majid, 1:247
Khan, Tariq, 2:421
Khar, Hina Rabbani, 2:*421*
Khieu Samphan, 1:*104*
Khmer Rouge, 1:101–105, *104*, 222, 223, **225**
Khomeini, Ruhollah (Ayatollah), 1:286, *287, 294*
  Iran leadership, 1:286, 287, 291–295
  Rushdie, Salman fatwa, 2:433
  Sunni-Shia conflict and, 1:299
Khrushchev, Nikita, 1:107, 129–130, 151, 154
Kibaki, Mwai, 2:327, 328–331, *332*
Kiir, Salva, 2:*496*, 498
Killing fields (Cambodia), 1:101, 103, *103*
Kim Dae-jung, 2:338
Kim Il-sung, 2:*337*
Kim Jong-il, 2:337, 338
Kim Jong-un, 2:337, 338, 339
Kim Yong-hyun, 2:334
King, Martin Luther, Jr., 2:398
Kingdom of Serbs, Croats, and Slovenes. *See* Yugoslavia
Kirchner, Néstor, 1:138
Kissinger, Henry, 1:182–183, 2:398, *415*
KLA (Kosovo Liberation Army), 2:342, 607–608
Koch, Edward, 1:114
Koje prison camp, 2:337
Kony, Joseph, 2:531, 533–535
Kony 2012 (Internet video), 2:534

M